The SEARCH
for Personal Freedom

VOLUME ONE

Introduction, the Greek and Roman Periods, Some Teachings of Jesus, and the Pulls of Life and Death in the Middle Ages.

THIRD EDITION

The SEARCH
for Personal Freedom

. . . A TEXT FOR A UNIFIED COURSE IN THE HUMANITIES

NEAL M. CROSS
Colorado State College

LESLIE DAE LINDOU
formerly of Colorado State College

ROBERT C. LAMM
Arizona State University

WM. C. BROWN COMPANY PUBLISHERS
Dubuque, Iowa

foreword

The reception of unified humanities courses, and textbooks for such courses, has been varied over the years. When the great books course at Columbia University was first inaugurated, when the integrated arts course at Stephens College and when the integrated humanities course at Colorado State College were first introduced, the idea was greeted with enthusiasm. The first lithographed edition of this book appeared almost exactly twenty years ago.

When the book appeared it was widely criticized as being superficial. This criticism was so strong that in a subsequent revision (1960), the authors felt it necessary to lead off with an introductory chapter, ostensibly for students but actually as an explanation to their academic colleagues. This chapter explained that the book, and the course which it represented, had a validity in its own right *as a unified humanities course*. Viewed as art history, music history, world literature, or history of philosophy, it was superficial, and remains so, without apology.

Let us reiterate. This book and this course are not histories of art, music, literature, or philosophy. Nor does the book represent the usual, subprofessional "introduction to" any of these disciplines, with the stress on learning the academic vocabulary of the fields so the student will be equipped to participate in more advanced courses without wasting time learning the elementary vocabulary.

The idea which underlies this book is twofold: The arts constitute an area of knowledge different from those of the natural sciences and the social studies; the arts are as important as either of the other two great areas of human understanding because they offer interpretations of the meaning of experience to the individual. The artist is a discoverer of new knowledge in the area of the meaning of experience, and his discoveries are as important as those of a natural scientist or a student of society. As the individual sees a wide variety of meanings in the happenings of his life he is more and more able to make sound value judgments. In the mid-twentieth century we need sound value judgments more than we need computers or nuclear devices.

Naturally, a single course cannot cover the field. The materials presented in this book are simply intended to give the student a start toward viewing the arts in this light, and to begin to give him some of the myriad meanings in a few of life's experiences. It is hoped that this work will cause him to begin to ask questions about things which he never knew were there to be questioned. And it is hoped, too, that he will be given the skills in thinking that will enable him to find some of the answers to his questions and eventually to formulate tentative and growing answers of his own through study and creation in the arts.

The book is organized chronologically, utilizing the traditional framework of the Greek, Roman, medieval, Renaissance, seventeenth and eighteenth centuries, and modern periods. In addition, some attempt is made to interpret the western world since 1914, which constitutes a new period in our history. For various reasons, the scope of the work is limited to the western world. At the beginning

of each of the units of work previously listed one will find two or three introductory chapters giving the background of the period. Then the music of the
time, some examples of the painting, sculpture, and architecture, and some
literary selections are given. The background chapters are the least important
part of the work. The chapters dealing with the arts, and the literary selections
are the most important parts. The background is included because the artists
worked within a certain milieu, and it is felt that the student needs to know
the limitations and the unique potentialities of those surroundings. Very frequently, however, unless strange or difficult concepts are introduced, the background
chapters can simply be assigned, tested over perhaps, and forgotten insofar as
class work is concerned. The greatest amount of time should be spent on the
works of art themselves.

The book organizes itself around a central idea: human freedom. Certainly
the zones for the human personality pose a central problem for a humanistic
study of the arts; furthermore, organization around a single great idea should
be a help to both teacher and student. One of the authors can remember back
to his freshman literature course when he read *Romeo and Juliet, Henry IV,*
Part I, *King Lear, Stones of Venice,* and *Sartor Resartus,* and probably a number
of other literary selections. They were good, but they didn't add up to anything.
Since one of the purposes of this book is to help the student find tentative and
growing answers to the meaning of life's experiences, it is hoped that the central
idea will help the cultural experience "add up."

As far as possible, the authors have tried to avoid using snippets of literary
selections. Whenever it has been necessary to cut a piece and to use only a
small part of a literary work, every attempt has been made to use a unit that
is complete within itself. Everybody's favorite pictures, musical selections, or
literary works cannot possibly be included. Furthermore, many of the authors'
selections may not be similar to the ones the individual teacher would make.
Tastes differ. The creative teacher is urged to use records and tapes of his own
choices, to use some of the thousands of available slides, and to introduce paperback editions of the literary selections which he thinks would aid his cause.

The authors wish to make certain personal acknowledgments. Joyce Anderson
Tibbetts made the drawing which serves as a headpiece for Chapter 4. Miss
Grace Baker made the drawings which we have used to illustrate the elements
and principles of design. Mr. Don Walters made the original drawings for the
chapter on symbolism in medieval art. Arline M. Cross made many of the designs
which appear throughout the text, and Nannette Lindou made the translation of
the selection from Rousseau's *Emile.* The authors wish to express their appreciation to these individuals for their gracious assistance.

acknowledgments

The authors are indebted to the following authors and publishers for permission to reprint selections from their works:

Associated Music Publishers, Inc. for selections from Carl Orff's *Carmina Burana*. Copyright © 1937 by B. Schott's Soehna, Mainz, Germany. Used by permission of Associated Music Publishers, Inc., sole U.S. Agent.

The Atlantic Monthly for selections from Francis H. Taylor's article, "Modern Art and the Dignity of Man," Vol. 182, No. 6 (December, 1948). Copyright © 1948, by The Atlantic Monthly Company, Boston, Mass. Reprinted with permission.

Boosey and Hawkes, Inc. for selections from Bartók's *Concerto for Orchestra* © 1946 by Hawkes & Son (London) Ltd. Reprinted by permission of Boosey and Hawkes, Inc. For selections from Stravinsky, *Le Sacre du Printemps*, © 1921 by Edition Russe de Musique; copyright assigned to Boosey and Hawkes, Inc., 1947. Reprinted by permission of Boosey and Hawkes, Inc.

Maurice A. Crane for permission to reprint his translations of two of the Odes of Horace.

Dell Publishing Co., Inc. for permission to reprint George Thomson's translations of the "Agamemnon" and "Eumenides." Reprinted from *Aeschylus* edited by Robert W. Corrigan. Translated by George Thomson. Copyright © 1965 by Dell Publishing Co., Inc. and used by permission of the publisher.

Desclee & Cie Editeurs S.A., Tournai, Belgium, for permission to reprint selections from the *Liber Usualis*, Copyright © 1961 by Desclee & Cie, Tournai.

E. P. Dutton & Co. Inc. for permission to reprint selections from Emile Male, *The Gothic Image: Religious Art in France of the XIII Century.*

Elkan-Vogel Co. for selections from DeBussy, *Prelude a L'Apres-Midi D'Un Faune*. Permission for reprint granted by Jean Jobert Editions, Paris; Copyright owners—Elkan-Vogel Co., Philadelphia, Pa., sole agents. For permission to reprint selections from DeBussy *La Cathedrale Engloutie* and *Voiles*, permission for reprint granted by Durand & Cie, Paris, copyright owner Elkan-Vogel Co., Philadelphia, Pa., sole agents.

The Estate of Albert Einstein for permission to reprint a paragraph from Einstein and Infeld, *The Evolution of Physics.*

Grove Press for permission to reprint a portion of Hilda Doolittle's poem, "Charioteer" from *Collected Poems of H.D.* Copyright © 1925.

Harcourt, Brace & World, Inc., for T. S. Eliot, "The Hollow Men." From *Collected Poems 1909-1962* by T. S. Eliot. Copyright, 1936, by Harcourt, Brace & World, Inc.; copyright © 1963, 1964 by T. S. Eliot. Reprinted by permission of the publishers. For E. E. Cummings, "anyone lived in a pretty how town," from *Poems 1923-1954* by E. E. Cummings. Copyright, 1940, by E. E. Cummings; renewed, 1968, by Marion Morehouse Cummings. Reprinted from *Poems 1923-1954* by E. E. Cummings, by permission of Harcourt,

Brace & World, Inc. For "The Abbey of Theleme" from the Urquhart-LeMotteux translation of *The Works of Francis Rabelais* edited by Albert Jay Nock and Catherine Rose Wilson, copyright, 1931, by Harcourt, Brace & World, Inc.; renewed, 1959, by Catherine Rose Wilson and Samuel A. Nock. Reprinted by permission of the publishers. For selections from Lewis Mumford, *The Condition of Man* and S. I. Hayakawa, *Language in Action* reprinted by permission of the publishers, Harcourt, Brace & World, Inc.

Curtis Brown, Ltd., New York, for permission to reprint from Herbert Read, *Art Now.*

Harper and Row, Publishers, for the lengthy selection from *Time Must Have a Stop* by Aldous Huxley. Copyright © 1944 by Aldous Huxley. For "The Door" from *The Second Tree From the Corner* by E. B. White, originally published in *The New Yorker.* Copyright © 1939 by E. B. White. Both selections reprinted by permission of Harper and Row, Publishers, Inc.

Holt, Rinehart and Winston, Inc., for permission to reprint "Stopping by Woods on a Snowy Evening," by Robert Frost. From *Complete Poems of Robert Frost.* Copyright 1923 by Holt, Rinehart and Winston, Inc. Copyright 1951 by Robert Frost. Reprinted by permission of Holt, Rinehart and Winston, Inc. For the selection from John Sewall, *A History of Western Art,* copyright 1961 by Holt, Rinehart and Winston, Inc., by permission of the publisher.

Houghton Mifflin Company for several selections from Henry Adams, *Mont St. Michel and Chartres*; for twenty-two lines from Isabel Butler's translation of *The Song of Roland*; for a brief selection from John Herman Randall's *The Making of the Modern Mind*; for a selection from John Livingston Lowes, *Convention and Revolt in Poetry*; and for the selection from the Bayard Taylor translation of Goethe's *Faust.* All of these are reprinted with the permission of the publisher, Houghton Mifflin Company.

MCA Music for the selection from Serge Prokofiev, Symphony No. 5. Copyright © 1946 by MCA Music, a division of MCA Inc. New York. Used by permission. All rights reserved.

The Museum of Modern Art for the paragraphs selected from *Cubism and Abstract Art* by Alfred H. Barr, Jr., copyright 1936 by the Museum of Modern Art, New York.

The National Council of the Churches of Christ in the U.S.A. for several selections from the Bible. The Bible text in this publication is from the Revised Standard Version of the Bible, copyrighted 1946 and 1952 by the Division of Christian Education of the National Council of the Churches of Christ in the U.S.A. and used by permission.

The Macmillan Company from W. B. Yeats, *Collected Poems,* "The Second Coming," copyright 1951 and used with the permission of The Macmillan Co.; for Oscar Levy, editor, *The Complete Works of Friedrich Nietzsche.* Used with the permission of Allen & Unwin, Ltd. London and The Macmillan Company, New York. For Seligman, ed.: *Encyclopedia of the Social Sciences* Vol. III Copyright 1931 by The Macmillan Company and used with their permission. For Seligman, ed.: *Encyclopedia of the Social Sciences* Vol. III Copyright 1934 by The Macmillan Company and used with their permission.

New American Library, Inc. for Plato's "Phaedo," from *Great Dialogues of Plato,* translated by W. H. D. Rouse and edited by Philip G. Rouse and Eric H. Warmington. Copyright © 1956, 1961 by John Clive Graves Rouse. Reprinted by arrangement with the New American Library, Inc., New York.

New Directions Publishing Corporation for "When all my five and country senses see," from Dylan Thomas, *Collected Poems.* Copyright 1939 by New Directions Publishing Corporation. Reprinted by permission of New Directions Publishing Corporation.

W. W. Norton and Co. for permission to reprint a selection from Oliver Strunk, *Source Readings in Music History.* Copyright © The W. W. Norton Co., New York.

Oxford University Press for "Antigone" and "Oedipus the King" from *Three Theban Plays by Sophocles,* new translation by Theodore Howard Banks. Copyright, 1956, by Theodore Howard Banks. Reprinted by permission of Oxford University Press, Inc.

"Bagpipe Music," by Louis MacNeice from *The Collected Poems of Louis MacNeice,* edited by E. R. Dodds, Copyright © The Estate of Louis MacNeice 1966. Reprinted by permission of Oxford University Press, Inc.

Random House, Inc., for "Shine Perishing Republic," from *Roan Stallion; Tamar; and Other Poems,* copyright 1925 and renewed 1953 by Robinson Jeffers, reprinted by permission of Random House, Inc.; for "For the Time Being," from *Collected Poetry of W. H. Auden,* copyright 1944 by W. H. Auden, reprinted by permission of Random House, Inc.

Ruth Lechlitner has given us permission to reprint her poem, "Only the Years."

Charles Scribner's Sons. Material from the following works is reprinted with the permission of Charles Scribner's Sons: *The Aeneid of Virgil,* pages 87-112, translated by Rolfe Humphries (Copyright 1951 Charles Scribner's Sons) and *The Petrified Forest,* pages 62-63, by Robert Sherwood (Copyright 1934, 1935 Robert Emmet Sherwood; renewal copyright © 1962, 1963 Madeline H. Sherwood). "A Clean, Well-Lighted Place" (Copyright 1933 Charles Scribner's Sons; renewal copyright © 1961 Ernest Hemingway) is reprinted with the permission of Charles Scribner's Sons from *Winner Take Nothing* by Ernest Hemingway.

Universal Edition A.G., Vienna, for permission to reprint an excerpt from Alban Berg, Concerto for Violin and Orchestra, 1936.

University of Chicago Press four lines from Elizabeth Wycoff translation of *Antigone,* from Grene and Lattimore, *Complete Greek Tragedies.*

Viking Press Inc. for permission to reprint a brief selection from Sheldon Cheney, *A New World History of Art,* 1943, and for a selection from James Joyce, *Portrait of the Artist as a Young Man,* copyright © by the Estate of James Joyce, reprinted by permission.

A. Watkins, Inc., New York, for permission to reprint *Hell* from Dorothy Sayers' translation of *Dante's Divine Comedy,* Copyright 1949, Dorothy L. Sayers.

Wilbur Daniel Steele and Harold Matson for permission to reprint Mr. Steele's story, "The Man Who Saw Through Heaven."

contents

unit **I**

the introductory unit

On Theories of History

This course involves freedom in six great periods of the history of man in the western world. Three questions naturally arise as we approach such a study. The first of these has to do with the value of such an historical approach. Why study the past when our life and our concern is with the present? A second question has to do with the meaning of the word freedom as it is used here. What do we mean when we speak of men finding their freedom within any given period of time? The third question deals with the dividing points in our historical study. Why, when history can be divided in so many ways, do we choose the six periods which we have? In this chapter we hope to answer these three questions, and to discuss our method of approach to each of the six great historical periods.

The first question is perhaps the most easily answered. Our history is a part of us. The ideas stated by the Greek philosophers Democritus or Heracleitus perhaps twenty-five hundred years ago have moved through our history, have been changed by later thinkers who were influenced by the circumstances of their times, and exist in our own time as active philosophies and codes for personal living which influence each one of us. The insights into the meanings of life of Michelangelo, of Sophocles, or of Beethoven are reinterpreted for each generation, and these new interpretations speak to our condition now perhaps even more fully than they did when those artists first composed their works of art. All of the great thought, all of the great meanings discovered by the artists of the past, have become more than part of our heritage; they have become a part of ourselves. If we would know ourselves at all, we must know some of the sources of our thought, our personalities, our ideas, our ways of looking at the myriad events of life. Through such an historical approach as the one made here we may see these forces beginning, changing, and developing into the forms they assume in our twentieth century life. Our history is a part of us.

Our second question deals with the meaning of such an expression as that of men "finding their freedom" within their period of history. In the first place, we must define freedom as an active process. It is not simply time to do nothing, time to waste, time to kill. We define freedom as the ability to accomplish one's purposes and desires. A man is free who knows what he wants to do and why he wants to do it. And then he must have enough skill and knowledge to go about the job of accomplishing his purpose with a minimum of frustration.

There have been times when the nature of the world has been so confusing to men that they were unable to accomplish their purposes without a great deal of floundering about. Slowly they have become accustomed to their world and have learned its ways. Then they were able to work toward their goals in freedom. And there have been periods when men were so accustomed to their world that they seem to have become bored with it. These we generally recognize as periods of decadence, when the setting of goals has been almost too much for men. One might ask how these things come about. Why do we have these changes in man's life and understanding of his world, particularly when the world itself, we are fairly sure, remains a constant factor?

This brings us to the whole question of philosophies of history. There are many of them. For example, one such philosophy ascribes all change to a process of accident. Such historians deny any purpose or plan in the changes of man's estate on his earth. It seems to such historians that things merely happen, and men respond with certain actions which serve as causative factors for other events and other actions. For such historians, man is merely muddling through his existence on this planet with no pre-established goal and no plan.

Other philosophers of history, St. Augustine, for example, have believed that even before man came to the earth, a goal had been established. For St.

Augustine this goal was the final establishment of the City of God on earth. He thought of each big change in history as a definite step toward this great purpose, and he would have arranged an educational system, a church, and many other human institutions to accord with this plan to further man's progress toward the City of God. Those who believe that a pattern and a goal are inherent in man's history are essentially religious philosophers, though their religion may take many forms.

A third general group of philosophies of history places great responsibility on man, for these philosophers deny any inherent pattern in history but assert that man himself, through his reason, must establish purposes and work toward them. The goals which they generally state are the goals of physical well-being. They envision a world in which all people are well-fed, clothed, and housed. They imagine a time when war as an instrument of international policy no longer exists, usually thinking in terms of some sort of world-state. They frequently postulate a time when each man has the right to express his opinions freely and to be heard, with the corollary of an educational system which will make every man sufficiently well-informed that his opinions are of value. But, they say, this is up to us. We can have it if we want it, but we must want it enough to work for it and establish it. No force outside of ourselves is working to bring this about, nor is any force except man's own greed and stupidity keeping him from it.

These, then, are some common philosophies of history. They are all attempts on the part of wise men to explain the great changes which occur in life on this planet and to explain the trends which seem to run through our racial life. Notice how, with the acceptance of each one, we almost automatically adopt a set of institutions to harmonize with the accepted philosophy. If we follow the pattern ascribed to St. Augustine, for example, we immediately exclude most of pagan learning since that would not lead directly to the City of God. In so doing, we begin to form a school system. Or, if we accept the philosophy which places responsibility on man, we would probably work toward democratic forms of government and toward some sort of league of nations or United Nations organization. If one studies these philosophies carefully enough, he observes that each one carries with it an implied set of human institutions: a political system which deals with the problem of justice among men; an educational system which gives men the kind of knowledge they need for the fulfillment of the purposes of history; a kind of church or religious organization in conformity with the basic philosophy; an economic system through which the needs for food, clothing, and shelter are provided, etc. Thus, each philosophy of history carries with it a set of institutions by which men's needs are met and into which men's lives are channeled.

Which of these—or other—philosophies of history is right? This is a question no one can answer, for each is an interpretation of events, and even the events, the "facts" of history, seem different as they are viewed from different points of view. One can find much evidence to support any one of these different philosophies, and until we know the inmost secrets of the workings of nature and the Mind of God we can never know which one is "right."

In this book we are adopting a very modified form of what is called the "Culture-Epoch" theory. We do not believe that it is more or less "right" than any other theory. But it does account for the great periods of change in the western world in most cases. In some cases, by the way, it does not seem to work, and in those cases we shall simply discard it for the moment. In general, however, for our purposes of teaching and learning it works better than any other; it seems as valid as any other explanation of change, and we shall use it as a general framework for our study.

A basic tenet of this philosophy of history is that all particular philosophies (the philosophy of law, ideas of religion, an economic theory, a philosophy of education, etc.) are based on the concept of reality which is held at any given time; and that in various periods of history people agree on a concept of reality. This very idea may seem strange to a student in the mid-twentieth century, for he is so accustomed to thinking of the solid things around him as "real" that he cannot imagine that anyone could think anything else. Or, if he is of a scientific bent, he may think of reality as being composed of atoms and electrons and the like. But even these are tangible things if we could only develop our senses to the point where we could be aware of them. But certainly, he would say, each tree, each rock, each table is "real."

But the student would be wrong in his thought that it is impossible to conceive of other than sense-apparent things as real. If we define reality as "unchanging", what happens to his concept of a real tree, a real stone, or even a real atom? These things all change; they are here today and gone tomorrow. If we accept permanence as a synonym for reality, then these things are no longer real. As a matter of fact, during the Middle Ages, God was accepted as the only reality, and the things of this world were regarded as of the least importance. And Plato thought of reality as consisting of certain Ideas or Patterns of things, perfect and unchanging, existing beyond the reach of the mind of mortal men. So it seems that reality can be thought of in many ways. Even in our own time it seems probable that we are witnessing a change in our concept of reality from those things which are present-to-our-senses (the view attributed above to the normal student) to some other concept.

Each period, however, adopts an idea of the nature of reality. For a long period of time this concept is almost universally held. Upon it, then, are built philosophies of law, religious philosophies, educational philosophies, economic theories, and the like. And upon these philosophies are constructed the actual institutions by which we live: our governments and legal systems, our various forms of religious organizations, our schools, our banks and our many ways of exchanging goods and services, and the like. When this is all accomplished life seems to run smoothly enough, for the concept of reality, the philosophies and theories which are built upon it, and the actual institutions which derive from these philosophies all seem to be in harmony. We might call this a period of balance, and if it lasts so long that people can find no important work to do, no goals to set, we may find that it becomes a period of decadence.

But always comes change. Usually some great intellectual giants see some new idea of reality. They discover in many ways—through scientific methods, through mathematical proof, or perhaps through philosophic speculation—that a new picture of reality is more valid than the accepted one. For many reasons their idea "catches on." Their proof seems so certain, their logic so inevitably right, that many other people accept this new basic idea. And then civilization is embarked on an entire new epoch, rebuilding basic philosophies and institutions on the new foundation. The change may be pictured in the following diagrams.

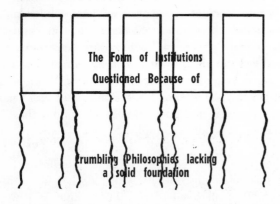

Govern-ments	Church	Ways of Ex-change	School	Other Insti-tutions
Philo-sophy of law	Ideas of reli-gion	Eco-nomic theory	Philo-sophy of Educa-tion	Other Philo-sophies

The Concept of Reality which is held at a given time

BALANCE ESTABLISHED ON A FIRM CONCEPT OF REALITY

The Form of Institutions Questioned Because of

Crumbling Philosophies lacking a solid foundation

THE CONCEPT OF REALITY HAS CHANGED. BASIC PHILOSOPHIES AND INSTITUTIONS CRUMBLE.

Institutions of Government, Church, Economic Arrangements, etc. Begin to Be Rebuilt in Accord with the New Philosophies.

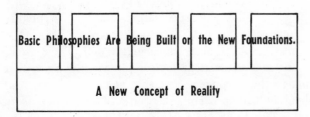

Basic Philosophies Are Being Built on the New Foundations.

A New Concept of Reality

A PERIOD OF CULTURAL ADJUSTMENT MOVING TOWARD A NEW BALANCE.

What we are picturing, then, is a world in which ultimate truth is never known, and perhaps never can be known. But men, using their highest intelligence, form a concept of what seems to be most real and most true. Such a concept of reality displaces an older one, and causes real confusion among men as they realize that the life of their whole period in history and that all the arrangements which they made to facilitate the processes of living and to satisfy their intellectual, physical, and spiritual needs are falsely grounded. Then, of course, comes the long, slow process of rebuilding. In the early stages of this rebuilding, life may be (and usually is) marked by the clashing of ideologies, with wars, with religious doubt and many other manifestations of chaos. Then directions and purposes emerge, and the time of adjustment may be a most exciting one. And finally comes a new balance in which all things seem to be in harmony and life seems to run smoothly. This, of course, will not last, for change seems to be the one permanent thing in all of life, and sooner or later a new concept of reality will probably upset the whole applecart of civilization once again.

Who makes all of these changes? The men who establish the new concepts of reality may be scientists like Sir Isaac Newton or Albert Einstein. They may be religious men like St. Augustine. They may be philosophers like Plato or Aristotle. They are the ones who question the ultimate nature of things, and they might be called the pure thinkers in that they take the universe apart as a small boy might take a watch apart and for the same reason—to see what makes it tick.

Then, one observes a number of other great minds who establish new theories in the various branches of knowledge. They are those who formulate philosophies of law, of religion, of education, or of economics in terms of the ideas of the great men who have developed the idea of Reality.

But in a time of chaos and confusion, who is it that determines the ultimate human values? This is the role of the artists whether they are writers, painters, sculptors, musicians, choreographers, or makers of motion pictures and television shows. Such men may or may not be aware of the basic problems of the nature of reality and the like, but they are always aware within themselves and within other people of the confusions and conflicts which upset human lives. And the artist is always the composer. It is he who seeks to bring order out of confusion insofar as the meanings of human life are concerned. So it is the great artists, men like Aeschylus, Sophocles, Dante, Shakespeare, Michelangelo, Beethoven, or Bach, who supply the final answers about man's purposes in the world.

Finally, it is the intellectual class, people who read books, who study science and religion and the social studies and the humanities, who reshape the institutions into usable forms. They are the ones who take all of the data at hand from all possible sources and turn that data into actual churches and schools, banks and governments. For these institutions are the crystallization of our fundamental ideas about the nature of reality and about our relation to God, the universe, other people, and ourselves. One can almost think of this intellectual class as the engineers in this total process of building a social structure within a culture-epoch, for they take the abstract ideas from the thinkers before them and turn those ideas into practical uses for men.

We recognize three very great changes within the history of Western Man which fulfill all of the descriptions of a culture-epoch given above. One of these was the rationalist period of the ancient Greeks which began before recorded history, reached its apex about the fifth century B.C., and declined during the next century. This same epoch, however, experienced a resurgence of life during Roman times, and continued until about the fifth century A.D. Then we see the triumph of the Idea of God as the concept of reality throughout the Middle Ages, lasting until about the fifteenth century. Finally we find a turning from this idea of reality to a sensate principle (that reality consisted only of those things which could be known through the senses) which marks the world up to the beginning of the twentieth century. Within this last period, we seem to detect two different ways of life which are of sufficient importance that we shall study them separately. The first of these is the period of the renaissance, lasting, let us say, from 1450 to 1650. Then we enter what is usually called the modern period, though, at the moment, it seems to be in a period of fundamental change.

In summary, can we make these statements which will underlie much of the thought of this course?

First, that men, to have freedom, must exercise their powers of intellect and emotion toward the ac-

complishment of their purposes. This is the definition of freedom which will be implied throughout the rest of this book. The capacity for freedom grows with each human experience. It is not a political or economic fact; politics and economics set a stage upon which personal freedom may thrive or dwindle. As people have new experiences they become more mature and acquire greater freedom. It may almost be said that the measure of personal freedom that one develops for himself and in himself is the measure of his humanity.

Second, implicit in the theory of history which we are adopting for our present purposes, is the idea that men have never known and probably do not now know the true nature of the world in which they live. From time to time, however, they discover facts or concepts which seem to be true. They act as if these facts and concepts were valid and find their freedom within that framework of seeming fact.

Third, we assume that human institutions are the crystallizations of our ways of living at any given time. They are man-made to facilitate our living. They change as our knowledge about the world and our design for life in the world changes, but since they are hardened and crystallized, they change more slowly than life itself changes, and sometimes they exert a deadening influence on men's lives.

Finally, and implied in all that has gone before, is the idea of the culture-epoch theory of change in the world which will be used, when it seems to fit, throughout the remainder of this book. It carries with it the idea of constant change in the world as our basic ideas of the nature of the world change. It implies that certain groups within a population are primarily responsible for change: the pure thinkers who give us our concepts of reality; the philosophers in each of the great areas of learning who formulate the structure of idea in these different areas; the artists who perform a great and important function in society by revealing meanings for life in times of confusion and chaos, who harmonize the conflicts which exist within individual lives and give those lives meaning, purpose, and direction; and finally the intellectuals who build the institutions by which we regulate many of the affairs of our every-day existence.

This same theory of history embodies a belief, which will be generally followed in this study, that each epoch has a beginning, a middle, and end.

The beginning is frequently chaotic and confused; the middle is often marked by the work of the great artists, and the end is usually one of harmony and balance. In the events of actual history, however, this does not seem always to be the case, and we shall not try to squeeze the facts of history into a scheme, which, like all theories of history, is but one of man's great interpretations of the problems of change, of cause and effect, which have moved through his life on the earth.

EXERCISES

1. In reading this chapter, the student's first job is to understand the idea of "reality." We are so accustomed to our present idea that it is very difficult to grasp any other idea of what is real.

2. In examining the modified culture-epoch theory which is to be used in this book, be sure to understand the three periods which are present in most epochs: the period of change and chaos, the period of adjustment, and the period of balance.

3. What is the role of each of the following groups of people in promoting change within an epoch: the pure thinkers, the artists, and the intellectuals?

4. At the end of a later chapter, one will find a story by Wilbur Daniel Steele entitled "The Man Who Saw Through Heaven." In it a single man experiences a fundamental change in his basic philosophy. Compare the stages of his personal change with the culture-epoch theory for mankind as a whole. Who represents the pure thinkers? How does art enter into the process of change? Through what stages does his thought, indeed, his entire personality, move from the beginning of the story to the end?

A Common Basis
for Understanding the Arts

Several years ago the writer read a paragraph which puzzled him, and which he could not believe. The paragraph, written by an important Shakespearian scholar and literary critic, made the statement that in his tragedies Shakespeare had made discoveries as important as those made by any scientist. Such an assertion is hard to accept, even by a person whose chief interest is a study of literature and the arts in general. It is only after some years of thought that the truth of the statement becomes apparent; yet this idea can give us a basis for understanding the arts, and is presented here for that purpose.

Let us put it this way: Two worlds exist. One is the world external to ourselves. It consists of the earth, the sun and moon, and the whole universe. It also consists of molecules and atoms. The studies of this world include physics, chemistry, biology, geology, geography, and the other sciences. Another world exists within the human personality and human experience. This last world is no less complicated, and is less well known than the first. Furthermore, discoveries within the realm of the personality are as important as are discoveries within the atom or the universe. Knowing the truth about ourselves and our experience is certainly as vital as knowing the truth about cosmic rays.

Now, it is obvious that the scientist investigates the world-outside-of-man. Because of the tremendous strides which the scientists have made in their discoveries and because their findings lie outside of us and are plain to our senses and minds, we have come to place a value on them higher than the value which we place on the humanistic discoveries. It is less apparent that the artist also makes discoveries. His findings are the discoveries within the world of human personality and experience.

In one respect artistic discovery differs from scientific discovery. To illustrate the point, one might well ask, "But if the great artists make discoveries about the human personality, and there have been so many artists, haven't all or most of the discoveries been made by now?" The answer is no. Artistic discoveries do not add to each other in any sort of arithmetical way, so that, at some time in the future, we can say that we have built a solid and complete structure of knowledge about the personality and its experience. In one respect this condition finds a similarity in scientific investigation, since the findings of a scientist in one stage of history are refined or discarded completely in another; yet each was regarded as truth in its own time.

The artist, however, deals with more relative material than the scientist, for artistic truth is largely individual. It depends as much upon the background and personality of the artist as it does upon the raw material of experience. One might take, for example, the treatment which two artists make of the same theme: let us say the futility of the life of a woman who, in herself, is a complete blank, but who moves from man to man, husband to husband, and lives only as she reflects these successive men. The student is referred to Dorothy Parker's story, "Big Blonde," and Chekov's story, "The Darling," for concrete evidence. Although the experience is the "same," the feeling of the two artists is quite different, and the experience of the reader, too, is very different as he re-lives the same thing in two different forms, created by two different artists. The reader might protest, "But one of them must be right about this kind of woman, and one of them must be wrong." Actually, both are right, and any other artist who treated the same material with different feelings might also be right. This discovery is almost entirely a personal matter, and the corollary is that the realm of truth in personality and experience, the area of truth in the arts, is inexhaustible. The person who appreciates any work of art grows with each new facet of experience which he lives through with the artist, and growth in this sense is limited only by the ability-for-experience of the beholder.

One may immediately wonder if the psychologists have not taken over the realm of the artists and beaten them at their own game, for the psychologists, too, are concerned with human personality and experience. Their discoveries have been nearly as earth-shaking as those of the scientists. The answer, however, remains in the negative. The psychologist, because of the very nature of his study, is on the outside, looking in. He may describe patterns of frustration and aggression; he may analyze the functions of the brain to discover that it is the pre-frontal lobe which is involved with many of our highest and most delicate emotions, but he is always describing from the outside. In reality, he is describing the raw material with which the artist works. One aspect of truth and meaning, perhaps the most important aspect, lies in personal experience with the raw data of the scientist and the psychologist. For example, we may come close to the idea of grief over the death of a loved one as we see that grief in a personal friend. We may form ideas about death as we read of it in essays and in scientific treatises. We do not really *know* about it until we have experienced, for ourselves, the death of a loved one—or lived through it in literature or one of the other arts. Then we know what it *really means*; its *truth*. It is the function of the artist to discover such truth and such meaning. His discoveries are as important as those of any scientist investigating the world-outside-of-men.

The triumph of science has been reached because of its methods, of which there are at least two. Of these, the one which is most common is called "the scientific method," and involves certain well recognized steps. First, the scientist becomes aware of a problem which involves raw materials which can be collected as data. He collects these data, and from observation makes an hypothesis. Then he gathers further data, observes these with great personal detachment, and emerges finally with a solution to his problem. This solution is one which can be checked by other scientists in other experiments. If such checking always yields the same answer, the scientist may be said to have discovered a portion of truth in his field. The second method, involving problems for which data cannot be gathered, uses a philosophic or logical method. In this case the scientist makes all the possible hypotheses and then checks to see which one is consistent. When only one is consistent, his conclusion is also accepted as true. With these methods the scientists have brought vast areas of knowledge into human ken.

Less well recognized is the fact that the artists in literature, painting, sculpture, music and the other arts also have a method. We may call it the method of intuition or insight. In much the same way that the scientist starts out, the artist becomes aware of a problem in the realm of human experience, or he senses some aspect of the human personality which is dark and unknown. He cannot, of course, collect data which he will put under the microscope, as the scientist does, for in the very process of putting it under the microscope, the human element will vanish. Instead, the artist has an insight or intuition about this truth of personality or experience. This insight usually takes the form of seeing undiscovered relationships between many experiences and aspects of personality, of which the one under consideration is the most important. Since it is a problem of relationships, the truth which he seeks takes the shape of arranging the materials of the personality in proper order with respect to each other. In other words, the form (arrangement and relationship) is as important as the outcome in the artistic truth. The next step in the artistic process is the arrangement of the human material in a form which leads inevitably to the conclusion which our artist has intuited. This is the process of selecting incidents in literature, of visual elements in painting and sculpture, of themes (call them tunes, if you want) in musical composition, and of arranging these so that they come out at the point which the artist has seen by insight. In other words, this is the step which we call *composition*, a term which is common to all the arts. But how can the artist check his results? That is the job of readers and critics. After the composition, the artist turns his creation loose in the world. Many people examine it. If it is composed in such a way that the audience (readers, lookers, or hearers) *live through* the experience themselves (remember our example of knowing the truth of grief over the death of a loved one), and find that the artist has made a true statement of the experience in all its relationships; then the discovery of the artist is accepted as a truth wrested from the dark ignorance of his world.

One caution: The test of the artistic truth cannot be made by the general public, although their criticism may be valuable. A scientist, for example, would not allow the validity of his conclusions to be tested by a plumber, a newsboy, and a meat-cutter. He asks that his truths be tested by the experiments of scientists who are his equals in scientific knowledge. There is a little difference between the scientist and the artist, but the difference is not too marked. We could argue that since the butcher, the baker, and the candle-stick maker are human personalities, they might be accepted as valid critics of the artist's discovery. To a certain extent this claim is true. On the other hand, certain people can read with more discernment than others. Some are excellent at understanding the language of painting, sculpture, or music. And, perhaps more important, some people are more sensitive than others to the problems of personality and experience. These people, those who can understand the medium of expression and who are sensitive to human problems, must constitute the group of judges for the validity of a work of art.

The next question for consideration is the nature of the raw materials for artistic investigation. The raw materials for scientific study are all around us. They are all growing things, all inanimate objects, the universe, and the elements, the molecules, and the atoms. It is easy to sense these. But the raw materials of the artist-discoverer are harder to see. Most obvious are the many facets of such emotions as love, hatred, jealousy, contentment, sudden apprehension of the beauty of nature or people, and other feelings of the same sort. As a matter of fact, these materials from life are so common that it is probable that the great bulk of art is made from them, but there is much more material which has been explored in literature, art, and music. Much of this the psychologists have discussed in learned treatises; the artists present it as experience which the members of the artistic audience may live through. It must be pointed out that the artist does not wait until he has read what some psychologist has written, for example, about the psychological experience which confronts a young prince who has been humanely educated, who faces a problem of evil involving the murder of his father, the king, and the unfaithfulness, even incest, of his mother. (In other words, the problem Shakespeare explored in *Hamlet*.) Rather, the artist feels this problem within himself and composes its elements and its solution. Psychology and literature may run parallel to each other; the former gives facts, the latter gives truth-to-life. This truth is achieved because we become personally involved in the work of literature, live through the complexities of the problem with all their attendant, opposing emotions, and sense the logic, the rightness, and the freedom of the solution when it is reached.

Let us return to our original statement: The artist is an explorer of the world-within-ourselves, and his discoveries are as important as those of any comparable scientist. Why has this been so little recognized? We are living in a time which places most of its values in external things. Life is measured largely in terms of possessions, seldom in terms of greatness of individual personality. It is science, as its discoveries are harnessed by engineering skill, which produces the material things which we value. Furthermore, the discoveries of science are apparent to our senses. It is easy to know when we or our neighbor has acquired a new car. It is extremely difficult to know when we or our neighbor has acquired the growth of personality which comes with the discovery of the peculiar welding of thought and action which we live in *Hamlet*. Because of reasons like these, art has become of less and less value in our age, and the importance of any discovery, scientific or humanistic, is only the importance that people give it in their minds. In the study we are now undertaking, we make the bold claim that the materialistic world has run its course. People have a need for the humanities. As soon as the need is realized, the artistic discoveries will be ranked as of equal importance with the scientific.

Perhaps one more consideration is necessary before we turn to examples of the explorations and discoveries of the artists. This consideration is that of the place and importance of form. Let us put it this way: Human experience is seldom simple or direct. Rather, its importance is frequently clouded with events of no importance, many of which are totally irrelevant. Perhaps the best illustration of this may be found in the artist who is painting a landscape. His purpose is not to make a direct copy from nature—a camera would do a better job than a human being. Rather, the painter is seeking to interpret an experience with beauty. The natural scene, however, is cluttered with objects detracting from the impression which the artist seeks. Consequently, he leaves many out, he rearranges in his mind and on his canvas the objects which he sees, so that the picture, when complete, is not a copy of nature, but a picture of beauty, with the natural objects selected and arranged to make the meaning clear. But no critic, nor commentator, perhaps not even the artist himself, could give us a definite, final statement as to what that

"meaning" is. Perhaps it is a sense of the importance of peace, quiet, repose; perhaps it is the wonder of organization, order, design; perhaps it is the sheer joy of contrasting colors, the delight in appearances of objects, their texture and feel. If it could be expressed definitely in words, the picture would not be necessary; but since it cannot, it is the only means by which the artist can share his delight in the world. And the imperative need to share it, to get it "said," is the quality that makes the artist; he does not only what he can, but what he *must*. Somehow, that creative urge, which everyone shares to some extent, is communicated to an audience; theorists of "aesthetic experience" do not agree on the "how": it helps little to say that the picture "speaks for itself." However little understood the process, the fact remains that people throughout the years have enjoyed (the word is too weak: *needed*) the making of pictures and the looking at them. The great point is that the good artist has made the picture do something to the beholder, partly through the subject-matter, partly through the form of the picture itself.

It is interesting that this element of form which all of the arts have in common, also gives them the "living-through" quality which we have noted as distinctive of artistic truth. For example, you will soon read a story called "The Man Who Saw Through Heaven." One reader's interpretation of the theme of the story might be stated in this way, "Men are afraid to live without the security of a belief in a Higher Being. So, when their absolute ideas of God are shattered by the light of science, they must go through the whole experience of the race, constructing God in the image of the highest living organism, until their final and highest conception is of a kind, loving, and personal God, much like the highest ideal of Man, the Father." Now such a statement of the meaning of the story is all right, but it is not very important. What *is* important is the process of the story which lets the reader live through the experience, seeing all that Mr. Diana felt as he struggled upward toward his final truth. It is the process, not the end result, which is important. It is the form, not the final statement, which yields artistic truth. This is not to say that the artists' final point is unimportant. It is to say that its importance lies in having gone through the experience with the artist and having arrived with him at the discovery which he finally wishes to communicate. With this in mind, let us examine some examples of art to see how the artist has discovered truth from the chaos and darkness of the human personality and its experiences.

A caution might well be stated before we launch upon the example. The caution is that we are speaking without the artist, and that the statements made about the meaning of a picture are only those of a single onlooker. With this in mind, we may go ahead.

Suppose the artist were interested in the ultimate tragedy of the human condition as was Picasso in his picture "The Tragedy." How does he convey his meaning? First one might discuss the element of color. The artist has used dark blues, black and pale green while the faces of his figures and all of the flesh tones are livid white. With this use of color he has created the somber effect which he wishes. One may note too the lines and repetition of lines. The figures are probably unduly elongated while the bent heads of the three figures each repeat an identical curve. A broken line starting vertically and then breaking and falling has the psychological effect of decay and desolation. These are the lines which Picasso has used. An interesting aspect of his painting is that he has broken the long vertical lines of his human figures with two horizontal lines: the breaking of the waves on the shore and the horizon line just above the center of the picture.

This picture is one of almost unrelieved gloom. A note of contrast is introduced with the white wavelets but that is all. The artist is here speaking not of any particular tragedy; there is no story which could be connected with this work of art. Instead he is concerned with the total tragedy of the human condition. This is borne out by the arrangement of arms held close to the body and in sharp right angles. It is as if the characters were hugging to themselves a sense of grief too profound to be expressed in words. It is interesting to trace the vertical lines in the woman's skirt, almost Greek in their simplicity, leading upward to the bent head. Then the eye moves to the bent head of the man and is carried down the sloping shoulders to the figure of the son and thence back down to the feet which carry the eye across again so that the central structural element is an elongated oval. Another interesting fact is the use of short straight lines and right angles to express what is perhaps a masculine quality since both the man and the boy have their arms arranged in this line pattern. The figure of the woman is essentially curved and monolithic. Picasso's arrangement of color and the repetitions involved are almost equal interest. The green of the earth and foreground is repeated in the coat of the boy and is followed by three different shades of blue. Above the horizon line we have a fairly light blue, the sea below it is darker, and the garments of the human figures are even darker. Here again he is expressing the element of *human* tragedy, since in the midst of the somber landscape it is the human figures which express the darkest and therefore the most tragic elements.

In all of this we have been discussing matters of form. We have been dealing with effects which might be talked of in terms of line, of color, of direction, of rhythm, of dominance, and of unity. Picasso has discovered a truth about life and humanity and has expressed this truth in terms of form.

The precautionary note which headed the discussion of the picture is an interesting one as it relates to the medium of the artist. Painting stands about midway between literature and music insofar as indefiniteness of meaning is concerned. Because literature uses words which have a fairly definite meaning in their context, the meaning is approximately clear. In literature there are some levels of meaning ranging deeper and deeper from the simple "story" meaning, and careful readers can uncover greater and greater depth of meaning as they read. In painting, the observer is much more on his own. As long as his interpretation does not violate the form of the painting, he can make his own meaning—or make none at all except an emotional response. The symbols of painting are much less definite than those of literature. It was for that reason that the precautionary note was placed before the discussion. The interpretation is a personal one; another person could give a different interpretation and still be "right." The variety of meanings is one of the glories of this art.

Music is almost pure form, and it is seldom that a definite "story" interpretation can be given to a musical selection. Most untutored listeners have one of two responses to music. When they think they are listening carefully and intelligently, they arrive at some sort of story, which usually sounds something like this: This person is in love, and then his girl leaves him, and right at the end she comes back and everything is dandy. The other listening attitude is simply to bathe in the sound, without distinguishing anything. Usually, such a listener finds his attention wandering off in a thousand directions before a musical selection of any length is finished. In other words, he finds himself paying attention to everything except the music.

But music, except for program music, which has a story to tell in sound and often employs sounds found in ordinary life, is pure form in sound. It is one of the "time arts," which makes it particularly elusive since, by the time it is heard, it is gone. Consequently, it makes greater demands on its audience, both in knowledge and attention, than do any of the other arts. The knowledgeable and attentive listener, however, finds that living through a musical selection yields as much meaning for life's experiences as does any of the other arts. In its structures one may find the grandeur of Bach, the intricate ornamentation of a Handel oratorio, the deceptively simple single line, horizontal melody of Gregorian chant, or the protest which is sometimes characteristic of good jazz. Whatever the significance of a musical selection, it is the composition that counts. As much as in any of the other arts, perhaps more, the musical composer must arrange his material so the listener lives through an experience which lies deeper than words or the recognizable subject matter of painting. It is this process of composition which leads to "living through," which is our concern in this chapter since it is the common basis for all the arts.

Let us try an example from literature to see how an artist gives form to his raw material in this art medium. Imagine, if you can, an entire civilization just emerging from an almost savage state; a people whose religious beliefs are in chaos. They have believed for generations and centuries in a god who was essentially whimsical—he alone did what he pleased, whenever he wished to act. Individuals and groups of people suffered from his whims or enjoyed good fortune from the same source. At any rate, there was nothing they could do about their deity except to be careful at all times for fear that they would offend him. But, we were saying, these people are emerging from savagery. They desire to go forward, and they are acquiring knowledge and skill which will carry them far—if they dare to use all of their new advantages. Over them, however, hangs the fearful image of their god whom they dare not displease.

Two other factors enter into the situation. The first is that these people recognize one power higher than their god. They may call it fate, destiny, or necessity. At any rate, it is a force in the universe, moving slowly and inexorably, carrying men and gods with it.

The other factor is the ideas which have been put forth by some philosophers. One philosopher has advanced the idea that the world is purely materialistic, and that there is no all-powerful being, except perhaps this force of necessity which brings about the happenings throughout the world in an almost accidental fashion. Another philosopher has proposed the idea that all things are moving and changing, but that the change is directed by a single great Wisdom or Mind. This, of course, rules out the old idea of the all-powerful, whimsical god. A third philosopher, discovering some of the great and seemingly universal truths of mathematics, has announced that the only reality in the world lies in mathematical relationships, which are sure and predictable.

Here, then, is the problem which the author faces. In the first place, the people are miserably confused because of a questioning of their old religious beliefs. They desire to make great forward strides toward civilization; yet their old religion urges them to be extremely cautious. They recognize the greatest force in the world, Destiny or Fate. Finally, a whole new series of upstart beliefs have arisen which challenge the traditions of centuries. What can a man believe in this confusion of ideas? This was the raw material which the Greek author, Aeschylus, formed into meaningful truths in his three plays dealing with the god who was friendly to men, Prometheus. How did he give the ideas form?

It is necessary here to state that the analyzer of this work of art has considerable leeway, and may give his imagination full reign. This is true because two of the plays have been lost. Only the second remains to guide the reader.

Perhaps in the first play he showed how the whimsical god, Zeus, came to power; that it was an act of cruelty and force, and that Zeus, himself, might be overthrown. Also in the first play the author might have shown the pitiable state of men under Zeus. A third idea which might have been introduced was that of the total power of Necessity, or Fate.

In the second play, we see the situation become clear. Two characters appear representing the whimsical god. They are interestingly enough, Strength and Force. One of them says, "Only Zeus is truly free." This, at the time it is spoken, is true, except, of course, for Fate. In the same play we see men endowed with certain gifts: ambition, ability to reason, language, mathematics, fire, and certain skills such as the ability to work metal, and the like. With these skills men will inevitably work their way toward their own freedom, and in so doing they will collide with the freedom of Zeus. It is the old problem of the irresistible force meeting the immovable object. What will happen?

In the third play, the problem must be resolved. And, you will remember, there remains one factor of the problem which has not yet been brought into action. We have the new philosophies yet to be heard from. It is quite possible that the author examined them, and decided that either the one which imagined a great Wisdom ruling the universe or the one which imagined reality in terms of mathematical relationships could save the situation. It seems probable that the other philosophy must have been discarded, since it provided a world which could never be counted on; it was as unpredictable and uncertain as the old rule of Zeus. But either one of the other two would provide regularity under which men could work and prosper. Suppose, then, that the Greek author brought out the fact that Fate or Destiny was either this Wisdom or the sum of mathematical relationships. Zeus would have to bow to the superior power, and men, free within the limits set by the new belief, could develop their freedom.

Thus does an author give form to ideas. He invents people to express the different points of view, and slowly but inevitably draws his forces together until a crisis stage is reached. Then, from the form which he has created, he shows how the situation may be resolved, the two points of view reconciled, and harmony restored. The individual who sees this play or reads it will live through this experience and emerge from it a greater man for having felt the problem work out in form, within himself.

In such fashion the artist, whatever his medium—music, painting, literature—has made *form* the vehicle of *idea*, has made the raw materials of his art acquire significance by arrangement and handling. It is a different kind of meaning from that of the scientist, which can be perceived and measured in an objective world; for this sort of meaning can be perceived only by the individual who can see the relationships the artist has formulated, and who can find them valid in terms of his own experience. It is not an easy process, sometimes; and just as the effectiveness of the scientist depends upon two things—the validity of his discovery, and the ability of the beholder to understand or comprehend it—so the effectiveness of the artist depends upon the validity of his discovery, and the sensitivity of the beholder to apprehend it. "I don't get it" is no refutation of either Einstein or Bach.

But what of the person who has no knowledge of the arts, and who doubts his own sensitivity? Must he leave all painting to the painters, all music to the musicians, all sculpture to the sculptors? The answer is a blunt "Yes," unless such individual is willing to work for at least a minimum of understanding, and for an increase of his own sensitivity; but the answer is an emphatic "No!" for the person who is willing to co-operate with the artist, and with his own capacities for enjoyment and appreciation of the arts. No amount of talking can compare with the actual hearing of a piece of music, the actual seeing of a picture, statue, or building, the actual reading of a book. To know that there are principles like unity, balance, harmony, transition, is to make the first step toward perceiving them; the next step is to experience the music, picture, or book.

Not everyone will derive the same kind or degree of satisfaction from a particular art form, obviously; but the educated person owes himself the obligation of knowing that "there is something in it," even if that "something" does not move him deeply. And perhaps, with deeper acquaintance and wider knowledge, that "something" will become clearer and of greater value than before.

To summarize: In this chapter we have made the assertion that the artist is an explorer and discoverer in the realm of the human personality, and that his discoveries are as important as the comparable discoveries in science. The scientist uses his appropriate methods, the artist uses the method of intuition. Where the scientist investigates the world-outside-of-men, the artist's raw material lies in the human personality and in human experience, with their vast and unknown reaches, their disrupting conflicts. The artist gives form to the component elements of personality and experience, and in so doing yields his artistic truth. No matter whether we speak of literature, of painting, of sculpture, of music, or any of the other arts, this concept of creating form out of chaos is the single common basis and foundation for all aesthetics.

EXERCISES

1.

Chopin: Prelude (7)

Andantino   Opus 28, #7

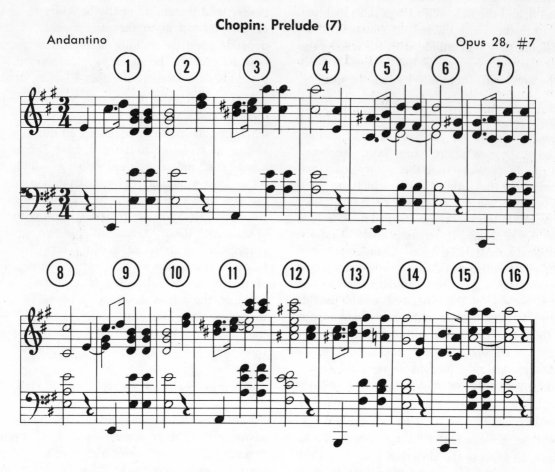

One *must* hear these sounds, preferably on the piano, as the composer intended; but at least with that "inward ear" that enables some people to read music as others read a poem. What is the mood the piece evokes—grave or gay? or something in between? What is the effect it produces: serenity? meditation? wistfulness? joy? sadness? The mood will probably vary not only from person to person, but from day to day with the same person! The point is not "What **does** this *mean*?"—with one definite, final, irrevocable an-

swer: but rather, how does *this* music accomplish, through its form, an effect upon the listener?

One notes, for one thing, a great deal of repetition: the rhythmic pattern is "la dum-ti ta, ta, dum" over and over, eight times in all. The second (repetition number one) group is higher than the first, the third still higher, the fourth lower, but not quite so low as the first time: and in the second half, the phrases make a different pattern—low to higher, low to higher, or to represent it graphically—

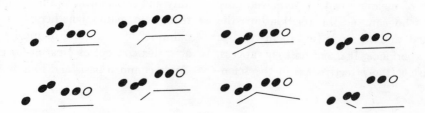

Only slight variations occur within the highly-repetitive six note phrase: sometimes the first two notes go up, or down, or remain the same; but with the last three, there is even less variety in the interval of the chord: it is mostly a sixth, or a third (which is only an upside-down sixth), until the "surprise" of measure 13, with its chord of many notes and strange harmony, followed by a downward-moving succession of intervals (fifth, sixth, seventh) in the next two measures. The expected (tonic) chord at the end is a welcome relief, a satisfying cadence (musical terms will be explained later), and we are content to stop.

The line of the melody throughout is contained within limited intervals: the last note of each phrase is not far distant from the first—the intervals are in each phrase a seventh, a fourth, a third, a fourth; a seventh, a seventh, a fourth—until the last phrase suddenly leaps one note over the octave. The effect is the release of something that has been held in for all the preceding measures, until at last it breaks out free.

The first four phrases are all on one of two chords—E-G#-B-D (the dominant) or A-C#-E (the tonic); the different pattern of the second half, with its varied chords in measures 13-14-15 ("modulation"), produce a strain that is relieved by return to the A-C#-E that we expect.

It is a wisp of a piece, slight, fragmentary, a mere breath—and yet it has achieved its own effect of wholeness and completeness. Suppose the composer had used a minor mode: try hearing it with all the C's natural, not sharped (except in measure 13). Try hearing it with the final phrase just like the fourth, on another position of the chord. Try hearing it in 4/4 rhythm, instead of 3/4. Try, in short, doing anything to the form beyond what the composer did with it; and you will hear it effectively ruined.

2.

Raphael painted his "Madonna della Seggiola" within a circle: why he did so does not especially matter—probably because he wanted to! But the decision once made, the problem of the arrangement within that circle was his to solve. How he did, the picture shows. Suppose that he had chosen some other arrangement of the Mother and Child: suppose he had (like Cimabue) presented her and the Babe face-on. Suppose he had turned the infant the other way. Being Raphael, he probably would have made a better design of it than these sketches would indicate! —but whatever the design he might have effected, the new picture would not have done what the present one does: it might have been better, or worse; it would certainly have been different. The "Madonna of the Chair" is what it is because it was designed the way it is; the flowing curves fitted together with their interweave of movement give the painting its quality of "cosiness" (if the word may be forgiven!), its intimately human appeal. The mother is not the "Virgin Enthroned", the baby is not God Incarnate, in this picture; the majesty and awe of the subsequent story are foregone to portray the most understandable, the most appealing of human relationships—simply Mother and Child.

Consider some other possible arrangements, not with a view of bettering or worsening Raphael's design, but in the hope of understanding more fully what this form, this arrangement, accomplishes. There's even a circle for you to try your hand in!

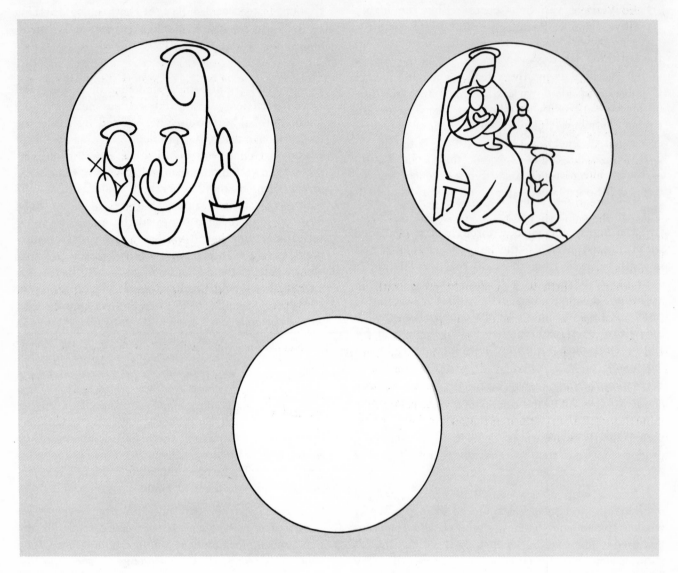

3.

Dirge in Woods

George Meredith

A wind sways the pines
    And below
Not a breath of wild air:
Still as the mosses that glow
On the flooring and over the lines
Of the roots here and there.
The pine-tree drops its dead:
They are quiet as under the sea.
    Overhead, overhead
Rushes life in a race
As the clouds the clouds chase:
    And we go,
And we drop like the fruits of the tree,
    Even we,
    Even so.

A Second Version

Pines in the wind are swaying.
    It is quiet down below;
Not one wild breath is straying
    Above the mosses that glow
Among the roots in wandering lines
    Upon the forest floor.
The needles quietly fall from the pines,
    Fall, and are no more.
As darkly green, as stilly quiet
    As under the sea, this place.
Look! overhead, in restless riot,
    The rushing clouds' wild chase!
But like the needles we shall fall,
    Nor run in life's swift race;
We all shall die—all, all.

A Third Version

> Above, wind in the pines;
> below, stillness—
> quiet as the mosses
> creeping over roots.
>   The pine needles drop, drop,
> quiet, dead.
> Overhead, the rushing clouds
> chasing each other.
>   We too die and become
> quiet: drop like dead leaves,
> like a dying wind
> vanish into silence.

Here are three ways of saying the same thing: or nearly the same thing. Yet two of these ways are definitely inferior, altho the words repeat, the ideas are like, and the "meaning" is similar. What makes the difference?

Perhaps a fourth way of straight prose, without versification, could convey the "meaning" more clearly, if by "meaning" we understand only the words and what they refer to; but there is—or should be—more to a poem than the words and their immediate, surface significance. For part of the stuff of the poem is its pattern, arrangement, design; the form is significant as well as the meanings of the words. It is to see better the effective form of one that we look at the other poorer versions.

Which one sounds most like a sermon, a teaching with a moral rather than like a poem? Which one is sing-song, so monotonous that your ear is distracted from meaning by the regularity of expected sound? Which one most effectively presents the three successive ideas, "Trees . . . Clouds . . . Ourselves"?

In the first version, what is gained by the short second line?

What is the effect of the succession of vowel sounds in "st*I*ll *A*s th*E* m*O*sses that gl*O*w"? (*the* is thə, not thi)

What is the effect of repeated sounds in "glow . . . flooring . . . over"?

Why is "overhead" repeated, and "clouds" (in the eleventh line)? Also the *r* sounds, and the sibilant *s*'s?

What is gained by the short line, "and we go"?

What is the effect of the near-repetition in the last two lines?

Again one might well ask, what does the poem gain by being a *poem*? It is not merely by the dictionary meanings of the words employed, but by the patterns of sound and arrangement, that the poet has achieved a meaning.

Reading the Literature Offered in the Humanities Course

One of the aims of the humanities course is to help students get more pleasure from their reading by developing the ability to get more meaning from literary works than they formerly did, for most people agree that an appreciation of literature as an art form is a valuable end in itself. In the second place, literary selections have been chosen here which yield their answers to the great questions of men concerning their relations to God, the universe, other men, and themselves. The development of new answers to these questions in each period of human history is one of the functions of artists in human society. This goal implies a principle of selection which has been used in choosing the literary works of this course. Those which have been chosen are nearly all serious works. They are chosen because the authors who wrote them had one or more of these questions in mind and were serious about proposing new answers. None of this is literature-to-entertain in the most shallow sense of that word. Not all literature needs to be read with the care which the selections in this course demand. The point is that this is all literature which has been found great by all sorts of readers in many ages. It is worth the most careful reading. The remarks about literature and the directions for specific reading which follow are designed to help you to appreciate this type of literature for itself and to help you find the ideas and meanings which will help you in the study of the humanities.

One might ask in the first place why an author writes. Obvious answers are that he wants to be rich and famous, and that he can achieve wealth and fame through writing. That is true, but for the sincere author (and artist of any kind) wealth and fame are goals of only secondary importance. Most writers say that they would have written books, plays, novels, essays, and stories even if they got no worldly rewards from them. Most authors do their work because they feel a sense of disturbance which will not leave them until they have put it down on paper.

The mental composure of an author is upset by a conflict of ideas, or by an idea which seems new to him. He puzzles about it as an inventor does until he finds a solution to his problem. He presents his work of art as his invention. Some of the greatest of the world's writers have made mental and emotional inventions or discoveries which rank in importance with the greatest mechanical ones. It is the work of some of these authors which is included in this course.

How Closely Should One Read Literature?

Many of us have developed habits of reading to get the general idea. When we consider the greatest of literature, this type of reading is not good enough. We can look at it this way: An author starts out with an entirely blank sheet of paper before him. He can put down on it whatever words he wants. For every word that an author writes, he has a choice of at least a hundred other words. For every sentence he has a choice of many different ways of saying almost the same thing. Yet an author consciously chooses to say exactly what he does, for he believes that he can accomplish his purpose best by using the words, the sentences, the paragraphs, and the larger blocks of organization in exactly the way that he finally puts them down. The writer, then, has a purpose for every word which he writes. If we wish to get his meaning fully, we must pay attention to each word and each sentence.

As a matter of fact, one of the best ways to read literature is to stop every once in a while to ask why the author said a thing as he did rather than in another way. For example, in the story which follows these explanatory pages we find the sentence given just below. Then we can see the same general idea as a less skillful writer might have written it. What is the difference?

The Author's Sentence:

"Accept as he would with the top of his brain the fact of a spherical earth zooming through space, deep in his heart he knew that the world lay flat from modern Illinois to ancient Palestine, and that the sky above it, blue by day and by night festooned with guiding stars for wise men, was the nether side of a floor on which the resurrected trod."

The Unskilled Writer's Sentence:

"Although he accepted in his mind the fact that the earth was a sphere travelling through space, yet in his deepest emotions he knew that it was flat and that the sky was the under-side of the floor of heaven."

Why, for example, does Mr. Steele say that the world "lay flat from modern Illinois to ancient Palestine" instead of simply saying that it was flat, as the other writer did? Perhaps he wanted to suggest an expanse of time, from the modern world back to the time of Christ, as well as an expanse of space. Why did he describe the sky as he did rather than plainly using the word *sky*, as the unskilled writer did? There is the possibility that while he was stating a fact about a man's belief concerning the physical structure of the earth he also wanted to suggest a religious significance to the belief. So he mentioned the stars and the wise men to flood our memories with the story of the birth of Christ. The two sentences differ in at least one more phase of meaning. The unskilled writer's sentence has no rhythm, while Steele's sentence reads in long undulations of sound. This kind of rhythm puts us in a philosophic frame of mind which creates the kind of atmosphere which he wanted. It is for such reasons that the author chose exactly the words he did, and arranged them as he did. For its purpose in the story it is a much better sentence than that of the unskilled writer. Perhaps this illustration makes the point that the literature for this course must be read very carefully if we are to get the author's meaning fully.

While You Are Reading, Stop and Think

The illustration given above suggests that there is as much meaning contained in the overtones and connotations of the words as there is in the words themselves. When the author spoke of "guiding stars for wise men," he intended that the reader should pause and let the memories of the Nativity come into his mind. Almost all literary writers choose words that have such connotative value, and which suggest all sorts of things to think about which lie outside of the story itself. The best reader is the one who sees the most relationships between the thing which he is reading and ideas, feelings, and facts which are suggested by the written words.

As a matter of fact, the incidents and plot of a story, a novel, or a play are frequently the least important parts of it. It is for this reason that the same story or plot can be used by many different authors, yet each literary work will be different. As an example, the story which you will read of the killing of a Greek king and his wife by the wife's son was used by all of the important Greek playwrights, and was also used by one of the contemporary French dramatists, Jean-Paul Sartre, in his play, *The Flies*. A member of an audience attending any one of these plays knows exactly what is going to happen. He is not paying his money to find out how the story comes out, for he knows that already. He attends the play to see what new meanings an author or an actor reveals in his interpretation of the incidents of the plot. This meaning is found in the new revelations of human character which the author finds and in the new relationships between the story and events and incidents in the outside world which the writer suggests. These types of meaning are gained only when a reader pauses and thinks carefully about what is written and lets his mind and imagination move freely about in the suggestions which the author's words and sentences give him.

There is at least one other kind of thinking which the reader must do if he is to read literature well. He must understand the author thoroughly. Such understanding comes only when one stops and thinks. Again an example is not out of order. In the play *Prometheus Bound* which you will read later, we find these three interesting speeches:

PROMETHEUS: Through me mankind ceased to foresee death.

THE CHORUS: What remedy could heal that sad disease?

PROMETHEUS: Blind hopes I made to dwell in them.

Here is a place to stop and think. How could blind hopes make men cease to foresee death? And why blind hopes rather than clear ones? Could the author mean something like this? "As long as men imagine that death is waiting for them just around the corner (as indeed it may be) they will do nothing. But if they have hope and ambition which is blind enough not to take death into consideration, they will live as if they were going to live forever. They will undertake great works, and make great plans and attempt to carry them out. If so, this gift of blind hope for the future and for the accomplishment of purposes does make men cease to foresee death, and is, in truth, a very great gift. Without it we would all live in fear and do nothing." Having stopped our reading to think through the meaning as carefully as this, the speeches acquire significance much beyond their length. It is only when we work out such meanings that great literature really shows its greatness.

How Much Meaning Is There in Literature?

It is a favorite statement of students that teachers of literature read meanings into it that authors never intended. To a certain extent this is true, for a piece of literature has many possible meanings, and they are, in part, at least, the product of the reader as well as of the writer. Such meanings, of course, depend upon the experience of the reader and the associations which he makes through the connotations of words and phrases, as that aspect of meaning has just been discussed. The more experience a reader has had, the more relationships he will see between the piece of literature and the world outside. It is for this reason that a person can read such a play as *Hamlet* over and over again, and with each reading get more meaning from it. We may conclude, then, that a piece of literature may have many meanings and many facets of meaning. They are partly the creation of the reader.

May we conclude, too, that the meaning depends entirely upon the reader? We think not. After all, the author has something to say about all of this. In his work he sets some boundaries beyond which the reader cannot go in his interpretation without violating these limits. A reader cannot safely say, "I don't see the meaning which you propose; therefore, it isn't there." Nor can he say, "I get such and such a meaning from this sentence and because I do, it's there." While the limits that the author sets are not absolute and do allow for wide interpretations, nevertheless, the limits are there.

Furthermore, we must try to come as close to the author's meaning as possible. After all, we are reading to gain new experience and new insights, not merely to catch a reflection of the experience and insights which we already have. The author has something to say. Many people have found it important. The best method of reading, then, is to get as close to the author's meaning as possible first, and then we may be free to agree or disagree or react in any other way that we like.

The way to discover the author's meaning is to read slowly and carefully in the manner already discussed. From our thoughts we can make partial judgments about meaning. Then we must carry these partial judgments in our mind as we read further. If they ring true throughout the whole course of the piece of literature, we can accept them as part of the author's intended meaning. If these meanings seem to be contradicted later in the work, we must stop and reorganize our meaning to fit the new situation. Fortunately a writer usually has a definite pattern or organization for his materials so that it is not difficult to follow the ideas through if we read carefully.

We might conclude with such a statement as this: Any sincere literary work is almost a little world within itself. It has its own mood, its own characters, and its own little history. As with all worlds, many discoveries and many meanings are to be found within it. The work itself is enriched as readers discover new meanings and new facets of meaning within it. Such new interpretations are valid as long as the reader stays within the framework provided by the author. The new meanings must check all the way through with the other facts, the mood, and the characters of the little world of the story, play, or poem. If they do, then both reader and literary selection are enriched by the discovery.

A Pattern for a Novel, a Short Story, Or a Play

To begin with, the action of a story, a play, or a novel usually takes place in a fairly short time. Usually there is quite a history of events leading up to the ones which the author is to describe. The reader should know this history if he is to understand the events which are to be related in the literary work. This is usually the first job of the author, and if the reader will examine many stories he will usually find the author takes time very early in the piece to tell as much as is needed about the characters and what has happened to them before the story opens.

Another part of the design of a story that is usually found quite early is a statement of a theme or problem which the author intends to work out. Frequently this theme is worked out in the conflict of two ideas. For example, in one of the Greek plays which you are soon to read, the theme may be stated in such a way as this: "What kind of power can be attributed to a God in the face of the growing power and maturity of mankind?" Then the author proceeds to take an absolute god who rules by fear and force and pit him against a symbol of maturing mankind. It is supposed that by the end of the play he will have worked out a solution which will allow both men and gods proper zones of action. The author seldom states his theme as badly as it has been stated above. More frequently he makes suggestions and gives hints which will lead the reader to think about the same problem which he has in mind. But if the reader proceeds carefully he can usually find the theme stated fairly early in the story or play or novel. As we have just said, it is frequently expressed in a conflict between two ideas.

The remainder of the literary work is usually devoted to the working out of the conflict between the ideas so that at the end one sees a synthesis of the opposing ideas into a new one, or the triumph of one of the ideas. The careful reader can watch the steps of the conflict and at the end can see how the writer brings his resolution of forces and ideas, and establishes harmony after the conflict.

One more word needs to be said about the conclusion. In great literature the conclusion is seldom if ever a "moral." The author simply reveals something new. A moral is a generalization about right or wrong in human conduct. Literature usually does not make such generalizations. Let us draw an analogy here. When Columbus discovered a vast new continent, his discovery had no implication of goodness and badness, and no generalization. What the discovery did was to open up new and unexplored realms for exploration, and as such it was a great awakening for the imaginations and thoughts of people. That is exactly what great literature does. It gives us whole new areas in which our minds, our imaginations, and our emotions may range and in which they may conduct new explorations.

General directions about the reading of literature may not be of much help in actual practice. It may be better to do a piece of reading to see how these directions work out. The story chosen for this practice has been selected for two reasons. In the first place, it is one of the best stories that the authors know. That in itself is good reason for including it here. Second, it is chosen because it is typical of the type of literature which is presented throughout this course. It deals with a very serious problem, that of the relation between the individual man and his God. It represents the period of chaos in the life of a man when old beliefs are crumbling, and new answers to the great questions of men must be found. The work of the pure thinkers, of the scientists in this case, is found in the information which the Reverend Hubert Diana discovers in the astronomical observatory. It is interesting too, that Diana finds his solution to the problem through artistic creation, for it is through his work as a sculptor that he finds his answer. If we understand this story thoroughly, we will understand much of what is said in this chapter.

The problem which is raised in the story is the conflict within an individual between an "old-time" religion and the findings of modern science. Let us see how the author resolves this conflict.

The Man Who Saw Through Heaven

Wilbur Daniel Steele

People have wondered (there being obviously no question of romance involved) how I could ever have allowed myself to be let in for the East African adventure of Mrs. Diana in search of her husband. There were several reasons. To begin with, the time and effort and money weren't mine; they were the property of the wheel of which I was but a cog, the Society through which Diana's life had been insured, along with the rest of that job lot of missionaries. The "letting in" was the firm's. In the second place, the wonderers have not counted on Mrs. Diana's capacity for getting things done for her. Meek and helpless. Yes, but God was on her side. Too meek, too helpless to move mountains herself, if those who happened to be handy didn't move them for her then her God would know the reason why. Having dedicated her all to making straight the Way, why should her neighbor cavil at giving a little? The writer for one, a colonial governor-general for another, railway magnates, insurance managers, *safari* leaders, the ostrich farmer of Ndua, all these and a dozen others in their turns have felt the hundred-ton weight of her thin-lipped meekness—have seen her in metaphor sitting grimly on the doorsteps of their souls.

A third reason lay in my own troubled conscience. Though I did it in innocence, I can never forget that it was I who personally conducted Diana's party to the Observatory on that fatal night in Boston before it sailed. Had it not been for that kindly intentioned "hunch" of mine, the astounded eye of the Reverend Hubert Diana would never have gazed through the floor of Heaven, and he would never have undertaken to measure the Infinite with the foot rule of his mind.

It all started so simply. My boss at the shipping-and-insurance office gave me the word in the morning. "Bunch of missionaries for the *Platonic* tomorrow. They're on our hands in a way. Show 'em the town." It wasn't so easy when you think of it: one male and seven females on their way to the heathen; though it was easier in Boston than it might have been in some other towns. The evening looked the simplest. My friend Krum was at the Observatory that semester; there at least I was sure their sensibilities would come to no harm.

On the way out in the street car, seated opposite to Diana and having to make conversation, I talked of Krum and of what I knew of his work with the spiral nebulae. Having to appear to listen, Diana did so (as all day long) with a vaguely indulgent smile. He really hadn't time for me. That night his life was exalted as it had never been, and would perhaps never be again. Tomorrow's sailing, the actual fact of leaving all to follow Him, held his imagination in thrall. Moreover, he was a bridegroom of three days with his bride beside him, his nerves at once assuaged and thrilled. No, but more. As if a bride were not enough, arrived in Boston, he had found himself surrounded by a very galaxy of womanhood gathered from the four corners; already within hours one could feel the chaste tentacles of their feminine dependence curling about the party's unique man: already their contacts with the world of their new lives began to be made through him; already they saw in part through his eyes. I wonder what he would have said if I had told him he was a little drunk.

In the course of the day I think I had got him fairly well. As concerned his Church he was at once an asset and a liability. He believed its dogma as few still did, with a simplicity, "the old-time religion." He was born that kind. Of the stuff of the fanatic, the reason he was not a fanatic was that, curiously impervious to little questionings, he had never been aware that his faith was anywhere attacked. A self-educated man, he had accepted the necessary smattering facts of science with a serene indulgence, as simply so much further proof of what the Creator could do when He put His Hand to it. Nor was he conscious of any conflict between these facts and the fact that there existed a substantial Heaven, geographically up, and a substantial Hot Place, geographically down.

So, for his Church, he was an asset in these days. And so, and for the same reason, he was a liability. The Church must after all keep abreast of the times. For home consumption, with modern congregations, especially urban ones, a certain streak of "healthy" skepticism is no longer amiss in the pulpit; it makes people who read at all more comfortable in their pews. A man like Hubert Diana is more for the cause than a hundred. But what to do with him? Well, such things arrange themselves. There's the Foreign Field. The blacker the heathen the whiter the light they'll want, and the solider the conception of a God the Father enthroned in a Heaven of which the sky above them is the visible floor.

And that, at bottom, was what Hubert Diana believed. Accept as he would with the top of his brain the fact of a spherical earth zooming through space, deep in his heart he knew that the world lay flat from modern Illinois to ancient Palestine, and that the sky above it, blue by day and by night festooned with guiding stars for wise men, was the nether side of a floor on which the resurrected trod.

I shall never forget the expression of his face when he realized he was looking straight through it that night. In the quiet dark of the dome I saw him remove his eye from the eyepiece of the telescope up there on the staging and turn it, in the ray of a hooded bulb, on the demon's keeper, Krum.

"What's that, Mr. Krum? I didn't get you!"

"I say, that particular cluster you're looking at—"

"This star, you mean?"

"You'd have to count awhile to count the stars describing their orbits in that 'star,' Mr. Diana. But what I was saying—have you ever had the wish I

used to have as a boy—that you could actually look back into the past? With your own two eyes?"

Diana spoke slowly. He didn't know it, but it had already begun to happen; he was already caught. "I have often wished, Mr. Krum, that I might actually look back into the time of our Lord. Actually. Yes."

Krum grunted. He was young. "We'd have to pick a nearer neighbor than *Messier* 79 then. The event you see when you put your eye to that lens is happening much too far in the past. The lightwaves thrown off by that particular cluster on the day, say, of the Crucifixion—*you* won't live to see them. They've hardly started yet—a mere twenty centuries on their way—leaving them something like eight hundred and thirty centuries yet to come before they reach the earth."

Diana laughed the queerest catch of a laugh. "And—and there—there won't be any earth here, then, to welcome them."

"*What?*" It was Krum's turn to look startled. So for a moment the two faces remained in confrontation, the one, as I say, startled, the other exuding visibly little sea-green globules of sweat. It was Diana that caved in first, his voice hardly louder than a whisper.

"W-w-will there?"

None of us suspected the enormousness of the thing that had happened in Diana's brain. Krum shrugged his shoulders and snapped his fingers. Deliberately. *Snap!* "What's a thousand centuries or so in the cosmic reckoning?" He chuckled. "We're just beginning to get out among 'em with the *Messier*, you know. In the print room, Mr. Diana, I can show you photographs of clusters to which, if you cared to go, traveling at the speed of light—"

The voice ran on; but Diana's eye had gone back to the eyepiece, and his affrighted soul had re-entered the big black tube sticking its snout out of the slit in the iron hemisphere. . . . "At the speed of light!" . . . . That unsuspected, that wildly chance found chink in the armor of his philosophy! The body is resurrected and it ascends to Heaven instantaneously. At what speed must it be borne to reach instantaneously that city beyond the ceiling of the sky? At a speed inconceivable, mystical. At, say (as he had often said to himself), *the speed of light.* . . . And now, hunched there in the trap that had caught him, black rods, infernal levers and wheels, he was aware of his own eye passing vividly through unpartitioned emptiness, *eight hundred and fifty centuries at the speed of light!*

"And still beyond these," Krum was heard, "we begin to come into the regions of the spiral nebulae. We've some interesting photographs in the print room, if you've the time."

The ladies below were tired of waiting. One had "lots of packing to do." The bride said, "Yes, I do think we should be getting along, Hubert, dear; if you're ready—"

The fellow actually jumped. It's lucky he didn't break anything. His face looked greener and dewier than ever amid the contraptions above. "If you—you and the ladies, Cora—wouldn't mind—if Mr.—Mr.—(he'd mislaid my name) would see you back to the hotel—" Meeting silence, he began to expostulate. "I feel that this is a rich experience. I'll follow shortly; I know the way."

In the car going back into the city Mrs. Diana set at rest the flutterings of six hearts. Being unmarried, they couldn't understand men as she did. When I think of that face of hers, to which I was destined to grow only too accustomed in the weary, itchy days of the trek into Kavirondoland, with its slightly tilted nose, its irregular pigmentation, its easily inflamed lids, and long moist cheeks, like those of a hunting dog, glorying in weariness, it seems incredible that a light of coyness could have found lodgment there. But that night it did. She sat serene among her virgins.

"You don't know Bert. You wait; he'll get a perfectly wonderful sermon out of all that to-night, Bert will."

Krum was having a grand time with his neophyte. He would have stayed up all night. Immured in the little print room crowded with files and redolent of acids, he conducted his disciple "glassy-eyed" through the dim frontiers of space, holding before him one after another the likenesses of universes sister to our own, islanded in immeasurable vacancy, curled like glimmering crullers on their private Milky Ways, and hiding in their wombs their myriad "coal-pockets," star-dust foetuses of which—their quadrillion years accomplished—their litters of new suns would be born, to bear their planets, to bear their moons in turn.

"And beyond these?"

Always, after each new feat of distance, it was the same. "And beyond?" Given an ell, Diana surrendered to a pop-eyed lust for nothing less than light-years. "And still beyond?"

"Who knows?"

"The mind quits. For if there's no end to these nebulae—"

"But supposing there is?"

"An end? But, Mr. Krum, in the very idea of an ending—"

"An end to what we might call this particular category of magnitudes. Eh?"

"I don't get that."

"Well, take this—take the opal in your ring there. The numbers and distances inside that stone may conceivably be to themselves as staggering as ours to us in our own system. Come! that's not so far-fetched. What are we learning about the structure of the atom? —a nucleus (call it a sun) revolved about it eternal orbits by electrons (call them planets, worlds). Infinitesimal; but after all what are bigness and littleness but matters of comparison? To eyes on one of those electrons (don't be too sure there aren't any) its tutelary sun may flame its way across a heaven a comparative ninety million miles away. Impossible for them to conceive of a boundary to their billions of atomic systems, molecular universes. In that category of magnitudes its diameter is infinity; once it has made the leap into our category and become an opal it is merely a quarter of an inch. That's right, Mr. Diana, you may well stare at it: between *now* and *now* ten thousand histories may have come and gone down there. . . . And just so the diameter of our own cluster of universes, going over into another category, may be. . ."

"May be a . . a ring . . a little stone . . in a . . a —ring."

Krum was tickled by the way the man's imagination jumped and engulfed it.

"Why not? That's as good a guess as the next. A ring, let's say, worn carelessly on the—well, say the tentacle—of s o m e vast organism—s o m e inchoate creature hobnobbing with its cloudy kind in another system of universes—which in turn—"

It is curious that none of them realized next day that they were dealing with a stranger, a changed man. Why he carried on, why he capped that night of cosmic debauch by shaving, eating an unremarkable breakfast, packing his terrestrial toothbrush and collars, and going up the gangplank in tow of his excited convoy to sail away, is beyond explanation—unless it was simply that he was in a daze.

It wasn't until four years later that I was allowed to know what had happened on that ship, and even then the tale was so disjointed, warped, and opinionated, so darkly seen in the mirror of Mrs. Diana's orthodoxy, that I had almost to guess what it was really all about.

"When Hubert turned irreligious. . . " T h a t phrase, recurrent on her tongue in the meanderings of the East African quest to which we were by then committed, will serve to measure her understanding. Irreligious! Good Lord! But from that sort of thing I had to reconstruct the drama. Evening after evening beside her camp fire (appended to the Mineral Survey Expedition Toward Uganda through the kindness—actually the worn-down surrender—of the Protectorate government) I lingered a while before joining the merrier engineers, watched with fascination the bumps growing under the mosquitoes on her forehead, and listened to the jargon of her mortified meekness and her scandalized faith.

There had been a fatal circumstance, it seems, at the very outset. If Diana could but have been seasick, as the rest of them were (horribly), all might still have been well. In the misery of desired death, along with the other contents of a heaving midriff, he might have brought up the assorted universes of which he had been led too rashly to partake. But he wasn't. As if his wife's theory was right, as if Satan was looking out for him, he was spared to prowl the swooping decks immune. Four days and nights alone. Time enough to digest and assimilate into his being beyond remedy that lump of whirling magnitudes and to feel himself surrendering with a strange n e w ecstasy to the drunkenness of liberty.

Such liberty! Given Diana's type, it is hard to imagine it adequately. The abrupt, complete removal of the toils of reward and punishment; the withdrawal of the surveillance of an all-seeing, all-knowing Eye; the windy assurance of being responsible for nothing, important to no one, no longer (as the police say) "wanted"! It must have been beautiful in those few days of its first purity, before it began to be discolored by his contemptuous pity for others, the mask of his inevitable loneliness and his growing fright.

The first any of them knew of it—even his wife —was in mid-voyage, the day the sea went down and the seven who had been sick came up. There seemed an especial Providence in the calming of the waters; it was Sunday morning and Diana had been asked to conduct the services.

He preached on the text: "For of such is the kingdom of Heaven."

"If our concept of God means anything it means a God all-mighty, Creator of all that exists, Director of the infinite, cherishing in His Heaven the saved souls of all space and all time."

Of course; amen. And wasn't it nice to feel like humans again, and real sunshine pouring up through the lounge ports from an ocean suddenly grown kind? . . . . But—then—what was Diana saying?

Mrs. Diana couldn't tell about it coherently even after a lapse of fifty months. Even in a setting as remote from that steamer's lounge as the equatorial bush, the ember-reddened canopy of thorn trees, the meandering camp fires, the chant and tramp somewhere away of Kikuyu porters dancing in honor of an especial largesse of fat zebra meat—even here her memory of that impious outburst was too vivid, too aghast.

"It was Hubert's look! The way he stared at us! As if you'd said he was licking his chops! . . . . That 'Heaven' of his!"

It seems they hadn't waked up to what he was about until he had the dimensions of his sardonic Paradise irreparably drawn in. The final haven of all right souls. Not alone the souls released from this our own tiny earth. In the millions of solar systems we see as stars how many millions of satellites must there be upon which at some time in their histories conditions suited to organic life subsist? Uncounted hordes of wheeling populations! Of men? God's creatures at all events, a portion of them reasoning. Weirdly shaped perhaps, but what of that? And that's only to speak of our own inconsiderable cluster of universes. That's to say nothing of other systems of magnitudes, where God's creatures are to our world what we are to the worlds in the atoms in our finger rings. (He had shaken his, here, in their astounded faces.) And all these, all the generations of these enormous and microscopic beings harvested through a time beside which the life span of our earth is as a second in a million centuries: all these brought to rest for an eternity to which time itself is a watch tick—all crowded to rest pellmell, thronged, serried, packed, packed to suffocation in layers unnumbered light-years deep. This must needs be our concept of Heaven if God is the God of the Whole. If, on the other hand—

The other hand was the hand of the second officer, the captain's delegate at divine worship that Sabbath day. He at last had "come to."

I don't know whether it was the same day or the next; Mrs. Diana was too vague. But here's t h e picture. Seven women huddled in the large stateroom on B deck, conferring in whispers, aghast, searching one another's eye obliquely even as they bowed their heads in prayer for some light—and all of a sudden the putting back of the door and the in-marching of the Reverend Hubert . . .

As Mrs. Diana tried to tell me, "You understand, don't you, he had just taken a bath? And he hadn't —he had forgotten to—"

Adam-innocent there he stood. Not a stitch. But I don't believe for a minute it was a matter of forgetting. In the high intoxication of his soul release, already crossed (by the second officer) and beginning to show his zealot claws, he needed some gesture stunning enough to witness to his separation, his unique rightness, his contempt of match-flare civilizations and infinitesimal taboos.

But I can imagine that stateroom scene: the gasps, the heads colliding in aversion, and Diana's six weedy feet of birthday suit towering in the shadows, and ready to sink through the deck I'll warrant, now the act was irrevocable, but still grimly carrying it off.

"And if, on the other hand, you ask me to bow down before a God peculiar to this one earth, this one grain of dust lost among the giants of space, watching its sparrows fall, profoundly interested in a speck called Palestine no bigger than the quadrillionth part of one of the atoms in the ring here on my finger—"

Really scared by this time, one of the virgins shrieked. It was altogether too close quarters with a madman.

Mad? Of course there was the presumption: "Crazy as a loon." Even legally it was so adjudged at the *Platonic's* first port of call, Algiers, where, when Diana escaped ashore and wouldn't come back again, he had to be given over to the workings of the French Law. I talked with the magistrate myself some forty months later, when, "let in" for the business as I have told, I stopped there on my way out.

"But what would you?" were his words. "We must live in the world as the world lives, is it not? Sanity is what? Is it, for example, an intellectual clarity, a balanced perception of the realities? Naturally, speaking out of court, your friend was of a sanity—of a sanity, sir—" Here the magistrate made with thumb and fingers the gesture only the French can make for a thing that is matchless, a beauty, a transcendent instance of any kind. He himself was Gallic, rational. Then, with a lift of shoulder: "But what would you? We must live in the world that seems."

Diana, impounded in Algiers for deportation, escaped. What after all are the locks and keys of this pinchbeck category of magnitudes? More remarkable still, there in Arab Africa, he succeeded in vanishing from the knowledge and pursuit of men. And of women. His bride, now that their particular mission had fallen through, was left to decide whether to return to America or to go on with two of the company, the Misses Brookhart and Smutts, who were bound for a school in Smyrna. In the end she followed the latter course. It was there, nearly four years later, that I was sent to join her by an exasperated and wornout Firm.

By that time she knew again where her husband-errant was—or where at least, from time to time in his starry dartings over this our mote of dust, he had been heard of, spoken to, seen.

Could we but have a written history of those years of his apostolic vagabondage, a record of the towns in which he was jailed or from which he was kicked out, of the ports in which he starved, of the ships on which he stowed away, presently to reveal himself in proselyting ardor, denouncing the earthlings, the fatelings, the dupes of bugaboo, meeting scoff with scoff, preaching the new revelation red-eyed, like an angry prophet. Or was it, more simply, like a man afraid?

Was that the secret, after all, of his prodigious restlessness? Had it anything in common with the swarming of those pale worms that flee the Eye of the Infinite around the curves of the stone you pick up in a field? Talk of the man without a country! What of the man without a universe?

It is curious that I never suspected his soul's dilemma until I saw the first of his mud-sculptures in the native village of Ndua in the province of Kasuma in British East. Here it was, our objective attained, we parted company with the government *safari* and shifted the burden of Way-straightening to the shoulders of Major Wyeside, the ostrich farmer of the neighborhood.

While still on the *safari* I put to Mrs. Diana a question that had bothered me: "Why on earth should your husband ever have chosen this particular neck of the woods to land up in? Why Kavirondoland?"

"It was here we were coming at the time Hubert turned irreligious, to found a mission. It's a coincidence, isn't it?"

And yet I would have sworn Diana hadn't a sense of humor about him anywhere. But perhaps it *wasn't* an ironic act. Perhaps it was simply that, giving up the struggle with a society blinded by "a little learning" and casting about for a virgin field, he had remembered this.

"I supposed he was a missionary," Major Wyeside told us with a flavor of indignation. "I went on that. I let him live here—six or seven months of it—while he was learning the tongue. I was a bit nonplused, to put it mildly, when I discovered what he was up to."

What things Diana had been up to the Major showed us in one of the huts in the native kraal—a round dozen of them, modeled in mud and baked. Blackened blobs of mud, that's all. Likenesses of nothing under the sun, fortuitous masses sprouting haphazard tentacles, only two among them showing pustules that might have been experimental heads. . . The ostrich farmer saw our faces.

"Rum, eh? Of course I realized the chap was anything but fit. A walking skeleton. Nevertheless, whatever it is about these beasties, there's not a nigger in the village has dared set foot inside this hut since Diana left. You can see for yourselves it's about to crash. There's another like it he left at Suki, above here. Taboo, no end!"

So Diana's "hunch" had been right. He had found his virgin field indeed, fit soil for his cosmic fright. A religion in the making, here before our eyes.

"This was at the very last before he left," Wyeside explained. "He took to making these mud pies quite of a sudden; the whole lot within a fortnight's time. Before that he had simply talked, harangued. He would sit here in the doorway of an evening with the niggers squatted around and harangue 'em by the hour. I knew something of it through my houseboys. The most amazing rot. All about the stars to begin with, as if these black baboons could half grasp *astronomy*! But that seemed all proper. Then there was talk about a something a hundred times as big and powerful as the world, sun, moon, and stars put together—some perfectly enormous stupendous awful being—but knowing how mixed the boys can get, it still seemed all regular—simply the parson's way of getting at the notion of an Almighty God. But no, they insisted, there wasn't any God. That's the point, they said; there *is no* God. . . Well, that impressed me as a go. That's when I decided to come down and get the rights of this star-swallowing monstrosity the beggar was feeding my labor on. And here he sat in the doorway with one of these beasties—here it is, this one—waving it furiously in the niggers' benighted faces. And do you know what he'd done?—you can see the mark here still on this wabble-leg, this tentacle business—he had taken off a ring he had and screwed it on just there. His ring, my word of honor! And still, if you'll believe it, I didn't realize he was just daft. Not until he spoke to me. 'I find,' he was good enough to enlighten me, 'I find I have to make it somehow concrete.' . . . 'Make what?'. . . 'Our wearer.' 'Our *what, where?*' . . . 'In the following category.' . . . His actual words, honor bright. I was going to have him sent down-country where he could be looked after. He got ahead of me though. He cleared out. When I heard he'd turned up at Suki I ought, I suppose, to have attended to it. But I was having trouble with leopards. And you know how things go."

From there we went to Suki, the Major accompanying. It was as like Ndua as one flea to its brother, a stockade inclosing round houses of mud, wattles, and thatch, and full of naked heathen. The Kavirondo are the nakedest of all African peoples and, it is said, the most moral. It put a great strain on Mrs. Diana; all that whole difficult anxious time, as it were detachedly, I could see her itching to get them into Mother Hubbards and cast-off Iowa pants.

Here too, as the Major had promised, we found a holy of holies, rather a dreadful of dreadfuls, "taboo no end," its shadows cluttered with hurlothrumbos of Diana's artistry. What puzzled me was their number. Why this appetite for experimentation? There was an uncertainty; one would think its effect on potential converts would be bad. Here, as in Ndua, Diana had contented himself at first with words and skyward gesticulations. Not for so long however. Feeling the need of giving his concept of the cosmic "wearer" a substance much earlier, he had shut himself in with the work, literally—a fever of creation. We counted seventeen of the nameless "blobs," all done, we were told, in seven days and nights before their maker had again cleared out. The villagers would hardly speak of him; only after spitting to protect themselves, their eyes averted, and in an undertone, would they mention him: "He of the Ring." Thereafter we were to hear of him only as "He of the Ring."

Leaving Suki, Major Wyeside turned us over (thankfully, I warrant) to a native who told us his name was Charlie Kamba. He had spent some years in Nairobi, running for an Indian outfitter, and spoke English remarkably well. It was from him we learned, quite casually, when our modest eight-load *safari* was some miles on its way, that the primary object of our coming was nonexistent. Hubert Diana was dead.

Dead nearly five weeks—a moon and a little—and buried in the mission church at Tara Hill.

Mission church! There was a poser for us. *Mission church?*

Well then, Charlie Kamba gave us to know that he was paraphrasing in a large way suitable to our habits of thought. We wouldn't have understood *his* informant's "wizard house" or "house of the effigy."

I will say for Mrs. Diana that in the course of our halt of lugubrious amazement she shed tears. That some of them were not tears of unrealized relief it would be hardly natural to believe. She had desired loyally to find her husband, but when she should have found him—what? This problem, sturdily ignored so long, was now removed.

Turn back? Never! Now it would seem the necessity for pressing forward was doubled. In the scrub-fringed ravine of our halt the porters resumed their

loads, the dust stood up again, the same caravan moved on. But how far it was now from being the same.

From that moment it took on, for me at least, a new character. It wasn't the news especially; the fact that Diana was dead had little to do with it. Perhaps it was simply that the new sense of something aimfully and cumulatively dramatic in our progress had to have a beginning, and that moment would do as well as the next.

Six villages: M'nann, Leika, Leikapo, Shamba, Tara and Little Tara, culminating in the apotheosis of Tara Hill. Six stops for the night on the road it had cost Diana as many months to cover in his singular pilgrimage to his inevitable goal. Or in his flight to it. Yes, his stampede. Now the pipers at that four-day orgy of liberty on the *Platonic's* decks were at his heels for their pay. Now that his strength was failing, the hosts of loneliness were after him, creeping out of their dreadful magnitudes, the hounds of space. Over all that ground it seemed to me we were following him not by the word of hearsay but, as one follows a wounded animal making for its earth, by the droppings of his blood.

Our progress had taken on a pattern; it built itself with a dramatic artistry; it gathered suspense. As though it were a story at its most breathless places "continued in our next," and I a reader forgetting the road's weariness, the dust, the torment of insects never escaped, the inadequate food, I found myself hardly able to keep from running on ahead to reach the evening's village, to search out the inevitable repository of images left by the white stranger who had come and tarried there awhile and gone again.

More concrete and ever more concrete. The immemorial compromise with the human hunger for a symbol to see with the eyes, touch with the hands. Hierarchy after hierarchy of little mud effigies—one could see the necessity pushing the man. Out of the protoplasmic blobs of Ndua, Suki, even M'nann, at Leikapo Diana's concept of infinity (so pure in that halcyon epoch at sea), of categories nested within categories like Japanese boxes, of an over-creature wearing our cosmos like a trinket, unawares, had become a mass with legs to stand on and a real head. The shards scattered about in the filth of the hut there (as if in violence of despair) were still monstrosities, but with a sudden stride of concession their monstrousness was the monstrousness of lizard and turtle and crocodile. At Shamba there were dozens of huge-footed birds.

It is hard to be sure in retrospect, but I do believe that by the time we reached Little Tara I began to see the thing as a whole—the foetus, working out slowly, blindly, but surely, its evolution in the womb of fright. At Little Tara there was a change in the character of the exhibits; their numbers had diminished, their size had grown. There was a boar with tusks and a bull the size of a dog with horns, and on a tusk and on a horn an indentation left by a ring.

I don't believe Mrs. Diana got the thing at all. Toward the last she wasn't interested in the huts of relics; at Little Tara she wouldn't go near the place; she was "too tired." It must have been pretty awful, when you think of it, even if all she saw in them was the mud-pie play of a man reverted to a child.

There was another thing at Little Tara quite as momentous as the jump to boar and bull. Here at last a mask had been thrown aside. Here there had been no pretense of proselyting, no astronomical lectures, no doorway harangues. Straightway he had arrived (a fabulous figure already, long heralded), he had commandeered a house and shut himself up in it and there, mysterious, assiduous, he had remained three days and nights, eating nothing, but drinking gallons of the foul water they left in gourds outside his curtain of reeds. No one in the village had ever seen what he had done and left there. Now, candidly, those labors were for himself alone.

Here at last in Tara the moment of that confession had overtaken the fugitive. It was he, ill with fever and dying of nostalgia—not these naked black baboon men seen now as little more than blurs—who had to give the Beast of the Infinite a name and a shape. And more and more, not only a shape, but a *shapeliness*. From the instant when, no longer able to live alone with nothingness, he had given it a likeness in Ndua mud, and perceived that it was intolerable and fled its face, the turtles and distorted crocodiles of Leikapo and the birds of Shamba had become inevitable, and no less inevitable the little Tara boar and bull. Another thing grows plain in retrospect: the reason why, done to death (as all the way they reported him) he couldn't die. He didn't dare to. Didn't dare to close his eyes.

It was at Little Tara we first heard of him as "Father Witch," a name come back, we were told,

from Tara, where he had gone. I had heard it pronounced several times before it suddenly obtruded from the native context as actually two English words. That was what made it queer. It was something they must have picked up by rote, uncomprehending; something then they could have had from no lips but his own. When I repeated it after them with a better accent they pointed up toward the north, saying "Tara! Tara!"—their eagerness mingled with awe.

I shall never forget Tara as we saw it, after our last blistering scramble up a gorge, situated in the clear air on a slope belted with cedars. A mid-African stockade left by some blunder in an honest Colorado landscape, or a newer and bigger Vermont. Here at the top of our journey, black savages, their untidy *shambas*, the very Equator, all these seemed as incongruous as a Gothic cathedral in a Congo marsh. I wonder if Hubert Diana knew whither his instinct was guiding him on the long road of his journey here to die. . .

He had died and he was buried, not in the village, but about half a mile distant, on the ridge; this we were given to know almost before we had arrived. There was no need to announce ourselves, the word of our coming had outrun us; the populace was at the gates.

"Our Father Witch! Our Father Witch!" They knew what we were after; the funny parrot-wise English stood out from the clack and clatter of their excited speech. "Our Father Witch! Ay! Ay!" With a common eagerness they gesticulated at the hilltop beyond the cedars.

Certainly here was a change. No longer the propitiatory spitting, the averted eyes, the uneasy whispering allusion to him who had passed that way: here in Tara they would shout him from the housetops, with a kind of civic pride.

We learned the reason for this on our way up the hill. It was because they were his chosen, the initiate.

We made the ascent immediately, against the village's advice. It was near evening; the return would be in the dark; it was a bad country for goblins; wouldn't tomorrow morning do? . . . . No, it wouldn't do the widow. Her face was set. . . And so, since we were resolved to go, the village went with us, armed with rattles and drums. Charlie Kamba walked beside us, sifting the information a hundred were eager to give.

These people were proud, he said, because their wizard was more powerful than all the wizards of all other villages "in the everywhere together." If he cared to he could easily knock down all the other villages in the "everywhere," destroying all the people and all the cattle. If he cared to he could open his mouth and swallow the sky and the stars. But Tara he had chosen. Tara he would protect. He made their mealies to grow and their cattle to multiply.

I protested, "But he is *dead* now!"

Charlie Kamba made signs of deprecation. I discerned that he was far from being clear about the thing himself.

Yes, he temporized, this Father Witch was dead, quite dead. On the other hand he was up there. On the other hand he would never die. He was longer than forever. Yes, quite true, he was dead and buried under the pot.

I gave it up. "How did he die?"

Well, he came to this village of Tara very suffering, very sick. The dead man who walked. His face was very sad. Very eaten. Very frightened. He came to this hill. So he lived here for two full moons, very hot, very eaten, very dead. These men made him a house as he commanded them, also a stockade. In the house he was very quiet, very dead, making magic two full moons. Then he came out and they that were waiting saw him. He had made the magic, and the magic had made him well. His face was kind. He was happy. He was full fed, these men said, without any eating. Yes, they carried up to him very fine food, because they were full of wonder and some fear, but he did not eat any of it. Some water he drank. So, for two days and the night between them, he continued sitting in the gate of the stockade, very happy, very full fed. He told these people very much about their wizard, who is bigger than everywhere and longer than forever and can, if he cares to, swallow the sky and stars. From time to time however, ceasing to talk to these people, he got to his knees and talked in his own strange tongue to Our Father Witch, his eyes held shut. When he had done this just at sunset of the second day he fell forward on his face. So he remained that night. The next day these men took him into the house and buried him under the pot. On the other hand Our Father Witch is longer than forever. He remains there still . . .

The first thing I saw in the hut's interior was the earthen pot at the northern end, wrong-side-up on the ground. I was glad I had preceded Mrs. Diana. I walked across and sat down on it carelessly, hoping so that her afflicted curiosity might be led astray. It gave me the oddest feeling, though, to think of what was there beneath my nonchalant sitting-portion—aware as I was of the Kavirondo burial of a great man—up to the neck in mother earth, and the rest of him left out in the dark of the pot for the undertakings of the ants. I hoped his widow wouldn't wonder about that inverted vessel of clay.

I needn't have worried. Her attention was arrested otherwheres. I shall not forget the look of her face, caught above me in the red shaft of sundown entering the western door, as she gazed at the last and the largest of the Reverend Hubert Diana's gods. That long, long cheek of hers, buffeted by sorrow, startled now and mortified—Not till that moment, I believe, had she comprehended the steps of mud-images she had been following for what they were, the steps of idolatry.

For my part, I wasn't startled. Even before we started up the hill, knowing that her husband had dared to die here, I could have told her pretty much what she would find.

This overlord of the cosmic categories that he had fashioned (at last) in his own image sat at the other end of the red-streaked house upon a bench—a throne?—of mud. Diana had been no artist. An ovoid two-eyed head, a cylindrical trunk, two arms, two legs, that's all. But indubitably man, man-size. Only one finger of one of the hands had been done with much care. It wore an opal, a two-dollar stone from Mexico, set in a silver ring. This was the hand that was lifted, and over it the head was bent.

I've said Diana was no artist. I'll take back the words. The figure was crudeness itself, but in the relation between that bent head and that lifted hand there was something which was something else. A sense of scrutiny one would have said no genius of mud could ever have conveyed. An attitude of interest centered in that bauble, intense and static, breathless and eternal all in one—penetrating to its bottom atom, to the last electron, to a hill upon it, and to a two-legged mite about to die. Marking (yes, I'll swear to the incredible) the sparrow's fall.

The magic was made. The road that had commenced with the blobs of Ndua—the same that commenced with our hairy ancestors listening to the night-wind in their caves—was run.

And from here Diana, of a sudden happy, of a sudden looked after, "full fed" had walked out—

But no; I couldn't stand that mortified sorrow on the widow's face any longer. She had to be made to see what she wanted to see. I said it aloud:

"From here, Mrs. Diana, your husband walked out—"

"He had sunk to idolatry. *Idolatry!*"

"To the bottom, yes. And come up its whole history again. And from here he walked out into the sunshine to kneel and talk with 'Our Father Which—'"

She got it. She caught it. I wish you could have seen the light going up those long, long cheeks as she got it:

"Our Father which art in Heaven, Hallowed be Thy Name!"

We went down hill in the darkness, protected against goblins by a vast rattling of gourds and beating of goat-hide drums.

EXERCISES

1. These are questions which might help you analyze both the composition and arrangement of the story, "The Man Who Saw Through Heaven," and help you find some of its meanings. You might use these questions, and similar ones, in analyzing other literary selections in this book.

First, let us look at the arrangement of materials.

a. How does Steele get in the necessary explanatory material?

b. Does he anywhere state the theme of this story very explicitly? If so, where?

c. If you were dividing the story into sections, about where would the dividing points be? Upon what basis are you making this division?

d. How does the "pace" of the story go? That is, where does the author deal with time very slowly, and where does he speed it up? What effects does he get by this change of pace?

Second, let us look at some of the devices which he uses to convey meaning.

a. The most recurrent symbol in the story is that of the opal in Diana's ring. Exactly what is it a symbol of? Why is a symbol necessary in this story?

b. Throughout much of the story, two emotions seem to be in conflict in Diana's personality. One of these is a sense of freedom; the other is fright. What is the connection between the two? Can you trace the changes in Diana's feeling of fright?

c. Is there any significance in the number of mud-images and the animals which he makes? The sequence is this: shapeless blobs of mud to reptiles (lizards, turtles, and crocodiles) to huge birds, to mammals (the boar and bull), to the single image of man, man-sized.

Third, let us try a comparison. Here is a poem which some people have said means the same thing as "The Man Who Saw Through Heaven." As exactly and specifically as possible, tell how much they have in common. To what extent does the difference in form make the meanings of the two different? Brunelleschi, by the way, was a fifteenth century Italian architect and sculptor. Perhaps his most famous work is the cupola which completes the cathedral church of Santa Maria del Fiore in Florence. But here's the poem. How much is its meaning the same, how much different from the meaning of the story?

Sky

Dilys Bennet Laing

Better than Brunelleschi
I can construct a dome:
the mind can warp space
to fit the eye's false frame.

Of edgeless emptiness
I vault me a blue prison,
its arc the meridian,
its lip the seen horizon.

Pantheon of my thought,
roof of the sight's illusion,
home for the frightened spirit
raised of the stones of vision.

For truth is beyond form,
but man, whose soul is simple,
must house the ineffable God
in the apparent temple.

2. In discussing the reading of literature in this chapter, we have dealt mainly with prose. Among the exercises some samples of poetry have been included. At the end of Chapter 2 some variations are given for George Meredith's poem, "Dirge in Woods." It might be profitable to look back at that exercise.

After looking at all the poetry exercises given thus far, can you make up some suggestions of your own for the careful reading of poetry?

3. Here, again, we might compare the writing of an expert and a rank amateur in terms of meanings which lie beyond pure sense meaning. Both the stanza from Matthew Arnold's "Dover Beach" and the paraphrase of it "mean" the same thing in that they deplore the loss of faith in the world. But what additional overtones and undertones of meaning does Arnold get? In what specific ways does he get them?

A. The Sea of Faith
Was once, too, at the full, and round earth's shore
Lay like the folds of a bright girdle furled.
But now I only hear
Its melancholy, long, withdrawing roar,
Retreating, to the breath
Of the night wind, down the vast edges drear
And naked shingles of the world.

B. Once men the world around believed
In other men and God.
But faith's now lost, men are deceived,
And earth's a dusty clod.

4. Or let's consider the matter of discovering valid or invalid meaning in a literary work. Here is Robert Frost's lovely poem, "Stopping by Woods on a Snowy Evening."

Whose woods these are, I think I know.
His house is in the village though;
He will not see me stopping here
To watch his woods fill up with snow.

My little horse must think it queer
To stop without a farmhouse near

Between the woods and frozen lake
The darkest evening of the year.

He gives the harness bells a shake
To ask if there is some mistake.
The only other sound's the sweep
Of easy wind and downy flake.

The woods are lovely, dark and deep.
But I have promises to keep,
And miles to go before I sleep,
And miles to go before I sleep.

Notice how the choice of words in a poem, once it is done, seems right, almost inevitable. In the twelfth line one accepts the word "easy" as an adjective describing the wind. What other adjectives could Robert Frost have chosen? Why do you suppose he selected the rather unusual word, "easy"?

In answering these questions, you might notice some of the music of the poem. For example, look at lines three and four. In line three we find the words *will* and *stopping*; in line four, the words *watch* and *fill*. Do you notice the cross-rhyme: *stop* and *watch*, *will* and *fill*? In lines seven and eight we have something of the same thing with the words *between* and *evening*. Now look at lines eleven and twelve to see why the choice of the word *easy*. You might notice the pattern of end-rhymes, too. Where does the word that ends line three of each stanza find its rhyme? What is the effect, and author's purpose, of having all four lines of the last stanza rhyme? As one begins to discover these rather hidden elements, a simple-seeming poem becomes a complicated fabric of rhyme and music, most of which has its effect on the reader even though he is not conscious of it.

An Introduction to Art
in a Humanities Course

Imagine three artists, on a fine sunny day, setting up their easels side by side to paint the same scene. Each, for reasons of his own, has wished to paint a particular tree on a particular knoll. Had they been "shutterbugs" instead of painters, using a camera instead of canvas and brushes, their pictures might conceivably have been so nearly identical that they could have been superimposed, one on top of the other. But—as you see below—that is not at all what happened!

The person at the left is copying the tree exactly as it is. The artist at the right has taken some liberties with nature; he has emphasized some of the rhythmic lines which he sees, he has romanticized the scene, but his painting is still recognizable as a tree. The painter in the center has taken those same rhythmic lines which we saw in the scene in nature and has translated them into a completely new abstract design.

This illustration brings up the question, What is art? The dictionary tells us that it is the "production or expression of what is beautiful, appealing, or of more than ordinary significance . . . skilled workmanship, execution, or agency (often opposed to nature)." It is exactly this last point which we wish to stress here. Art is a process and a product of creation by people. Another definition which may give us an insight into our subject is the one given by James Joyce in his novel, *Portrait of the Artist as a Young Man*: "'Art,' said Stephen, 'is the human disposition of sensible or intelligible matter for an esthetic end.'"[1] He continues to point out that it must have "wholeness" (let us call it individuality), "harmony" (a satisfactory relationship between all its parts), and "radiance" (a sort of inner significance).

At any rate, art is the *human* arrangement of matter to express beauty or significance, and very often the two are synonymous. The materials that a painter or sculptor or architect works with are always the same: line, value, shape, form, color, and texture. The principles which he uses in combining these elements, too, are the same: repetition, opposition, symmetry, transition, and dominance. The effects which he achieves through the development of these principles lie in terms of rhythm, harmony and proportion, and unity. Let us add that very often, for shock value in communicating his significance, the individual artist avoids these last three, but the very conscious violation of them affirms the reality of their existence.

Perhaps the important point is that by using these elements, principles and effects of design, the artist seeks to create beauty or significance. But what is beauty and significance? Between different artists the idea of these will vary; between different schools of expression one will find wide variation; in different cultures (think of some Chinese painting as compared with Italian renaissance painting) the concept of beauty differs; at different times in the development of western civilization, the prevailing thought about the nature of beauty and significance has been different from that idea at other times.

The Elements of Design

Later in this chapter we can see illustrations of different styles in our changing concepts of beauty. At this time it would perhaps be well to pause to look more carefully at the principles and elements of design. Following is a reproduction of Breughel's picture called "Winter" or "Hunters in the Snow." Perhaps the first thing that strikes the viewer is the multiplicity of shapes and figures throughout the picture. One sees the skaters on the ponds at the right, jagged rocks above them, a blazing fire on the left, a long landscape in deep perspective and the many short curved lines of the tails and legs of the hunting dogs. Breughel's purpose is obviously to convey two moods, one of general bleakness, the other of warmth and human activity. The picture is essentially composed of triangles and squares. From the lower right hand corner the line of the hill leading toward the fire produces the largest of the triangles. Another one was created with the slope of the hill beyond the houses and leading down into the valley. The two ponds form the central square while the valley itself going into the background is a long rectangle. In contrast to this we have a multitude of vertical lines: trees, houses, the rocky cliffs, and the like.

The colors represent an interesting contrast. The sky is green with a suggestion of bleakness and the same green is reflected in the skating ponds. Although the white of the snow dominates the picture it is contrasted with some reds which one finds in the houses, two of the dogs, one hunter's costume, and the building at the lower right which is evidently a mill. The textures are even more varied and interesting. We have the smooth textures of the ponds and the sky and the rough textures of the small trees and shrubbery which emphasize the slanting lines of the triangles. Below one sees the varied short vertical lines of the trees and the variegated texture created by the figures of the hunters and their dogs. This use of texture is certainly not the least of the means the painter has employed in this study in contrast. The wispy feathery foliage is very different from the liquidity of the ponds and the sky. These are qualities

[1]James Joyce, *Portrait of the Artist as a Young Man* (New York: The Viking Press, 1965), p. 207.

COLORPLATE 1. The Tragedy
by Pablo Picasso

Courtesy The National Gallery of Art,
Washington, D.C., Chester Dale Collection

COLORPLATE 2. Winter (Return of the Hunters) by Pieter Brueghel

COLORPLATE 4. Nude Descending a Staircase—
No. 2–DuChamp

COLORPLATE 3. Louis XIV–Rigaud

COLORPLATE 5. Self-Portrait by Vincent van Gogh

that one can almost tactilely perceive. Not the least of the elements which Breughel has used to convey his mood are the shapes of the half dozen or so birds perched desolately on the bare branches or flying as if suspended as a dot of gloom in the middle of the picture. These black birds almost make one shiver physically as one views the scene.

All of this discussion has centered upon the elements and principles of design. We have discussed color, texture, line, and shape. We have been concerned with rhythms, opposition and all of the other principles. Yet somehow these abstract ideas end up as an expresion of Breughel's love for his native land, of his delight of the infinite variety of it and of the sense of human warmth and delight in the midst of a bleak landscape.

Yet, the means of his communication have been relatively simple: line, value, shape, form, color, texture. These make meaningful the space with which any painter is concerned; these are the elements of all graphic design. Any one of them could be made the subject of long and serious study; but it is something, at least, to know that they exist, and to try to be aware of their function when one looks at their organization into a picture. These are the things with which an artist works.

Artists say that there are only four kinds of lines: vertical lines, horizontal lines, slanting lines, and curved lines. For our purposes, however, this distinction is not necessary. We can simply say that the

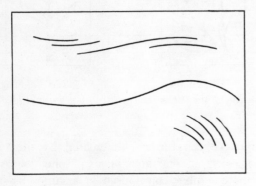

Curved lines, horizontal direction suggest beauty and repose.

artist can organize his space with lines. There is another meaning to this word, however, which the artist uses, and which we should know. He might speak of the essential line or *direction* of the picture

or statue or design. By this word he suggests the way in which the eye moves within the composition. For example, curved lines suggest calm beauty. When their direction is essentially horizontal, we have the added emotion of repose. On the other hand, straight lines suggest vigor and energy, particularly when their direction is upward. Sharp angles, which bring in the principle of opposition, suggest strife and vigor. Confusion may be created by a seemingly unplanned mixture of the various types of line and direction.

Value means the darkness or lightness of the colors. It is used for opposition and to produce dominance.

An artist also uses texture to organize his space, and texture refers to the impression of roughness or

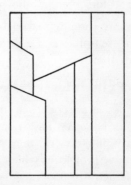

Vertical and slanting lines, in opposition, general direction upward, suggest energy and vigor.

smoothness which he gives to surfaces. Here, again, he makes use of an emotional-psychological effect, for a smooth surface usually gives the impression of coolness, while a rough surface suggests warmth. One of the best places to observe the use of texture in design is in the fabrics which are used for various types of clothing. We suppose that an overcoat could be given a very smooth finish, but most overcoats are not treated that way because the maker wishes them to appear warm. If you wish to observe a use of different textures in pictures, compare the silk-smooth textures in the portrait of Louis XIV with the rough texture of the Van Gogh Self-Portrait.

Little need be said of the various flat shapes which the artist uses. They are essentially circles and ovals, squares, rectangles, and triangles. It is through the use of such shapes that the artist builds his basic design. These shapes come into being, of course, when lines are brought together.

Exactly the same thing is true of the three-dimensional forms which the artist uses. They are spheres, cylinders, cubes, and pyramids. They come into being as the artist suggests perspective in his drawing and makes his shapes seem three-dimensional.

Another element which artists use in organizing space is color. There are six standard colors: red, orange, yellow, green, blue, and violet. Each of these may have variations of intensity and value. These six and their variations are available for the painter. Here again the artist can count on gaining certain emotional effects by the various use of color; for we recognize that most blues and greens, for example, are cool colors, while red, yellow, and orange are warm colors. Warm and cool, however, are relative, for this quality depends upon the relationships which exist with other colors used in the picture.

These, then, are the raw materials of the painter, the designer, the sculptor, and the architect. What principles govern their use?

The Principles of Design

The principles are repetition, opposition, symmetry, transition, balance, and dominance. When these are properly put to work, they produce rhythm, harmony, and unity: properties which are not so much principles as characteristics of good design.

It has already been said that the direction of lines is important. One of the ways in which direction is created is through repetition, the first of the principles which we wish to discuss here. It is this which gives us a sense of what comes next. For example, the design below has repetition:

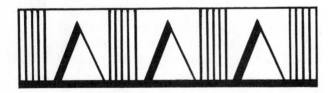

Repetition yields a sense of order, which seems to be desirable psychologically. One caution should be stated here, however. Too much repetition is monotonous. Most of us know this from experience, having been driven to distraction by a wallpaper design which repeats itself in a seemingly endless progression around the room. Or you have experienced the same

monotony when you get a tune in your mind that will not stop going over and over. It is here that the principle of opposition should come in.

Opposition means exactly what the word says. It is line or color or texture or value or one of the other elements which is used to oppose another. The principle of opposition is illustrated in the design above, for the vertical and slanting lines are opposed, as are the values in the triangular shapes. If we had simply repeated the vertical lines across the space, which would have been one illustration of repetition, the design would not have been interesting. Or if we had made a series of triangles all the way across, they, too, would have become monotonous. By the opposition we have made a relationship or a comparison possible, and this relationship enlivens the design.

Still another principle is that of symmetry or balance. A design should not appear to be top-heavy, bottom-heavy, or lop-sided. It would seem from this that a good design should have exactly the same units in one part as another, yet this is not the case, for balance can be produced in many ways. For example, with occult balance (assymmetry) we do not use units of the same size, but we arrange them so that they appear to be equipoised:

Occult Balance   *Absolute Balance*
(assymmetry)   *(bisymmetry)*

Balance can further be created by the use of bright colors in one area, a small one, let us say, with more somber colors used in a larger balancing area. Balance, too, can be achieved through differences in value in the shapes and forms. In other words, it is through the use of the elements that the artist achieves a sense of symmetry.

Transition, the fourth of the principles to be discussed, is the process of getting from one thing to another. One of the most common examples can be seen in nature in the leaves of a locust or ash tree, which make a transition from large to small shapes. Below we see a transition from vertical to horizontal lines by use of the diminishing tree-shapes, and then the curved line of the hill which completes the transition.

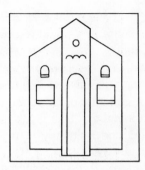

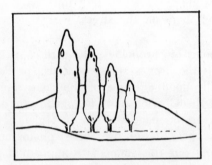

Dominance, a fifth principle, means that one thing should stand out more than others. Dominance is aided by the general direction of the design which should lead the eye inevitably to the point of dominance. It may be aided by color, for the single idea may be made to stand out in that way. This can frequently be seen in cartoons which are printed in black-and-white with the exception of the single key to the humor which is printed in color so that the eye goes to that object before one is through looking, and consequently the reader gets the point of the drawing. Whether the purpose of the painting is to give a mood, to tell a story, to mirror nature, or to present an abstract pattern, all of the elements and all of the lesser principles must lead up to the big principle of dominance.

When the principles are followed, the resulting picture or design has rhythm, harmony and proportion, and unity. As the term is used here, rhythm is more than mere repetition. It is a sense of movement throughout the whole design which makes it come alive, and which holds it together.

Harmony and proportion mean that the parts of the picture are right for each other. Rather than using words for this, the illustration in the next column reveals the meaning as we look at a good example of harmony or proportion and a poor one.

A final characteristic of good design, and a result of the proper working out of the principles which we

have discussed, is unity. This simply means that the whole thing must hang together. Each part must look as if it belonged to every other part of the design; as if it made a real and definite contribution, at the appropriate place, to the working out of the meaning which the artist wished to express. Below are examples of unity and lack of unity:

These, then, are the principles and elements of design. Written as they are, they may seem abstract and difficult. They occur, however, in design wherever you may look. They function as designers plan dress designs and the patterns of clothing, in wall-paper and linoleum, in the arrangement of a business letter on a page, and, perhaps most commonly of all, in the arrangement of an advertisement. Examine a full-page, color advertisement in a national magazine. You will see all of these elements used, and the principles followed. Why are advertising agencies so careful to observe these principles? It is because they know that the advertisement will not look right if they do not. The person who is reading the advertisement will be vaguely disturbed if the thing isn't right.

The principles are not laid down by an authority. They are really psychological principles. We feel a rightness about some things, and a wrongness about others. These principles are really a statement of the sense of rightness that people feel.

How to Look at a Work of Art

There are many ways of looking at and appreciating a work of art. One of the most usual ways is to make up a story which lies behind a picture or to find a moral in the picture. One can, for example, look at a picture of mountain peaks and come up with such a moral as, "Isn't God's masterpiece in nature wonderful, and isn't little man insignificant after all." A second way of looking at a work of art is to let it remind you of some scene in your own past so you lose yourself in the revery of your own experience. The picture or statue has been a stepping stone toward one's own nostalgic past. The kinds of art which provoke these two responses usually aren't very good; this is usually called calendar art simply because it is found on advertising calendars which aim at an immediate, sentimental appeal. Pictures of babies, dogs, and obvious motherhood are particularly fine subjects for this type of art.

These two types of appreciation are very much like the "bath in sound" appreciation of music which is discussed in Chapter 5. Notice that these types of appreciation depend almost entirely on the subject matter of the picture and lead back into the past experience of the viewer. If art is to be considered as exploration and discovery, appreciation of these types is not good enough.

Perhaps the best way to look at a work of art is the same method suggested for music in the next chapter: First, really look at it and report what you see. Then draw whatever valid conclusions you can from your accurate observation. At the end of this chapter, you will find a sort of checklist to guide your looking at a picture, statue, or architectural example to see it for what it is.

Given here are five examples of works of art; for purposes of comparison we have chosen pictures all representing the same subject matter: the human body, or at least, the human face. They are drawn from different periods in western history, and represent different styles and techniques. What can we notice about them? Perhaps first we might notice the degree, or level of abstraction.

Degrees of Abstraction

One could make many distinctions among the various levels of abstraction as they are revealed in art. Here we shall make only three, which we may call photographic realism, idealization, and complete abstraction. These are represented in the pictures of the tree at the head of this chapter.

With our present group of portrayals of the human form, the first level of abstraction is shown in the statue of the Roman couple. Very little need be said about this particular style since the statue reveals it all. This seems to be a very real picture of the man and the woman, exactly as they must have appeared. If we met them on the street, we would recognize them.

In point of chronology, the earliest of our illustrations is the bronze statue of Zeus (or Poseidon). An equally good example of the same thing is the statue of the Charioteer of Delphi in our discussion of Greek art on page 91. At first glance it would seem that these statues are almost photographic representation, but this immediate impression probably results from custom rather than accurate observation. These statues represent idealization, and most statues we know use the same degree of abstraction found in these two. (General Sherman never looked so good as he does on his sculptured horse.) Notice the musculature of Zeus. This is uncommon, to say the least. Notice, too, his perfect balance and the calmness of his face. Observe the straightness of nose, the peculiar way the nose is joined to the smooth, globular forehead. The arm, if dropped, would come almost to the knee. Or, examine the charioteer. He is represented just after the race, yet his face is calm. The long area from waist to the bottom of the chiton is fluted, and is made almost in the shape of a Greek column. Again we have the globular forehead.

After such an examination one realizes that these statues have come a long way from photographic realism. They represent an idea personified (power in the case of Zeus; inner strength rather than outward emotion for the charioteer). Of this type of idealization, one art critic has said, "Had the process of abstracting and idealizing been carried further along the same line, Fifth Century sculpture would have arrived at something very close to modern cubism."[1]

A third level of abstraction is represented by Duchamp's *Nude Descending a Staircase* (No. 2). This

[1]John Ives Sewall, *A History of Western Art* (New York: Holt, Rinehart & Winston, Inc., 1961), p. 121.

ROMAN MAN AND WIFE

STATUE OF ZEUS

is scarcely contemporary art since it was painted in 1912 and created a furor at the time, but this is still a portrayal of the human figure. Upon closer study we see that the figure is in motion, and that we see it in several poses at the same time. Further, we see it from different perspectives, as we *would* see it in at least three different poses on the staircase. Most important of all, however, we are aware that the figure itself has been broken down into planes and geometric shapes, almost completely destroying the qualities of the figure which we would call human. This picture is a forerunner or early example of cubism.

We can have, then, at least three levels of abstraction in art—and we are right back to the three paintings of the tree with which this chapter started. The first level is photographic representation as represented by the Roman statue of the man and his wife. The second level may be called idealization, in which the subject matter is still quite recognizable but which has been altered to present an idea rather than a photograph. Finally, we come to the third level of complete abstraction, in which the subject matter has become completely unrecognizable and the pattern or shape or color, the structure, in other words, has become totally important in itself.

Different Techniques in Painting

A second characteristic of a work of art is its technique, and there are many techniques which could be described. Only two are chosen here, and they may be illustrated by the portrait of Louis XIV and the Van Gogh Self-Portrait.

The first picture comes from the late seventeenth century, and is a development of the painting of the renaissance. The perspective is carefully created, and the portrait is made dramatic through use of light and shadow to reveal the dominant area. Furthermore, the colors are carefully mixed to recreate exactly the colors of the garments which the king was wearing. Although the eye goes back through the use of perspective, the surface is flat and highly polished. One could rub his hand across it with little sense of texture of the canvas itself.

The Van Gogh Self-Portrait is an example of late *impressionism*. Let it be noted that this term has a special significance in art and does not simply mean, as in the common usage, the artist's impression of his subject matter.

Impressionism is the name given to a technique in painting designed to give more life and light to a painting. The painters who have been called impressionists were particularly concerned with light and color. In order to make these more brilliant, one of their methods was to leave their paints relatively unmixed, and to put the unmixed paints side-by-side on the canvas. For example, a painter who copies nature mixes red and blue when he wants purple. The impressionist would put strokes of red and blue very close together on the canvas, and let the eye of the beholder blend the two. The effects of light thus achieved are much more brilliant than the painters of nature-as-it-appears can get, partially because the person who looks at the picture is, to some extent, creating it with his own eyes. In this way the brilliance of each of the colors remains, a brilliance which would otherwise be killed in the mixing of the paints.

Styles of Different Periods in Western Culture

Another point to consider as one examines various works of art is the period in which a work was created, and the typical style and subject matter of the different periods. Here are a few hints which may help in making a good guess about the period of composition.

Of course, no Greek painting of the classical period (about 450 B.C.) remains to us, and we must consider here only sculpture and architecture. The sculpture is almost totally devoted to statues of Gods, mythological material, and athletes. At the high point of Greek civilization it is idealized, revealing the idea of inner strength rather than external emotion. Even in the pediment sculpture where action is portrayed, we usually find that the action is caught at a turning point so that the moment is static, frozen for an instant of time. The poet, Keats, caught this sense of the static nature of Greek art almost perfectly, and a complete understanding of the poem "Ode on a Grecian Urn" (see Cleanth Brooks' critical essay, "Keats's Sylvan Historian," for a complete analysis of the poem) will give one a fine awareness of the nature of this type of art.

Greek architecture is almost always given over to temples to the gods. The structure is always of the post and lintel type (see p. 92 for further definition), and the design is always balanced and predictable. Lines are horizontal rather than vertical; the concept is rational rather than emotional.

The uses of Roman architecture (the subject matter) are much more varied than the Greek. The dates are from about 250 B.C. to 450 A.D. There are many temples to the gods or to deified Roman emperors, many colosseums, some public meeting halls or law courts (called basilicas), some houses and apartment houses, and some aqueducts. The style sometimes follows the late Greek, with a highly ornamented post and lintel structure; more often it uses the rounded arch and the dome as its basic structural principle. Size and massiveness are noticeable characteristics of Roman building.

Roman sculpture consists almost entirely of portrait statues, usually of the emperors or of wealthy Romans. In style it varies from photographic representation as seen in the statues of the Roman married couple to idealization which is best shown in the statue of Augustus Haranguing His Troops on page 227. Particularly in such statues as this last one, the Roman debt to Greek artists is apparent.

Turning to the Middle Ages (450 A.D. to 1450 A.D.), we find a number of different styles of architecture: the romanesque, which is an adaptation of the basilica in Rome; Norman, which, as its name suggests, was originally a Scandanavian type of architecture which entered France and England with the invasions of the northmen early in the Middle Ages and evolved there into a distinctive style; and a strong Byzantine influence which emanated from the Italian city of Ravenna on the Adriatic Sea when that city became the capital of the Roman Empire. The really distinctive architecture of the Middle Ages, however, is the Gothic, which in many ways formed a synthesis of the earlier styles. The prime characteristic of the Gothic is height. Until this time the main architectural line had been horizontal; now the vertical line supplanted it. The most important structural element of the Gothic is the pointed arch. This, and the flying buttress (an outside-the-walls prop which took the shape of half a pointed arch) allowed for thin walls and the use of a great deal of stained glass in magnificent windows. While Gothic architecture was used in many types of buildings, guildhalls, for example, its crowning use was in the Gothic church, or cathedral. While most early styles of architecture had been rational and predictable, the Gothic, with its great height and vertical lines, is essentially energetic and emotional.

We find little independent, free-standing sculpture during the Middle Ages; most of the statues exist as part of the churches. One characteristic of the stone carving is the overall design: Columns are frequently covered with abstract, geometric designs. As part of the columns one finds elongated, often emaciated statues, their length increasing the vertical direction

of the structure itself. One finds other examples of statuary in many places about the church, perhaps chiefly under the pointed arch over the doorways. This is not elongated as are the archetonic statues on the pillars, but in most cases seem to be statuary in motion, a far cry from the frozen-moment of Greek sculpture.

In the Middle Ages too we find almost our first examples of painting—the subject matter is always religious. A chief characteristic of medieval painting is its lack of perspective. Frequently the painters use the Byzantine device of a solid background of gold against which their two dimensional figures are set (see for example Martini's "The Annunciation" on Colorplate 6).

Closely allied to painting in the Middle Ages is the art of stained glass. One of the glories of the Gothic churches is the great areas of window, usually telling a story from the Bible or from the lives of the saints, which reads from bottom to top in a manner not unlike the comic strip of today. While one might say much about this art (and much will be said in a later chapter) its chief characteristic, the feature most sought after by the makers of the glass, was color. Here, probably for the first time in western civilization, we find the full exploitation of the glory of color.

From the Renaissance (roughly 1450-1650) onward, we find so many styles of art that only a few can be mentioned here. A few instances of the new freedom in art can be mentioned. In painting we find the artists of the Renaissance studying and developing fully the possibilities of perspective. They used color richly and freely. Many new types of subject matter were opened for the artist: Landscapes for their own beauty were first painted at this time; the rediscovered classic art of the Romans and Greeks inspired a return to mythology. This classic interest and a revived study of anatomy brought about a new interest in the human form as a subject for art. Whereas earlier architecture had expressed itself in buildings devoted to religion, with the Renaissance we find many new types of structures, chiefly the palace, as a subject for architectural achievement.

One of the most important styles following the Renaissance was the Baroque, which aimed, more than anything else, at grandeur. The portrait of Louis XIV earlier in the chapter is a good example of the type. The Baroque painter used canvasses of tremendous size. Rubens, for example, painted a series of pictures dealing with the marriage of Henry IV of France and Maria de Medici, each of which is

13 feet by 9 feet, 8½ inches in size. Portrait painting, begun in the Renaissance, offered one of the great new possibilities for Baroque artists since kings, noblemen, and rich merchants paid handsomely for portraits. The chief characteristics of the style are seen in the Rigaud portrait: great curving lines, large areas of solid color, rounded, classic arches as background, and extensive use of light and shadow, all to produce a sense of richness and grandeur.

Baroque architecture was reserved almost entirely for churches and palaces. Other buildings would have been too small to accommodate its grandness. The Baroque architect frequently drew upon classic design and classic rationalism as a basis for his structure, with rows of Corinthian columns and a Greek pediment, or he used Roman arches and domes. In the arrangement of a landscape with broad avenues, lanes of trees, small lakes and the like, he utilized a rational principle, frequently that of the wheel with the central building at the hub, from which the avenues radiated like spokes. At this point, however, the nod toward classicism ended. The facade of the structure showed frequent niches for statuary, where the full play of light and shadow could be utilized. One art critic has said that the architect conceived of his building as a piece of sculpture and created it as if it were a statue.

The interior of the Baroque building is full of grand salons and ballrooms, magnificent staircases designed to show off the personages descending the stairs, and bedrooms the size of a small barn. This is architecture for display.

Omitting mention here of the Dutch masters who painted solid burghers and honest pictures of common people doing common tasks, the next style to consider is the Romantic, which reached its height in the late eighteenth century. Only the romantic painters will be considered. Their most usual subjects were nature, common people (usually peasants) and children. The style seems to be that of the photographic realist, but was usually made highly sentimental. This type of art lends itself to "associational" appreciation (the viewer can be plunged into nostalgic memories of his own experience), or to story-value appreciation (in which the viewer makes up a story about the scene in the picture). The romantics employed all the standard themes which are sure to evoke an emotional response in the viewer: the grandeur of nature, motherhood, the innocence of childhood and others of the same sort.

With the twentieth century come most of the experiments in abstract painting. These will be dis-

cussed in the unit on the twentieth century, and a few of them can only be named here. The common ones are cubism, surrealism, dadaism, and abstract expressionism. Whatever the school, or style of these contemporary artists, their aim is to break through the ordinary appearances of things and to find a truth or reality which lies beyond the surface, either in dream or symbolism, or perhaps in the mathematical purity of the cubists, a type of truth which has been exciting from the time of the first mathematical discoverers.

New materials have had a great impact on art, particularly in architecture where the use of structural steel, concrete, and glass has made possible the great skyscrapers which seem to be the greatest contribution to architecture of the twentieth century. New materials, however, have had their influence on the other arts; witness sculpture made from steel and sometimes from scrap iron, frequently welded together. Or consider the various forms of pop and op art in which the commonest materials are utilized in making a picture.

Except where such appreciation is obviously demanded by the artist, as in the case of some romantic painting, one should try to avoid the associational or story-value types of understanding of art in this course. The structure (including use of color and the subject matter) reveal the idea of beauty which the painter, the sculptor, or the architect held. In other words, the student is encouraged to look carefully at a work of art under consideration, and to report what he actually sees. From such careful observation, he can draw valid conclusions about the significance of the work of art, including the discovery about the meaning of human experience which the artist wished to convey. The check sheets which follow may serve as a help in this first understanding of art objects. Later in the course, with more practice, these observations will become automatic and the student will go ahead to a more sophisticated understanding of the space arts.

EXERCISES

Given below are two check sheets. Look at a number of buildings, paintings, and statues (or slides showing pictures of these) and fill out the check sheets for each work of art.

Check Sheet for Architecture

1. What is the subject matter? (religious building, palace office building, etc.) _____

_____

2. What is the building material?_____

3. Is the structure symmetrical or assymetrical?___
_____

4. Is the essential direction horizontal or vertical?
_____

5. Is there any suggestion of classical influence? (Greek post-and-lintel, Roman arches and domes)
_____

6. Are the lines straight?_____ Long or short? _____

7. Are most of the lines curved? _____ Are the curves long and sweeping or short and choppy? _____

8. How much ornamentation on the structure, and what kind?_____

9. Does the ornamentation contribute to the structural idea or is it added purely for decorative purposes?_____

10. Are the shapes and forms geometric or irregular? _____

11. What kinds of windows? _____ What is the relation of the windows in relation to the plan of the entire building?_____

Conclusions:

a. From our discussion of styles, what do you think is the approximate date of the building? _____
_____

b. Is the structure predictable? (After having seen a part, do you know what comes next?) _____
_____

c. Is the psychological effect one of rest and repose, vigor and energy, logical efficiency, or some other?_____

d. On the basis of the conclusions above, did the architect seem to think of beauty as intellectual or emotional?_____

e. From all the above, how would you define the architect's conception of beauty? _____

Check Sheet for Painting and Sculpture

1. What is the subject matter? (landscape, portrait, etc.)_____

2. What is the medium? (oil, water color, bronze, etc.) _____

3. Which of the three levels of abstraction discussed —or other levels? _____

4. Is the work symmetrical or assymetrical?_____

5. Is the essential direction horizontal, vertical, or circular? _____

6. Are the lines straight? _____ Are the shapes and forms geometric or haphazard?___
_____ . If straight lines predominate, are they long harmonious ones, or are they short and in opposition to each other? _____

7. Are most of the lines curved? _____ If so, are the curves long and sweeping or short and choppy? _____

8. What are the predominant colors? _____

9. Are the colors used in large areas, or small, rather spotty ones? _____

10. Where does the eye enter the picture, and in what direction does it move through it? _____
_____

11. In sculpture, is it free standing, low or high relief? _____

12. If it is free standing, is the composition harmonious from all aspects as one walks around it?
_____

13. Does the picture or statue portray action, the Greek "frozen-moment," or a subject at rest?
_____

14. Is the technique in painting like the Renaissance technique, impressionist, or some form of complete abstraction?

Conclusions:

a. What is the approximate date of the work?_____
_____

b. What is the appropriate type of appreciation for this work? (story value, association, formal analysis, etc.) _____

c. Is the psychological effect one of rest and repose, vigor and energy, or some other? _____

d. What was the artist's purpose? (portrayal of grandeur, photographic reproduction, formal composition, etc.) _____

e. Did the artist consider beauty to be emotional or intellectual?_____

f. From all the above, how would you define the artist's conception of beauty?_____
_____

An Introduction to Music Listening

Because this text is concerned with the education of the musical amateur within the framework of an integrated study of the humanities, primary emphasis will be placed on a study of music as:

1. a nonverbal art of structured sound moving in time;
2. a social art reflecting the mores and modes of life of past and present cultures.

The other areas of musical study are best left to the scientists, psychologists and professionals in the various fields of musical composition and performance. These areas will be included only to the extent necessary to assist in the acquisition of the skills and knowledge leading to the development of perceptive and intelligent listening.

Listening is developed by listening; music is learned from music; musical experience is gained only by listening to music. Reading or hearing a lecture *about* music is undoubtedly a prerequisite for developing a knowledgeable awareness of music in all its aspects, but by no means a substitute for the actual musical experience. In this respect, music differs little from other art forms. Just as verbal descriptions and even blueprints of a notable piece of architecture can do no more than prepare one for *experiencing* the building as one moves about, in and through the actual structure, so does music require the *hearing* of the various combinations of musical sounds and silences, colors and textures, as they, in a manner of speaking, move about, in and through the conscious and even subconscious aural perceptions of the listener.

Experiencing music involves a varying combination of *sensory, emotional,* and *intellectual* responses. The lively beat of a stirring march can literally increase the pulse rate of a parade watcher (sensory response). Listening to a somber funeral march can bring about feelings of depression and sadness (emotional response). The organized sounds of the tonal architecture of a complex symphonic composition can appeal directly to an intellectual awareness of unity, varied repetition and coherent and logical structure (intellectual response); these responses, however, rarely if ever exist independently. The same symphonic composition can also stimulate the physical response of the listener in passages with great excitement and volume (sensual response), can remind him of a familiar song of his own past, thus releasing memories associated with that particular song (emotional-associational response), and can produce feelings of joy or sorrow (emotional response) while also appealing intellectually to his sense of order and logic.

Because of wide variations in the physical make-up of different individuals and the uniqueness of individual experiences, the sensory and especially emotional responses can be as many and varied as there are people in the audience. On the other hand, the intellectual response will tend to vary according to the amount of knowledge and experience that each person brings to the music. It follows then that people can be educated to a greater intellectual awareness of the various elements of music without losing either their inherent physical responses or experiential emotional and associational responses. There is no such thing as knowing so much as to spoil the music, a frequently heard rationale for *not* studying music; nor is there any known limit to what people can learn about music, as attested to by veteran concert artists who, in their own words, study Bach and Mozart all their lives.

A European exposed to his first American baseball game would undoubtedly respond physically and emotionally to the roar of the crowd after a grand-slam home run; however, he would not know *why* there was excitement or realize the significance of this sudden and dramatic four-run addition. In other words, he would react to the crowd, but not to the actual event since he would not understand the event nor would he have any knowledge of the rules or purpose of the game. Also, there would not be any understanding of the logical progression of balls, strikes, outs, home base, batting order, fielding position, or the other myriad details of the all-American game. In short, the bewildered European would not understand the procedures about which some knowledge is mandatory if the game is to be comprehensible; he would not appreciate the game because he does not *know* the game. And no one has ever claimed that too much knowledge of baseball has spoiled the game!

To summarize: Music is a form of communication which has existed in every culture known to man. The responses to music are sensory, emotional, and intellectual. The sensory responses seem to be common to all mankind. The emotional responses are dependent on the beliefs, customs, and conventions of society and on the unique experiences of the individual. The intellectual response can range from zero (a "tonal bath") up to and including the ability of a Mozart to not only perceive and understand everything happening in a piece of music he heard only once, but the technical ability to write down the entire piece from memory, as he heard it, and as it was. This is not to suggest that everyone, or even anyone, can be educated and trained to this fantastic level of achievement. There is no limit, however, to the amount of pleasurable understanding to be derived from listening to music; the more knowledge you bring to listening the more you will hear, the more you will understand, and the more pleasure you will receive. Appreciation results not from attitude or exposure, but from knowledge, and a genuine, knowledgeable appreciation of music as both social and nonverbal art is one of the goals of this book.

The Listening Experience

Listening to music begins and ends with the question: What do you hear? This is an objective question which has nothing whatever to do with a story you may think the music is telling, random associations the music may invoke, or any meaning you may attribute to the music. The question, What do you hear? can be taken literally. If you heard, for example, a recording of a baritone singing a French song accompanied by a tuba and a piccolo it is likely that "what you hear" is tuba and piccolo accompanying a baritone song in the language of France, providing of course that you could hear and recognize French, songs, baritone voices, tubas, and piccolos.

Assuming you cannot read music and you have no knowledge of musical terminology (or think you have no such knowledge) it is nevertheless possible to hear, recognize and identify many basic, important elements in a piece of music. The following outline represents the initial stage in an objective approach to music listening. Part A specifies some basic categories of things to listen for; Part B, three conclusions which could be drawn from the information in Part A.

LISTENING GUIDE (FIRST STAGE)

1. Listening outline
    a. Medium
       (1) Vocal
           (a) Text: English, Latin, German, French, other
       (2) Instrumental
       (3) Vocal and instrumental
    b. Tempo: very slow, slow, moderate, fast, very fast
    c. Loudness: soft, medium loud, loud, combination
    d. Number of performers
       (1) Solo
       (2) Ensemble
           (a) Small (2 to 5 performers)
           (b) Medium (6 to 20)
           (c) Medium large (21 to 59)
           (d) Large (60 to 100 or more)
    e. Rhythm
       (1) Regular beat (or pulsation)
       (2) Pulsation seems to be either irregular or indistinct
    f. Texture
       (1) One melody, unaccompanied
       (2) Melody with accompaniment
       (3) Simultaneous melodies (two or more)
    g. Form: sacred, secular
2. Conclusions
    a. Possible period: 600-1450 A.D.; 1450-1600; 17th century; 18th century; 19th century; 20th century
    b. Possible style: symphony; concerto; sonata; mass; cantata; oratorio; opera; jazz; art song; folk song; madrigal; other
    c. Possible national origin: England; France; Germany; Italy; Hungary; United States; Austria; other

EXERCISES

Your first listening experiences based on the Listening Guide will preview some of the musical

selections to be studied, music which includes a variety of styles and a time span of about ten centuries. For best results, your listening should be as objective as possible and follow this pattern:

A. Listening Outline
    1. Write a column of Arabic numerals from 1 through 7.
    2. Follow the Listening Guide, writing down your answers for each number.
    3. Always determine the medium first. It is best to answer each question in the order given but you may prefer following your own sequence. In this case, try to do it the same way every time.
    4. Do *not* leave any blank spaces. Incorrect guesses are better than no answer at all. Follow the procedures; correct answers come later as your continued listening experiences are reinforced by an increasing fund of factual knowledge about music and its materials.

B. Conclusions
    After concluding the seven categories make a column of three numerals and hazard a guess as to approximately *when* the music might have been written, the *type* or *style* it may be, and the possible national *origin* of the composer (check the Listening Guide for the possibilities).

The goal of the Listening Guide is to provide you with enough concrete information to make these three educated guesses. Up to this point, it is presumed that you have comparatively little information on which to base conclusions; however you can make some logical deductions based on what you are able to hear when coupled with the following information:

1. The language used in a song usually identifies the country. Names of places (New York, London, etc.) can help pinpoint a country.
2. The use of Latin usually (but not always) indicates some kind of sacred music.
3. Symphony orchestras, string quartets, and pianos did not exist before the eighteenth century.
4. Opera did not exist before the seventeenth century.
5. Jazz did not exist before about 1890 and is still mostly of American origin.
6. A cappella (unaccompanied) choral music was common in the sixteenth century, but became quite rare until revived in the twentieth century.
7. Solo songs (with instrumental accompaniment) were numerous through the sixteenth century but declined for the next two centuries. They be-

came important again in the nineteenth and twentieth centuries. The instrument used for the accompaniment provides a valuable clue.

The outline for each listening selection reads as follows (consult the Listening Guide for categories, choices, etc.):

Record I

A. Listening Outline
   1.
   2.
   3.
   4.
   5.
   6.
   7.

B. Conclusions
   1.
   2.
   3.

Record II
   (etc.)

Fundamentals of Music

The first experiences in objective listening help prove that everyone possesses the ability to identify some of the characteristics of music as outlined in the Listening Guide. Increased knowledge and awareness of the materials of music can only serve to increase the listening capabilities. Fortunately, there is no regression in listening-learning experiences, only progression!

The basic materials of music (notes, melodies, chords, etc.) are no less susceptible to study and analysis than are the materials of language (alphabet, words, phrases, etc.). Learning to read a language is a necessary preamble to reading a nursery rhyme, a newspaper or the plays of Shakespeare. Learning to read music is just as obviously a prerequisite for studying a popular song, polka, symphony or opera. It might be argued, however, that since listening is the primary activity when viewing *Hamlet* or hearing Beethoven's *Fifth Symphony*, the ability to read either English or music is a supplementary capability which is not really necessary for the understanding of either the play or symphony. After all, anyone, whether literate or not, can get *something* out of these performances. Something yes, but how much, or how little?

Both drama (on the stage) and music are time arts, that is they take place over a period of time and when that segment of time has elapsed there is no more than a remembrance of things past. They exist only in performance; all else is secondary.

How are all the interlocking complexities of *Hamlet* and the *Fifth Symphony* to be studied? When orchestral conductors have been known to study the score of the Beethoven symphony in infinite detail over a period of years, just how much can the musical amateur expect to hear and comprehend in a single performance leasting some twenty minutes?

When beginning a study of *Hamlet* an English literature class would expect to read the play, check on word meanings, and analyze symbols, character description and development, plot and structure before arriving at some understanding of what the play was all about. The next step would be to attend an actual performance of the play followed by discussion and additional analysis, plus the additional possibility of evaluating the performance itself. Repeated trips to the theatre would of course deepen their understanding of the play. No less could logically be expected in terms of the *Fifth Symphony*.

On the other hand, to *write* as well as Shakespeare or Beethoven is a requirement which is not practical. The creation of literature or music must necessarily be left to the labors of a chosen few. To go still further, to act in the play or perform the music are endeavors for the few rather than the many. Our goal is to acquire an understanding of the elements of music (rhythm, melody, harmony and tone color), and how they are combined into meaningful units. The procedure, then, will be to commence with the characteristics of sound, and work our way through the elements of music, musical notation, and principles of organization until we arrive at a comprehensive understanding of the language of music.

Characteristics of Sound

Musical sounds, or tones result from a vibrating string (piano or column of air (trumpet). Setting a string into vibration or motion by striking it will generate sound waves which radiate from the source in an expanding sphere. When these physical disturbances of the air (sound waves) reach the ear, they are perceived as a *tone*, or musical pitch (highness or lowness of sound). A specific pitch is heard because strings and air columns vibrate in a regular pattern at a fixed rate. Irregular patterns of vibrations such as the squeak of chalk on a blackboard or the rattle of pots and pans are heard as noise.

Using the single note of middle C on the piano (see piano keyboard illustration below), striking it firmly, and holding it for five seconds can demonstrate all four characteristics of musical tones:

physical characteristic	*psychological characteristic*
frequency ——————→	pitch
amplitude ——————→	intensity or loudness
duration ——————→	duration (note value)
overtone structure ——→	tone color or timbre

The *frequency* of middle C is the number of complete vibrations the string will make in one second, in this case 256 cps (cycles per second). These 256 vibrations are heard as a musical *pitch*, or tone. The *amplitude* refers to the size of the vibration; the farther the string is displaced from its position of rest, the greater the amplitude of vibration and the *louder* the tone that is heard. In terms of this illustration a *duration* of five seconds has been prescribed which means simply that the tone has a length, or duration of five seconds. The *overtone structure* of a set of piano strings (middle C has three strings) is that characteristic by which we know we are hearing a piano rather than a violin or harp; we hear the *tone color* which results from the overtone series.

The *overtone series* is a physical phenomenon common to all vibrating strings and air columns. Strings, for example, vibrate throughout their entire length and give the *fundamental tone*, or the pitch that we actually hear. In addition, the string vibrates in segments: halves, thirds, fourths and so forth. Each segment produces its own pitch, each of which is higher and softer than the fundamental pitch. This can be illustrated as follows:

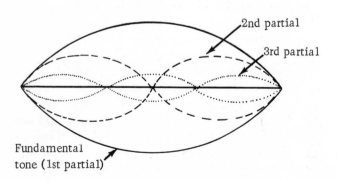

2nd partial

3rd partial

Fundamental tone (1st partial)

Using middle C as the fundamental tone (1st partial), the 2nd partial is 'c' above middle C and the 3rd partial is 'g' above that 'c'. These overtones proceed in a regular pattern upward from the fundamental pitch until they pass out of audible range. The pattern of overtones never changes but the relative strength (loudness) of the individual partials varies, depending on whether the vibrating body is string or air column and how this body is set in motion.[1]

Musical Notation

Pitch

The essential elements of our notational system were devised some ten centuries ago and subsequently altered and augmented to become a reasonably efficient means of communicating the composer's intentions to listener and performer. The system is based on the first seven letters of the alphabet and can best be illustrated by using a segment of the piano keyboard. The pitches range from low to high, from A through G in a repeating A—G pattern.[2]

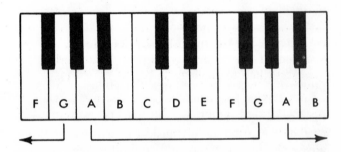

In order to know which of the eight A's available on the piano is the intended note the following is necessary:

1. use a musical *staff* of five lines and four spaces;

2. use a symbol for a musical pitch, i.e., *note*;

3. place the notes on the staff;

---

[1]Overtones are discussed further in connection with Greek music and musical instruments. Also see *Overtone Series* in Appendix I.

[2]The pattern A—G (rather than C—B) is used simply because it begins with the first letter of the alphabet.

4. indicate by means of a *clef sign* the *names* of the notes.

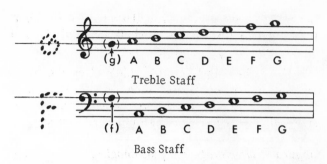

Treble Staff

Bass Staff

Clef (French, *key*) implies that the key to precise placement of the notes is the establishment of the letter name of *one* of the lines or spaces of the staff. There are two clefs in common use. Both are ornamental symbols derived from the letters G and F. The solid lines are the present clef signs and the dotted lines their original form.

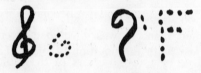

The clefs are placed on the staff to indicate the location of the letters they represent. Although the clef sign can specify G or F on any staff line or space, they are usually confined to one location on the staff. The lower portion of the G clef curls around the second line to indicate the location of G; the two dots of the F clef are placed above and below the fourth line to show that this is the F line.

Once the five-line staff has received its pitch designations of G or F, the *staff* is subsequently identified as *treble,* or *bass staff.*

Both these staffs (or staves) are segments of a complete system of eleven lines and ten spaces called the *great staff*:

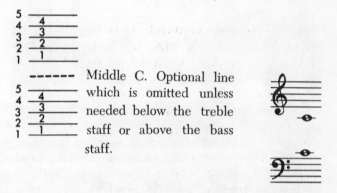

Middle C. Optional line which is omitted unless needed below the treble staff or above the bass staff.

A rising sequence of two sets of pitches (A through G) would look like this on:

1. Individual staves

2. The piano keyboard

3. The great staff

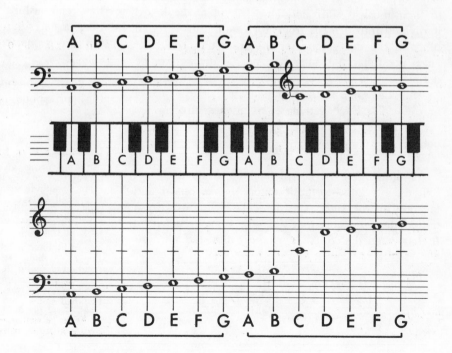

Leger lines are short lines used to indicate the pitch of notes which lie above or below:

1. Treble or bass staff

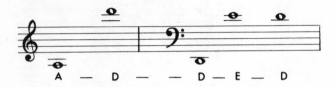

2. The great staff (with the two sets of lines separated for greater clarity in reading)

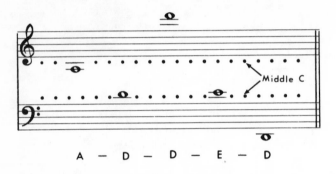

Letter Designations

With only seven letters for pitches and eighty-eight pitches available on the piano keyboard it is necessary to have a system by which musical pitches can be pinpointed by letter name without reference to their musical staff notation. The piano keyboard is divided into *octaves* from, for example c^1 through b^1, with the next higher octave from c^2 through b^2 (also notated c''–b'') and so on. An *octave* can be defined as the distance between two adjacent pitches bearing the *same* letter name: c^1–c^2 (or c''), c^2–c^3 or c''–c'''). Each set of seven pitches also has an octave name; c^1–d^1–e^1–f^1–g^1–a^1–b^1 is the one-line octave.[3]

Following is the complete pitch designation system as it relates to position on the keyboard and location on the staff. The numeral '8' followed by a dotted line indicates that the note *sounds* an octave *higher* when the "8 . . . ." is *above* the staff and an

octave *lower* when the "8 . . . ." is *below* the staff.

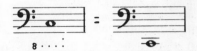

Loudness (Intensity)

Composers did not indicate how loud or how soft the music was to be performed until about the year 1600. This particular element will therefore be taken up in conjunction with musical development in the seventeenth century.

Duration

The notation of the length of time of musical sounds (and silences) was developed in conjunction, more or less, with the notation of pitch. The modern *note-value* system consists of fractional parts of a whole unit, or *whole note* (𝅝), expressed in mathematical terms as 1/1.[4] A *half note* (𝅗𝅥) is one-half the whole unit, or ½; a *quarter note* (𝅘𝅥) is one-quarter the unit, or ¼ and so forth.

The *name* of the note value indicates the *number* of notes in the whole-note unit: There are four quarter notes ($4 \times ¼ = 1/1$), eight eighth notes ($8 \times ⅛ = 1/1$, etc.).

With note values smaller than the whole note the relationships remain constant: There are two quarter notes in a half note ($2 \times ¼ = ½$), two eighth notes in a quarter note ($2 \times ⅛ = ¼$), etc.

The following reference chart (to be consulted as necessary) outlines the entire system (including the corresponding durations of *silences* known as *rests*).

[3]The names given to the octaves have no special significance; they are merely used for identification. For example, there is nothing great about the Great Octave or small about the Small Octave. The terms simply identify specific sets of pitches. The outline of pitch identification (nomenclature) is a *reference chart*, to be referred to when necessary (particularly in connection with Greek Music).

[4]Rhythmic notation is both relative and fixed. The duration of a whole note is dependent on the tempo (speed) and notation of music. It may have a duration of one second, eight seconds or something in between. The *interior* relationships, however, never vary. A whole note has the same duration as two half notes, four quarter notes and so forth. The mathematical relationship is fixed and precise.

REFERENCE CHART: PITCH NOMENCLATURE

REFERENCE CHART:
NOTE AND REST VALUES

Note Value	Symbol	Rest Value	Symbol
Double whole note		Double whole-note rest	
Whole note (basic unit)		Whole (note) rest	
Half note		Half rest	
Quarter note		Quarter rest	
Eighth note		Eighth rest	
Sixteenth note		Sixteenth rest	
Thirty-second note		Thirty-second rest	
Sixty-fourth note		Sixty-fourth rest	

Rhythmic notation uses certain conventional symbols and terms including *notehead, stem, flag, beam, tie, dot,* and *double dot*:

Notes may be:

beamed for easier reading (if all notes have flags);

tied over to the next note (continuation of tone);

dotted to increase their value; the augmentation dot adds half the value to the note it augments;

dotted half note

dotted quarter note

double dotted to increase their value still further; the second dot adds half the value of the first dot.

double-dotted half note

double-dotted quarter note

Rhythm

Rhythm, one of the four elements of music is easier to hear than define. It can be heard in the complex noise patterns of a large city, the click of train wheels on rails, a Ping-pong game or the castanets of a Spanish dancer. Essentially, rhythm is the organization of musical time, i.e., everything that takes place with respect to the duration of sound and silence, musical tones and noise, accent and non-accent, tension and relaxation.

Rhythm is the name of the whole and is not to be confused with *beat,* which results from a certain regularity of the rhythmic patterns. Beat, or pulse can be compared with heart beat, or pulse rate. The beat will usually be steady, but it may temporarily speed up or slow down. It may be *explicit* (the uniform thump of a bass drum in a marching band) or *implicit* (resulting from combinations of rhythmic patterns). As soon as one duration follows another there will be rhythm but not necessarily beat. Certain types of music (such as Gregorian chant) do not produce the regular pulsation called beat.

When beats are produced by the music in a repeating pattern of accents the result is *meter.* *Metered* music is *measured* music, with groupings of two, three or four beats (or combinations of these) in each *measure,* or *bar.*

Duple Meter (two beats per measure)

First beat stressed (accented)

Example:

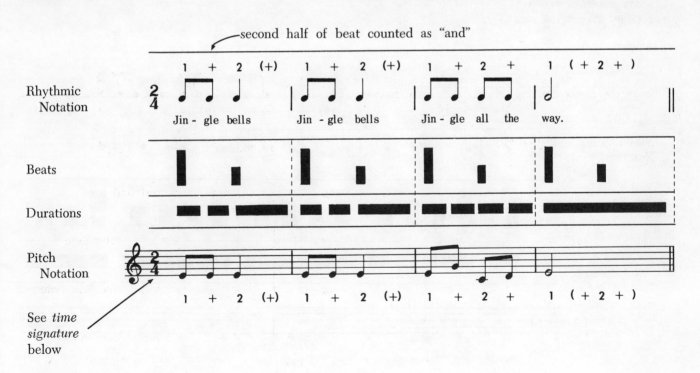

Triple Meter (three beats to a measure or bar)

First beat accented

Example:

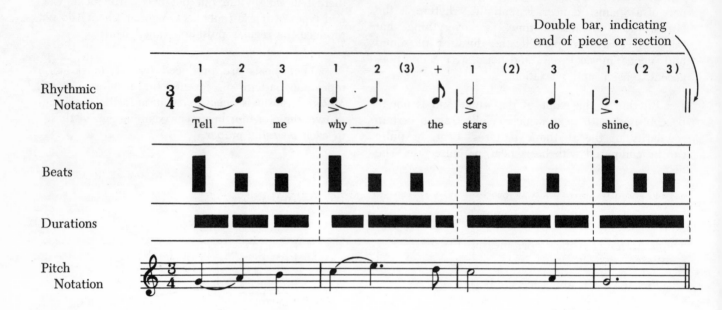

Quadruple Meter (four beats to a bar)

Primary accent (>) on '1'
Secondary accent (>) on '3'

Example:

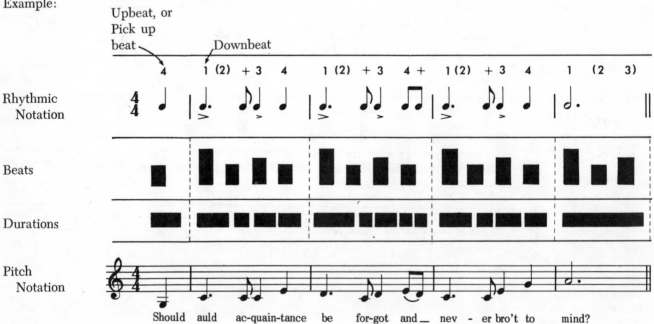

Beat Patterns

The most effective way to recognize meters is to trace the metrical patterns in the air using a *conductor's beat.*

Duple meter

downbeat upbeat

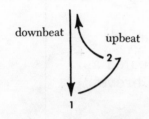

downbeat   upbeat

Triple meter

downbeat   upbeat

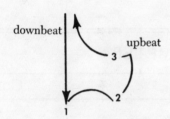

downbeat   upbeat

Quadruple meter

downbeat   upbeat

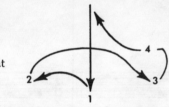

Time Signatures (Meter Signatures)

Metrical (measured) music usually includes two numerals at the beginning of a piece to indicate *meter* and *unit of beat:*

$\frac{2}{4}$ = duple meter

$\frac{2}{4}$ = ♩ unit of beat (quarter note receives one beat)

The *time signature* also indicates whether the meter is *simple* or *compound.*

Simple meter (beats divided into *two* equal parts)

simple duple meter   *simple triple* meter

N.B. The lower numeral can be replaced by the unit of beat:

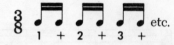   etc.

Compound meter (beats divided into *three* equal parts)

compound duple meter   *compound triple* meter

one and uh two and uh   one and uh two and uh three and uh

Alternate time signatures:

$\frac{6}{8} = \frac{2}{♩.}$ $\frac{9}{4} = \frac{3}{♩.}$ etc.

Examples:

Simple duple

Fath'r and I went down to camp a - long with Cap - tain Good - 'in,

Compound duple

For he's a jol - ly good fel - low, for he's a jol - ly good fel - low,

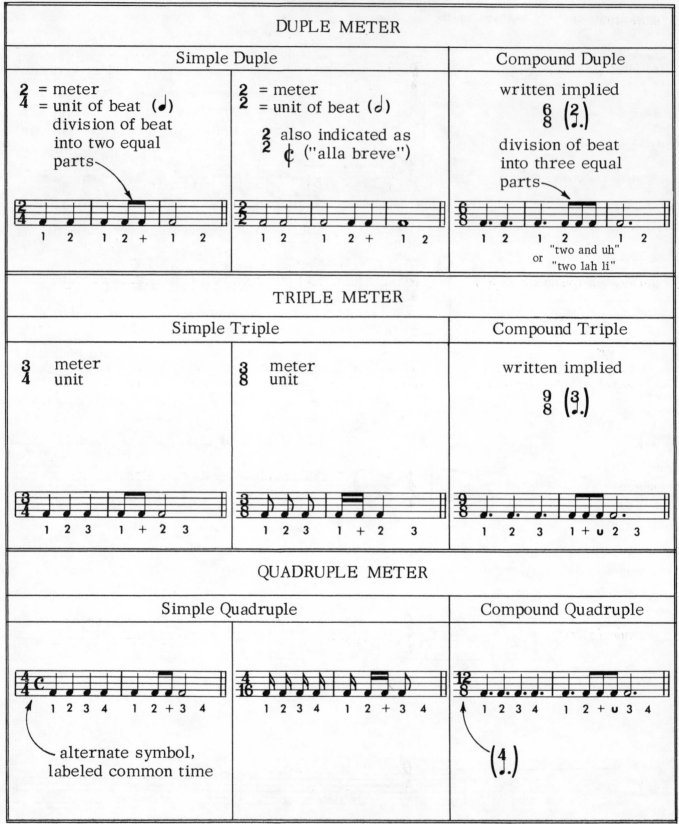

Melody

A melody is a horizontal organization of pitches or, simply, a succession of musical tones. Melodies may move with:

conjunct (stepwise) motion

disjunct (skipping) motion

disjunct and conjunct motion

In addition to describing the types of melodic motion, melodies may also be described by the range they encompass: the distance between the lowest and highest notes of a particular melody. *Ranges* may be:

narrow

medium (average)

wide

Harmony

Harmony exists when two or more pitches are sounded simultaneously. It can also be described as a vertical organization of pitches. Because harmony was developed during the Middle Ages it will be discussed in greater detail in conjunction with the development of medieval music.

REFERENCE CHART: HARMONY

Six different vertical organizations (individual harmonies):

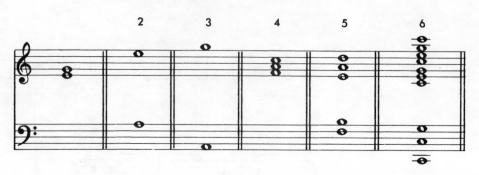

Horizontal organization (melody) combined with harmony:

MUSICAL EXAMPLES FOR EXERCISES IN LISTENING

Listening Outline

Bach, Johann Sebastian, *Fugue in G minor*

1. Instrumental: pipe organ
2. Moderate
3. Medium loud
4. Solo
5. Regular beat
6. Simultaneous melodies
7. Secular

Conclusions

1. Period: 18th century
2. Style: fugue
3. Germany

Bartók, Béla, *Concerto for Orchestra*, 4th Movement

1. Instrumental: orchestra
2. Slow-fast-slow
3. Combination
4. Large ensemble
5. Regular beat
6. Melodies with accompaniment
7. Secular

1. 20th century
2. Concerto (symphony)
3. Hungary (United States)

Beethoven, Ludwig van, Symphony No. 5, 3rd Movement (scherzo)

1. Instrumental: orchestra
2. Fast
3. Combination
4. Large ensemble
5. Regular beat
6. Melodies with accompaniment
7. Secular

1. 19th century
2. Symphony
3. Germany (Austria)

Bennet, John, *Thyrsis, Sleepest Thou?*

1. Vocal, English text
2. Fast
3. Medium loud
4. Medium ensemble (chorus)
5. Regular beat
6. Simultaneous melodies
7. Secular

1. 16th century
2. Madrigal
3. England

Brahms, Johannes, Symphony No. 3, 3rd Movement

1. Instrumental: orchestra
2. Moderate
3. Soft—loud
4. Large ensemble
5. Regular beat
6. Melodies with accompaniment
7. Secular

1. 19th century
2. Symphony
3. Germany

Debussy, Claude, *Voiles* (Sails)

1. Instrumental: piano
2. Slow
3. Soft
4. Solo
5. Indistinct beat
6. Melodies with accompaniment
7. Secular

1. 20th century
2. Piano solo
3. France

Gabrieli, Giovanni, *Et ecclesiis*

1. Vocal and instrumental
2. Moderate
3. Soft—loud
4. Chorus, organ, brass (large)
5. Regular beat
6. Melody and accompaniment
7. Sacred

1. 16th century
2. Motet
3. Italy (Venice)

Haydn, Franz Joseph, Quartet in F Major, 2nd Movement

1. Instrumental: strings
2. Slow
3. Soft—medium loud
4. Small ensemble (string quartet)

1. 18th century
2. String quartet
3. Austria

5. Regular beat
6. Melody with accompaniment
7. Secular

Scarlatti, Domenico, *Sonata*, Longo 104

1. Instrumental: harpsichord
2. Fast—very fast
3. Medium loud
4. Solo
5. Regular beat
6. Melody with accompaniment
7. Secular

1. 18th century
2. Harpsichord solo
3. Italy

Schubert, Franz, *Gretchen am Spinnrade* ("Margaret at the Spinning Wheel")

1. Vocal and instrumental
2. Moderate
3. Medium loud
4. Vocal solo with piano accom.
5. Regular beat
6. Melody with accompaniment
7. Secular

1. 19th century
2. Song
3. Germany

——————————, Jazz: "Kyrie Eleison" from *Jazz Suite on the Mass Texts*

1. Vocal and instrumental
2. Moderate
3. Medium loud—loud
4. Chorus with medium ensemble
5. Regular beat
6. Melody with accompaniment and simultaneous melodies
7. Sacred

1. 20th century
2. Mass; Jazz
3. United States

——————————, Jazz: *This Here*

1. Instrumental
2. Moderate
3. Medium loud
4. Small ensemble
5. Regular beat
6. Melody with accompaniment
7. Secular

1. 20th century
2. Jazz
3. United States

——————————, Sequence: *Victimae paschali laudes*

1. Vocal
2. Moderate
3. Medium soft
4. Solo and chorus
5. No regular beat
6. One melody, unaccompanied
7. Sacred

1. 600-1450 A.D.
2. Sequence (liturgical)
3. Western Europe

_____, Spiritual: *Didn't It Rain*

1. Vocal and instrumental
2. Moderately fast
3. Loud
4. Solo and medium ensemble
5. Regular beat
6. Melody with accompaniment
7. Sacred

1. 19th century
2. Spiritual (folk song)
3. United States

_____, Trouvère song: *Or la truix*

1. Vocal
2. Moderate
3. Medium soft
4. Solo
5. Regular beat
6. One melody, unaccompanied
7. Secular

1. 600-1450 A.D.
2. Trouvère song
3. France

RECORD LIST

Following are some suggested recordings for the music used in Exercises in Listening. Because records are constantly going out of print alternate selections are given wherever possible. Records are listed by composer, composition, title of record album (if different from the title of the composition, performer or performing group, record company and catalog number. All records are 12 inches, 33⅓ LP's unless specified otherwise. Catalog numbers for monophonic records are listed first, followed by the stereo number (if any).

1. Bach, J. S., Fugue in G minor, Schweitzer, Angel COLC-89.
   or: Recordings of Bach's organ works by Biggs, Weinrich, Richter, Walcha, Dupré, etc.
2. Bartók, B., *Concerto for Orchestra*, Ormandy, Philadelphia Orch., Columbia ML-6026; MS-6626.
   or: Szell, Cleveland Orch., Columbia ML-6215; MS-6815.
      Bernstein, N.Y. Phil., Columbia ML-5471; 6040.
      Leinsdorf, Boston Sym., Victor LM-2643; LSC-2643.
3. Beethoven, L. v., Symphony No. 5, Ormandy, Philadelphia Orch., Columbia ML-5098.
   or: Munch, Boston, Sym., Victor VIC-1035; VICS-1035.
      Bernstein, N.Y. Phil., ("How a Great Symphony Was Written"), Columbia ML-5868; MS-6468.
      (and many others).
4. Bennet, John, "Thyrsis, Sleepest Thou?", *Masterpieces of Music before 1750*, Vol. 2, Haydn Society 9039 (3 volume set, 9038/9040).
5. Brahms, J., Symphony No. 3, Reiner, Chicago Sym., Victor LM-2209; LSC-2209.

   or: Szell, Cleveland Orch., Columbia ML-6085; MS-6685.
      Karajan, Vienna Phil., London 9318; 6249.
6. Debussy, C., "Voiles," *Preludes for Piano*, Books One and Two, Horowitz, Columbia ML-5941; MS-6541.
   or: Casadesus, 2-Columbia ML-4977/8.
      Gieseking, 2-Angel 35066, 35249.
      Bachauer, Mercury 50391; 90391.
7. Gabrieli, G., "Et Ecclesiis," *History of Music in Sound*, Vol. 4, Victor LM-6029.
   or: Stokowski, Victor LM-1721.
8. Haydn, F. J., Quartet in F Major, Allegri Quartet, Westminster 19111; 17111.
   or: Amadeus Quartet, Westminster 9033.
      Janacek Quartet, London 9385; 6385.
9. Scarlatti, D., Sonata in C Major, Longo 104, Valenti, Harpsichord, 3-Westminster 1010; S-1010.
   or: Kirkpatrick, 4-Columbia SL-221.
      Landowska, 2-Angel COLH-73, 304.
10. Schubert, F., "Gretchen am Spinnrade," *A Lieder Recital by Schwarzkopf and Fischer*, Angel 35022.
    or: *Marian Anderson Sings Beloved Schubert Songs*, Victor LM-98.
11. Jazz: "Kyrie Eleison" from *Jazz Suite on the Mass Texts*, Victor LPM-3414; LSP-3414.
12. Jazz: "This Here," Cannonball Adderly, *Quintet in San Francisco*, Riverside 311; 1157.
    or: Cannonball Adderly, *Greatest Hits*, Riverside 416; 9416.
13. Sequence, "Victimae paschali laudes," *Masterpieces of Music before 1750* (henceforth referred to as *Masterpieces*), 3 volumes, Haydn Society 9038/9040.
14. Spiritual, "Didn't It Rain," *Newport 1958: Mahalia Jackson*, Columbia CL-1244; CS-8071.
    or: Mahalia Jackson, *Greatest Hits*, Columbia CL-2004; CS-8804.
15. Trouvère song, "Or la truix," *Masterpieces*.

unit II

the search for
freedom in Greece

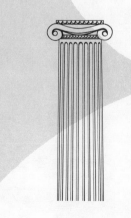

Some Foundations for Greek Culture: The Tyranny of Tradition and Nature in Greece

One of the theses of this unit is that the triumph of Greek civilization and the brilliant culture which flourished in the fifth century came only after a victory over the forces of nature and of tradition. Much of the land area of the Greek peninsula has never been productive. It is laced with mountains upon which sheep graze, but which will support little other agriculture. Even in the valleys the land is rocky. From very early references, we know that land-erosion has always been a problem in this land. The task of wresting a bare existence from such soil

has always been a difficult one, although the sea offered possibilities for fishing and for trade. The earliest civilization in Greece was almost a twofold one; in the narrow rocky valleys we find small groups of people living as tribes or clans, making their living from agriculture, which consisted mainly of the raising of sheep and goats. Near the sea another type of culture, centered around fishing and trading, was also apparent. In either case, life was hard.

The earliest period of Greek life is usually known as the Archaic period. We may date it from 900 B.C. to 500 B.C.

"Full is the earth of ills, and full no less are the waters.

Freely diseases among mankind by day and in darkness

Hither and thither may pass, and bring much woe upon mortals,—

Voiceless, since of speech high-counseling Zeus has bereft them."

The quotation is from Hesiod, a poet who lived in the ninth century B.C., who described the life of the Greek farmer of his time. According to his reports, it was a dull, dreary life, filled with work, and with little reward for the labor.

It would seem that nature, superstition, and tradition bound the early Greek during this long period. His land was poor, and his horizon narrow. The earliest governmental groups were clans related throughout by blood ties. It was a civilization which looked backward, for the most vital of their religions was ancestor worship. Indeed, as one examines the answer which these people made to the questions of their relation to God and the universe, one can well understand that there was little opportunity for individuality. Ancestor worship is essentially a reactionary belief, judging all human conduct by past experience. New ideas would have little chance. In addition, of course, these people had their Olympian gods, usually representing the forces of nature. The fact that they imagined these gods as being entirely capricious and unpredictable suggests their lack of knowledge about the laws of nature.

In the relations between the individual and the group there seems to be little more freedom for human action. The ruler of the clan, the oldest free man of the group, bore the title of both king and priest. With his authority as temporal ruler bolstered by his religious power, clothed as it was with superstition

and fear, there was little chance for any disobedience to his will. The very fact that the members of the clan were all related had a further stifling influence upon the individual, we must suppose. A college student can perhaps understand this if he imagines living in a group entirely composed of uncles, aunts, sisters, cousins, and all the other relatives. There would be little chance for him to live his own life.

When we look at the question of the individual's purpose for living, the answer seems to be simple. The person worked, worshipped, fought with neighbors, and eventually died. We may get some of the flavor of this life from Hesiod, again, who writes:

"Truly, the gods keep hid from mortals the means of subsistence."

The picture of this period of culture seems black indeed. This was the time of the simple Doric hut which is diagrammed in a later chapter, the time of the carving of the archaic statues, so straight and unnatural, and the time exemplified by the chorus in Aeschylus' Agamemnon.

But the picture was not wholly gloomy. The ruler was advised by a council composed of all the free men in the clan, and later, when several clans banded together into a tribe, we see two advisory bodies grow up: a senate, composed of the elders of the several clans, and a larger advisory group consisting of all the free men within the tribe. These advisory groups eventually gained sufficient power to promote the king-priest to the position of priest alone, and to select a king, usually for a term of a year, from their own group. There is the possibility of progress here.

Perhaps even more important is the fact that these people probably did not want to remain within the suffocating boundaries which we have noticed. Not only did their myths deal with a seemingly unknowable and unpredictable universe, but also with the magnificent Greek heroes such as Agamemnon. These were the men who thrust aside the narrow bounds of archaic existence and invaded the territory and sphere of action which was reserved for gods alone. That these men invariably met their doom because of their rash acts makes little difference. The important thing is that they were the heroes to be admired and followed. Furthermore, these people were creative. While their statues were narrow and traditional, yet they showed the desire to make something new. It was this spirit which led the Greeks into the period of great liberty.

The record of this early time shows it to be a half dozen centuries of ignorance but of questioning. The world around these early men was new and fresh. Each day's dawning brought new and unpredictable experience, new questions about the nature of things. There were no answers, or rather, there were only the answers which the people could give in the light of their limited knowledge. The eclipse, the rain, the flood, the rising and setting of sun and moon, and the clouds rolling down from Mount Ida to obscure the battlefield: all these phenomena could only be answered with the sentence, "It is the whim of the Gods." An ignorant people, tribesmen living according to the laws of the tribe, the important thing about them was that they were asking questions. The infinite mystery of the world lay around them, and they, with eager and childlike curiosity, asked questions and demanded answers of that world. That the answers were wrong, that they ended in every case with the inscrutable gods, is unimportant. The intellectual curiosity which prompted the questions was the seed from which grew answers ever more right, allowing wider and wider zones for human action.

The Iliad Interprets the Early Period of Chaos

It was the poet Homer, writing of the Trojan War, who gives us the best artistic interpretation of the spirit of man in this early phase of the period of chaos which we call archaic. The first of his two epic poems deals with the closing phases of that war, while the second, the *Odyssey*, tells of the return of Odysseus from the struggle. It is the first of these poems, the *Iliad*, which we wish to discuss here.

The story of the *Iliad* is an account of the events of fifty-two days in the ninth year of the Trojan War. The occasion of the poem is the quarrel between Agamemnon and Achilles. Agamemnon has refused to accept a ransom for his captive, Chryseis, from her father, Chryses, priest of Apollo; and the priest prays for Apollo's wrath to be visited upon the Greeks. It is, and the Greeks suffer in battle. The chiefs are then called into council by Achilles, to find what has angered the god, and a soothsayer tells them the reason for the sun-god's wrath. Achilles urges Agamemnon to give the maiden up; but the king refuses. When Achilles presses the point, Agamemnon agrees, but angrily takes away from Achilles, Briseis, Achilles' captive. Achilles, sulking, prays Zeus to wreak his wrath upon Agamemnon, and Achilles himself refuses to fight.

The tide of battle now turns against the Greeks; they are forced to build a wall about their ships to protect them from the Trojans. Zeus favors the Trojans until Achilles is pacified, but the other gods are not unanimous. Hera even tries to circumvent Zeus' decree by causing him to slumber so that the Greeks may be at least temporarily successful; but he wakes and gives new victory to the Trojans. In Book XVI comes the crucial episode. Patroklus, Achilles' friend, begs the hero to return to the fight and throw the Trojans back to their walls. Failing in this entreaty, Patroklus borrows Achilles' armor and goes into the fray, hoping to make the Trojans think that Achilles has returned. Patroklus is slain, and Achilles' grief is great enough to cause him to return to the struggle. Thetis, Achilles' mother, procures new armor for the hero, forged by the god, Hephaestus, and Achilles goes into battle. There follows a search for the Trojan hero, Hector, and in Book XXII the two mighty warriors engage in single combat. Achilles wins and shamefully abuses the body of Hector by tying it to his chariot and dragging it nine times around the walls of Troy. The poem ends with the funeral of Patroklus and the ransom of Hector's body by his father, Priam, King of Troy.

"Thus held they funeral for Hector, tamer of horses."

It is a temptation to linger over the literary value of the epics, the beauty of phrase, the vividness of imagery, the poetic power; but our concern with the epics here is not the concern of *belles lettres*. It is rather with a very limited but exceedingly important aspect of the author's view of men and their conduct. In the poems, men and gods move together in bewildering proximity. Deities are constantly intervening in behalf of mortals, or turning their divine anger against them. Yet despite these Olympian interventions, despite the operation of what seems to be caprice and whim, the dominant note is that man is responsible for his own destiny. There are times when he seems a plaything, the shuttlecock of irresponsible players, but *in the main* he is his own agent. The idea is not presented in black and white clarity; it does not have the Hebraic intensity of sin-and-punishment cause and effect. It is as if the maker of the poem, uncertain of all the reasons underlying the events which happen to man—

remember that these gods were heightened ideas of natural phenomena—could yet see that many times the forces affecting the individual are those he himself has set in motion.

The gods are gods, men are men; both have their own desires and wishes. Within the pattern of the will of the gods, often neither just nor fair, though generally their interest is the good of men, within that pattern, man is largely responsible for his own fate. It is thus that the zone of freedom in human conduct was established. What happens to man is, more often than not, the consequence of choices he has made. If he is intelligent, wise in his choices, just and fair in his dealings, his lot is probably good although even his best efforts and endeavors may sometimes run counter to *diké*, "The Way Things Are," and he may become the victim of forces beyond reason or control. Yet for the most part his *fate* is his character.

Achilles' withdrawal from the fight is a case in point. Wounded in his vanity (more vulnerable than his heel!), he prays Zeus, in a moment of pique, that the Greeks may suffer because they do not appreciate him. His prayer, like his wrath, is unworthy of him, and the consequences of it go far beyond his expectations. Patroklus, fighting in the armor of Achilles, had been warned not to pursue the Trojans once they had turned from the ships; but his reckless ardor led him into the bad choice of actions like those of his superiors, and he is killed. Hector, the noblest warrior of them all, is the victim whose lot we most deplore; yet even Hector, personally as near blameless as a man can be, is up against the Way Things Are; he is a Trojan, and Troy has merited destruction. Agamemnon, not once but many times, has revealed himself as a man who forges his own doom, for it was his pride which led to the sacrifice of his daughter, Iphigenia, and later to the quarrel with Achilles. His tragedy lies less in what happens to him (violent death at the hands of his wife) than in being the kind of man to whom tragedy must come. His violence, his failure to make good choices, show him as one who runs counter to the Way Things Are.

Thus in these early poems one sees the reaching toward the discovery of an idea about the nature of man: that despite Chance, or Fate, or the caprice of the gods, or whatever name one gives to the powers arrayed against him, man himself, in his own purposes and choices, is the instrument of his own destiny.

The zone of safe action was a narrow one, and only the man who risked little was sure—or reasonably sure—of a long life. Thus did Thetis, mother of Achilles, have a choice of a long and, we suspect, dull life for her son or a short but glorious one. She chose the latter, for the narrow zone did not allow for great individualism. While the Greeks respected the crafty and intelligent man, the man who never overreached himself and who lived long within the limits, they loved their tragic heroes, for they were men whose boldness defied the narrow limits. For proof we need but count the stories which are told of Agamemnon and those which are told of the intelligent and long-lived Odysseus. The Greeks recognized the inevitable necessity of The Way Things Are, but their deep love for great individual action pushed constantly against the limits of the zone of action, and made for the great freedom which the Greeks finally enjoyed.

The archaic statues, narrow, stiff, and straight, may be taken as symbols of this time. Carved as they were in the tradition of tree-trunk sculpture, they were limited to the narrow bounds of the tree's diameter, bounds imposed by nature which, as yet, the Greeks had to accept as they found it. It is the same nature which caused the clouds to rise from the river Scamander or which caused the dust of the Trojan plain to obscure both the pursued victim and the haughty pursuer in the battle before Ilium. These were the forces of nature which were interpreted as all-powerful gods. The archaic statue, man's attempt to create shape and shapeliness *of his own*, was thus constrained by the limits of nature. The important thing is that man was trying to create his own order, and would continue trying. In that unceasing effort he was to learn to work more fully with these forces which at one time bound him, and in the fullness of that work, to expand the zone of his own area of life.

EXERCISES

1. One writer has suggested that the realization of freedom depends upon the achievement of five conditions of life. He lists these as follows:

a. The banishment of superstition. What effect would superstition have upon the life of people? What would be the best cure for it?

b. The right for all people to express their ideas and to have these ideas accepted or rejected on their own merit. What happens to this condition in a caste society? What does an unequal distribution of money do for this condition?

c. A certain amount of unselfishness on the part of all people so that they can see that what they do for the general good is also for their own good.

d. A relatively large amount of leisure time. This condition is an interesting one. How much leisure is good? How much leisure would work against a good society?

e. A critical pride which avoids smugness, which sees areas of improvement.

It would be interesting to take this list of conditions for freedom and see how many of them were present in archaic Greek society, and then to trace their development as that development is discussed in the next two chapters. For example, what would be the effects of each one of the political reforms which is discussed? What would be the effect of the victory over the Persians? Of the discovery of the silver mines near Athens?

Men, Events, and Ideas Leading to Classical Greek Culture

The long roll of the centuries after the Heroic Age, one differing little from another, reached a climax in Greece shortly before the middle of the fifth century B.C. A succession of illustrious men, of remarkable events, and of startlingly new ideas brought about a great change. It is the purpose of this chapter to look at the work of some of those men, to review some of the great events, and to discuss some of those great ideas. Then we shall look at the dramatist Aeschylus, who more than any other was aware of the changes going on and helped to foster them.

About the year 621 B.C. the archon or ruler of Athens, Draco, published a set of laws. That sounds like an unremarkable statement, until one realizes that here for the first time was an opportunity for men to know exactly where they stood in relation to the law, not at the whim or caprice of the ruler. There are few real facts known about the Code of Draco, except that the penalty for almost all crimes was death; indeed, the severity of the laws has made the word "Draconian" the synonym for unreasonable severity. Yet the notion that the laws should be published and made known is a step toward the knowledge which was to make men free.

Draco's code, of course, did little to reduce the inequalities within the population; the stranglehold of the rich was not affected, nor was poverty of the very poor alleviated. Particularly evil was the custom of borrowing money on the security of the debtor's person, for defaulters thereby became slaves. Because of this practice, thousands of former freemen had become slaves.

A second reformer, Solon, who became archon in 594, undertook to relieve the inequalities of Athens by drastic economic reforms. He cancelled all debts, so that the entire city-state could begin anew, from an economic standpoint; he freed all slaves who had gone into slavery because of debt, and abolished the law that made such slavery possible; he established a graduated income tax, designed to maintain a greater degree of economic equality than had existed before; and he regulated the amount of land that one individual might own, in some cases confiscating parts of the great estates that had grown up. He introduced the law that sons of Athenians killed in battle should be reared at the public expense. In short, it was Solon more than any other individual who established a degree of equality among his people, a condition of prime importance if men are to be free. There are many other contributions from Solon to the growth of Athenian democracy; suffice it to say that his name has become the synonym for a wise lawgiver.

He was aided in his effort by a succeeding ruler, Peisistratus, who made the laws of Solon more effective. While Solon's laws had freed many men, the laws had not given these men land. Peisistratus created small farms out of the land which had been taken from the large holdings and distributed them among the freed people. With this reform, many more people were able to meet the property qualifications for voting, and consquently many more people had an active voice in the government. Not the least of Peisistratus' reforms lay in the collection of much of the literature of Greece, and in providing festivals for the people in which these poems were recited. When the people realized their common culture and tradition, their sense of pride in their land grew accordingly, and tended to transfer loyalty from the small clan or tribe to the whole city-state, Athens.

The last of the great reformers was Cleisthenes, at the end of the sixth century B.C.; he has been called the father of Athenian democracy. Perhaps his most important change was to abolish the old blood clans and to substitute artificial political units in their place. He retained small political groups which he called *demes*, and retained the idea of the tribe, for his law stated that a "tribe" was to be composed of ten "demes." These ten demes, however, were situated in various parts of the city of Athens, so that each tribe had within it people of all classes and political parties of the city-state. He increased the power of the assembly, a group composed of all the free citizens of Athens, and enlarged the senate to five hundred members (ten members of each of the fifty tribes which made up the city's population). Cleisthenes' new laws placed the actual executive power of government in the hands of a committee of ten generals who were elected yearly by the assembly. This committe-of-ten was headed by a commander-in-chief whose term, like that of the committee members, was for one year. Cleisthenes increased the citizenship greatly by extending the franchise and admitting to full citizenship all of the foreign merchants who lived in Athens, thus introducing new blood and new ideas into the government of his state.

Thus it was that politics became purely secular in Athens, divorced from blood ties or religion. It was now possible for the individual to assert himself in dealing with other men, since an individual act was no longer to be censored by the group consisting entirely of uncles, aunts, sisters, brothers, or cousins. Neither did a political act have religious significance, and a man or woman could do as he pleased in the matter of government without running the risk of being considered impious or sacrilegious. Following the reforms of Solon and Peisistratus, a great middle class had been established, so that there could be freedom of expression among all free men of the city-state.

Among the remarkable events, the most striking is the repulse of invasions from Persia, twice in a decade. The battle of Marathon, 490 B.C., stopped the advance of an overwhelming Oriental army; and the battle of Salamis, 480 B.C., was the turning point of a second invasion. These two victories, Marathon by land, Salamis by sea, were the occasion of great patriotic pride; the David-and-Goliath story of the defeat of a mighty empire by a handful of city-states was like the effect in England, much later, of the defeat of the Spanish Armada. These wars had all the ideological implications of the struggle of freemen against totalitarian aggressors; for the Persian emperors were the most powerful in the East, and their armies, if not the best-trained, were certainly the most numerous in the world. The Greeks were not a military group of states, and their victories against impossible odds yielded them tremendous pride in their achievement. It is hardly too much to say that the victory over the Persians made possible a Western European world, without the threat of

Oriental despotisms. Small wonder that the Greeks were now ready to enter an era of unprecedented achievement.

Another of the remarkable events was the discovery, just at this time, of rich silver mines near Athens. The income from these mines was used in part to build a navy which brought all the products of the world to Athens, and made the city a thriving commercial center. It was this increase of wealth which was to provide the leisure needed for freedom, as well as means for the construction of rich public buildings during the reign of Pericles, of which the Athenians were justly proud.

In the realm of ideas, also, there is change and development. Out of the welter of superstition and fear which represented the forces of nature and tradition were emerging ideas about the universe and the world of nature. The thinkers who were concerned with these problems might be called philosopher-scientists, in that they wondered about the nature of the world, apparently with little thought about the gods; yet before they had finished, they had done much to diminish, if not to banish, the Olympian deities.

These philosopher-scientists began their work by wondering about some of the questions that might concern any one of us if the information were not already available and largely taken for granted. For example, seeds, with the aid of water and certain minerals, become grass; the grass, eaten by a cow, becomes meat; the meat eaten by a man becomes part of his human substance, which thus becomes part of the cycle of earth-into-grass-into-meat-into-human-into-earth. Change there is, all the way through; but what directs the process of change? What common element or elements are there in all things that make it possible for the seed to undergo such transformations, on its way to becoming seed again?

Think for a moment of a brand new baby named, perhaps, John Jones. It is a wrinkled, hairless, crying little bundle, already an individual. Fifteen years later, John Jones is tall, with black wavy hair, and an almost uncontrollable voice which breaks at the most inopportune and embarrassing times. Does any single shred remain of the baby flesh, bones, or skin in this John Jones? Yet he is still the "same" person. Shortly he will become bald, paunchy, and near-sighted; still later he will be old, bent, and wrinkled, possibly leaning on a cane for support. He does not look the same as he did in any of the earlier phases of his life, nor is any part of his physical make-up the same; yet we still recognize him as John Jones. At what stage of life is he *really* John Jones? If he is really John Jones all his life long, what is the element or characteristic that remains constant through all the years and their changes which makes him the *same* person?

The problem is a complex one: what is the relation of Appearance and Reality, of Unity and Diversity, of the One and the Many? What is the nature of Reality? Is it the changing, or the constant? It is easy to see how, from questions of the kind, the Greek philosopher-scientists were led into a speculation about the possibility of some one thing, some common element, some World-Stuff or Universal Substance, that would explain the fixed within the flux, the unchanging in the apparently constantly changing.

The Ionian Philosophers

The first group of these philosopher-scientists lived not in Greece, but in the Greek settlement across the Aegean on the coast of Asia Minor known as Ionia, in the city of Miletus. They are called the Ionian or Milesian School. The first name of importance is that of Thales, who lived at almost exactly the same time as did Draco: in other words, at the beginning of the questioning time that preceded the great Periclean day. Thales and his fellow Ionians were all concerned with the question, "Is there a single substance that underlies all the varied appearances of the world of nature, a World-Stuff, a common element that makes up all things? What is the nature of the universal substance?"

In his speculation about this universal substance, Thales advanced the idea that water seemed to fill all the qualifications. All living things are dependent upon it; furthermore, water changes its form under different conditions, and does not always present the same appearance. Normally a liquid, it becomes a solid when it freezes, a vapor when it is heated; yet through all its changes it is still the one thing—water. Under different conditions, why could not water assume still more varied forms and appearances? Is it not the best explanation of the unity that underlies the variety of the world of appearances?

However naive such an answer seems to a modern, the important concern is not the answer: it is the question itself, an attempt to make coherent and whole the experience of the world. Whether Thales was thinking literally or figuratively may be doubtful, but that he was *thinking* is what matters. The line of inquiry he opened was to occupy the minds of philosophers ever after: how can one account for the consistency in a changing world, the Unity-in-Diversity, the problem of the One and the Many? We may reject his answer, —water—, but we are still concerned with his question.

Another of the Ionian philosophers asked a question which is of great importance: "Granted a World-Stuff, what is the process by which the universal element changes into all things?" This man was Anaximander, who did little but ask his question. He said that the common element in all things was nothing so simple as water, or air, or earth, but that it was "The Boundless," an unbounded, all-inclusive substance, from which things "separated out." One can see that Anaximander did nothing more than put names to things which remain unknown and unidentified; but he did ask the question. And philosophers and scientists ever since have been dealing with the same problem.

From the Ionian School came another later philosopher, still looking for the single stuff or substance of the world. This man, Heracleitus, found his Universal Substance in fire, for the flame—though a recognizable "thing"—is yet never the same, always changing and "becoming." The process of change is the central point in his philosophy, and he has made it memorable by his statement that one can never step into the same river twice; the river, though still there, is not the "same" as at the first step. If the point seems difficult, think back on John Jones, who is always the same person—yet never the same; he is constantly changing, yet however changing, constant. This, argued Heracleitus, is the condition and the process of everything in the world; all is in a process of becoming, growing-being-decaying all at the same time.

Heracleitus made one other point which is of great importance. He asked himself what it is that directed the constant, yet orderly, change of the world; he could not bring himself to believe that the change was haphazard or illogical. (John Jones, for all his changing, never changes into a tree, or a rock, or a bird; the process of his change has some consistent direction.) Heracleitus was forced to assume a controlling force in the world which he called

"logos,"[1] a word which we translate as "reason." Here is really a startling idea: for if the world is essentially reasonable, and in the nature of things figs do not grow from thistles, nor grapes from thorns—what, then, happens to the Olympian Gods? A second question presents itself: If this is a reasonable world, what chance has man for progress in it? Would he not have a great chance if only he could come to some understanding of the reason, or reasonability, of the whole?

The Eleatic Philosophers

The whole tenor of thought of these Ionian philosophers, it will be seen, is in the direction of emphasizing the changing quality of the world; however much they look for a single Universal Substance, the real problem is its change into the varied appearances of the world. A point of view directly opposed to these Milesians sprang up in another far-distant Greek colony, this time in Italy, in the city of Elea. The notion of perpetual change, of constant "becoming," was apparently repellent to a group known as the "Eleatics"; among them two men, Parmenides and Zeno, are remembered for their opposition to the idea of change and for their stress upon permanence, unchangingness, as the characteristic of reality.

These men began by pointing out the fallibility of the senses. The eye can easily be deceived, the ear is not always reliable—in short, the senses are not to be trusted; too often they give false reports of experience. Only the mind, independent of sensual experience, can perceive reality; the testimony of the senses does not matter. The eye sees the stick thrust into water "bend"; the mind knows it does not bend. Zeno illustrated his opposition to the idea of change and his contempt for sensual evidence by his famous "paradoxes." Imagine a race between the swift-footed Achilles and a tortoise. Achilles, for all his speed, can never overtake his reptilian rival; in order to pass the

---

[1]The word *logos* means at its simplest level *word* (cf. Latin *verbum*). But there is something mysterious about the *word* to people in an early stage of intellectual development: even an individual's name is a closely guarded secret, for if one's enemy should know it, the knowledge would give him power over the individual, so powerful is the word. Hence the developed meaning from the root "logos" as we find it in *logic*, and the like—the idea of power, control; and in the form *-ology*, the meaning of organization, the control and arrangement of what we know. It is in this direction that the word moves when St. John begins the Last Gospel, "In the beginning was—the Word (Logos)."

tortoise, he would first have to cover half the distance between himself and the tortoise, then half the remaining distance—then half of *that* remainder. However small the half that is left, half of that remainder is still a quantity; and poor Achilles would spend forever halving halves! Or consider an arrow in flight toward a target. Will it ever reach its mark? Never; such "change" is only apparent, not real. There is an infinite number of points-in-space between the arrow and the target: the arrow, at any such point, is motionless; yet its whole apparent "flight" is the sum of a series of motionless points. That one sees Achilles pass the tortoise, that one hears the "plunk" of the arrow hitting the target—such evidence is unreliable, for the senses are notorious liars, not to be relied upon; the mind rejects such change as unreal.

Such a philosophic position may seem difficult to take seriously at first; yet one must consider it. Much in our modern point of view would seem to support the Eleatic mistrust of the senses as the guides to reality. For instance, we look at a leaf, and say that its color is green; yet we know that the leaf reflects the sun's rays, absorbing all but the yellow and blue. These it reflects to our eyes. What we see, then, is reflected light rays; we do not actually know much about the "reality" of the leaf. Is there here a conflict between our "common sense" and our theoretical knowledge? The importance of the Eleatic view, for our purposes, is the insistence upon the intellect, not the senses, as the means to a comprehension of reality. It is a way of looking at things that requires great courage, and has important personal consequences for those who accept it.

The Mediators

It is hard to imagine a more polar opposition than these two schools of thought, the Ionian and the Eleatic, the former placing its emphasis on the idea of change, the latter on the idea of permanence.

Between these opposed views stands the work of two men who are generally called "The Mediators." One of them was Empedocles, who tried to reconcile the opposites; in his view, the Ionian philosophers were on the right track in their search for "universal substance," but had not included enough. He contended there are four such permanent stuffs, themselves unchanging, but combining so as to produce all other things; these four are earth, air, fire, and water. But the Eleatic view is retained, and perman-

ence re-established, by the unchanging nature of the elements, whatever their combination. Variety and uniformity, change and permanence are thus reconciled.

The other "mediator," Anaxagoras, improves on Empedocles' view by assuming, not four, but an indefinite number of elements: as many as are necessary to account for different kinds of things. (The view is strongly reminiscent of Anaximander's "Boundless.")

Earlier it was said that the inquiry of these philosopher-scientists would lead to important religious implications, and here we see one aspect of these implications, for Heracleitus came very close to the idea of the single omnipotent, omniscient, and omnipresent God. Another aspect of the religious implication of the scientific philosophy can be seen in the thinking of still another philosopher-scientist, Democritus.

Democritus started his philosophy by stating that the universal element was atoms. This is as if he had taken the "boundless" of Anaximander and broken it up into indivisible pieces. These pieces, he said, are variously shaped; some round, others square, others with knobs on them, still others with hooks. Now then, said Democritus, since the beginning of time these atoms have been drifting and falling through space, with no direction and no purpose. He called the force which directed their falling and drifting "Necessity," which, as he used it, is almost synonymous with our word accident. Frequently in their aimless drift these atoms cling together because of the variation in their shape. When they do so, they may take the forms which we know as wood or mineral, bone or flesh. The atoms so joined together may drift apart, too, and it is by this drifting together and apart that Democritus accounted for change in the world.

There are many more aspects of this philosophy which could be considered. The religious significance is the only one which will concern us here. In the first place, since the atoms were there since the beginning of time, they needed no creator. In the second place, any gods there might be are of little importance, since they, too, are made of the atomic drift, and—subject to the law of Necessity—are no more permanent than the things which appear in the physical world. In other words, this is a completely materialistic philosophy which starts from the same point as did that of Heracleitus, but ends with extremely different conclusions. How should a man conduct his life in this accidental world? That is one of the great questions which the Greeks had to answer (if they accepted the thinking of Democritus) and which people ever since who have accepted materialism have had to adjust to. One can see how these ideas upset the archaic ideas of tradition and natural forces which seemed to be enemies of human freedom.

Pythagoras

At approximately the same time that the early Ionian philosophers were seeking the one thing which made up all of nature, another Greek who lived in the town of Crotona in Southern Italy attacked the same problem from a slightly different point of view. Instead of seeking to find unity in material (the universal element of the Ionians), Pythagoras sought unity in the idea of form. Perhaps this idea needs some illustration.

As one considers the ideas of Democritus, one might be struck with at least one doubt. As his atoms drifted through space, endlessly, and without any guidance other than Necessity, they fall into the shapes we know. If we accept this as true, it may seem strange to us that the shapes are so uniform. Some kinds of atoms seem to fall into the shapes of trees, other kinds of atoms cling together in the shapes of men. Each tree or each man is different; yet they conform to a sufficiently uniform pattern that we recognize each object as a member of its general group. If the whole process of formation occurs by accident, such uniformity seems improbable, even impossible. How can one account for it? May it not be that there is somewhere the *pattern* or *idea* of a man, or a tree, or any of the other of the millions of things in the world, and that matter (atoms in the present case) takes the shape of this idea, and falls into this pattern? This is the idea of form as existing apart from matter. It is simply an abstract idea of pattern, existing without any substance itself, but shaping matter into the things which we recognize. It was at this point of highly abstract thinking that Pythagoras attacked the problem of unity-in-diversity which we illustrated with our two examples of seed to grass to flesh to mineral to grass, and the story of the development of John Jones.

Most of us know Pythagoras best for his theorem in geometry that the square of the hypotenuse of a right triangle is equal to the sum of the squares of the other two sides. This was one of his contributions to the already flourishing deductive science of mathematics which was to be edited and collected by Euclid two centuries later in such a form that it remains as the basis for the geometry which we study in school today. It is not this contribution to mathematics which concerns us here, but the type of idea that Pythagoras was dealing with, for he concluded that the idea of form or pattern, as we have been discussing it, existed in mathematical relationships. This is not hard to understand, when we reflect that this relationship between the sides of a right triangle exists for all such triangles, whether they be large or small, whether a side be very long or very short. In other words, this mathematical relationship is a universal one for all right triangles. Could it be that it is the idea or pattern for right triangles?

Even in the idea of number itself we can find some interesting speculations, for number is purely abstract, yet it can apply to everything which we can see and recognize. Take "two-ness" for example. The number two is pure idea. It does not exist in any material form. Yet it can apply to all kinds of substance, and we can have two electrons or two hippopotamuses. This relationship can apply to all things, though it exists as idea only. Or we might look at another field in which Pythagoras was a pioneer: music. Here he observed that the strings of a stringed instrument vibrated when they were plucked. Further, he discovered that if one cut the length of the string exactly in half and plucked it with the same force, the vibrations were of the same length as before, but exactly twice as fast. Even further, when the shortened string was plucked, the sound produced was the same note as was produced with the long string, but an octave higher than that note. Here was an interesting mathematical relationship which Pythagoras investigated thoroughly, and in doing so he laid the foundation for much of the study of the scientific aspects of music.

One could continue the consideration of Pythagoras at great length, for he was the founder of a rather important religion, and developed many theories about human conduct. These, however, are only interesting as antiquities. What is important for us is that wherever he looked, Pythagoras saw mathematical relationships uniting the material things of the world. He stated the belief that we would not find the basic principle of unity in material things such as atoms or elements of material, but that we would find it in *form,* the pure idea of any material thing, the abstract pattern which gives material substance its shape. Throughout all of man's thinking we find this idea recurring time and time again.

A Summary

These, then, are some of the big new ideas that were troubling the Greeks. To people brought up in the tradition of absolute government in which political acts were always involved with religion, the new freedoms created by Solon, Peisistratus, and Cleisthenes; the new pride and wealth which came about as a result of the victories over the Persians and the discovery of the silver mines—these things must have been exciting, but disturbing. Particularly upsetting were the new ideas about the world and the gods, introduced by the philosophers. Should a person overthrow his belief in the old gods and accept the single Reason or Logos of Heracleitus; should he forsake the old gods and take up the materialism and the accidental universe of Democritus; or should he believe that the unity of the world and the patterns for all things lay in the abstract ideas of form which existed somewhere beyond the earth, but which gave all substance form as we know it? What was *real*? Could our senses be trusted to tell us the truth, or should we deny them and trust only the intellect, as the Eleatics proposed? These questions must have been as upsetting to the Athenian as are the clashes of rival political and economic systems, as disturbing as the theories of Einstein and the scientists in our own day.

According to the culture epoch-theory, the period of chaos in which the Greeks had lived for centuries was now coming to an end with the work of the "Pure Thinkers"—in this case, the philosophers. A coming period of adjustment would find the promulgation of such ideas through the work of the Artists, to be followed in turn by the Intellectuals who would fashion these ideas into better institutions, or ways of accomplishing purposes and desires, that would achieve a period of balance.

The pattern fits very well the actual happenings in Greece. It was to the artists that Athenians turned for their answers. The whole great possibility of a free people lay before the citizens of Athens; and it was an artist, the dramatist Aeschylus, who caught the dream and communicated it to his people in his tragedies.

Aeschylus: Democracy in Its Morning

It was in this time of great upheaval and of great possibility that Aeschylus wrote of the possibilities which he saw for his city, starting with the old ideas of human and divine zones of action and showing how these have changed. In *Prometheus Bound* he is treating of the nature of the relationship between God and Man. More broadly interpreted, he is attempting to define the relationship between stern power and regulation on one hand and individual freedom on the other. Prometheus, like Agamemnon, is the kind of man the Greeks loved. He is a man of great soul and great deeds, magnanimous and magnificent. Directly opposed to him in the play is Hermes, a god who has seen the way things are, and who has tempered his attitudes and actions accordingly, fitting himself to the limits of freedom allowed by the ruler of heaven. Zeus is a new ruler, having only recently and with the aid of Prometheus, led a successful revolt against Kronus. As a new and absolute ruler, he represents stern justice, issuing strict rules which all of his subjects, both divine and human, must obey without question. All power lies with the king in this scheme of things, and Power and Force are his agents. In the face of this order of things, Prometheus has believed that mankind, given the responsibility of knowledge and power, could grow to maturity and wield that power wisely.

Prometheus, the Magnificent, defied the limits set by Zeus, to give power to men whom he saw as babies, viewing each phenomenon as separate rather than in its proper relationships. Each change of seasons they regarded as a miracle, for example, and they could not foresee that the cycle would continue. To aid these child-men, Prometheus gave them blind hope; thus ambition and incentive for effort would occupy them so that they would not foresee and give continual contemplation to death. To make possible the fruition of these efforts he gave them fire from which would come all of the arts. He gave them reason that they might make observations and draw conclusions about the things which they saw; that they might begin to see the relationships between things such as the changes of the seasons and the course of the stars. Number, the language of relationships, was one of his gifts, and language, by which experience could be communicated, was another. He gave them horses and ships and medicine.

These are the tools by which man matures in that they enable him to have more power and make wider choices. Every choice involves the element of values: which of two or more alternatives is the better, which is the worse? Such a question is always answered when a choice is made. It is the knowledge of good and evil, and involves the choices by which men mature.

What conclusion does Aeschylus draw in this struggle between strict organization based on force and power and Prometheus' idea of power shared for the development of freedom among men? The question cannot be answered with certainty, for the last play of the three is lost. Lacking the answer which Aeschylus gave, we can make some shrewd guesses. These things we know: Zeus will fall unless Prometheus divulges his secret. Zeus did not fall. Prometheus would not yield his secret under torture. Man's power increased. Clearly there must have been some reconciliation between Zeus and Prometheus with man as the beneficiary.

By no stretch of the imagination could Zeus have become a God of Love. Not only was that totally alien to his character, but to the Greek character, as well. We must remember that they were rationalists, through and through. But Aeschylus did have a great amount of raw material upon which to draw. For example, he had the philosophies of Heracleitus, of the materialists such as the forerunners of Democritus, of Pythagoras, and of the Eleatics from which he might draw some solution to his problem. Further, he had already established the fact that Zeus was not completely free. He was in bondage to the "fates, triform, and unforgetting furies"; and to Necessity.

Aeschylus would scarcely have drawn upon the philosophy of the materialists, for these philosophers viewed Necessity as almost the same as Accident. Nor would the author have selected the philosophy of the Eleatics with its denial of change and of the human senses. Aeschylus was nothing if not a believer in change. But he might have taken the idea of *Logos* of Heracleitus or the reality of mathematical relationships which Pythagoras had propounded and called one of these Necessity. Such an arrangement, to which Zeus himself was subject, would provide an orderly and predictable universe in which both men and gods might work out their freedoms.

As the problem of the establishment of justice (freedom) between men and the gods is treated by Aeschylus in *Prometheus Bound*, so is the problem of the establishment of justice in human interaction considered in the *Oresteia*. The accepted idea at the beginning of the trilogy is approximately that found in the *Iliad*. The chorus of Argive elders frequently speaks of the limits beyond which a man cannot go with safety:

> We know, we elders, that in wealth
> Excessive lies no guarantee of grace:
> Its pride begets disease, not health;
> Save us from pride, O guardian of the race!

and again:

> Hope is gone; in mouldy ruin
> Always ends our mortal clay.

Thus do these people of Argos live, believing that there is a sphere of activity allotted to men, another to the gods, while over all is Fate, controlling both. Men can never be sure exactly what their sphere of action is and where its limits lie, so they must walk warily, assuming as unpretentious a role as possible. Within such a scheme of things there is little place for individualism, for the grooves of mass action are worn smooth. These beliefs and customs are the beliefs of the blood-clan which flourished at the time of Homer.

Agamemnon, of course, is the tragic hero. He has dared beyond the limits of human action. He has determined his own fate by the sacrifice of Iphigenia. But the incident which actually brings on his doom is one of the little things, an act which takes unto mortal men that which is right for the gods only. Agamemnon walks on a red-dyed carpet, an offense to the zone of men's actions, an act by which he over-reaches himself. Because of it, quite as much as because of the human transgressions of Iphigenia's sacrifice and the bringing home of Cassandra, either of which would excite Clytemnestra, the woman, to murder, Agamemnon is killed.

By Agamemnon's death, the dilemma of the trilogy is brought into sharp focus. Orestes, by tribal law, must kill his mother. This is justice by revenge: an eye for an eye, a tooth for a tooth. Not only is it law, but Orestes is commanded to do the deed by Apollo, who promises dire consequences if Orestes refuses. But if Orestes does the murder, he will be hounded by the Furies, also a part of the tribal mores, probably invented to strengthen blood clans by preventing strife and bloodshed within the clan itself. Orestes is damned if he does and damned if he doesn't. The reaction of the people, the chorus, to this is the reaction of children; for in this city of Mycenae they are like the child-people whom Prometheus described. Before the act of revenge, they are hot for it, with no thought of consequences. Following the death of Clytemnestra, they speak of the dark consequences of the curse on the House of Atreus, even before Orestes is set upon by the Furies. Limited in knowledge and power by their fear and their blind fatalism, one thing at a time is enough for them.

In *Eumenides,* the problem is presented in its broadest scope, no longer as a single incident of a particular prince killing a particular mother. In this last play of the trilogy, it becomes the problem for all men and may be stated thus: If the old justice-through-fear (represented by the Furies) is overthrown, then anarchy will reign. Children will murder their parents wholesale, and civil strife will be the rule rather than the exception. On the other hand, if justice-through-fear is maintained, then men will never grow to manhood. It is Athena, goddess of wisdom, who sees the problem thus and states it clearly. The solution takes place in Athens, not without reason. In the first place Athens is *a* city, where men are congregated in groups, where ideas are held and expressed, where the need for human justice, because of this very congregation of men and the conflict of ideas, is greater than in any rural place; in the second place, because Athens is *the* city in which Aeschylus saw the hope for human freedom about to blossom, the city which was to lead the world in the development of a quality of life which would accomplish the necessary compromise between the greatest human freedom and the necessary curbs imposed by society so that the freedom might exist for all: a democracy.

The easy path for Athena and for Aeschylus would have been to free Orestes forthwith, and trample upon the old ideas of fear. Aeschylus, however much of an optimist he was, was not that optimistic. He knew people well enough to know that some form of fear was necessary to curb some men. A wiser choice needed to be made.

The decision which Athena reached was the establishment of a permanent court of justice, where cases could be decided on the basis of reason and

sworn evidence. Fear was not completely dissolved, but it was fear of men's law, which was written and known, rather than fear of the mysterious unknown. Men, in other words, defined the limits of their own sphere of activity, their own zone, and could proceed surely and with freedom within it. The principle of law was stated here:

> Let no one be uncurbed by law
> Or curbed by tyranny.

Thus was the compromise worked out between fear and freedom; thus the rough zone of men's cooperation. The instrument by which it was administered was Athena's specialty, persuasion, the way in which reason is communicated. It is the way in which civilized men make their way, supplanting force.

The task of defining the limits of man's activities, however, is not finished, for fear of the law is not a sufficient curb to keep men within those limits. Something deeper within each person is the only force which can maintain the law. As Athena changes the immortal hags who have pursued the slayer from the Furies to the Gracious Ones (Eumenides) she speaks of them as household gods, without whose blessing the land will never prosper. Could this be the dawn of conscience which Aeschylus is describing? For conscience is the knowledge of right and wrong, of good and evil, residing within each person, which disciplines and restrains his actions. It is the necessary adjunct to formal and established courts of law. It is this conscience which enables men and women to make wise choices, the responsibility of the power and knowledge which Athena has just given them.

This, then, is a play like the statue of the Charioteer of Delphi. It represents man springing from the old and archaic forms. Yet he is a new man, proud and powerful, free both from the smothering tradition, and the fear of an unexplainable nature. Yet he is sufficiently proud of himself as human being that he will control himself. He stands tall and free.

If this is true, then Aeschylus' trilogy is the story of the triumph of wisdom over fear in the governing of men's affairs. Here is the path by which men may create and perpetuate their way of freedom. The fact remains that it is not a thing completely finished. The process of perpetuation will be a continuous one, and the way will remain good only so long as men make their choices with the idea that man, all mankind, is the measure of all things. If this accomplishment was made as suggested here, then the triumphal chorus in praise of the great city of Athens, the home of freedom, is justified.

This, then, is the set of answers which Aeschylus made to the chaos brought about by new ideas which upset old ways. The courts of Athens had been established before Aeschylus wrote. It was his function as artist in the period of primary adjustment to show the people the meaning of their new freedom. That he succeeded is revealed in the moment of high culture which followed in his city.

EXERCISES

1. Why is it a contradiction in terms to speak of "splitting the atom"? What did the Greek mean by the word "atom"?

2. The text suggests certain conditions necessary for the development of freedom:

a. the banishment of su-
perstition;
b. the right to express
ideas;
c. fairly even distribu-
tion of wealth;
d. reasonable unselfish-
ness;
e. a reasonable amount
of leisure; and
f. pride in one's self and
one's nation.

Did any of the following make specific contribution to the achieving of these conditions?—Draco; Solon; Peisistratus; Cleisthenes; Themistocles.

3. Do you find any similarity of thought between either the Ionians or the Eleatics, and Christianity?

4. We have seen how the history of Greek philosophical thought runs something like this: "On the one hand . . . but, on the other . . . yet, taking one thing with another . . ." so that it makes a pattern like that below. Which philosophers would you arrange along such a pattern? Is there one who stands outside it almost completely?

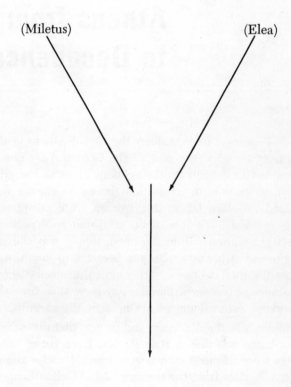

(Miletus)   (Elea)

Athens from Golden Age to Decadence

Whenever one considers the city of Athens at the time of Pericles (the peak of the Golden Age) one is tempted to exaggerate the good qualities of the city. One is tempted to forget that the entire culture was based on slave labor, that women were completely disregarded in the life of the city, that rival political factions warred within the town, that it was the enlightened Athenians who put Socrates to death, and that the final decline of Athenian culture came about because of traitors within the city more than from the work of external enemies. One sees the magnificent buildings of the Acropolis, and forgets that the Athenian home was only a rude shelter. Even these buildings were financed with money which Pericles almost literally stole from the treasury of the Delian League, which had become the Athenian Empire. All of these accusations are true and must not be forgotten.

On the other hand, one sees here a small city state with a population of about sixty-five to seventy thousand people. Yet within the space of two centuries, certainly no more than that, this town produced three of the world's greatest tragic dramatists, one of the world's greatest writers of dramatic comedy, two of the most renowned philosophers and a half dozen of lesser rank. In this city were produced a type of architecture which has been an inspiration to the world ever since, and sculpture which is no less famous. The atmosphere of the city must have been alive with interest in those days.

We may picture Athens in those days as a small but beautiful city. On every hand rose the temples and public meeting places whose beauty we still admire. It is known that the Greeks cultivated their bodies, so that we can imagine on every side well-proportioned, handsome men talking or engaged in athletic games. The life was largely an outdoor existence (the reason for the poor houses, which were little more than sleeping places), and games, worship, and political meetings were carried on in the public squares and on the porches of the beautiful buildings. Yearly dramatic festivals were held, at which all of the free Athenian citizens gathered to see the great explorations of the human personality such as the *Oedipus the King* of Sophocles or *Antigone*. Here, too, were played the tragedies of Euripides, such as the *Medea*, a study of pent-up despair and anger. These must have been great moments in the city's life.

All this was the vision of Aeschylus become a reality for a brief second in the total stream of time, but a second so important that it is remembered and celebrated up to our own time. This reality manifested itself in a quality of life, seldom if ever equalled since, in which the guiding principle was that man is the measure of all things. A name which we can apply to this idea is the achievement of *human values*. By that term is meant that nothing was done for itself, but only insofar as it contributed to an increase in the quality of life, the excitement and satisfaction of the process of living itself. Perhaps the finest example of this idea is found in Athenian athletics, which were practiced by every free Athenian man. In athletic contests, however, the race was not always to the swift, nor the prize to him who threw the discus farthest. Rather it went to the man who achieved satisfactory performance and who showed the best form in what he was doing. The goal of Greek athletics, then, was not the highest jump, the farthest throw, or the fastest run (achievements which are meaningless, when we think about them for a minute), but in the development of the good body, for the Greeks realized that a good body was one of the factors which led to a good life in general.

Pericles' memorial oration furnishes many examples of this principle as it was idealized in Athens. Wealth was no longer regarded with suspicion, as it had been by the chorus of *Agamemnon*, which continually muttered against the acquisition of too much luxury, since too great a display might offend the gods. Instead, Pericles boasts that the city has wealth and uses it freely for the improvement of the conditions of living. In saying this, he is simply saying that the Athenians have matured so that they can use the instrument of wealth (potentially dangerous, potentially beneficial) freely for its best uses.

Nor, he says, are Athenians afraid of amusement, again, either good or bad, depending upon its type and use. He asserts that the Athenians were sufficiently mature to know the proper sphere for enjoyments of all sorts; they could use them freely, knowing always where to stop and having sufficient sense and sufficient pride to stop there. Athens had military strength, he said, but he continued with the idea that they did not waste the years of their youth in nothing but military training, which might make the young men useless for other things. Rather the Athenian depended upon the love of the city and its way of life to inspire the soldiers with the courage necessary to win their battles, and the diversified training of the Athenians to make soldiers intelligent individuals, capable of adapting themselves to any circumstance of war. Nor, said Pericles, do the Athenians shut out new ideas, but welcome them instead. Ideas, like all else, are potentially dangerous or potentially good. The Athenian was wise enough in their use to profit by them.

Pride was the characteristic of these Athenians; pride in the fact that every citizen was sufficiently sophisticated that he could use the knowledge and power which were common property, and which were provided with sufficient political equality that all men shared in the government, for the good of the people within the city. No longer was there a snivelling subservience and craven fear such as we saw in the chorus of *Agamemnon*. The Athenians had given themselves power and responsibility and had learned to use it. The use of it is as important as the possession of it, and Pericles makes much of the sense of responsibility which the Athenian citizen felt for expressing his opinions and for taking part in public affairs. Given power, a man must have within him the compulsion to use it, not to hoard it, and to use it for the public good. This is the secret of the compromise which the Athenians made in these great years, the factor which maintained the balance of the time, the regulating mechanism which kept men within their new zone of action.

The principles of Greek art such as those embodied in the Parthenon furnish as good an illustration of these ideas as do any spoken words. The classic form of the building is strict; the architect and the builders allowed themselves no wild exuberance, no excessive ornamentation to make the building pretty. Yet strict as were the classic rules, they were wide enough to allow the builder his individual expression; this work of art, then, is like the ideal of a democratic state.

Such, then, was the great age of Athens. The quality of life embodied freedom, pride, and responsibility. Each man had all the power of his manhood, power which he held in check by his own choice, for his own individual good and for the good of the group. The greatness of this high period depended upon a most delicate balance, a discipline self-imposed upon each man. Such a balance is most difficult to maintain.

The Beginning of Decadence

The teachers of Athens during this high period were the Sophists, and their failure to maintain the balance just discussed was also the failure of the city itself. It is really the admission that men were not yet able to support as much freedom as they had allowed themselves. These men abandoned all concepts of a Divinity, and adopted the materialism and atomism of Democritus as their basic belief. From that point, they developed their most famous teaching, that "man is the measure of all things." If this needs explanation, it simply means that there is no higher power than men, and that the whole purpose of life is to live well. This, you will observe, is an extremely practical philosophy.

In their early teaching, the Sophists were high minded men, who held the highest ideals. Plato, in his dialogue named after the leader of the group, Protagoras, causes him to say, "The lesson which I have to teach is prudence and good counsel, both in respect to domestic matters, that the man may manage his household aright, and in respect to public affairs, that he may be thoroughly qualified to take part, both by deed and word, in the business of the state." In order to achieve these goals, the Sophists were principally concerned with teaching the arts of thinking and of oratory.

Although these teachers were at first very high minded men, their doctrine of man as the measure can be easily perverted to become a dangerous philosophy. It is satisfactory as long as one takes the word *man* to mean all men; it is dangerous when we take the word

to mean *I*. For when it becomes a completely selfish doctrine, the self-discipline which was revealed in the Charioteer, and which was boasted of by Pericles, is destroyed. As we pointed out, the Athenian balance depended upon the ability of the individual Athenian to control and discipline himself. Although the Sophists' teachings are not necessarily bad in themselves, they are inherently dangerous in leading to selfishness, skepticism about the possibility of knowledge, and the pursuit of completely utilitarian purposes.

Against the teachings that led to such conclusions came the opposition of one of the most fascinating figures of ancient Greece: Socrates, "the gadfly of Athens," as he liked to call himself; "the ugliest of men, and the wisest." Although he never wrote a word of philosophy, no one Greek ever exerted a greater influence upon philosophical thought than Socrates. Angered at the pretensions of the Sophists, he claimed that he was wise only in that he knew his ignorance. Irritated by loose thinking and general statements, he would ask the speaker, "What do you mean?" Then he would proceed, often by the very Sophistical methods he despised, to involve his unfortunate victim in a maze of contradiction and qualification that made it abundantly clear that the speaker did not know what he was talking about. For Socrates, the admission of ignorance was the beginning of wisdom.

Although it is all but impossible to say definitely, "Socrates thought thus and so" (for all we know of the man is hearsay, largely from his two pupils, Xenophon and Plato), yet a little can be pieced out about him. He did not, like the Sophists, make truth only a matter of expediency: "This is the point in which, as I think, I am superior to men in general, and in which I might, perhaps, fancy myself wiser than other men—that whereas I know but little of the world below, I do not suppose that I know. But I *do* know . . . that injustice and disobedience to a better, whether god or man, is evil and dishonorable, and I will never fear or avoid a possible good rather than a certain evil." He was not a systematic or dogmatic philosopher, advancing set opinions; he was rather a questioner, a lover of wisdom. He, too, believed that man is the measure, but with a difference: "man" for him meant not the isolated individual of the Sophists, but men, mankind, the race. He had great faith in the essential and common quality of man's humanity: his reason or common sense. His interest was always in promoting the good actions of men. To arrive at any conclusions, he felt, one must classify and make distinctions, thereby avoiding the error of ignorance, and arriving at true opinions. The end of this process, according to Socrates, is happiness, which is not only the avoidance of ignorance and its fruits, but the virtue which comes from knowledge. To know rightly, to make right choices is virtue; for virtue alone can satisfy the reason. Knowledge and virtue are inseparables. And happiness is the result of worthiness that comes when enlightenment and knowledge result, as necessarily they must in this highest good, which we have called virtue.

These ideas, one sees immediately, are the very ideas which had made Athens great; they are the ideas which had brought about the golden age. But the type of thinking which the Sophists brought about was already triumphant in destroying the heart of this civilization, and Socrates was put to death by the democratic processes in Athens which he had loved so much. His influence was strong, however, upon his pupil and successor, Plato, who, in turn, passed the same teaching on to Aristotle, the student of Plato.

By Plato's time, the selfish doctrine of the Sophists was clearly victorious over other more stern philosophies, and Plato sought to restore the broken balance of his civilization. In his formal philosophy he borrowed much from the Eleatic philosophers, who, you remember, denied the validity of the senses and insisted that only the mind was to be trusted in the search for truth. He also borrowed the idea of form as different from substance from Pythagorean philosophy. Plato's formal philosophy may be stated something like this:

In the first place, he believed that reality existed, not in the earthly manifestations of things, but in the ideas or patterns or forms of them. Here we recognize something taken from both the Eleatics and from Pythagoras. In other words Plato believed that the trees, the rocks, or the men and women we see are but the reflections of the idea-trees, the idea-rocks, and the idea-men and women which are truly reality. Next, he believed that there existed higher and higher forms of these ideas, at the top of which was the idea which he called The Good. The wise man is one, Plato would say, who seeks to know reality, and who is not happy with the reflections of it. So the wise man is the one who studies philosophy so that he may get a glimpse of the essence of all things. This, of course, leads to the idea that death is a desirable state, since it frees the soul of the wise man from his body, and makes greater knowledge of reality possible.

But death is not the goal of life; it is only an event which happens in good time, and which men who have lived well should welcome rather than fear. In the meantime one must do one's work and seek truth here on earth. This idea of working with men, too, has an important place in Plato's thinking. He believed that men had three characteristics: appetite, spirit, and wisdom. When the first two are properly balanced and controlled by wisdom, we see the emergence of the highest of human virtues, according to Plato, and that is justice. Accordingly he names four great human virtues. They are temperance, courage, wisdom, and justice. These, may it be noted in passing, were later to be combined with the Hebrew virtues of faith, hope, and love to become the seven great virtues of the Christian religion, for Plato's philosophy has had almost as much influence on Christianity as did the teachings of Jesus.

Plato would continue to say that in some men there is an excess of appetite, with the result that this quality overshadows all the rest; in some men spirit takes too great a proportion of their being, with the result that they are foolhardy. Only when the two faculties are controlled by reason and held in a careful relation to each other and to wisdom itself, does the good and just man appear. Upon this basis Plato makes a classification of men in the formation of an imaginary state. At the very bottom he places the slaves, who simply do not exist as men at all. Next he places the craftsmen and farmers and merchants, essentially, he says, the men of appetite. These men, he believes, should receive little or no education, and should have no voice in the running of the government. The next class is that of the soldiers. They are men of spirit. They should receive enough education to train them for their work, and enough of the liberal arts to keep them from being savage toward their own countrymen; beyond that they should not be educated, and they, too, should not have any political power. It is only when we come to the highest class, the men of wisdom and justice, that we find the rulers. They should receive the most careful education in order to develop their powers, and then they should be made absolute rulers. Plato had some justice on his side. He saw many states ruled by men of appetite or by men who were foolhardy. In each case the state was operating to the harm of the people in it. He was trying to find some way in which justice might be insured within a nation.

Following Plato, many different schools of philosophy sprang up, all of them endeavoring to create a good way of life in the midst of a world that was crumbling around them. Offshoots of the Academy and Plato's teaching were such schools as the Cynics and the Stoics; another group, following the materialism of Democritus, were the Epicureans; but these philosophies are so much more important to the Roman world than to the Greek that discussion of them will be reserved for a later chapter.

One of the greatest challenges to Plato's views, yet curiously derived from his teachings, was to come much later than the Periclean period. It was the work of Plato's one-time pupil, Aristotle (384-322 B.C.), whose birthplace in the north of Greece at Stageirus has given him the name of "the Stagirite," and whose custom of lecturing as he walked up and down with his students has given his other nickname, "the Peripatetic Philosopher." Aristotle is one of the most extraordinary men of all time; the keenness of his intellect, the range of his interests and studies, the staggering amount of information and speculation in his enormous collection of writings, rouse the admiration and awe of any who read of his work. With Plato, he was to shape the course of Western thought; these two men are two of the most powerful influences that have come to us out of antiquity.

Plato, the mathematician and poet, was always more interested in theory than in fact; his concern is with principle and law that is universal and unchanging, like the theorems of geometry; his philosophy, like that of the Eleatics, insists upon the superiority of the mind over the fallacious senses. Aristotle, son of a physician, was always deeply concerned with biology; his concern is with visible change, growth, and development; his outlook is that of the scientist, always willing to subject theory to the test of actuality. Plato's quest for the Permanent, the Idea or Form, rather than the actuality of experience, led him into a dualism that separates theory and practice; Aristotle, profoundly interested in the changing life about him, tried to reconcile the two. Perhaps the difference could be expressed in this way: when Plato wished to discuss his ideas of the State, he wrote the *Republic,* a theoretical speculation that constructs the wholly imaginary idea of a State; when Aristotle wished to

discuss his ideas of the State, he and his students collected and studied the constitutions of 158 Greek city-states, as a prelude to the work known as "Politics."

It is an impossible task, and not to the present purpose, to make mention of the multitude of Aristotle's writings; only two of his ideas concern us here. One is his view of the nature of reality; the other is idea of the conduct of life in the light of that view.

For Aristotle, the abstract "Idea" or "Form" of Plato's teaching could not be separated from the matter or substance by which it was known; the two must somehow come together as different aspects of the same thing. Thus Plato's "ideal" chair did not exist for Aristotle apart from the actual wood-and-metal which composed it. A brick is a brick only when the "idea" *brick* and the clay composing it come together; then the brick is "real." The brick then may become the matter or substance of another "idea," and become house; and the house, in turn, may be substance to the idea of town or city. At every stage, the union of Substance and Form, of Matter and Idea, is necessary to constitute "reality"; but there is a progression, upwards or downwards, the substance that Plato is not concerned with becoming for Aristotle the basis for higher, more complex realities when it is *informed* by Idea or Form. Such, at least, is the direction of the difference between the two men; Plato's static view becomes more dynamic in Aristotle's teaching.

The process of change (which Plato never satisfactorily explains; his nearest approach to explanation may be found in his "Allegory of the Cave," p. 211) is accounted for, by Aristotle, in his theory of *enteleche.* (The Greek word is made of the particles *en,* "within"; *telos,* "purpose or end"; and *echaia,* "having, possessing.") That is to say, it is in the nature of things that they have within them a goal, a destiny, to fulfill: the seed becomes the plant, for that is its "enteleche"; the clay becomes the brick, for that is its "enteleche." The movement upward through increasing complexity is the "enteleche" of the universe; and the cause of the process, drawing all things toward their own perfection, is God, the First Cause, who moved all things without being moved: the "Unmoved Mover," in Aristotle's phrase.

The motive power of Aristotle's God is apparently not love, as Christianity might contend, nor will, as Judaism might argue; it is rather that there seems to be a cosmic yearning toward perfection, and that perfection is, by definition, God. Aristotle's customary view of the necessity for the union of both form and matter to constitute reality here breaks down (or more kindly, "transcends itself"?), for such a God must be pure form, with none of the inherent weakness or imperfection of the material;[1] God is the only instance where pure form is separated from matter.

How does one lead the Good Life? It is interesting to note that Aristotle makes no apology for thinking that it must begin with sufficient means; he holds no ascetic views on the matter, and quite matter-of-factly begins with an assumption of enough material possession to allow one the choice of doing as he would. Granted, however, the adequate wealth, what does one *do*? The *enteleche* of which he speaks implies that there is a goal, or end, reached when the person or thing is functioning *properly*—that is, in accord with its own inner purposes; when conditions permit such functioning, there is a highest good, a *summum bonum*, attained. The enteleche of man, then, would lead him to his own *summum bonum*, his own best functioning, the worthy and proper fulfillment of his humanity. And since man is for Aristotle the "rational animal," that fulfillment would be the life of reason. When he is living harmoniously, using his mind, functioning in family and state (for Aristotle also calls man a "political"—i.e., social animal), he has achieved his greatest good. Such a life has two implications, among many others, that concern us here.

One is that such a life will be a life of virtue, or excellence. But virtues may fail by being deficient, or by being carried to excess; the middle ground between is what is to be desired. Courage, for instance, is a virtue: but it may be perverted through deficiency into cowardice, or no less perverted by being carried to the excess of foolhardiness, mere rashness. Generosity is a virtue, but it can be carried to the excess of prodigality and wastefulness, or perverted through deficiency to stinginess. To mediate between extremes, to discover the "Golden Mean,"—which it is to be noted is a relative and not an absolute matter—that is to achieve virtue.

The other implication, then, is that man's best use of reason is in the life of contemplation. He must have time to read, to talk, to think about the whole

idea of excellence, that he may achieve the high-mindedness that is his *summum bonum;* the word that Aristotle uses is "magnanimity." Such a quality is not to be won in the heat and dust of the market place; though the good man will perform his duties as a member of society, still the life of action is not as good as the life of contemplation.

Plato and Aristotle, for all their differences, are at one in their emphasis upon the importance of the intellect in the realization of the Good Life; and they are both of tremendous importance in the later development of Christianity. One must wait for the Middle Ages, indeed, to see how aspects of Aristotelian thought are woven into the very pattern of Western civilization.

Aristotle, however, scarcely belongs to the Athenian epoch. By the time when Aristotle flourished, the Macedonian emperors had conquered all of Greece, and the center of learning had changed to the city of Alexandria in Africa. If we are to sum up the Athenian epoch we should return for a moment to Plato.

In Plato's lifetime the delicate balance which had made Athens great was upset. The Athenians began to regard democracy as a government, embodied in laws and assemblies. As such, it was a thing complete and finished. With the job done, each Athenian could work upon his own selfish interests, feeling that he had no duty to his city. The Sophists misapplied the maxim of man as the measure of all things to mean only that the individual's pleasure was the measure. Inequalities in wealth grew up, and people became suspicious of each other. The new statues showed stress and strain. The new discus thrower was trying to set new distance records, forgetting the purpose of his exercise. The result of all of these things was disorder and confusion.

Plato, seeing the evils, sought to reconstruct a new justice and a new freedom, and he turned to a totalitarian state and a philosophy of absolutes as the desperate remedy for the confusion which he saw about him. Plato's idea of the state resembles almost exactly the

---

[1] "Such then is the principle upon which depend the heavens and the world of nature. And its life (i.e., the principle, or God) is like the best that we enjoy, and enjoy but for a short time; for it is ever in this state, which we cannot be. And if then God is always in that good state in which we sometimes are, this compels our wonder; and if in a better state, then this compels it yet more. And God *is* in a better state. We say therefore, that God is a living being, eternal, most good; so that life and a continual eternal existence belong to God; for this *is* God." (Aristotle, *Metaphysics*, XII, 7.)

caste system found among the Hindus. With the exception that in Plato's *Republic* the wise always succeeded to rule, it was the system found in Sparta, and Sparta produced nothing worth remembering except a good army.

Plato's justice, then, is a stern and inflexible order. In it, every person is catalogued and classified in unchanging categories. It has the advantage of being ruled by wisdom, but the power of the state is concentrated entirely in the hands of these wise men. The result would be efficient, no doubt, but would only serve to cause the mass of men to revert to their childlike innocence. This is Plato's new order, his state.

There is, however, one interesting paragraph in the *Republic* which deserves further consideration. In it, Socrates says:

> In heaven there is laid up a pattern of such a city, and he who desires may behold this, and beholding, govern *himself*[2] accordingly. But whether there really is or ever will be such an one is of no importance to him; for he will act according to the laws of that city and of no other.

Plato's Republic, then, can exist within an individual as well as within a city-state. If we accept this idea only, then a completely new light is shed on the matter. According to this, a man may conduct himself, developing his appetites and his courage to the full, and governing both with wisdom. Thus interpreted, and it is the best interpretation, Plato's ideas lead to the development of a strong, self-reliant, independent, and free man. This would be a true return to the balance of the Golden Age of Athens. Fortunately the great wheel of change allows no return, and by the time of Plato and Aristotle the wheel had begun to turn on.

Here, then, is the story of the Greek epoch. In the beginning man was uncertain and afraid. He had his narrow zone of action; the gods had theirs. And no man knew just where the boundaries lay. Only the heroes, magnanimous and magnificent, dared live as individuals—and they were always tragic heroes. Then came the philosopher-scientists, making

new discoveries about the world. Light was shed on man's dark journey, and he transferred his thought from the framework of a religion of fear to secular thought. New ideas about government spurred him, in his search for freedom and for justice, to find new ways of getting along with other men, and to find new and nobler purposes for individual existence. It is Aeschylus who makes articulate these hopes and ideals, and their realization follows for the brief period of Periclean Athens. Freedom and justice were established on the basis of human values. Men, knowing the boundaries of their zone, were able to walk proudly and live well. But any such balance is delicate. Here it fell when men *assumed* their liberty—that is, took it for granted—and forgot the discipline and the responsibility which must accompany it. The result was a shift to the Spartan ideal of sternness and totalitarianism, with limits imposed still by men, but by men of authority. This was the civilization which led into the best that the Roman empire could later produce.

Exercises

1. Aristotle's idea of *virtue* as a mean between extremes implies that every virtue has not one opposite, but two. What are the opposites for *temperance?* for *love?* for *generosity?* for *wisdom?* Extend the list . . .

2. "I shall not pay my taxes to the archons of Athens this year. It is my money, and I shall do what I will with it. After all, man is the measure of all things; I am a man; and since this is my opinion, I find it good and sufficient."

Imagine that you are Socrates, and comment on the above.

3. Obviously the interested student should read farther in these philosophies and in Greek literature in general. The limits of size preclude the inclusion of Plato's *Republic* or Aristotle's *Ethics*. Or, what one of the authors regards as the most shocking play in all literature, Euripides' *Bachae*. Good modern translations in paperback editions are readily available.

---

[2] The italics are the authors.

The Search for Freedom as Reflected in Greek Art

Very roughly, the history of Greek art can be divided into three parts. In the first, called the *archaic period*, the men of Greece were still at war with the elements of nature, and eked out a scanty victory through the provision of rude shelter in their building, and were unable to create their image of beauty because of the tyranny of nature and the bondage of a tradition in sculpture. The second period, called the *classic period*, marks a complete victory within the forces of nature, so that men were able to work with it rather than against it. A new and completely Greek tradition emerged, in which Greek men found a new freedom. They were able to build their temples exactly as they wanted them; they were able to cut the stone of their statues to reveal their ideal of beauty. The third period, usually called the *decadent period*, reveals men no longer at war with nature or tradition, but fighting a losing battle in their own spirits. They had become so adept at their craft that the inner drive for creation was gone. The temptation to make something "pretty" just because they had sufficient skill to make it that way was so strong that their work was over-elaborate. The tyranny of too much skill was as great a bondage for true and great creative work as was the tyranny of nature and tradition in the archaic period.

At first these Greek men sought shelter, and the simplest form of shelter is what is known as "post and lintel" architecture. For the ends of the building, one simply puts two posts in the ground, and places

Archaic Art Form

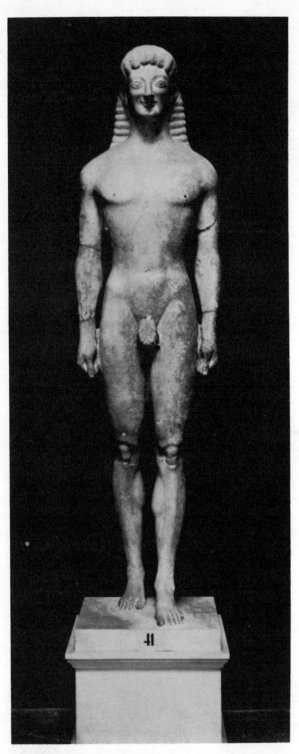

Underwood & Underwood

THE "APOLLO" OF TENEA
PROBABLY THE STATUE FOR A YOUNG MAN'S TOMB

a beam across them. On top of the beam, or "lintel," one builds a flat roof, and one fills in the space between posts with a built-up wall. This provides shelter. But nature makes other demands upon the builder. In the first place, if the distance between posts is too great, the weight of the roof will break the lintel, and the building will fall. In the second, in a country of

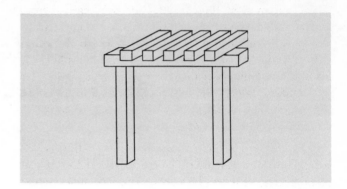

much rain, a flat roof is not satisfactory. On the post and lintel architecture, however, one can build a sloping roof. From such simple problems as this, essentially a part of man's struggle against nature, emerged the basic features of Greek temple architecture. The posts became Greek columns, mathematically spaced to give adequate support to the roof; the lintel remains; the ends of the roof-joists, too, remain largely as a decorative feature and are now called triglyphs, while the space between them which can be used for decorative purposes is called the metope; and above these we have the triangle under the sloping roof which was to furnish the area for some of the best of Greek relief sculpture.

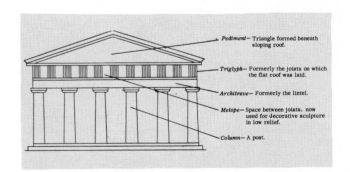

Pediment— Triangle formed beneath sloping roof.

Triglyph— Formerly the joists on which the flat roof was laid.

Architrave— Formerly the lintel.

Metope— Space between joists, now used for decorative sculpture in low relief.

Column— A post.

While this evolution in building was going on, an evolution from the construction of a cave-entrance to post-and-lintel hut architecture to the temple building pictured above, a similar development was taking place in sculpture. Here, as in building, nature first imposed limitations on the artist, for there is one tradition that the first material, used for carving figures was wood. Carving in wood, of course, meant that one must cut with the grain of the wood. Cutting across it would weaken the statue to such an extent that an outstretched arm, for example, would easily break off. Then, too, most of the early statues were carved from the trunks of trees, which meant that the carved figure must be of such a size and shape as to fit within the trunk of the tree. The hand of tradition placed a further bondage upon the archaic Greek sculptor, for the culture which he inherited came largely from Egypt, so that he knew only to make his creation in the stiff, straight style of that civilization.

It was from this archaic style that the Greek learned to know freedom. When he began to work in stone instead of wood, he learned to carve outstretched arms and hands; and within the straight lines of the archaic style he learned the art of delicate curvature which suggests a living quality and a calmly disciplined strength which was the glory of Greek sculpture. The beginning of this change is seen in the bronze statue, the Charioteer of Delphi.

The American poet, Hilda Doolittle, has described her reaction to this statue in such a way as to reveal its meaning better than other words can do. Below is given a part of her poem, "Charioteer."

"In that manner (archaic) he finished the statue of his brother. It stands mid-way in the hall of laurels.

> Only the priest
> of the inmost house
> has such height,
> only the faun
> in the glade
> such light, strong ankles,
> only the shade of the bay-tree
> such rare dark
> as the darkness
> caught under the fillet
> that covers your brow,
> only the blade
> of the ash-tree
> such length, such beauty
> as thou,
> O my brother. . .

> I will fashion a statue
> of him, of my brother
> out of thought
> and the strength of my wrist
> and the fire of my brain. . .

Ewing Galloway   CHARIOTEER OF DELPHI

When death comes,
instead of a vision
(I will catch it in bronze)
you will stand
as you stood at the end,
(as the herald announced it,
proclaiming aloud,
"Achaea has won,")
in-reining them now,
so quiet,
not turning to answer
the shout of the crowd."

        H. D., *Charioteer*

Aeschylus depicted a new freedom for men as they worked with the gods in *Prometheus,* and a new freedom in their dealings with others in *The Eumenides.* Cleisthenes had already removed blood-ties and superstition from government. The Ionian philosophers were questing for more knowledge about the universe. What these people did in their fields, the sculptor of the Charioteer did in his. He placed a new pattern of freedom where all people could see it.

The sculptor is still working in the archaic manner, the composition is still up-and-down, but with what a difference! The size of the area at the bottom as compared to the other areas gives the composition balance and stability. The little rhythms of the folds in the sleeves furnish variety, and are picked up by the folds of the waist-garment and carried down to the simple, sweeping and rhythmic lines of the chiton. So, too, does the outer line of the arm come up, over the shoulder, and down to the ground in a great sweeping rhythm. What is the main line or direction here? It is the beginning of the flame-shaped curve. Notice that the figure is not exactly straight, but from the top of the head, through the V of the neck, and thence to the bottom of the garment, we have a line like a much elongated S.

What kind of a man is here? He has just guided four horses through a race, and has emerged as the victor. The shouts of the crowd ring around him. He is unmoved, calm. Where does his strength lie?

The Development of Classic Architecture

The foregoing discussion has made a few pointed suggestions about the evolution of Greek art during the archaic period; a period marked by the bondages which nature and tradition imposed upon the creative artist. It has also indicated the ways in which these artists found a freedom in expression which was to result in the classic period of Greek art. Let us return

to the subject of architecture to see how it fared during this time and then turn again to sculpture.

The form of the Greek temple emerged from its function, which was markedly different from that of the present-day church. In Greece the congregation, if any, assembled outside the temple itself, so that there was little need for a large room. In the early temples there was but one room. Later two rooms developed, one for the statue of the god or goddess to whom the temple was dedicated, and a second room for the treasury of the temple. At either end of this room porches extended outward, and it was from these that the priests conducted any public services which were held. The central room of the temple was called the cella, while the porch at the front was known as the pronaus; the rear porch was called the opisthodomos.

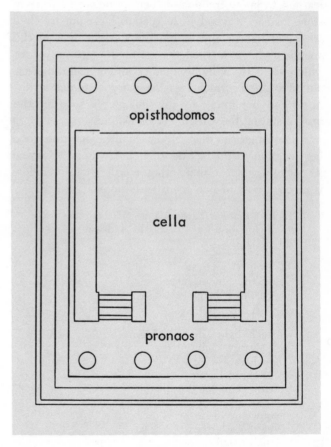

The simple floor plan given here is that of the Temple of the Wingless Victory at Athens. While this floor plan shows columns at the front and the rear of the temple only, later temples, such as the Parthenon, had a row of columns down each of the sides as well.

During the classic period, three important styles or "orders" of architecture developed. In point of time, the first of these is the Doric order, which is the simplest of the three, and had been widely used in hut building of the archaic period. At that time its columns had seemed stubby and clumsy, more nearly barrel-shaped than anything else. In later times, however, the column was lengthened until it acquired the balance and grace which we find in the columns of the Parthenon. The column had no decorative base. It was made with an *entasis* or slight bulge, so that its thickest point was found about a third of the distance from the base. From that point it tapered up to its very simple capital, which was a curved stone somewhat resembling a cushion. Above was a squared stone serving as a base for the lintel.

The Ionic order was the second of the great Greek styles of architecture. It is more ornate than the Doric, in that its column was longer and more slender, and its capital, as in the following diagram, was more decorative. It is of interest that in this scroll we recognize a form from nature, although no one is sure whether it was copied from a ram's-horn or from a shell like that of a snail. Between the two scrolls we have a typical egg-and-dart decoration.

The Corinthian order was even later in its development, and was much more ornate. As a matter of fact, it more properly belongs to the period of decadence. It can be recognized by its extremely long, slender shaft, and by its capital which is profusely decorated with stylized acanthus leaves and other ornamental figures. Because of the slenderness of the column it seems almost too brittle to support the weight of a great building.

DORIC   IONIC   CORINTHIAN

THE GREEK ORDERS OF ARCHITECTURE

Greek Classic Art

In the sculpture of the classic period, we find such great names as Phidias, the designer of the Parthenon, and Praxitiles, Myron, and several others. These were individual creators whose works have been preserved for us. The statues, like the buildings, had their beginnings in the forms of the archaic period, though the workers were now carving stone, ivory, and gold instead of wood. The forms which they created, however, still maintain much of the straightness and simplicity of the older works.

The difference between the sculpture of the archaic period and that of the classic period consists in the very delicate use of the curve to suggest life and strength. In the Charioteer of Delphi, for example, we find the archaic style used, but with a new freedom which the artist gave himself, a freedom to extend the lines of the garments and to create rhythms by the use of flutings and folds, very similar to the flutings on the Doric columns. In much of the statuary, too, we find the curve of the flame, an elongated "S" curve, as the direction around which the composition was formed.

None of the statues shows any great activity on the part of the subject. The Greeks believed that inner strength was more important than outward show, and, through the use of the inherited forms plus the addition of the delicate curvatures spoken of here, achieved that sense of calm and inner force which they sought. The same may be said of their buildings; the Parthenon, for example, appears straight and right simply because there are no straight lines in it. We have already spoken of the entasis or slight bulge of the Doric column. This same principle was carried out in the whole of the construction of the building, so that we get the sense of strength, of rightness, of balance, and of life because of the nicely calculated curve of the lines.

In the Athena, note the balance between the curved line to the left of the skirt and a similar one at the right from shoulder to waist. From the facial features, what was the character of the goddess? What Greek ideal of beauty is noticeable here?

Ewing Galloway

ATHENA LEMNIA

Ewing Galloway

THE DISCUS THROWER
CORCORAN ART GALLERY BY MYRON OF ATHENS

In the Discobolus, are two opposing, though simple and sweeping lines: one from the discus, through the shoulder, down the left arm and right leg; the other from the head, through the body and left leg. This man is not going to throw the discus very far. Why throw a discus, if not to develop a good body (a Greek ideal)?

Ewing Galloway

THE FIGURES OF HESTIA, DIONE, AND APHRODITE FROM
THE EAST PEDIMENT OF THE PARTHENON

Here the rhythmic lines flow from left to right. One group flows over the knees of the figures, another group over their breasts. These lines suggest the curve of an Ionic capital. Here the artist had to fit his composition into the triangle of the pediment; and within those limits he created an interesting, simple, and beautiful composition.

Ewing Galloway   PARTHENON FROM THE NORTHWEST

Said Pericles, "We are lovers of the beautiful, yet simple in our tastes, and we cultivate the mind without loss of manliness. Wealth we employ, not for talk and ostentation, but when there is a real use for it . . . To sum up: I say that Athens is the school of Hellas, and that the individual Athenian in his own person seems to have the power of adapting himself to the most varied forms of action with the utmost versatility and grace."

PERICLES

VATICAN, ROME

What Pericles said in words, the Parthenon says in marble. Here we have a building in perfect proportion, each area of which complements each other area. (Note. This does not mean that we should copy it today. The spirit which produced it, we might well copy, but we must remember that the best composition for Athens in the fifth century B.C. cannot be good for the world in the twentieth century.) Each line is gently curved to give the sense of balance and rightness which the total structure achieves. It is rich in ornamentation, but tastefully so, which means that the ornament has a vital function in the whole design. "Wealth we employ . . . when there is a real use for it."

It is a temple, designed to glorify a god. Yet its lines bring it to earth and to men. Athena was the goddess who said, in Aeschylus' phrase, "Let no man be uncurbed by law, or curbed by tyranny." This temple justly and fitly honors such a goddess of wisdom and justice, who was concerned with the development of maturity in her people.

It was during the time of Pericles that this brief moment of balance came into being. It was he who had the Parthenon built as a symbol of all that Athens stood for. The artist portrays him as a man of intellect and ability to act, a man who was, perhaps, kind, but certainly just in his dealings. The helmet which he wears in this bust is a symbol of the fact that he was a general.

As we know, this period of balance did not last, but soon gave way to the time of decadence, when men passed the boundary between sincerity and artfulness.

We have stressed throughout this discussion of classic Greek art the use of natural forms. It would seem that the curve of the Doric capital is a line borrowed from certain flower petals. The curve of the Ionic capital is the curve of the ram's-horn. The curve of the classic statues is that of a flame. The shape and features of the Greek temple are those which sprang from the hard realities of post and lintel construction. The triglyphs, for example, were the former ends of joists, and the pediment was a necessity created to provide a slope to the roof for adequate drainage. These give definite limits to the work of the craftsman, and would seem to constitute a bondage to creative effort. The glory of classic sculpture and of classic architecture was that the artist achieved his freedom within the disciplines imposed upon him. He learned to do exactly what he wanted to do by working within these limits. With their help, not in spite of the limitations, he created a harmony and rightness of design, function, and decoration. These aspects of the work, design, function, and decoration, were integrated, and integrity and honesty are still closely related.

Decadent Greek Art

Turning to the decadent forms, let us first ask what we mean when we speak of this time as one in which skill in craftsmanship was so great that the artists were no longer able to achieve their purposes. Maybe a comparison would help to clarify the point. Have you ever known a person who was so clever, so facile with conversation and manners, so "slick," that you wondered if there was any genuine character and personality behind the smooth front? You have known such a person? Then you know exactly what we are talking about. The art of the decadent period represents exactly that "slickness."

In this third period of Greek art, the buildings are no longer the balanced and harmonious structures of the Parthenon type. Rather they are the tall, overly-delicate Corinthian order which gives a sense of being too brittle to be solid. In contrast with the calm assurance of power which we see in the Charioteer of Delphi, we see the stress and the turmoil of the Laocoön Group, whose line is distorted and grotesque. Instead of the Athena of Lemnia, whose face and figure suggest calm beauty and justice, we have the Apollo Belvedere, who is nothing more than a very pretty man. The creation of these new statues and new buildings took skill; more, probably than the artists of the classic period possessed, but that very skill was their undoing. Their products show the same "slickness" which we noted above, and betray a lack of inward strength and integrity.

One sign of the passage from balance to decadence may be seen in the Corinthian temple below. For the most part, Corinthian architecture found its peak in Rome. Certainly this temple is thrust high in the air; more so than one of the more simple types such as the Parthenon. Its columns are exactly straight, and their slenderness is very graceful. Is it appropriate, or even emotionally satisfying, in a great building?

Ewing Galloway   TEMPLE OF OLYMPIAN ZEUS   ATHENS—GREEK AND ROMAN

Ewing Galloway

APOLLO BELVEDERE
VATICAN, ROME

A "slick" statue, very pretty. What did the Greeks now think of their gods? Compare this face with that of Athena Lemnia.

Underwood-Stratton

LAOCOÖN
VATICAN, ROME

Notice the complexity of line, and the obvious exertion on the face of the father and two sons. Notice, too, the bulging muscles. What is this new idea in portraying strength? Compare this with the Charioteer. Does the confusion of line reflect a similar confusion of thought on the part of the people?

EXERCISES

1. *Vocabulary.* In order to understand this chapter and to discuss it intelligently, you will need to know the meanings of the following words and others:

architrave	entasis
triglyph	archaic
metope	ethos
pediment	pathos
post and lintel	

2. Be able to explain the three orders of Greek architecture.

3. What were the chief differences between the archaic, classic, and decadent forms of sculpture and architecture?

4. More important than any of the factual questions above (though the facts are necessary first), can you understand and discuss the spirit that brought the Greeks from simple post and lintel huts to the glory of a Parthenon; from the narrow archaic sculpture to a discus thrower? And can you see the spirit that led from those forms to an Apollo Belvedere and a Temple of Olympian Zeus?

Greek Music

"After music our youth are to be educated by gymnastics? Certainly." The question from Glaucon and the answer by Socrates cover the essentials of the educational philosophy of Plato's *Republic* and of Greece during the Golden Age. The balanced combination of music and gymnastics provides for harmonious adjustment of body and soul, a healthy mind in a healthy body. Overemphasizing gymnastics makes men "more brutal than they should be." Overemphasizing music makes men "softer than is good for them."

For the Greeks music implied the following: 1. the art of singing and playing music, 2. "of the muses," (all of the arts), 3. study of the scientific basis of music (acoustics and music theory), 4. music (acoustics) as a key to understanding the harmony of the universe (the Pythagorean "music of the spheres"), 5. performing and listening to music as part of the ethical training necessary to inculcate virtue and "sobriety in the soul."

Acoustical and mathematical principles form the basis for all considerations of Greek music. Pythagoras (sixth century B.C.) is traditionally credited with discovering that the relationship of musical tones depends on the relative sizes of strings or air columns producing the tones. Perhaps Pythagoras first noted the differences in pitch produced by blacksmith's hammers or the differences in pitch of the shields which the smiths were hammering into shape, but the acoustical principles can be demonstrated by using, as did the Greeks, a vibrating string.

Assume there are two strings of equal diameter and stretched to the same tension. String x is 12 cm.

long, while string y is 6 cm. long. String y is *half* as long as x and will therefore have *twice* as many vibrations. If x has a *frequency* (vibrations per second or cps) of 64, then y will have a frequency of 128; in other words, y is to x as 128 is to 64 $(y/x = 128/64 = 2/1)$.

If x has Great C as its pitch then y will sound c (small c) an octave higher. In other words C–c is an octave with a *frequency ratio* of 2/1 and all octaves will have a 2/1 relationship of their frequencies.

	Vibrations/sec. Frequency	Ratio	Notation
y_____	128	2	
x____12 cm.	64	1	

The Greeks exploited their knowledge of the mathematical relationships of vibrating bodies, but they were not aware, for example, that string x vibrated not only throughout its entire length but simultaneously in halves, thirds, fourths and so forth to produce the same mathematical relationships *within* a string as the Greeks had observed *between* strings.[1]

An octave is one of many *musical intervals*, the difference in pitch between any two notes. Musical intervals are usually designated by *number* and *quality*. The *numerical* size of an interval is obtained by counting every line and space between two notes,

including the line or space on which each note rests. The numerical size of a 2/1 octave is *eight*[2] and the *quality* is *perfect*.[3] The 2/1 octave is therefore a *perfect octave* (abbreviated as P8).

Musical Intervals: Numerical size

Harmonic interval
(notes sounded together)

Melodic interval
(notes sounded in succession)

The next note in the overtone series above the octave is g[1], which lies a fifth above c[1]. The ratio is 3/2 and the interval is a *perfect fifth* (P5). The next note is c[2], which forms the interval of a P4 (perfect fourth) with g[1].[4]

The mathematical relationships of these four notes form the basis of Greek music in theory and practice. The fundamental intervals are P8, P5, P4; all other intervals are derived from these. In terms of ratios the system can be expressed as 1:2:3:4 and can be summarized as follows:

Vibrating Strings		Frequency	Ratio	Number of Partial
3 cm._____	c[2] g[1]	512	4	4
4 cm._____		384	3	3
6 cm._____	c[1]	256	2	2
12 cm._____ Fundamental Note	c	128	1	1

[1]Physicist Joseph Sauveur (1653-1716) is generally credited with being the first to prove scientifically that one string or air column vibrated in multiple segments to produce the fixed sequence of higher and softer tones known as the *overtone series*.
[2]*Octave* is derived from the Latin word for "eight." The Greeks called an octave a *diapason*, meaning "through all the strings (of a lyre)," an instrument with the range of an octave.
[3]Intervals are *perfect*, according to the Greeks, when their sounds tend to blend together.
[4]Consult the Reference Chart: Pitch Nomenclature (p. 53) for precise location of all of these notes.

Instruments

Lyre, kithara and *aulos*, each with its own special function, were the principle instruments of classical Greece. *Lyre* and *kithara* were different-sized plucked string instruments of similar construction which represented Apollo, the god of light, music, poetry, healing and so forth. The *aulos* consisted of two short tubes joined together in a mouthpiece with a double reed; it represented the emotional and expressive aspects of life presided over by Dionysus, god of wine and drama.

Lyre and kithara were dominant in Greek music to the same extent that the ideas they represented tended to dominate Greek thought: a balanced unity of opposing concepts[5] but with mind taking precedence over matter, soul over body, rational over nonrational, intellectual over emotional, classicism over romanticism, idealism over realism. Dorian (Apollonian) instruments and music were to provide ethical instruction and control over Phrygian (Dionysian) instruments and music.

Characteristics and functions of these instruments can be summarized as follows:

REFERENCE CHART:
GREEK MUSICAL INSTRUMENTS

Instrument	LYRE	KITHARA	AULOS
Basic form			
Tone production	string instrument	string instrument	wind instrument
Played	plucking	plucking	blowing through double reed into twin pipes
Size	small, hand-held	larger than lyre, hand-held	small, hand-held
Number of strings or air columns	usually seven strings	usually eleven strings	two pipes with up to eleven tone holes
Performance by:	amateurs (usually aristocrats)	professional musicians	professionals and amateurs
function	primarily to accompany solo songs	accompany solo and group singing	solo instrument and accompany group singing
location	home, school	social and public gatherings, plays	plays, orgiastic religious ceremonies, elegies
Tone quality	light, delicate, serene	louder than lyre but still delicate	loud, nasal, penetrating
Ethos (ethical quality)	intellectual, Dorian, Apollonian	intellectual, Dorian, Apollonian	emotional, Phrygian, Dionysian

---

[5]Essentially Platonic dualism: Reality=The Ideas and Phenomena.

Musical Scale

A musical scale is a graduated series of pitches formed by reducing the tonal materials of music to a one-octave ladder of ascending or descending pitches. A scale can be understood as the supply of notes used to make music, or a theoretical series culled from existing music and placed in an orderly arrangement indicating the tones (or building blocks) out of which the music is made. A scale, as such, will rarely appear in actual music. The following melody, however, is a convenient exception:

To determine the tonal foundation (scale) of music, a melody, for example, can be studied to discover which tones are used consistently and, moreover, which seem to be the most important. The consistently used pitches are then written down as a scale beginning and ending with the most important tone, for instance, the note which tends to be used more often, tends to appear on strong beats and frequently concludes sections of the composition. The following melody has the scale tones circled the first time they appear (regardless of octave); the most important tone is marked each time it appears:

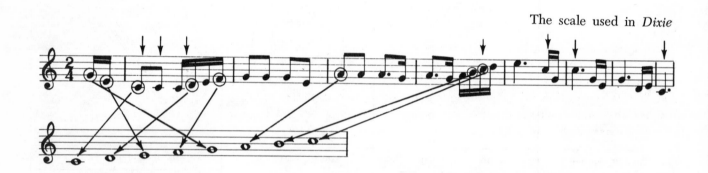

The eight basic tones (seven plus the octave) are scaled from low to high (or high to low). The scales illustrated above (they are the same scale) are *diatonic* scales because *each* of the seven letter names (c–d–e–f–g–a–b–c) is used only once. The octave duplication is used to round off the scale.

Scale constructions are described in terms of *half steps* (semitones) and *whole steps* (whole tones or, simply, tones) between each *degree* (note) of a scale. A half step (semitone) is the distance from one note to the *next available note,* whether that note is black or white on the keyboard. A whole step (tone) consists naturally enough of two semitones (half steps). On the keyboard the distance

e–f is a semitone (white to white). From c to the next available note above is from white to black (half step), or it can be called (for reasons which will be made clear later) a half step from c to *c-sharp* (c♯). From c♯ to the next available note (black to white) is another semitone; thus, the distance from c to d (white to white) is a *tone* (whole tone) because there is a black note (c♯) in between.

Following are keyboard and music notation illustrations of the semi- and whole-tone relationships. When a scale uses all twelve tones in the octave (all white and black keys) it is said to be *chromatic,* made up entirely of semitones.

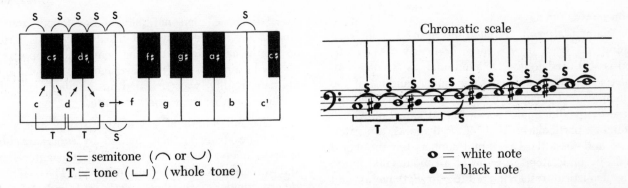

S = semitone (⌢ or ⌣)
T = tone (⌴) (whole tone)

○ = white note
● = black note

Semi- and whole-tones can be counted up *or* down. When going *up* a semitone from c the black key is c♯; however, when going *down* from d the next lower note is called *d-flat* (d♭). The *same* black note will be either C♯ or d♭ depending, in general, on whether it is approached from above or below. Each black note has *two* names: c♯ or d♭, d♯ or e♭ and so forth.

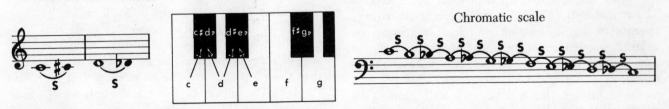

Scale Tuning

Accurate tuning is a practical necessity in all music. The tuning procedure can be best understood by briefly describing a modern procedure. When a technician *tunes* a piano he first adjusts the tensions of the strings of a[1] so this tone will agree (be in tune) with his tuning fork. He then selects the tones of the one-line octave[6] and "lays the temperament" by adjusting these twelve tones so each is an *equal* semitone away from its neighbor. He then moves outside the one-line octave and tunes in octaves by making c[2] blend with c[1], d[2] with d[1], e[2] with e[1] and so on.

1. Tune to tuning fork.
2. Tune in equal semitones

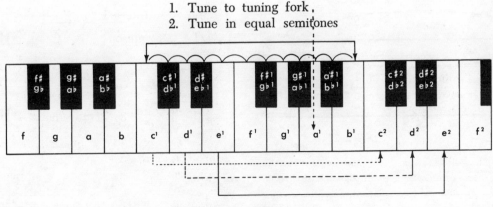

3. Tune in octaves

The type of tuning described is called *equal temperament* because the pitches have been tempered (adjusted) so they form *equal* semitones.[7]

---

[6]See Reference Chart: Pitch Nomenclature on p. 53.

[7]Equal temperament is the standardized tuning for modern musical instruments. It is briefly introduced here in order to provide a point of reference for Greek and medieval tuning practices.

Pythagorean Tuning

Named after its reputed inventor, Pythagorean tuning has been in existence for nearly 3000 years, and is still used today. Detailed analysis is not essential for our purposes, but some understanding of the principles of Pythagorean tuning is necessary because these help illuminate some mainstreams of Greek thought, particularly that of Pythagoras, Socrates, Plato and Aristotle. Greek philosophers felt the world could be understood in terms of a fundamental unity. The acoustical research credited to Pythagoras and his successors provided welcome *proof* of the existence of basic unity in the natural world.

A *monochord*, also ascribed to Pythagoras, was the device used to work out the tuning, in conjunction with the necessary mathematical computations. The monochord (Greek *monos*, one; *chorde*, string) consists of a single string stretched lengthwise on a large wooden resonator and fastened securely at each end of the resonating box. Any note could be produced (after plucking the string) by sliding a movable bridge (fret) back and forth under the string, after first determining mathematically where the string was to be divided. The ratios between the various string lengths, as discussed earlier in this chapter, also apply to a single string which can be divided to produce shorter string lengths.

Pythagoras' personal religion developed from a kind of mystical ecstasy, but his theology was based on mathematics and the mathematical proportions of a vibrating string. For Pythagoras the nature of ultimate reality was revealed in *number*, and the cardinal number was *one*, or *unity*.

The full length of a vibrating string stands for *unity*. The string is then divided by *superparticular ratios*, namely, those ratios in which the antecedent and consequent differ by *unity* (one). The essential superparticular ratios were 2/1, 3/2 and 4/3, all differing by one and all related to the *oneness* (1/1) of the entire string.

The full length of the string is a unison (1/1) and represents unity, or *perfection*. The superparticular ratios of 2/1, 3/2 and 4/3 all differ by one (unity) and are therefore degrees of perfection. Because they stand nearest to unity the P8, P5 and P4 are *perfect consonances*. The P8 (2/1) is more perfect than the P5 (3/2), and the P5 more perfect than the P4 (4/3). The unison, however, is the only true perfection and everything is related to it.

To summarize: The perfect consonances are unison, P8, P5 and P4. All other intervals are either imperfect consonances or dissonances.[8]

REFERENCE CHART:
DIVISIONS OF A VIBRATING STRING

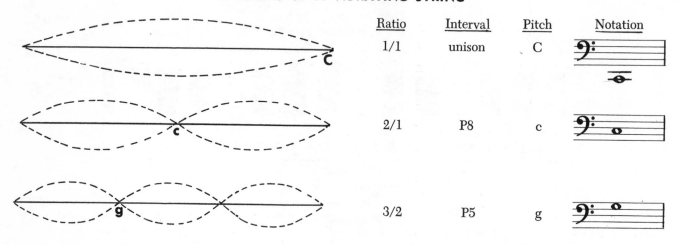

Ratio	Interval	Pitch	Notation
1/1	unison	C	
2/1	P8	c	
3/2	P5	g	

---

[8]Additional superparticular ratios would be 5/4 and 6/5, which will eventually be added to the system as *imperfect consonances*. Larger superparticular ratios (9/8, 10/9, 16/15) and nonsuperparticular ratios (81/64, 256/243, etc.) are *dissonances*.

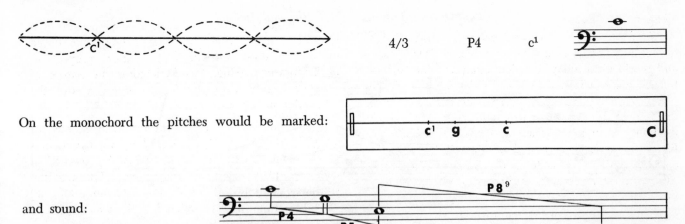

$$4/3 \qquad P4 \qquad c^1$$

On the monochord the pitches would be marked:

and sound:

Once the framework of consonances has been established, it becomes necessary to devise a procedure for *tuning a scale*. The most important notes are known, but placement of the remaining notes is a necessity for the performing musician.

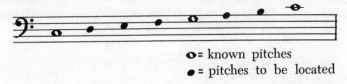

○ = known pitches
● = pitches to be located

Following his conception of an all-pervading unity Pythagoras chose to build the scale by utilizing a single procedure. He selected the *perfect fifth* (3/2) because it produced the first note (g) to actually differ in pitch from the fundamental note (C) and its octave duplications (c and c¹). He added fifths, one on top of another, to get the necessary pitches and then subtracted octaves to place the notes in the same octave with the known pitches. The final result of pitch relationships (by ratios) for the white notes of the Small Octave looks like this:[10]

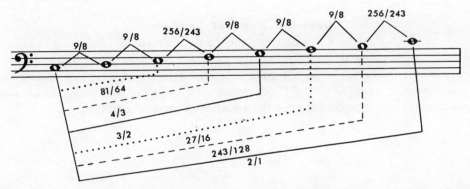

In summary, Pythagorean tuning was possibly derived as much from performance practice (the way musicians actually played and sang) as it was from theory. It was the *theory*, however, that fascinated the Greeks. Using only one procedure (adding up perfect fifths), Pythagoras could move from the *unity* of the fundamental string to achieve the *diversity* of the scale.[11] Pythagorean tuning possessed

for the Greeks the twin virtues of logic (backed up by scientific evidence) and the beautiful simplicity of a single procedure.

---

[9] These ratios may also be indicated as 1:2:3:4 (1:2:3:4).

[10] See Appendix II for the mathematical procedures which lead to these ratios.

[11] Reflecting the unity of ultimate reality and the diversity of the visible world.

Pythagorean Tuning: Add Fifths and Reduce
to a Single Octave

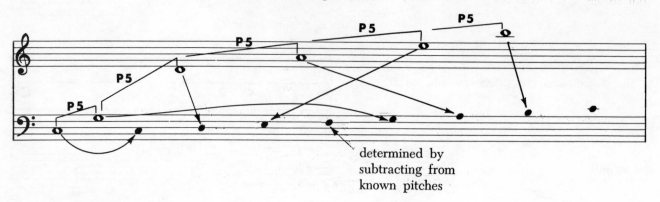

determined by
subtracting from
known pitches

Applied Tuning

The seven-stringed lyre could be tuned to a variety of pitches, but the diatonic scale on e¹ (e¹–d¹–c¹–b–a–g–(f)–e) was standard. The missing note (f) was obtained by *stopping* the string: A finger was placed near the end of the e string to shorten the string and raise the pitch a semitone. All strings were the same length, but with larger diameters for the lower strings (as in modern violin and guitar).

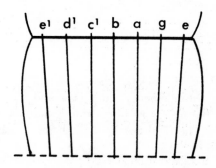

Greater Perfect System

The scale e¹ to e to which the lyre was tuned was the *Dorian octave*, the basic tonal arrangement around which the Greeks built an elaborate structure called the *Greater Perfect System* (GPS), one of the most complete theories of music ever devised. The GPS furnished a logical frame of reference for the music of the period. As such it is still another example of the Greek passion for reducing everything to an ultimate unity; in this case to a single comprehensive explanation for the varieties of musical practice.

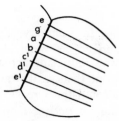

---

[12]The scale is in descending order (high to low pitch). The Greeks, however, described this as an *ascending* scale because e¹ was the lowest string when the lyre was held in playing position. This literal description of high and low *strings* led to considerable confusion when scholars of the early Christian era attempted to unravel some of the complexities of Greek music.

The Greater Perfect System was built from a nucleus of the *Dorian tetrachord* (*tetrachordos,* having four strings) consisting of two tones and a semitone.

Dorian tetrachord

The *Dorian octave* is composed of two Dorian tetrachords joined by a whole tone.

Dorian octave

The Greater Perfect System consists of the Dorian octave plus a tetrachord at each end:

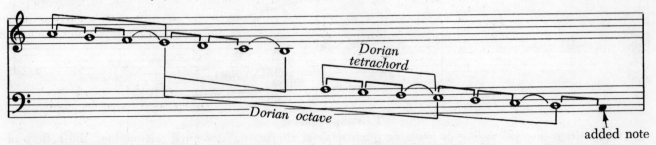

added note

The system included all the diatonic pitches used by lyre, kithara and aulos. The low A (added note) was not part of any portion of the system. Its sole purpose was to round the system off to two complete octaves (a^1 to A), and thus further exemplify Greek preoccupation with balance, order and unity.

Greek Modes

A composition played on a lyre tuned to the Dorian octave and using the notes of this octave is said to be in *Dorian mode. Mode* may be defined as the *manner* in which musical tones are arranged in a scale, or to put it another way, mode refers to *arrangements* of tones and semitones in scales. The four principle *Greek modes* are as follows:

REFERENCE CHART: GREEK MODES
Tones and Semitones

Mode	Letter Names	Between Pitches	Notation
Dorian	e^1 to e	T T S T T T S	
Phrygian	d^1 to d	T S T T T S T	
Lydian	c^1 to c	S T T T S T T	
Mixolydian	b to B	T T T S T T S	

In addition there are three related modes which are treated as lower versions of the four principle modes and which are named by using the prefix *hypo* (lower): Hypodorian, Hypophrygian, Hypolydian, (*lower* always means low strings of the lyre when held in playing position).

The seven modes formed the Greater Perfect System, a system which was "greater" because it explained the variety of musical practices and "perfect" because it symbolized unity. The following chart indicates the top string and one-octave range of the seven modes of the Greater Perfect System:

REFERENCE CHART: DIATONIC MODES
IN THE GREATER PERFECT SYSTEM

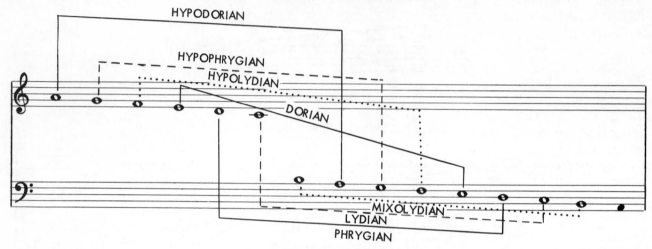

Transposition

Transposition involves raising or lowering pitch *without* altering interior pitch relationships, the pattern of tones and semitones. For example, a composition using the diatonic scale of C–C could be transposed by raising the pitch level while at the same time maintaining the identical pattern of tones and semitones. Because C^2–C^1 uses only white notes (on the piano) a new pitch level of d^2–d^1 must use some black notes in order to maintain the tone-semitone arrangement.

Greek instrumentalists had to transpose all modes (except Dorian) to the Dorian octave in which their lyres were tuned. All modes could be played between e^1 and e by adjusting the tone-semitone arrangement to conform to the desired modal pattern and then stopping the strings to get the correct notes.

Phrygian mode (transposed UP to the Dorian octave)

Phrygian mode (untransposed white notes from the GPS)

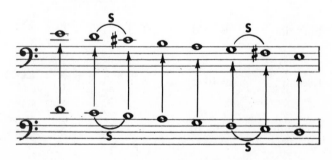

Performance of Music

Greek music was always bound up with drama and dance and was indispensable for the proper presentation of poetry. Accompanying themselves on the lyre, singers presented recitations, rhapsodies, odes, lyric songs and epic poetry of Homer. Trained choruses sang the choral parts of Greek drama accompanied by kithara and aulos. Modern performances of Greek dramas do not include music, a practice almost comparable to operatic presentations without music. The music for *Oedipus the King, Agamemnon* and others has been lost, for reasons which will be explained later.

Melody, rhythm and tone color (but not harmony) were the elements of Greek music. Rhythm was directly related to the rhythm and meter of poetry. The predominant tone color was the delicate string tone of lyre and kithara. The aulos, with its emotional and exciting tone, was used most effectively with songs of mourning and dramatic portions of religious ceremonies.

Melody was by far the most elaborately developed of the three elements. Because the Greeks practiced more than one tuning with seven different modes and used, in addition to the Dorian tetrachord previously illustrated, two other types of tetachords,[13] the same melody could appear in many different forms. For example, a melody could be performed in Dorian mode with Pythagorean tuning and diatonic tetrachords; then the mode could be changed, *or* the tuning, *or* the tetrachord, *or* any two of these, *or* even all three. Theoretically, it was possible to perform one melody in approximately 100,000 different variants. This staggering number of possibilities undoubtedly helps account for Greek fascination with the development and exploitation of melody.[14] These manifold melodic possibilities more than made up for the absence of harmony, that fourth element of music which did not begin its development until fourteen or fifteen centuries after the Golden Age.[15]

Musical Notation

Almost all the written music of ancient Greece has been lost. Historians have tended to belittle the importance of music in Greek life, contending that a literate society which valued music would have certainly left a musical heritage. They argued, not illogically, that a civilization which leaves behind only five or six complete compositions and a like number of fragments can hardly be interested in that particular art form. To further compound these misconceptions there has been a tendency to min-

imize the purely musical importance of the essays on music in such literary sources as Euclid, Plato, Aristotle, Aristoxenus, Plutarch, Quintilianus, Nichomachus, Ptolemy and others.

Music in all its aspects was so important that music theory and music notation reached a high stage of development; in fact, the notation was so well developed that later generations were unable to read it!

Because few Greek works survived in their original forms, posterity has had to rely on surviving copies of these works. When reproducing a Greek drama, for example, a scholar would copy the text but omit the accompanying intricate alphabet which symbolized the music. The Greek musical alphabet died out under Roman rule, and there was not an adequate notational system to take its place. There was no point, for the copyist, in copying a dead musical system and no possibility of transcribing Greek notation into another set of symbols. The net result of this dilemma was the copyists' omission of a musical system which had become incomprehensible, and the loss of Greek music forever.[16]

Musical Examples

No music has survived from the Periclean age. From a later period the "First Delphic Hymn" (c. 138 B.C.) is the most extended work known. Like much of Greek music it is in *quintuple* meter (a combination of triple and duple meters). The piece has three major sections of which a portion of the first section is reproduced below. The example is *diatonic* (Greater Perfect System) and is in the

---

[13]The Dorian tetrachord could be divided into three different kinds, or *genera*: the diatonic version already discussed plus the *chromatic* and *enharmonic* varieties. All three *genera* were extended throughout the Greater Perfect System.

Dorian tetrachords		midway between f and e
Genus Diatonic	Chromatic	Enharmonic

[14]In terms of present-day possibilities a melody could be played on the piano in one tuning (equal temperament) and with possibly a dozen different scales or modes in general use.

[15]The twelve tones of a chromatic scale on the piano give little indication of the pitches available for Greek melodies. Within one octave the Greeks could choose from about two dozen pitches, none of which (except the octave) coincided with the piano pitches.

[16]Not even surviving manuscripts could tell the whole story because the Greeks are credited with improvising much of their music.

Phrygian mode. Other sections of the piece are considerably more elaborate with chromatic tetrachords and the like. The text setting is *syllabic* (a syllable for each note) except where the note beams  indicate two notes to a syllable.[17]

First Delphic Hymn c. 138 B.C.[18]

Translation of the first two sections of the text is as follows:

Hark, ye fair-armed daughters of the loud thundering Zeus who dwell in the deep forests of Helicon! Hasten thither, to praise in song your brother Phoebus, of the golden locks, who high above the rocky dwellings of the two-peaked Parnassus, surrounded by the august daughters of Delphi, betakes himself to the waters of limpid Kastalis, visiting at Delphi the prophetic crag.

Lo, the famous Attica, with its great city, which, thanks to the prayer of the arms-bearing Triton, inhabits an unassailable region. On holy altars Hephaestus consumes the thighs of bullocks; together Arabian incense rises toward Olympus. The oboe [aulos] shrilly sounding brings forth music with varied melodies and the golden sweet-voiced kithara sounds with hymns.

This segment of the "First Delphic Hymn" provides the first opportunity for a consideration of the *formal structure* of a piece of music, for example, the parts of the composition and their place in the total design (form) of the music. In music, as in the other arts, the structural details can be studied objectively and systematically to determine what they are and how they operate within the basic design to make the whole greater than the sum of its parts.

One of the important aspects of music is the *motive*, which is defined as the smallest coherent musical idea. Motives may be rhythmic and/or melodic (or harmonic). Using "The Battle Hymn of the Republic" as an illustration we can extract the smallest coherent rhythmic unit of ♩. ♪ and then indicate its use as a motive in the first four measures of the piece:

The melodic motive (the pattern used most frequently) is a three-note group descending the interval of a 3rd.

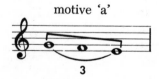

___

[17] This music exists in recorded form but usually in the equal temperament of the piano keyboard, a practice which does no justice whatever to the song as originally performed. Many of the Greek tunings gave a oriental flavor to the music.

[18] T. Reinach, *La Musique grecque,* 1926, p. 177.

The basic motive is used in several variations:

1. Basic

2. Same interval of a 3rd but ascending rather than descending (*inverted*) and with the middle note omitted

3. Inverted

4. Middle note omitted

In terms of the motive and its variations the first four measures can be outlined as follows:

Both the rhythmic and melodic motives can now be indicated in connection with the actual melodic line:[19]

Battle Hymn of the Republic

One or more motives combine to make a *phrase,* which is a unit of melody or, to put it another way, a musical thought. Because it is necessary to remember the beginning of a phrase until the end is heard (in order to hear the musical thought) phrases are rarely longer than eight measures in moderate tempo (24 to 32 beats).

The segment of the "Battle Hymn" given above is a phrase. If you will sing, hum or whistle through this first phrase you will find yourself taking a good breath at the end as you prepare to sing the second phrase (which is not given).

The *phrase structure* for the verse and chorus of the "Battle Hymn" is as follows:

verse   refrain

4 + 4   4 + 4

The + indicates that the phrases go together to make a *period,* which consists of two or three (sometimes four) phrases which make a complete musical idea. The phrase structure therefore indicates that the piece in question has two periods of two phrases each. The phrase structure can also be illustrated with the first verse and chorus of the text:

Phrase 1

> Mine eyes have seen the glory of the coming of the Lord, He is trampling out the vintage where the grapes of wrath are stored.

---

[19]The use of **x** and **a** is purely arbitrary and for reasons of ready identification. Any set of symbols will suffice so long as it is simple and logical. When the analysis symbols have become more complicated than the music they have defeated their purpose.

Phrase 2

He has loosed the fateful lightning of his terrible swift sword; His truth goes marching on.

Phrase 3

Glory, glory, hallelujah. Glory, glory, hallelujah.

Phrase 4

Glory, glory, hallelujah, his truth is marching on.

Finally, a *cadence* is a formula which occurs at the ends of phrases and which separates one phrase from another. A cadence may be momentary (at the end of a phrase) or permanent (at the end of a piece). The "Battle Hymn" has a cadence at the end of each of the four phrases, three momentary and one permanent.

Form (design, structure) refers to the plan of construction of a piece of music, including such structural items as motives, phrases and periods. If architecture can be termed "frozen music" then music can be described as "tonal architecture."

The following basic units of language and music can illustrate the above terminology if it is kept in mind that language and music are very complex and the "equivalents" are therefore only broad generalizations:

Music	Language
note	letter
motive	word (or syllable)
phrase	phrase (or sentence)
period	paragraph (or sentence)
cadence	punctuation mark
formal structure	syntax

Following is the "First Delphic Hymn" with a brief analysis:[20]

Performance Time: :30[21]

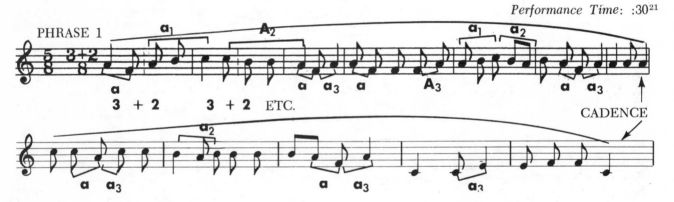

ANALYSIS:

Quintuple meter is, in this case, a combination of triple plus duple as indicated by the $3 + 2$ and the dotted bar line.

Phrase 1 is 7 measures in length; phrase 2 is 5 measures long. The *phrase structure* is $7 + 5$.

The basic *motive* is a falling third which is used throughout the piece.

---

[20]When analyzing music the question invariably arises: Did the composer consciously choose, for example, the consistent use of motives as in the "Delphic Hymn" or was this basic unity merely accidental? The answer in almost every case is that a composer, painter or poet probably organizes his work subconsciously or even instinctively. In cases where a composer has consciously and deliberately tried to weld his music together the result has often been mechanical rather than musical.

The sole purpose in searching for and labeling motives, phrases, periods, and the like is to take some of the mystery out of music, show that it is made of many small pieces which are easy to recognize and hear once they have been pointed out. From the motives and phrases one can move to the perception of larger structural units and eventually to whole symphonies, sonatas, concertos, jazz suits and such.

[21]Performance time will be given for each musical example, in this case, thirty seconds. Since music is the movement of sound in time the performance time of each illustration is an important factor.

a₁ is motive *a* varied (ascending with the third filled in).

a₂ is the original motive in another variation (going down but with the third filled in).

a₃ is motive *a inverted* (going up instead of down).

The mode of this segment is Phrygian with cadences on a¹ and c¹.

The "Song of Seikolos" was found engraved on a tombstone in Asia Minor. It can be transcribed into a modern equivalent of eight measures of music. Probably because the song is an epitaph the meter is duple with none of the irregularity so typical of Greek meters. The beams and also the slurs in measures 4 and 6 indicate one syllable to these two- or three-note groups. Following are text, the song and a brief analysis of the formal structure:

As long as you live, be cheerful; let nothing grieve you. For life is short, and time claims its tribute.

Seikolos Song (1st century A.D.)[22]

Time: :20

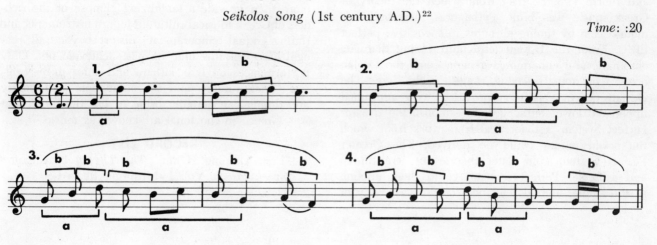

ANALYSIS:

Phrase structure: four 2-bar phrases with momentary cadence at measure 4 and final cadence at measure 8. Phrase structure can be indicated as four 2-bar phrases dividing into two 4-bar sections to make one 8-bar piece.

$$2 \ \overbrace{\underbrace{4 + 4}^{8}}_{+ \ 2 \ 2 +} \ 2$$

Primary motivic device (motive **a**): interval of a perfect fifth used at high and low extremes of melody line.

Secondary motive **b**: interval of a third used consistently throughout.

Characteristic rhythm: ♪ ♩ appears six times.

Phrygian mode d² to d¹ (untransposed) with cadences on f¹ and d¹.

---

[22]*Ibid.*, p. 193.

Summary

A proper balance of instruction in music and gymnastics provided the educational foundation for the citizens of ancient Greece. The study of music included the arts in general and music in particular with special reference to its scientific basis (acoustics) and the comprehensive theory and tuning of music built on that basis. Music was also expected to further ethical instruction, which was designed to encourage rational behaviour and intellectual control.

Through acoustics the Greeks determined the mathematical relationships of sounding bodies and built a theory resting on the conception of the unity and perfection of the vibrating string. This eventually led to the metaphysical concept of a unified universe which could be perceived and understood by the rational logic of those philosophers who could go beyond the sensory data of the material world.

Derived from the unison of the vibrating string were the so-called perfect intervals of octave, fifth and fourth (P8, P5, P4) from which the theory of Greek music was built. Pythagoras then built his model scale by tuning all notes in successive perfect fifths. From the Dorian tetrachord (using diatonic, chromatic and enharmonic *genera*) came the Dorian octave, or actual playing range of the lyre. The Dorian octave was then provided with additional upper and lower tetrachords to establish the Greater Perfect System, a theoretical framework from which the seven modes could be derived. The Greater Perfect System (plus later theories of lyre tuning and a Lesser Perfect System) could then function as the single, unified reference for the vast body of existing music, to provide, in other words, a theoretical unity for the multiplicity of musical practices.

Music performance was allied with drama, dance and especially poetry. Principle tone colors were the golden sounds of lyre or kithara (the instruments of Apollo) and the dark and pungent tone of the aulos (the instrument of Dionysus). Rhythm was almost entirely dependent on the rhythm and meter of poetry. Melody was developed to a fine art of subtle nuances selected from a vast range of compounded variations in tunings, modes and tetrachords. Harmony as such was unknown, but the melodic element has reigned supreme and unmatched by developments in Western music up to the present day.

The specialized art and craft of music notation achieved a notable degree of clarity and precision, almost all of which was lost during the centuries of copying and recopying Greek manuscripts. The precious little Greek music remaining can do no more than provide a tantalizing glimpse of the richness of Greek musical culture. Modern instruments and tuning (equal temperament) distort beyond all recognition even this hint of past achievements. Only performances on lyre, kithara and aulos in the original Greek tunings and in conjunction with poetry and drama can actually bring to life the glory that was Greece in the tonal art known as music.

RECORD LIST

1. "First Delphic Hymn," *The Theory of Classical Greek Music*, Vol. 1, Musurgia Records.
2. "Seikolos Song," *ibid*.

TIME CHART FOR GREEK CIVILIZATION

Time	Government and Politics	Philosophers—Scientists	Literature and Art
900 B.C.	Achaean Civilization. Blood Clans. Trojan War about 300 years before. Lycurgus molds Spartan law: two kings; young men in constant military training.		
850 B.C.			
750 B.C.			*Iliad* and *Odyssey* of Homer. Hesiod writes *Theogony* and *Works and Days*.
700 B.C.	Revision of Spartan Constitution. Ephors rule.		
650-550 B.C.	Draco's Code: Written law. 621 B.C. Solon (638-558). Cancelled all debt; freed debt-slaves, established graduated income tax. Peisistratus (605-527 B.C.). Redistributed land. Established national rather than local religious celebrations.	Ionian Philosophers a. Thales (water as world-stuff). b. Anaximander (the Boundless; separating out). c. Anaximenes. Pythagoras (580-500 B.C.). Form found in numerical relationships.	Sappho: woman lyric poet. Archaic statues such as Egyptian-like Apollo. Thespis: original dramatist.
550-500 B.C.	Cleisthenes (c. 507). Abolished blood clans substituting political demes. Assembly of all free Athenians. Senate of 500 members; ten generals administer law.	Heraclitus (535-475). "No thing abides." Fire as world-element. *Logos* or *Reason* rules change.	
500-450 B.C.	Persian Wars 491-480 B.C. Themistocles (514-449 B.C.) Income from silver mines used for fleet which defeated Persia and made Athens supreme sea power.	The Eleatic Philosophers. a. Parmenides (510-?). b. Zeno (488-?). Nothing changes. Our senses lie to us. Only reason can be trusted. The Mediators: Many elements. Change occurs by combination. Democritus (460?-362?).	Charioteer of Delphi. Pindar (522-448). Odes to victors in Olympic games. Aeschylus (525-456). First tragic dramatist. Celebrated greatness of men and Athens

Time	Government and Politics	Philosophers—Scientists	Literature and Art
450-400 B.C.	Pericles (490-429). Ruled in Athens 443-429. The height of Athenian glory. Rebuilt city after Persian Wars.	All things made of atoms which drift through space following no law but necessity. Completely materialistic.	Sophocles (496-406). Second tragic dramatist.
			Euripides (480-406). Third tragic dramatist.
		Socrates (469-399). Teacher of Plato.	Herodotus (484-425). Historian of Persian Wars.
			Thucydides (471-400). Historian of Peloponnesian Wars.
			Aristophanes (448-380). Writer of comic drama satirizing life of Athens.
	Peloponnesian Wars (431-404)	Plato (427-347). Reality lies in the idea or essence of things. Virtues of temperance, **courage**, wisdom, from which comes highest good, justice.	Phidias (500-432). Designer of Parthenon, statue of Athena, v a r i o u s pediment ornamentation, etc.
		The Sophists.	Myron (480-407). Famed sculptor.
400-350 B.C.		Aristotle (384-322). Collected and wrote down all wisdom of his time. Principle of *enteleche* or *purposivity*. All things exist as they are, but move into higher forms. There must be a *summum bonum* or highest good.	Polycletus (460-412). Famed sculptor.
			Demosthenes (383-322). Orations to arouse Athenians against Phillip.
		Epicureans – Pleasure the highest good.	
350-232 B.C.	Rome conquers Greece 232 B.C.	Stoics—Virtue the highest good.	Apollo Belvedere.
			Venus of Milo.

Prometheus Bound

Aeschylus

This play is the second of three in which Aeschylus dealt with the problem of the clash between an absolute God who ruled by power, force and fear, and mankind which was growing in many skills and in reasoning ability. Obviously the two forces will be in conflict unless an understanding can be reached which will allow proper zones for action for each. Thus he is treating the problem of man's relation to God, one of the questions which we have spoken of as fundamental for human freedom. Aeschylus was trying to interpret for the people of Athens the importance and the meaning of a change from the old Olympian gods to a new idea of divine power.

In order to understand this play, which deals entirely with the gods, it is necessary to know a little of the development of the gods and something of the myths about the gods. Briefly this can be told as follows: In the beginning was Chaos, composed of void, mass, and darkness. From Chaos emerged a male god, Uranus, who represented the heavens, and a female god, Gaea, who represented earth. These gods had three types of offspring, one of which was the Titans, who represented earthquakes and other cataclysms of the earth. Kronos, one of the Titans, led a revolt against his father and overthrew him. (It is interesting that from the drops of blood of Uranus sprang the fearful hags known as The Furies, gods whose duty it was to pursue anyone who had shed the blood of his kindred. It was this type of superstition which held the blood clans together). Kronos took his sister Rhea (another representation of the earth-goddess) for a wife, and from this union came the Olympian gods, Zeus, Demeter, Hera, Pluto, Poseidon, and Vesta. Zeus soon led a revolt against his father, and with the aid of the Titan, Prometheus, managed to shut up the older gods in Tartarus, the underworld.

Zeus then took over the task of reigning in heaven and earth, taking Hera as his wife. These are the group of gods referred to in the play as the "new gods in heaven." Kronos and his group were the "old gods." It is to be noticed and emphasized that Prometheus, a Titan, together with Oceanus, another Titan, aided Zeus. The rest of the group fought on the side of Kronos. Prometheus was given the task of creating man, which he did by rolling dust together. However, Prometheus favored man so much that he gave him many gifts. It was for this that Zeus had Prometheus chained to a massive cliff for all eternity. Prometheus, however, knows the secret which reveals the way in which Zeus will be overthrown. If Prometheus would reveal his secret, Zeus might free him from the rock. Thus we see the conflict of the play.

Read this play as a conflict between an absolute god (Zeus) and the champion of men (Prometheus). The play which follows this one and which brought about a solution to the problem is lost. When you finish this one, noticing carefully the powers which men have acquired, you might try writing a sketch (or a full play) of the type which Aeschylus might have written.

(Scene:—A rocky gorge in Scythia. Power and Force enter, carrying Prometheus as a captive. They are accompanied by Hephaestus.)

POWER:

To this far region of the earth, this pathless wilderness of Scythia, at last we are come. O Hephaestus, thine is the charge, on thee are laid the Father's commands in never-yielding fetters linked of adamant to bind this miscreant to the high-ridged rocks. For this is he who stole the flame of all-working fire, thy own bright flower, and gave to mortal men. Now for the evil done he pays this forfeit to the gods; so haply he shall learn some patience with the reign of Zeus and put away his love for human kind.

HEPHAESTUS:

O Power and Force, your share in the command of Zeus is done, and for you nothing remains; but I— some part of courage still is wanting to bind with force a kindred god to this winter-bitten gorge. Yet must I summon daring to my heart, such dread dwells in the Father's word.—(to Prometheus) O high magnanimous son of prudent Themis, against thy will and mine with brazen bonds no hand can loose I bind thee to this unvisited lonely rock. No human voice will reach thee here, nor any form of man be seen. Parched by the blazing fires of the sun thy skin shall change its pleasant hue; grateful to thee the starry-kirtled night shall come veiling the day, and grateful again the sun dispelling the morn's white frost. Forever the weariness of unremitting pain shall waste thy strength, for he is not born who can deliver thee. See now the profit of thy human charity: thou, a god not fearing the wrath of the gods, hast given to mortal men honors beyond their due; and therefore on this joyless rock thou must keep vigil, sleepless and weary-clinging, with unbended knees, pouring out thy ceaseless lamentations and unheeded cries; for the mind of Zeus knows no turning, and ever harsh the hand that newly grasps the sway.

POWER:

It may be so, yet why seek delay in vainly spent pity? Feel you no hatred for this enemy of the gods, who hath betrayed to mortals your own chief honor?

HEPHAESTUS:

Kinship and old fellowship will have their due.

POWER:

'Tis true, but where is strength to disobey the Father's words? Fearest thou not rather this?

HEPHAESTUS:

Ever merciless thou art, and steeped in cruelty.

POWER:

It healeth nothing to weep for him. Take not up an idle burden wherein there is no profit.

HEPHAESTUS:

Alas, my cherished craft, thrice hateful now!

POWER:

Why hateful? In simple sooth thy art hath no blame for these present ills.

HEPHAESTUS:

Yet would it were another's, not mine!

POWER:

All toil alike in sorrow, unless one were lord of heaven; none is truly free, save only Zeus.

HEPHAESTUS:

This task confirms it; I can nothing deny.

POWER:

Make haste then to bind him in fetters, lest the Father detect thee loitering.

HEPHAESTUS:

Behold the chain; it is ready to hand.

POWER:

Strongly with thy hammer, strongly weld it about his hands; make him fast to the rock.

HEPHAESTUS:

The work goes on, it is well done.

POWER:

Harder strike them, tighter draw the links, leave nothing loose; strange skill he hath to find a way where none appeared.

HEPHAESTUS:

One arm is fastened, and none may loose it.

POWER:

Fetter the other, make it sure; he shall learn how all his cunning is folly before Zeus.

HEPHAESTUS:

Save now my art hath never wrought harm to any.

POWER:

Now strongly drive the biting tooth of the diamond-hard wedge straight through his breast.

HEPHAESTUS:
Alas, Prometheus! I groan for thy pangs.

POWER:
Dost thou shrink? Wilt thou groan for the foes of Zeus? Take heed, lest thou groan for thyself.

HEPHAESTUS:
Thou lookest upon a spectacle grievous to the eye.

POWER:
I look upon one suffering as he deserves.—Now about his sides strain tight the girth.

HEPHAESTUS:
It must needs be done; yet urge me not overmuch.

POWER:
Yet will I urge and harry thee on.—Now lower; with force constrain his legs.

HEPHAESTUS:
'Tis even done; nor was the labor long.

POWER:
Weld fast the galling fetters; remember that he who appraises is strict to exact.

HEPHAESTUS:
Cruel thy tongue, and like thy cruel face.

POWER:
Be thine the tender heart! Rebuke not my bolder mood, nor chide my austerity.

HEPHAESTUS:
Let us go; now the clinging web binds all his limbs.

(*Hephaestus departs.*)

POWER:
There, wanton, in thy insolence! Now for thy creatures of a day filch divine honors. Tell me, will mortal men drain for thee these tortures? Falsely the gods call thee Prometheus, the Contriver, for no cunning contrivance shall help thee to slip from this bondage.

(*Power and Force depart.*)

PROMETHEUS: (*alone, chanting*)
O air divine, and O swift-winged winds!
Ye river fountains, and thou myriad-twinkling
Laughter of ocean waves! O mother earth!
And thou, O all-discerning orb o' the sun!—
To you, I cry to you; behold what I,
A god, endure of evil from the gods.

Behold, with what dread torments
I through the slow-revolving
Ages of time must wrestle;
Such hideous bonds the new lord
Of heaven hath found for my torture.
Woe! woe! for the present disasters
I groan, and for those that shall come;
Nor know I in what far sky
The dawn of deliverance shall rise.

Yet what is this I say? All future things
I see unerring, nor shall any chance
Of evil overtake me unaware.
The will of Destiny we should endure
Lightly as may be, knowing still how vain
To take up arms against Necessity.
Silent I cannot keep, I cannot tongue
These strange calamities. Lo, I am he
Who, darkly hiding in a fennel reed
Fountains of fire, so secretly purloined
And gave to be the teacher of all arts
And giver of all good to mortal men.
And now this forfeit for my sin I pay,
Thus lodged in fetters under the bare sky.
(*The Chorus of the Daughters of Oceanus enter, drawn in a winged car.*)

PROMETHEUS:
Ah me! ah me!
O all ye children of Tethys,
Daughters of father Oceanus
Who ever with tide unwearied
Revolveth the whole world round,—
Behold now prisoned in chains
On the dizzy verge of this gorge
Forever I keep sad watch.

CHORUS:
I see, O Prometheus, thy body
In the toils and torture of bondage
Withering here on this rock;
And a mist as of terror, a cloud
Of tears o'erveils my eyes:
New helmsmen guide in the heavens,
And Zeus unlawfully rules
With new laws, and the might of old
He hath banished to uttermost darkness.

PROMETHEUS:
Would that me too he had hurled,
Bound in these cruel, unyielding
Bonds, down, down under earth,

Beneath wide Hades, where go
The tribe of innumerable dead,
Down to the infinite depths
Of Tartarus! There no god,
No mortal would gloat o'er my ruin.
Now like a toy of the winds
I hang, my anguish a joy
To my foes.

CHORUS:

Who of the gods is so hardened
To whom is thy sorrow a joy?
Who save only Zeus
But feels the pang of thy torments?
But he, ever savage of soul
Swayeth the children of heaven;
Nor ever will cease till his heart
Is satiate grown, or another
Snatches the empire by guile.

PROMETHEUS:

Ay, and this Lord of the blessed
Shall call in the fulness of time
Upon me whom he tortures in bondage,
Shall implore me to utter the plot
That will rob him of honour and throne.
No sweet-lipped charm of persuasion
Then shall allure me, and never
In cringing fear of his threats
The knowledge will I impart,
Till first he has loosened these bonds,
And for all my anguish he too
Hath humbled his neck unto judgment.

CHORUS:

Bold art thou, and calamity
Softens thee not, but ever
Thy thought is quick on thy tongue.
Terror pierceth my heart,
And fearing I ask what shore,
O wanderer tempest-tost,
Far-off of peace shall receive thee!
Stern is the son of Kronos,
And deaf his heart to beseeching.

PROMETHEUS:

I know of his hardness, I know
That justice he holds in his palm;
Yet his pride shall be humbled, I think;
His hardness made soft, and his wrath
Shall bow to the blows of adversity;

He, too, in milder mood
Shall come, imploring of me
The friendship I willingly grant.

LEADER OF THE CHORUS:

Unfold to us the whole story. For what crime does Zeus so shamefully and bitterly torture you? Tell us, if there is no harm in telling.

PROMETHEUS:

Painful are these things to relate, painful is silence, and all is wretchedness. When first the gods knew wrath, and faction raised its head amongst them, and some would tear old Kronos from his throne that Zeus might take his place, and others were determined that Zeus should never reign over the gods, then I with wise counsel sought to guide the Titans, children of Earth and Sky,—but all in vain. My crafty schemes they disdained, and in their pride of strength thought it were easy to make themselves lords by force. Often to me my mother Themis (or call her Earth, for many names she hath, that being one) had foretold in oracles what was to be, with warning that not by might or brutal force should victory come, but by guile alone. So I counselled them, but they turned their eyes from me in impatience. Of the courses which then lay open, far the best, it seemed, was to take my mother as my helper and to join my will with the will of Zeus. By my advice the cavernous gloom of Tartarus now hides in night old Kronos and his peers. Thus the new tyrant of heaven took profit of me, and thus rewards me with these torments. 'Tis the disease of tyranny, no more, to take no heed of friendship. You ask why he tortures me; hear now the reason. No sooner was he established on his father's throne than he began to award various offices to the different gods, ordering his government throughout. Yet no care was in his heart for miserable men, and he was fain to blot out the whole race and in their stead create another. None save me opposed his purpose; I only dared; I rescued mankind from the heavy blow that was to cast them in Hades. Therefore I am bowed down by this anguish, painful to endure, pitiable to behold. Mercy I had for mortals, but found no mercy for myself: So piteously I am disciplined, an ignoble spectacle for Zeus.

LEADER:

Fashioned of rock is he, and iron is his heart, O Prometheus, who feels not indignation at thy disasters. Rather would I not have seen them at all, and seeing them I am sore of heart.

PROMETHEUS:
To my very friends I am a spectacle of pity.

LEADER:
Yet it may be—did thy transgressions end there?

PROMETHEUS:
Through me mankind ceased to foresee death.

LEADER:
What remedy could heal that sad disease?

PROMETHEUS:
Blind hopes I made to dwell in them.

LEADER:
O merciful boon for mortals.

PROMETHEUS:
And more than all I gave them fire.

LEADER:
And so in their brief life they are lords of flaming fire?

PROMETHEUS:
Through it they will learn many arts.

LEADER:
And was it for crimes like this Zeus—

PROMETHEUS:
Tortures me, and ceases not nor relents.

LEADER:
And is there no goal to the struggle before thee?

PROMETHEUS:
There is none, save when it seems to him good.

LEADER:
When shall it so seem? What hope? Seest thou not thy error? That thou hast erred, I say in sorrow and with sorrow to thee. But enough of that; seek thou some release from the conflict.

PROMETHEUS:
How easy for one who fares in pleasant ways to admonish those in adversity. But all this I knew; with open eyes, with willing mind, I erred; I do not deny it. Mankind I helped, but could not help myself. Yet I dreamed not that here in this savage solitary gorge, on this high rock, I should waste away beneath such torments. Yet care not to bewail these present disasters; but descend to the earth, and hear of the woes to come and all that is to be. I pray you heed my word; have compassion on one who is now caught in the toils; for sorrow flitteth now to one and now to another, and visiteth each in his turn.

CHORUS: (singing)
We list to your words, O Prometheus.—
Lo, with light foot I step
From the swift-rushing car; the pure air,
The highway I leave of the birds;
And now to the rugged earth
I descend. I listen, I wait
For thy story of pain and disaster.
        (Oceanus enters, borne on a winged horse.)

OCEANUS:
To thee I come, O Prometheus;
Borne on this swift-winged bird
That knoweth the will of his rider
And needeth no curb, from afar
I have flown a wearisome way,
Weary but ended at last.
I am grieved with thy grief; I am drawn
By our kinship, and even without it
Thee more than all others I honor.
I speak simple truth, and my tongue
Knows not to flatter in idleness.
Nay, tell me what aid I may render;
For never thy lips shall avow
Oceanus failed thee in friendship.

PROMETHEUS:
Ho! What is this I look upon? What then, art thou too come to stare upon my ruin? What new daring has brought thee from thy ocean stream and thy rock-roofed unbuilded caverns hither to our earth, the mother of iron? Art thou come to view my fate with indignation for my calamities? Behold the spectacle! Behold me, the friend of Zeus, who helped him to a throne, now bowed down by his torments.

OCEANUS:
I see, Prometheus; and, though thou art thyself cunning in device, I would admonish thee to prudence. Learn to know thyself, put on the habit of new ways, for there is a new tyrant among the gods. If still thou hurlest forth these harsh and biting words, perchance from afar off, Zeus, sitting above, may hear thee, and thy present burden of sorrows will seem as the sport of children. But, O wretched sufferer, put away thy moody wrath, and seek some respite from thy ills. My advice may sound as the trite sayings of old, yet thou thyself canst see what are the wages of too bold a tongue. Thou hast not

learned humility, nor to yield to evils, but rather wouldst add others new to thy present store. Take me for thy teacher and kick not against the pricks, for there rules in heaven an austere monarch who is responsible to none. Now I will go and make trial to win thy release from this grievous state. Do thou keep thy peace, and restrain thy blustering speech. Or knowest thou not in thy wisdom what penalties overtake an idle tongue?

PROMETHEUS:

I give you joy that, having shared and dared with me, you have still kept yourself free of blame. I bid you trouble not your peace; his will is immutable and you cannot persuade him. Even beware, lest by your going you bring sorrow upon yourself.

OCEANUS:

It is clear your words dismiss me home.

PROMETHEUS:

Your tears for me might win hatred for yourself.

OCEANUS:

His hatred you mean, who newly wears the sovereignty?

PROMETHEUS:

Ay, his; beware that you vex not his heart.

OCEANUS:

Your calamity, Prometheus, is my teacher.

PROMETHEUS:

Be gone, take yourself off, keep your present mind.

OCEANUS:

I am gone even with your urgent words. See, the winged beast flutters the broad path of the air; gladly would he bend the weary knee in his stall at home.

(*Oceanus departs as the Chorus begins its song.*)

CHORUS:

I mourn, O Prometheus, for thee,
I wail for thy hapless fate;
And tears in a melting flood
Flow down from the fount of my eyes,
Drenching my cheeks. O insolent
Laws, O sceptre of Zeus,
How over the gods of old
Ye wield despotic might!

Lo, all the land groans aloud;
And the people that dwell in the West

Lament for thy time-honored reign
And the sway of thy kindred, Prometheus.

PROMETHEUS:

Think not I am silent through pride or insolence; dumb rage gnaws at my very heart for this outrage upon me. Yet who but I established these new gods in their honours? But I speak not of this, for already you are aware of the truth. Rather listen to the sad story of mankind, who like children lived until I gave them understanding and a portion of reason; yet not in disparagement of men I speak, but meaning to set forth the greatness of my charity. For seeing they saw not, and hearing they understood not, but like as shapes in a dream they wrought all the days of their life in confusion. No houses of brick raised in the warmth of the sun they had, nor fabrics of wood, but like the little ants they dwelt underground in the sunless depth of caverns. No certain sign of approaching winter they knew, no harbinger of flowering spring or fruitful summer; ever they labored at random, till I taught them to discern the seasons by the rising and the obscure setting of the stars. Numbers I invented for them, the chiefest of all discoveries; I taught them the grouping of letters, to be a memorial and record of the past, the mistress of the arts and mother of the Muses. I first brought under the yoke beasts of burden, who by draft and carrying relieved men of their hardest labors; I yoked the proud horse to the chariot, teaching him obedience to the reins, to be the adornment of wealth and luxury. I too contrived for sailors seafaring vessels with their flaxen wings. Alas for me! such inventions I devised for mankind, but for myself I have no cunning to escape disaster.

LEADER OF THE CHORUS:

Sorrow and humiliation are your portion: you have failed in understanding and gone astray; and like a poor physician falling into sickness you despond and know not the remedies for your own disease.

PROMETHEUS:

Hear but the rest, and you will wonder more at my inventions and many arts. If sickness visited them, they had no healing drug, no salve or soothing potion, but wasted away for want of remedies, and this was my greatest boon; for I revealed to them the mingling of bland medicaments for the banishing of all diseases. And the secret treasures of the earth, all benefits to men, copper, iron, silver, gold,—who but I could boast their discovery? No one, I ween, unless in idle vaunting. Nay, hear the whole matter in a word,—all human arts are from Prometheus.

LEADER:
Care not for mortals overmuch, whilst you neglect your own profit. Indeed, I am of good hope that yet some day, freed from bondage, you shall equal the might of Zeus.

PROMETHEUS:
Not yet hath all-ordaining Destiny decreed my release; but after many years, broken by a world of disaster and woe, I shall be delivered. The craft of the forger is weaker far than Necessity.

LEADER:
Who then holds the helm of Necessity?

PROMETHEUS:
The Fates triform and the unforgetting Furies.

LEADER:
And Zeus, is he less in power than these?

PROMETHEUS:
He may not avoid what is destined.

LEADER:
What is destined for Zeus but endless rule?

PROMETHEUS:
Ask not, neither set thy heart on knowing.

LEADER:
Some solemn secret thou wouldst clothe in mystery.

PROMETHEUS:
Speak no more of it; the time is not yet to divulge it, and the secret must still be deeply shrouded. Harbouring this I shall one day escape from this outrage and ignominy of bondage.

At this point, a long episode (here omitted) introduces Io, another victim of divine wrath. Beloved of Zeus, hated consequently by Hera, transformed into a heifer and tormented by a gadfly, she is being driven out of Europe and into Asia, crossing at the Bosphorus ("cow-crossing"). The point of the episode is twofold; it increases sympathy for Prometheus by showing the injustice of the gods to a fellow-sufferer, and it provides Prometheus a chance to foretell that from Io's progeny, after a dozen generations, his eventual deliverer will come.

PROMETHEUS:
Yet shall Zeus himself, the stubborn of soul, be humbled, for the union he purposes in his heart

shall hurl him to outer darkness from his throne of supremacy. Then at last the curse of his father Kronos shall be fulfilled to the uttermost, the curse that he swore when thrown from his ancient seat. All this I know and how the curse shall work, and I only of the gods may point out a refuge from these disasters. Therefore let him sit boldly now, trusting in his thunders that reverberate through the sky, and wielding fiery darts in his hands; they shall avail him naught nor save him from falling in ruin unendurable. A mighty wrestler he is preparing against himself, an irresistible champion, who shall search out a fire more terrible than his lightning and a roaring noise to drown his thunder, and who shall break in pieces that sea-scourge and shaker of the earth, the trident-spear of Poseidon. And Zeus, broken on this rock, shall learn how far apart it is to rule and be a slave.

LEADER OF THE CHORUS:
Thy bodings against Zeus are but thy own desire.

PROMETHEUS:
I speak what is to be, and that is my desire.

LEADER:
Must we look for one to reign above Zeus?

PROMETHEUS:
Troubles more grievous to bear shall bow his neck.

LEADER:
Thou tremblest not to utter such words?

PROMETHEUS:
Why should I tremble whose fate is not to die?

LEADER:
Yet he might still harder torments inflict.

PROMETHEUS:
So let him! I am prepared for all.

LEADER:
Yet the wise bow down to Nemesis.

PROMETHEUS:
So worship, flatter, adore the ruler of the day; but I have no thought in my heart for Zeus. Let him act, let him reign his little while as he will; for he shall not long rule over the gods.—(*Hermes enters.*) But I see here the lackey of Zeus, the servant of the new tyrant. No doubt he has come with tidings of some new device.

HERMES:

Thee, the wise, the bitter beyond bitterness, the thief of fire, who hast revolted against the gods and betrayed their honours to thy creatures of a day,—to thee I speak. The Father bids thee declare the chance of wedlock thou vauntest, that shall bereave him of his sceptre; and this thou art to state clearly and not involve thy speech in riddles. Put me not, O Prometheus, to double my journey; thou seest that Zeus is not appeased by dubious words.

PROMETHEUS:

Haughty thy speech and swollen with pride, as becomes a servant of the gods. Ye are but young in tyranny, and think to inhabit a citadel unassaulted of grief; yet have I not seen two tyrants fall therefrom? And third I shall behold this present lord cast down in utter ruin. Do I seem to cower and quail before these new gods? Hardly, I think; there is no fear in me. But do you trudge back the road you came; for all your pains of asking are in vain.

HERMES:

Yet forget not such insolence has brought you to this pass of evil.

PROMETHEUS:

Be assured I would not barter my hard lot for your menial service.

HERMES:

It is better no doubt to serve this rock than to be the trusted herald of Zeus.

PROMETHEUS:

I but answered insult with insult.

HERMES:

You seem to glory in your present state.

PROMETHEUS:

What, I? So might I see my enemies glory,—and you among them!

HERMES:

You blame me too for your calamities?

PROMETHEUS:

In simple sooth I count all the gods my foes, who requited my benefits with injuries.

HERMES:

Your madness I see is a deep-rooted disease.

PROMETHEUS:

If hatred of foes is madness, I am mad.

HERMES:

Who could endure you in prosperity!

PROMETHEUS:

Alas, prosperity!

HERMES:

Zeus has not learned that cry, alas.

PROMETHEUS:

Time growing ever older, teaches all things.

HERMES:

It has not taught you wisdom yet.

PROMETHEUS:

Else I should hardly talk with you, a slave.

HERMES:

It seems you will not answer the Father's demands.

PROMETHEUS:

My debt of gratitude I fain would pay.

HERMES:

You have reviled and scorned me as a child.

PROMETHEUS: (*in supreme anger*)

And are you not simpler than a child if you hope to learn aught from me? There is no torment or contrivance in the power of Zeus to wring this utterance from me, except these bonds are loosened. Therefore let him hurl upon me the red lightning, let him confound the reeling world with tempest of white-feathered snow and subterranean thunders; none of these things shall extort from me the knowledge that may ward off his overthrow.

HERMES:

Consider if you shall profit by this.

PROMETHEUS:

I have considered long since and formed my plan.

HERMES:

Yet subdue thyself in time, rash fool, to regard thy present ills in wisdom.

PROMETHEUS:

You vex me to no purpose, as one might waste his words on a wave of the sea. Dream not that ever in fear of Zeus's will I shall grow woman-hearted, and raise my supine hands in supplication to my hated foe for deliverance from these bonds;—it is not in my nature.

HERMES:

Though I speak much, my words will all be wasted; my appeals have no power to soften and appease your heart, but champing the bit like a new-yoked colt you are restive and struggle against the reins. There is no strength of wisdom in your savage mood, for mere self-will in a foolish man avails nothing. And consider, if thou disregard my words, what a tempest of evils, wave on wave inevitable, shall break upon thee; for first the Father will smite this rugged cliff with rending of thunder and hurtling fires, and in its harsh and rock-ribbed embrace enfold thy hidden body. Then after a weary age of years once more thou shalt come forth to the light; and the winged hound of Zeus, the ravening eagle, with savage greed shall tear the mighty ruin of thy limbs, feasting all day an uninvited guest, and glutting his maw on thy black-gnawed liver. Neither look for any respite from this agony, unless some god shall appear as a voluntary successor to thy toils, and of his own free will goeth down to sunless Hades and the dark depths of Tartarus. Therefore take heed; for my words are not vain boasting, but all too truly spoken. The lips of Zeus know not to utter falsehood, but all that he saith he will accomplish. Do thou consider and reflect, and regard not vaunting pride as better than wise counsel.

LEADER:

To us Hermes seems to utter words not untimely; for he admonishes you to abandon vaunting pride and seek for wise counsel. Obey him; it is shameful for a wise man to go astray.

PROMETHEUS: (chanting)

All this ere he uttered his message
I knew; yet feel no dishonor
In suffering wrong from a foe.
Ay, let the lightning be launched
With curled and forked flame
On my head; let the air confounded
Shudder with thunderous peals
And convulsion of raging winds;
Let tempests beat on the earth
Till her rooted foundations tremble;
The boisterous surge of the sea
Leap up to mingle its crest
With the stars eclipsed in their orbs;
Let the whirling blasts of Necessity
Seize on my body and hurl it

Down to the darkness of Tartarus,—
Yet all he shall not destroy me!

HERMES:

I hear the delirious cries
Of a mind unhinged; his prayer
Is frenzy, and all that he doth.—
But ye who condole with his anguish,
Be quick, I implore, and depart,
Ere the deafening roar of the thunder
Daze and bewilder your senses.

CHORUS:

Waste not thy breath in vain warnings,
Nor utter a word unendurable;
For who art thou in the pathway
Of evil and falsehood to guide me?
Better I deem it to suffer
Whate'er he endures; for traitors
My soul abhorreth, their shame
I spew from my heart as a pest.

HERMES:

Yet remember my counsel in season,
And blame not your fortune when caught
In the snare of Disaster, nor cry
Unto Zeus that he throws you unwarned
Into sorrow. Yourselves take the blame;
Foretaught and with eyes unveiled
You walk to be snared in the vast
And implicate net of Disaster.

(*Hermes goes out. A storm bursts, with thunder and lightning. The rocks are sundered; Prometheus slowly sinks from sight, while the Chorus scatters to right and left.*)

PROMETHEUS:

Lo, in grim earnest the world
Is shaken, the roar of thunders
Reverberates, gleams the red lightning,
And whirlwinds lick up the dust.
All the blasts of the winds leap out
And meet in tumultuous conflict,
Confounding the sea and the heavens.
'Tis Zeus who driveth his furies
To smite me with terror and madness.
O mother Earth all-honored,
O Air revolving thy light
A common boon unto all,
Behold what wrongs I endure.

EXERCISES

1. In the early part of the play, Power says, "None is truly free, save only Zeus." Look through the rest of the play to find out how exact this statement is. Is Zeus himself completely free?

2. Study the speeches about Man and blind hopes rather carefully. In his "Essay on Man," Alexander Pope wrote:

Hope humbly then; with trembling pinions soar;
Wait the great teacher Death, and God adore.
What future bliss he gives not thee to know.
But gives that hope to be thy blessing now.
Hope springs eternal in the human breast;
Man never is, but always to be, blest.

In what ways are Pope's ideas on hope and death similar to those of Aeschylus? In what ways dissimilar?

In the introduction to *The Condition of Man,* Lewis Mumford writes of man as building his civilizations as a child builds sand-castles on the beach. The civilizations are always destroyed with the rising of the tide, but Man continues to build each day anew. Man, says Mumford, is the only one of the animals who consciously can impose work on himself.

Does this statement of Mumford's have any relation to Aeschylus' statement about Death and blind hopes? What, exactly?

So now can you explain why this gift of blind hope (why *blind,* by the way?) is important to mankind?

3. Notice the pattern of Prometheus's gifts. We might arrange them in this way: Blind hopes, a portion of reason (why only a portion?), language, numbers, fire, etc. If so, and remembering that according to the legend, fire was the only gift that Prometheus gave to man, what seems to be the idea that Aeschylus had about man's development? Why, for example, didn't he give them Cadillacs, yachts, and garbage disposals?

In the same preface referred to above, Mumford makes the point that man creates things, which may or may not be of too great importance, but that in making things, man himself grows. Does this idea have anything to do with this series of Promethean gifts?

4. Having considered all of these factors, you might speculate on the solution which Aeschylus may have worked out for his problem in the third play. For example, what are the limits of the power of Zeus, of Prometheus, of Man? What ideas of the philosophers did Aeschylus have to work with? In developing some sort of a solution, you need not be afraid of altering the status of the gods. See, for example, what Aeschylus did to the Furies in *Eumenides.*

AGAMEMNON

Aeschylus

This is the first of a series of three plays by Aeschylus, called the *Oresteia*. Exactly as Aeschylus explored the question of the relation of men to God and the universe in *Prometheus Bound,* he investigates in these plays the question of man's relation to other men. He is asking the question, "What is justice?" In the first of the plays he presents the old idea of justice and men's freedom of choice as it probably existed in the period of chaos. In the second of the plays (omitted here) he carries the question further. In the last of the series he presents a new idea of justice and explains the meaning of it to his Athenian audience as they approached the period of balance in their epoch. To understand this series of plays, one needs to know a little about the history of the dynasty of kings who ruled in the land of Argos. Since Atreus was one of the early kings in this dynasty, the family line is called the House of Atreus.

Atreus, ruler of the kingdom of Argos, quarreled with his brother Thyestes, and banished him. Later, Thyestes sought reconciliation. Atreus pretended forgiveness and invited his brother to a feast. Secretly, however, he killed the two elder sons of Thyestes, and served them as roast meats to their father, who unwittingly ate the flesh. When he discovered the treachery of Atreus, however, he again departed from Argos with his remaining son, Egistheus, leaving behind him an abiding curse on all the house of Atreus.

The sons of Atreus, Agamemnon and Menelaus, married the sisters, Clytemnestra and Helen, daughters of the King of Lacedemon. Helen left her husband, fleeing to Troy with Paris, and Agamemnon rallied all the forces of Greece to help his brother win her back. The fleet could not leave from Aulis because of adverse winds; the seer, Calchas, interpreted omens to mean that the winds would change when Agamemnon sacrificed his daughter, Iphigenia. That sacrifice was made.

While the war was in progress and Agamemnon fighting before Troy, Egistheus returned to Argos and became Clytemnestra's lover. He roused discontent among the people and became powerful.

These plays, then, develop a new idea of justice and freedom in the period in which Aeschylus lived. The first one presents the old ideas which made the tragedy of Agamemnon possible. Watch for those ideas.

The Greeks had arranged a series of beacons stretching from Troy to the Grecian mainland to be kindled as a token of victory over Troy. It is with their imminent flaming that the play opens.

Characters   *Watchman*

Chorus of Old Men

Clytemnestra

Herald

Agamemnon

Cassandra

Aegisthus

Captain of the Guard

The scene is the entrance to the palace of the Atreidae.
Before the doors stand shrines of the gods.
[*A* WATCHMAN *is posted on the roof.*]

Watchman

I've prayed God to release me from sentry duty
All through this long year's vigil, like a dog
Couched on the roof of Atreus, where I study
Night after night the pageantry of this vast
Concourse of stars, and moving among them like
Noblemen the constellations that bring
Summer and winter as they rise and fall.
And I am still watching for the beacon signal
All set to flash over the sea the radiant
News of the fall of Troy. So confident
Is a woman's spirit, whose purpose is a man's.
Every night, as I turn in to my stony bed,
Quilted with dew, not visited by dreams,
Not mine—no sleep, fear stands at my pillow
Keeping tired eyes from closing once too often;
And whenever I start to sing or hum a tune,
Mixing from music an antidote to sleep,
It always turns to mourning for the royal house,
Which is not in such good shape as it used to be
But now at last may the good news in a flash
Scatter the darkness and deliver us! [*The beacon flashes.*]
O light of joy, whose gleam turns night to day,
O radiant signal for innumerable
Dances of victory! Ho there! I call the queen,
Agamemnon's wife, to raise with all the women
Alleluias of thanksgiving through the palace
Saluting the good news, if it is true
That Troy has fallen, as this blaze portends:
Yes, and I'll dance an overture myself.
My master's dice have fallen out well, and I
Shall score three sixes for this nightwatching. [*A pause.*]
Well, come what will, may it soon be mine to grasp
In this right hand my master's, home again!
      [*Another pause.*]
The rest is secret. A heavy ox has trodden
Across my tongue. These walls would have tales to tell
If they had mouths. I speak only to those
Who are in the know, to others—I know nothing.
[*The* WATCHMAN *goes into the palace. Women's cries are*
heard. Enter CHORUS OF OLD MEN.]

Chorus

It is ten years since those armed prosecutors of Justice,
Menelaus and Agamemnon, twin-sceptred in God-given

sovranty, embarked in the thousand ships crying war,
like eagles with long wings beating the air over a robbed
mountain nest, wheeling and screaming for their lost
children. Yet above them some god, maybe Apollo or
Zeus, overhears the sky-dweller's cry and sends after the
robber a Fury. [CLYTEMNESTRA *comes out of the palace*
and unseen by the elders places offerings before the
shrines.] Just so the two kings were sent by the greater
king, Zeus, for the sake of a promiscuous woman to fight
Paris, Greek and Trojan locked fast together in the dusty
betrothals of battle. And however it stands with them
now, the end is unalterable; no flesh, no wine can appease God's fixed indignation.

As for us, with all the able-bodied men enlisted and
gone, we are left here leaning our strength on a staff;
for, just as in infancy, when the marrow is still unformed,
the War-god is not at his post, so it is in extreme old
age, as the leaves fall fast, we walk on three feet, like
dreams in the daylight. [*They see* CLYTEMNESTRA.]

O Queen, what news? what message sets light to the
altars? All over the town the shrines are ablaze with
unguents drawn from the royal stores and the flames
shoot up into the night sky. Speak, let us hear all that
may be made public, so healing the anxieties that have
gathered thick in our hearts; let the gleam of good news
scatter them! [CLYTEMNESTRA *goes out to tend the other*
altars of the city.]

Strength have I still to recall that sign which greeted
      the two kings
Taking the road, for the prowess of song is not yet spent.
I sing of two kings united in sovranty, leading
Armies to battle, who saw two eagles
Beside the palace
Wheel into sight, one black, and the other was
      white-tailed,
Tearing a hare with her unborn litter.
Ailinon cry, but let good conquer!

Shrewdly the priest took note and compared each
      eagle with each king,
Then spoke out and prefigured the future in
      these words:
"In time the Greek arms shall demolish the fortress
      of Priam;
Only let no jealous God, as they fasten
On Troy the slave's yoke,
Strike them in anger; for Artemis[1] loathes the rapacious
Beagles of Zeus that have slaughtered the frail hare.
Ailinon cry, but let good conquer!
O Goddess, gentle to the tender whelp of fierce lions
As to all young life of the wild,
So now fulfil what is good in the omen and mend
      what is faulty.
And I appeal unto the Lord Apollo,
Let not the north wind hold the fleet storm-bound,
Driving them on to repay that feast with another,
Inborn builder of strife, feud that fears no man, it
      is still there,

---

[1] Artemis is the goddess of the hunt and all wild things.
In this context, the hare is the city of Troy.

Treachery keeping the house, it remembers, revenges,
   a child's death!"
Such, as the kings left home, was the seer's revelation.
Ailinon cry, but let good conquer!

Zeus, whoe'er he be, if so it best
Please his ear to be addressed,
So shall he be named by me.
All things have I measured, yet
None have found save him alone,
Zeus, if a man from a heart heavy-laden
Seek to cast his cares aside.

Long since lived a ruler of the world,[2]
Puffed with martial pride, of whom
None shall tell, his day is done;
Also, he who followed him
Met his master and is gone.
Zeus the victorious, gladly acclaim him;
Perfect wisdom shall be yours;

Zeus, who laid it down that man
Must in sorrow learn and through
Pain to wisdom find his way.
When deep slumber falls, remembered wrongs
Chafe the bruised heart with fresh pangs, and no
Welcome wisdom meets within.
Harsh the grace dispensed by powers immortal,
Pilots of the human soul.

Even so the elder prince,[3]
Marshal of the thousand ships,
Rather than distrust a priest,
Torn with doubt to see his men
Harbor-locked, hunger-pinched, hard-oppressed,
Strained beyond endurance, still
Watching, waiting, where the never-tiring
Tides of Aulis ebb and flow:

And still the storm blew from mountains far north,
With moorings windswept and hungry crews pent
In rotting hulks,
With tackling all torn and seeping timbers,
Till Time's slow-paced, enforced inaction
Had all but stripped bare the bloom of Greek manhood.
And then was found but one
Cure to allay the tempest—never a blast so bitter—
Shrieked in a loud voice by the priest, "Artemis!"
   striking the Atreidae with dismay, each with
   his staff smiting the ground and weeping.

And then the king spoke, the elder, saying:
"The choice is hard—hard to disobey him,
And harder still
To kill my own child, my palace jewel,
With unclean hands before the altar
Myself, her own father, spill a maid's pure blood.
I have no cnoice but wrong.
How shall I fail my thousand ships and betray
   my comrades?
So shall the storm cease, and the men eager for war
   clamor for that virginal blood righteously! So
   pray for a happy outcome!"

And when he bowed down beneath the harness
Of cruel coercion, his spirit veering
With sudden sacrilegious change,
He gave his whole mind to evil counsel.
For man is made bold with base-contriving
Impetuous madness, first cause of much grief.
And so then he slew his own child
For a war to win a woman
And to speed the storm-bound fleet from the
   shore to battle.

She cried aloud "Father!", yet they heard not;
A girl in first flower, yet they cared not,
The lords who gave the word for war.
Her father prayed, then he bade his vassals
To seize her where swathed in folds of saffron
She lay, and lift her up like a yearling
With bold heart above the altar,
And her lovely lips to bridle
That they might not cry out, cursing the House
   of Atreus,

With gags, her voice sealed with brute force
   and crushed.
And then she let fall her cloak
And cast at each face a glance that dumbly craved
   compassion;
And like a picture she would but could not greet
Her father's guests, who at home
Had often sat when the meal was over,
The cups replenished, with all hearts enraptured
To hear her sing grace with clear unsullied voice for
   her loving father.

The end was unseen and unspeakable.
The task of priestcraft was done.
For Justice first chastens, then she presses home
   her lesson.
The morrow must come, its grief will soon be here,
So let us not weep today.
It shall be made known as clear as daybreak.
And so may all this at last end in good news,
For which the queen prays, the next of kin and stay
   of the land of Argos. [CLYTEMNESTRA appears
   at the door of the palace.]
Our humble salutations to the queen!
Hers is our homage, while our master's throne
Stands empty. We are still longing to hear
The meaning of your sacrifice. Is it good news?

Clytemnestra
Good news! With good news may the morning rise
Out of the night—good news beyond all hope!
My news is this: The Greeks have taken Troy.

---

[2]The reference here is to Uranus and Kronos, both kings of the gods. Zeus led a successful revolt against Kronos so that Zeus could become king.

[3]This refers to the beginning of the Trojan War when the Greek fleet was delayed in the harbor of Aulis. In order to appease Artemis and secure favorable winds, Agamemnon, "the elder prince," followed the prophecy of the seer, Calchas, and sacrificed his daughter, Iphigenia.

Chorus
What? No, it cannot be true! I cannot grasp it.

Clytemnestra
The Greeks hold Troy—is not that plain enough?

Chorus
Joy steals upon me and fills my eyes with tears.

Clytemnestra
Indeed, your looks betray your loyalty.

Chorus
What is the proof? Have you any evidence?

Clytemnestra
Of course I have, or else the Gods have cheated me.

Chorus
You have given ear to some beguiling dream.

Clytemnestra
I would not come screaming fancies out of my sleep.

Chorus
Rumors have wings—on these your heart has fed.

Clytemnestra
You mock my intelligence as though I were a girl.

Chorus
When was it? How long is it since the city fell?

Clytemnestra
In the night that gave birth to this dawning day.

Chorus
What messenger could bring the news so fast?

Clytemnestra
The God of Fire, who from Ida sent forth light
And beacon by beacon passed the flame to me.
From the peak of Ida first to the cliff of Hermes
On Lemnos, and from there a third great lamp
Was flashed to Athos, the pinnacle of Zeus;
Up, up it soared, luring the dancing fish
To break surface in rapture at the light;
A golden courier, like the sun, it sped
Post-haste its message to Macistus, thence
Across Euripus, till the flaming sign
Was marked by the watchers on Messapium,
And thence with strength renewed from piles of heath
Like moonrise over the valley of Asopus,
Relayed in glory to Cithaeron's heights,
And still flashed on, not slow the sentinels,
Leaping across the lake from peak to peak,
It passed the word to burn and burn, and flung
A comet to the promontory that stands
Over the Gulf of Saron, there it swooped
Down to the Spider's Crag above the city,
Then found its mark on the roof of this house of Atreus,
That beacon fathered by Ida's far-off fires.
Such were the stages of our torch relay,

And the last to run is the first to reach the goal.
That is my evidence, the testimony which
My lord has signaled to me out of Troy.

Chorus
Lady, there will be time later to thank the Gods.
Now I ask only to listen: speak on and on.

Clytemnestra
Today the Greeks have occupied Troy.
I seem to hear there a very strange street-music.
Pour oil and vinegar into one cup, you will see
They do not make friends. So there two tunes are heard.
Slaves now, the Trojans, brothers and aged fathers,
Prostrate, sing for their dearest the last dirge.
The others, tired out and famished after the
    night's looting,
Grab what meal chance provides, lodgers now
In Trojan houses, sheltered from the night frosts,
From the damp dews delivered, free to sleep
Off guard, off duty, a blissful night's repose.
Therefore, provided that they show due respect
To the altars of the plundered town and are not
Tempted to lay coarse hands on sanctities,
Remembering that the last lap—the voyage home—
Lies still ahead of them, then, if they should return
Guiltless before God, the curses of the bereaved
Might be placated—barring accidents.
That is my announcement—a message from my master.
May all end well, and may I reap the fruit of it!

Chorus
Lady, you have spoken with a wise man's judgment.
Now it is time to address the gods once more
After this happy outcome of our cares.

Thanks be to Zeus and to gracious Night, housekeeper
of heaven's embroidery, who has cast over the towers of
Troy a net so fine as to leave no escape for old or
young, all caught in the snare! All praise to Zeus, who
with a shaft from his outstretched bow has at last
brought down the transgressor!

"By Zeus struck down!" The truth is all clear
With each step plainly marked. He said, Be
It so, and so it was. A man denied once
That heaven pays heed to those who trample
Beneath the feet holy sanctities. He lied wickedly;
For God's wrath soon or late destroys all sinners filled
With pride, puffed up with vain presumption,
And great men's houses stocked with silver
And gold beyond measure. Far best to live
Free of want, without grief, rich in the gift of wisdom.
Glutted with gold, the sinner kicks
Justice out of his sight, yet
She sees him and remembers.

As sweet temptation lures him onwards
With childlike smile into the death-trap,
He cannot help himself. His curse is lit up
Against the darkness, a bright baleful light.
And just as false bronze in battle hammered turns
    black and shows

Its true worth, so the sinner time-tried stands condemned.
His hopes take wing, and still he gives chase, with
  foul crimes branding all his people.
He cries to deaf heaven, none hear his prayers.
Justice drags him down to hell as he calls for succor.
Such was the sinner Paris, who
Rendered thanks to a gracious
Host by stealing a woman.

She left behind her the ports all astir
With throngs of men under arms filing onto shipboard;
She took to Troy in lieu of dowry death.
A light foot passed through the gates and fled,
And then a cry of lamentation rose.
The seers, the king's prophets, muttered darkly:
"Bewail the king's house that now is desolate,
Bewail the bed marked with print of love that fled!"
Behold, in silence, without praise, without reproach,
They sit upon the ground and weep.
Beyond the wave lies their love;
Here a ghost seems to rule the palace!
Shapely the grace of statues,
Yet they can bring no comfort,
Eyeless, lifeless and loveless.

Delusive dream shapes that float through the night
Beguile him, bringing delight sweet but unsubstantial;
For, while the eye beholds the heart's desire,
The arms clasp empty air, and then
The fleeting vision fades and glides away
On silent wing down the paths of slumber.
The royal hearth is chilled with sorrows such as these,
And more; in each house from end to end of Greece
That sent its dearest to wage war in foreign lands
The stout heart is called to steel itself
In mute endurance against
Blows that strike deep into the heart's core:
Those that they sent from home they
Knew, but now they receive back
Only a heap of ashes.

The God of War holds the twin scales of strife,
Heartless gold-changer trafficking in men,
Consigning homeward from Troy a jar of dust
  fire-refined,
Making up the weight with grief,
Shapely vessels laden each
With the ashes of their kin.
They mourn and praise them saying, "He
Was practiced well in sword and spear,
And he, who fell so gallantly—
All to avenge another man's wife":
It is muttered in a whisper
And resentment spreads against each of the
  royal warlords.
They lie sleeping, perpetual
Owners each of a small
Holding far from their homeland.

The sullen rumors that pass mouth to mouth
Bring the same danger as a people's curse,
And brooding hearts wait to hear of what the night
  holds from sight.

Watchful are the Gods of all
Hands with slaughter stained. The black
Furies wait, and when a man
Has grown by luck, not justice, great,
With sudden turn of circumstance
He wastes away to nothing, dragged
Down to be food in hell for demons.
For the heights of fame are perilous.
With a jealous bolt the Lord Zeus in a flash shall
  blast them.
Best to pray for a tranquil
Span of life and to be
Neither victor nor vanquished.

—The news has set the whole town aflame.
Can it be true? Perhaps it is a trick.
—Only a child would let such fiery words
Kindle his hopes, then fade and flicker out.
—It is just like a woman
To accept good news without the evidence.
—An old wives' tale, winged with a woman's wishes,
Spreads like wildfire, then sinks and is forgotten.

We shall soon know what the beacon signifies,
Whether it is true or whether this joyful daybreak
Is only a dream sent to deceive us all.
Here comes a messenger breathless from the shore,
Wearing a garland and covered in a cloud
Of dust, which shows that he has news to tell,
And not in soaring rhetoric of smoke and flame,
But either he brings cause for yet greater joy,
Or else,—no, let us abjure the alternative.
Glad shone the light, as gladly break the day!

[*Enter* HERALD

Herald

O joy! Argos, I greet you, my fatherland!
Joy brings me home after ten years of war.
Many the shattered hopes, but this has held.
Now I can say that when I die my bones
Will lie at rest here in my native soil.
I greet you joyfully, I greet the Sun,
Zeus the All-Highest, and the Pythian King,[4]
Bending no more against us his fatal shafts,
As he did beside Scamander—that was enough,
And now defend us, Savior Apollo; all
The Gods I greet, among them Hermes, too,
Patron of messengers, and the spirits of our dead,
Who sent their sons forth, may they now prepare
A joyful welcome for those whom war has spared.
Joy to the palace and to these images
Whose faces catch the sun, now, as of old,
With radiant smiles greet your sovran lord,
Agamemnon, who brings a lamp to lighten you
And all here present, after having leveled
Troy with the mattock of just-dealing Zeus,
Great son of Atreus, master and monarch, blest
Above all living men. The brigand Paris
Has lost his booty and brought down the house of Priam.

---

[4]Apollo.

Chorus
Joy to you, Herald, welcome home again!

Herald
Let me die, having lived to see this day!

Chorus
Your yearning for your country has worn you out.

Herald
So much that tears spring to the eyes for joy.

Chorus
Well, those you longed for longed equally for you.

Herald
Ah yes, our loved ones longed for our safe return.

Chorus
We have had many anxieties here at home.

Herald
What do you mean? Has there been disaffection?

Chorus
Never mind now. Say nothing and cure all.

Herald
Is it possible there was trouble in our absence?

Chorus
Now, as you said yourself, it would be a joy to die.

Herald
Yes, all has ended well. Our expedition
Has been successfully concluded, even though in part
The issue may be found wanting. Only the Gods
Prosper in everything. If I should tell you all
That we endured on shipboard in the night watches,
Our lodging the bare benches, and even worse
Ashore beneath the walls of Troy, the rains
From heaven and the dews that seeped
Out of the soil into lice-infested blankets;
If I should tell of those winters, when the birds
Dropped dead and Ida heaped on us her snows;
Those summers, when unruffled by wind or wave
The sea slept breathless under the glare of noon—
But why recall that now? It is all past,
Yes, for the dead past never to stir again.
Ah, they are all gone. Why count our losses? Why
Should we vex the living with grievance for the dead?
Goodbye to all that for us who have come back!
Victory has turned the scale, and so before
This rising sun let the good news be proclaimed
And carried all over the world on wings of fame:
"These spoils were brought by the conquerors of Troy
And dedicated to the Gods of Greece."
And praise to our country and to Zeus the giver
And thanks be given. That is all my news.
[CLYTEMNESTRA *appears at the palace door.*

Chorus
Thank God that I have lived to see this day!
This news concerns all, and most of all the queen.

Clytemnestra
I raised my alleluia hours ago,
When the first messenger lit up the night,
And people mocked me saying, "Has a beacon
Persuaded you that the Greeks have captured Troy?
Truly a woman's hopes are lighter than air."
But I still sacrificed, and at a hundred
Shrines throughout the town the women chanted
Their endless alleluias on and on,
Singing to sleep the sacramental flames,
And now what confirmation do I need from you?
I wait to hear all from my lord, for whom
A welcome is long ready. What day is so sweet
In a woman's life as when she opens the door
To her beloved, safe home from war? Go and tell him
That he will find, guarding his property,
A wife as loyal as he left her, one
Who in all these years has kept his treasuries sealed,
Unkind only to enemies, and knows no more
Of other men's company than of tempering steel. [*Exit.*]

Herald
Such a protestation, even though entirely true,
Is it not unseemly on a lady's lips?

Chorus
Such is her message, as you understand,
Full of fine phrases plain to those who know.
But tell us now, what news have you of the king's
Co-regent, Menelaus? Is he too home again?

Herald
Lies cannot last, even though sweet to hear.

Chorus
Can you not make your news both sweet and true?

Herald
He and his ships have vanished. They are missing.

Chorus
What, was it a storm that struck the fleet at sea?

Herald
You have told a long disaster in a word.

Chorus
Has no one news whether he is alive or dead?

Herald
Only the Sun, from whom the whole earth draws life.

Chorus
Tell us about the storm. How did it fall?

Herald
A day of national rejoicing must not be marred
By any jarring tongue. A messenger who comes
With black looks bringing the long prayed-against
Report of total rout, which both afflicts
The state in general and in every household leaves
The inmates prostrate under the scourge of war—
With such a load upon his lips he may fitly
Sing anthems to the Furies down in hell;
But when he greets a prospering people with
News of the war's victorious end—how then

Shall I mix foul with fair and find words to tell you
Of the blow that struck us out of that angry heaven?
    Water and Fire, those age-old enemies,
Made common cause against the homebound fleet.
Darkness had fallen, and a northerly gale
Blew up and in a blinding thunderstorm
Our ships were tossed and buffeted hull against hull
In a wild stampede and herded out of sight;
Then, at daybreak, we saw the Aegean in blossom
With a waving crop of corpses and scattered timbers.
Our ship came through, saved by some spirit, it seems,
Who took the helm and piloted her, until
She slipped under the cliffs into a cove.
There, safe at last, incredulous of our luck,
We brooded all day, stunned by the night's disaster.
And so, if any of the others have survived,
They must be speaking of us as dead and gone.
May all yet end well! Though it is most to be expected
That Menelaus is in some great distress,
Yet, should some shaft of sunlight spy him out
Somewhere among the living, rescued by Zeus,
Lest the whole house should perish, there is hope
That he may yet come home. There you have the truth.

Chorus

Tell us who invented that
Name so deadly accurate?
Was it one who presaging
Things to come divined a word
Deftly tuned to destiny?
Helen—hell indeed she carried
To men, to ships, to a proud city, stealing

From the silk veils of her chamber, sailing seaward
With the Zephyr's breath behind her;
And they set forth in a thousand ships to hunt her
On the path that leaves no imprint,
Bringers of endless bloodshed.

So, as Fate decreed, in Troy,
Turning into keeners kin,
Furies, instruments of God's
Wrath, at last demanded full
Payment for the stolen wife;
And the wedding song that rang out
To greet the bride from beyond the broad Aegean
Was in time turned into howls of imprecation
From the countless women wailing
For the loved ones they had lost in war for her sake,
And they curse the day they gave that
Welcome to war and bloodshed.

An old story is told of an oxherd who reared at his
    hearth a lion-cub, a pet for his children,
Pampered fondly by young and old with dainty
    morsels begged at each meal from his master's table.

But Time showed him up in his true nature after his
    kind—a beast savaging sheep and oxen,
Mad for the taste of blood, and only then they knew
    what they had long nursed was a curse from
    heaven.

And so it seemed then there came to rest in Troy
A sweet-smiling calm, a clear sky, seductive,

A rare pearl set in gold and silver,
Shaft of love from a glancing eye.
She is seen now as an agent
Of death sent from Zeus, a Fury
Demanding a bloody bride-price. [*Enter* CLYTEMNESTRA]

From ancient times people have believed that when
A man's wealth has come to full growth it breeds
And brings forth tares and tears in plenty.
No, I say, it is only wicked deeds
That increase, fruitful in evil.
The house built on justice always
Is blest with a happy offspring.

And yet the pride bred of wealth often burgeons anew
In evil times, a cloud of deep night,
Spectre of ancient crimes that still
Walks within the palace walls,
True to the dam that bore it.

But where is Justice? She lights up the smoke-
    darkened hut.
From mansions built by hands polluted
Turning to greet the pure in heart,
Proof against false praise, she guides
All to its consummation. [*Enter* AGAMEMNON *in a
    chariot followed by another chariot carrying*
    CASSANDRA *and spoils of war.*]

Agamemnon, conqueror, joy to our king! How shall my
greeting neither fall short nor shoot too high? Some men
feign rejoicing or sorrow with hearts untouched; but
those who can read man's nature in the book of the
eyes will not be deceived by dissembled fidelity. I
declare that, when you left these shores ten years ago to
recover with thousands of lives one woman, who eloped
of her own free will, I deemed your judgment misguided;
but now in all sincerity I salute you with joy. Toil happily
ended brings pleasure at last, and in time you shall learn
to distinguish the just from the unjust steward.

Agamemnon

First, it is just that I should pay my respects
To the land of Argos and her presiding Gods,
My partners in this homecoming as also
In the just penalty which I have inflicted on
The city of Troy. When the supreme court of heaven
Adjudicated on our cause, they cast
Their votes unanimously against her, though not
Immediately, and so on the other side
Hope hovered hesitantly before it vanished.
The fires of pillage are still burning there
Like sacrificial offerings. Her ashes
Redolent with riches breathe their last and die.
For all this it is our duty to render thanks
To the celestial powers, with whose assistance
We have exacted payment and struck down
A city for one woman, forcing our entry
Within the Wooden Horse, which at the setting
Of the Pleiads like a hungry lion leapt
Out and slaked its thirst in royal blood.
As to your sentiments, I take due note
And find that they accord with mine. Too few

Rejoice at a friend's good fortune. I have known
Many dissemblers swearing false allegiance.
One only, though he joined me against his will,
Once in the harness, proved himself a staunch
Support, Odysseus, be he now alive or dead.
All public questions and such as concern the Gods
I shall discuss in council and take steps
To make this triumph lasting; and if here or there
Some malady comes to light, appropriate
Remedies will be applied to set it right.
Meanwhile, returning to my royal palace,
My first duty is to salute the Gods
Who led me overseas and home again.
Victory attends me; may she remain with me!

Clytemnestra

Citizens of Argos, councillors and elders,
I shall declare without shame in your presence
My feelings for my husband. Diffidence
Dies in us all with time. I shall speak of what
I suffered here, while he was away at the war,
Sitting at home, with no man's company,
Waiting for news, listening to one
Messenger after another, each bringing worse
Disasters. If all his rumored wounds were real,
His body was in shreds, shot through and through.
If he had died—the predominant report—
He was a second Geryon, an outstretched giant
With three corpses and one death for each,
While I, distraught, with a knot pressing my throat,
Was rescued forcibly, to endure still more.

And that is why our child is not present here,
As he should be, pledge of our marriage vows,
Orestes. Let me reassure you. He lives
Safe with an old friend, Strophius, who warned me
Of various dangers—your life at stake in Troy
And here a restive populace, which might perhaps
Be urged to kick a man when he is down.

As for myself, the fountains of my tears
Have long ago run dry. My eyes are sore
After so many nights watching the lamp
That burnt at my bedside always for you.
If I should sleep, a gnat's faint whine would shatter
The dreams that were my only company.

But now, all pain endured, all sorrow past,
I salute this man as the watchdog of the fold,
The stay that saves the ship, the sturdy oak
That holds the roof up, the longed-for only child,
The shore despaired-of sighted far out at sea.
God keep us from all harm! And now, dearest,
Dismount, but not on the bare ground! Servants,
Spread out beneath those feet that have trampled Troy
A road of royal purple, which shall lead him
By the hand of Justice into a home unhoped-for,
And there, when he has entered, our vigilant care
Shall dispose of everything as the Gods have ordained.

Agamemnon

Lady, royal consort and guardian of our home,
I thank you for your words of welcome, extended
To fit my lengthy absence; but due praise
Should rather come from others; and besides,
I would not have effeminate graces unman me

With barbarous salaams and beneath my feet
Purple embroideries designed for sacred use.
Honor me as a mortal, not as a god.
Heaven's greatest gift is wisdom. Count him blest
Who has brought a long life to a happy end.
I shall do as I have said, with a clear conscience.

Clytemnestra

Yet tell me frankly, according to your judgment.

Agamemnon

My judgment stands. Make no mistake about that.

Clytemnestra

Would you not in time of danger have vowed such
an act?

Agamemnon

Yes, if the priests had recommended it.

Clytemnestra

And what would Priam have done, if he had won?

Agamemnon

Oh, he would have trod the purple without a doubt.

Clytemnestra

Then you have nothing to fear from wagging tongues.

Agamemnon

Popular censure is a potent force.

Clytemnestra

Men must risk envy in order to be admired.

Agamemnon

A contentious spirit is unseemly in a woman.

Clytemnestra

Well may the victor yield a victory.

Agamemnon

Do you set so much store by your victory?

Clytemnestra

Be tempted, freely vanquished, victor still!

Agamemnon

Well, if you will have it, let someone unlace
These shoes, and, as I tread the purple, may
No far-off god cast at me an envious glance
At the prodigal desecration of all this wealth!
Meanwhile, extend your welcome to this stranger.
Power tempered with gentleness wins God's favor.
No one is glad to be enslaved, and she
Is a princess presented to me by the army,
The choicest flower culled from a host of captives.
And now, constrained to obey you, setting foot
On the sacred purple, I pass into my home.

Clytemnestra

The sea is still there, nothing can dry it up,
Renewing out of its infinite abundance

Unfailing streams of purple and blood-red dyes.[5]
So too this house, the Gods be praised, my lord.
Has riches inexhaustible. There is no counting
The robes I would have vowed to trample on,
Had some oracle so instructed, if by such means
I could have made good the loss of one dear soul.[6]
So now your entry to your hearth and home
Is like a warm spell in the long winter's cold,
Or when Zeus from the virgin grape at last
Draws wine, coolness descends upon the house
(For then from the living root the new leaves raise
A welcome shelter against the burning Dog-Star)
As man made perfect moves about his home.
        [*Exit* AGAMEMNON.]
Zeus, perfecter of all things, fulfil my prayers
And fulfil also your own purposes! [*Exit.*]

Chorus
What is this delirious dread,
Ominous, oracular,
Droning through my brain with unrelenting
Beat, irrepressible prophet of evil?
Why can I not cast it out
Planting good courage firm
On my spirit's empty throne?
In time the day came
When the Greeks with anchors plunged
Moored the sloops of war, and troops
Thronged the sandy beach of Troy.

So today my eyes have seen
Safe at last the men come home.
Still I hear the strain of stringless music,
Dirge of the Furies, a choir uninvited
Chanting in my heart of hearts.
Mortal souls stirred by God
In tune with fate divine the shape
Of things to come; yet
Grant that these forebodings prove
False and bring my fears to naught.

If a man's health be advanced over the due mean,
It will trespass soon upon sickness, who stands
Next neighbor, between them a thin wall.
So does the vessel of life
Launched with a favoring breeze
Suddenly founder on reefs of destruction.
Caution seated at the helm
Casts a portion of the freight
Overboard with measured throw;
So the ship may ride the storm.
Furrows enriched each season with showers
        from heaven
Banish hunger from the door.
But if the red blood of a man spatters the ground,
        dripping and deadly, then who
Has the magical power to recall it?
Even the healer who knew
Spells to awaken the dead,
Zeus put an end to his necromancy.
Portions are there preordained,
Each supreme within its own
Province fixed eternally.

That is why my spirit groans
Brooding in fear, and no longer it hopes to unravel
Mazes of a fevered mind.
[*Enter* CLYTEMNESTRA.

Clytemnestra
You, too, Cassandra, come inside! The merciful
Zeus gives you the privilege to take part
In our domestic sacrifice and stand
Before his altar among the other slaves there.
Put by your pride and step down. Even Heracles
Submitted once to slavery, and be consoled
In serving a house whose wealth has been inherited
Over so many generations. The harshest masters
Are those who have snatched their harvest out of hand.
You shall receive here what custom prescribes.

Chorus
She is speaking to you. Caught in the net, surrender.

Clytemnestra
If she knows Greek and not some barbarous language,
My mystic words shall fill the soul within her.

Chorus
You have no choice. Step down and do her will.

Clytemnestra
There is no time to waste. The victims are
All ready for the knife to render thanks
For this unhoped-for joy. If you wish to take part,
Make haste, but, if you lack the sense to understand,—
        [*To the* CHORUS.]
Speak to her with your hands and drag her down.

Chorus
She is like a wild animal just trapped.

Clytemnestra
She is mad, the foolish girl. Her city captured,
Brought here a slave, she will be broken in.
I'll waste no words on her to demean myself. [*Exit.*]

Cassandra
Oh! oh! Apollo!

Chorus
What blasphemy, to wail in Apollo's name!

Cassandra
Oh! oh! Apollo!

Chorus
Again she cries in grief to the god of joy!

Cassandra
Apollo, my destroyer! a second time!

---

[5]The purple dye was extracted from seaweed. It was very rare, therefore very expensive; a color reserved for the gods.

[6]Iphigenia.

Chorus

Ah, she foresees what is in store for her.
She is now a slave, and yet God's gift remains.

Cassandra

Apollo, my destroyer! What house is this?

Chorus

Do you not know where you have come, poor girl?
Then let us tell you. This is the House of Atreus.

Cassandra

Yes, for its very walls smell of iniquity,
A charnel house that drips with children's blood.[7]

Chorus

How keen her scent to seize upon the trail!

Cassandra

Listen to them as they bewail the foul
Repast of roast meat for a father's mouth!

Chorus

Enough! Reveal no more! We know it all.

Cassandra

What is it plotted next? Horror unspeakable,
A hard cross for kinsfolk.
The hoped-for savior is far away.

Chorus

What does she say? This must be something new.

Cassandra

Can it be so—to bathe one who is travel-tired,
And then smiling stretch out
A hand followed by a stealthy hand!

Chorus

She speaks in riddles, and I cannot read them.

Cassandra

What do I see? A net!
Yes, it is she, his mate and murderess!
Cry alleluia, cry, angels of hell, rejoice,
Fat with blood, dance and sing!

Chorus

What is the Fury you have called upon?
Helpless the heart faints with the sinking sun.
Closer still draws the stroke.

Cassandra

Ah, let the bull[8]beware!
It is a robe she wraps him in, and strikes!
Into the bath he slumps heavily, drowned in blood.
Such her skilled handicraft.

Chorus

It is not hard to read her meaning now.
Why does the prophet's voice never have good to tell,
Only cry woes to come?

Cassandra

Oh, pitiful destiny! Having lamented his,
Now I lament my own passion to fill the bowl.
Where have you brought me? Must I with him die?

Chorus

You sing your own dirge, like the red-brown bird
That pours out her grief-stricken soul,
Itys, Itys! she cries, the sad nightingale.

Cassandra

It is not so; for she, having become a bird,
Forgot her tears and sings her happy lot,
While I must face the stroke of two-edged steel.

Chorus

From whence does this cascade of harsh discords
Issue, and where will it at last be calmed?
Calamity you cry—O where must it end?

Cassandra

O wedding day, Paris accurst of all!
Scamander,[9] whose clear waters I grew beside!
Now I must walk weeping by Acheron.

Chorus

Even a child could understand.
The heart breaks, as these pitiful cries
Shatter the listening soul.

Cassandra

O fall of Troy, city of Troy destroyed!
The king's rich gifts little availed her so
That she might not have been what she is now.

Chorus

What evil spirit has possessed
Your soul, strumming such music upon your lips
As on a harp in hell?

Cassandra

Listen! My prophecy shall glance no longer
As through a veil like a bride newly-wed,
But bursting towards the sunrise shall engulf
The whole world in calamities far greater
Than these. No more riddles, I shall instruct,
While you shall verify each step, as I
Nose out from the beginning this bloody trail.
Upon this roof—do you see them?—stands a choir—
It has been there for generations—a gallery
Of unmelodious minstrels, a merry troop
Of wassailers drunk with human blood, reeling
And retching in horror at a brother's outraged bed.
Well, have I missed? Am I not well-read in
Your royal family's catalogue of crime?

---

[7]She refers to Thyestes' banquet. See introduction.
[8]Agamemnon.
[9]Scamander is a river near Troy; Acheron is the river of the underworld.

Chorus

You come from a far country and recite
Our ancient annals as though you had been present.

Cassandra

The Lord Apollo bestowed this gift on me.

Chorus

Was it because he had fallen in love with you?

Cassandra

I was ashamed to speak of this till now.

Chorus

Ah yes, adversity is less fastidious.

Cassandra

Oh, but he wrestled strenuously for my love.

Chorus

Did you come, then, to the act of getting child?

Cassandra

At first I consented, and then I cheated him.

Chorus

Already filled with his gift of prophecy?

Cassandra

Yes, I forewarned my people of their destiny.

Chorus

Did your divine lover show no displeasure?

Cassandra

Yes, the price I paid was that no one listened to me.

Chorus

Your prophecies seem credible enough to us.

Cassandra

Oh!
Again the travail of the prophetic trance
Runs riot in my soul. Do you not see them
There, on the roof, those apparitions—children
Murdered by their own kin, in their hands
The innards of which their father ate—oh
What a pitiable load they carry! For that crime
Revenge is plotted by the fainthearted lion,[10]
The stay-at-home, stretched in my master's bed
(Being his slave, I must needs call him so),
Lying in wait for Troy's great conqueror.
Little he knows what that foul bitch with ears
Laid back and rolling tongue intends for him
With a vicious snap, her husband's murderess.
What abominable monster shall I call her—
A two-faced amphisbaene or Scylla that skulks
Among the rocks to waylay mariners,
Infernal sea-squib locked in internecine
Strife—did you not hear her alleluias
Of false rejoicing at his safe return?
Believe me or not, what must be will be, and then
You will pity me and say, She spoke the truth.

Chorus

The feast of Thyestes I recognized, and shuddered,
But for the rest my wits are still astray.

Cassandra

Your eyes shall see the death of Agamemnon.

Chorus

No, hush those ill-omened lips, unhappy girl!

Cassandra

There is no Apollo present, and so no cure.

Chorus

None, if you speak the truth; yet God forbid!

Cassandra

Pray God forbid, while they close in for the kill!

Chorus

What man is there who would plot so foul a crime?

Cassandra

Ah, you have altogether misunderstood.

Chorus

But how will he do it? That escapes me still.

Cassandra

And yet I can speak Greek only too well.

Chorus

So does Apollo, but his oracles are obscure.

Cassandra

Ah, how it burns me up! Apollo! Now
That lioness[11] on two feet pours in the cup
My wages too, and while she whets the blade
For him promises to repay my passage money
In my own blood. Why wear these mockeries,
This staff and wreath, if I must die, then you
Shall perish first and be damned. Now we are quits!
Apollo himself has stripped me, looking upon me
A public laughingstock, who has endured
The name of witch, waif, beggar, castaway,
So now the god who gave me second sight
Takes back his gift and dismisses his servant,
Ready for the slaughter at a dead man's grave.
Yet we shall be avenged. Now far away,
The exile[12] shall return, called by his father's
Unburied corpse to come and kill his mother.
Why weep at all this? Have I not seen Troy fall,
And those who conquered her are thus discharged.
I name this door the gate of Hades: now
I will go and knock, I will take heart to die.
I only pray that the blow may be mortal,
Closing these eyes in sleep without a struggle,
While my life blood ebbs quietly away.

---

[10] Aegisthus.
[11] Clytemnestra.
[12] Orestes.

Chorus
O woman, in whose wisdom is so much grief,
How, if you know the end, can you approach it
So gently, like an ox that goes to the slaughter?

Cassandra
What help would it be if I should put it off?

Chorus
Yet, while there is life there's hope—so people say.

Cassandra
For me no hope, no help. My hour has come.

Chorus
You face your end with a courageous heart.

Cassandra
Yes, so they console those whom life has crossed.

Chorus
Is there no comfort in an honorable death?

Cassandra
O Priam, father, and all your noble sons! [*She approaches the door, then draws back.*]

Chorus
What is it? Why do you turn back, sick at heart?

Cassandra
Inside there is a stench of dripping blood.

Chorus
It is only the blood of their fireside sacrifice.

Cassandra
It is the sort of vapor that issues from a tomb.
I will go now and finish my lament
Inside the house. Enough of life! O friends!
I am not scared. I beg of you only this:
When the day comes for them to die, a man
For a man, woman for woman, remember me!

Chorus
Poor soul condemned to death, I pity you.

Cassandra
Yet one word more, my own dirge for myself.
I pray the Sun, on whom I now look my last,
That he may grant to my master's avengers
A fair price for the slave-girl slain at his side.
O sad mortality! when fortune smiles,
A painted image; and when trouble comes,
One touch of a wet sponge wipes it away. [*Exit.*]

Chorus
And her case is even more pitiable than his.

Human prosperity never rests but always craves more,
till blown up with pride it totters and falls. From the
opulent mansions pointed at by all passersby none warns
it away, none cries, "Let no more riches enter!" To him
was granted the capture of Troy, and he has entered his
home as a god, but now, if the blood of the past is on

him, if he must pay with his own death for the crimes
of bygone generations, then who is assured of a life
without sorrow?

Agamemnon
Oh me!

Chorus
Did you hear?

Agamemnon
Oh me, again!

Chorus
It is the King. Let us take counsel!
1 I say, raise a hue and cry!
2 Break in at once!
3 Yes, we must act.
4 *They* spurn delay.
5 They plot a tyranny.
6 Must we live their slaves?
7 Better to die.
8 Old men, what can we do?
9 We cannot raise the dead.
10 His death is not yet proved.
11 We are only guessing.
12 Let us break in and learn the truth!
[*The doors are thrown open and* CLYTEMNESTRA *is seen standing over the bodies of* AGAMEMNON *and* CASSANDRA, *which are laid out on a purple robe.*]

Clytemnestra
All that I said before to bide my time
Without any shame I shall now unsay. How else
Could I have plotted against an enemy
So near and seeming dear and strung the snare
So high that he could not jump it? Now the feud
On which I have pondered all these years has been
Fought out to its conclusion. Here I stand
Over my work, and it was so contrived
As to leave no loophole. With this vast dragnet
I enveloped him in purple folds, then struck
Twice, and with two groans he stretched his legs,
Then on his outspread body I struck a third blow,
A drink for Zeus the Deliverer of the dead.
There he lay gasping out his soul and drenched me
In these deathly dew-drops, at which I cried
In sheer delight like newly-budding corn
That tastes the first spring showers. And so,
Venerable elders, you see how the matter stands.
Rejoice, if you are so minded. I glory in it.
With bitter tears he filled the household bowl;
Now he has drained it to the dregs and gone.

Chorus
How can you speak so of your murdered king?

Clytemnestra
You treat me like an empty-headed woman.
Again, undaunted, to such as understand
I say—commend or censure, as you please—
It makes no difference—here is Agamemnon,
My husband, dead, the work of this right hand,
Which acted justly. There you have the truth.

Chorus

Woman, what evil brew have you devoured to take
On you a crime that cries out for a public curse?
Yours was the fatal blow, banishment shall be yours,
Hissed and hated of all men.

Clytemnestra

Your sentence now for me is banishment,
But what did you do then to contravene
His purpose, when, to exorcise the storms,
As though picking a ewe-lamb from his flocks,
Whose wealth of snowy fleeces never fails
To increase and multiply, he killed his own
Child, born to me in pain, my best-beloved?
Why did you not drive *him* from hearth and home?
I bid you cast at me such menaces
As make for mastery in equal combat
With one prepared to meet them, and if, please God,
The issue goes against you, suffering
Shall school those grey hairs in humility.

Chorus

You are possessed by some spirit of sin that stares
Out of your bloodshot eyes matching your bloody hands.
Dishonored and deserted of your kin, for this
Stroke you too shall be struck down.

Clytemnestra

Listen! By Justice, who avenged my child,
By the Fury to whom I vowed this sacrament,
No thought of fear shall enter through this door
So long as the hearth within is kindled by
Aegisthus, faithful to me now as always.
Low lies the man who insulted his wedded wife,
The darling of the Chryseids at Troy,
And stretched beside him this visionary seer,
Whom he fondled on shipboard, both now rewarded,
He as you see, and she swanlike has sung
Her dying ditty, his tasty side dish, for me
A rare spice to add relish to my joy.

Chorus

Oh, for the gift of death
To bring the long sleep that knows no waking,
Now that my lord and loyal protector
Breathes his last. For woman's sake
Long he fought overseas,
Now at home falls beneath a woman's hand.
    Helen, the folly-beguiled, having ravaged the city of
        Troy,
    She has set on the curse of Atreus
    A crown of blood beyond ablution.

Clytemnestra

Do not pray for death nor turn your anger against one
    woman as the slayer of thousands!

Chorus

Demon of blood and tears
Inbred in two women single-hearted!
Perched on the roof he stands and preens his
Sable wings, a carrion-crow.
Loud he croaks, looking down
Upon the feast spread before him here below.

Clytemnestra

Ah now you speak truth, naming the thrice-fed demon,
    who, glutted with blood, craves more, still young
    in his hunger.

Chorus

When will the feast be done?
Alas, it is the will of Zeus,
Who caused and brought it all to pass.
Nothing is here but was decreed in heaven.

Clytemnestra

It was not my doing, nor am I Agamemnon's wife, but a
    ghost in woman's guise, the shade of the banqueter
    whom Atreus fed.

Chorus

How is the guilt not yours?
And yet the crimes of old may well
Have had a hand, and so it drives
On, the trail of internecine murder.

Clytemnestra

What of *him?* Was the guilt not his, when he killed the
    child that I bore him? And so by the sword he
    has fallen.

Chorus

Alas, the mind strays. The house is falling.
A storm of blood lays the walls in ruins.
Another mortal stroke for Justice' hand
Will soon be sharpened.
    Oh me, who shall bury him, who sing the dirge?
    Who shall intone at the tomb of a blessed spirit
    A tribute pure in heart and truthful?

Clytemnestra

No, I'll bury him, but without mourners. By the waters
    of Acheron Iphigenia is waiting for him with a kiss.

Chorus

The charge is answered with countercharges.
The sinner must suffer: such is God's will.
The ancient curse is bringing down the house
In self-destruction.

Clytemnestra

That is the truth, and I would be content that the spirit
    of vengeance should rest, having absolved the house
    from its madness.

[*Enter* AEGISTHUS *with a bodyguard.*

Aegisthus

Now I have proof that there are Gods in heaven,
As I gaze on this purple mesh in which
My enemy lies, son of a treacherous father.
His father, Atreus, monarch of this realm,
Was challenged in his sovran rights by mine,
Thyestes, his own brother, and banished him
From hearth and home. Later he returned
A suppliant and found sanctuary, indeed
A welcome; for his brother entertained him
To a feast of his own children's flesh, of which

My father unsuspecting took and ate.
Then, when he knew what he had done, he fell
Back spewing out the slaughtered flesh and, kicking
The table to the floor, with a loud cry
He cursed the House of Pelops. That is the crime
For which the son lies here. And fitly too
The plot was spun by me; for as a child
I was banished with my father, until Justice
Summoned me home. Now let me die, for never
Shall I live to see another sight so sweet.

Chorus
Aegisthus, if it was you who planned this murder,
Then be assured, the people will stone you for it.

Aegisthus
Such talk from the lower benches! Even in dotage
Prison can teach a salutary lesson.
Better submit, or else you shall smart for it.

Chorus
You woman, who stayed at home and wallowed in
His bed, you plotted our great commander's death!

Aegisthus
Orpheus led all in rapture after him.[13]
Your senseless bark will be snuffed out in prison.

Chorus
You say the plot was yours, yet lacked the courage
To raise a hand but left it to a woman!

Aegisthus
As his old enemy, I was suspect.
Temptation was the woman's part. But now
I'll try my hand at monarchy, and all
Who disobey me shall be put in irons
And starved of food and light till they submit.

Chorus
Oh, if Orestes yet beholds the sun,
May he come home and execute them both!

Aegisthus
Ho, my guards, come forward, you have work to do.

Captain of the Guard
Stand by, draw your swords!

Chorus
We are not afraid to die.

Aegisthus
Die! We'll take you at your word.

Clytemnestra
Peace, my lord, and let no further wrong be done.
Captain, sheathe your swords. And you, old men,
Go home quietly. What has been, it had to be.
Scars enough we bear, now let us rest.

Aegisthus
Must I stand and listen to their threats?

Chorus
Men of Argos never cringed before a rogue.

Aegisthus
I shall overtake you yet—the day is near.

Chorus
Not if Orestes should come home again.

Aegisthus
Vain hope, the only food of castaways.

Chorus
Gloat and grow fat, blacken justice while you dare!

Aegisthus
All this foolish talk will cost you dear.

Chorus
Flaunt your gaudy plumes and strut beside your hen!

Clytemnestra
Pay no heed to idle clamor. You and I,
Masters of the house, shall now direct it well.

---

[13]That is: You are not Orpheus, whose music caused
people to follow him.

EXERCISES

1. It might be interesting to read through the speeches of the Chorus without any reference to the other speeches or action of the play. What is your impression of their attitude toward life in general? Do you find many examples of their speaking proverbial wisdom? It is one theme of this discussion of the Greeks that, in their early cultural development, they were bound by tradition and nature. Does this speaking in proverbs have any relation to this theme?

2. Cassandra, of course, is trying to arouse the Chorus to action. Quite aside from the mythical problem of the curse of Apollo which caused everyone to disbelieve her prophecies, can you see any other reason why she cannot get these men to act? For example, why, when she was left alone in the chariot, knowing that she faced death as soon as she entered the palace, did she not run away? Certainly the members of the Chorus would not stop her.

3. Below is given a little chart dealing with the levels of human freedom of action. It might be interesting to place the characters somewhere above or below the dividing line. Where would you place the Chorus throughout the play? Do they stand still, or does their position fluctuate? Where would you place Cassandra? Agamemnon? Clytemnestra?

4. When the Chorus is telling of the death of Iphigenia, they speak of her "swathed in folds of saffron." Later they say, "Night . . . who has cast over the towers of Troy a net so fine." Still later, Agamemnon walks on a purple "web," or "net." Why did Aeschylus use this image throughout the play? Does it have any significance beyond its literal meaning?

5. Notice that *Agamemnon* has its beginning in the darkness in the country town of Mycenae. *The Eumenides*, the third play of the trilogy, ends in the bright sunlight of Athens. Does this symbolism have any significance?

The area of conduct in which men are free to accomplish their purposes and desires.

The Dividing Line ─────────────────────────

A not-quite-human level where men's ideas of justice are bound by tradition and nature.

Eumenides

Aeschylus

This is the third play of the *Oresteia*. In the second one (*Choephori*, or The Libation Bearers), Orestes has returned to Argos, recognized his sister, Electra, and the two of them have planned and carried out the murder of Aegisthus and Clytemnestra. In the second play, the two ideas of justice became more apparent, for Orestes felt qualms about the murder of his mother. His sense of filial duty in carrying out revenge, as well as the fact that Apollo had commanded him to the deed, triumphed over his own conscience. Immediately after the murder he was set upon by the old hags, goddesses descended from the blood of Uranus, whose duty it was to pursue those who had killed their own kindred.

The old idea of justice, revenge or retaliation, was presented in *Agamemnon;* we see here the development of a new idea of justice and freedom for the city of Athens. Watch how this is handled. When you have finished the play, stop a while and think about the ways in which men can live under this new concept.

Characters   *Prophetess*

Apollo

Orestes

Ghost of Clytemnestra

Chorus of Furies

Athena

Escort of Women

Before the temple of Apollo at Delphi.
[*Enter the* PRIESTESS.

Priestess
First among all the gods to whom this prayer
Shall be addressed is the first of prophets, Earth;[1]
And next her daughter, Themis, who received
The oracular shrine from her; third, another
Daughter, Phoebe, who having settled here
Bestowed it as a birthday gift, together
With her own name, on Phoebus; whereupon,
Leaving his native isle of Delos and landing
In Attica, he made his way from there
Attended by the sons of Hephaestus, who tamed
The wilderness and built a road for him;
And here Zeus, having inspired him with his art,
Set him, the fourth of prophets, on this throne,
His own son and interpreter, Apollo.
Together with these deities I pay
Homage to Athena and to the nymphs that dwell
In the Corycian caves on the rugged slopes
Of Parnassus,[2] where Dionysus led
His troop of frenzied Bacchants to catch and kill
King Pentheus like a mountain-hare; and so,
After calling on Poseidon and the springs
Of Pleistus, watering this valley, and last
On Zeus the All-Highest, who makes all things perfect,
I take my seat on the oracular throne,
Ready to be consulted. Let all Greeks
Approach by lot according to the custom
And I shall prophesy to them as God dictates. [*She
enters the temple, utters a loud cry, and returns.*]
O horror, horror! I have been driven back
Strengthless, speechless, a terror-struck old woman,
By such a sight as was never seen before.
Entering the shrine I saw at the navel-stone
In the posture of a suppliant a man
Who held an olive-branch and an unsheathed sword
In hands dripping with blood; and all round him,
Lying fast asleep, a gruesome company
Of women—yet not women—Gorgons rather;
And yet not Gorgons; them I saw once in a picture
Of the feast of Phineus: these are different.
They have no wings, and are all black, and snore,
And drops ooze from their eyes, and the rags they wear
Unutterably filthy. What country could
Have given such creatures birth, I cannot tell.
Apollo is the master of this house,
So let him look to it, healer, interpreter,

Himself of other houses purifier.
[*The inside of the temple is revealed, as described, with*
APOLLO *and* HERMES *standing beside* ORESTES.

Apollo
I will keep faith, at all times vigilant,
Whether at your side or far away, and never
Mild to your enemies, whom you now see
Subdued by sleep, these unloved virgins, these
Children hoary with age, whose company
Is shunned by God and man and beast, being born
For evil, just as the abyss from which they come
Is evil, the bottomless pit of Tartarus.
Yet you must fly before them, hotly pursued,
Past island cities and over distant seas,
Enduring all without faltering, until
You find sanctuary in Athena's citadel,
And there, embracing her primeval image, you
Shall stand trial, and after healing words
From me, who commanded you to kill your mother,
You shall be set free and win your salvation.

Orestes
O Lord Apollo, you have both wisdom and power,
And, since you have them, use them on my behalf!

Apollo
Remember, endure and have no fear! And you,
Hermes, go with him, guide him, guard his steps,
An outcast from mankind, yet blest of Zeus.
[*Exeunt* HERMES *and* ORESTES. *Enter the ghost of*
CLYTEMNESTRA.

Clytemnestra
Oho! asleep! What good are you to me asleep?
While I, deserted and humiliated,
Wander, a homeless ghost. I warn you that
Among the other spirits of the dead
(The taunt of murder does not lose its sting
In the dark world below) I am the accused
And not the accuser, with none to defend me,
Brutally slain by matricidal hands.
Look on these scars, and remember all
The wineless offerings which I laid upon
The hearth for you at many a solemn midnight—
All now forgotten, all trampled underfoot!
And *he* is gone! Light as a fawn he skipped
Out of your snare and now he laughs at you.
Oh hear me! I am pleading for my soul!
O goddesses of the underworld, awake!
I, Clytemnestra, call you now in dreams!

Chorus
Mu!

---

[1] Earth, Themis, Phoebe, and Phoebus Apollo are the gods
who have prophesied at the Oracle of Delphi.

[2] Mount Parnassus stands beside Delphi. King Pentheus of
Thebes was killed by the female worshippers of Dionysus
either here or on Mount Kithaeron. For this story and one
of the most shocking plays in literature, read Euripides' *The
Bacchae.*

Clytemnestra

Ah, you may mew, but he is fled and gone.
He has protectors who are no friends of mine.

Chorus

Mu!

Clytemnestra

Still so drowsy, still so pitiless?
Orestes has escaped, the matricide!

Chorus

Oh, oh!

Clytemnestra

Still muttering and mumbling in your sleep!
Arise, do evil! is not that your task?

Chorus

Oh, oh!

Clytemnestra

How sleep and weariness have made common cause
To disenvenom the foul dragon's rage!

Chorus

Oh, oh! where is the scent? Let us mark it down!

Clytemnestra

Yes, you may bay like an unerring hound,
But still you are giving chase only in your dreams.
What are you doing? Rise, slothful slugabeds,
Stung by the scourge of my rebukes, arise
And blow about his head your bloody breath,
Consume his flesh in bellifuls of fire!
Come on, renew the chase and hunt him down! [*Exit*]

Chorus

We have been put to shame! What has befallen us?
The game has leapt out of the snare and gone.
In slumber laid low, we let slip the prey.

Aha, son of Zeus! pilferer, pillager!
A God, to steal away the matricide!
A youth to flout powers fixed long ago!

In dream I felt beneath the heart a swift
Charioteer's sharp lash.
Under the ribs, under the flank
It rankles yet, red and sore,
Like the public scourger's blow.

This is the doing of the younger gods.
Dripping with death, red drops
Cover the heel, cover the head.
Behold the earth's navel-stone
Thick with heavy stains of blood!

His own prophetic cell he has himself defiled,
Honoring mortal claims, reckless of laws divine,
And dealing death to Fates born of old.
He injures us and yet *him* he shall never free,
Not in the depths of hell, never shall he have rest
But suffer lasting torment below.

Apollo

Out, out! Be off, and clear this holy place
Of your foul presence, or else from my golden bow
Shall spring a snake of silver and bite so deep
That from your swollen bellies you shall spew
The blood which you have sucked! Your place is where
Heads drop beneath the axe, eyes are gouged out,
Throats slit, and men are stoned, limbs lopped, and boys
Gelded, and a last whimper heard from spines
Spiked writhing in the dust. Such celebrations,
Which fill heaven with loathing, are your delight.
Off with you, I say, and go unshepherded,
A herd shunned with universal horror!

Chorus

O Lord Apollo, hear us in our turn!
You are not an abettor in this business.
You are the culprit. On you lies the whole guilt.

Apollo

Explain yourselves. How do you make that out?

Chorus

It was at your command that he killed his mother.

Apollo

I commanded him to take vengeance for his father.

Chorus

So promising the acceptance of fresh blood.

Apollo

I promised to absolve him from it here.

Chorus

Why do you insult the band that drove him here?

Apollo

This mansion is not fit for your company.

Chorus

But this is the task that has been appointed to us.

Apollo

What is this privilege that you are so proud of?

Chorus

To drive all matricides from hearth and home.

Apollo

And what of a woman who has killed her husband?

Chorus

That is not manslaughter within the kin.

Apollo

So then you set at naught the marriage-bond
Sealed by Zeus and Hera, and yet what tie
Is stronger, joined by Fate and watched over
By Justice, than the joy which Aphrodite
Has given to man and woman? If you let those
Who violate that covenant go unpunished,
You have no right to persecute Orestes.

Why anger here, and there passivity?
On this in time Athena shall pass judgment.

Chorus

We shall give chase and never let him go.

Apollo

Pursue him then, and make trouble for yourselves.

Chorus

No words of yours can circumscribe our powers.

Apollo

I would not have your powers even as a gift.

Chorus

Then take your proud stand by the throne of Zeus.
Meanwhile a mother's blood is beckoning to us,
And we must go and follow up the trail.

Apollo

And I will still safeguard the suppliant.
A wrong unheard-of in heaven and on earth
Would be his protest, if I should break faith.
[*A year passes. Before a shrine of Athena at Athens. Enter*
ORESTES.

Orestes

O Queen Athena, I have come here in obedience
To the Lord Apollo. Grant me sanctuary,
An outcast, yet with hands no longer sullied, for
The edge of my pollution has been worn
Off on countless paths over land and sea;
And now, in accordance with his word, present
Before your image, I entreat you to
Receive me here and pass the final judgment.

Chorus

Step where our dumb informer leads the way;
For as the hounds pursue a wounded fawn,
So do we dog the trail of human blood.
How far we have traveled over land and sea,
Faint and footsore but never to be shaken off!
He must be somewhere here, for I smell blood.

—Beware, I say, beware!
Look on all sides for fear he find some escape!
—Ah, here he is, desperate,
Clasping that image awaiting trial.
—It cannot be! The mother's blood
That he has spilt is irrecoverable.
—Ravenous lips shall feed upon his living flesh
And on his blood—a lush pasturage.
—And others shall he see in hell, who wronged
Parents, guests or gods;
For Hades is a stern inquisitor of souls,
Recording all things till the hour of judgment.

Orestes

Taught by long suffering, I have learnt at what
Times it is right to keep silence and when
To break it, and in this matter a wise

Instructor has charged me to speak. The stain
Of matricide has been washed out in the flow
Of swine's blood by Apollo. I could tell
Of many who have given me lodging and no
Harm has befallen them from my company;
And now with lips made pure I call upon
Athena to protect me and so join
Our peoples as allies for all time to come.
Wherever she may be, on Libyan shores
Or by the stream of Trito, where she came
To birth, or like a captain keeping watch
On the heights of Phlegra against some enemy,
O may she come—far off, she can still hear me—
And from my sufferings deliver me!

Chorus

Neither Apollo nor Athena can
Save your soul from perdition, a feast for fiends.
Have you no answer? Do you spurn us so,
Fattened for us, our consecrated host?

Let us dance and declare in tune with this grim music
the laws which it is ours to enforce on the life of man.
It is only those that have blood on their hands who need
fear us at all, but from them without fail we exact
retribution.

Mother Night, your children cry! Hear, black Night!
It is ours to deal by day and dark night judgment.
The young god Apollo has rescued the matricide!
    Over the blood that has been shed
    Maddening dance, melody desperate, deathly,
    Chant to bind the soul in hell,
    Spell that parches flesh to dust.

This the Fates who move the whole world through
Have assigned to us, a task for all future ages,
To keep watch on all hands that drip red with
    kindred blood.
    Over the blood that has been shed
    Maddening dance, melody desperate, deathly,
    Chant to bind the soul in hell,
    Spell that parches flesh to dust.

Such are the powers appointed us from the beginning,
None of the Gods of Olympus to eat with us, while we
Take no part in the wearing of white—no,
Other pleasures are our choice—
    Wrecking the house, hunting the man,
    Hard on his heels ever we run,
    And though his feet be swift we waste and wear
        him out.

Hence it is thanks to our zealous endeavor that from such
Offices Zeus and the Gods are exempted, and yet he
Shuns us because we are covered in blood, not
Fit to share his majesty.
    Wrecking the house, hunting the man,
    Hard on his heels ever we run,
    And though his feet be swift we waste and wear
        him out.

Glories of men, how bright in the day is their splendor,

Yet shall they fade in the darkness of hell,
Faced with our grisly attire and dancing
Feet attuned to sombre melodies.
   Nimble the feet leap in the air,
   Skip and descend down to the ground,
   Fugitive step suddenly tripped up in fatal confusion.

Caught without knowing he stumbles, his wickedness
    blinds him,
Such is the cloud of pollution that hangs
Over him and on his house, remembered
Many generations after him.
   Nimble the feet leap in the air,
   Skip and descend down to the ground,
   Fugitive step suddenly tripped up in fatal confusion.

Our task is such. With long memories
We keep constant watch on human sin.
What others spurn is what we prize,
Our heaven their hell, a region of trackless waste,
Both for the quick and dead, for blind and seeing too.

What wonder then that men bow in dread
At these commandments assigned to us
By Fate—our ancient privilege?
We are not without our own honors and dignities,
Though we reside in hell's unfathomable gloom.

[*Enter* ATHENA.

Athena
I heard a distant cry, as I was standing
Beside Scamander to take possession of
The lands which the Achaean princes have
Bestowed on my people in perpetuity;
And thence I have made my way across the sea
In wingless flight; and now, as I regard
Before my shrine this very strange company,
I cannot but ask, in wonder, not in fear,
Who you may be. I address you all in common,
This stranger here who is seated at my image,
And you, who are not human in appearance
Nor yet divine; but rather than speak ill
Without just cause let me receive your answer.

Chorus
Daughter of Zeus, your question is soon answered.
We are the dismal daughters of dark Night,
Called Curses in the palaces of hell.

Athena
I know your names then and your parentage.

Chorus
And now let us inform you of our powers.

Athena
Yes, let me know what office you perform.

Chorus
We drive the matricide from hearth and home.

Athena
Where? In what place does his persecution end?

Chorus
A place where joy is something quite unknown.

Athena
Is that your hue and cry against this man?

Chorus
Yes, because he dared to kill his mother.

Athena
Was he driven to it perhaps against his will?

Chorus
What force could drive a man to matricide?

Athena
It is clear there are two parties to this case.

Chorus
We challenged him to an ordeal by oath.

Athena
You seem to seek only the semblance of justice.

Chorus
How so? Explain, since you are so rich in wisdom.

Athena
Do not use oaths to make the wrong prevail.

Chorus
Then try the case yourself and give your judgment.

Athena
Will you entrust the verdict to my charge?

Chorus
Yes, a worthy daughter of a worthy father.

Athena
Stranger, what is your answer? Tell us first
Your fatherland and family and what
Misfortune overtook you, and then answer
The charge against you. If you have taken your stand
Here as a suppliant with full confidence
In the justice of your cause, now is the time
To render on each count a clear reply.

Orestes
O Queen Athena, first let me remove one doubt.
I am not a suppliant seeking purification.
I was already cleansed before I took
This image in my arms, and I can give
Evidence of this. The manslayer is required
To keep silent until he has been anointed
With sacrificial blood. That has been done,
And I have traveled far over land and sea
To wear off the pollution. So, having set
Your mind at rest, let me tell you who I am.
I come from Argos, and my father's name—
For asking me that I thank you—was Agamemnon,
The great commander, with whom not long ago
You wiped out Troy. He died an evil death,

Murdered on his return by my blackhearted
Mother, who netted him in a bath of blood.
And therefore I, restored from banishment,
In retribution for my father's death,
I killed my mother; and yet not I alone—
Apollo too must answer for it, having
Warned me what anguish would afflict me if
I should fail to take vengeance on the guilty.
Whether it was just or not, do you decide.

Athena

This is too grave a case for mortal minds,
Nor is it right that I should judge an act
Of blood shed with such bitter consequences,
Especially since you have come to me
As one already purified, who has done no wrong
Against this city. But your opponents here
Are not so gentle, and, if their plea
Should be rejected, the poison dripping from
Their angry bosoms will devastate my country.
The issue is such that, whether I let them stay
Or turn them out, it is fraught with injury.
But be it so. Since it has come to this,
I will appoint judges for homicide,
A court set up in perpetuity.
Do you prepare your proofs and witnesses,
Then I, having selected from my people
The best, will come to pass a final judgment. [*Exit.*]

Chorus

Now the world shall see the downfall of old
    commandments made
Long ago, if the accurst matricide should win his case.
Many a bitter blow awaits parents from their own
    children in the times to come.

We who had the task to watch over human life shall now
Cease to act, giving free rein to deeds of violence.
Crime shall spread from house to house like a plague,
    and whole cities shall be desolate.

Then let no man stricken cry
Out in imprecation, "Oh
Furies!" Thus shall fathers groan,
Thus shall mothers weep in vain,
Since the house of righteousness
Lies in ruins, overthrown.

Times there are when fear is good,
Keeping watch within the soul.
Needful too are penalties.
Who of those that have not nursed
Wholesome dread within them can
Show respect to righteousness?

Choose a life despot-free, yet restrained by rule of law.
God has appointed the mean as the master in all things.
Wickedness breeds pride, but from wisdom is
    brought forth
Happiness prayed for by all men.

So, we say, men must bow down before the shrine
    of Right.

Those who defy it shall fail; for the ancient
    commandments
Stand—to respect parents and honor the stranger.
Only the righteous shall prosper.
The man who does what is right by choice,
    not constraint,
Shall prosper always; the seed of just men shall
    never perish.
Not so the captain who ships a load of ill-gotten gains.
Caught in the gathering storm his proud sail shall be
    torn from the masthead.

He cries to deaf ears, no longer able to ride
The gale, and meanwhile his guardian spirit is
    close beside him
And scoffs to see him despair of ever again making port,
Dashed on the reefs of Justice, unlooked-on
    and unlamented.

[*Enter* ATHENA *with the* JUDGES, *followed by citizens of
Athens.*

Athena

Herald, give orders to hold the people back,
Then sound the trumpet and proclaim silence.
For while this new tribunal is being enrolled,
It is right that all should ponder on its laws,
Both the litigants here whose case is to be judged,
And my whole people for all generations.

[*Enter* APOLLO.

Chorus

Apollo, what is there here that concerns you?
We say you have no authority in this matter.

Apollo

I come both as a witness, the accused
Having been a suppliant at my sanctuary
And purified of homicide at my hands,
And also to be tried with him, for I too
Must answer for the murder of his mother.
Open the case, and judge as you know how.

Athena

The case is open. You shall be first
    to speak. [*To the* CHORUS.]
The prosecutors shall take precedence
And first inform us truthfully of the facts.

Chorus

Many in number, we shall be brief in speech.
We beg you to answer our questions one by one.
First, is it true that you killed your mother?

Orestes

I killed her. That is true, and not denied.

Chorus

So then the first of the three rounds is ours.

Orestes

You should not boast that you have thrown me yet.

Chorus

Next, since you killed her, you must tell us how.

Orestes
Yes, with a drawn sword leveled at the throat.

Chorus
Who was it who impelled or moved you to it?

Orestes
The oracle of this God who is my witness.

Chorus
The God of prophecy ordered matricide?

Orestes
Yes, and I have not repented it to this day.

Chorus
You *will* repent it, when you have been condemned.

Orestes
My father shall defend me from the grave.

Chorus
Having killed your mother, you may well trust the dead!

Orestes
She was polluted by a double crime.

Chorus
How so? Explain your meaning to the judges.

Orestes
She killed her husband and she killed my father.

Chorus
She died without bloodguilt, and you still live.

Orestes
Why did you not hunt her when she was alive?

Chorus
She was not bound by blood to the man she killed.

Orestes
And am I then bound by blood to my mother?

Chorus
Abandoned wretch, how did she nourish you
Within the womb? Do you repudiate
The nearest and dearest tie of motherhood?

Orestes
Apollo, give your evidence. I confess
That I did this deed as I have said.
Pronounce your judgment: was it justly done?

Apollo
Athena's appointed judges, I say to you,
Justly, and I, as prophet, cannot lie.
Never from my prophetic shrine have I
Said anything of city, man or woman
But what my father Zeus has commanded me.
This plea of mine must override all others,
Since it accords with our great father's will.

Chorus
Your argument is, then, that Zeus commanded you
To charge Orestes with this criminal act
Regardless of the bond between son and mother?

Apollo
It is not the same, to murder a great king,
A woman too to do it, and not in open
Fight like some brave Amazon, but in such
Manner as I shall now inform this court.
On his return from battle, bringing home
A balance for the greater part of good,
She welcomed him with fine words and then, while
He bathed, pavilioned him in a purple robe
And struck him down and killed him—a man and king
Whom the whole world had honored. Such was
        the crime
For which she paid. Let the judges take note.

Chorus
According to your argument Zeus gives
Precedence to the father; yet Zeus it was
Who cast into prison his own father Kronos.
Judges, take note, and ask him to explain.

Apollo
Abominable monsters, loathed by gods
And men, do you not understand that chains
Can be unfastened and prison doors unlocked?
But once the dust has drunk a dead man's blood,
He can never rise again—for that no remedy
Has been appointed by our almighty Father,
Although all else he can overturn at will
Without so much effort as a single breath.

Chorus
See what your plea for the defendant means.
Is this not what he did—to spill his mother's
Blood on the ground? And shall he then be allowed
To live on in his father's house? What public
Altar can he approach and where find fellowship?

Apollo
The mother is not a parent, only the nurse
Of the seed which the true parent, the father,
Commits to her as to a stranger to
Keep it with God's help safe from harm. And I
Have proof of this. There can be a father
Without a mother. We have a witness here,
This daughter of Olympian Zeus, who sprang
Armed from her father's head, a goddess whom
No goddess could have brought to birth. Therefore,
Out of goodwill to your country and your people
I sent this suppliant to seek refuge with you,
That you, Athena, may find in him and his
A faithful ally for all time to come.

Athena
Enough has now been spoken. Are you agreed
That I call on the judges to record
Their votes justly according to their conscience?

Apollo

Our quiver is empty, every arrow spent.
We wait to hear the issue of the trial.

Athena

And has my ruling your approval too?

Chorus

Sirs, you have heard the case, and now declare
Judgment according to your solemn oath.

Athena

Citizens of Athens, hear my declaration
At this first trial in the history of man.
This great tribunal shall remain in power
Meeting in solemn session on this hill,
Where long ago the Amazons encamped
When they made war on Theseus, and sacrificed
To Ares—hence its name:[3] Here reverence
For law and inbred fear among my people
Shall hold their hands from evil night and day,
Only let them not tamper with the laws,
But keep the fountain pure and sweet to drink.
I warn you not to banish from your lives
All terror but to seek the mean between
Autocracy and anarchy; and in this way
You shall possess in ages yet unborn
An impregnable fortress of liberty
Such as no people has throughout the world.
With these words I establish this tribunal
Grave, quick to anger, incorruptible,
And always vigilant over those that sleep.
Let the judges now rise and cast their votes.[4]

Chorus

We charge you to remember that we have
Great power to harm, and vote accordingly.

Apollo

I charge you to respect the oracles
Sanctioned by Zeus and see that they are fulfilled.

Chorus

By interfering in what is not your office
You have desecrated your prophetic shrine.

Apollo

Then was my Father also at fault when he
Absolved Ixion, the first murderer?

Chorus

Keep up your chatter, but, if our cause should fail,
We shall lay on this people a heavy hand.

Apollo

Yes, you will lose your case, and then you may
Spit out your poison, but it will do no harm.

Chorus

Insolent youth mocks venerable age.
We await the verdict, ready to let loose
Against this city our destructive rage.

Athena

The final judgment rests with me, and I
Announce that my vote shall be given to Orestes.
No mother gave me birth, and in all things
Save marriage I commend with all my heart
The masculine, my father's child indeed.
Therefore I cannot hold in higher esteem
A woman killed because she killed her husband.
If the votes are equal, Orestes wins.
Let the appointed officers proceed
To empty the urns and count the votes.

Orestes

O bright Apollo, how shall the judgment go?

Chorus

O black mother Night, are you watching this?

Orestes

My hour has come—the halter or the light.

Chorus

And ours—to exercise our powers or perish.

Apollo

Sirs, I adjure you to count carefully.
If judgment errs, great harm will come of it,
Whereas one vote may raise a fallen house.

Athena

He stands acquitted on the charge of bloodshed,
The human votes being equally divided.

Orestes

Lady Athena, my deliverer,
I was an outcast from my country, now
I can go home again and live once more
In my paternal heritage, thanks to you
And to Apollo and to the third, the Savior,
Who governs the whole world. Before I go
I give my word to you and to your people
For all posterity that no commander
Shall lead an Argive army in war against
This city. If any should violate this pledge,
Out of the graves which shall then cover us
We would arise with adverse omens to
Obstruct and turn them back. If, however,
They keep this covenant and stand by your side,
They shall always have our blessing. And so farewell!
May you and your people always prevail
Against the assaults of all your enemies! [*Exit.*]

Chorus

Oho, you junior gods, since you have trod under foot
The laws of old and robbed us of our powers,

---

[3]The hill and the court which met on it were called the Areopagus.

[4]It is understood that the members of the jury are dropping their votes into an urn during the next eight speeches.

We shall afflict this country
With damp contagion, bleak and barren, withering
    up the soil,
Mildew on bud and birth abortive. Venomous pestilence
Shall sweep your cornlands with infectious death.
To weep?—No! To work? Yes! To work ill and lay low
    the people!
So will the maids of Night mourn for their stolen honors.

Athena
Let me persuade you to forget your grief!
You are not defeated. The issue of the trial
Has been determined by an equal vote.
It was Zeus himself who plainly testified
That Orestes must not suffer for what he did.
I beg you, therefore, do not harm my country,
Blasting her crops with drops of rank decay
And biting cankers in the early buds.
Rather accept my offer to stay and live
In a cavern on this hill and there receive
The adoration of my citizens.

Chorus
Oho, you junior gods, etc.

Athena
No, *not* dishonored, and therefore spare my people!
I too confide in Zeus—why speak of that?—
And I alone of all the Olympian gods
Know of the keys which guard the treasury
Of heaven's thunder. But there is no need of that.
Let my persuasion serve to calm your rage.
Reside with me and share my majesty;
And when from these wide acres you enjoy
Year after year the harvest offerings
From couples newly-wed praying for children,
Then you will thank me for my intercession.

Chorus
How can you treat us so?
Here to dwell, ever debased, defiled!
Hear our passion, hear, black Night!
For the powers once ours, sealed long, long ago
Have by the junior gods been all snatched away.

Athena
You are my elders, and therefore I indulge
Your passion. And yet, though not so wise as you,
To me too Zeus has granted understanding.
If you refuse me and depart, believe me,
This country will yet prove your heart's desire,
For as the centuries pass so there will flow
Such glory to my people as will assure
To all divinities worshipped here by men
And women gathered on festive holidays
More honors than could be yours in any other
City throughout the world. And so, I beg you,
Keep from my citizens the vicious spur
Of internecine strife, which pricks the breast
Of manhood flown with passion as with wine!
Abroad let battle rage for every heart
That is fired with love of glory—that shall be theirs
In plenty. So this is my offer to you—

To give honor and receive it and to share
My glory in this country loved by heaven.

Chorus
How can you, etc.

Athena
I will not weary in my benedictions,
Lest it should ever be said that you, so ancient
In your divinity, were driven away
By me and by my mortal citizens.
No, if Persuasion's holy majesty,
The sweet enchantment of these lips divine,
Has power to move you, please, reside with me.
But, if you still refuse, then, since we have made
This offer to you, it would be wrong to lay
Your hands upon us in such bitter rage.
Again, I tell you, it is in your power to own
This land attended with the highest honors.

Chorus
Lady Athena, what do you offer us?

Athena
A dwelling free of sorrow. Pray accept.

Chorus
Say we accept, what privileges shall we have?

Athena
No family shall prosper without your grace.

Chorus
Will you ensure us this prerogative?

Athena
I will, and bless all those that worship you.

Chorus
And pledge that assurance for all time to come?

Athena
I need not promise what I will not perform.

Chorus
Your charms are working, and our rage subsides.

Athena
Here make your dwelling, where you shall win friends.

Chorus
What song then shall we chant in salutation?

Athena
A song of faultless victory—from land and sea,
From skies above let gentle breezes blow
And breathing sunshine float from shore to shore;
Let crops and cattle increase and multiply
And children grow in health and happiness,
And let the righteous prosper; for I, as one
Who tends flowers in a garden, cherish fondly
The seed that bears no sorrow. That is your part,
While I in many a battle shall strive until

This city stands victorious against all
Its enemies and renowned throughout the world.

Chorus

We accept; we agree to dwell with you
Here in Athens, which by grace of Zeus
Stands a fortress for the gods,
Jeweled crown of Hellas. So
With you now we join in prayer
That smiling suns and fruitful soils unite to yield
Lifelong joy, fortune fair,
Light and darkness reconciled.

Athena

For the good of my people I have given homes in the city to these deities,[5] whose power is so great and so slowly appeased; and, whenever a man falls foul of them, apprehended to answer for the sins of his fathers, he shall be brought to judgment before them, and the dust shall stifle his proud boast.

Chorus

Free from blight may the early blossom deck
Budding trees, and may no parching drought
Spread across the waving fields.
Rather Pan in season grant
From the flocks and herds a full
Return from year to year, and from the rich
Store which these gods vouchsafe
May the Earth repay them well!

Athena

Guardians of my city, listen to the blessings they bring, and remember that their power is great in heaven and hell, and on earth too they bring to some glad music and to some lives darkened with weeping.

Chorus

Free from sudden death that cuts
Short the prime of manhood, blest
In your daughters too, to whom
Be granted husband and home, and may the dread Fates
Keep them safe, present in every household,
Praised and magnified in every place!

Athena

Fair blessings indeed from powers that so lately were averted in anger, and I thank Zeus and the spirit of persuasion that at last there is no strife left between us, except that they vie with me in blessing my people.

Chorus

Peace to all, free from that
Root of evil, civil strife!
May they live in unity,
And never more may the blood of kin be let flow!
Rather may all of them bonded together
Feel and act as one in love and hate!

Athena

From these dread shapes, so quick to learn a new music, I foresee great good for my people, who, if only they repay their favors with the reverence due, shall surely establish the reign of justice in a city that will shine as a light for all mankind.

[*Enter* ESCORT OF WOMEN, *carrying crimson robes and torches.*

Chorus

Joy to you all in your justly appointed riches,
Joy to all the people blest
With the Virgin's love, who stands
Next beside her Father's throne!
Wisdom man has learnt at last.
Under her protection this
Land enjoys the grace of Zeus.

Athena

Joy to you also, and now let me lead you in torchlight to your new dwelling place! Let solemn oblations speed you in joy to your home beneath the earth, and there imprison all harm while still letting flow your blessings!

Chorus

Joy to you, joy, yet again we pronounce our blessing,
Joy to all the citizens,
Gods and mortals both alike.
While you hold this land and pay
Homage to our residence,
You shall have no cause to blame
Chance and change in human life.

Athena

I thank you for your gracious salutations,
And now you shall be escorted in the light
Of torches to your subterranean dwelling,
Attended by the sacristans of my temple
Together with this company of girls
And married women and others bowed with years.
Women, let them put on these robes of crimson,
And let these blazing torches light the way,
That the goodwill of our new co-residents
Be shown in the manly prowess of your sons!

[*The* CHORUS *put on the crimson robes and a procession is formed led by young men in armor, with the* CHORUS *and the escort following, and behind them the citizens of Athens. The rest is sung as the procession moves away.*

Chorus of the Escort

Pass on your way, O powers majestic,
Daughters of darkness in happy procession!
People of Athens, hush, speak fair!

Pass to the caverns of earth immemorial
There to be worshipped in honor and glory!
People of Athens, hush, speak fair!

Gracious and kindly of heart to our people,
Come with us, holy ones, hither in gladness,
Follow the lamps that illumine the way!
O sing at the end alleluia!

Peace to you, peace of a happy community,
People of Athens! Zeus who beholds all
Watches, himself with the Fates reconciled.
O sing at the end alleluia!

---

[5]This is the transition of the awful goddesses from the *Erinyes* (The Furies) to the *Eumenides* (the Gracious Ones).

EXERCISES

1. Of course all that one has to do to understand this play almost completely is to understand the difference in the meaning of the word *justice* as it is first used in the play by the Furies and as it is used by Athena in her last speech of the play. That difference in meaning is worth analyzing in class. To do so, here are some questions which may guide your discussion:

a. Insofar as the structure of the play is concerned— and its significance—why can Orestes leave when two-thirds of the play is over?

b. The Furies insist that *fear* is a necessary part of the idea of justice that people hold. How right are they?

c. The real turning point of the play probably comes when Athena gives her final instructions to the jury:

>   Here reverence
> For law and inbred fear among my people

Shall hold their hands from evil night and day,
Only let them not tamper with the laws,
But keep the fountain pure and sweet to drink.
I warn you not to banish from your lives
All terror but to seek the mean between
Autocracy and anarchy; and in this way
You shall possess in ages yet unborn
An impregnable fortress of liberty. . .

What principles are involved in this statement?

d. The actual role of the Eumenides (as they are changed from the Furies) is never made entirely clear. From the evidence in the play itself, what seems to be their role in the maintenance of a new type of justice?

2. What difference in the lives of the people of Athens will be found as they change from the old idea of justice to the new? In what way will the new idea allow for personal freedom?

Pericles' Memorial Oration

This portion of Pericles' famous oration is taken from the history of the Peloponnesian War as written by Thucydides. Pericles made this address at the public funeral of a group of Athenian young men who had been killed in the war.

As a method of study, you might ask yourself what questions about human life had been raised previously in the plays of Aeschylus. In the *Agamemnon* the chorus railed against great wealth or great action, insisting that the most humble life was the best. In *Eumenides* we observed the question of whether justice should be by reason or by stern revenge within the family. The question of the conflict between maturing man and an absolute god who ruled through fear had been raised. Other questions which we have not yet seen in the literature, but which were present in the Greek mind (and in our own) are whether the state needs to protect itself by universal military training or not, and whether a life of cultural pursuits does not enfeeble people in a nation. Perhaps the greatest question for our time and theirs is whether a democracy can really function. The argument on the one side is that an absolute government gets things done quickly and efficiently, while in a democracy, people talk so much that they have no time for action.

You will find some of the answers in which the Athenians believed in the following selection.

. . . Before I praise the dead, I should like to point out by what principles of action we rose to power, and under what institutions and through what manner of life our empire became great. For I conceive that such thoughts are not unsuited to the occasion, and that this numerous assembly of citizens and strangers may profitably listen to them.

Our form of government does not enter into rivalry with the institutions of others. We do not copy our neighbors, but are an example to them. It is true that we are called a democracy; for the administration is in the hands of the many and not of the few. But while the law secures equal justice to all alike in their private disputes, the claim of excellence is also recognized; and when a citizen is in any way distinguished, he is preferred to the public service, not as a matter of privilege, but as the reward of merit. Neither is poverty a bar, but a man may benefit his country whatever be the obscurity of his condition. There is no exclusiveness in our public life, and in our private intercourse we are not suspicious of one another, nor angry with our neighbor if he does what he likes; we do not put on sour looks at him, which

though harmless are not pleasant. While we are thus unconstrained in our private intercourse, a spirit of reverence pervades our public acts: we are prevented from doing wrong by respect for authority and for the laws; having an especial regard to those which are ordained for the protection of the injured, as well as to these unwritten laws which bring upon the transgressor of them the reprobation of the general sentiment.

And we have not forgotten to provide for our weary spirits many relaxations from toil; we have regular games and sacrifices throughout the year; at home the style of our life is refined; and the delight which we daily feel in all these things helps to banish melancholy. Because of the greatness of our city the fruits of the whole earth flow in upon us; so that we enjoy the goods of other countries as freely as of our own.

Then again, our military training is in many respects superior to that of our adversaries. Our city is thrown open to the world; and we never expel a foreigner, or prevent him from seeing or learning anything of which the secret, if revealed to an enemy, might profit him. We rely not upon management of trickery, but upon our own hearts and hands. And in the matter of education whereas they from early youth are always undergoing laborious exercises which are to make them brave, we live at ease, and yet are equally ready to face the perils which they face . . .

If, then, we prefer to meet danger with a light heart but without laborious training, and with a courage which is gained by habit and not enforced by law, are we not greatly the gainers? Since we do not anticipate the pain, although, when the hour comes, we can be as brave as those who never allow themselves to rest; and thus too our city is equally admirable in peace and in war. For we are lovers of the beautiful, yet simple in our tastes, and we cultivate the mind without loss of manliness. Wealth we employ, not for talk and ostentation, but when there is a real use for it. To avow poverty with us is no disgrace; the true disgrace is in doing nothing to avoid it. An Athenian citizen does not neglect the State because he takes care of his own household; and even those of us who are engaged in business have a very fair idea of politics. We alone regard a man who takes no interest in public affairs, not as a harmless but as a useless character; and if few of us are originators, we are all sound judges, of a policy. The great impediment to action is, in our opinion, not discussion, but the want of that knowledge which is gained by discussion preparatory to action. For we have a peculiar power of thinking before we act, and of acting too; whereas other men are courageous from ignorance but hesitate upon reflection. And they are surely to be esteemed the bravest spirits, who, having the clearest sense both of the pains and the pleasures of life, do not on that account shrink from danger. In doing good, again we are unlike others; we make our friends by conferring, not by receiving favors. Now he who confers a favor is the firmer friend, because he would fain by kindness keep alive the memory of an obligation; but the recipient is colder in his feelings, because he knows that in requiting another's generosity he will not be winning gratitude, but only paying a debt. We alone do good to our neighbors not upon a calculation of interest, but in the confidence of freedom and in a frank and fearless spirit.

To sum up: I say that Athens is the school of Hellas, and that the individual Athenian in his own person seems to have the power of adapting himself to the most varied forms of action with the utmost versatility and grace. This is no passing and idle word, but truth and fact; and the assertion is verified by the position to which these qualities have raised the State. For in the hour of trial, Athens alone among her contemporaries is superior to the report of her. No enemy who comes against her is indignant at the reverses which he sustains at the hands of such a city; no subject complains that his masters are unworthy of him. And we shall assuredly not be without witnesses: there are mighty monuments of our power, which will make us the wonder of this and of succeeding ages; we shall not need the praises of Homer or of any other panegyrist, whose poetry may please for the moment although his representation of the facts will not bear the light of day. For we have compelled every land and every sea to open a path for our valor, and have everywhere planted eternal memorials of our friendship and of our enmity. Such is the city for whose sake these men nobly fought and died: they could not bear the thought that she might be taken from them; and every one of us who survive should gladly toil on her behalf.

EXERCISES

1. The chorus of *Agamemnon* cautions against the evils of wealth. We, too, have a proverb about money and evil. How have the Greeks grown since Aeschylus wrote of the earlier populace? How would Pericles argue with our own proverb?

2. What stand would Pericles take on the question of universal military training?

3. Here is raised an old question about men of words and men of action. It is frequently said that the democratic ways are terribly slow because people spend their time talking and never act. Is a compromise between words and action possible?

4. Why does Pericles speak of the individual Athenian when he is making a summary of the government?

Oedipus the King

Sophocles

This play is perhaps the best known of all the Greek tragedies since it was taken by Aristotle in his volume, *Poetics*, as a model for this form of drama. All of the classic elements of tragedy are here: a man of great stature who falls from high station to low because of a fatal flaw in his personality; the unity of time (one day) and of place (the exterior of the royal palace at Thebes); the calling forth of the emotions of pity and fear in the spectator; and the final sense of catharsis. This last might be defined as the sense that the action has worked itself out to its one inevitable conclusion. In doing so, the emotions of pity and fear are purged in the spectator, so that he is left at peace. We feel that the ending, though tragic, is right, and that there is no more to be said or done.

In order to understand the play, one should know some of the mythology which lies in its background. The city of Thebes was founded by Cadmus, as we are reminded frequently in the speeches. The history which follows is not of immediate concern until we come to the reign of King Laius and his queen, Jocasta. Two things happened at that time. First, Laius set out on a journey and was murdered on the road by unknown assailants. In the meantime a fearful monster known as the Sphinx (to whom frequent references are made in the play) established itself outside the gate of Thebes and demanded a yearly tribute from the city. This was to continue until someone could solve the riddle which the Sphinx proposed to every passer-by. The riddle, we might think, is a simple one, for it was the old one, "What goes on four legs in the morning, on two legs at noon, and on three legs in the evening?" The answer, of course, is *Man*. The riddle and its answer in this play are symbolic of the idea that the one who could solve the riddle knew the nature of man.

To the city at this time came a young man, Oedipus, supposedly the son of the king and queen of Corinth. The Sphinx posed her riddle and he gave the right answer readily, thus freeing the city of the monster and the tribute she demanded. The king being dead, the people of the city chose Oedipus as their king. As was the custom, he married Jocasta who bore him two sons and two daughters. It is several years after this when the play begins.

One question that this play might bring up in the mind of a spectator is whether Oedipus is the victim of fate, or whether he is a man with free will whose character is his fate and produces his doom. Probably one will not find a clear answer to this question. In this connection one might ask what is the fatal flaw in Oedipus' character. Is it his sudden anger? Is it his impulsiveness in all of his actions, an impulsiveness which might be of great value to a ruler who must make quick decisions? Or is it his search for truth which will not be turned aside even when his wife and the chorus suggest that he should leave well-enough alone? This last, again, would be a good quality in most men. Another interesting point is that of clear vision: Oedipus sees all things clearly; Tiresias is blind and sees truth with a sort of inner sight. Which one beholds more clearly? And why is the wound which Oedipus inflicts upon himself not only *an* appropriate one, but *the* appropriate one?

OEDIPUS THE KING

Characters in the Play

OEDIPUS, *King of Thebes*

JOCASTA, *Queen of Thebes, wife and mother of* OEDIPUS

CREON, *brother of* JOCASTA

TIRESIAS, *a prophet*

BOY, *attendant of* TIRESIAS

PRIEST OF ZEUS

SHEPHERD

FIRST MESSENGER, *from Corinth*

SECOND MESSENGER

CHORUS *of Theban elders*

ATTENDANTS

OEDIPUS THE KING

SCENE: *Before the doors of the palace of* OEDIPUS *at Thebes. A crowd of citizens are seated next to the two altars at the sides. In front of one of the altars stands the* PRIEST OF ZEUS.

Enter OEDIPUS

OEDIPUS:

Why are you here as suppliants, my children,
You in whose veins the blood of Cadmus flows?
What is the reason for your boughs of olive,
The fumes of incense, the laments and prayers
That fill the city? Because I thought it wrong,
My children, to depend on what was told me,
I have come to you myself, I, Oedipus,
Renowned in the sight of all. (*to* PRIEST) Tell me—you are
Their natural spokesman—what desire or fear
Brings you before me? I will gladly give you   10
Such help as is in my power. It would be heartless
Not to take pity on a plea like this.

PRIEST:

King Oedipus, you see us, young and old,
Gathered about your altars: some, mere fledglings
Not able yet to fly; some, bowed with age;
Some, priests, and I the priest of Zeus among them;
And these, who are the flower of our young manhood.
The rest of us are seated—the whole city—
With our wreathed branches in the market places,
Before the shrines of Pallas, before the fire   20
By which we read the auguries of Apollo.
Thebes, as you see yourself, is overwhelmed
By the waves of death that break upon her head.
No fruit comes from her blighted buds; her cattle
Die in the fields; her wives bring forth dead children.
A hideous pestilence consumes the city,
Striking us down like a god armed with fire,
Emptying the house of Cadmus, filling full
The dark of Hades with loud lamentation.
I and these children have not thronged your altars   30
Because we hold you equal to the immortals,
But because we hold you foremost among men,
Both in the happenings of daily life
And when some visitation of the gods
Confronts us. For we know that when you came here,
You freed us from our bondage, the bitter tribute
The Sphinx wrung from us by her sorceries.
And we know too that you accomplished this

Without foreknowledge, or clue that we could furnish.
We think, indeed, some god befriended you,   40
When you renewed our lives. Therefore, great king,
Glorious in all men's eyes, we now beseech you
To find some way of helping us, your suppliants,
Some way the gods themselves have told you of,
Or one that lies within our mortal power;
For the words of men experienced in evil
Are mighty and effectual. Oedipus!
Rescue our city and preserve your honor,
Since the land hails you as her savior now
For your past service. Never let us say   50
That when you ruled us, we were lifted up
Only to be thrown down. Restore the state
And keep it forever steadfast. Bring again
The happiness and good fortune you once brought us.
If you are still to reign as you reign now,
Then it is better to have men for subjects
Than to be king of a mere wilderness,
Since neither ship nor town has any value
Without companions or inhabitants.

OEDIPUS:

I pity you, my children. Well I know   60
What hopes have brought you here, and well I know
That all of you are suffering. Yet your grief,
However great, is not so great as mine.
Each of you suffers for himself alone,
But my heart feels the heaviness of my sorrow,
Your sorrow, and the sorrow of all the others.
You have not roused me, I have not been sleeping.
No. I have wept, wept long and bitterly,
Treading the devious paths of anxious thought;
And I have taken the only hopeful course   70
That I could find. I have sent my kinsman, Creon,
Son of Menoeceus, to the Pythian home[1]
Of Phoebus Apollo to find what word or deed
Of mine might save the city. He has delayed
Too long already, his absence troubles me;
But when he comes, I pledge myself to do
My utmost to obey the god's command.

PRIEST:

Your words are timely, for even as you speak
They sign to me that Creon is drawing near.

OEDIPUS:

O Lord Apollo! Grant he may bring to us   80
Fortune as smiling as his smiling face.

PRIEST:

Surely he brings good fortune. Look! The crown
Of bay leaves that he wears is full of berries.

OEDIPUS:

We shall know soon, for he is close enough
To hear us. Brother, son of Menoeceus, speak!
What news? What news do you bring us from the god?

Enter CREON

CREON:

Good news. If we can find the fitting way
To end this heavy scourge, all will be well.

OEDIPUS:

That neither gives me courage nor alarms me.
What does the god say? What is the oracle?   90

CREON:

If you wish me to speak in public, I will do so.
Otherwise let us go in and speak alone.

OEDIPUS:

Speak here before everyone. I feel more sorrow
For their sakes than I feel for my own life.

CREON:

Then I will give the message of Lord Phoebus:
A plain command to drive out the pollution

---

[1]That is the oracle at Delphi.

Here in our midst, and not to nourish it
Till our disease has grown incurable.

OEDIPUS:

  What rite will purge us? How are we corrupted?

CREON:

  We must banish a man, or have him put to death   100
To atone for the blood he shed, for it is blood
That has brought this tempest down upon the city.

OEDIPUS:

  Who is the victim whose murder is revealed?

CREON:

  King Laius, who was our lord before you came
To steer the city on its proper course.

OEDIPUS:

  I know his name well, but I never saw him.

CREON:

  Laius was killed, and now we are commanded
To punish his killers, whoever they may be.

OEDIPUS:

  How can they be discovered? Where shall we look
For the faint traces of this ancient crime?   110

CREON:

  In Thebes, the god said. Truth can be always found:
Only what is neglected ever escapes.

OEDIPUS:

  Where was King Laius murdered? In his home,
Out in the fields, or in some foreign land?

CREON:

  He told us he was journeying to Delphi.
After he left, he was never seen again.

OEDIPUS:

  Was no one with King Laius who saw what happened?
You could have put his story to good use.

CREON:

  The sole survivor fled from the scene in terror,
And there was only one thing he was sure of.   120

OEDIPUS:

  What was it? A clue might lead us far
Which gave us even the faintest glimmer of hope.

CREON:

  He said that they were violently attacked
Not by one man but by a band of robbers.

OEDIPUS:

  Robbers are not so daring. Were they bribed
To commit this crime by some one here in Thebes?

CREON:

  That was suspected. But in our time of trouble
No one appeared to avenge the death of Laius.

OEDIPUS:

  But your King was killed! What troubles could you have had
To keep you from searching closely for his killers?   130

CREON:

  We had the Sphinx. Her riddle made us turn
From mysteries to what lay before our doors.

OEDIPUS:

  Then I will start fresh and again make clear
Things that are dark. All honor to Apollo
And to you, Creon, for acting as you have done
On the dead King's behalf. So I will take
My rightful place beside you as your ally,
Avenging Thebes and bowing to the god.
Not for a stranger will I dispel this taint,
But for my own sake, since the murderer,   140
Whoever he is, may strike at me as well.
Therefore in helping Laius I help myself.
Come, children, come! Rise from the altar steps,
And carry away those branches. Summon here
The people of Cadmus. Tell them I mean to leave
Nothing undone. So with Apollo's aid
We may at last be saved—or meet destruction.

                             Exit OEDIPUS

PRIEST:

  My children, let us go. The King has promised
The favor that we sought. And may Lord Phoebus

Come to us with his oracles, assuage   150
Our misery, and deliver us from death.

                        Exeunt. Enter CHORUS

CHORUS:

  The god's great word, in whose sweetness we ever rejoice,
    To our glorious city is drawing nigh,
  Now, even now, from the gold of the Delphic shrine.
    What next decree will be thine,
  Apollo, thou healer, to whom in our dread we cry?
    We are anguished, racked, and beset by fears!
  What fate will be ours? One fashioned for us alone,
    Or one that in ancient time was known
    That returns once more with the circling years?   160
  Child of our golden hope, O speak, thou immortal voice!

  Divine Athene, daughter of Zeus, O hear![2]
    Hear thou, Artemis! Thee we hail,
  Our guardian goddess throned in the market place.
    Apollo, we ask thy grace.
  Shine forth, all three, and the menace of death will fail.
    Answer our call! Shall we call in vain?
  If ever ye came in the years that have gone before,
    Return, and save us from plague once more,
    Rescue our city from fiery pain!   170
  Be your threefold strength our shield. Draw near to us now, draw near!

  Death is upon us. We bear a burden of bitter grief.
  There is nothing can save us now, no device that our thought can frame.
    No blossom, no fruit, no harvest sheaf
    Springs from the blighted and barren earth.
  Women cry out in travail and bring no children to birth;
    But swift as a bird, swift as the sweep of flame,
    Life after life takes sudden flight
  To the western god, to the last, dark shore of night.
    Ruin has fallen on Thebes. Without number her children are
        dead;   180
  Unmourned, unattended, unpitied, they lie polluting the ground.
    Grey-haired mothers and wives new-wed
    Wail at the altars everywhere,
  With entreaty, with loud lament, with clamor filling the air.
    And songs of praise to Apollo, the healer, resound.
    Athene, thou knowest our desperate need.
  Lend us thy strength. Give heed to our prayer, give heed!

  Fierce Ares has fallen upon us. He comes unarrayed for war,
  Yet he fills our ears with shrieking, he folds us in fiery death.
    Grant that he soon may turn in headlong flight from our land,   190
  Swept to the western deep by the fair wind's favoring breath,
    Or swept to the savage sea that washes the Thracian shore.
  We few who escape the night are stricken down in the day.
  O Zeus, whose bolts of thunder are balanced within thy hand,
  Hurl down thy lightning upon him! Father, be swift to slay!

  Save us, light-bringing Phoebus! The shower of thine arrows let fly;
  Loose them, triumphant and swift, from the golden string of thy bow!
  O goddess, his radiant sister, roaming the Lycian glade,
  Come with the flash of thy fire! Artemis, conquer our foe!
    And thou, O wine-flushed god to whom the Bacchantes cry,   200
  With thy brilliant torch ablaze amid shouts of thy maenad train,
    With thy hair enwreathed with gold, O Bacchus, we beg thine aid
  Against our destroyer Ares, the god whom the gods disdain!

                           Enter OEDIPUS

OEDIPUS:

  You have been praying. If you heed my words
And seek the remedy for your own disease,

---

[2]These appeals to the gods are understandable, chiefly as cries of despair. Ares, referred to in line 188, is the God of War and here chiefly suggests destruction. Bacchus or Dionysus (line 200) was the patron god of Thebes, and his devotees, the bacchantes, held wild revels in the streets of the city.

The gods will hear your prayers, and you will find
Relief and comfort. I myself know nothing
About this story, nothing about the murder,
So that unaided and without a clue
I could not have tracked it down for any distance.   210
And because I have only recently been received
Among you as a citizen, to you all,
And to all the rest, I make this proclamation:
Whoever knows the man who killed King Laius,
Let him declare his knowledge openly.
If he himself is guilty, let him confess
And go unpunished, except for banishment.
Or if he knows the murderer was an alien,
Let him by speaking earn his due reward,
And thanks as well. But if he holds his tongue,   220
Hoping to save himself or save a friend,
Then let him hear what I, the King, decree
For all who live in Thebes, the land I rule.
No one shall give this murderer shelter. No one
Shall speak to him. No one shall let him share
In sacrifice or prayer or lustral rites.
The door of every house is barred against him.
The god has shown me that he is polluted.
So by this edict I ally myself
With Phoebus and the slain. As for the slayer,   230
Whether he had accomplices or not,
This is my solemn prayer concerning him:
May evil come of evil; may he live
A wretched life and meet a wretched end.
And as for me, if I should knowingly
Admit him as a member of my household,
May the same fate which I invoked for others
Fall upon me. Make my words good, I charge you,
For love of me, Apollo, and our country
Blasted by the displeasure of the gods.   240
You should not have left this guilt unpurified,
Even without an oracle to urge you,
When a man so noble, a man who was your King,
Had met his death. Rather, it was your duty
To seek the truth. But now, since it is I
Who hold the sovereignty that once was his,
I who have wed his wife, who would have been
Bound to him by the tie of having children
Born of one mother, if he had had a child
To be a blessing, if fate had not struck him down—   250
Since this is so, I intend to fight his battle
As though he were my father. I will leave
Nothing undone to find his murderer,
Avenging him and all his ancestors.
And I pray the gods that those who disobey
May suffer. May their fields bring forth no harvest,
Their wives no children; may the present plague,
Or one yet worse, consume them. But as for you,
All of you citizens who are loyal to me,
May Justice, our champion, and all the gods   260
Show you their favor in the days to come.

CHORUS:

King Oedipus, I will speak to avoid your curse.
I am no slayer, nor can I point him out.
The question came to us from Phoebus Apollo;
It is for him to tell us who is guilty.

OEDIPUS:

Yes. But no man on earth is strong enough
To force the gods to act against their will.

CHORUS:

There is, I think, a second course to follow.

OEDIPUS:

If there is yet a third, let me know that.

CHORUS:

Tiresias, the prophet, has the clearest vision   270
Next to our Lord Apollo. He is the man
Who can do most to help us in our search.

OEDIPUS:

I have not forgotten. Creon suggested it,
And I have summoned him, summoned him twice.
I am astonished he is not here already.

CHORUS:

The only rumors are old and half-forgotten.

OEDIPUS:

What are they? I must find out all I can.

CHORUS:

It is said the King was killed by travelers.

OEDIPUS:

So I have heard, but there is no eye-witness.

CHORUS:

If fear can touch them, they will reveal themselves   280
Once they have heard so dreadful a curse as yours.

OEDIPUS:

Murderers are not terrified by words.

CHORUS:

But they can be convicted by the man
Being brought here now, Tiresias. He alone
Is godlike in his knowledge of the truth.

Enter TIRESIAS,[4] *led by a* BOY

OEDIPUS:

You know all things in heaven and earth, Tiresias:
Things you may speak of openly, and secrets
Holy and not to be revealed. You know,
Blind though you are, the plague that ruins Thebes.
And you, great prophet, you alone can save us.   290
Phoebus has sent an answer to our question,
An answer that the messengers may have told you,
Saying there was no cure for our condition
Until we found the killers of King Laius
And banished them or had them put to death.
Therefore, Tiresias, do not begrudge your skill
In the voice of birds or other prophecy,
But save yourself, save me, save the whole city,
Save everything that the pestilence defiles.
We are at your mercy, and man's noblest task   300
Is to use all his powers in helping others.

TIRESIAS:

How dreadful a thing, how dreadful a thing is wisdom,
When to be wise is useless! This I knew
But I forgot, or else I would never have come.

OEDIPUS:

What is the matter? Why are you so troubled?

TIRESIAS:

Oedipus, let me go home. Then you will bear
Your burden, and I mine, more easily.

OEDIPUS:

Custom entitles us to hear your message.
By being silent you harm your native land.

TIRESIAS:

You do not know when, and when not to speak.   310
Silence will save me from the same misfortune.

OEDIPUS:

If you can be of help, then all of us
Kneel and implore you not to turn away.

---

[3]This whole passage is filled with dramatic irony: that is, the audience understands the words in another sense than the speaker means them.

[4]Tiresias is a blind prophet, a priest of Apollo. He seems to have been almost infinitely old, and was both masculine and feminine. Consequently his wisdom was almost without bounds. Priests often made their prophecies after observing flights of birds, listening to the cries of birds, observing the entrails of sacrificial animals, etc.

TIRESIAS: None of you know the truth, but I will never
Reveal my sorrow—not to call it yours.

OEDIPUS: What are you saying? You know and will not speak?
You mean to betray us and destroy the city?

TIRESIAS: I refuse to pain you. I refuse to pain myself.
It is useless to ask me. I will tell you nothing.

OEDIPUS: You utter scoundrel! You would enrage a stone!
Is there no limit to your stubbornness?

TIRESIAS: You blame my anger and forget your own.

OEDIPUS: No one could help being angry when he heard
How you dishonor and ignore the state.   320

TIRESIAS: What is to come will come, though I keep silent

OEDIPUS: If it must come, your duty is to speak.

TIRESIAS: I will say no more. Rage to your heart's content.

OEDIPUS: Rage? Yes, I will rage! I will spare you nothing.
In the plot against King Laius, I have no doubt
That you were an accomplice, yes, almost
The actual killer. If you had not been blind,
I would have said that you alone were guilty.

TIRESIAS: Then listen to my command! Obey the edict
That you yourself proclaimed and never speak,   330
From this day on, to me or any Theban.
You are the sinner who pollutes our land.

OEDIPUS: Have you no shame? How do you hope to escape
The consequence of such an accusation?

TIRESIAS: I have escaped. My strength is the living truth.

OEDIPUS: This is no prophecy. Who taught you this?

TIRESIAS: You did. You forced me to speak against my will.

OEDIPUS: Repeat your slander. Let me learn it better.

TIRESIAS: Are you trying to tempt me into saying more?
I have spoken already. Have you not understood?   340

OEDIPUS: No, not entirely. Give your speech again.

TIRESIAS: I say you are the killer, you yourself.

OEDIPUS: Twice the same insult! You will pay for it.

TIRESIAS: Shall I say more to make you still more angry?

OEDIPUS: Say what you want to. It will make no sense.

TIRESIAS: You are living in shame with those most dear to you,
As yet in ignorance of your dreadful fate.

OEDIPUS: Do you suppose that you can always use
Language like that and not be punished for it?

TIRESIAS: Yes. I am safe, if truth has any strength.   350

OEDIPUS: Truth can save anyone excepting you,
You with no eyes, no hearing, and no brains!

TIRESIAS: Poor fool! You taunt me, but you soon will hear
The self-same insults heaped upon your head.

OEDIPUS: You live in endless night. What can you do
To me or anyone else who sees the day?

TIRESIAS: Nothing. I have no hand in your destruction.
For that, Apollo needs no help from me.

OEDIPUS: Apollo! Is this your trick, or is it Creon's?

TIRESIAS: Creon is guiltless. The evil is in you.   360

OEDIPUS: How great is the envy roused by wealth, by kingship,
By the subtle skill that triumphs over others
In life's hard struggle! Creon, who has been
For years my trusted friend, has stealthily
Crept in upon me anxious to seize my power,
The unsought gift the city freely gave me.
Anxious to overthrow me, he has bribed
This scheming mountebank, this fraud, this trickster,
Blind in his art and in everything but money!
Your art of prophecy! When have you shown it?   370
Not when the watch-dog of the gods was here,
Chanting her riddle. Why did you say nothing,
When you might have saved the city? Yet her puzzle
Could not be solved by the first passer-by.
A prophet's skill was needed, and you proved
That you had no such skill, either in birds
Or any other means the gods have given.
But I came, I, the ignorant Oedipus,
And silenced her. I had no birds to help me.
I used my brains. And it is I you now   380
Are trying to destroy in the hope of standing
Close beside Creon's throne. You will regret
This zeal of yours to purify the land,
You and your fellow-plotter. You seem old;
Otherwise you would pay for your presumption.

CHORUS: Sir, it appears to us that both of you
Have spoken in anger. Anger serves no purpose.
Rather we should consider in what way
We best can carry out the god's command.

TIRESIAS: King though you are, I have a right to answer   390
Equal to yours. In that I too am king.
I serve Apollo. I do not acknowledge
You as my lord or Creon as my patron.
You have seen fit to taunt me with my blindness.
Therefore I tell you this: you have your eyesight
And cannot see the sin of your existence,
Cannot see where you live or whom you live with,
Are ignorant of your parents, bring disgrace
Upon your kindred in the world below
And here on earth. And soon the double lash   400
Of your mother's and father's curse will drive you headlong
Out of the country, blinded, with your cries
Heard everywhere, echoed by every hill
In all Cithaeron. Then you will have learned
The meaning of your marriage, learned in what harbor,
After so fair a voyage, you were shipwrecked.
And other horrors you could never dream of
Will teach you who you are, will drag you down
To the level of your children. Heap your insults
On Creon and my message if you choose to.   410
Still no one ever will endure the weight
Of greater misery than will fall on you.

OEDIPUS: Am I supposed to endure such talk as this,
Such talk from him? Go, curse you, go! Be quick!

TIRESIAS: Except for your summons I would never have come.

OEDIPUS: And I would never have sent for you so soon
If I had known you would prove to be a fool.

TIRESIAS: Yes. I have proved a fool—in your opinion,
And yet your parents thought that I was wise.

OEDIPUS: What parents? Wait! Who was my father? Tell me!   420

TIRESIAS:
>Today will see your birth and your destruction.

OEDIPUS:
>You cannot speak unless you speak in riddles!

TIRESIAS:
>And yet how brilliant you are in solving them!

OEDIPUS:
>You sneer at me for what has made me great.

TIRESIAS:
>The same good fortune that has ruined you.

OEDIPUS:
>If I have saved the city, nothing else matters.

TIRESIAS:
>In that case I will go. Boy, take me home.

OEDIPUS:
>Yes, let him take you. Here, you are in the way.
>Once you are gone, you will give no further trouble.

TIRESIAS:
>I will not go before I have said my say,   430
>Indifferent to your black looks. You cannot harm me.
>And I say this: the man whom you have sought,
>Whom you have threatened, whom you have proclaimed
>The killer of King Laius—he is here.
>Now thought an alien, he shall prove to be
>A native Theban, to his deep dismay.
>Now he has eyesight, now his wealth is great;
>But he shall make his way to foreign soil
>Blinded, in beggary, groping with a stick.
>In his own household he shall be shown to be   440
>The father of his children—and their brother,
>Son to the woman who bore him—and her husband,
>The killer and the bedfellow of his father.
>Go and consider this; and if you find
>That I have been mistaken, you can say
>That I have lost my skill in prophecy.

Exeunt OEDIPUS *and* TIRESIAS

CHORUS:

What man is this the god from the Delphic rock denounces,
>Whose deeds are too shameful to tell, whose murderous hands
>>are red?
Let his feet be swifter now than hooves of horses racing
>The storm-clouds overhead.   450
For Zeus's son, Apollo, leaps in anger upon him,
>Armed with lightning to strike and slay;
And the terrible Fates, unflagging, relentless,
>Follow the track of their prey.

The words of the god have flashed from the peaks of snowy Parnassus,
>Commanding us all to seek this killer as yet unknown.
Deep in the tangled woods, through rocks and caves he is roaming
>Like a savage bull, alone.
On his lonely path he journeys, wretched, broken by sorrow,
>Seeking to flee from the fate he fears;   460
But the voice from the center of earth that doomed him
>Inescapably rings in his ears.
Dreadful, dreadful those words! We can neither approve nor
>>deny them.
>Shaken, confounded with fears, we know not what to say.
Nothing is clear to us, nothing—what is to come tomorrow,
>Or what is upon us today.
If the prophet seeks revenge for the unsolved murder of Laius,
>Why is Oedipus charged with crime?
Because some deep-rooted hate divides their royal houses?
>The houses of Laius and Oedipus, son of the King of Corinth?   470
>There is none that we know of, now, or in ancient time.

From Zeus's eyes and Apollo's no human secret is hidden;
>But man has no test for truth, no measure his wit can devise.
Tiresias, indeed, excels in every art of his office,
>And yet we too may be wise.
Though Oedipus stands accused, until he is proven guilty
>We cannot blacken his name;
>For he showed his wisdom the day the wingéd maiden faced him.

He triumphed in that ordeal, saved us, and won our affection.
We can never believe he stooped to an act of shame.   480

Enter CREON

CREON:
>Thebans, I come here outraged and indignant,
>For I have learned that Oedipus has accused me
>Of dreadful crimes. If, in the present crisis,
>He thinks that I have wronged him in any way,
>Wronged him in word or deed, then let my life
>Come to a speedy close. I cannot bear
>The burden of such scandal. The attack
>Ruins me utterly, if my friends, and you,
>And the whole city are to call me traitor.

CHORUS:
>Perhaps his words were only a burst of anger,   490
>And were not meant as a deliberate insult.

CREON:
>He *did* say that I plotted with Tiresias?
>And that the prophet lied at my suggestion?

CHORUS:
>Those were his words. I cannot guess his motive.

CREON:
>Were his eyes clear and steady? Was his mind
>Unclouded, when he brought this charge against me?

CHORUS:
>I cannot say. To see what princes do
>Is not our province. Here comes the King himself.

Enter OEDIPUS

OEDIPUS:
>So you are here! What brought you to my door?
>Impudence? Insolence? You, my murderer!   500
>You, the notorious stealer of my crown!
>Why did you hatch this plot? What kind of man,
>By heaven, what kind of man, could you have thought me?
>A coward or a fool? Did you suppose
>I would not see your trickery take shape,
>Or when I saw it, would not counter it?
>How stupid you were to reach for royal power
>Without a troop of followers or rich friends!
>Only a mob and money win a kingdom.

CREON:
>Sir, let me speak. When you have heard my answer,   510
>You will have grounds on which to base your judgment.

OEDIPUS:
>I cannot follow all your clever talk.
>I only know that you are dangerous.

CREON:
>That is the issue. Let me explain that first.

OEDIPUS:
>Do not explain that you are true to me.

CREON:
>If you imagine that a blind self-will
>Is strength of character, you are mistaken.

OEDIPUS:
>As you are, if you strike at your own house,
>And then expect to escape all punishment.

CREON:
>Yes, you are right. That would be foolishness.   520
>But tell me, what have I done? How have I harmed you?

OEDIPUS:
>Did you, or did you not, urge me to summon
>Tiresias, that revered, that holy prophet?

CREON:
>Yes. And I still think my advice was good.

OEDIPUS:
>Then answer this: how long ago was Laius—

CREON:
>Laius! Why how am I concerned with him?

OEDIPUS:
>How many years ago was Laius murdered?

CREON:
>So many they cannot easily be counted.

OEDIPUS:
>And was Tiresias just as cunning then?

CREON:
>As wise and honored as he is today. 530

OEDIPUS:
>At that time did he ever mention me?

CREON:
>Not in my hearing. I am sure of that.

OEDIPUS:
>And the murderer—a thorough search was made?

CREON:
>Yes, certainly, but we discovered nothing.

OEDIPUS:
>Then why did the man of wisdom hold his tongue?

CREON:
>I cannot say. Guessing is not my habit.

OEDIPUS:
>One thing at least you need not guess about.

CREON:
>What is it? If I know it, I will tell you.

OEDIPUS:
>Tiresias would not have said I murdered Laius,
>If you two had not put your heads together. 540

CREON:
>You best know what he said. But now I claim
>The right to take my turn in asking questions.

OEDIPUS:
>Very well, ask. You never can find me guilty.

CREON:
>Then answer this: my sister is your wife?

OEDIPUS:
>I cannot deny that fact. She is my wife.

CREON:
>And in your rule she has an equal share?

OEDIPUS:
>She has no wish that goes unsatisfied.

CREON:
>And as the third I stand beside you both?

OEDIPUS:
>True. That position proves your treachery.

CREON:
>No. You would see, if you thought the matter through 550
>As I have done. Consider. Who would choose
>Kingship and all the terrors that go with it,
>If, with the same power, he could sleep in peace?
>I have no longing for a royal title
>Rather than royal freedom. No, not I,
>Nor any moderate man. Now I fear nothing.
>Every request I make of you is granted,
>And yet as king I should have many duties
>That went against the grain. Then how could rule
>Be sweeter than untroubled influence? 560
>I have not lost my mind. I want no honors
>Except the ones that bring me solid good.
>Now all men welcome me and wish me joy.
>Now all your suitors ask to speak with me,
>Knowing they cannot otherwise succeed.
>Why should I throw away a life like this
>For a king's life? No one is treacherous
>Who knows his own best interests. To conspire
>With other men, or to be false myself,
>Is not my nature. Put me to the test. 570
>First, go to Delphi. Ask if I told the truth
>About the oracle. Then if you find
>I have had dealings with Tiresias, kill me.
>My voice will echo yours in passing sentence.
>But base your verdict upon something more
>Than mere suspicion. Great injustice comes
>From random judgments that bad men are good
>And good men bad. To throw away a friend
>Is, in effect, to throw away your life,
>The prize you treasure most. All this, in time, 580
>Will become clear to you, for time alone
>Proves a man's honesty, but wickedness
>Can be discovered in a single day.

CHORUS:
>Sir, that is good advice, if one is prudent.
>Hasty decisions always lead to danger.

OEDIPUS:
>When a conspiracy is quick in forming,
>I must move quickly to retaliate.
>If I sat still and let my enemy act,
>I would lose everything that he would gain.

CREON:
>So then, my banishment is what you want? 590

OEDIPUS:
>No, not your banishment. Your execution.

CREON:
>I think you are mad.   OE.: I can protect myself.

CREON:
>You should protect me also.   OE.: You? A traitor?

CREON:
>Suppose you are wrong?   OE.: I am the King. I rule.

CREON:
>Not if you rule unjustly.   OE.: Thebes! Hear that!

CREON:
>Thebes is my city too, as well as yours.

CHORUS:
>No more, no more, sirs! Here is Queen Jocasta.
>She comes in time to help make peace between you.

Enter JOCASTA

JOCASTA:
>Oedipus! Creon! How can you be so foolish?
>What! Quarrel now about a private matter 600
>When the land is dying? You should be ashamed.
>Come, Oedipus, come in. Creon, go home.
>You make a trivial problem too important.

CREON:
>Sister, your husband has made dreadful threats.
>He claims the right to have me put to death
>Or have me exiled. He need only choose.

OEDIPUS:
>Yes. I have caught him at his treachery,
>Plotting against the person of the King.

CREON:
>If I am guilty, may it be my fate
>To live in misery and to die accursed. 610

JOCASTA:
>Believe him, Oedipus, believe him, spare him—
>I beg you by the gods—for his oath's sake,
>For my sake, for the sake of all men here.

CHORUS:
>Consent, O King. Be gracious. Hear us, we beg you.

OEDIPUS: What shall I hear? To what shall I consent?

CHORUS: Respect the evidence of Creon's wisdom,
>Respect the oath of innocence he has taken.

OE.:   You know what this means?   CH.: Yes.   OE.: Tell me again what
>you ask for.

CHORUS: To yield, to relent.
>He is your friend and swears he is not guilty. 620
>Do not act in haste, convicting him out of hand.

OEDIPUS: When you ask for this, you ask for my destruction;
>You sentence me to death or to banishment.
>Be sure that you understand.

CHORUS:
>No, by Apollo, no!
>If such a thought has ever crossed my mind,
>Then may I never find

A friend to love me or a god to save;
And may dark doom pursue me to the grave.
  My country perishes, and now new woe   630
Springs from your quarrel, one affliction more
Has come upon us, and my heart is sore.

OEDIPUS:
  Let him go free, even though that destroys me.
  I shall be killed, or exiled in disgrace.
  Not his appeal but yours aroused my pity.
  I shall hate him always, no matter where he is.
CREON:
  You go beyond all bounds when you are angry,
  And are sullen when you yield. Natures like yours
  Inflict their heaviest torments on themselves.
OEDIPUS:
  Go! Go! Leave me in peace! CR.: Yes, I will go.   640
  You have not understood, but in the sight
  Of all these men here I am innocent.

                                          Exit CREON

CHORUS: Take the King with you, Madam, to the palace.
JOCASTA: When I have learned what happened, we will go.
CHORUS: The King was filled with fear and blind suspicion.
  Creon resented what he thought injustice.
JOC.: Both were at fault? CH.: Both. JOC.: Why was the King
              suspicious?
CHORUS: Do not seek to know.
  We have said enough. In a time of pain and trouble
  Inquire no further. Let the matter rest.   650
OEDIPUS: Your well meant pleading turned me from my purpose,
  And now you come to this. You fall so low
      As to think silence best.

CHORUS:
      I say again, O King,
  No one except a madman or a fool
      Would throw aside your rule.
  For you delivered us; your single hand
  Lifted the load from our belovéd land.
      When we were mad with grief and suffering,
  In our extremity you found a way   660
  To save the city, as you will today.
JOCASTA:
  But tell *me*, Oedipus, tell *me*, I beg you,
  Why you were so unyielding in your anger.
OEDIPUS:
  I will, Jocasta, for I honor you
  More than I do the elders. It was Creon's plotting.
JOCASTA:
  What do you mean? What was your accusation?
OEDIPUS:
  He says I am the murderer of King Laius.
JOCASTA:
  Did he speak from first-hand knowledge or from hearsay?
OEDIPUS:
  He did not speak at all. His lips are pure.
  He bribed Tiresias, and that scoundrel spoke.   670
JOCASTA:
  Then you can rid your mind of any fear
  That you are guilty. Listen to me. No mortal
  Shares in the gods' foreknowledge. I can give you
  Clear proof of that. There came once to King Laius
  An oracle—I will not say from Phoebus,
  But from his priest—saying it was his fate
  That he should be struck down by his own child,
  His child and mine. But Laius, as we know,
  Was killed by foreign robbers at a place
  Where three roads came together. As for the child,   680
  When it was only three days old, its father
  Pierced both its ankles, pinned its feet together,
  And then gave orders that it be abandoned

On a wild mountainside. So in this case
Phoebus did not fulfill his oracle. The child
Was not its father's murderer, and Laius
Was not the victim of the fate he feared,
Death at his son's hands, although just that fate
Was what the seer predicted. Pay no heed
To prophecies. Whatever may be needful   690
The god himself can show us easily.
OEDIPUS:
  What have you said, Jocasta? What have you said?
  The past comes back to me. How terrible!
JOCASTA:
  Why do you start so? What has happened to you?

OEDIPUS: It seemed to me—I thought you said that Laius
  Was struck down where three roads came together.

JOCASTA: I did. That was the story, and still is.

OEDIPUS: Where was it that this murder was committed?

JOCASTA: In Phocis, where the road from Thebes divides,
  Meeting the roads from Daulia and Delphi.

OEDIPUS: How many years ago did this occur?

JOCASTA: The news of it was published here in Thebes
  Not long before you came to be our king.

OEDIPUS: Is this my fate? Is this what the gods decreed?

JOCASTA: What have I said that has so shaken you?

OEDIPUS: Do not ask me yet. Tell me about King Laius.
  What did he look like? Was he young or old?

JOCASTA: His build was not unlike yours. He was tall.
  His hair was just beginning to turn grey.

OEDIPUS: I cannot bear the thought that I called down
  A curse on my own head unknowingly.

JOCASTA: What is it, Oedipus? You terrify me!

OEDIPUS: I dread to think Tiresias had clear eyesight;   710
  But tell me one thing more, and I will know.

JOCASTA: And I too shrink, yet I will answer you.

OEDIPUS: How did he travel? With a few men only,
  Or with his guards and servants, like a prince?

JOCASTA: There were five of them in all, with one a herald.
  They had one carriage in which King Laius rode.

OEDIPUS: It is too clear, too clear! Who told you this?

JOCASTA: The only servant who escaped alive.

OEDIPUS: And is he still here now, still in the palace?

JOCASTA: No. When he came home and found Laius dead   720
  And you the reigning king, he pleaded with me
  To send him where the sheep were pasturing,
  As far as possible away from Thebes.
  And so I sent him. He was a worthy fellow
  And, if a slave can, deserved a greater favor.
OEDIPUS:
  I hope it is possible to get him quickly.
JOCASTA:
  Yes, that is easy. Why do you want to see him?
OEDIPUS:
  Because I am afraid, deadly afraid
  That I have spoken more than I should have done.
JOCASTA:
  He shall come. But Oedipus, have I no right   730
  To learn what weighs so heavily on your heart?
OEDIPUS:
  You shall learn everything, now that my fears
  Have grown so great, for who is dearer to me

OEDIPUS:

Than you, Jocasta? Whom should I speak to sooner,
When I am in such straits? King Polybus
Of Corinth was my father. Meropé,
A Dorian, was my mother. I myself
Was foremost among all the citizens,
Till something happened, strange, but hardly worth
My feeling such resentment. As we sat   740
One day at dinner, a man who had drunk too much
Insulted me by saying I was not
My father's son. In spite of being angry,
I managed to control myself. Next day
I asked my parents, who were both indignant
That he had leveled such a charge against me.
This was a satisfaction, yet the thing
Still rankled, for the rumor grew widespread.
At last I went to Delphi secretly.   750
Apollo gave no answer to my question
But sent me off, anguished and terrified,
With fearful prophecies that I was fated
To be my mother's husband, to bring forth
Children whom men could not endure to see,
And to take my father's life. When I heard this
I turned and fled, hoping to find at length
Some place where I would know of Corinth only
As a far distant land beneath the stars,
Some place where I would never have to see
The infamies of this oracle fulfilled.   760
And as I went on, I approached the spot
At which you tell me Laius met his end.
Now this, Jocasta, is the absolute truth.
When I had come to where the three roads fork,
A herald met me, walking before a carriage,
Drawn by two colts, in which a man was seated,
Just as you said. The old man and the herald
Ordered me off the road with threatening gestures.
Then as the driver pushed me to one side,
I struck him angrily. And seeing this,   770
The old man, as I drew abreast, leaned out
And brought his driver's two-pronged goad down hard
Upon my head. He paid a heavy price
For doing that. With one blow of my staff
I knocked him headlong from his chariot
Flat on his back. Then every man of them
I killed. Now if the blood of Laius flowed
In that old stranger's veins, what mortal man
Could be more wretched, more accursed than I?
I whom no citizen or foreigner   780
May entertain or shelter, I to whom
No one may speak, I, I who must be driven
From every door. No other man has cursed me,
I have brought down this curse upon myself.
The hands that killed him now pollute his bed!
Am I not vile, foul, utterly unclean?
For I must fly and never see again
My people or set foot in my own land,
Or else become the husband of my mother
And put to death my father Polybus,   790
To whom I owe my life and my upbringing.
Men would be right in thinking that such things
Have been inflicted by some cruel fate.
May the gods' high and holy majesty
Forbid that I should see that day. No! No!
Rather than be dishonored by a doom
So dreadful may I vanish from the earth.

CHORUS:

Sir, these are terrible things, but there is hope
Until you have heard what the one witness says.

OEDIPUS:

That is the one remaining hope I have,   800
To wait for the arrival of the shepherd.

JOCASTA:

And when he *has* arrived, what can he do?

OEDIPUS:

He can do this. If his account agrees
With yours, I stand acquitted of this crime.

JOCASTA:

Was what I said of any consequence?

OEDIPUS:

You said his story was that robbers killed
King Laius. If he speaks of the same number,
Then I am not the murderer. One man
Cannot be several men. But if he says
One traveler, single-handed, did the deed,   810
Beyond all doubt the evidence points to me.

JOCASTA:

I am quite certain that was what he said.
He cannot change now, for the whole of Thebes
Heard it, not I alone. In any case,
Even supposing that his story *should*
Be somewhat different, he can never make
Laius's death fulfill the oracle.
Phoebus said plainly Laius was to die
At my son's hands. However, that poor child
Certainly did not kill him, for it died   820
Before its father. I would not waste my time
In giving any thought to prophecy.

OEDIPUS:

Yes, you are right. And yet have someone sent
To bring the shepherd here. Make sure of this.

JOCASTA:

I will, at once. Come, Oedipus, come in.
I will do nothing that you disapprove of.

                                   Exeunt OEDIPUS *and* JOCASTA

CHORUS:

May piety and reverence mark my actions;
May every thought be pure through all my days.
May those great laws whose dwelling is in heaven
Approve my conduct with their crown of praise: 830
Offspring of skies that overarch Olympus,
Laws from the loins of no mere mortal sprung,
Unslumbering, unfailing, unforgetting,
Filled with a godhead that is ever young.

Pride breeds the tyrant. Insolent presumption,
Big with delusive wealth and false renown,
Once it has mounted to the highest rampart
Is headlong hurled in utter ruin down.
But pour out all thy blessings, Lord Apollo,
Thou who alone hast made and kept us great,   840
On all whose sole ambition is unselfish,
Who spend themselves in service to the state.
Let that man be accursèd who is proud,
In act unscrupulous, in thinking base,
Whose knees in reverence have never bowed,
In whose hard heart justice can find no place,
Whose hands profane life's holiest mysteries,
How can he hope to shield himself for long
From the gods' arrows that will pierce him through?
If evil triumphs in such ways as these,   850
Why should we seek, in choric dance and song,
To give the gods the praise that is their due?

I cannot go in full faith as of old,
To sacred Delphi or Olympian vale,
Unless men see that what has been foretold
Has come to pass, that omens never fail.
All-ruling Zeus, if thou art King indeed,
Put forth thy majesty, make good thy word,
Faith in these fading oracles restore!
To priest and prophet men pay little heed;   860
Hymns to Apollo are no longer heard;
And all religion soon will be no more.

                                                Enter JOCASTA

JOCASTA:

Elders of Thebes, I thought that I should visit
The altars of the gods to offer up
These wreaths I carry and these gifts of incense.

The King is overanxious, overtroubled.
He is no longer calm enough to judge
The present by the lessons of the past,
But trembles before anyone who brings
An evil prophecy. I cannot help him.   870
Therefore, since thou art nearest, bright Apollo,
I bring these offerings to thee. O, hear me!
Deliver us from this defiling curse.
His fear infects us all, as if we were
Sailors who saw their pilot terrified.

Enter MESSENGER

MESSENGER:
Sirs, I have come to find King Oedipus.
Where is his palace, can you tell me that?
Or better yet, where is the King himself?
CHORUS:
Stranger, the King is there, within his palace.
This is the Queen, the mother of his children.   880

MESSENGER:
May all the gods be good to you and yours!
Madam, you are a lady richly blessed.
JOCASTA:
And may the gods requite your courtesy.
But what request or message do you bring us?
MESSENGER:
Good tidings for your husband and your household.
JOCASTA:
What is your news? What country do you come from?
MESSENGER:
From Corinth. And the news I bring will surely
Give you great pleasure—and perhaps some pain.
JOCASTA:
What message can be good and bad at once?
MESSENGER:
The citizens of Corinth, it is said,   890
Have chosen Oedipus to be their King.
JOCASTA:
What do you mean? Their King is Polybus.
MESSENGER:
No, madam. Polybus is dead and buried.
JOCASTA:
What! Dead! The father of King Oedipus?
MESSENGER:
If I speak falsely, let me die myself.
JOCASTA (*to* ATTENDANT):
Go find the King and tell him this. Be quick!
What does an oracle amount to now?
This is the man whom Oedipus all these years
Has feared and shunned to keep from killing him,
And now we find he dies a natural death!   900

Enter OEDIPUS

OEDIPUS:
My dear Jocasta, why have you sent for me?
JOCASTA:
Listen to this man's message, and then tell me
What faith you have in sacred oracles.
OEDIPUS:
Where does he come from? What has he to say?
JOCASTA:
He comes from Corinth and has this to say:
The King, your father, Polybus is dead.
OEDIPUS (*to* MESSENGER):
My father! Tell me that again yourself.
MESSENGER:
I will say first what you first want to know.
You may be certain he is dead and gone .
OEDIPUS:
How did he die? By violence or sickness?   910

MESSENGER:
The scales of life tip easily for the old.
OEDIPUS:
That is to say he died of some disease.
MESSENGER:
Yes, of disease, and merely of old age.
OEDIPUS:
Hear that, Jocasta! Why should anyone
Give heed to oracles from the Pythian shrine,
Or to the birds that shriek above our heads?
They prophesied that I must kill my father.
But he is dead; the earth has covered him.
And I am here, I who have never raised
My hand against him—unless he died of grief,   920
Longing to see me. Then I might be said
To have caused his death. But as they stand, at least,
The oracles have been swept away like rubbish.
They are with Polybus in Hades, dead.
JOCASTA:
Long ago, Oedipus, I told you that.
OEDIPUS:
You did, but I was blinded by my terror.
JOCASTA:
Now you need take these things to heart no longer.
OEDIPUS:
But there is still my mother's bed to fear.
JOCASTA:
Why should you be afraid? Chance rules our lives,
And no one can foresee the future, no one.   930
We live best when we live without a purpose
From one day to the next. Forget your fear
Of marrying your mother. That has happened
To many men before this in their dreams.
We find existence most endurable
When such things are neglected and forgotten.
OEDIPUS:
That would be true, Jocasta, if my mother
Were not alive; but now your eloquence
Is not enough to give me reassurance.
JOCASTA:
And yet your father's death is a great comfort.   940

OEDIPUS:
Yes, but I cannot rest while she is living.
MESSENGER:
Sir, will you tell me who it is you fear?
OEDIPUS:
Queen Meropé, the wife of Polybus.
MESSENGER:
What is so terrible about the Queen?
OEDIPUS:
A dreadful prophecy the gods have sent us.
MESSENGER:
Are you forbidden to speak of it, or not?
OEDIPUS:
It may be told. The Lord Apollo said
That I was doomed to marry my own mother,
And shed my father's blood with my own hands.
And so for years I have stayed away from Corinth,   950
My native land—a fortunate thing for me,
Though it is very sweet to see one's parents.
MESSENGER:
Was that the reason you have lived in exile?
OEDIPUS:
Yes, for I feared my mother and my father.
MESSENGER:
Then since my journey was to wish you well,
Let me release you from your fear at once.
OEDIPUS:
That would deserve my deepest gratitude.
MESSENGER:
Sir, I *did* come here with the hope of earning
Some recompense when you had gotten home.

OEDIPUS:
     No. I will never again go near my home.   960
MESSENGER:
     O son, son! You know nothing. That is clear—
OEDIPUS:
     What do you mean, old friend? Tell me, I beg you.
MESSENGER:
     If that is why you dare not come to Corinth.
OEDIPUS:
     I fear Apollo's word would be fulfilled.
MESSENGER:
     That you would be polluted through your parents?
OEDIPUS:
     Yes, yes! My life is haunted by that horror.
MESSENGER:
     You have no reason to be horrified.

OEDIPUS:
     I have no reason! Why? They are my parents.
MESSENGER:
     No. You are not the son of Polybus.
OEDIPUS:
     What did you say? Polybus not my father?   970
MESSENGER:
     He was as much your father as I am.
OEDIPUS:
     How can that be—my father like a stranger?
MESSENGER:
     But he was *not* your father, nor am I.
OEDIPUS:
     If that is so, why was I called his son?
MESSENGER:
     Because he took you as a gift, from me.
OEDIPUS:
     Yet even so, he loved me like a father?
MESSENGER:
     Yes, for he had no children of his own.
OEDIPUS:
     And when you gave me, had you bought or found me?
MESSENGER:
     I found you in the glens of Mount Cithaeron.
OEDIPUS:
     What could have brought you to a place like that?   980
MESSENGER:
     The flocks of sheep that I was tending there.
OEDIPUS:
     You went from place to place, hunting for work?
MESSENGER:
     I did, my son. And yet I saved your life.
OEDIPUS:
     How? Was I suffering when you took me up?
MESSENGER:
     Your ankles are the proof of what you suffered.
OEDIPUS:
     That misery! Why do you speak of that?
MESSENGER:
     Your feet were pinned together, and I freed them.
OEDIPUS:
     Yes. From my cradle I have borne those scars.
MESSENGER:
     They are the reason for your present name.[5]
OEDIPUS:
     Who did it? Speak! My mother, or my father?   990
MESSENGER:
     Only the man who gave you to me knows.
OEDIPUS:
     Then you yourself did not discover me.
MESSENGER:
     No. A man put you in my arms, some shepherd.
OEDIPUS:
     Do you know who he was? Can you describe him?
MESSENGER:
     He was, I think, one of the slaves of Laius.

OEDIPUS:
     The Laius who was once the King of Thebes?
MESSENGER:
     Yes, that is right. King Laius was his master.
OEDIPUS:
     How could I see him? Is he still alive?
MESSENGER:
     One of his fellow Thebans would know that.
OEDIPUS:
     Does anyone here know who this shepherd is?   1000
     Has anyone ever seen him in the city
     Or in the fields? Tell me. Now is the time
     To solve this mystery once and for all.
CHORUS:
     Sir, I believe the shepherd whom he means
     Is the same man you have already sent for.
     The Queen, perhaps, knows most about the matter.
OEDIPUS:
     Do you, Jocasta? You know the man we summoned.
     Is he the man this messenger spoke about?
JOCASTA:
     Why do you care? What difference can it make?
     To ask is a waste of time, a waste of time!   1010
OEDIPUS:
     I cannot let these clues slip from my hands.
     I must track down the secret of my birth.
JOCASTA:
     Oedipus, Oedipus! By all the gods,
     If you set any value on your life,
     Give up this search! I have endured enough.
OEDIPUS:
     Do not be frightened. Even if my mother
     Should prove to be a slave, and born of slaves,
     This would not touch the honor of your name.
JOCASTA:
     Listen, I beg you! Listen! Do not do this!
OEDIPUS:
     I cannot fail to bring the truth to light.   1020
JOCASTA:
     I know my way is best for you, I know it!
OEDIPUS:
     I know your best way is unbearable.
JOCASTA:
     May you be saved from learning who you **are**!
OEDIPUS:
     Go, someone. Bring the shepherd. As for her,
     Let her take comfort in her noble birth.
JOCASTA:
     You are lost! Lost! That is all I can call you now!
     That is all I will ever call you, ever again!
                    Exit JOCASTA

CHORUS:
     What wild grief, sir, has driven the Queen away?
     Evil, I fear, will follow from her silence,
     A storm of sorrow that will break upon us.   1030
OEDIPUS:
     Then let it break upon us I must learn
     My parentage, whatever it may be.
     The Queen is proud, far prouder than most women,
     And feels herself dishonored by my baseness.
     But I shall not be shamed. I hold myself
     The child of Fortune, giver of all good.
     She brought me forth. And as I lived my life,
     The months, my brothers, watched the ebb and flow
     Of my well-being. Never could I prove
     False to a lineage like that, or fail   1040
     To bring to light the secret of my birth.

---

[5]The name *Oedipus* means "swollen foot."

CHORUS:

    May Phoebus grant that I prove a true prophet!
      My heart foreknows what the future will bring:
    At tomorrow's full moon we shall gather, in chorus
      To hail Cithaeron, to dance and sing
    In praise of the mountain by Oedipus honored,
      Theban nurse of our Theban King.

    What long-lived nymph was the mother who bore you?
      What god whom the joys of the hills invite
    Was the god who begot you? Pan? or Apollo?   1050
      Or Hermes, Lord of Cylené's height?
    Or on Helicon's slope did an oread place you
      In Bacchus's arms for his new delight?

OEDIPUS:

    Elders, I think I see the shepherd coming
    Whom we have sent for. Since I never met him,
    I am not sure, yet he seems old enough,
    And my own slaves are the men bringing him.
    But you, perhaps, know more of this than I,
    If any of you have seen the man before.

CHORUS:

    Yes, it is he. I know him, the King's shepherd,   1060
    As true a slave as Laius ever had.

Enter SHEPHERD

OEDIPUS:

    I start with you, Corinthian. Is this man
    The one you spoke of?   MESS.: Sir, he stands before you.

OEDIPUS:

    Now you, old man. Come, look me in the face.
    Answer my questions. You were the slave of Laius?

SHEPHERD:

    Yes, but not bought. I grew up in his household.

OEDIPUS:

    What was the work that you were given to do?

SHEPHERD:

    Sheep-herding. I have always been a shepherd.

OEDIPUS:

    Where was it that you took your sheep to pasture?

SHEPHERD:

    On Mount Cithaeron, or the fields near by.   1070

OEDIPUS:

    Do you remember seeing this man there?

SHEPHERD:

    What was he doing? What man do you mean?

OEDIPUS:

    That man beside you. Have you ever met him?

SHEPHERD:

    No, I think not. I cannot recollect him.

MESSENGER:

    Sir, I am not surprised, but I am sure
    That I can make the past come back to him.
    He cannot have forgotten the long summers
    We grazed our sheep together by Cithaeron,
    He with two flocks, and I with one—three years,
    From spring to autumn. Then, for the winter months,   1080
    I used to drive my sheep to their own fold,
    And he drove his back to the fold of Laius.
    Is that right? Did it happen as I said?

SHEPHERD:

    Yes, you are right, but it was long ago.

MESSENGER:

    Well then, do you remember you once gave me
    An infant boy to bring up as my own?

SHEPHERD:

    What do you mean? Why do you ask me that?

MESSENGER:

    Because the child you gave me stands before you.

SHEPHERD:

    Will you be quiet? Curse you! Will you be quiet?

OEDIPUS (*to* SHEPHERD):

    You there! You have no reason to be angry.   1090
    You are far more to blame in this than he.

SHEPHERD:

    What have I done, my Lord? What have I done?

OEDIPUS:

    You have not answered. He asked about the boy.

SHEPHERD:

    Sir, he knows nothing, nothing at all about it.

OEDIPUS:

    And you say nothing. We must make you speak.

SHEPHERD:

    My Lord, I am an old man! Do not hurt me!

OEDIPUS (*to* GUARDS):

    One of you tie his hands behind his back.

SHEPHERD:

    Why do you want to know these fearful things?

OEDIPUS:

    Did you, or did you not, give him that child?

SHEPHERD:

    I did. I wish that I had died instead.   1100

OEDIPUS:

    You will die now, unless you tell the truth.

SHEPHERD:

    And if I speak, I will be worse than dead.

OEDIPUS:

    You seem to be determined to delay.

SHEPHERD:

    No. No! I told you that I had the child.

OEDIPUS:

    Where did it come from? Was it yours or not?

SHEPHERD:

    No, it was not mine. Someone gave it to me.

OEDIPUS:

    Some citizen of Thebes? Who was it? Who?

SHEPHERD:

    Oh! Do not ask me that! Not that, my Lord!

OEDIPUS:

    If I must ask once more, you are a dead man.

SHEPHERD:

    The child came from the household of King Laius.   1110

OEDIPUS:

    Was it a slave's child? Or of royal blood?

SHEPHERD:

    I stand on the very brink of speaking horrors.

OEDIPUS:

    And I of hearing horrors—but I must.

SHEPHERD:

    Then hear. The child was said to be the King's.
    You can best learn about this from the Queen.

OEDIPUS:

    The Queen! She gave it to you?   SHEP.: Yes, my Lord.

OEDIPUS:

    Why did she do that?   SHEP.: So that I should kill it.

OEDIPUS:

    Her own child?   SHEP.: Yes, she feared the oracles.

OEDIPUS:

    What oracles?   SHEP.: That it must kill its father.

OEDIPUS:

    Then why did you give it up to this old man?   1120

SHEPHERD:

    I pitied the poor child. I thought the man
    Would take it with him back to his own country.
    He saved its life only to have it come
    At last to this. If you should be the man
    He says you are, you were born miserable.

OEDIPUS:

    All true! All, all made clear! Let me no longer
    Look on the light of day. I am known now
    For what I am—I, cursed in being born,
    Cursed in my marriage, cursed in the blood I shed.

Exit OEDIPUS

CHORUS:

Men are of little worth. Their brief lives last   1130
    A single day.
They cannot hold elusive pleasure fast;
    It melts away.
All laurels wither; all illusions fade;
Hopes have been phantoms, shade on air-built shade,
    Since time began.
Your fate, O King, your fate makes manifest
Life's wretchedness. We can call no one blessed,
    No, not one man.

Victorious, unerring, to their mark   1140
    Your arrows flew.
The Sphinx with her curved claws, her riddle dark,
    Your wisdom slew.
By this encounter you preserved us all,
Guarding the land from death's approach, our tall,
    Unshaken tower.
From that time, Oedipus, we held you dear,
Great King of our great Thebes, without a peer
    In place and power.

But now what sadder story could be told?   1150
    A life of triumph utterly undone!
What fate could be more grievous to behold?
    Father and son
Both found a sheltering port, a place of rest,
    On the same breast.
Father and son both harvested the yield
    Of the same bounteous field.
How could that earth endure such dreadful wrong
    And hold its peace so long?
All-seeing time condemned your marriage lot;   1160
    In ways you least expected bared its shame—
Union wherein begetter and begot
    Were both the same.
This loud lament, these tears that well and flow,
    This bitter woe
Are for the day you rescued us, O King,
    From our great suffering;
For the new life and happiness you gave
    You drag down to the grave.

Enter SECOND MESSENGER

SECOND MESSENGER:

Most honored elders, princes of the land,   1170
If you are true-born Thebans and still love
The house of Labdacus,[6] then what a burden
Of sorrow you must bear, what fearful things
You must now hear and see! There is no river—
No, not the stream of Ister or of Phasis—
That could wash clean this house from the pollution
It hides within it or will soon bring forth:
Horrible deeds not done in ignorance,
But done deliberately. The cruelest evils
Are those that we embrace with open eyes.   1180

CHORUS:

Those we already know of are enough
To claim our tears. What more have you to tell?

SECOND MESSENGER:

It may be briefly told. The Queen is dead.

CHORUS:

Poor woman! oh, poor woman! How? What happened?

SECOND MESSENGER:

She killed herself. You have been spared the worst,
Not being witnesses. Yet you shall learn
What her fate was, so far as I remember.
When she came in, almost beside herself,
Clutching her hair with both her hands, she rushed
Straight to her bedroom and slammed shut the doors   1190
Behind her, screaming the name of Laius—
Laius long dead, but not her memory
Of their own child, the son who killed his father,

The son by whom his mother had more children.
She cursed the bed in which she had conceived
Husband by husband, children by her child,
A dreadful double bond. Beyond this much
I do not know the manner of her death,
For with a great cry Oedipus burst in,
Preventing us from following her fate   1200
To its dark end. On him our gaze was fixed,
As in a frenzy he ran to and fro,
Calling: 'Give me a sword! Give me a sword!
Where is that wife who is no wife, that mother,
That soil where I was sower and was sown?'
And as he raved, those of us there did nothing,
Some more than mortal power directed him.
With a wild shriek, as though he had some sign,
He hurled himself against the double doors,
Forcing the bars out of their loosened sockets,   1210
And broke into his room. There was the Queen,
Hanged in a noose, still swinging back and forth.
When he saw this, the King cried out in anguish,
Untied the knotted cord in which she swung,
And laid the wretched woman on the ground.
What happened then was terrible to see.
He tore the golden brooches from her robe,
Lifted them up as high as he could reach,
And drove them with all his strength into his eyes,
Shrieking, 'No more. no more shall my eyes see   1220
The horrors of my life—what I have done,
What I have suffered. They have looked too long
On those whom they ought never to have seen.
They never knew those whom I longed to see.
Blind, blind! Let them be blind!' With these wild words
He stabbed and stabbed his eyes. At every blow,
The dark blood dyed his beard, not sluggish drops,
But a great torrent like a shower of hail.
A two-fold punishment of two-fold sin
Broke on the heads of husband and of wife.   1230
Their happiness was once true happiness,
But now disgrace has come upon them, death,
Sorrow, and ruin, every earthly ill
That can be named. Not one have they escaped.

CHORUS:

Is he still suffering? Has he found relief?

SECOND MESSENGER:

He calls for someone to unbar the doors
And show him to all Thebes, his father's killer,
His mother's—no, I cannot say the word;
It is unholy, horrible. He intends
To leave the country, for his staying here
Would bring down his own curse upon his house.   1240
He has no guide and no strength of his own.
His pain is unendurable. This too
You will see. They are drawing back the bars.
The sight is loathsome and yet pitiful.

Enter OEDIPUS

CHORUS:

Hideous, hideous! I have seen nothing so dreadful,
    Ever before!
    I can look no more.
Oedipus, Oedipus! What madness has come upon you?
    What malignant fate
    Has leaped with its full weight,   1250
Has struck you down with an irresistible fury,
    And born you off as its prey?
        Poor wretch! There is much that I yearn
        To ask of you, much I would learn;
But I cannot. The sight of you fills me with horror!
    I shudder and turn away.

---

[6]Labdacus was a grandson of Cadmus and the father of
Laius.

OEDIPUS:
Oh, Oh! What pain! I cannot rest in my anguish!
 Where am I? Where?
Where are my words? They die away as I speak them,
 Into thin air.   1260
 What is my fate to be?

CHORUS: A fate too fearful for men to hear of, for men to see.

OEDIPUS: Lost! Overwhelmed by the rush of unspeakable darkness!
 It smothers me in its cloud.
  The pain of my eyes is piercing.
The thought of my sins, the horrors that I have committed,
 Racks me without relief.

CHORUS: No wonder you suffer, Oedipus, no wonder you cry aloud
 Under your double burden of pain and grief.

OEDIPUS: My friend, my friend! How steadfast you are, how ready 1270
 To help me in my great need!
  I feel your presence beside me.
Blind as I am, I know your voice in the blackness
 Of my long-lasting night.

CHORUS: How could you put out your eyes, still another infamous deed?
 What god, what demon, induced you to quench their light?

OEDIPUS: It was Apollo, my friends, who brought me low,
Apollo who crushed me beneath this unbearable burden;
 But it was my hand, mine, that struck the blow.
 Why should I see? What sight could have given me pleasure?

CHORUS: These things are as you say.

OEDIPUS: What is there now to love? What greeting can cheer me?
 Lead me away,
Quickly, quickly! O lead me out of the country
To a distant land! I am beyond redemption
Accursed, beyond hope lost, the one man living
 Whom all the gods most hate.

CHORUS: Would we had never heard of your existence,
 Your fruitless wisdom and your wretched fate.

OEDIPUS: My curses be upon him, whoever freed   1290
My feet from the cruel fetters, there on the mountain,
 Who restored me from death to life, a thankless deed.
 My death would have saved my friends and me from anguish.

CHORUS: I too would have had it so.

OEDIPUS: Then would I never have been my father's killer.
 Now all men know
That I am the infamous son who defiled his mother,
 That I shared the bed of the father who gave me being.
And if there is sorrow beyond any mortal sorrow,
 I have brought it upon my head.   1300

CHORUS: I cannot say that you have acted wisely.
 Alive and blind? You would be better dead.

OEDIPUS:
Give me no more advice, and do not tell me
That I was wrong. What I have done is best.
For if I still had eyesight when I went
Down to the underworld, how could I bear
To see my father and my wretched mother?
After the terrible wrong I did them both,
It would not have been punishment enough
If I had hanged myself. Or do you think   1310
That I could find enjoyment in the sight
Of children born as mine were born? No! No!
Nor in the sight of Thebes with its towered walls
And sacred statues of the gods. For I—
Who is so wretched?—I, the foremost Theban,
Cut myself off from this by my own edict
That ordered everyone to shun the man
Polluting us, the man the gods have shown

To be accursed, and of the house of Laius.
Once I laid bare my shame, could I endure   1320
To look my fellow-citizens in the face?
Never! Never! If I had found some way
Of choking off the fountain of my hearing,
I would have made a prison of my body,
Sightless and soundless. It would be sweet to live
Beyond the reach of sorrow. Oh, Cithaeron!
Why did you give me shelter rather than slay me
As soon as I was given to you? Then
No one would ever have heard of my begetting.
Polybus, Corinth, and the ancient house   1330
I thought my forebears'! You reared me as a child.
My fair appearance covered foul corruption,
I am impure, born of impurity.
Oh, narrow crossroad where the three paths meet!
Secluded valley hidden in the forest,
You that drank up my blood, my father's blood
Shed by my hands, do you remember all
I did for you to see? Do you remember
What else I did when I came here to Thebes?
Oh marriage rites! By which I was begotten,   1340
You then brought forth children by your own child,
Creating foulest blood-relationship:
An interchange of fathers, brothers, sons,
Brides, wives, and mothers—the most monstrous shame
Man can be guilty of. I should not speak
Of what should not be done. By all the gods,
Hide me, I beg you, hide me quickly somewhere
Far, far away. Put me to death or throw me
Into the sea, out of your sight forever.
Come to me, friends, pity my wretchedness.   1350
Let your hands touch me. Hear me. Do not fear,
My curse can rest on no one but myself.

CHORUS:
Creon is coming. He is the one to act
On your requests, or to help you with advice.
He takes your place as our sole guardian.

OEDIPUS:
Creon! What shall I say? I cannot hope
That he will trust me now, when my past hatred
Has proved to be so utterly mistaken.

Enter CREON

CREON:
I have not come to mock you, Oedipus,
Or to reproach you for any evil-doing.   1360
(*to* ATTENDANTS) You there. If you have lost all your respect
For men, revere at least the Lord Apollo,
Whose flame supports all life. Do not display
So nakedly pollution such as this,
Evil that neither earth nor holy rain
Nor light of day can welcome. Take him in,
Take him in, quickly. Piety demands
That only kinsmen share a kinsman's woe.

OEDIPUS:
Creon, since you have proved my fears were groundless,
Since you have shown such magnanimity   1370
To one so vile as I, grant my petition.
I ask you not for my sake but your own.

CREON:
What is it that you beg so urgently?

OEDIPUS:
Drive me away at once. Drive me far off.
Let me not hear a human voice again.

CREON:
I have delayed only because I wished
To have the god reveal to me my duty.

OEDIPUS:

But his command was certain: put to death
The unholy parricide. And I am he.

CREON:

True. But as things are now, it would be better   1380
To find out clearly what we ought to do.

OEDIPUS:

An oracle for a man so miserable?

CREON:

Yes. Even you will now believe the god.

OEDIPUS:

I will. Creon, I charge you with this duty.
Accept it, I entreat you. Give to her
Who lies within such burial as you wish,
For she belongs to you. You will perform
The proper obsequies. But as for me,
Let not my presence doom my father's city,
But send me to the hills, to Mount Cithaeron,   1390
My mountain, which my mother and my father
Chose for my grave. So will I die at last
By the decree of those who sought to slay me.
And yet I know I will not die from sickness
Or anything else. I was preserved from death
To meet some awful, some mysterious end.
My own fate does not matter, only my children's.
Creon, my sons need give you no concern,
For they are men, and can find anywhere
A livelihood. But Creon, my two girls!   1400
How lost, how pitiable! They always ate
Their daily bread with me, at my own table,
And had their share of everything I touched.
Take care of them! O Creon, take care of them!
And one thing more—if I could only touch them
And with them weep. O prince, prince, grant me this!
Grant it, O noble Creon! If I touched them,
I could believe I saw them once again.

Enter ISMENE *and* ANTIGONE

What! Do I hear my daughters? Hear them sobbing?
Has Creon had pity on me? Has he sent them,   1410
My children, my two darlings? Is it true?

CREON:

Yes. I have had them brought. I knew how much
You used to love them, how you love them still.

OEDIPUS:

May the gods bless you, Creon, for this kindness;
And may they guard you better on your journey
Than they have guarded me. Children, where are you?
Come to your brother's hands, the hands that made
Your father's clear eyes into what these are—
Your father, who saw nothing and knew nothing,
Begetting you where he had been conceived.   1420
I cannot see you, but I weep for you,
Weep for the bitter lives that you must lead

Henceforward. Never, never will you go
To an assembly with the citizens,
Or to a festival, and take your part.
You will turn back in tears. And when you come
To the full bloom of womanhood, what man
Will run the risk of bringing on himself
Your shame, my daughters, and your children's shame?
Is there one evil, one, that is not ours?   1430
'Your father killed his father; he begot
Children of his own mother; she who bore you
Bore him as well.' These are the taunts, the insults
That you will hear. Who, then, will marry you?
No one, my children. Clearly it is your fate
To waste away in barren maidenhood.
Creon, Creon, their blood flows in your veins.
You are the only father left to them;
They have lost both their parents. Do not let them
Wander away, unmarried, destitute,   1440
As miserable as I. Have pity on them,
So young, so utterly forlorn, so helpless
Except for you. You are kind-hearted. Touch me
To tell me that I have your promise. Children,
There is so much, so much that I would say,
If you were old enough to understand it,
But now I only teach you this one prayer:
May I be given a place in which to live,
And may my life be happier than my father's.

CREON:

Come, come with us. Have done with further woe.   1450

OE.: Obedience is hard. CR.: No good in life endures beyond
                                its season.

OE.: Do you know why I yield? CR.: When I have heard your
                                reason I will know.

OE.: You are to banish me. CR.: The gods alone can grant you
                                that entreaty.

OE.: I am hated by the gods. CR.: Then their response to you
                                will not be slow.

OE.: So you consent to this? CR.: I say no more than I have
                                said already.

OE.: Come, then, lead me away. CR.: Not with your children.
                                You must let them go.

OE.: Creon, not that, not that! CR.: You must be patient.
                                Nothing can restore
                                Your old dominion. You are King no more.

Exeunt CREON, OEDIPUS, ISMENE, *and* ANTIGONE

CHORUS:

Behold him, Thebans: Oedipus, great and wise,
Who solved the famous riddle. This is he   1460
    Whom all men gazed upon with envious eyes,
Who now is struggling in a stormy sea,
    Crushed by the billows of his bitter woes.
Look to the end of mortal life. In vain
    We say a man is happy, till he goes
Beyond life's final border, free from pain.

EXERCISES

1. The final chorus of the play is an interesting one to compare with some of the passages in the *Prometheus* play. What difference in outlook do you find between the final chorus above and the Aeschylus chorus on page 130.

> Ay, let the lightning be launched
> With curled and forked flame
> On my head; let the air confounded
> Shudder with thunderous peals
> And convulsion of raging winds;
> Let tempests beat on the earth
> Till her rooted foundations tremble;
> The boisterous surge of the sea

> Leap up to mingle its crest
> With the stars eclipsed in their orbs;
> Let the whirling blasts of Necessity
> Seize on my body and hurl it
> Down to the darkness of Tartarus—
> Yet all he shall not destroy me!

Is there any significant difference in the idea of fate in the two dramas?

2. One real question which arises after reading the *Oedipus* is whether the king is brought to his doom through the workings of an inexorable fate, whether he is brought low through a flaw in his own character, or whether the downfall is the result of the interweaving of the two forces. What evidence can you find in the play itself to support any of these positions?

Antigone

In terms of the history of Thebes, *Antigone* is the third of the three Theban plays written by Sophocles. In point of time, *Antigone* was written first, probably produced in 442 B.C. *Oedipus the King* was probably written about 427 B.C., although the exact date is unknown. *Oedipus at Colonus* was written much later, when Sophocles was a very old man. It is not given here although it is very much worth reading.

As far as Theban history is concerned, the plays occur in this order: *Oedipus the King, Oedipus at Colonus* (which tells of the death of Oedipus and his being raised to the level of the gods), and *Antigone.*

From the end of *Oedipus the King* we can imagine the long years of the blind old man's wandering. He was guided during these years by his daughter, Antigone, and aided by Ismene, who brought them news from Thebes. Finally, the two reach the town of Colonus, a suburb of Athens, where Oedipus dies.

In the meantime, the throne of Thebes was first occupied by Eteocles and Polyneices, the two sons of Oedipus, advised by Creon. The two sons quarreled, however, and Polyneices was banished. Eteocles ruled alone. Polyneices went to Argos where he raised an army to attack Thebes and regain the throne. In the battle which followed, the two brothers met each other at the gate of Thebes, fought, and both were killed. Creon then assumed the kingship. It is on the day following this, when Eteocles has been given proper burial and Creon has declared that Polyneices as an enemy of the state shall not be buried, that the play opens.

On the surface this play seems to be structured the same as *Oedipus the King,* with Creon as the tragic hero. Perhaps, however, both Antigone and Creon are tragic heroes. Give this some thought as you read the play. The most usual interpretation of *Antigone* is that it involves a conflict between the man-made laws of the state and the eternal laws of the gods. On the other hand, one Greek scholar, Moses Hadas, suggests that the play is really Creon's since the Greeks at the time of Sophocles had little concern for the gods or their eternal laws. This, too, is a problem to consider throughout your reading. What *is* the central problem?

CHARACTERS IN THE PLAY

CREON, *King of Thebes, brother of* JOCASTA, *the mother and wife of* OEDIPUS

EURYDICE, *Queen of Thebes, wife of* CREON

HAEMON, *son of* CREON

ANTIGONE }
ISMENE } *daughters of* OEDIPUS *and* JOCASTA

TIRESIAS, *a prophet*

BOY, *attendant of* TIRESIAS

GUARD

MESSENGER

CHORUS *of Theban Elders*

ATTENDANTS

SCENE: *Courtyard of the royal palace at Thebes. Daybreak.*

Enter ANTIGONE *and* ISMENE

ANTIGONE:
 Dear sister! Dear Ismene! How many evils
 Our father, Oedipus, bequeathed to us!
 And is there one of them—do you know of one
 That Zeus has not showered down upon our heads?
 I have seen pain, dishonor, shame, and ruin,
 I have seen them all, in what we have endured.
 And now comes this new edict by the King
 Proclaimed throughout the city. Have you heard?
 Do you not know, even yet, our friends are threatened?
 They are to meet the fate of enemies. 10

ISMENE:
 Our friends, Antigone? No, I have heard
 Nothing about them either good or bad.
 I have no news except that we two sisters
 Lost our two brothers when they killed each other.
 I know the Argive army fled last night,
 But what that means, or whether it makes my life
 Harder or easier, I cannot tell.

ANTIGONE:
 This I was sure of. So I brought you here
 Beyond the palace gates to talk alone.

ISMENE:
 What is the matter? I know you are deeply troubled. 20

ANTIGONE:
 Yes, for our brothers' fate. Creon has given
 An honored burial to one, to the other
 Only unburied shame. Eteocles
 Is laid in the earth with all the rites observed
 That give him his due honor with the dead.
 But the decree concerning Polyneices
 Published through Thebes is that his wretched body
 Shall lie unmourned, unwept, unsepulchered.
 Sweet will he seem to the vultures when they find him,
 A welcome feast that they are eager for. 30
 This is the edict the good Creon uttered
 For your observance and for mine—yes, mine.
 He is coming here himself to make it plain
 To those who have not heard. Nor does he think it
 Of little consequence, because whoever
 Does not obey is doomed to death by stoning.
 Now you can show you are worthy of your birth,
 Or bring disgrace upon a noble house.

ISMENE:
 What can I do, Antigone? As things are,
 What can I do that would be of any help? 40

ANTIGONE:
 You can decide if you will share my task.

ISMENE:
 What do you mean? What are you planning to do?

ANTIGONE:
 I intend to give him burial. Will you help?

ISMENE:
 To give him burial! Against the law?

ANTIGONE:
 He is our brother. I will do my duty,
 Yours too, perhaps. I never will be false.

ISMENE:
 Creon forbids it! You are too rash, too headstrong.

ANTIGONE:
 He has no right to keep me from my own.

ISMENE:
 Antigone! Think! Think how our father perished
 In scorn and hatred when his sins, that he 50
 Himself discovered, drove him to strike blind
 His eyes by his own hand. Think how his mother,
 His wife—both names were hers—ended her life
 Shamefully hanging in a twisted noose.
 Think of that dreadful day when our two brothers,
 Our wretched brothers, fought and fell together,
 Each slayer and each slain. And now we too,
 Left all alone, think how in turn we perish,
 If, in defiance of the law, we brave
 The power of the commandment of a king. 60
 O think Antigone! We who are women
 Should not contend with men; we who are weak
 Are ruled by the stronger, so that we must obey
 In this and in matters that are yet more bitter.
 And so I pray the dead to pardon me
 If I obey our rulers, since I must.
 To be too bold in what we do is madness.

ANTIGONE:
 I will not urge you. And I would not thank you
 For any help that you might care to give me.
 Do what you please, but I will bury him, 70
 And if I die for that, I shall be happy.
 Loved, I shall rest beside the one I loved.
 My crime is innocence, for I owe the dead
 Longer allegiance than I owe the living.
 With the dead I lie forever. Live, if you choose,
 Dishonoring the laws the gods have hallowed.

ISMENE:
 No, I dishonor nothing. But to challenge
 Authority—I have not strength enough.

ANTIGONE:
 Then make that your excuse. I will go heap
 The earth above the brother that I love. 80

ISMENE:
 O Sister, Sister! How I fear for you!

ANTIGONE:
 No, not for me. Set your own life in order.

ISMENE:
 Well then, at least, tell no one of your plan.
 Keep it close hidden, as I too will keep it.

ANTIGONE:
 Oh! Publish it! Proclaim it to the world!
 Then I will hate you less than for your silence.

ISMENE:
 Your heart is hot for deeds that chill the blood.

ANTIGONE:
 I know that I give pleasure where I should.

ISMENE:
 Yes, if you can, but you will try in vain.

ANTIGONE:
 When my strength fails, then I shall try no longer. 90

ISMENE:

A hopeless task should never be attempted.

ANTIGONE:

Your words have won their just reward: my hatred
And the long-lasting hatred of the dead.
But leave me and the folly that is mine
To undergo the worst that can befall me.
I shall not suffer an ignoble death.

ISMENE:

Go then, Antigone, if you must go.
And yet remember, though your act is foolish,
That those who love you do so with all their hearts.

Exeunt ANTIGONE *and* ISMENE. *Enter* CHORUS

CHORUS:

Sunbeam, eye of the golden day, on Thebes the seven-gated,   100
On Dircé's¹ streams you have dawned at last, O fairest of light.

Dawned on our foes, who had come enflamed by the quarrel of
Polyneices,
Shone on their glittering arms, made swifter their headlong flight.
From Argos they came with their white shields flashing,
Their helmets, crested with horsehair, agleam:
An army that flew like a snow-white eagle
Across our borders with shrilling scream.

Above our roofs it soared, at our gates with greedy jaws it was gaping;
But before their spears tasted our blood, and before our circle of
towers
Felt the flame of their torches, they turned to flight. The foes of the
Theban dragon   110
Found the surge and clamor of battle too fierce for their feebler
powers.
For Zeus, who abhors a proud tongue's boasting,
Seeing their river of armor flow
Clashing and golden, struck with his lightning
To silence the shout of our foremost foe.

He crashed to the earth with his torch, who had scaled the top of our
ramparts,
Raging in frenzy against us, breathing tempestuous hate,
Raging and threatening in vain. And mighty Ares, our ally,
Dealing havoc around him, apportioned to other foemen their fate.
For at seven portals, their seven leaders,   120
Down to the earth their bronze arms threw
In tribute to Zeus, the lord of the battle;
Save the fated brothers, the wretched two,
Who went to their common doom together,
Each wielding a spear that the other slew.

Now glorious Victory smiles upon jubilant Thebes rich in chariots.
Let us give free rein to our joy, forgetting our late-felt war;
Let us visit in night-long chorus the temples of all the immortals,
With Bacchus,² who shakes the land in the dances, going before.
But behold! The son of Menoeceus approaches,   130
Creon, the new-crowned King of the land,
Made King by new fortunes the gods have allotted.
What step has he pondered? What has he planned
To lay before us, his council of elders,
Who have gathered together at his command?

Enter CREON

CREON:

Elders of Thebes, our city has been tossed
By a tempestuous ocean, but the gods
Have steadied it once more and made it safe.
You, out of all the citizens, I have summoned,
Because I knew that you once reverenced   140
The sovereignty of Laius, and that later,
When Oedipus was King and when he perished,
Your steadfast loyalty upheld his children.
And now his sons have fallen, each one stained
By his brother's blood, killed by his brother's hand,
So that the sovereignty devolves on me,
Since I by birth am nearest to the dead.
Certainly no man can be fully known,

Known in his soul, his will, his intellect,
Until he is tested and has proved himself   150
In statesmanship. Because a city's ruler,
Instead of following the wisest counsel,
May through some fear keep silent. Such a man
I think contemptible. And one whose friend
Has stronger claims upon him than his country,
Him I consider worthless. As for me,
I swear by Zeus, forever all-beholding,
That I would not keep silence, if I saw
Ruin instead of safety drawing near us;
Nor would I think an enemy of the state   160
Could be my friend. For I remember this:
Our country bears us all securely onward,
And only while it sails a steady course
Is friendship possible. Such are the laws
By which I guard the greatness of the city.
And kindred to them is the proclamation
That I have made to all the citizens
Concerning the two sons of Oedipus:

Eteocles, who has fallen in our defence,
Bravest of warriors, shall be entombed   170
With every honor, every offering given
That may accompany the noble dead
Down to their rest. But as for Polyneices,
He came from exile eager to consume
The city of his fathers with his fire
And all the temples of his fathers' gods,
Eager to drink deep of his kindred's blood,
Eager to drag us off to slavery.
To this man, therefore, nothing shall be given.
None shall lament him, none shall do him honor.   180
He shall be left without a grave, his corpse
Devoured by birds and dogs, a loathsome sight.
Such is my will. For never shall the wicked
Be given more approval than the just,
If I have power to stop it. But whoever
Feels in his heart affection for his city
Shall be rewarded both in life and death.

CHORUS:

Creon, son of Menoeceus, it has pleased you
So to pass judgment on our friend and foe.
And you may give commands to all of us,   190
The living and the dead. Your will is law.

CREON:

Then see that this command is carried out.

CHORUS:

Sir, lay that burden on some younger man.

CREON:

Sentries have been assigned to guard the body.

CHORUS:

Then what additional duty would you give us?

CREON:

Never to countenance the disobedient.

CHORUS:

Who is so stupid as to long for death?

CREON:

Death is indeed the punishment. Yet men
Have often been destroyed by hope of gain.

Enter GUARD

GUARD:

My Lord, I cannot say that I have hurried,   200
Or that my running has made me lose my breath.

----

¹Here the reference is to a spring of water near Thebes.
Dircé was a former queen in Thebes who was tied to the
horns of a bull and died at the spring bearing her name.

²Bacchus, or Dionysus was the native god of Thebes and
therefore the patron of the city.

I often stopped to think, and turned to go back.
I stood there talking to myself: 'You fool,'
I said, 'Why do you go to certain death?'
And then: 'You idiot, are you still delaying?
If someone else tells Creon, you will suffer.'
I changed my mind this way, getting here slowly,
Making a short road long. But still, at last,
I did decide to come. And though my story
Is nothing much to tell, yet I will tell it.   210
One thing I know. I must endure my fate,
But nothing more than that can happen to me.

CREON:

What is the matter? What is troubling you?

GUARD:

Please let me tell you first about myself.
I did not do it. I did not see who did.
It is not right for me to be punished for it.

CREON:

You take good care not to expose yourself.
Your news must certainly be something strange.

GUARD:

Yes, it is strange—dreadful. I cannot speak.

CREON:

Oh, tell it, will you? Tell it and go away!   220

GUARD:

Well, it is this. Someone has buried the body,
Just now, and gone—has sprinkled it with dust
And given it other honors it should have.

CREON:

What are you saying? Who has dared to do it?

GUARD:

I cannot tell. Nothing was to be seen:
No mark of pickaxe, no spot where a spade
Had turned the earth. The ground was hard and dry,
Unbroken—not a trace of any wheels—
No sign to show who did it. When the sentry
On the first watch discovered it and told us,   230
We were struck dumb with fright. For he was hidden
Not by a tomb but a light coat of dust,
As if a pious hand had scattered it.
There were no tracks of any animal,
A dog or wild beast that had come to tear him.
We all began to quarrel, and since no one
Was there to stop us, nearly came to blows.
Everyone was accused, and everyone
Denied his guilt. We could discover nothing.
We were quite willing to handle red-hot iron,   240
To walk through fire, to swear by all the gods
That we were innocent of the deed itself,
And innocent of taking any part
In planning it or doing it. At last
One of us spoke. We trembled and hung our heads,
For he was right; we could not argue with him,
Yet his advice was bound to cause us trouble.
He told us all this had to be reported,
Not kept a secret. We all agreed to that.
We drew lots for it, and I had no luck.   250
I won the prize and was condemned to come.
So here I stand, unwilling, because I know
The bringer of bad news is never welcome.

CHORUS:

Sir, as he spoke, I have been wondering.
Can this be, possibly, the work of gods?

CREON:

Be silent! Before you madden me! You are old.
Would you be senseless also? What you say
Is unendurable. You say the gods
Cared for this corpse. Then was it for reward,
Mighty to match his mighty services,   260
That the gods covered him? He who came to burn
Their pillared temples and their votive offerings,

Ravage their land, and trample down the state.
Or is it your opinion that the gods
Honor the wicked? Inconceivable!
However, from the first, some citizens
Who found it difficult to endure this edict,
Muttered against me, shaking their heads in secret,
Instead of bowing down beneath the yoke,
Obedient and contented with my rule.   270
These are the men who are responsible,
For I am certain they have bribed the guards
To bury him. Nothing is worse than money.
Money lays waste to cities, banishes
Men from their homes, indoctrinates the heart,
Perverting honesty to works of shame,
Showing men how to practice villainy,
Subduing them to every godless deed.
But all those men who got their pay for this
Need have no doubt their turn to pay will come.   280
(*to the* GUARD) Now, you. As I still honor Zeus the King,
I tell you, and I swear it solemnly,
Either you find the man who did this thing,
The very man, and bring him here to me,
Or you will not just die. Before you die,
You will be tortured until you have explained
This outrage; so that later when you steal
You will know better where to look for money
And not expect to find it everywhere.
Ill-gotten wealth brings ruin and not safety.   290

GUARD:

Sir, may I speak? Or shall I merely go?

CREON:

You can say nothing that is not offensive.

GUARD:

Do I offend your hearing or your heart?

CREON:

Is it your business to define the spot?

GUARD:

The criminal hurts your heart, and I your ears.

CREON:

Still talking? Why, you must have been born talking!

GUARD:

Perhaps. But I am not the guilty man.

CREON:

You are. And what is more you sold yourself.

GUARD:

You have judged me, sir, and have misjudged me, too.

CREON:

Be clever about judging if you care to.   300
But you will say that treachery leads to sorrow
Unless you find the man and show him to me.

Exit CREON

GUARD:

Finding him is the best thing that could happen.
Fate will decide. But however that may be,
You never are going to see me here again.
I have escaped! I could not have hoped for that.
I owe the gods my thanks for guarding me.

Exit GUARD

CHORUS:

Many the marvelous things; but none that can be
More of a marvel than man! This being that braves
With the south wind of winter the whitened streaks of the sea,   310
  Threading his way through the troughs of engulfing waves.
And the earth most ancient, the eldest of all the gods,
  Earth, undecaying, unwearied, he wears away with his toil;
Forward and back with his plowshare, year after year, he plods,
  With his horses turning the soil.

Man in devising excels. The birds of the air,
  That light-minded race, he entangles fast in his toils.
Wild creatures he catches, casting about them his snare,
  And the salt-sea brood he nets in his woven coils.

The tireless bull he has tamed, and the beast whose lair   320
  Is hidden deep in the wilds, who roams in the wooded hills.
He has fitted a yoke that the neck of the shaggy-maned horse
        will bear;
  He is master of all through his skills.

He has taught himself speech, and wind-like thought, and the lore
  Of ruling a town. He has fled the arrows of rain,
The searching arrows of frost he need fear no more,
  That under a starry sky are endured with pain.
Provision for all he has made—unprovided for naught,
  Save death itself, that in days to come will take shape.
From obscure and deep-seated disease he has subtly wrought   330
  A way of escape.

Resourceful and skilled, with an inconceivable art,
  He follows his course to a good or an evil end.
When he holds the canons of justice high in his heart
  And has sworn to the gods the laws of the land to defend,
Proud stands his city,[3] without a city is he
  Who with ugliness, rashness, or evil dishonors the day.
Let me shun his thoughts. Let him share no hearthstone with me,
  Who acts in this way!

CHORUS:
  Look there! Look there! What portent can this be?   340
  Antigone! I know her, it is she!
  Daughter of Oedipus a prisoner brought?
  You defied Creon? You in folly caught?

              Enter GUARD *with* ANTIGONE

GUARD:
  She did it. Here she is. We caught this girl
  As she was burying him. Where is the King?

CHORUS:
  Leaving the palace there, just as we need him.

              Enter CREON

CREON:
  Why do you need my presence? What has happened?

GUARD:
  My Lord, no one should take a solemn oath
  Not to do something, for his second thoughts
  Make him a liar. I vowed not to hurry back.   350
  I had been battered by your storm of threats.
  But when a joy comes that exceeds our hopes,
  No other happiness can equal it.
  So I have broken my vow. I have returned,
  Bringing this girl along. She was discovered
  Busy with all the rites of burial.
  There was no casting lots, no, not this time!
  Such luck as this was mine and no one else's.
  Now sir, take her yourself, examine her,
  Convict her, do what you like. But as for me,   360
  I have the right to a complete acquittal.

CREON:
  This is the girl you caught? How? Where was she?

GUARD:
  Burying the dead man, just as I have told you.

CREON:
  Do you mean that? Or have you lost your mind?

GUARD:
  Your order was that he should not be buried.
  I saw her bury him. Is that all clear?

CREON:
  How was she seen? You caught her in the act?

GUARD:
  This was what happened. When we had gotten back,
  With your threats following us, we swept away
  The dust that covered him. We left him bare,   370
  A rotting corpse. And then we sat to windward,

Up on the hillside, to avoid the stench.
All of us were alert, and kept awake
Threatening each other. No one could get careless.
So the time passed, until the blazing sun
Stood at the zenith, and the heat was burning.
Then suddenly the wind came in a blast,
Lifting a cloud of dust up from the earth,
Troubling the sky and choking the whole plain,
Stripping off all the foliage of the woods,   380
Filling the breadth of heaven. We closed our eyes
And bore the affliction that the gods had sent us.
When it had finally stopped, we saw this girl.
She wailed aloud with a sharp, bitter cry,
The cry a bird gives seeing its empty nest
Robbed of its brood. And she too, when she saw
The naked body, was loud in her lament
And cursed the men who had uncovered him.
Quickly she sprinkled him with dust, and then
Lifting a pitcher, poured out three libations   390
To do him honor. When we ran and caught her,
She was unterrified. When we accused her
Both of her earlier and her present act,
She made no effort to deny the charges.
I am part glad, part sorry. It is good
To find that you yourself have gotten clear,
But to bring trouble on your friends is hard.
However, nothing counts except my safety.

CREON (*to* ANTIGONE):
  You there. You, looking at the ground. Tell me.
  Do you admit this or deny it? Which?   400

ANTIGONE:
  Yes, I admit it. I do not deny it.

CREON (*to* GUARD):
  Go. You are free. The charge is dropped.

              Exit GUARD

              Now you,
  Answer this question. Make your answer brief.
  You knew there was a law forbidding this?

ANTIGONE:
  Of course I knew it. Why not? It was public.

CREON:
  And you have dared to disobey the law?

ANTIGONE:
  Yes. For this law was not proclaimed by Zeus,
  Or by the gods who rule the world below.
  I do not think your edicts have such power
  That they can override the laws of heaven,   410
  Unwritten and unfailing, laws whose life
  Belongs not to today or yesterday
  But to time everlasting; and no man
  Knows the first moment that they had their being.
  If I transgressed these laws because I feared
  The arrogance of man, how to the gods
  Could I make satisfaction? Well I know,
  Being a mortal, that I have to die,
  Even without your proclamations. Yet
  If I must die before my time is come,   420
  That is a blessing. Because to one who lives,
  As I live, in the midst of sorrows, death
  Is of necessity desirable.
  For me, to face death is a trifling pain
  That does not trouble me. But to have left
  The body of my brother, my own brother,

---

[3]Elizabeth Wyckoff's translation of these lines reads: *When he honors the laws of the land and the gods' sworn right high indeed is his city.* In comparing the two translations, what is the difference in their significance?

Lying unburied would be bitter grief.
And if these acts of mine seem foolish to you,
Perhaps a fool accuses me of folly.
CHORUS:
The violent daughter of a violent father,   430
She cannot bend before a storm of evils.
CREON (*to* ANTIGONE):
Stubborn? Self-willed? People like that, I tell you,
Are the first to come to grief. The hardest iron,
Baked in the fire, most quickly flies to pieces.
An unruly horse is taught obedience
By a touch of the curb. How can you be so proud?
You, a mere slave! (*to* CHORUS) She was well schooled already
In insolence, when she defied the law.
And now look at her! Boasting, insolent,
Exulting in what she did. And if she triumphs
And goes unpunished, I am no man—she is.   440
If she were more than niece, if she were closer
Than anyone who worships at my altar,
She would not even then escape her doom,
A dreadful death. Nor would her sister. Yes,
Her sister had a share in burying him.
(*to* ATTENDANT) Go bring her here. I have just seen her, raving,
Beside herself. Even before they act,
Traitors who plot their treason in the dark
Betray themselves like that. Detestable!
(*to* ANTIGONE) But hateful also is an evil-doer   450
Who, caught red-handed, glorifies the crime.
ANTIGONE:
Now you have caught me, will you do more than kill me?
CREON:
No, only that. With that I am satisfied.
ANTIGONE:
Then why do you delay? You have said nothing
I do not hate. I pray you never will.
And you hate what I say. Yet how could I
Have won more splendid honor than by giving
Due burial to my brother? All men here
Would grant me their approval, if their lips
Were not sealed up in fear. But you, a king,   460
Blessed by good fortune in much else besides,
Can speak and act with perfect liberty.
CREON:
All of these Thebans disagree with you.
ANTIGONE:
No. They agree, but they control their tongues.
CREON:
You feel no shame in acting without their help?
ANTIGONE:
I feel no shame in honoring a brother.
CREON:
Another brother died who fought against him.
ANTIGONE:
Two brothers. The two sons of the same parents.
CREON:
Honor to one is outrage to the other.
ANTIGONE:
Eteocles will not feel himself dishonored.   470
CREON:
What! When his rites are offered to a traitor?
ANTIGONE:
It was his brother, not his slave, who died.
CREON:
One who attacked the land that he defended.
ANTIGONE:
The gods still wish those rites to be performed.
CREON:
Are the just pleased with the unjust as their equals?
ANTIGONE:
That may be virtuous in the world below.
CREON:
No. Even there a foe is never a friend.

ANTIGONE:
I am not made for hatred but for love.
CREON:
Then go down to the dead. If you must love,
Love them. While I yet live, no woman rules me.   480
CHORUS:
Look there. Ismene, weeping as sisters weep.
The shadow of a cloud of grief lies deep
On her face, darkly flushed; and in her pain
Her tears are falling like a flood of rain.

Enter ISMENE *and* ATTENDANTS

CREON:
You viper! Lying hidden in my house,
Sucking my blood in secret, while I reared,
Unknowingly, two subverters of my throne.
Do you confess that you have taken part
In this man's burial, or deny it? Speak.
ISMENE:
If she will recognize my right to say so,   490
I shared the action and I share the blame.
ANTIGONE:
No. That would not be just. I never let you
Take any part in what you disapproved of.
ISMENE:
In your calamity, I am not ashamed
To stand beside you, beaten by this tempest.
ANTIGONE:
The dead are witnesses of what I did,
To love in words alone is not enough.
ISMENE:
Do not reject me, Sister! Let me die
Beside you, and do honor to the dead.
ANTIGONE:
No. You will neither share my death nor claim   500
What I have done. My death will be sufficient.
ISMENE:
What happiness can I have when you are gone?
ANTIGONE:
Ask Creon that. He is the one you value.
ISMENE:
Do you gain anything by taunting me?
ANTIGONE:
Ah, no! By taunting you, I hurt myself.
ISMENE:
How can I help you? Tell me what I can do.
ANTIGONE:
Protect yourself. I do not grudge your safety.
ISMENE:
Antigone! Shall I not share your fate?
ANTIGONE:
We both have made our choices: life, and death.
ISMENE:
At least I tried to stop you. I protested.   510
ANTIGONE:
Some have approved your way; and others, mine.
ISMENE:
Yet now I share your guilt. I too am ruined.
ANTIGONE:
Take courage. Live your life. But I long since
Gave myself up to death to help the dead.
CREON:
One of them has just lost her senses now.
The other has been foolish all her life.
ISMENE:
We cannot always use our reason clearly.
Suffering confuses us and clouds our minds.
CREON:
It clouds your mind. You join in her wrong-doing.
ISMENE:
How is life possible without my sister?   520

CREON:

> Your sister? You have no sister. She is dead.

ISMENE:

> Then you will kill the wife your son has chosen?

CREON:

> Yes. There are other fields that he can plow.

ISMENE:

> He will not find such an enduring love.

CREON:

> A wicked woman for my son? No, never!

ANTIGONE:

> O Haemon, Haemon! How your father wrongs you!

CREON:

> You and your marriage! Let me hear no more!

CHORUS:

> You are unyielding? You will take her from him?

CREON:

> Death will act for me. Death will stop the marriage.

CHORUS:

> It seems, then, you have sentenced her to death.   530

CREON:

> Yes. And my sentence you yourselves accepted.
> Take them inside. From now on, they are women,
> And have no liberty. For even the bold
> Seek an escape when they see death approaching.

Exeunt ANTIGONE, ISMENE, *and* ATTENDANTS

CHORUS:

> Blesséd the life that has no evil known,
> For the gods, striking, strike down a whole race—
>   Doomed parent and doomed child both overthrown.
> As when the fierce breath of the winds of Thrace
>   Across the darkness of the sea has blown
> A rushing surge; black sand from deep below   540
>   Comes boiling up; wind-beaten headlands moan,
> Fronting the full shock of the billow's blow.

> The race of Oedipus, from days of old,
> To long dead sorrows add new sorrows' weight.
>   Some god has sent them sufferings manifold.
> None may release another, for their fate
>   Through generations loosens not its hold.
> Now is their last root cut, their last light fled,
>   Because of frenzy's curse, words overbold,
> And dust, the gods' due, on the bloodstained dead.   550

> O Zeus, what human sin restricts thy might?
> Thou art unsnared by all-ensnaring sleep
>   Or tireless months. Unaging thou dost keep
> Thy court in splendor of Olympian light.
>   And as this law was true when time began,
> Tomorrow and forever it shall be:
>   Naught beyond measure in the life of man
>   From fate goes free.

> For hope, wide-ranging, that brings good to some,
> To many is a false lure of desire   560
>   Light-minded, giddy; and until the fire
> Scorches their feet, they know not what will come.
>   Wise is the famous adage: that to one
> Whom the gods madden, evil, soon or late,
>   Seems good;[4] then can he but a moment shun
>   The stroke of fate.

> But Haemon comes, of your two sons the last.
> Is his heart heavy for the sentence passed
>   Upon Antigone, his promised bride,
> And for his hope of marriage now denied?   570

Enter HAEMON

CREON:

> We soon shall know better than seers could tell us.
> My son, Antigone is condemned to death.

Nothing can change my sentence. Have you learned
Her fate and come here in a storm of anger,
Or do you love me and support my acts?

HAEMON:

> Father, I am your son. Your greater knowledge
> Will trace the pathway that I mean to follow.
> My marriage cannot be of more importance
> Than to be guided always by your wisdom.

CREON:

> Yes, Haemon, this should be the law you live by!   580
> In all things to obey your father's will.
> Men pray for children round them in their homes
> Only to see them dutiful and quick
> With hatred to requite their father's foe,
> With honor to repay their father's friend.
> But what is there to say of one whose children
> Prove to be valueless? That he has fathered
> Grief for himself and laughter for his foes.
> Then, Haemon, do not, at the lure of pleasure,
> Unseat your reason for a woman's sake.   590
> This comfort soon grows cold in your embrace:
> A wicked wife to share your bed and home.
> Is there a deeper wound than to find worthless
> The one you love? Turn from this girl with loathing,
> As from an enemy, and let her go
> To get a husband in the world below.
> For I have found her openly rebellious,
> Her only out of all the city. Therefore,
> I will not break the oath that I have sworn.
> I will have her killed. Vainly she will invoke   600
> The bond of kindred blood the gods make sacred.
> If I permit disloyalty to breed
> In my own house, I nurture it in strangers.
> He who is righteous with his kin is righteous
> In the state also. Therefore, I cannot pardon
> One who does violence to the laws or thinks
> To dictate to his rulers; for whoever
> May be the man appointed by the city,
> That man must be obeyed in everything,
> Little or great, just or unjust. And surely   610
> He who was thus obedient would be found
> As good a ruler as he was a subject;
> And in a storm of spears he would stand fast
> With loyal courage at his comrade's side.
> But disobedience is the worst of evils.
> For it is this that ruins cities; this
> Makes our homes desolate; armies of allies
> Through this break up in rout. But most men find
> Their happiness and safety in obedience.
> Therefore we must support the law, and never   620
> Be beaten by a woman. It is better
> To fall by a man's hand, if we must fall,
> Than to be known as weaker than a girl.

CHORUS:

> We may in our old age have lost our judgment,
> And yet to us you seem to have spoken wisely.

HAEMON:

> The gods have given men the gift of reason,
> Greatest of all things that we call our own.
> I have no skill, nor do I wish to have it,
> To show where you have spoken wrongly. Yet
> Some other's thought, beside your own, might prove   630
> To be of value. Therefore it is my duty,
> My natural duty as your son, to notice,
> On your behalf, all that men say, or do,

------

[4]To quote the Wyckoff translation again: *The bad becomes the good to whom a god would doom.* Does this apply to Creon? to Antigone? or both? Your decision on who is the tragic hero of the play may depend on your answer to the question.

Or find to blame. For your frown frightens them,
So that the citizen dares not say a word
That would offend you. I can hear, however,
Murmurs in darkness and laments for her.
They say: 'No woman ever less deserved
Her doom, no woman ever was to die
So shamefully for deeds so glorious.   640
For when her brother fell in bloody battle,
She would not let his body lie unburied

To be devoured by carrion dogs or birds.
Does such a woman not deserve reward,
Reward of golden honor?' This I hear,
A rumor spread in secrecy and darkness.
Father, I prize nothing in life so highly
As your well-being. How can children have
A nobler honor than their father's fame
Or father than his son's? Then do not think   650
Your mood must never alter; do not feel
Your word, and yours alone, must be correct.
For if a man believes that he is right
And only he, that no one equals him
In what he says or thinks, he will be found
Empty when searched and tested. Because a man
Even if he be wise, feels no disgrace
In learning many things, in taking care
Not to be over-rigid. You have seen
Trees on the margin of a stream in winter: 660
Those yielding to the flood save every twig,
And those resisting perish root and branch.
So, too, the mariner who never slackens
His taut sheet overturns his craft and spends
Keel uppermost the last part of his voyage.
Let your resentment die. Let yourself change.
For I believe—if I, a younger man,
May have a sound opinion—it is best
That men by nature should be wise in all things.
But most men find they cannot reach that goal;   670
And when this happens, it is also good
To learn to listen to wise counselors.

CHORUS:
Sir, when his words are timely, you should heed them.
And Haemon, you should profit by his words.
Each one of you has spoken reasonably.

CREON:
Are men as old as I am to be taught
How to behave by men as young as he?

HAEMON:
Not to do wrong. If I am young, ignore
My youth. Consider only what I do.

CREON:
Have you done well in honoring the rebellious?   680

HAEMON:
Those who do wrong should not command respect.

CREON:
Then that disease has not infected her?

HAEMON:
All of our city with one voice denies it.

CREON:
Does Thebes give orders for the way I rule?

HAEMON:
How young you are! How young in saying that!

CREON:
Am I to govern by another's judgment?

HAEMON:
A city that is one man's is no city.

CREON:
A city is the king's. That much is sure.

HAEMON:
You would rule well in a deserted country.

CREON:
This boy defends a woman, it appears.   690

HAEMON:
If you are one. I am concerned for you.

CREON:
To quarrel with your father does not shame you?

HAEMON:
Not when I see you failing to do justice.

CREON:
Am I unjust when I respect my crown?

HAEMON:
Respect it! When you trample down religion?

CREON:
Infamous! Giving first place to a woman!

HAEMON:
But never to anything that would disgrace me.

CREON:
Each word you utter is a plea for her.

HAEMON:
For you, too, and for me, and for the gods.

CREON:
You shall not marry her this side of death.   700

HAEMON:
Then if she dies, she does not die alone.

CREON:
What! Has it come to this? You threaten me?

HAEMON:
No. But I tell you your decree is useless.

CREON:
You will repent this. You! Teaching me wisdom!

HAEMON:
I will not call you mad. You are my father.

CREON:
You woman's slave! Your talk will not persuade me.

HAEMON:
Then what you want is to make all the speeches.

CREON:
So. Now by all the gods in heaven above us,
One thing is certain: you are going to pay
For taunting and insulting me. (to ATTENDANTS) Bring out   710
That hated object. Let her die this moment,
Here, at her bridegroom's feet, before his eyes.

HAEMON:
No, you are wrong. Not at my feet. And never
Will you set eyes upon my face again.
Rage, rave, with anyone who can bear to listen.
                                                    Exit HAEMON

CHORUS:
Sir, he is gone; his anger gives him speed.
Young men are bitter in their agony.

CREON:
Let him imagine more than man can do,
Or let him do more. Never shall he save
These two girls; they are going to their doom.   720

CHORUS:
Do you intend to put them both to death?

CREON:
That was well said. No, not the innocent.

CHORUS:
And the other? In what way is she to die?

CREON:
Along a desolate pathway I will lead her,
And shut her, living, in a rocky vault
With no more food than will appease the gods,
So that the city may not be defiled.
Hades, who is the only god she worships,
May hear her prayers, and rescue her from death.
Otherwise she will learn at last, though late,   730
That to revere the dead is useless toil.
                                                    Exit CREON

CHORUS:
None may withstand you, O love unconquered,
    Seizing the wealth of man as your prey,
In the cheek of a maiden keeping your vigil,
    Till night has faded again to day.
You roam the wilds to men's farthest dwellings,
    You haunt the boundless face of the sea.

No god may escape you, no short-lived mortal
  From the madness that love inflicts may flee.
You twist our minds until ruin follows.   740
  The just to unrighteous ways you turn.
You have goaded kinsman to strive with kinsman
  Till the fires of bitter hatred burn.
In the eyes of a bride you shine triumphant;
  Beside the eternal laws your throne
Eternal stands, for great Aphrodite, [5]
  Resistless, works her will on her own.

But now I too am moved. I cannot keep
  Within the bounds of loyalty. I weep
When I behold Antigone, the bride,   750
  Nearing the room where all at last abide.

Enter ANTIGONE, *guarded*

ANTIGONE:
  See me, my countrymen! See with what pain
I tread the path I shall not tread again,
Looking my last upon the light of day
  That shines for me no more.
Hades, who gives his sleep to all, me, living, leads away
  To Acheron's [6] dark shore.
Not mine the hymeneal chant, not mine the bridal song,
For I, a bride, to Acheron belong.

CHORUS:
  Glorious, therefore, and with praise you tread   760
The pathway to the deep gulf of the dead.
You have not felt the force of fate's decrees,
Struck down by violence, wasted by disease;
But of your own free will you choose to go,
Alone of mortals, to the world below.

ANTIGONE:
  I know how sad a death she suffered, she
Who was our guest here, Phrygian Niobe. [7]
Stone spread upon her, close as ivy grows,
  And locked her in its chains.
Now on her wasted form, men say, fall ceaselessly the
      snows,   770
  Fall ceaselessly the rains;
While from her grieving eyes drop tears, tears that
      her bosom steep.
And like hers, my fate lulls me now to sleep.

CHORUS:
  She was a goddess of the gods' great race;
Mortals are we and mortal lineage trace.
But for a woman the renown is great
In life and death to share a godlike fate.

ANTIGONE:
  By our fathers' gods, I am mocked! I am mocked! Ah! why, [8]
You men of wealth, do you taunt me before I die?   780
O sacred grove of the city! O waters that flow
From the spring of Dircé! Be witness; to you I cry.
What manner of woman I am you know
And by what laws, unloved, unlamented, I go
To my rocky prison, to my unnatural tomb.
  Alas, how ill-bestead!
No fellowship have I; no others can share my doom,
Neither mortals nor corpses, neither the quick nor the dead.

CHORUS:
  You have rushed forward with audacious feet
And dashed yourself against the law's high seat.   790
That was a grievous fall, my child, and yet
In this ordeal you pay your father's debt.

ANTIGONE:
  You have touched on the heaviest grief that my heart
    can hold:

Grief for my father, sorrow that never grows old
For our famous house and its doom that the fates have spun.
My mother's bed! Ah! How can its horrors be told?
My mother who yielded her love to one
Who was at once my father and her son.
  Born of such parents, with them henceforth I abide,
    Wretched, accursed, unwed.   800
  And you, Polyneices, you found an ill-fated bride,
And I, the living, am ruined by you, the dead.

CHORUS:
  A pious action may of praise be sure,
But he who rules a land cannot endure
An act of disobedience to his rule.
Your own self-will you have not learned to school.

ANTIGONE:
  Unwept, unfriended, without marriage song,
Forth on my road I miserable am led;
  I may not linger. Not for long
Shall I, most wretched, see the holy sun.   810
My fate no friend bewails, not one;
  For me no tear is shed.

Enter CREON

CREON:
  Do you not know that singing and lamentation
Would rise incessantly as death approached,
If they could be of service? Lead her away!
Obey my orders. Shut her in her grave
And leave her there, alone. Then she can take
Her choice of living in that home, or dying.
I am not stained by the guilt of this girl's blood,
But she shall see the light of day no longer.   820

ANTIGONE:
  O tomb! O cavern! Everlasting prison!
O bridal-chamber! To you I make my way
To join my kindred, all those who have died
And have been greeted by Persephone. [9]
The last and far most miserable of all,
I seek them now, before I have lived my life.
Yet high are the hopes I cherish that my coming
Will be most welcome to my father; welcome,
Mother, to you; and welcome to you, Brother.
For when you died I ministered to you all,   830
With my own hands washed you and dressed your bodies,
And poured libations at your graves. And now,
Because I have given to you, too, Polyneices,
Such honors as I could, I am brought to this.
And yet all wise men will approve my act. [10]
Not for my children, had I been a mother,
Not for a husband, for his moldering body,
Would I have set myself against the city
As I have done. And the law sanctions me.
Losing a husband, I might find another.   840
I could have other children. But my parents
Are hidden from me in the underworld,
So that no brother's life can bud and bloom
Ever again. And therefore, Polyneices,
I paid you special honor. And for this

---

[5]The goddess of love.

[6]Acheron is the river of sorrows; the river of the underworld.

[7]A queen of Thebes, wife of King Amphion. Apollo and Artemis killed all her children, and she, of her own desire returned to her native land and was turned to stone that weeps.

[8]Has the chorus mocked or taunted her? What does this speech reveal about her state of mind?

[9]The goddess of the underworld.

[10]Lines 835 to 847 with their legalistic argument are probably spurious, added by a later author or actor.

Creon has held me guilty of evil-doing,
And leads me captive for my too great boldness.
No bridal bed is mine, no bridal song,
No share in the joys of marriage, and no share
In nursing children and in tending them.   850
But thus afflicted, destitute of friends,
Living, I go down to the vaults of death.
What is the law of heaven that I have broken?
Why should I any longer look to the gods,
Ill-fated as I am? Whose aid should I invoke,
When I for piety am called impious?
If this pleases the gods, then I shall learn
That sin brought death upon me. But if the sin
Lies in my judges, I could wish for them
No harsher fate than they have decreed for me.   860

CHORUS:

Still the storm rages; still the same gusts blow,
Troubling her spirit with their savage breath.

CREON:

Yes. And her guards will pay for being slow.

ANTIGONE:

Ah! With those words I have drawn close to death.

CREON:

You cannot hope that you will now be freed
From the fulfillment of the doom decreed.

ANTIGONE:

O Thebes, O land of my fathers, O city!
O gods who begot and guarded my house from of old!
They seize me, they snatch me away!
Now, now! They show no pity.   870
They give no second's delay.
You elders, you leaders of Thebes, behold me, behold!
The last of the house of your kings, the last.
See what I suffer. See the doom
That is come upon me, and see from whom,
Because to the laws of heaven I held fast.

Exeunt ANTIGONE *and* GUARDS

CHORUS:

This likewise Danaë [11] endured:
The light of heaven she changed for a home brass-bound,
In a tomb-like chamber close immured.
And yet, O my child, her race was with honor crowned,   880
And she guarded the seed of Zeus gold-showered.
But naught from the terrible power of fate is free·
Neither war, nor city walls high-towered,
Nor wealth, nor black ships beaten by the sea.

He too bowed down beneath his doom,
The son of Dryas, swift-angered Edonian king,
Shut fast in a rocky prison's gloom.
How he roused the god with his mad tongue's mocking sting,
As his frenzy faded, he came to know;
For he sought to make the god-filled maenads mute,   890
To quench the Bacchic torches' glow,
And angered the Muses, lovers of the flute.

By the double sea and the dark rocks steely blue
The beach of Bosporus lies and the savage shore
Of Thracian Salmydessus. There the bride
Of Phineus, whose fierce heart no mercy knew,
Dealt his two sons a blow that for vengeance cried;
Ares beheld her hand, all stained with gore,
Grasping the pointed shuttle that pierced through
Their eyes that saw no more.   900

In misery pining, their lot they lamented aloud,
Sons of a mother whose fortune in marriage was ill.
From the ancient line of Erechtheus her blood she traced;
Nurtured in caves far-distant and nursed in cloud,
Daughter of Boreas, daughter of gods, she raced
Swift as a steed on the slope of the soaring hill.
And yet, O child, O child, she also bowed
To the long-lived fates' harsh will.

Enter TIRESIAS *and* BOY

TIRESIAS:

Elders of Thebes, we have come to you with one
Finding for both the pathway that we followed,   910
For in this fashion must the blind be guided.

CREON:

What tidings, old Tiresias, are you bringing?

TIRESIAS:

I will inform you, I the seer. Give heed.

CREON:

To ignore your counsel has not been my custom.

TIRESIAS:

Therefore you kept Thebes on a steady course.

CREON:

I can bear witness to the help you gave.

TIRESIAS:

Mark this. You stand upon the brink of ruin.

CREON:

What terrible words are those? What do you mean?

TIRESIAS:

My meaning is made manifest by my art
And my art's omens. As I took my station   920
Upon my ancient seat of augury,
Where round me birds of every sort come flocking,
I could no longer understand their language.
It was drowned out in a strange, savage clamor,
Shrill, evil, frenzied, inarticulate.
The whirr of wings told me their murderous talons
Tore at each other. Filled with dread, I then
Made trial of burnt sacrifice. The altar
Was fully kindled, but no clear, bright flame
Leaped from the offering; only fatty moisture   930
Oozed from the flesh and trickled on the embers,
Smoking and sputtering. The bladder burst,
And scattered in the air. The folds of fat
Wrapping the thigh-bones melted and left them bare.
Such was the failure of the sacrifice,
That did not yield the sign that I was seeking.
I learned these things from this boy's observation;
He is my guide as I am guide to others.
Your edict brings this suffering to the city,
For every hearth of ours has been defiled   940
And every altar. There the birds and dogs
Have brought their carrion, torn from the corpse
Of ill-starred Polyneices. Hence, the gods
Refuse our prayers, refuse our sacrifice,
Refuse the flame of our burnt-offerings.
No birds cry clearly and auspiciously,
For they are glutted with a slain man's blood.
Therefore, my son, consider what has happened.
All men are liable to grievous error;   950
But he who, having erred, does not remain
Inflexible, but rather makes amends
For ill, is not unwise or unrewarded.
Stubborn self-will incurs the charge of folly.
Give to the fallen the honors he deserves
And do not stab him. Are you being brave
When you inflict new death upon the dead?
Your good I think of; for your good I speak,
And a wise counselor is sweet to hear
When the advice he offers proves of value.

CREON:

Old man, all of you shoot your arrows at me   960
Like archers at a target. You have used
Even the art of prophecy in your plotting.
Long have the tribe of prophets traded in me,
Like a ship's cargo. Drive whatever bargain

---

[11]See any good mythology for these specific references.
In general they refer to others who have been shut up in caves
or prisons. (Danaë's prison was made of brass.)

May please you, buy, sell, heap up for yourself
Silver of Sardis, gold of India. Yet
I tell you this: that man shall not be buried,
Not though the eagles of Zeus himself should bear
The carrion morsels to their master's throne.
Not even from the dread of such pollution   970
Will I permit his burial, since I know
There is no mortal can defile the gods.
But even the wisest men disastrously
May fall, Tiresias, when for money's sake
They utter shameful words with specious wisdom.

TIRESIAS:
Ah! Do men understand, or even consider—

CREON:
Consider what? Doubtless some platitude!

TIRESIAS:
How precious beyond any wealth is prudence.

CREON:
How full of evil is the lack of prudence.

TIRESIAS:
Yet you are sick, sick with that same disease.   980

CREON:
I will not in reply revile a prophet.

TIRESIAS:
You do. You say my prophecy is false.

CREON:
Well, all the race of seers are mercenary.

TIRESIAS:
And love of base wealth marks the breed of tyrants.

CREON:
Are you aware that you address your King?

TIRESIAS:
I made you King by helping you save Thebes.

CREON:
Wise in your art and vicious in your acts.

TIRESIAS:
Do not enrage me. I should keep my secret.

CREON:
Reveal it. Speak. But do not look for profit.

TIRESIAS:
You too will find no profit in my words.   990

CREON:
How can you earn your pay? I will not change.

TIRESIAS:
Then know this. Yes, be very sure of it.
Only a few more times will you behold
The swift course of the chariot of the sun
Before you give as payment for the dead
Your own dead flesh and blood. For you have thrust
A living soul to darkness, in a tomb
Imprisoned without pity. And a corpse,
Belonging to the gods below you keep
Unpurified, unburied, unrevered.   1000
The dead are no concern either of yours
Or of the gods above, yet you offend them.
So the avengers, the destroyers, Furies
Of Hades and the gods, lurking in ambush,
Wait to inflict your sins upon your head.
Do you still think my tongue is lined with silver?
A time will come, and will not linger coming,
That will awaken in your house the wailing
Of men and women. Hatred shakes the cities,
Hatred of you. Their sons are mangled corpses,   1010
Hallowed with funeral rites by dogs or beasts
Or birds who bear the all-polluting stench
To every city having hearth or altar.
You goaded me, and therefore like an archer
I shoot my angry arrows at your heart,
Sure arrows; you shall not escape their sting.
Boy, lead me home. Let him expend his rage
On younger men, and let him learn to speak
With a more temperate tongue, and school his heart
To feelings finer than his present mood.   1020

Exeunt TIRESIAS *and* BOY

CHORUS:
Sir, he is gone, with fearful prophecies.
And from the time that these dark hairs have whitened,
I have known this: never has he foretold
Anything that proved false concerning Thebes.

CREON:
I also know it well, and it dismays me.
To yield is bitter. But to resist, and bring
A curse upon my pride is no less bitter.

CHORUS:
Son of Menoeceus, listen. You must listen.

CREON:
What should I do? Tell me, I will obey.

CHORUS:
Go. Free the girl. Release her from the cavern,   1030
And build a tomb for the man you would not bury.

CREON:
So that is your advice—that I should yield?

CHORUS:
Sir, you should not delay. The gods are swift
In cutting short man's folly with their curse.

CREON:
How hard it is to change! Yet I obey.
I will give up what I had set my heart on.
No one can stand against the blows of fate.

CHORUS:
Go. Go yourself. These things are not for others.

CREON:
I will go this moment. Guards there! All of you!
Take up your axes. Quick! Quick! Over there.   1040
I imprisoned her myself, and I myself
Will set her free. And yet my mind misgives me.
Never to break the ancient law is best.

Exit CREON

CHORUS:
   Thou art known by many a name.
  O Bacchus! To thee we call.
  Cadmean Semele's[12] glory and pride,
Begotten of Zeus, whose terrible lightnings flame,
   Whose thunders appall.
Bacchus, thou dost for us all in thy love provide.
  Over Icaria thou dost reign,   1050
  And where the worshippers journey slow
  To the rites of Eleusis, where mountains shield
The multitudes crossing Demeter's welcoming plain.
Thou makest this mother-city of maenads thine own,
  A city beside the rippling flow
Of the gentle river, beside the murderous field
  Where the teeth of the dragon were sown.

   In the torches' wind-blown flare
  Thou art seen, in their flicker and smoke,
Where the two-fold peaks of Parnassus gleam,   1060
Corycian nymphs, as they move through the ruddy glare,
   Thee, Bacchus, invoke.
They move in their dance beside the Castalian stream.
  O Bacchus, guardian divine!
  Down from the slopes of Nysa's hills
  Where a mantle of ivy covers the ground,
From headlands rich with the purple grape and the vine,
Thou comest to us, thou comest. O be not long!
  Thy triumph the echoing city fills.
The streets are loud with thy praises; the highways
   resound,   1070
  Resound with immortal song.

---

[12]Semele was the mother of Bacchus, or Dionysus. Through
line 171 this choral song describes the spread of the worship
of Dionysus to Eleusis (near Athens) and Delphi (Parnassus).
The chief characteristic of this worship is the troop of frenzied
women, the maenads.

Thou honorest highly our Theban city,
   Thou, and thy mother by lightning slain.
Our people sicken. O Bacchus have pity!
   Across the strait with its moaning wave,
Down from Parnassus, come thou again!
   Come with thy healing feet, and save!

O thou who leadest the stars in chorus,
   Jubilant stars with their breath of fire,
Offspring of Zeus, appear before us!   1080
   Lord of the tumult of night, appear!
With the frenzied dance of thy maenad choir,
   Bacchus, thou giver of good, draw near!

Enter MESSENGER

MESSENGER:
   You of the house of Cadmus and Amphíon,
   No man's estate can ever be established
   Firmly enough to warrant praise or blame.
   Fortune, from day to day, exalts the lucky
   And humbles the unlucky. No one knows
   Whether his present lot can long endure.
   For Creon once was blest, as I count blessings;   1090
   He had saved this land of Cadmus from its foes;
   He was the sovereign and ruled alone,
   The noble father of a royal house.
   And now, all has been lost. Because a man
   Who has forfeited his joy is not alive,
   He is a living corpse. Heap, if you will,
   Your house with riches; live in regal pomp.
   Yet if your life is unhappy, all these things
   Are worth not even the shadow of a vapor
   Put in the balance against joy alone.   1100
CHORUS:
   What new disaster has the King's house suffered?
MESSENGER:
   Death. And the guilt of death lies on the living.
CHORUS:
   The guilt of death! Who has been killed? Who killed him?
MESSENGER:
   Haemon is killed, and by no stranger's hand.
CHORUS:
   He killed himself? Or did his father kill him?
MESSENGER:
   He killed himself, enraged by his murderous father.
CHORUS:
   Tiresias! Now your prophecy is fulfilled.
MESSENGER:
   Consider, therefore, what remains to do.
CHORUS:
   There is the Queen, wretched Eurydice.
   Perhaps mere chance has brought her from the palace;   1110
   Perhaps she has learned the news about her son.
Enter EURYDICE
EURYDICE:
   Thebans, I heard you talking here together
   When I was on my way to greet the goddess,
   Pallas Athene, and to pray to her.
   Just as I loosed the fastening of the door,
   The words that told of my calamity
   Struck heavily upon my ear. In terror
   I fell back fainting in my women's arms.
   But now, repeat your story. I shall hear it
   As one who is not ignorant of grief.   1120
MESSENGER:
   My Lady, I will bear witness to what I saw,
   And will omit no syllable of the truth.
   Why should I comfort you with words that later
   Would prove deceitful? Truth is always best.
   Across the plain I guided my Lord Creon
   To where unpitied Polyneices lay,

A corpse mangled by dogs. Then we besought
Hecate, goddess of the roads, and Pluto
To moderate their wrath, and to show mercy.
We washed the dead with ceremonial water.   1130
Gathering the scattered fragments that remained,
With fresh-cut boughs we burned them. We heaped up
A mound of native earth above·his ashes.
Then we approached the cavern of Death's bride,
The rock-floored marriage-chamber. While as yet
We were far distant, someone heard the sound
Of loud lament in that unhallowed place,
And came to tell our master. As the King
Drew near, there floated through the air a voice,
Faint, indistinct, that uttered a bitter cry.   1140
The King burst out in anguish: 'Can it be
That I, in my misery, have become a prophet?

Will this be the saddest road I ever trod?
My son's voice greets me. Quickly, slaves! Go quickly!
When you have reached the sepulcher, get through
The opening where the stones are wrenched away,
Get to the mouth of the burial chamber. Look,
See if I know his voice—Haemon's, my son's—
Or if I am deluded by the gods.'
We followed our despairing master's bidding   1150
And in the farthest recess of the tomb
We found Antigone, hanging, with her veil
Noosed round her neck. And with her we found Haemon,
His arms flung round her waist, grieving aloud
For his bride lost in death, his ruined marriage,
His father's deeds. But when his father saw him,
Creon cried piteously and going in,
Called to him brokenly: 'My son, my son,
What have you done? What are you thinking of?
What dreadful thing has driven you out of your mind?   1160
Son, come away. I beg you. I beseech you.'
But Haemon glared at him with furious eyes
Instead of answering, spat in his face,
And drew his sword. His father turned to fly
So that he missed his aim. Immediately,
In bitter self-reproach, the wretched boy
Leaned hard against his sword, and drove it deep
Into his side. Then while his life yet lingered,
With failing strength he drew Antigone close;
And as he lay there gasping heavily,   1170
Over her white cheek his blood ebbed away.
The dead lie clasped together. He is wedded,
Not in this world but in the house of Death.
He has borne witness that of all the evils
Afflicting man, the worst is lack of wisdom.

Exit EURYDICE

CHORUS:
   What does that mean? Who can interpret it?
   The Queen has gone without a single word.
MESSENGER:
   It startles me. And yet I hope it means
   That hearing these dreadful things about her son,
   She will not let herself show grief in public   1180
   But will lament in private with her women.
   Schooled in discretion, she will do no wrong.
CHORUS:
   How can we tell? Surely too great a silence
   Is no less ominous than too loud lament.
MESSENGER:
   Then I will enter. Perhaps she is concealing
   Some secret purpose in her passionate heart.
   I will find out, for you are right in saying
   Too great a silence may be ominous.

Exit MESSENGER. *Enter* CREON *with* ATTENDANTS,
carrying the body of HAEMON *on a bier*

CHORUS:
   Thebans, look there! The King himself draws near,
   Bearing a load whose tale is all too clear.   1190

This is a work—if we dare speak our thought—
That not another's but his own hands wrought.

CREON:

    O, how may my sin be told?
The stubborn, death-fraught sin of a darkened brain!
    Behold us here, behold
Father and son, the slayer and the slain!
    Pain, only pain
Has come of my design.
    Fate struck too soon; too soon your spirit fled.
    My son, my young son, you are lying dead   1200
Not for your folly, but for mine, for mine.

CHORUS:

    Sir, you have come to learn the right too late.

CREON:

    My lesson has been bitter and complete.
Some god has struck me down with crushing weight,
Filling my heart with cruelty and hate,
    Trampling my happiness beneath his feet.
    Grief, bitter grief, is man's fate.

Enter MESSENGER

MESSENGER (*indicating* HAEMON):

    Your load is heavy, Sir, but there is more.
That is the burden you are bearing now.
Soon you must bear new woe within your house.   1210

CREON:

    And what worse misery can follow this?

MESSENGER:

    Your wife is dead, a mother like her son.
Poor woman, by her own hand she has died.

CREON:

    By her own hand she died.
Death, spare me! Can you never have your fill?
    Never be satisfied?
Herald of evil, messenger of ill,
    Your harsh words kill,
They smite me now anew.
    My wife is dead—You tell me my wife is dead.   1220
    Death after death is heaped upon my head.
Speak to me, boy. Is what you tell me true?

MESSENGER:

    It is no longer hidden. Sir, look there.
        (*The body of* EURYDICE *is disclosed
        through the palace doors*)

CREON:

    Another horror that makes blind mine eyes!
What further agony has fate in store?
My dead son's body in my arms I bore,
    And now beside him his dead mother lies.
    I can endure no more.

MESSENGER:

    There at the altar with a keen-edged knife
She stabbed herself; and as her eyes were darkened,   1230
She wailed the death of Megareus, her son,
Who earlier had met a noble fate;
She wailed for Haemon; then, with her last breath,
You, as the slayer of your sons, she cursed.

CREON:

    I am shaken with terror, with terror past belief.
Is there none here to end my anguish? None?
    No sword to pierce me? Broken with my grief,
So steeped in agony that we are one.

MESSENGER:

    Sir, as she died, she burdened you with guilt,
Charging you with the death of both your sons.   1240

CREON:

    And by what act of violence did she die?

MESSENGER:

    Hearing the shrill lament for Haemon's fate,
Deep in her heart she drove the bright blade home.

CREON (*to* HAEMON):

    I am your slayer, I alone.
I am guilty, only I.
    I, and none other, must atone.
Lead me away. The truth I own.
    Nothing is left, except to die.

CHORUS:

    If anything can be good, those words are good.
For when calamity has come upon us,   1250
The thing that is the briefest is the best.

CREON:

    Draw near me, death! O longed for death, draw near!
Most welcome destiny, make no delay.
    Tell me my last hour, my last breath, is here.
I have no wish to see another day.

CHORUS:

    Such things are yet to come. We are concerned
With doing what must needs be done today.
The future rests in other hands than ours.

CREON:

    That is my whole desire. That is my prayer.

CHORUS:

    No. Do not pray. Men must accept their doom.   1260

CREON:

    My life's work there before me lies.
My folly slew my wife, my son.
    I know not where to turn mine eyes.
All my misdeeds before me rise.
    Lead me away, brought low, undone.
                Exit CREON

CHORUS:

    The crown of happiness is to be wise.
Honor the gods, and the gods' edicts prize.
They strike down boastful men and men grown bold.
Wisdom we learn at last, when we are old.

EXERCISES

1. In considering the structure of the play, consider the placement of the choral odes. How do they create the play's structure?

2. As far as the central question about the meaning of the play and the tragic hero, consider lines 334-336 (and the alternative translation), and lines 563-565 and its alternate translation. If these lines apply both to Creon and Antigone, would we have a double tragedy?

3. Where do you find Creon's justification for his first decision not to bury Polyneices? How valid is his justification?

4. Where do you find Antigone's justification for burying Polyneices? Is her reasoning sound?

5. At the first of the play, the chorus supports Creon. Are they sincere? What evidence from the play can you find to support your answer?

6. The final speech of the chorus may summarize the entire meaning of the play. If this is true, what is that final meaning, and how do all the earlier events and important speeches lead to this?

7. Sometimes in modern production, Creon is played as a tyrant, made almost insane by his furious anger. How do you visualize him? How do you visualize Antigone?

8. A very interesting minor character is the guard who reports Polyneices' burial. What kind of a character do you think he is?

Phaedo
Plato

The scene of this dialogue is a small town in the Peloponnesus to which Phaidon (Phaedo) has gone some time after the death of Socrates. Here he encounters Echecrates, a former student of Socrates. Echecrates asks Phaedo about the death, and the remainder of the dialogue ensues. Except in a few instances which are so designated, Phaedo is the speaker, recounting all of the conversation of Socrates' last day.

The central problem of this dialogue is the fate of the soul after the death of the body, and in the discussion Socrates touches on most of the doctrines which he had developed during his life-time. Some of the ideas which the reader might notice are these: (1) the idea of the separateness of soul and body; (2) the "Platonic" virtues; (3) the doctrine of opposites and of the ebb and flow of all things from their opposites; (4) the concept of the soul's recollection as evidence of the pre-existence of the soul; (5) the whole thought about reincarnation of the soul; (6) and the concept that the soul is not simply a harmony of the various qualities which make up the body.

You might also notice the extent to which Socrates builds his philosophy on the thought of earlier philosopher-scientists, particularly the Eleatics.

PHAEDO (Phaidon)

The Death of Socrates, 399 B.C.

Echecrates, Phaidon.

Apollodoros, Socrates, Cebes, Simmias, Criton.

ECHECRATES: Were you there yourself, Phaidon, with Socrates, on the day when he took the poison in prison, or did you hear about it from someone?

PHAIDON: I was there myself, Echecrates.

ECHECRATES: Then what was it our friend said before his death? And how did he end? I should be glad to hear. You see no one at all from our part of the world[1] goes now to visit in Athens, and no visitor has come to us from there this long time who might be able to tell us properly what happened; all they could say was, he took the poison and died; no one could tell us anything about the other details.

PHAIDON: Then you never heard how things went at the trial?

ECHECRATES: Yes, somebody did bring news of that, and we were surprised how long it seemed between the sentence and his death. Why was that, Phaidon?

PHAIDON: It was just a piece of luck, Echecrates; for the day before the trial it so happened that the wreath was put on the poop of the ship which the Athenians send to Delos.

ECHECRATES: What ship is that?

PHAIDON: That is the ship, as the Athenians say, in which Theseus once went off to Crete with those "twice seven," you know, and saved them and saved himself.[2] The Athenians vowed to Apollo, so it is said, that if the lives of these were saved, they would send a sacred mission every year to Delos; and they do send it still, every year ever since that, to honour the god. As soon as the mission has begun, then, it is their law to keep the city pure during that time, and to put no one to death before the ship arrives at Delos and comes back again here; this often takes some time, when the winds happen to delay them. The beginning of the mission is when the priest of Apollo lays a wreath on the poop of the ship, and this happened, as I say, the day before the trial. Accordingly Socrates had a long time in prison between the trial and his death.

ECHECRATES: Then what about the death itself, Phaidon? What was said or done, and which of his friends were with him? Or did the magistrates forbid their presence, and did he die alone with no friends there?

PHAIDON: Oh no, friends were with him, quite a number of them.

ECHECRATES: That's just what I want to know; please be so kind as to tell me all about it as clearly as possible, unless you happen to be busy.

PHAIDON: Oh, I have plenty of time, and I will try to tell you the whole story; indeed, to remember Socrates, and what he said himself, and what was said to him is always the most precious thing in the world to me.

ECHECRATES: Well, Phaidon, those who are going to hear you will feel the same; pray try to tell the whole story as exactly as you can.

PHAIDON: I must say I had the strangest feeling being there. I felt no pity, as one might, being present at the death of a dear friend; for the man seemed happy to me, Echecrates, in bearing and in speech. How fearlessly and nobly he met his end! I could not help thinking that divine providence was with that man as he passed from this world to the next, and on coming there also it would be well with him, if ever with anyone that ever was. For this reason I felt no pity at all, as one might at a scene of mourning; and yet not the pleasure we used to have in our philosophic discussions. The conversation was certainly of that sort, but I really had an extraordinary feeling, a strange mixture of pleasure and pain at once, when I remembered that then and there that man was to make his end. And all of us who were present were very much in the same state, sometimes laughing, sometimes shedding tears, and one of us particularly, Apollodoros —no doubt you know the man and his ways.

ECHECRATES: Oh yes, of course.

PHAIDON: Well, he behaved quite as usual, and I was broken down myself, and so were others.

ECHECRATES: But who were they, Phaidon?

PHAIDON: Of our countrymen[3] there was this Apollodoros I have mentioned, and Critobulos and his father, and, besides, Hermogenes and Epigenes and Aischines and Antisthenes; there was also Ctesippos the Paianian and Menexenos, and others of our countrymen; but Plato was ill, I think.

ECHECRATES: Were any foreigners present?

PHAIDON: Yes, Simmias the Theban and Cebes and Phaidondes; and from Megara, Eucleides and Terpsion.

ECHECRATES: Oh, were not Aristippos and Cleombrotos present?

PHAIDON: No, they were said to be in Aegina.

ECHECRATES: Was anyone else there?

PHAIDON: I think these are about all who were present.

ECHECRATES: Very well; tell me, what did you talk about?

PHAIDON: I will try to tell you the whole story from the beginning. You see we had been accustomed during all the former days to visit Socrates, myself and the rest. We used to gather early at the court where the trial had been, for that was near the prison. We always waited until the prison was opened, passing the time together, for it was not opened early; and when it was opened we went in to Socrates and generally spent the day with him. That day, however, we gathered earlier than usual; for the day before, after we left the prison in the evening, we learnt that the ship had come in from Delos; so we warned one another to come as early as possible. to the usual place. We came early, then, and the porter who used to answer the door came out to us, and told us to wait and not to go in till he gave the word; for, he said, "The Eleven[4] are knocking off his fetters and informing him that he must die today."

After a short while he came back and told us to go in. So we went in, and found Socrates just released, and Xanthippe,[5] you know her, with his little boy, sitting beside him. Then when Xanthippe saw us, she cried out in lamentation and said as women do, "O Socrates! Here is the last time your friends will speak to you and you to them!"

---

[1]Phlius, a small town in the Peloponnesus (Morea)about sixty miles from Athens.

[2]In Athenian legend, Athens because of a past misdeed had to send seven youths and seven maidens every ninth year to King Minos in Crete to be devoured by the Minotaur. Theseus of Athens went to Crete and killed the monster.

[3]Athenians.

[4]In charge of the prison and of executions.

[5]Socrates' wife.

Socrates glanced at Criton and said quietly, "Please let someone take her home, Criton."

Then some of Criton's people led her away crying and beating her breast. Socrates sat up on his bed, and bent back his leg and rubbed it with his hand, and said while he rubbed it, "How strange a thing it seems, my friends, that which people call pleasure! And how wonderful is its relation to pain, which they suppose to be its opposite; both together they will not come to a man, yet if he pursues one of the pair, and catches it, he is almost compelled to catch the other, too; so they seem to be both hung together from one head. I think that Aesop would have made a fable, if he had noticed this; he would have said they were at war, and God wanted to make peace between them and could not, and accordingly hung them together by their heads to the same thing, and therefore whenever you get one, the other follows after. That's just what it seems like to me; first came the pain in my leg from the irons, and here seems to come following after it, pleasure."

Cebes took up here, and said, "Upon my word, Socrates, I am much obliged to you for reminding me. About your poems, I mean, when you put into verse Aesop's fables, and the prelude for Apollo; many people have asked me, for example Euenos, the other day, what on earth put it in your mind to make those poems after you came into prison, although you never made any before. Then if you care that I should be able to answer Euenos, next time he asks me, and I'm sure he will, tell me what to say."

"Tell him then, Cebes," he said, "just the truth: that I did not want to rival him or his creations when I did it, for I knew it would not be easy; but I was trying to find out the meaning of certain dreams, and getting it off my conscience, in case they meant to command me to attempt that sort of composition. The dreams went like this: In my past life, the same dream often used to come to me, in different shapes at different times, but saying the same thing, 'Socrates, get to work and compose music!' [6] Formerly I took this to mean what I was already doing; I thought the dream was urging and encouraging me, as people do in cheering on their own men when they are running a race, to compose—which, taking philosophy to be the highest form of composition, I was doing already; but now after the trial, while the festival was putting off my execution, I thought that, if the dream should really command me to work at this common kind of composition, I ought not to disobey the dream but to do so. For it seemed safer not to go away before getting it off my conscience by composing poetry, and so obeying the dream. So first of all I composed in honour of the god [7] whose festival this was; after the god, I considered that a poet must compose fiction if he was to be a poet, not true tales, and I was no fiction-monger, and therefore I took the fictions that I found to my hand and knew, namely Aesop's, and composed the first that came. Then tell Euenos that, Cebes, and bid him farewell, and tell him to follow me as soon as he can, if he is sensible. I am going away, as it seems, today; for so the Athenians command."

"What advice, Socrates," he said, "to give to Euenos! I have often met the man; from what I have seen of him so far he will be the last man to obey!"

"Why," said he, "is not Euenos a philosopher?"

"I think so," said Simmias.

"Then Euenos will be willing enough, and so will everyone who goes properly into the subject. But perhaps he will not do violence to himself; for they say that is not lawful."

As he spoke, he let down his legs on to the ground, and sat thus during the rest of the talk. Then Cebes asked him, "What do you mean, Socrates, by saying, that it is not lawful for a man to do violence to himself, but that the philosopher would be willing to follow the dying?"

"Why, Cebes," he said, "have not you and Simmias heard all about such things from Philolaos, when you were his pupils?"

"Nothing clear, Socrates."

"Well truly, all I say myself is only from hearsay; however, what I happen to have heard I don't mind telling you. Indeed, it is perhaps most proper that one who is going to depart and take up his abode in that world should think about the life over there and say what sort of life we imagine it to be: for what else could one do with the time till sunset?"

"Well then, why pray do they say it is not lawful for a man to take his own life, my dear Socrates? I have already heard Philolaos myself, as you asked me just now, when he was staying in our parts, and I have heard others too, and they all said we must not do that; but I never heard anything clear about it."

"Well, go on trying," said Socrates, "and perhaps you may hear something. It might perhaps seem surprising to you if in this one thing, of all that happens to a human being, there is never any exception—if it never chances to a man amongst the other chances of his life that sometimes for some people it is better to die than to live; but it does probably seem surprising to you if those people for whom it *is* better to die may not rightly do this good to themselves, but must wait for some other benefactor."

And Cebes answered, with a light laugh. "True for ye, by Zeus!" using his native Doric.

"Indeed, put like this," said Socrates, "it would seem unreasonable; but possibly there is a grain of reason in it. At least, the tale whispered in secret about these things is that we men are in a sort of custody, and a man must not release himself or run away, which appears a great mystery to me and not easy to see through. But I do think, Cebes, it is right to say the gods are those who take care of us, and that we men are one of the gods' possessions—don't you think so?"

"Yes, I do," said Cebes.

"Then," said he, "if one of your own possessions, your slave, should kill himself, without your indicating to him that you wanted him to die, you would be angry with him, and punish him if there were any punishment?"

"Certainly," said he.

"Possibly, then, it is not unreasonable in that sense, that a man must not kill himself before God sends on him some necessity, like that which is present here now."

"Yes indeed, that seems likely," said Cebes. "But you said just now, Socrates, that philosophers ought cheerfully to be willing to die; that does seem unreasonable, at least if there is reason in what we have just said, that God is he who cares for us and we are his possessions. That the wisest men should not object to depart out of this service in which we are overseen by the best overseers there are, gods, there is no reason in that. For I don't suppose a wise man thinks he will care better for himself when he is free. But a foolish man might well believe that he should run away from an owner; and he would not remember that from a good one he ought not to run away but to stay as long as he could, and so he would thoughtlessly run away, while the man of sense would desire always to be with one better than himself. Indeed, in this case, Socrates, the opposite of what was said would be likely: It is proper that wise men should object to die, and foolish men should be glad."

Socrates, hearing this, was pleased, I thought, at the way Cebes dealt with the matter; and, glancing away at us, he said, "Cebes is always on the hunt for arguments, and won't believe straight off whatever one says."

And Simmias added, "But I tell you, Socrates, I think I now see something in what Cebes says, myself; for what could men want, if they are truly wise, in running away from owners better than themselves, and lightly shaking them off? And I

---

[6]"Music" included poetry.

[7]Apollo.

really think Cebes is aiming his argument at you, because you take it so easily to leave both us and good masters, as you admit yourself, gods!"

"Quite right," said he. "I think I must answer this before you just as if you were a court!"

"Exactly," said Simmias.

"Very well," said he, "I will try to convince you better than I did my judges. I believe, my dear Simmias and Cebes, that I shall pass over first of all to other gods, both wise and good, secondly to dead men better than those in this world; and if I did not think so, I should do wrong in not objecting to death; but, believing this, be assured that I hope I shall find myself in the company of good men, although I would not maintain it for certain; but that I shall pass over to gods who are very good masters, be assured that if I would maintain for certain anything else of the kind, I would with certainty maintain this. Then for these reasons, so far from objecting, I have good hopes that something remains for the dead, as has been the belief from time immemorial, and something much better for the good than for the bad."

"Then," said Simmias, "do you mean to keep this idea to yourself and go away with it, or will you give us a share? This good find seems to be a case of findings is sharings[8] between us, and don't forget you are on your defence, to see if you can convince us."

"Well, I'll try," he said.

"But first I see Criton here has been wanting to say something ever so long; let's ask what it is."

"Only this," Criton said, "the man who is to give you the poison keeps telling me to advise you not to talk too much. He says people get hotter by talking, and nothing like that ought to accompany the poison; otherwise people who do that often have to take two or three potions."

And Socrates said, "Oh, let him be; he must just be ready to give me two, or three if necessary."

"I guessed as much," said Criton, "but he keeps bothering me."

"Oh, let him be," said he. "Now then, I want to give the proof at once, to you as my judges, why I think it likely that one who has spent his life in philosophy should be confident when he is going to die, and have good hopes that he will win the greatest blessings in the next world when he has ended: so Simmias and Cebes my judges, I will try to show how this could be true.

"The fact is, those who tackle philosophy aright are simply and solely practising dying, practising death, all the time, but nobody sees it. If this is true, then it would surely be unreasonable that they should earnestly do this and nothing else all their lives, yet when death comes they should object to what they had been so long earnestly practising."

Simmias laughed at this, and said, "I don't feel like laughing just now, Socrates, but you have made me laugh. I think the many if they heard that would say, 'That's a good one for the philosophers!' And other people in my city would heartily agree that philosophers are really suffering from a wish to die, and now they have found them out, that they richly deserve it!"

"That would be true, Simmias," said Socrates, "except the words 'found out.' For they have not found out in what sense the real philosophers wish to die and deserve to die, and what kind of death it is. Let us say good-bye to them," he went on, "and ask ourselves: Do we think there is such a thing as death?"

"Certainly," Simmias put in.

"Is it anything more than the separation of the soul from the body?" said Socrates. "Death is, that the body separates from the soul, and remains by itself apart from the soul, and the soul, separated from the body, exists by itself apart from the body. Is death anything but that?"

"No," he said, "that is what death is."

"Then consider, my good friend, if you agree with me here, for I think this is the best way to understand the question we are examining. Do you think it the part of a philosopher to be earnestly concerned with what are called pleasures, such as these—eating and drinking, for example?"

"Not at all," said Simmias.

"The pleasures of love, then?"

"Oh no."

"Well, do you suppose a man like that regards the other bodily indulgences as precious? Getting fine clothes and shoes and other bodily adornments—ought he to price them high or low, beyond whatever share of them it is absolutely necessary to have?"

"Low, I think," he said, "if he is a true philosopher."

"Then in general," he said, "do you think that such a man's concern is not for the body, but as far as he can he stands aloof from that and turns towards the soul?"

"I do."

"Then firstly, is it not clear that in such things the philosopher as much as possible sets free the soul from communion with the body, more than other men?"

"So it appears."

"And I suppose, Simmias, it must seem to most men that he who has no pleasure in such things and takes no share in them does not deserve to live, but he is getting pretty close to death if he does not care about pleasures which he has by means of the body."

"Quite true, indeed."

"Well then, what about the actual getting of wisdom? Is the body in the way or not, if a man takes it with him as companion in the search? I mean, for example, is there any truth for men in their sight and hearing? Or as poets are forever dinning into our ears, do we hear nothing and see nothing exactly? Yet if these of our bodily senses are not exact and clear, the others will hardly be, for they are all inferior to these, don't you think so?"

"Certainly," he said.

"Then," said he, "when does the soul get hold of the truth? For whenever the soul tries to examine anything in company with the body, it is plain that it is deceived by it."

"Quite true."

"Then is it not clear that in reasoning, if anywhere, something of the realities becomes visible to it?"

"Yes."

"And I suppose it reasons best when none of these senses disturbs it, hearing or sight, or pain, or pleasure indeed, but when it is completely by itself and says good-bye to the body, and so far as possible has no dealings with it, when it reaches out and grasps that which really is."

"That is true."

"And is it not then that the philosopher's soul chiefly holds the body cheap and escapes from it, while it seeks to be by itself?"

"So it seems."

"Let us pass on, Simmias. Do we say there is such a thing as justice by itself, or not?"

"We do say so, certainly!"

"Such a thing as the good and beautiful?"

"Of course!"

"And did you ever see one of them with your eyes?"

"Never," said he.

"By any other sense of those the body has did you ever grasp them? I mean all such things, greatness, health, strength, in short everything that really is the nature of things whatever they are: Is it through the body that the real truth is perceived? Or is this better—whoever of us prepares himself most completely and most exactly to comprehend each thing which he examines would come nearest to knowing each one?"

---

[8] A proverb.

"Certainly."

"And would he do that most purely who should approach each with his intelligence alone, not adding sight to intelligence, or dragging in any other sense along with reasoning, but using the intelligence uncontaminated alone by itself, while he tries to hunt out each essence uncontaminated, keeping clear of eyes and ears and, one might say, of the whole body, because he thinks the body disturbs him and hinders the soul from getting possession of truth and wisdom when body and soul are companions—is not this the man, Simmias, if anyone, who will hit reality?"

"Nothing could be more true, Socrates," said Simmias.

"Then from all this," said Socrates, "genuine philosophers must come to some such opinion as follows, so as to make to one another statements such as these: 'A sort of direct path, so to speak, seems to take us to the conclusion that so long as we have the body with us in our enquiry, and our soul is mixed up with so great an evil, we shall never attain sufficiently what we desire, and that, we say, is the truth. For the body provides thousands of busy distractions because of its necessary food; besides, if diseases fall upon us, they hinder us from the pursuit of the real. With loves and desires and fears and all kinds of fancies and much rubbish, it infects us, and really and truly makes us, as they say, unable to think one little bit about anything at any time. Indeed, wars and factions and battles all come from the body and its desires, and from nothing else. For the desire of getting wealth causes all wars, and we are compelled to desire wealth by the body, being slaves to its culture; therefore we have no leisure for philosophy, from all these reasons. Chief of all is that if we do have some leisure, and turn away from the body to speculate on something, in our searches it is everywhere interfering, it causes confusion and disturbance, and dazzles us so that it will not let us see the truth; so in fact we see that if we are ever to know anything purely we must get rid of it, and examine the real things by the soul alone; and then, it seems, after we are dead, as the reasoning shows, not while we live, we shall possess that which we desire, lovers of which we say we are, namely wisdom. For if it is impossible in company with the body to know anything purely, one thing of two follows: either knowledge is possible nowhere, or only after death; for then alone the soul will be quite by itself apart from the body, but not before. And while we are alive, we shall be nearest to knowing, as it seems, if as far as possible we have no commerce or communion with the body which is not absolutely necessary, and if we are not infected with its nature, but keep ourselves pure from it, until God himself shall set us free. And so, pure and rid of the body's foolishness, we shall probably be in the company of those like ourselves, and shall know through our own selves complete incontamination, and that is perhaps the truth. But for the impure to grasp the pure is not, it seems, allowed.' So we must think, Simmias, and so we must say to one another, all who are rightly lovers of learning; don't you agree?"

"Assuredly, Socrates."

"Then," said Socrates, "if this is true, my comrade, there is great hope that when I arrive where I am travelling, there if anywhere I shall sufficiently possess that for which all our study has been pursued in this past life. So the journey which has been commanded for me is made with good hope, and the same for any other man who believes he has got his mind purified, as I may call it."

"Certainly," replied Simmias.

"And is not purification really that which has been mentioned so often in our discussion, to separate as far as possible the soul from the body, and to accustom it to collect itself together out of the body in every part, and to dwell alone by itself as far as it can, both at this present and in the future, being freed from the body as if from a prison?"

"By all means," said he.

"Then is not this called death—a freeing and separation of soul from body?"

"Not a doubt of that," said he.

"But to set it free, as we say, is the chief endeavour of those who rightly love wisdom, nay of those alone, and the very care and practice of the philosophers is nothing but the freeing and separation of soul from body, don't you think so?"

"It appears to be so."

"Then, as I said at first, it would be absurd for a man preparing himself in his life to be as near as possible to death, so to live, and then when death came, to object?"

"Of course."

"Then in fact, Simmias," he said, "those who rightly love wisdom are practising dying, and death to them is the least terrible thing in the world. Look at it in this way: If they are everywhere at enmity with the body, and desire the soul to be alone by itself, and if, when this very thing happens, they shall fear and object—would not that be wholly unreasonable? Should they not willingly go to a place where there is good hope of finding what they were in love with all through life (and they loved wisdom), and of ridding themselves of the companion which they hated? When human favourites and wives and sons have died, many have been willing to go down to the grave, drawn by the hope of seeing there those they used to desire, and of being with them; but one who is really in love with wisdom and holds firm to this same hope, that he will find it in the grave, and nowhere else worth speaking of —will he then fret at dying and not go thither rejoicing? We must surely think, my comrade, that he will go rejoicing, if he is really a philosopher; he will surely believe that he will find wisdom in its purity there and there alone. If this is true, would it not be most unreasonable, as I said just now, if such a one feared death?"

"Unreasonable, I do declare," said he.

"Then this is proof enough," he said, "that if you see a man fretting because he is to die, he was not really a philosopher, but a philosoma—not a wisdom-lover but a body-lover. And no doubt the same man is money-lover and honours-lover, one or both."

"It certainly is so, as you say," he replied.

"Then, Simmias," he said, "does not what is called courage belong specially to persons so disposed as philosophers are?"

"I have no doubt of it," said he.

"And the same with temperance, what the many call temperance, not to be agitated about desires but to hold them lightly and decently; does not this belong to those alone who hold the body lightly and live in philosophy?"

"That must be so," he said.

"You see," said he, "if you will consider the courage and temperance of others, you will think it strange."

"How so, Socrates?"

"You know," said he, "that everyone else thinks death one of the greatest evils?"

"Indeed I do," he said.

"Then is it not fear of greater evils which makes the brave endure death, when they do?"

"That is true."

"Then fear, and fearing, makes all men brave, except philosophers. Yet it is unreasonable to become brave by fear and cowardice!"

"Certainly."

"And what of the decent men? Are they not in the same case? A sort of intemperance makes them temperate! Although we say such a thing is impossible, nevertheless with that self-complacent temperance they are in a similar case; because they fear to be deprived of other pleasures, and because they desire them, they abstain from some because they are mastered by others. They say, of course, intemperance is 'to be ruled by pleasures'; yet what happens to them is, to master some pleasures and to be mastered by others, and this is much the same as what was said just now, that in a way intemperance has made them temperate."

"So it seems."

"Bless you, Simmias! This is hardly an honest deal in virtue—to trade pleasure for pleasure, and pain for pain, and fear for fear, and even greater for less, as if they were current coin; no, the only honest currency, for which all these must be traded, is wisdom, and all things are in truth to be bought with this and sold for this.[9] And courage and temperance and justice and, in short, true virtue, depend on wisdom, whether pleasure and fear and all such things are added or taken away. But when they are deprived of wisdom and exchanged one for another, virtue of that kind is no more than a make-believe,[10] a thing in reality slavish and having no health or truth in it; and truth is in reality a cleansing from all such things, and temperance and justice and courage, and wisdom itself, are a means of purification. Indeed, it seems those who established our mystic rites were no fools; they in truth spoke with a hidden meaning long ago when they said that whoever is uninitiated and unconsecrated when he comes to the house of Hades will lie in mud, but the purified and consecrated when he goes there will dwell with gods. Indeed, as they say in the rites, 'Many are called but few are chosen',[11] and these few are in my opinion no others than those who have loved wisdom in the right way. One of these I have tried to be by every effort in all my life, and I have left nothing undone according to my ability; if I have endeavoured in the right way, if we have succeeded at all, we shall know clearly when we get there; very soon, if God will, as I think. There is my defence before you gentlemen on the bench, Simmias and Cebes, showing that in leaving you and my masters here, I am reasonable in not fretting or being upset, because I believe that I shall find there good masters and good comrades. So if I am more convincing to you in my defence than I was to the Athenian judges, I should be satisfied."

When Socrates had thus finished, Cebes took up the word: "Socrates," he said, "on the whole I think you speak well; but that about the soul is a thing which people find very hard to believe. They fear that when it parts from the body it is nowhere any more; but on the day when a man dies, as it parts from the body, and goes out like a breath or a whiff of smoke, it is dispersed and flies away and is gone and is nowhere any more. If it existed anywhere, gathered together by itself, and rid of these evils which you have just described, there would be great and good hope, Socrates, that what you say is true; but this very thing needs no small reassurance and faith, that the soul exists when the man dies, and that it has some power and sense."

"Quite true," said Socrates, "quite true, Cebes; well, what are we to do? Shall we discuss this very question, whether such a thing is likely or not?"

"For my part," said Cebes, "I should very much like to know what your opinion is about it."

Then Socrates answered, "I think no one who heard us now could say, not even a composer of comedies, that I am babbling nonsense and talking about things I have nothing to do with! So if you like, we must make a full enquiry.

"Let us enquire whether the souls of dead men really exist in the house of Hades or not. Well, there is the very ancient legend which we remember, that they are continually arriving there from this world, and further that they come back here and are born again from the dead. If that is true, and the living are born again from the dead, must not our souls exist there? For they could not be born again if they did not exist; and this would be sufficient proof that it is true, if it should be really shown that the living are born from the dead and from nowhere else. But if this be not true, we must take some other line."

"Certainly," said Cebes.

"Then don't consider it as regards men only," he said; "if you wish to understand more easily, think of all animals and vegetables, and, in a word, everything that was birth, let us see if everything comes into being like that, always opposite from opposite and from nowhere else; whenever there happens to be a pair of opposites, such as beautiful and ugly, just and unjust, and thousands of others like these. So let us enquire whether everything that has an opposite must come from its opposite and from nowhere else. For example, when anything becomes bigger, it must, I suppose, become bigger from being smaller before."

"Yes."

"And if it becomes smaller, it was bigger before and became smaller after that?"

"True," he said.

"And again, weaker from stronger, and slower from quicker?"

"Certainly."

"Very well, if a thing becomes worse, is it from being better, and more just from more unjust?"

"Of course."

"Have we established that sufficiently, then, that everything comes into being in this way, opposite from opposite?"

"Certainly."

"Again, is there not the same sort of thing in them all, between the two opposites two becomings, from the first to the second, and back from the second to the first; between greater and lesser increase and diminution, and we call one increasing and the other diminishing?"

"Yes," he said.

"And being separated and being mingled, growing cold and growing hot, and so with all; even if we have sometimes no names for them, yet in fact at least it must be the same everywhere, that they come into being from each other, and that there is a becoming from one to the other?"

"Certainly," said he.

"Well then," he said, "is there something opposite to being alive, as sleeping is opposite to being awake?"

"There is," he said.

"What?"

"Being dead," he said.

"Well, all these things come into being from each other, if they are opposites, and there are two becomings between each two?"

"Of course."

"Then," said Socrates, "I will speak of one of the two pairs that I mentioned just now, and its becomings; you tell me about the other. My pair is sleeping and being awake, and I say that being awake comes into being from sleeping and sleeping from being awake, and that their becomings are falling asleep and waking up. Is that satisfactory?"

"Quite so."

"Then you tell me in the same way about life and death. Do you not say that to be alive is the opposite of to be dead?"

"I do."

"And that they come into being from each other?"

"Yes."

"From the living, then, what comes into being?"

"The dead," he said.

"And what from the dead?"

"The living, I must admit."

"Then from the dead, Cebes, come living things and living men?"

"So it appears," he said.

[9]Plato's text is doubtful here, and in the next two sentences.
[10] σκιαγραφαι, literally, a shadow-drawing.
[11]The Greek means "Wand-bearers are many, inspired mystics are few."

"Then," said he, "our souls exist in the house of Hades."

"It seems so."

"Well, of the two becomings between them, one is quite clear. For dying is clear, I suppose, don't you think so?"

"Oh yes," said he.

"Then what shall we do?" he said. "Shall we refuse to grant in return the opposite becoming; and shall nature be lame in this point? Is it not a necessity to grant some becoming opposite to dying?"

"Surely it is," he said.

"What is that?"

"Coming to life again."

"Then," said he, "if there is coming to life again, this coming to life would be a being born from the dead into the living."

"Certainly."

"It is agreed between us, then, in this way also that the living are born from the dead, no less than the dead from the living: and since this is true, there would seem to be sufficient proof that the souls of the dead must of necessity exist somewhere, whence we assume they are born again."

"It seems to me, Socrates," he answered, "from our admissions that must of necessity be true."

"Another way of looking at this, Cebes," he said, "shows, as I think, that we were right to make those admissions. If opposites did not return back continually to replace opposites, coming into being just as if going round in a circle, but if birth were something going direct from the opposite once only into the exact opposite and never bent back and returned back again to its original, be sure that in the end all things would get the same form and go through the same process, and becomings would cease."

"How do you mean?" he asked.

"What I mean is nothing difficult to understand," said he.

"For example, if there were falling asleep, but waking up did not return back in its place, coming into being from the sleeping, be sure that in the end Endymion[12] would be nowhere and this would show his story to be nonsense, because everything else would be in the same state as he, fast asleep. And if everything were combined and nothing split up, the result would be the Chaos of Anaxagoras, 'all things together.' In the same way, my dear Cebes, if everything died that had any life, and when it died, the dead things remained in that state and never came to life again, is it not absolutely necessary that in the end all things would be dead and nothing alive? For if the living things came into being from things other than the dead, and the living died, all things must be swallowed up in death, and what device could possibly prevent it?"

"Nothing could possibly prevent it, Socrates, and what you say I think perfectly true."

"Yes, Cebes," he said, "I think this is all perfectly true, and we are not deceived in admitting what we did; but in fact coming to life again is really true, and living persons are born from the dead, and the souls of the dead exist."[13]

"Another thing," said Cebes, putting in, "you know that favourite argument of yours, Socrates, which we so often heard from you, that our learning is simply recollection: that also makes it necessary, I suppose, if it is true, that we learnt at some former time what we now remember; but this is impossible unless our soul existed somewhere before it was born in this human shape. In this way also the soul seems to be something immortal."

Then Simmias put in, "But, Cebes, what are the proofs of this? Remind me, for I don't quite remember now."

"There is one very beautiful proof," said Cebes, "that people, when asked questions, if they are properly asked, say of themselves everything correctly; yet if there were not knowledge in them, and right reason, they would not be able to do this. You see, if you show someone a diagram or anything like that, he proves most clearly that this is true."

Socrates said, "If you don't believe this, Simmias, look at it in another way and see whether you agree. You disbelieve, I take it, how what is called learning can be recollection?"

"Disbelieve you," said Simmias, "not I! I just want to have an experience of what we are now discussing—recollection. I almost remember and believe already from what Cebes tried to say; yet none the less I should like to hear how *you* were going to put it."

"This is how," he answered. "We agree, I suppose, that if anyone remembers something he must have known it before at some time."

"Certainly," he said.

"Then do we agree on this also, that when knowledge comes to him in such a way, it is recollection? What I mean is something like this: If a man has seen or heard something or perceived it by some other sense, and he not only knows that, but thinks of something else of which the knowledge is not the same but different, is it not right for us to say he remembered that which he thought of?"

"How do you mean?"

"Here is an example: Knowledge of a man and knowledge of a lyre are different."

"Of course."

"Well, you know about lovers, that when they see a lyre or a dress or anything else which their beloved uses, this is what happens to them: they know the lyre, and they conceive in the mind the figure of the boy whose lyre it is? Now this is recollection; just as when one sees Simmias, one often remembers Cebes, and there would be thousands of things like that."

"Thousands, indeed!" said Simmias.

"Then is that sort of thing," said he, "a kind of recollection? Especially when one feels this about things which one had forgotten because of time and neglect?"

"Certainly," he said.

"Very well then," said Socrates. "When you see a horse in a picture, or a lyre in a picture, is it possible to remember a man? And when you see Simmias in a picture, to remember Cebes?"

"Yes indeed."

"Or when you see Simmias in a picture, to remember Simmias himself?"

"Oh yes," said he.

["These being either like or unlike?"

"Yes."

"It makes no difference," he said. "Whenever, seeing one thing, from sight of this you think of another thing whether like or unlike, it is necessary," he said, "that that was recollection."

"Certainly."][14]

"Does it not follow from all this that recollection is both from like and from unlike things?"

"It does."

"But when a man remembers something from like things, must this not necessarily occur to him also—to reflect whether anything is lacking or not from the likeness of what he remembers?"

"He must."

---

[12]The Moon fell in love with Endymion, most beautiful of men, and kept him in a perpetual sleep on Mt. Latmos, so that she could embrace him nightly.

[13]Socrates' theory of a conservation of life is somewhat like our familiar theory of the conservation of energy.

[14]The bracketed passage has been transposed from 74 C-D of the Greek text, where it would appear to be meaningless.

194

Plato—Phaedo

"Consider then," he said, "if this is true. We say, I suppose, there is such a thing as the equal, not a stick equal to a stick, or a stone to a stone, or anything like that, but something independent which is alongside all of them, the equal itself, equality; yes or no?"

"Yes indeed," said Simmias, "upon my word, no doubt about it."

"And do we understand what that is?"

"Certainly," he said. "Where did we get the knowledge of it? Was it not from such examples as we gave just now, by seeing equal sticks or stones and so forth, from these we conceived that, which was something distinct from them? Don't you think it is distinct? Look at it this way also: Do not the same stones or sticks appear equal to one person and unequal to another?"

"Certainly."

"Well, did the really-equals ever seem unequal to you, I mean did equality ever seem to be inequality?"

"Never, Socrates."

"Then those equal things," said he, "are not the same as the equal itself."

"Not at all, I think, Socrates."

"Yet from these equals," he said, "being distinct from that equal, you nevertheless conceived and received knowledge of that equal?"

"Very true," he said.

"Well," said he, "how do we feel about the sticks as compared with the real equals we spoke of just now; do the equal sticks seem to us to be as equal as equality itself, or do they fall somewhat short of the essential nature of equality; or nothing short?"

"They fall short," he said, "a great deal."

"Then we agree on this: When one sees a thing, and thinks, 'This which I now see wants to be like something else—like one of the things that are, but falls short and is unable to be such as that is, it is inferior,' it is necessary, I suppose, that he who thinks thus has previous knowledge of that which he thinks it resembles but falls short of?"

"That is necessary."

"Very well, do we feel like that or not about equal things and the equal?"

"Assuredly we do."

"It is necessary then that we knew the equal before that time when, first seeing the equal things, we thought that all these aim at being such as the equal, but fall short."

"That is true."

"Well, we go on to agree here also: we did not and we could not get a notion of the equal by any other means than by seeing or grasping, or perceiving by some other sense. I say the same of equal and all the rest."

"And they are the same, Socrates, for what the argument wants to prove."

"Look here, then; it is from the senses we must get the notion that all these things of sense aim at that which is the equal, and fall short of it; or how do we say?"

"Yes."

"Then before we began to see and hear and use our other senses, we must have got somewhere knowledge of what the equal is, if we were going to compare with it the things judged equal by the senses and see that all things are eager to be such as that equal is, but are inferior to it."

"This is necessary from what we agreed, Socrates."

"Well, as soon as we were born we saw and heard and had our other senses?"

"Certainly."

"Then, we say, we must have got knowledge of the equal before that?"

"Yes."

"Before we were born, then, it is necessary that we must have got it."

"So it seems."

"Then if we got it before we were born and we were born having it, we knew before we were born and as soon as we were born, not only the equal and the greater and the less but all the rest of such things? For our argument now is no more about the equal than about the beautiful itself, and the good itself, and the just and the pious, and I mean everything which we seal with the name of 'that which is,' the essence, when we ask our questions and respond with our answers in discussion. So we must have got the proper knowledge of each of these before we were born."

"That is true."

"And if having got the knowledge, in each case, we have not forgotten, we must continue knowing this and know it through life; for to know is, having got knowledge of something, to keep it and not to lose it; dropping knowledge, Simmias, is what we call forgetfulness, isn't it?"

"Just so, Socrates," he said.

"But, I think, if we got it before birth, and lost it at birth, and if afterwards, using our senses about these things, we recover the knowledge which once before we had, would not what we call learning be to recover our own knowledge? And this we should rightly call recollection?"

"Certainly."

"For, you see, it has been shown to be possible that a man perceiving something, by sight or hearing or some other sense, thinks, from this perception, of some other thing which he has forgotten, to which he compares this as being like or unlike. So as I say, there is choice of two things: either we were all born knowing them and we all know them throughout life; or afterwards those who we say learn just remember, and nothing more, and learning would be recollection."

"That is certainly true, Socrates."

"Which do you choose then, Simmias? Were we born knowing, or do we remember afterwards what we had got knowledge of before?"

"I can't choose all at once, Socrates."

"Another question, then; you can choose, and have some opinion about this. When a man knows anything, could he give an account of what he knows or not?"

"He must be able to do that, Socrates."

"Do you think that all could give account of the matters we have been discussing?"

"I would that they could," said Simmias, "but so far from that, I fear that tomorrow at this time there may be no one left in the world able to do that properly."

"Then, Simmias, you don't think that all know them?"

"Oh, no!"

"Then are they trying to remember what they once learnt?"

"It must be so."

"When did our souls get the knowledge of these things? For surely it is not since we became human beings."

"Certainly not."

"Then before."

"Yes."

"So, Simmias, our souls existed long ago, before they were in human shape, apart from bodies, and then had wisdom."

"Unless, indeed, we get all these knowledges at birth, Socrates; for this time is still left."

"Very well, my comrade; at what other time do we lose them? For we are not born having them, as we admitted just now. Do we lose them at the very same time as we get them? Can you suggest any other time?"

"Oh no, Socrates, I did not see I was talking nonsense."

"Is this the case then, Simmias?" he asked. "If all these exist which we are always harping on, the beautiful and the good and every such essence; and if we refer to these essences all the things which our senses perceive, finding out that the essences existed before and are ours now, and compare our sensations with them, it necessarily follows that, just as these exist, so our soul must have existed before our birth; but if they do not exist, this argument will be worthless. Is this true, and is there equal necessity that these things exist and our souls did before our birth, or if they do not exist, neither did our souls?"

"I am quite convinced, Socrates," said Simmias, "that there is the same necessity; our argument has found an excellent refuge when it maintains equally that our soul exists before we are born, and the essences likewise which you speak of. Nothing is clearer to me than this, that all such things exist most assuredly, beauty and good and the others which you named; and I think it has been sufficiently proved."

"And what thinks Cebes?" said Socrates. "We must convince Cebes too."

"It is good enough for him," said Simmias, "as I believe; but he is the most obstinate man in the world at disbelieving what is said; however, I believe he really is convinced that our soul existed before our birth.

"Yet will it exist after death too?" he went on. "I don't think myself that has been proved yet, Socrates. We are confronted still with what Cebes said just now: Can it be that when the man dies his soul is scattered abroad and that is the end of it, as so many say? For supposing it is composed from somewhere or other, and comes into existence before it even enters a human body; what hinders it, when it has entered and finally got rid of that body, from ending at that moment also, and being itself destroyed?"

"Well said, Simmias," said Cebes. "It does seem that half of what ought to be proved has been proved, that our soul exists before our birth; it must also be proved that when we die it will exist no less than before our birth, if the proof is to be completed."

"It has been proved already, my dear Simmias and Cebes," said Socrates, "if you choose to combine this argument with what we agreed to before it, that all the living comes from the dead. For if the soul exists before, and if it is necessary that when coming into life and being born it comes from death and from nothing else at all, it must certainly be necessary that it exists even when one dies, since it must be born again. Well then, what you said has in fact been proved already. Still, I think you and Cebes would be glad to investigate this argument yet further, and you seem to me to have the fear which children have—that really, when it leaves the body, the wind blows it away and scatters it, especially if anyone dies not in calm weather but in a great tempest."

Cebes laughed, and said, "Then think we are afraid of that, Socrates," he said, "and try to convince us against it; or better, don't think *we* are afraid, but imagine there is a kind of child in us which has such fears; then let us try to persuade this child not to fear death as if it were a bogey."

"No," said Socrates, "you must sing incantations over it every day, until you charm it out."

"My dear Socrates," he said, "where shall we get a good charmer of such things, since you are leaving us?"

"Hellas is a big place, my dear Cebes," he replied, "and there are many good men in it, and there are many barbarian nations too; and you must search through them all looking for such a charmer; you must spare neither money nor pains, since you could not spend money on anything more important. And you must not forget to search among yourselves; for perhaps you could not easily find any better able than yourselves to do that."

"Oh, that shall be done, of course," said Cebes; "but let us go back to where we left off—if you would like to."

"But certainly I should like to," he said; "of course I should!"

"That's well said," said Cebes.

"Very well then," said Socrates, "we must ask ourselves what sorts of things properly undergo this; I mean, what sorts of things are dissolved and scattered, for what sorts

we must fear such an end, and for what not; next we must consider which sort the soul belongs to. We shall know then whether to be confident or fearful for our own soul."

"True," he said.

"Isn't it to the composite, which is by nature compounded, that dissolution is proper—I mean it is dissolved just as it was composed? And, on the other hand, an uncompounded thing, if indeed such exists, is least of all things naturally liable to dissolution?"

"That seems to me correct," said Cebes.

"Then what is always the same and in the same state is likely to be the uncompounded, but what is always changing and never keeps in the same state is likely to be the compounded?"

"I think so."

"Let us turn to what we have discussed already," he said. "This essence which we describe in all our questions and answers as existing—is it always in the same state or does it change? I mean the equal itself, the beautiful itself, everything which exists by itself, that which is—does it admit of any changes whatever? Or is it true that each thing that so exists, being of one form and itself alone, is always in the same state, and never admits of any change whatever in any way or at any time or in any place?"

"It must necessarily be always in the same state," said Cebes.

"And what of the many particulars, men or horses or dresses or what you will, things equal or beautiful and so forth, all that have the same name as those essences? Are they always in the same state; or, quite opposite to the essences, are they not constantly changing in themselves and in relation to each other, and, one might say, never keep in the same state?"

"That again is right," said Cebes, "they never keep in the same state."

"These, then, you could touch or see or perceive by the other senses, but those which continue in the same state cannot be grasped by anything except intellectual reasoning, and such things are unseen[15] and not visible?"

"Certainly that is true," he said.

"Shall we lay down, then, that there are two kinds of existing things, one visible, one unseen?"

"Yes," he said.

"And the unseen is always in the same state, but the visible constantly changing?"

"Yes to that also," he said.

"Now come," said he, "in ourselves one part is body and one part soul?"

"Just so," he said.

"Then which kind do we say the body would be more like and akin to?"

"The visible," he said, "that is clear to anyone."

"And the soul—is it visible, or unseen?"

"Not visible to mankind at least, Socrates," he said.

"But when we say visible and not visible, we mean to human senses, don't we?"

"Yes, we do."

"Then what of the soul—do we say that is visible or invisible?"

"Not visible."

"Unseen, then?"

"Yes."

"Then soul is more like to the unseen, and body to the visible."

---

[15]The word used is ἀειδής, unseen or without form. Plato introduces it here because it sounds significantly like the word Ἀιδης, Hades, suggesting that the unchanging essences are immaterial and belong to the other world.

"It surely must be."

"Now you remember that we were saying some time ago that the soul, when it has the body to help in examining things, either through sight or hearing or any other sense— for to examine something through the body means through the senses—then it is dragged by the body towards what is always changing, and the soul goes astray and is confused and staggers about like one drunken because she is taking hold of such things."

"Certainly."

"But when she examines by herself, she goes away yonder to the pure and everlasting and immortal and unchanging; and being akin to that, she abides ever with it, whenever it becomes possible for her to abide by herself. And there she rests from her wanderings, and while she is amongst those things she is herself unchanging because what she takes hold of is unchanging: and this state of the soul has the name of wisdom?"

"Most excellent and true, Socrates."

"Then which of the two kinds is she more like and more akin to, judging from what we said before and what we are saying now?"

"Everyone, even the most ignorant, would admit, I think, Socrates," he said, "from that way of reasoning, that soul is wholly and altogether more like the unchanging than the changing."

"And the body?"

"More like the changing."

"Look at it in this way also: When soul and body are together, our nature assigns the body to be slave and to be ruled, and the soul to be ruler and master; now, then, further, which of the two seems to be like the divine, and which like the mortal? Don't you think the divine is naturally such as to rule and to guide, and the mortal such as to be ruled and to be a slave?"

"I do."

"Then which is the soul like?"

"It is clear, Socrates, that the soul is like the divine, and the body like the mortal."

"Consider now, Cebes, whether it follows from all that we have said, that the soul is most like the divine and immortal and intellectual and simple and indissoluble and self-unchangeable, but on the contrary, the body is most like the human and mortal and manifold and unintellectual and dissoluble and ever-changing. Can we say anything to contradict that, my dear Cebes, or is that correct?"

"We cannot contradict it."

"Very well. This being so, is it not proper to the body to be quickly dissolved, but on the contrary to the soul to be wholly indissoluble or very nearly so?"

"Of course."

"You understand, then," he said, "that when the man dies, the visible part of him, the body—that which lies in the visible world, and which we call the corpse, for which it is proper to dissolve and disappear—does not suffer any of this at once but instead remains a good long time, and if a man dies with his body in a nice condition and age, a very long time. For if the body is shrivelled up and mummified like the mummies in Egypt it lasts almost whole, for an incredibly long time. And some portions of the body, even when it decays, bones and sinews and so forth, may almost be called immortal."

"Yes."

"But the soul, the 'unseen' part of us, which goes to another place noble and pure and unseen like itself, a true unseen Hades, to the presence of the good and wise God, where, if God will, my own soul must go very soon—shall our soul, then, being such and of such nature, when released from the body be straightway scattered by the winds and perish, as most men say? Far from it, my dear Simmias! This is much

more likely: If it is pure when it gets free, and drags nothing of the body with it, since it has no communion with the body in life if it can help it, but avoids the body and gathers itself into itself, since it is always practising this—here we have nothing else but a soul loving wisdom rightly, and in reality practising death—don't you think this would be a practice of death?"

"By all means."

"Then, being thus, it goes away into the unseen, which is like itself, the divine and immortal and wise, where on arrival it has the opportunity to be happy, freed from wandering and folly and fears and wild loves and all other human evils, and, as they say of the initiated, really and truly passing the rest of time with the gods. Is that what we are to say, Cebes?"

"Yes indeed," said Cebes.

"But if contrariwise, I think, if it leaves the body polluted and unpurified, as having been always with it and attending it and in love with it and bewitched by it through desires and pleasures, so that it thinks nothing to be true but the bodily —what one could touch and see and drink and eat and use for carnal passion; if what is darksome to the eyes and 'unseen' but intellectual and to be caught by philosophy, if this, I say, it is accustomed to hate and fear and flee; do you think a soul in that state will get away pure and incorrupt in itself?"

"By no possible means whatever," he said.

"No, I think it is interpenetrated by the bodily, which the association and union with it of the body has by constant practice made ingrained."

"Exactly."

"A heavy load, my friend, we must believe that to be, heavy and earthy and visible; and such a soul with this on board is weighed down and dragged back into the visible world, by fear of the unseen, Hades so-called, and cruises[16] about restless among tombs and graves, where you know shadowy apparitions of souls have often been seen, phantoms such as are produced by souls like this, which have not been released purely, but keep something of the visible, and so they are seen."

"That is likely, Socrates."

"Indeed it is likely; and likely that these are not the souls of the good, but souls of the mean, which are compelled to wander about such places as a penalty for their former way of life, which was evil; and wander they must until by desire for the bodily which is always in their company they are imprisoned once more in a body. And they are imprisoned, as is likely, into the same habits which they had practised in life before."

"What sort of habits do you mean, Socrates?"

"It is likely, for example, that those who have practised gluttony and violence and drunkenness and have not taken heed to their ways enter the bodies of asses and suchlike beasts, don't you think so?"

"Very likely indeed."

"Those, again, who have preferred injustice and tyrannies and robberies, into the bodies of wolves and hawks and kites; or where else do we say they would go?"

"No doubt," said Cebes, "they pass into creatures like these."

"Then it is clear," said he, "that the rest go wherever they do go, to suit their own likenesses and habits?"

"Quite clear, of course," he said.

"Then of these the happiest people," he said, "and those who go to the best place, are those who have practised the public and political virtues which they call temperance and justice, got from habit and custom without philosophy and reason?"

---

[16]Literally "rolls about" (like a ship at sea).

"How are these happiest, pray?"

"Why, isn't it likely that they pass into another similar political and gentle race, perhaps bees or wasps or ants; or even into the same human race again, and that there are born from them decent men?"

"Yes, that is likely."

"But into the family of gods, unless one is a philosopher and departs wholly pure, it is not permitted for any to enter, except the lover of learning. Indeed, it is for the sake of this purity, Simmias and Cebes, my two good comrades, that those who truly seek wisdom steadfastly abstain from all bodily desires and refuse to give themselves over to them, not from having any fear of ruin of their home or of poverty, as the money-loving multitude has; and again, not from being afraid of dishonour, or a bad reputation for wickedness, as the honour-lovers and power-lovers are; that is why these abstain from them."

"No, Socrates," said Cebes, "that would not be proper."

"Not at all, by heaven," said he. "Therefore those who care at all for their own soul and do not live just serving[17] the body say good-bye to everyone of that kind and walk not after guides who know not where they are going; for they themselves believe they must not act contrary to philosophy, and its deliverance and purification, and so they turn to philosophy and follow by the way she leads them."

"How, Socrates?"

"I will tell you," he said.

"The lovers of learning understand," said he, "that philosophy found their soul simply imprisoned in the body and welded to it, and compelled to survey through this as if through prison bars the things that are, not by itself through itself, but wallowing in all ignorance; and she saw that the danger of this prison came through desire, so that the prisoner himself would be chief helper in his own imprisonment. As I say then, lovers of learning understand that philosophy, taking possession of their soul in this state, gently encourages it and tries to free it, by showing that surveying through the eyes is full of deceit, and so is perception through the ears and the other senses; she persuades the soul to withdraw from these, except so far as there is necessity to use them, and exhorts it to collect itself together and gather itself into itself, and to trust nothing at all but itself, and only whatever of the realities each in itself the soul itself by itself can understand; but that whatever of what varies with its environs the soul examines through other means, it must consider this to be no part of truth; such a thing, philosophy tells it, is a thing of the senses and of the visible, but what it sees itself is a thing of the intellect and of the 'unseen.' So the soul of the true philosopher believes that it must not oppose this deliverance, and therefore abstains from pleasures and desires and griefs and fears as much as possible, counting that when a man feels great pleasure or fear or pain or desire, he suffers not only the evil that one might think (for example, being ill or squandering money through his desires), but the greatest and worst of all evils, which he suffers and never counts."

"What is that, Socrates?" asked Cebes.

"That the soul of every man suffers this double compulsion: At the same time as it is compelled to feel great pleasure or pain about anything, it is compelled also to believe that the thing for which it specially feels this is most clearly real and true, when it is not. These are generally the visible things, aren't they?"

"Certainly."

"Then in this state especially the soul is imprisoned by the body?"

"Pray how?"

"Because each pleasure and pain seems to have a nail, and nails the soul to the body and pins it on and makes it bodily, and so it thinks the same things are true which the body says are true. For by having the same opinion as the body, and liking the same things, it is compelled, I believe, to adopt the same ways and the same nourishment, and to become such as never could come pure to the house of Hades, but would always go forth infected by the body; so it would fall again quickly into another body and there be sown and grown, and therefore would have neither part nor lot in communion with the divine and pure and simple."

"Most true, indeed," said Cebes.

"So then it is for these reasons, Cebes, that those who rightly love learning are decent and brave, not for the reasons which the many give; what do you think?"

"Certainly not."

"No indeed. Such would be the reasoning of the philosopher. His soul would not think it right that philosophy should set her free, and that while being set free she herself should surrender herself back again in bondage to pleasures and pains, and so perform the endless task of a Penelope unweaving the work of her loom.[18] No, she thinks she must calm these passions; and, following reason and keeping always in it, beholding the true and the divine and the certain, and nourishing herself on this, his soul believes that she ought to live thus, as long as she does live, and when she dies she will join what is akin and like herself, and be rid of human evils. After nurture of this kind there is nothing to fear, my dear Simmias and Cebes, and she need not expect in parting from the body to be scattered about and blown away by the winds, and to be gone like a bird and be nowhere any more."

There was a long silence after Socrates had ended; Socrates himself was deep in these thoughts, or appeared to be, and so were most of us. But Cebes and Simmias whispered together a bit, and when Socrates noticed them he said, "What's the matter? Surely you don't think our argument has missed anything? Indeed, there are a good many suspicions and objections, if one is to go through it thoroughly. If, then, you are considering something else, I say nothing; but if you are at all puzzled about what we have been saying, don't hesitate to speak yourselves. Go through it, and see if you think it might have been improved; and take me with you through it again if you think I can help you any more at all in your difficulties."

Simmias answered, "Well then, Socrates, I will tell you the truth. We have been puzzled for a long time, both of us, and each pushes on the other and bids him ask; because we wish to hear and don't want to be a nuisance, in case you are feeling unhappy about the present misfortune!"

Socrates laughed gently as he heard this, and said. "Bless me, my dear Simmias! Surely I could hardly persuade others that I don't think the present fortune a misfortune, when I can't persuade even you, but you fear I am more fretful now than I have been in my past life. Apparently it seems to you that I'm a worse prophet than the swans. When they perceive that they must die, you know, they sing more and better than they ever did before, glad to be going away into the presence of that god whose servants they are. But men tell lies against them because they fear death themselves, and they say that the swans are mourning their death and singing a dirge for sorrow; men don't take into account that no bird ever sings when it is hungry or cold or feels any other pain, not the swallow or the hoopoe or even the nightingale, which they say all sing a dirge for sorrow. But I don't be-

---

[17]This word is doubtful in the Greek text.

[18]Penelope prolonged her task for three years by unweaving at night what she wove by day. *Odyssey* xix. Bodily indulgence is unweaving and the soul would have to weave it up again.

lieve those birds do sing in sorrow, nor do the swans, but these, I think, because they belong to Apollo, are prophets and know beforehand the good things in the other world, and sing and rejoice on that day far more than ever before. Indeed I think myself that I am the swans' fellow-slave, and sacred to the same god, and I think I have prophecy from my master no less than they have, and I depart from life no more dispirited than they do. No, as far as that matters, you should speak and ask what you will, so long as we have leave of the Athenian Board of Eleven."

"Good," said Simmias, "then I will speak out, and tell you my difficulty, and Cebes too, where he does not accept all you have said. For I think, as perhaps you do, Socrates, that to know the plain truth about such matters in this present life is impossible, or at least very difficult; but only a very soft man would refuse to test in every possible way what is said about them, and would give up before examining them all over till he was tired out. I think a man's duty is one of two things: either to be taught or to find out where the truth is, or if he cannot, at least to take the best possible human doctrine and the hardest to disprove, and to ride on this like a raft over the waters of life and take the risk; unless he could have a more seaworthy vessel to carry him more safely and with less danger, some divine doctrine to bring him through. So now I will not be ashamed to ask, since you tell me yourself to do it; and I shall not blame myself afterwards because I did not now say what I think. Well, my opinion is, Socrates, when I consider what has been said in my own mind and with Cebes here, that it is not quite satisfactory."

Socrates said, "Perhaps, my comrade, your opinion is true. But say where it is not satisfactory."

"Here," said he: "That one could say the same about harmony[19] and a harp with strings; that the harmony is invisible and bodiless and all-beautiful and divine on the tuned harp; but the harp itself and the strings are bodies and bodily and composite and earthy and akin to the mortal. So when someone breaks the harp, or cuts and bursts the strings, suppose he should maintain by the same argument as yours that it is necessary the harmony should still exist and not perish; for it would be just as impossible that the harp should still exist when the strings are broken, and the strings should still exist which are of mortal kind, as that the harmony should perish —harmony, which is of the same kith and kin as the divine and immortal, perishing before the mortal; no, he would say, the harmony must necessarily exist somewhere, and wood and strings must rot away first, before anything could happen to the harmony! Well, Socrates, I think you yourself must have noticed that we conceive the soul to be something like this—that our body being tuned and held together by hot and cold and dry and wet and suchlike, our soul is a kind of mixture and harmony of these very things, when they are well and harmoniously mixed together. If, then, our soul is a kind of harmony, it is plain that when the body is slackened inharmoniously or too highly strung, by diseases and other evils, the soul must necessarily perish, although it is most divine, just as the other harmonies do, those in sounds and those in all the works of craftsmen, but the relics of each body will remain until it rots or is burnt. Then consider what we must answer to this argument, if anyone claims that the soul is a mixture of the things in the body, and at what is called death, it is the first to perish."

Socrates gazed at us with his eyes wide open, as he usually did, and said, smiling, "What Simmias says is quite fair. Then if any of you is readier than I am, why didn't he reply? I think he tackles the question neatly. But before the answer comes, I think we ought to hear Cebes first, what fault he, too, has to find with our argument. Then there will be a little time and we can consider what to say; afterwards, when we have heard them, we ought to agree with them if they seem to be in tune with us, or if not, we should continue as before to defend our

doctrine. Come along, Cebes," he said, "speak! What worried you?"

"I'll tell you," said Cebes. "I think the argument is where it was, and has the same objection which I made before. That our soul existed before it came into this form, I do not retract; it was a nice, neat proof, and quite satisfactory, if I may say so without offence; but that when we are dead the soul will still exist somewhere, I can't say the same of that. However, I do not agree with the objection of Simmias, that the soul is not stronger and much longer-lasting than the body; for I think it is very far superior in all those respects. 'Well,' the argument might say to me, 'why do you still disbelieve? You can see when the man is dead the weaker part still existing, and don't you think the longer-lasting must necessarily survive during this time?' Well, see if you think anything of this answer of mine; really, it seems that I also want a simile, like Simmias. I think all this is very much the same as saying as follows of a weaver who died old: The man is not dead but exists somewhere safe and sound, and here is a proof one might offer— here is the cloak which he wove himself, and used to wear, safe and sound, and it has not perished. If someone disbelieved, one might ask him, 'Which kind of thing is longer-lasting, a man, or a cloak in use and wear?' If the answer was, 'A man lasts longer than a cloak,' one might imagine that this proved that the man was certainly safe and sound, since the shorter-lasting thing had not perished. But I don't think that is right, Simmias; just consider what I have to say now. Everyone would understand that such an argument is silly; for this weaver had woven and worn out many such cloaks and died later than all except the last, when he died before it, yet for all that a man is neither inferior to a cloak nor weaker. Soul and body might admit of the same simile, and one might fairly say the same about them, I think, that the soul is long-lasting, the body weaker and shorter-lasting; but one might say more, that each of the souls wears out many bodies, especially if it lives many years. For if the body wastes and perishes while the man still lives, but the soul always weaves anew what is worn away, it would, however, be necessary that when the soul perished it would happen to be wearing the last body and it would perish before this last only, and when the soul perished, the body would show at once the nature of its weakness and would quickly rot and vanish in decay. This argument, then, is not yet enough to give confidence that when we die our soul exists somewhere. For if one should grant your supporter even more than what you say, and admitted to him not only that our souls existed in the time before our birth, but that nothing hindered the souls of some of us from still existing when we die, and continuing to exist, and from being born and dying again and again, for so strong is its nature that the soul endures being born many times: one might admit that, and yet never admit that it does not suffer in these many births, and at last in one of its deaths does not perish outright. But one might say that no one knows which death and dissolution of the body brings death of the soul; for it is impossible for any one of us to distinguish it beforehand. Now if this is correct, it follows that anyone who is confident about death is foolish in his confidence, unless he can show that the soul is wholly immortal and imperishable; for if he cannot show this, it is necessary that he who is about to die must always fear for his soul lest at the present separation from the body it may utterly perish."

When we had heard these two we were very unhappy, as we told one another afterwards. We had been firmly convinced by the earlier arguments, and now we seemed to be thrown back by the speakers into confusion and disbelief; we distrusted not only the earlier arguments but those which were coming, and we thought that either we were worthless judges, or else there could be nothing to trust in the whole thing.

---

[19]Or tune.

ECHECRATES: By heaven, Phaidon, I feel with you. As I heard you tell such a story, I felt like asking myself, "Then what argument can we trust any longer?" That one seemed quite convincing when Socrates spoke, but now it has fallen into distrust. This notion has a wonderful hold of me and always did, that our soul is a kind of harmony, and when you spoke of it I was, one might say, reminded that I had once thought so too. Now again we must start from the beginning, for I very much want another argument to persuade me that the soul of the dead does not die with him. Tell me this in heaven's name, how did Socrates follow up the discussion? Was he also put out like the rest of you? Did he show it or not? If not, did he quietly defend the reasoning? And did he defend it enough, or too little? Tell us the whole story as exactly as you can.

PHAIDON: Well, I must say, Echecrates, I always wondered at Socrates, but I never wondered at him more than when I was with him then. To have something to say was perhaps no novelty in that man; but what most surprised me was, how pleasant and friendly and respectful he was in welcoming the speculations of the young men, and then how sharply he saw how we were affected by what was said, and then how well he treated us, and rallied us like a lot of beaten runaways, and headed us back to follow the argument and examine it along with him.

ECHECRATES: Well, how?

PHAIDON: I will tell you. I happened to be sitting on his right hand, on a low stool beside his bed, and his seat was much higher than mine. Then he stroked my head and pinched together the hair on my neck—he used occasionally to play with my hair—and said, "Tomorrow perhaps, Phaidon, you'll cut off this pretty hair." [20]

"It seems like it, Socrates," I said.

"Well, you won't, if you will listen to me."

"But why?" said I.

"Today," he said, "you shall cut off this, and I mine, at least if our argument comes to its latter end and we can't bring it to life again. In fact if I were you, and if the argument escaped me, I would swear an oath like the Argives,[21] never to let my hair grow long again till I renew the fight with Simmias and Cebes and beat their argument."

"But Socrates," I said, "two to one! Not even Heracles could be a match for two, as they say!" [22]

"Then," he said, "call me in as your Ioleos, while there is daylight still."

"I call you to help, then," said I, "not as Heracles did to Ioleos; but like an Ioleos to Heracles."

"That will be the same thing," he said. "But first let us be careful against a danger."

"What is the danger?" said I.

"Don't let us be 'misologues,' hating argument as misanthropes hate men; the worst disease one can have is to hate arguments. Misology and misanthropy come in the same way. Misanthropy is put on from believing someone too completely without discrimination, and thinking the man to be speaking the truth wholly and wholesomely, and then finding out soon afterwards that he is bad and untrustworthy and quite different; when this happens often to a man, especially from those he thought to be his closest and truest friends, at last, after so many knocks, he hates everybody, and believes there is no soundness in anyone at all. Haven't you noticed that happening?"

"Oh yes," I said.

"Then that is an ugly thing," he said, "and it is clear such a man tries to deal with men when he has no skill in human affairs. For if he had that technical skill when he dealt with them, he would take them as they are, and believe that the very good and very bad are few, but most are betwixt and between."

"What do you mean?" I asked.

"As with very big and very small men. Don't you think the rarest thing is to find a very big or a very small man, or dog, or anything else? So with quick and slow, ugly and handsome, white and black? Don't you see that in all these the extremes are few and rare, but the betweens plenty and many?"

"Oh, yes, indeed," I said.

"Then," said he, "if there were a competition in wickedness, there, too, the prize-winners would be few?"

"Quite likely," I said.

"Yes, quite likely," said he, "but in that respect arguments are not like men. I have been following your lead so far, but I think the likeness lies in this: when a person without technical skill in words believes an argument to be true, and soon afterwards thinks it false, sometimes when it is and sometimes when it is not, and so again one person after another—and especially those who spend their time arguing against each other—you know that in the end they think they are the wisest men in the world, and that they alone understand how there is nothing sound and wholesome either in practical affairs or in arguments, but all real things are just like a Euripos,[23] a tide moving up and down and never remaining the same."

"That is truly stated indeed," I said.

"Then, Phaidon," he said, "it would be a pitiable disease, when there *is* an argument true and sound and such as can be understood, if through the pain of meeting so many which seem sometimes to be true and sometimes not, instead of blaming himself and his own clumsiness a man should in the end gladly throw the blame from himself upon the arguments, and for the rest of his life should continually hate and abuse them, and deprive himself of the truth and the knowledge of what is real."

"Yes, I do declare," said I, "it would be pitiable."

"First, then, let us be careful," he said, "and let us not admit into our souls the belief that there really is no health or soundness in arguments. Much rather let us think that we are not sound ourselves, let us be men and take pains to become sound: you and the others to prepare you for all your coming life, I to prepare myself for death. For in fact as regards this very matter I am just now no philosopher, I am a philovictor— I want to win, as much as the most uneducated men do. Such men, you know, when there is difference of opinion, care nothing how the truth stands in a question, but do their very best to make their audience believe whatever they have laid down. Just now I am the same as they are, with only one difference: I shall do my very best to convince of the truth—not my audience, except by the way, but to convince myself that what seems true to me is perfectly true. For, my dear comrade, see how selfishly I reckon it up! If what I say is really true, then it is well to be convinced; but if for the dead nothing remains, then at least for just this time before death, I shall not be disagreeable to you here by lamentations. And this ignorance[24] of mine will not last, which would be an evil thing, but very soon it will perish. Thus prepared, then," he said, "my dear Simmias and Cebes, I proceed to the question; but you, if you please, do not be anxious about Socrates, not a bit, but be very anxious about truth; if you think I say anything true, agree with me, and if not, oppose me with all your might, that my eagerness may not deceive both myself and you—I don't want to be like a bee and leave my sting in you when I go.

---

[20] In mourning for Socrates.

[21] Herodotos, I. 82. They swore not to let their hair grow till they reconquered Thyreai.

[22] A proverb. Heracles was fighting the hydra, and saw a crab coming up to help the hydra. He then called in Ioleos.

[23] The strait between Euboia and the mainland, where there are several "tides" or currents of water every day.

[24] Another reading is "folly."

"Forward, now," he went on. "First remind me what you said, if I don't seem to remember. Simmias, as I think, disbelieves, and fears that the soul, although something more divine and beautiful than the body, may perish before the body like a sort of harmony. Cebes I thought admitted with me that soul was at least longer-lasting than body, but everyone must doubt whether the soul has already worn out many bodies, and now, leaving the last body, it may perish itself; and death may be just this, the destruction of soul, since body is perishing continually and never stops. Are not these the matters which we must consider, Simmias and Cebes?" Both agreed to this. "Well, do you reject all the earlier arguments, or only some?"

"Some only," they replied.

"And what of that one," said he, "when we said learning was recollection, and that therefore our soul must exist somewhere before being imprisoned in the body?"

"That one," said Cebes, "seemed to me wonderfully convincing, and I abide by it now as by no other argument."

"Yes, and so do I, too," said Simmias, "and I should be surprised if I could ever think otherwise about that."

Socrates answered, "Well, my good friend from Thebes," he said, "you must think otherwise, if the notion holds that harmony is a thing composite, and soul is a harmony arising from all the elements strung and tuned in the body. For you will not allow yourself to say that a composite harmony existed before the elements from which it had to be composed—eh, Simmias?"

"Oh dear me no, Socrates!"

"You perceive, then," said he, "that this is what you really affirm, when you say that the soul existed before it came into human shape and body, and that it existed composed of things which did not exist. But see, harmony is not such a thing as you likened it to; no, first the harp and the strings and their tones not yet harmonised come into being, and last of all the harmony is composed, and it is first to perish. Then how will your argument be in tune[25] with that?"

"It will not," said Simmias.

"And yet," said he, "it ought to be in tune with the argument about harmony, if with any at all."

"So it ought," said Simmias.

"Then your argument," he said, "is not in tune. But look here: Which of the two do you choose—is learning recollection, or is the soul a harmony?"

"I much rather choose the first," said he. "Perhaps the other came without proof from a likely comparison that looked good, which makes most people pleased with it; but I am conscious that arguments proved from likelihood are humbugs, and if we are not careful they deceive us, in geometry and everything else. But the argument about recollection and learning has been shown to stand on a good foundation. What was said, I think, was that our soul existed before coming into the body just as that essence exists which has the name of 'real being.' This I have accepted, I am convinced, with right and sufficient reason. I must therefore refuse now, as it seems, to accept for myself or anyone else that account of the soul which calls it a harmony."

"Very well, Simmias," said he. "What do you think of this: Is it proper for a harmony, or any other composite thing, to exist in any other state than the state of its component parts?"

"No," he said.

"Again, it cannot do, or be done to, anything else than they do or are done to?" He said no. "Then it is proper that a harmony does not lead the things which compose it, but follows?" He agreed. "Then a harmony cannot be moved and cannot sound or do anything else in opposition to its own parts?"

"Impossible," he said.

"Well, is not each harmony naturally so much a harmony according as it is harmonised?"

"I don't understand," he said.

"Listen," said he, "if it is more harmonised and more intensely, supposing that to be possible, would it be more a harmony and more intense, and if less harmonised and less intensely, would it be less a harmony and less intense?"

"Certainly."

"Is this true, then, of soul—that even in the smallest degree one soul can be more intensely and more completely, or less intensely and less completely, that very thing, a soul, than another is?"

"Not in the least," he said.

"Very well, then," he said, "in God's name: Is it said that one soul has sense and virtue and is good, but another has folly and wickedness and is bad, and is this true?"

"Quite true," he said.

"Then what will they say, those who lay down that soul is harmony, what will they say these things are which are in the souls, virtue and vice? Will they say these are yet another harmony, and a discord? And say that one soul is harmonised, the good one, and, being itself harmony, has in it another harmony, but the other is discordant itself and has in it no other harmony?"

"I can't say," said Simmias, "but it is clear that one who laid that down would say something of that kind."

"But we agreed before," said Socrates, "that one soul is not more or less soul than other; that means it is agreed that one is not more or less harmony than another, nor to a greater or less degree that another. Is that so?"

"Certainly."

"But that which is neither more nor less harmony has been neither more nor less harmonised. Is that true?"

"That is true."

"When it is neither more nor less harmonised, can it partake of harmony to a greater or less degree, or only the same?"

"The same."

"Then soul, since one is no more than another what we actually mean by soul, consequently is neither more nor less harmonised?"

"Just so."

"In this condition, it would have no greater share of discord or harmony?"

"No, indeed."

"Then in this condition one would not partake of vice or virtue more than another, if vice is discord and virtue harmony?"

"No more."

"Rather I think, Simmias, according to right reasoning, no soul will partake of vice, if it is really harmony; for harmony which is wholly this very thing harmony could never partake of discord."

"Never, surely."

"Nor could soul partake of vice, if it is wholly soul."

"How could it, after what we admitted?"

"By this our reasoning then, all souls of all living creatures will be equally good, if they are equally and actually souls."

"I think so, Socrates," he said.

"Do you think that is correct," said he, "and do you think our argument would have come to this state, if the foundation were right, that is, that soul is harmony?"

"Not in the least," he said.

"Well now," said Socrates, "of all that there is in man, would you say anything rules but soul, especially a wise one?"

"No, not I."

"A soul which gives way to the feelings of the body, or one that even opposes them? I mean something like this—suppose fever be in the body and thirst, would you say soul drags it in the opposite way, so as not to drink, and if hunger be in it,

---

[25]Literally, "sing together," i.e., accord.

not to eat? And we see the soul opposing the body in thousands of other things, don't we?"

"We do."

"Well then; did we not moreover agree earlier, that if it be indeed a harmony it would never sound a tune opposing the elements from which it arises, according as they are strung tight or loose, and twangled, and however else they are treated? It must follow these, it could never lead them?"

"Yes," he said, "we did agree. Of course."

"Very well: Don't we see it now doing the very opposite, leading all the things from which it is said to be composed, and opposing almost always all through life, a tyrant in every way, punishing them sometimes harshly and with bodily pain, that is, through gymnastic and physic, sometimes gently, giving now threats and now advice, talking to desires and angers and fears just as if it was different from them and they from it? Remember, too, Homer's lines in the Odyssey, where he says somewhere of Odysseus[26]

> Striking his chest, he thus reproached his heart,
> My heart, bear up! You have borne worse than this!

Do you think when he composed this he regarded the soul as a kind of harmony, something to be led by the body's feelings? —surely not, but as something able to lead these and play the tyrant, something much more divine than a harmony!"

"Yes indeed, Socrates, I agree," he said.

"Then, my good sir," he said, "it is quite wrong altogether to say that the soul is a harmony; for it appears we should contradict Homer, the divine poet, and ourselves too."

"Just so," he said.

"So much for that, then," said Socrates. "Our Theban Harmonia[27] has been appeased, it seems, pretty well; but what of Cadmos? My dear Cebes," he said, "how shall we appease Cadmos? What argument will do?"

"You'll find one, I think," said Cebes; "this one at least, against the harmony, was amazingly unexpected. When Simmias was telling what he was puzzled about, I wondered very much if anyone could deal with his argument at all, and to my surprise it couldn't stand your argument's first attack. I shouldn't wonder if the same happened to the argument of Cadmos."

"My good man," said Socrates, "don't tempt Providence, or some evil eye may overturn the argument which is coming. But God will care for that; let us charge into the fray like Homeric heroes, and try if there's anything in your contention. This is the sum of what you seek: You demand that it be proved that our soul is imperishable and immortal, if a student of philosophy, being about to die, and being confident, and believing that after death he will be better off in that world than if he had lived to the end a different life, is not to be found foolish and senseless in this confidence. But to show that the soul is something strong and godlike and existed before we were born men, all this you say may be no more than to indicate, not immortality, but that the soul is something long-lasting, and that it existed somewhere before for an immeasurable time, and knew and did many things; but it is not really any more immortal, but in fact its entry into the body of a man was the beginning of destruction for it, like a disease; it lives this life in distress, and last of all, at what is called death, it perishes. So there is no difference at all, you say, whether it comes once into the body or often, at least as regards our feeling of fear; for fear is proper, if one is not senseless, for him that knows not and cannot prove that the soul is immortal. That is very much what you say, Cebes; and I repeat it often on purpose that nothing may escape us; pray add or subtract if you wish."

And Cebes replied, "No, there is nothing I wish to add or subtract now; that is what I do say."

Socrates was silent for some time, thinking to himself; then he said, "That is no trifle you seek, Cebes; we are bound to discuss generally the cause of generation and destruction. If you allow me, I will run through my own experience in these matters. Then if anything of what I shall say seems useful, you shall use it to prove whatever you may say."

"By all means," Cebes said.

"Then listen, and I will tell you. When I was a young man, Cebes, I was most amazingly interested in the lore which they call natural philosophy. For I thought it magnificent to know the causes of everything, why it comes into being and why it is destroyed and why it exists; I kept turning myself upside down to consider things like the following: Is it when hot and cold get some fermentation in them, as some said,[28] that living things are bred? Is it the blood by which we think,[29] or air[30] or fire;[31] or whether it is none of these, but the brain is what provides the senses of hearing and sight and smell, and from these arise memory and opinion, and from memory and opinion in tranquillity comes knowledge; again I considered the destructions of these things, and what happens about heaven and earth. At last I believed myself as unfitted for this study as anything could be. I will tell you a sufficient proof: I found myself then so completely blinded by this study that I unlearned even what I used to think that I knew—what I understood clearly before, as I thought and others thought—about many other things and particularly as to the reason why man grows. I used to think that this was clear to all—by eating and drinking; for when from his foods flesh was added to flesh, and bones to bones, and in the same way the other parts each had added to them what was their own, then what was the little mass before became great later, and so the small man became big. That is what I believed then; isn't it a natural opinion?"

"I think so," said Cebes.

"Look next at this, then. I believed that when a big man stood by a small man, it was correct enough to suppose that he was bigger by the head, and so horse and horse; more clearly still, I thought ten was greater than eight because two was added to it, and the two-cubit bigger than the one-cubit because it overreached it by half."

"But now," said Cebes, "what do you think about them?"

"I'm very far, I swear, from thinking I know the cause of any of these things, for I can't agree with myself, even when one is added to one, either that the one to which it was added has become two, or the one which was added has become two, or that the one added and the one it was added to become two, by the adding of the one to the other; for I am surprised that when they were apart from each other each was one and they were not then two, but when they approached each other this was the cause of their becoming two, the meeting, their being near together. Or again, if a one is cut in half I cannot be convinced any longer that this, the cutting, was the cause of its becoming two; then it was because they were brought close together and one was added to the other, now because one is taken away and separated from the other. Nor can I even convince myself any longer that I know how the one is generated, or in a word how anything else is generated or perishes or exists; I can't do it by this kind of method, but I am muddling along with another of my own[32] and I don't allow this one at all.

"Well, I heard someone reading once out of a book, by Anaxagoras he said, how mind is really the arranger and cause of all things; I was delighted with this cause, and it seemed to me in a certain way to be correct that mind is the cause of all, and I thought that if this is true, mind arranging

---

[26]*Odyssey* xx. 17.
[27]Wife of Theban Cadmos in Greek story.
[28]Anaximandros, Anaxagoras and others.
[29]Empedocles.
[30]Anaximenes.
[31]Heracleitos.
[32]The logical method.

all things places everything as it is best. If, therefore, one wishes to find out the cause of anything, how it is generated or perishes or exists, what one ought to find out is how it is best for it to exist or to do or feel everything; from this reasoning, then, all that is proper for man to seek about this and everything is only the perfect and the best; but the same man necessarily knows the worse, too, for the same knowledge includes both. Reasoning thus, then, I was glad to think I had found a teacher of the cause of things after my own mind in Anaxagoras: I thought he would show me first whether the earth is flat or round, and when he had shown this, he would proceed to explain the cause and the necessity, by showing that it was better that it should be such; and if he said it was in the middle of the universe, he would proceed to explain how it was better for it to be in the middle; and if he would explain all these things to me, I was prepared not to want any other kind of cause. And about the sun too I was equally prepared to learn in the same way, and the moon and stars besides, their speed as compared with one another, their turnings, and whatever else happens to them, how these things are better in each case for them to do or to be done to. For I did not believe that, when he said all this was ordered by mind, he would bring in any other cause for them than that it was best they should be as they are. So I thought that, when he had given the cause for each and for all together, that which is best for each, he would proceed to explain the common good of all; and I would not have sold my hopes for anything, but I got his books eagerly as quick as I could, and read them, that I might learn as soon as possible the best and the worse.

"Oh, what a wonderful hope! How high I soared, how low I fell! When as I went on reading I saw the man using mind not at all; and stating no valid causes of the arrangement of all things, but giving airs and ethers[33] and waters as causes, and many other strange things. I felt very much as I should feel if someone said, 'Socrates does by mind all he does'; and then, trying to tell the causes of each thing I do, if he should say first that the reason why I sit here now is, that my body consists of bones and sinews, and the bones are hard and have joints between them, and the sinews can be tightened and slackened, surrounding the bones along with flesh and the skin which holds them together; so when the bones are uplifted in their sockets, the sinews slackening and tightening make me able to bend my limbs now, and for this cause I have bent together and sit here; and if next he should give you other such causes of my conversing with you, alleging as causes voices and airs and hearings and a thousand others like that, and neglecting to give the real causes. These are that since the Athenians thought it was better to condemn me, for this very reason I have thought it better to sit here, and more just to remain and submit to any sentence they may give. For, by the Dog! these bones and sinews, I think, would have been somewhere near Megara or Boeotia long ago, carried there by an opinion of what is best, if I had not believed it better and more just to submit to any sentence which my city gives than to take to my heels and run. But to call such things causes is strange indeed. If one should say that unless I had such things, bones and sinews and all the rest I have, I should not have been able to do what I thought best, that would be true; but to say that these, and not my choice of the best, are the causes of my doing what I do (and when I act by mind, too!), would be a very far-fetched and slovenly way of speaking. For it shows inability to distinguish that the real cause is one thing, and that without which the cause could not be a cause is another thing. This is what most people seem to me to be fumbling after in the dark, when they use a borrowed name for it and call it cause! And so one man makes the earth remain under the sky, if you please, by putting a rotation about the earth; another thinks it is like the bottom of a flat kneading-trough and puts the air underneath to support it; but they never look for the power which has placed things so that they are in the best

possible state, nor do they think it has a divine strength, but they believe they will some time find an Atlas[34] more mighty and more immortal and more able than ours to hold all together, and really they think nothing of the good which must necessarily bind and hold all things together. How glad I should be to be anyone's pupil in learning what such a cause really is! But since I have missed this, since I could not find it myself or learn it from another, would you like me to show you, Cebes," he said, "how I managed my second voyage in search for the cause?"

"Would I not!" said he: "more than anything else in the world!"

"Well then," he said, "it occurred to me after all this—and it was then I gave up contemplating the realities—that I must be careful not to be affected like people who observe and watch an eclipse of the sun. What happens to them is that some lose their sight, unless they look at his reflection in water or something of that sort. This passed through my mind, and I feared that I might wholly blind my soul by gazing at practical things[35] with my eyes and trying to grasp them by each of the senses. So I thought I must take refuge in reasoning, to examine the truth of the realities. There is, however, something not like in my image; for I do not admit at all that one who examines the realities by reasoning makes use of images, more than one who examines them in deeds and facts. Well anyway, this is how I set out; and laying down in each case the reasoning which I think best fortified, I consider as true whatever seems to harmonise with that, both about causes and about everything else, and as untrue whatever does not. But I wish to make it clearer, for I think you do not understand yet."

"Indeed I do not," said Cebes, "not well."

"Well, this is what I mean," he said, "nothing new, but the same as I have been saying all this time in our conversation, and on other occasions. I am going to try to show you the nature of the cause, which I have been working out. I shall go back to the old song and begin from there, supposing that there exists a beautiful something all by itself, and a good something and great and all the rest of it; and if you grant this and admit it, I hope from these to discover and show you the cause, that the soul is something immortal."

"I grant it to you," said Cebes; "pray be quick and go on to the end."

"Then consider," he said, "what follows, and see if you agree with me. What appears to me is, that if anything else is beautiful besides beauty itself, what makes it beautiful is simply that it partakes of that beauty; and so I say with everything. Do you agree with such a cause?"

"I agree," said he.

"Very well," he said, "I can no longer recognise or understand all those clever causes we heard of; and if any one tells me that anything is beautiful because it has a fine flowery colour or shape or anything like that, I thank him and let all that go; for I get confused in all those, but this one thing I hold to myself simply and completely, and foolishly perhaps, that what makes it beautiful is only that beauty, whether its presence or a share in it or however it may be with the thing, for I am not positive about the manner, but only that beautiful things are beautiful by that beauty. For this I think to be the safest answer to give to myself or anyone else, and clinging to this I think I shall never fall, but it is a safe answer for me and everyone else, that by that beauty all beautiful things are beautiful. Don't you think so?"

"I do."

"And by greatness the great things are great, and the greater greater, and by smallness small things are small?"

---

[33] Air is the lower air about the earth, ether the upper air of heaven.

[34] The Titan who upheld the heavens.

[35] Natural phenomena, etc.

"Yes."

"So you would not accept it if you were told that one person was greater than another by a head, or less by the same, but you would protest that you say every greater is greater than another because of greatness alone, and the smaller is smaller by reason of smallness alone; you would fear, I think, that a contradictory reasoning might meet you if you said someone is greater or less by a head, first that the same thing is making the greater greater and the lesser lesser, and next that a small thing like a head is making the greater greater, which is a monstrosity—that a small thing should make anyone great. Would you not fear that?"

And Cebes said, with a laugh, "I should!"

"So," said he, "you would not dare to say that ten is more than eight by two, but you would say it is more by number and because of number?—and the two-cubit measure greater than the cubit not by half, but by length? For you would fear the same each time."

"Certainly," he said.

"Well, if one has been added, you would be careful not to say the addition caused the two, or if one is divided, the division caused the two. And you would shout that you do not know how each thing comes to be, except by partaking of its own proper essence, whatever each partakes of; in these examples, you see for instance no other cause for becoming two but partaking of twohood, and whatever is to be two must partake of this, and of onehood whatever is to be one, while these splittings and addings and such niceties you would just bow to and let them go, leaving cleverer men than you to answer. For you would be frightened of your own shadow, as people say, your inexperience, and you would cling to that safe supposition,[36] and so you would answer. If anyone should attack the supposition itself, you would let him be and would not answer, until you examined the consequences to see if they were in agreement or discord together; and when you must give account of that supposition itself, you would do it in the same way by supposing another supposition, whichever seemed best of the higher suppositions, until you came to something satisfactory; at the same time you would not make a muddle like the dialecticians, by confusing arguments about the beginning with arguments about the consequences of the beginning, if you wished to find out something of reality. For those people, perhaps, think and care nothing at all about this; they are clever enough to make a mess of the whole business and yet to be pleased with themselves; but if you are a true philosopher, I believe you would do as I say."

"Very true," said Simmias and Cebes together.

ECHECRATES: Reasonable too, I do declare, Phaidon. Amazingly cléar he makes it, as anyone with a grain of sense can see.

PHAIDON: Yes indeed, Echecrates, and all of them thought so who were present.

ECHECRATES: So do we who were not present, but are hearing of it now. But what was said after that?

PHAIDON: As I think, when this was granted, and all agreed that each of these ideal qualities has a kind of existence, and the particular things that partake of them get their name from them, next he asked: "Well then," said he, "if that is what you agree, when you say Simmias is bigger than Socrates, and smaller than Phaidon, you say that both are in Simmias, both bigness and smallness?"

"I do."

"But all the same you agree that for Simmias to overtop Socrates is not true as the words describe it. For Simmias, I suppose, does not naturally overtop Socrates by being Simmias, but by the bigness which he happens to have; nor does he overtop Socrates because Socrates is Socrates, but because Socrates has smallness as against the other's bigness."

"True."

"Nor again is he overtopped by Phaidon because Phaidon is Phaidon, but because Phaidon has bigness as against the smallness of Simmias?"

"That is right."

"Thus, then, Simmias has the title of being both small and great, being between both, in the first case submitting his smallness for the other's bigness to surpass, in the second offering his bigness which surpasses the other's smallness. At the same time," he said, smiling, "I seem to speak like a lawyer's deed, but that is very much how things are." He said yes. "I say this," he added, "because I want you to agree with me. For it appears to me that bigness itself never consents to be big and small at the same time, and not only that, even the bigness in us never accepts smallness and will not be surpassed; but one of two things, it must either depart and retreat whenever its opposite, smallness, comes near, or else must perish at its approach; it does not consent to submit and receive the smallness, and so to become other than what it was. Just so I, receiving and submitting to smallness, am still the man I am, I'm still this same small person; but the bigness in me, being big, has not dared to become small! In the same way, the smallness in us does not want to become or be big, nor does any other of the opposites, being still what it was, want to become and be the opposite; but either it goes away or it is destroyed in this change."

"Certainly," said Cebes, "that is what I think."

One of those present, hearing this, said—I do not clearly remember who it was— "Good heavens, didn't we admit in our former discussion the very opposite of what we are saying now—that the greater came from the less and the less from the greater, and in fact this is how opposites are generated, from opposites? Now it seems to be said that this could never be."

Socrates bent down his head to listen, and said, "Spoken like a man! I thank you for reminding me, but you don't understand the difference between what we are saying now and what we said then. For then we said that the practical opposite thing is generated from its practical opposite, but now we are saying that the opposite quality itself could never become the quality opposite to itself, either in us or in nature. Then, my friend, we were speaking of things which have opposites, these being named by the name of their (opposite) qualities, but now we are speaking of the opposite qualities themselves, from which being in the things, the things are named: those qualities themselves, we say, could never accept generation from each other." Then, with a glance at Cebes, he added, "Is it possible that you too, Cebes, were disturbed by what our friend spoke of?"

"No, not by this," replied Cebes, "but I don't deny that I get disturbed a good deal."

"Well, then, are we agreed," said Socrates, "simply on this, that nothing will ever be opposite to itself?"

"Quite agreed," he said.

"Here is something else," he said, "see if you will agree to this. You speak of hot and cold?"

"Yes."

"Is it the same as fire and snow?"

"Not at all."

"But the hot is something other than fire, and the cold other than snow?"

"Yes."

"Well, I suppose you agree that snow receiving fire (to use our former way of putting it) will never be what it was, snow, and also be hot, but when the hot approaches it will either retreat from it or be destroyed."

"Certainly."

"Fire, also, when the cold approaches, will either go away from it or be destroyed, but it will never endure to receive the coldness and still be what it was, fire, and cold too."

---

[36]I.e., the "safe answer."

"True," said he.

"Then it is possible," he said, "with some such things, that not only the essence is thought worthy of the same name forever, but something else also is worthy, which is not that essence but which, when it exists, always has the form of that essence. Perhaps it will be a little clearer as follows. Odd numbers must always be called odd, I suppose, mustn't they?"

"Yes."

"Of all things do we use this name only for oddness, for that is what I ask, or is there something else, not oddness, but what must be called always by that name because its nature is never to be deserted by oddness? For example, triplet and so forth. Now consider the triplet: Don't you think it should be called always both by its own name and also by the name of odd, although oddness is not the same as triplet? Still it is the nature of triplet and quintet and half of all the numbers, that each of them is odd although it is not the same thing as oddness; so also two and four and all the other row of numbers are each of them always even, although none is the same thing as evenness; do you agree?"

"Of course," he said.

"Now attend, this is what I want to make clear. It seems that not only those real opposites do not receive each other, but also things which not being opposites of each other yet always have those real opposites in them, these also do not look like things which receive that reality which is opposite to the reality in them, but when it approaches they either are destroyed or retire. We shall say, for example, that a triplet will be destroyed before any such thing happens to it, before it remains and becomes even, while it is still three?"

"Certainly," said Cebes.

"Nor, again," he said, "is twin the opposite of triplet."

"Not at all."

"Then not only the opposite essences do not remain at the approach of each other, but some other things do not await the approach of the opposites."

"Very true," he said.

"Then shall we distinguish what sorts of things these are," he said, "if we can?"

"Certainly."

"Then, Cebes, would they be those which compel whatever they occupy not only to get their own essence but also the essence of some opposite?"

"How so?"

"As we said just now. You know, I suppose, that whatever the essence of three occupies must necessarily be not only three but odd."

"Certainly."

"And the essence opposite to that which does this we say could never come near such a thing."

"It could not."

"And what has done this? Was not it oddness?"

"Yes."

"And opposite to this is the essence of even?"

"Yes."

"Then the essence of even will never approach three."

"No."

"So three has no part in the even."

"None."

"Then the triplet is uneven."

"Yes."

"Now for my distinction. What things, not being opposite to something, yet do not receive the opposite itself which is in that something? For instance now, the triplet is not the opposite to the even, yet still does not receive it because it always brings the opposite against it; and a pair brings the opposite against the odd, and fire against cold, and so with very many others. Just look then, if you distinguish thus, not only the opposite does not receive the opposite, but that also which brings anything opposite to whatever it approaches never

receives the opposite to that which it brings. Recollect once more; there's no harm to hear the same thing often. Five will not receive the essence of even, or its double ten the essence of odd; yet this same double will not receive the essence of odd, although it is not opposite to anything. Again, one and a half and other such things with a half in them will not receive the essence of whole, nor will one-third and all such fractions, if you follow and agree with me in this."

"I do agree certainly, and I follow."

"Once more, then," he said, "go back to the beginning. And don't answer the questions I ask, till I show you how. I want something more than the first answer I mentioned, the safe one; I see a new safety from what we have been saying now. If you ask me what must be in any body if that body is to be hot, I will not give you that safe answer, the stupid answer, 'Heat,' but a more subtle answer from our present reasoning, 'Fire'; or if you ask what must be in a body if it is to be diseased, I will not answer 'Disease,' but 'Fever'; or if you ask what must be in a number if it is to be odd, I will not say 'Oddness,' but 'Onehood,' and so forth. Now then, do you know clearly enough what I want?"

"Oh yes," he said.

"Answer then," said he, "what must be in a body if it is to be living?"

"Soul," said he.

"Is this always true?

"Of course," he said.

"Well now, whatever the soul occupies, she always comes to it bringing life?"

"She does, indeed," he said.

"Is there an opposite to life, or not?"

"There is."

"What?"

"Death."

"Then soul will never receive the opposite to that which she brings, as we have agreed already."

"Most assuredly," said Cebes.

"Well, what name did we give just now to that which did not receive the essence of the even?"

"Uneven," he said.

"And what name to that which does not receive what is just, or to that which does not receive music?"

"Unmusical," he said, "and unjust the other."

"Very well. What do we call that which does not receive death?"

"Immortal," he said.

"And the soul does not receive death?"

"No."

"Then the soul is a thing immortal?"

"It is," he said.

"Very well," said he. "Shall we say this has been proved? Or what do you think?"

"Proved, and amply proved, Socrates."

"Now then, Cebes," he said, "if the uneven were necessarily imperishable, would not three be imperishable?"

"Of course."

"And if the not-hot were necessarily imperishable, when someone brought a hot thing to snow, the snow would retire safe and unmelted? For it would not be destroyed, nor would it remain and receive the heat."

"Quite true," he said.

"So also if the not-cold were imperishable, when something cold was brought to fire, the fire would not be quenched or destroyed, but it would go away safe."

"That is necessary," he said.

"And is it equally necessary to say that of the immortal? If the immortal is also imperishable, it is impossible for the soul to be destroyed when death comes to it; for death it will never receive, by our argument, and it will never be dead, just as we showed that the three would never be even, nor the odd be even, nor indeed would fire, or the heat in the fire, ever be cold. But someone might say, 'The odd will not become even, when the even comes near, as we have agreed, but what is to hinder its being destroyed and an even being made instead?' In answer to the man who said that, we could not maintain that it is not destroyed; for the uneven is not imperishable; since if that had been granted us we could easily maintain that when the even approached, the odd, and the three, go clean off; and we could do the same about fire and heat and all the rest, couldn't we?"

"Certainly.

"So about the immortal, if we agree that this is imperishable, the soul would be imperishable as well as immortal; but if we do not, we need a new argument."

"There's no need of that in this case," said he, "nothing could escape destruction if the immortal, which is everlasting, could be destroyed."

"God himself, I think," said Socrates, "and the very essence of life, and whatever else is immortal, would be admitted by all never to suffer destruction."

"Yes, admitted by all indeed," he said, "by men of course and still more, I think, by the gods."

"Then, since the immortal is also imperishable, the soul if it is immortal would be imperishable too?"

"That must certainly be."

"So when death approaches a man, the mortal in him dies, as it seems, but the immortal part goes away undestroyed, giving place to death."

"So it seems."

"Then beyond all doubt, Cebes," he said, "soul is immortal and imperishable, and in fact our souls will exist in the house of Hades."

"I have nothing else to say to the contrary, Socrates," he answered, "and I cannot disbelieve you in any way."

"But now if Simmias has something to say, or anyone else, it is well not to be silent. I don't know what better opportunity we could have; we can't put it off now; there is only this chance if anyone wishes to say or hear more about such matters as this."

"No, indeed," said Simmias, "I can't find anything myself to disbelieve after what has been said. But in the momentous matter which we are discussing, I do distrust human weakness, and I am compelled to have a little incredulity in my mind about what we say."

"Not only that, Simmias," said Socrates; "you are quite right, and you ought still to scrutinise our first suppositions and see if you can trust them; and if you test them sufficiently, you will follow our reasoning, I think, as well as it is possible for man to follow it; and if only this be made clear, you will seek nothing further."

"True," he said.

"Well, here is something more, gentlemen," said Socrates, "that we ought to understand. If the soul is immortal, she needs care, not only for the time which we call life, but for all time, and the danger indeed would seem to be terrible if one is ready to neglect her. For if death were release from everything, a great blessing it would be for evil men to be rid of the body and their own wickedness along with the soul. But since, as things are, she appears to be immortal, there could be no escape from evil for her and no salvation, except that she should become as good and wise as possible. For when the soul comes to Hades she brings with her nothing but her education and training; and this is said to do the greatest help or hurt to the dead man at the very beginning of his course thither. What men say is this. At death the guardian spirit of each, to whom each was allotted for life, undertakes to lead each to a certain place; there those gathered must stand their trial, and then pass on to the house of Hades with the guide whose duty it is to conduct them hence to that place. When they have met there what they must meet with, and remained such time as they should, another guide again brings them back after many long periods of time. The journey is not as Telephos describes in Aeschylus, for he says that a simple way leads to Hades, but this appears to me neither simple nor single. If so, there would be no need of guides, for no one could miss one way to anywhere. But really, it seems to have many breaks and branches; I judge by the pious offerings made to the dead among us.[37] The wise and decent soul follows and understands the circumstances; but the soul which has desire for the body, as I said once before, flutters about it for a long time and about the visible world, resisting much and suffering much, and the appointed spirit drags her away by force not easily. When she comes where the others are, the unpurified soul, which has done deeds like herself, which has touched unjust murders, or done other such deeds which are akin to these and are the acts of kindred souls, is avoided by all; each one turns from her and will neither be fellow-traveller nor guide, but she wanders by herself in complete helplessness, until certain times come: when they come she is carried by necessity to her proper dwelling place. But the soul which has passed through life purely and decently finds gods for fellow-travellers and leaders, and each soul dwells in her own proper dwelling place. There are many wonderful regions in the earth, and the earth itself is not of such a quality or such a size as it is thought to be by those who are accustomed to describe the earth, so a certain man has convinced me."

Then Simmias asked, "What is this you say, Socrates? I have heard much about the earth myself, but not this story that convinced you. So I should be very glad to hear it."

He answered, "Why indeed, Simmias, I am afraid I lack a Glaucos' handbook[38] to tell you all that! But truly I think it is too hard for Glaucos' book, and besides me not perhaps being equal to it, at the same time even if I understood it, my life, Simmias, seems to me insufficient for such a long story. But what I believe to be the shape of the earth and its regions, I can tell you, there's nothing to hinder that."

"Well," said Simmias, "that will do."

"I believe, then," said he, "that first, if it is round and in the middle of the heavens, it needs nothing to keep it from falling, neither air nor any other such necessity, but the uniformity of the heavens[39] themselves alike all through, is enough to keep it there, and the equilibrium of earth itself; for a thing in equilibrium and placed in the middle of something which is everywhere alike will not incline in any direction, but will remain steady and in like condition. First I believe that," he said.

"Quite right too," said Simmias.

"Next, I believe it is very large indeed, and we live in a little bit of it between the Pillars of Heracles[40] and the river Phasis,[41] like ants or frogs in a marsh, lodging round the sea, and that many other people live in many other such regions. For there are everywhere about the earth many hollows of all sorts in shape and size, into which have collected water and mist and air; but the earth itself is pure and lies in the pure heavens where the stars are, which is called ether by most of those who are accustomed to explain such things; of which all this is a sediment, which is always collecting into

---

[37] Food and the like were laid on shrines where roads joined; he therefore assumes that the roads below were like that.

[38] A proverb: probably some discoverer or inventor.

[39] The universe is homogeneous and of one density, so there is no reason why the earth should move this way or that.

[40] Mts. Calpe and Abyla, on the straits of Gibraltar; Calpe is the modern Rock of Gibraltar.

[41] The river Rion which flows into the eastern part of the Black Sea.

the hollows of the earth. We then, who lodge in its hollows, know nothing about it, and think we are living upon the earth; as if one living deep on the bottom of the sea should think he was at the top, and, seeing through the water sun and stars, should think the sea was heaven, but from sluggishness and weakness should never come to the surface and never get out and peep up out of the sea into this place, or observe how much more pure and beautiful it is than his own place, and should never have heard from anyone who saw it. This very thing has happened to us; for we live in a hollow of the earth and think we live on the surface, and call the air heaven, thinking that the stars move through that and that is heaven; but the fact is the same, from weakness and sluggishness we cannot get through to the surface of the air, since if a man could come to the top of it, and get wings and fly up, he could peep over and look, just as fishes here peep up out of the sea and look round at what is here, so he could look at what is there, and if his nature allowed him to endure the sight, he could learn and know that that is the true heaven and the true light and the true earth. For this earth and the stones and all the place here are corrupted and corroded, as things in the sea are by the brine so that nothing worth mention grows in the sea, and there is nothing perfect there, one might say, but caves and sand and infinite mud and slime wherever there is any earth, things worth nothing at all as compared with the beauties we have; but again those above as compared with ours would seem to be much superior. But if I must tell you a story, Simmias, it is worth hearing what things really are like on the earth under the heavens."

"Indeed, Socrates," said Simmias, "we should be glad to hear this story."

"It is said then, my comrade," he went on, "that first of all the earth itself looks from above, if you could see it, like those twelve-patch leathern balls,[42] variegated, with strips of colour of which the colours here, such as are used by painters, are a sort of specimens; but there the whole earth is made of such as these, and much brighter and purer than these; one is sea purple wonderfully beautiful, one is like gold, the white is whiter than chalk or snow, and the earth is made of these and other colours, more in number and more beautiful than any we have seen. For indeed the very hollows full of water and mist present a colour of their own as they shine in the variety of other colours, so that the one whole looks like a continuous coloured pattern. Such is the earth, and all that grows in it is in accord, trees and flowers and fruits; and again mountains and rocks in like manner have their smoothness and transparency and colours more beautiful, and the precious stones which are so much valued here are just chips of those, sard and jaspers and emerald and so forth, but there every single one is such and they are still more beautiful. The cause of that is that those stones are pure and not corroded or corrupted as ours are by the rot and brine of stuff which has gathered here, which bring ugliness and disease on stones and earth and everything else, living creatures and plants. But the real earth is adorned with all these and with gold and silver and all such things as these. For there they are clearly to be seen, being many in number and large and all over the earth, so that to see it is a sight for happy spectators. Animals there are on it many and various, and men too, some living inland, some round the air as we do round the sea, some in islands surrounded by the flowing air near the mainland; in a word, what water and sea are to us for our use, the air is to them, and what the air is to us, ether is to them. The seasons have such temperature that the people there are free from disease and live a much longer time than we do, and in sight and hearing and intelligence and so forth they are as different from us as air is different from water and ether from air in purity. Groves of the gods also they have and sanctuaries, and the gods really dwell in them, and there are between them and the gods voices and prophecies and perceptions and other such communions; sun and moon and stars are seen by them as they are, and their happiness in all other respects is according.

"This, then, is the nature of the whole earth and all that is about it; but there are many regions in it and hollows of it all round, some deeper and spreading wider than the one we live in, some deeper but having their gap smaller than ours, some again shallower in depth than ours and wider; but these are all connected together by tunnels in many places narrower or wider, and they have many passages where floods of water run through from one to another as into a mixing-bowl, and huge rivers ever flowing underground both of hot waters and cold, where also are masses of fire and great rivers of fire, and many rivers of liquid mud, some clearer, some muddier, like the rivers of mud which run in Sicily before the lava,[43] and the lava itself. And each of these regions is filled with this, according as the overflow comes in each case. All these things are moved up and down by a sort of seesaw which there is in the earth, and the nature of this seesaw movement is this. One of the chasms in the earth is largest of all, and, besides, it has a tunnel which goes right through the earth, the same which Homer speaks of when he says,

Far, far away, where is the lowest pit
Beneath the earth,[44]

and which elsewhere he and many other poets have called Tartaros. For into this chasm all the rivers flow together, and from this again they flow out, and they are each like the earth through which they flow. The cause which makes all the streams run out from there and run in is that this fluid has no bottom or foundation to rest on. So it seesaws and swells up and down, and the air and wind about it do the same; for they follow with it, both when the rivers move towards that side of the earth, and when they move towards this side, and just as the breath always goes in and out when men breathe, so there, too, the wind is lifted up and down with the liquid and makes terrible tempests both coming in and going out. Therefore whenever the water goes back into the place which is called 'down,' it rushes in along those rivers and fills them up like water pumped in; but when, again, it leaves that part and moves this way, it fills up our region once more, and when the rivers are filled they flow through the channels and through the earth, and, coming each to those places where their several paths lead, they make seas and lakes and rivers and fountains. After that they sink into the earth again, some passing round larger regions and more numerous, some round fewer and smaller, and plunge again into Tartaros, some far below their source, some but little, but all below the place where they came out. Some flow in opposite where they tumbled out, some in the same place; and there are others which go right round the earth in a circle, curling about it like serpents once or many times, and then fall and discharge as low down as possible. It is possible from each side to go down as far as the centre, but no farther, for beyond that the opposite part is uphill from both sides.

"All these rivers are large, and they are of many kinds; but among these many are four in especial. The greatest of these, and the outermost, running right round, is that called Ocean; opposite this and flowing in the contrary direction is Acheron, the River of Pain, which flows through a number of desert places, and also flowing under the earth comes to the Acherusian Lake, to which come the souls of most of the dead, and when they have remained there certain ordained times, some

---

[42]Leathern balls with coloured patches. He is thinking also of the twelve Signs of the Zodiac, hence twelve.

[43]From Mount Etna in eruption.

[44]Iliad viii. 14.

longer and some shorter, they are sent out again to birth in living creatures. The third of these rivers issues forth in the middle, and near its issue it falls into a large region blazing with much fire, and makes a lake larger than our[45] sea, boiling with water and mud; from there it moves round turbid and muddy, and rolls winding about the earth as far as another place at the extreme end of the Acherusian Lake, without mingling with the water; when it has rolled many times round it falls into a lower depth than Tartaros. This is what they call Pyriphlegethon, the River of Burning Fire, and its lava streams blow up bits of it wherever they are found on the earth. Opposite this again the fourth river discharges at first into a region terrible and wild, it is said, all having the colour of dark blue; this they call the Stygian, the River of Hate, and the lake which the river makes they call Styx. But the river, falling into this and receiving terrible powers in the water, plunges beneath the earth and, rolling round, moves contrary to Pyriphlegethon and meets it in the Acherusian Lake on the opposite side. The water of this, too, mixes with none, but this also goes round and falls into Tartaros opposite to Pyriphlegethon. The name of this, as the poets say, is Cocytos, the River of Wailing.

"Such is the nature of the world. So when the dead come to the place whither the spirit conveys each, first the judges divide them into those who have lived well and piously, and those who have not. And those who are thought to have been between the two travel to the Acheron, then embark in the vessels which are said to be there for them, and in these come to the lake, and there they dwell, being purified from their wrongdoings; and after punishment for any wrong they have done they are released, and receive rewards for their good deeds each according to his merit. But those who are thought to be incurable because of the greatness of their sins, those who have done many great acts of sacrilege or many unrighteous and lawless murders or other such crimes, these the proper fate throws into Tartaros whence they never come out. Those who are thought to have committed crimes curable although great, if they have done some violence to father or mother, say, from anger, and have lived the rest of their lives in repentance, or if they have become manslaughterers in some other such way, these must of necessity be cast into Tartaros; but when they have been cast in and been there a year the wave throws them out, the manslaughterers by way of Cocytos, the patricides and matricides by way of Pyriphlegethon; and when they have been carried down to the Acherusian Lake, there they shriek and call to those whom they slew or treated violently, and, calling on them, they beg and beseech them to accept them and let them go out into the lake; if they win consent, they come out and cease from their sufferings; if not, they are carried back into Tartaros and from there into the rivers again, and they never cease from this treatment until they win the consent of those whom they wronged: for this was the sentence passed on them by the judges. But those who are thought to have lived in especial holiness, they are those who are set free and released from these places here in the earth as from a prison house, and come up into the pure dwelling place and are settled upon earth. Of these same, again, those who have purified themselves enough by philosophy live without bodies altogether forever after, and come into dwellings even more beautiful than the others, which it is not easy to describe nor is there time enough at this present. But for the reasons which we have given, Simmias, we must do everything so as to have our share of wisdom and virtue in life; for the prize is noble and the hope great.

"No sensible man would think it proper to rely on things of this kind being just as I have described; but that, since the soul is clearly immortal, this or something like this at any rate is what happens in regard to our souls and their habitations—that this is so seems to me proper and worthy of the risk of believing; for the risk is noble. Such things he must sing like a healing charm to himself, and that is why I have lingered so long over the story. But these are the reasons for a man to be confident about his own soul, when in his life he has bidden farewell to all other pleasures, the pleasures and adornments of the body, thinking them alien and such as do more harm than good, and has been earnest only for the pleasure of learning; and having adorned the soul with no alien ornaments, but with her own—with temperance and justice and courage and freedom and truth, thus he awaits the journey to the house of Hades, ready to travel when the doom ordained shall call. You indeed," he said, "Simmias and Cebes and all, hereafter at some certain time shall each travel on that journey: but me—'Fate calls me now,' as a man might say in a tragedy, and it is almost time for me to travel towards the bath; for I am sure you think it better to have a bath before drinking the potion, and to save the women the trouble of washing a corpse."

When he had spoken, Criton said, "Ah well, Socrates, what injunctions have you for these friends or for me, about your children or anything else? What could we do for you to gratify you most?"

"What I always say, Criton," he said, "nothing very new: Take good care of yourselves, and you will gratify me and mine and yourselves whatever you do, even if you promise nothing now. But if you neglect yourselves, and won't take care to live your lives following the footsteps, so to speak, of both this last conversation and those we have had in former times, you will do no good even if you promise ever so much at present and ever so faithfully."

"Then we will do our best about that," he said; "but how are we to bury you?"

"How you like," said he, "if you catch me and I don't escape you." At the same time, laughing gently and looking towards us, he said, "Criton doesn't believe me, my friends, that this is I, Socrates now talking with you and laying down each of my injunctions, but he thinks me to be what he will see shortly, a corpse, and asks, if you please, how to bury me! I have been saying all this long time, that when I have drunk the potion, I shall not be here then with you; I shall have gone clear away to some bliss of the blest, as they call it. But he thinks I am talking nonsense, just to console myself, yes and you too. Then go bail for me to Criton," he said, "the opposite of the bail he gave to those judges. He gave bail that I would remain; you please, give bail that I will not remain after I die, but I shall get off clear and clean, that Criton may take it more easily, and may not be vexed by seeing my body either being burnt or buried; don't let him worry for me and think I'm in a dreadful state, or say at the funeral that he is laying out or carrying out or digging in Socrates. Be sure, Criton, best of friends," he said, "to use ugly words not only is out of tune with the event, but it even infects the soul with something evil. Now, be confident and say you are burying my body, and then bury it as you please and as you think would be most according to custom."

With these words, he got up and retired into another room for the bath, and Criton went after him, telling us to wait. So we waited discussing and talking together about what had been said, or sometimes speaking of the great misfortune which had befallen us, for we felt really as if we had lost a father and had to spend the rest of our lives as orphans. When he had bathed, and his children had been brought to see him—for he had two little sons, and one big—and when the women of his family had come, he talked to them before Criton and gave what instructions he wished. Then he asked the women and children to go, and came back to us. It was

---

[45]The Mediterranean.

now near sunset, for he had spent a long time within. He came and sat down after his bath, and he had not talked long after this when the servant of the Eleven came in, and standing by him said, "O Socrates! I have not to complain of you as I do of others, that they are angry with me, and curse me, because I bring them word to drink their potion, which my officers make me do! But I have always found you in this time most generous and gentle, and the best man who ever came here. And now too, I know well you are not angry with me, for you know who are responsible, and you keep it for them. Now you know what I came to tell you, so farewell, and try to bear as well as you can what can't be helped."

Then he turned and was going out, with tears running down his cheeks. And Socrates looked up at him and said, "Farewell to you also, I will do so." Then, at the same time turning to us, "What a nice fellow!" he said. "All the time he has been coming and talking to me, a real good sort, and now how generously he sheds tears for me! Come along, Criton, let's obey him. Someone bring the potion, if the stuff has been ground; if not, let the fellow grind it."

Then Criton said, "But, Socrates, I think the sun is still over the hills, it has not set yet. Yes, and I know of others who, having been told to drink the poison, have done it very late; they had dinner first and a good one, and some enjoyed the company of any they wanted. Please don't be in a hurry, there is time to spare."

But Socrates said, "Those you speak of have very good reason for doing that, for they think they will gain by doing it; and I have good reasons why I won't do it. For I think I shall gain nothing by drinking a little later, only that I shall think myself a fool for clinging to life and sparing when the cask's empty.[46] Come along," he said, "do what I tell you, if you please."

And Criton, hearing this, nodded to the boy who stood near. The boy went out, and after spending a long time, came in with the man who was to give the poison[47] carrying it ground ready in a cup. Socrates caught sight of the man and said, "Here, my good man, you know about these things; what must I do?"

"Just drink it," he said, "and walk about till your legs get heavy, then lie down. In that way the drug will act of itself."

At the same time, he held out the cup to Socrates, and he took it quite cheerfully, Echecrates, not a tremble, not a change in colour or looks; but looking full at the man under his brows, as he used to do, he asked him. "What do you say about this drink? What of a libation to someone?[48] Is that allowed, or not?"

He said, "We only grind so much as we think enough for a moderate potion."

"I understand," he said, "but at least, I suppose, it is allowed to offer a prayer to the gods and that must be done, for good luck in the migration from here to there. Then that is my prayer, and so may it be!"

With these words he put the cup to his lips and, quite easy and contented, drank it up. So far most of us had been able to hold back our tears pretty well; but when we saw him begin drinking and end drinking, we could no longer. I burst into a flood of tears for all I could do, so I wrapped up my face and cried myself out; not for him indeed, but for my own misfortune in losing such a man and such a comrade. Criton had got up and gone out even before I did, for he could not hold the tears in. Apollodoros had never ceased weeping all this time, and now he burst out into loud sobs, and by his weeping and lamentations completely broke down every man there except Socrates himself. He only said, "What a scene! You amaze me. That's just why I sent the women away, to keep them from making a scene like this. I've heard that one ought to make an end in decent silence. Quiet yourselves and endure."

When we heard him we felt ashamed and restrained our tears. He walked about, and when he said that his legs were feeling heavy, he lay down on his back, as the man told him to do; at the same time the one who gave him the potion felt him, and after a while examined his feet and legs; then pinching a foot hard, he asked if he felt anything; he said no. After this, again, he pressed the shins; and, moving up like this, he showed us that he was growing cold and stiff. Again he felt him, and told us that when it came to his heart, he would be gone. Already the cold had come nearly as far as the abdomen, when Socrates threw off the covering from his face—for he had covered it over—and said, the last words he uttered, "Criton," he said, "we owe a cock to Asclepios;[49] pay it without fail."

"That indeed shall be done," said Criton. "Have you anything more to say?"

When Criton had asked this, Socrates gave no further answer, but after a little time, he stirred, and the man uncovered him, and his eyes were still. Criton, seeing this, closed the mouth and eyelids.

This was the end of our comrade, Echecrates, a man, as we would say, of all then living we had ever met, the noblest and the wisest and most just.

Study Guide for Plato's PHAEDO

This dialogue is rather difficult reading, particularly the questions asked by Simmias and Cebes and the somewhat complicated answers developed by Socrates. The outline of questions is intended to serve as a guide for your reading.

1. What is Socrates' argument against suicide?
2. Socrates gives two major reasons for the philosopher welcoming death.
    a. The quest for knowledge.
       (1) How does he define death?
       (2) What is the single goal of the philosopher?
       (3) What are we accepting as the concept of reality?
       (4) What can we say about the body and the senses in our search for truth and reality?
       (5) What part of the human being can be trusted in the search for truth?
       (6) This answer is not in the reading, but what human quality would Socrates probably equate with soul?
       (7) Therefore, why should the philosopher welcome death?
    b. What seems to be the afterlife for the lover of wisdom?

---

[46] There's a proverb:
Cask full or failing, drink; but in between
Spare if you like; sparing at bottom's mean.

Hesiod, *Works and Days*, 368

[47] The poison was hemlock.

[48] The custom was for the butler to spill a drop into the cup which the drinker then spilt on the ground as a libation with a prayer; then the butler filled and the man drank.

[49] A thank-offering to the god of healing. The cock is the poor man's offering. The touching beauty and restraint of this account is heightened still more, if Plato, who was ill and unable to be present at the death of his dearest friend, took this last request to have been made for his sake.

3. The question of immortality of the soul.
   a. The doctrine of opposites.
      (1) State as briefly as you can this doctrine in its simplest form.
      (2) What are the two *processes* (not things) involved?
      (3) What is the opposite of life?
      (4) What is the process involved in life and death?
      (5) Then what must be true of souls if they can emerge into life?
      (6) How does Socrates' doctrine of "conservation of life" apply to this problem?
   b. The doctrine of "learning as recollection."
      (1) What is true if someone remembers something?
      (2) When we see or think of one thing, what frequently happens?
      (3) When we see two things or recollect them, what other intangible thing may we recollect? What is an example of this new recollection?
      (4) What is the difference between the equal and unequal things and the relationship which we recollect?
      (5) How and when do we know these qualities? And how do we know the "things"?
      (6) When did we acquire our senses and our knowledge of the essences?
      (7) What are the two alternatives in our knowledge of the essences?
      (8) What is the test of "knowing a thing"? How does this apply to the essences?
      (9) Where did our knowledge of the essences come from?
   c. Granting the existence of the soul before birth, can we be sure it continues to exist after the death of the body?
      (1) What already accepted conclusions can we use? How do they work in this new problem?
      (2) Further analysis of the question. What is permanent and what sorts of things are dissolved and scattered?
      (3) How do we know these two kinds of things?
      (4) What is another way of classifying the two kinds of things, then?
      (5) What is the composition of the human being?
      (6) What is the nature of the soul and what is its duty?
      (7) What can we say of the immortality of the soul?
   d. Socrates' idea of the soul in Hades.
      (1) What is his picture of the good and the bad soul after death?
      (2) What is the action of bodily desires on the human?
      (3) What of the pure soul's fear of disintegration?
   e. The problem of the soul as a harmony (Simmias' question).
      (1) Using the comparison of the lyre, how is this question stated?
      (2) What is the definition of a harmony?
      (3) Which one of the earlier-proved doctrines are we to accept as true?
      (4) What did that doctrine prove?
      (5) But what can we say about the coming-into-being of the harmony of a lyre? What, then, of soul and body?
      (6) State briefly the second proof dealing with the similarity of the harmony with the physical things harmonized.
   f. Cebes' question: Is the soul simply tougher than the body but not immortal? Does it wear out several bodies but finally disintegrate?
      (1) What previous conclusion can we grant?
      (2) How does a particular thing possess a certain quality?
      (3) What can we say of various naturalistic explanations?
      (4) What can we say of a quality and its opposite?
      (5) What objection is raised to the argument in 4, and how does Socrates answer the objection?
      (6) What can we agree on, then?
      (7) How can we define the new class of things which Socrates speaks of now? What of *two, three,* and their qualities?
      (8) How shall we define this class of things we have just discussed?
      (9) What is the relation between body and soul? What does a soul do to matter?
      (10) Assuming that soul is one of the class of things mentioned above, what is the opposite of living?
      (11) And what will this class of things do in the face of their opposite?
      (12) Then what of the soul when death approaches?

(13) What do we call something which will not receive death?

(14) But what if the soul does not retreat when death approaches, but is destroyed by that approach?

g. (Let's skip Socrates' picture of the world and go on.) What is the state of the soul after death? But first, what care should we take of our soul during life?

EXERCISES

1. In the Eighteenth Century, the English romantic poet, Wordsworth, wrote the following stanza in his poem "Ode, Intimations of Immortality from Recollections of Early Childhood." To what extent does the thought expressed here correspond to one of Plato's ideas? To what extent is it different? Read the rest of the Ode to see if you can find other significant differences between the thought of Wordsworth and that of Socrates.

Our birth is but a sleep and a forgetting.
The Soul that rises with us, our life's Star,
   Hath had elsewhere its setting,
     And cometh from afar:
   Not in entire forgetfulness,
   And not in utter nakedness,
But trailing clouds of glory do we come
   From God, who is our home:
Heaven lies about us in our infancy!
Shades of the prison-house begin to close
   Upon the growing boy,
But He beholds the light, and whence it flows,
   He sees it in his joy;
The Youth, who daily farther from the east
   Must travel, still is Nature's Priest,
   And by the vision splendid
   Is on his way attended;
At length the Man perceives it die away,
And fade into the light of common day.

2. In an earlier chapter of this book some of the thoughts of the Eleatic philosophers is outlined. To what extent does Socrates draw upon that thought? To what extent does his thought resemble that of Pythagoras?

The Allegory of the Cave

This story represents Plato's idea about absolute reality in the universe, and the world that appears to our senses. What should the student of philosophy, who glimpses reality, do? This is taken from Book VII of the *Republic*. Socrates and Glaucon are talking.

And now, I said, let me show in a figure how far our nature is enlightened or unenlightened;—Behold! human beings living in an underground den, which has a mouth open towards the light and reaching all along the den; here they have been from their childhood, and have their legs and necks chained so that they cannot move and can only see before them, being prevented by the chains from turning round their heads. Above and behind a fire is blazing at a distance, and between the fire and the prisoners there is a raised way, like the screen which marionette players have in front of them, over which they show the puppets.

I see.

And do you see, I said, men passing along the wall carrying all sorts of vessels, and statues and figures of animals made of wood and stone and various materials, which appear over the wall? Some of them are talking, others silent.

You have shown me a strange image, and they are strange prisoners.

Like ourselves, I replied; and they see only their own shadows, or the shadows of one another, which the fire throws on the opposite wall of the cave?

True, he said; how could they see anything but the shadows if they were never allowed to move their heads?

And of the objects which are being carried in like manner they would only see the shadows?

Yes, he said.

And if they were able to converse with one another, would they not suppose that they were naming what was actually before them?

Very true.

And suppose further that the prison had an echo which came from the other side, would they not be sure to fancy when one of the passers-by spoke that the voice which they heard came from the passing shadow?

No question, he replied.

To them, I said, the truth would be literally nothing but the shadows of the images.

That is certain.

And now look again, and see what will naturally follow if the prisoners are released and disabused of their error. At first, when any of them is liberated and compelled suddenly to stand up and turn his neck round and walk and look towards the light, he will suffer sharp pains; the glare will distress him, and he will be unable to see the realities of which in his former state he had seen the shadows; and then conceive someone saying to him, that what he saw before was an illusion, but that now, when he is approaching nearer to being and his eye is turned towards more real existence, he has a clearer vision,—what will be his reply? And you may further imagine that his instructor is pointing to the objects as they pass and requiring him to name them—will he not be perplexed? Will he not fancy that the shadows which he formerly saw are truer than the objects which are now shown to him?

Far truer.

And if he is compelled to look straight at the light, will he not have a pain in his eyes which will make him turn away to take refuge in the objects of vision which he can see, and which he will conceive to be in reality clearer than the things which are now being shown to him?

True, he said.

And suppose once more, that he is reluctantly dragged up a steep and rugged ascent, and held fast until he is forced into the presence of the sun himself, is he not likely to be pained and irritated? When he approaches the light his eyes will be dazzled, and he will not be able to see anything at all of what are now called realities.

Not all in a moment, he said.

He will require to grow accustomed to the sight of the upper world. And first he will see the shadows best, next the reflections of men and other objects in the water, and then the objects themselves; then he will gaze upon the light of the moon and the stars and the spangled heaven; and he will see the sky and the stars by night better than the sun or the light of the sun by day?

Certainly.

Last of all he will be able to see the sun,[1] and not mere reflections of it in the water, but he will see it in its own proper place, and not in another; and he will contemplate it as it is.

Certainly.

He will then proceed to argue that this is it which gives the season and the years, and is the guardian of all that is in the visible world, and in a certain way the cause of all things which he and his fellows have been accustomed to behold?

Clearly, he said, he would first see the sun and then reason about it.

And when he remembered his old habitation, and the wisdom of the den and his fellow-prisoners, do you not suppose that he would congratulate himself on the change and pity them?

Certainly, he would.

And if they were in the habit of conferring honours among themselves on those who were quickest to observe the passing shadows and to remark which of them went before, and which followed after, and which were together; and who were therefore best able to draw conclusions as to the future, do you think that he would care for such honors and glories, or envy the possessors of them? Would he not say with Homer,

"Better to be the poor servant of a poor master," and to endure anything, rather than think as they do and live after their manner?

Yes, he said, I think that he would rather suffer anything than entertain these false notions and live in this miserable manner.

Imagine once more, I said, such an one coming suddenly out of the sun to be replaced in his old situation; would he not be certain to have his eyes full of darkness?

To be sure, he said.

And if there were a contest, and he had to compete in measuring the shadows with the prisoners who had never moved out of the den, while his sight was still weak, and before his eyes had become steady (and the time which would be needed to acquire this new habit of sight might be very considerable), would he not be ridiculous? Men would say of him that up he went and came back without his eyes; and that it was better not even to think of ascending; and if any one tried to loose another and lead him up to the light, let them only catch the offender, and they would put him to death.

No question, he said.

This entire allegory, I said, you may now append, dear Glaucon, to the previous argument; the prison-house is the world of sight, the light of the fire is the sun, and you will not misapprehend me if you interpret the journey upwards to be the ascent of the soul into the intellectual world according to my poor belief, which, at your desire, I have expressed—whether rightly or wrongly God knows. But whether true or false, my opinion is that in the world of knowledge the idea of good appears last of all, and is seen only with an effort; and when seen, is also inferred to be the universal author of all things beautiful and right, parent of light and of the lord of light in this visible world, and the immediate source of reason and truth in the intellectual; and that this is the power upon which he who would act rationally either in public or private life must have his eye fixed.

I agree, he said, as far as I am able to understand you.

Moreover, I said, you must not wonder that those who attain to this beatific vision are unwilling to descend to human affairs; for their souls are ever hastening into the upper world where they desire to dwell; which desire of theirs is very natural, if our allegory may be trusted.

Yes, very natural.

And is there anything surprising in one who passes from divine contemplations to the evil state of man, misbehaving himself in a ridiculous manner; if, while his eyes are blinking and before he has become accustomed to the surrounding darkness, he is compelled to fight in courts of law, or in other places, about the images or the shadows of images of justice, and is endeavoring to meet the conceptions of those who have never yet seen absolute justice?

---

[1]Imagine that the sun is Plato's idea of The Good.

Anything but surprising, he replied.

Anyone who has common sense will remember that the bewilderments of the eyes are of two kinds, and arise from two causes, either from coming out of the light or from going into the light, which is true of the mind's eye, quite as much as of the bodily eye; and he who remembers this when he sees anyone whose vision is perplexed and weak, will not be too ready to laugh; he will first ask whether that soul of man has come out of the brighter life, and is unable to see because unaccustomed to the dark, or having turned from darkness to the day is dazzled by excess of light.

The business of us who are the founders of the State will be to compel the best minds to attain that knowledge which we have already shown to be the greatest of all—they must continue to ascend until they arrive at the good; but when they have ascended and seen enough we must not allow them to do as they do now.

What do you mean?

I mean that they remain in the upper world; but this must not be allowed; they must be made to descend again among the prisoners in the den, and partake of their labors and honors, whether they are worth having or not.

A QUESTION:

Why does Plato insist that the one who has gone through all of the difficulties involved in coming to see and know the true light *must* return to the cave, that he must even partake of the labors and honors of the people in the cave, even though he recognizes that these are foolish?

Rome

The Failure of Professionalism

CHAPTER

11

Rome: The Failure
of Professionalism

Throughout our study of Greek culture the point was made that this was essentially a rationalistic civilization. That is, the Greeks in all of their wonderings about the nature of things, in all of their concern about justice and the proper ways for people to live in harmony with other people; in all of these problems and others, too, they trusted their minds to find answers. They were not mystics; nor did their emotions have much place in the finding of answers to their questions. Even the Ideas or Essences which Plato postulated were intellectual concepts, lacking the clothing, the color, or the warmth of spiritual or emotional qualities.

Roman civilization continued the rationalism of the Greeks—but with a great difference. As a matter of fact these two great periods in the history of Western civilization might well be studied together under the general heading of "Classical" civilization. The twentieth century philosopher of history, Arnold Toynbee, points out that in any dying epoch we can usually see efforts to bring back the ebbing strength of the old time, and to restore the broken balance. He makes the point that the whole classical period, including the histories of both Greece and Rome, constitutes a single epoch, and that the Roman period was but one of the resurgences of life in the dying epoch rather than an attempt to establish a new way of doing things.

The most obvious difference between the cultural life of Greece and Rome is that the Greeks used their intellects to explore the great philosophic problems of human life and used their artistic creativity to delve into the mysteries of human character and personality. The Romans were much more practical. They devoted their intellectual efforts to the developmnt of government and law; to engineering problems like the building of roads and aqueducts; to philosophies which dealt with the practical, everyday problems of conduct. As a result, the Romans conquered most of the world that they knew of, and they established law, relative peace, and relative comfort throughout that world. Most of their artistic product and most of their philosophic thought was borrowed or copied from the Greeks.

In point of time, Roman culture may be dated from about 500 B.C., when the early kings were overthrown and we begin to have some historical records, to some time in the fifth century A.D. when Rome was sacked by northern invaders at least twice, and the fact of the Roman Empire in the West was shattered, although the tradition of the Empire continued for centuries more. The earliest period with which we are concerned here is the period of the Republic, which lasted in spite of civil war at its end, until 30 B.C. when Octavius took the title of Caesar Augustus and assumed the position of Emperor of Rome.

The Empire continued, though it was frequently badly shaken, until the "Fall" of Rome in the fifth century A.D. The usual dates for this fall are either 410 or 476 A.D.

The Period of the Republic

As it was in the beginning of the Greek period, it was, too, in Rome. We start out with a long and quiet period of history in which relative peace and tradition hold sway. As was true in Greece, the original governments were clan and tribe groups, ruled over by the elders who were, in turn, advised by a senate. Below these groups was the body of free men who, in the beginning, had little voice in the government. During the course of two centuries, however, the common men took over the power of the nobility until, in the year 27 B.C. the old nobility had lost almost all political authority. During this same time, too, Rome had expanded its borders by warfare and by treaty until all of Italy was united under the leadership of Rome in the year 270 B.C.

The virtues which these people revered were duty and simplicity. It is interesting, again, to make a comparison with the virtues which Plato spoke of,

—temperance, courage, wisdom, and justice,—and the virtues which the Christians preached—faith, hope, and love,—with these two ideals of duty and simplicity which the Romans tried to achieve. As much as anything else, this presents the contrast with the intellectual and secular Greek, the spiritual Christian, and the stern, professional Roman with a job to do.

The people themselves were a quiet, but stern and unimaginative group. For the most part they were farmers, holding small and not too prosperous plots of ground. It is interesting, however, and important, that in this early time the farmers were independent; the man owned his land and worked on it. Such a life is satisfying, and in the later days of the empire, the Romans looked back upon the life of the early Republic as the ideal time in all of Roman history. It was under conditions such as these that the virtues which they revered could best be practiced.

Nowhere are the traits of these people so clearly revealed as in their religion. Their two most immediate gods were Janus and Tellus. The first of these was a god who presided over gates and doorways, and as such, was the guardian of the home. He was two-faced, so that he might look outward to perceive enemies from without, and at the same time look into the house, to preserve the stability of the home from strife within. Tellus was the goddess of fertility, and in consequence was the protector of the crops. In addition to these two gods, the Romans of this early period had a group of gods who were virtues personified; such gods as Fortune, Faith (in the sense of keeping one's word), Boundaries, and others.

If, as one Greek writer said, we make our gods in our own image, one can get an excellent picture of the early Italian from these deities. Notice, first, that they were completely practical. None of these gods is frivolous or useless. In the second place, each is associated with some aspect of farm and home life. Later, when these people grew more sophisticated, and when their knowledge of the world increased, they borrowed the entire imaginative Greek pantheon for their more imaginative moods, but in this beginning, practicality and lack of imagination were most evident. These are the qualities which were to make Rome the great government that it became.

Into this quiet rural life, however, came a greater chaos than the Greeks had ever known, and for a period of a century and a half, following the year

264 B.C., Rome embarked on a career of world conquest. That it was succesful, we all know, for the boundaries of Rome at its height included all of North Africa, Spain, Britain, much of France, and all of Middle and Southern Europe to the Danube River, and from the Mediterranean region east to include all of Greece and Asia Minor. The most immediate problem which these conquests raised was that of government, for the old city-state type which had sufficed fairly well while Rome contained itself in Italy was no longer satisfactory. The immediate solution was to send military governors to the provinces, governors who were left on their own to produce order. Under these early governors the colonies were exploited and taxed to the very limit of their ability to pay. The governors, of course, became immensely wealthy.

After such a period in the provinces, the governor would return to Italy to try to gain power there. For nearly a hundred years Rome was in a state of semi-civil war because of the rival claims of these generals.

Of as great importance as the small civil wars which kept the country in a state of chaos was the breakdown of the old agricultural system which occurred at the same time, and resulted from the new wealth which came from the colonies. As money became more plentiful, it also became collected in the hands of a fairly small class of large landowners, who bought more and more of the small independent farms. Thus they built their great estates. Now wealth was not the only import from the colonies, for the conquering generals brought many slaves with them, and the new landlords found that it was more profitable to operate with slave labor than they could by hiring the farmers whose land they had bought. As a result, the free men were dispossessed, and many of them went to Rome, where they formed a mass of as many as three hundred and fifty thousand unemployed. They depended upon the government for their food and amusement, and consequently were the dupes of any general or would-be dictator who needed backing. By promising these people more food and bigger amusements, he could gain their support. The presence of this unemployed mob at the center of government increased the civil unrest of the period.

Clearly two of the institutions by which the Romans had lived during the time of the early Re-

public failed them. The government was no longer able to carry out its functions, and failed to serve the needs of the people, and the economic institutions had failed. The simple answers to man's questions of his relationships to his world were no longer adequate for the more complex world which the Roman had made for himself. Quite as important as this came the question about man's purpose in life. Up until this time each man had conceived his purpose simply. He had thought that when he did his work, raised his crops, raised his family, and paid proper respect to his practical gods, that his purpose in life was fulfilled. In the early times of relatively frugal living, the virtues of duty and simplicity came easily. The new prosperity threatened to destroy this entire conception of the proper way of life; for the dispossessed farmers there was no duty to be done and no incentive for the simple and dignified way of life which had formerly existed. For the wealthy, the ideas of simplicity seemed to hold value no longer. The relations between the individual and other men in the old days had been simple. Each man was relatively independent of others, and in that simple agricultural life there was little problem in the maintenance of this free and independent state for everyone. Now, with new conquests and new wealth, that free and moderate relationship had come to an end.

As if this were not enough, the question of man's relation to God was brought into question. The old gods lost their force as the way of life which they symbolized fell into discard. New wealth, new ways. And the far-spreading Romans encountered many new forms of worship as they ranged through the world, and they brought many of these back to Rome. From Greece they brought Epicureanism and Stoicism, as well as many of the mystery cults which had sprung up during the decadent period. From Egypt came the cult of Isis. And there were many others, such as the cult of Mithra from Persia. The effects of these various cults, religions, philosophies, and beliefs were to be felt later in the development of the epoch, but at first they challenged all of the old beliefs of the people.

World conquest, then, proved that the simple way of life of the early Republic was no longer adequate. At the very heart of the empire, the city of Rome was plunged into a time of chaos, and it seemed as if this nation could not stand the strains which threatened to tear it apart. Remedies, both desperate and rapid, were needed to save the culture.

The Period of Empire

The quick and desperate remedy came with the five year rule of Julius Caesar, who seized power in Rome in 49 B.C. In order to cure some of the economic ills of his empire, he made a bankruptcy law, not unlike that of today, so that the whole nation could begin over again in an economic sense. In order to disperse the mob of unemployed men in Rome, he made it a law that landlords must employ one free laborer for every two slaves whom they held. In order to decrease this mob even further, he sent many of them out of the city to establish towns in the provinces. He also established a new coinage system, created an equal and fair tax system, and kept his own administration on a careful and economical budget. In order to create greater equality among people, he increased the number of Roman citizens. Through the establishment of a public library and in other ways, he raised the cultural level of the city. Finally he provided that the governors of the provinces should be trained and honest men, receiving a fixed salary, and maintaining a position subordinate to the government in Rome.

It will immediately be seen that Caesar's reforms were designed to bring about some of the conditions of freedom which were discussed at the beginning of the unit on Greece. Further, they resemble greatly the reforms of Solon in Athens. They did much to create order out of confusion, and to correct the evils which we have seen as the disruptive forces in the earlier period.

After a brief rule, Caesar was murdered by conspirators, and civil war again broke out, but the direction of the epoch had been set, and when Caesar Augustus ascended the throne and took the title of Emperor in 31 B.C. there was little change in the high type of administration.

One can scarcely praise the accomplishments of the Roman government sufficiently. Rome itself became a city of great grandeur, for the state built many impressive public buildings. The Roman legions maintained peace and order throughout the known world. The Roman military highways stretched out in every direction from the hub city, highways which were so well built that some of them are in use today. In the provinces wherever the Romans settled, they brought with them their efficiency and their way of life. From all of the measurable aspects of civiliza-tion, the world reached a peak which it never again attained until the nineteenth century. These are the accomplishments of the Roman mind and attitude.

With the rule and order established by Julius Caesar and the Emperor Augustus, the new way of life became a fact. However, the artist, in the person of Vergil, did present new answers to the questions, but only after the institutions embodying those answers had already come into being. Vergil's purpose in the *Aeneid* is much more to establish than to propose the answers to mankind's questions.

Vergil's epic tells the story of the founding of Rome, which, according to his legend, was accomplished by Aeneas, a Trojan fleeing after the Greeks had taken and destroyed the city of Troy. In so doing, he makes Aeneas the symbol of all the virtues that the Roman revered, the professional doing his duty with a fixity of purpose which never allowed a moment's deviation from the path toward his goal and which never allowed any other conflicting choices to interfere with the one great choice which had been imposed upon him.

We may cite two examples to illustrate our meaning. Aeneas and his party come to Carthage after their flight from Troy, and here are royally met and entertained by Dido, the queen of that city. She asks Aeneas to tell his story, and as he recounts the adventures which have befallen them, she finds herself falling in love with this wanderer. He, too, is strongly attracted to her, and would have stayed in Carthage if he had been a free man. But he was bound by his duty; reminded by the gods of the mission he has to fulfill, Aeneas left the Carthaginian queen with whom he had fallen in love, giving up his own desires. Early in the morning, before anyone was astir, he gathered his band and made off in his ships for Italy.

Later, after the group had landed in Italy, they were opposed by a native leader, Turnus, who was in every respect a great man. Vergil takes pains to point out this quality of greatness; Turnus was no unworthy opponent of the heroic Aeneas. Nor is Turnus' destruction due to his own shortcomings or faults. It is Aeneas' duty to get rid of him as an obstacle in the way of duty; and Aeneas does his duty. One could point to other instances in which the job to be done over-rules all other considerations of humanity. The pathetic part of it all is that Vergil recognizes that these choices must be made, and deplores the fact that from many aspects what seems to be a better choice for the individual must be disregarded in order to advance the business at hand.

This choice of a way of life is almost exactly the opposite of that which the Athenians made. You will remember that Pericles stressed their diversity of training, their amateur interest in politics, and their concern for the amusement and edification of their citizens. In their military training, for example, he spoke of their choice of the citizen soldier who combined enough of the talents in his own person that he was able to conduct himself well as a citizen, and at the same time be valiant and resourceful when he was forced to war. The basis of the Athenian way of life was in the individual Athenian.

The basis of the Roman way was in the institutions which were established, and the greatest of these was the State. The emperor made himself god, and was literally worshipped as divine throughout the empire. After that worship, the individuals were free to believe as they wished; but the universal church and the universal state was Rome. Establish strong institutions, said the Romans, man them with efficient professionals whose job it is to run them with stern and impartial justice, and the individuals will either be made good, or will be regulated into goodness if they do not choose it of their own free will.

The results of this system were nothing short of marvelous. We have already pointed out the prosperity which came because of the new order. Most important of all was the Roman system of law, for the mother-city soon realized that within a world state composed of all races and kinds of men, a single uniform law would not work. Consequently the government of Rome made a systematic collection of local ideas of justice and local customs throughout the entire empire. From this they built some fundamental laws which applied to the whole, but made them sufficiently flexible that local ways could be incorporated. And if the law failed, the legions were present to see that order was maintained.

What effect does this way of life have on the lives of the people? For the really "noble" Roman, and there were many of them, both men and women, it provided high purposes and real opportunity for achievement. For such a man as Julius Caesar, Cicero, or Marcus Aurelius, and many whose names are not known, the system provided a good life, for these men were the professionals who had the jobs to do. For the many, it was a hollow life which allowed no possibility for growth.

Roman art furnishes a good analogy to the whole problem of life. To begin with, the production of art works, either literary or in architecture or sculpture, was very small in volume; nothing to compare with the product of the single city of Athens. The names of individual sculptors are almost unknown; we have the name of one architect, Vitruvius, who wrote a very extensive work on architecture; and we know less than a dozen names of writers of imaginative literature, and most of them are second rate at best. The big art was the art which pertained to the state; the *Aeneid*, and the great architecture. All of this was professional work, usually done by slaves brought from Greece who retained the dregs of Hellenistic culture.

Most of the people of the Roman Empire simply had nothing to do with art in any form. It was reserved for the professionals who did their jobs adequately.

Again, we may turn to the field of athletics. In Greece the playing of games was a common recreation for most of the men. Many people were concerned with athletics, and many got the benefits of sports.

In Rome, athletics was the province of the professional athlete. That they were good, there is no question. They no doubt ran faster and hurled javelins, weighty shot, and discuses farther than the Greeks did. As professionals they should. For the most of the people, however, this area of living was reserved for the professional athlete. The average Roman only watched his sports; he did not participate.

So it was in all fields. The Roman professionals did such a good job that the great mass of men had little challenge in their own lives, and lived secluded, narrow lives. They, themselves, specialized in their crafts, and knew little beyond them. In the cities there came again the great rabble of unemployed, who were fed and amused at state expense to keep them happy. They were the ones for whom the motto "Bread and Circuses" was invented.

For the mass of people, the intellectuals as well as the rabble, life was a hollow episode. There was work to do, but life ended with that. The question of one's relation to God went unanswered, for the official god was the ruling emperor, and many emperors could scarcely be worshipped. Religion demands some sort of mystic element, and the worship of an emperor or a state failed to supply that element. We see here the paradox of people doing a job supremely well, and yet the people themselves were rotting. This is simply to say that in Rome, as in twentieth century America, human values were lost to material values. In the face of this poverty of life, many turned to completely sensual living, trying in every way to find some new way of increasing and sharpening the appetites so that they might find new ways of satisfying them. The writer Petronius writes in disgust of the orgies which he had observed, of the effort to fill lives with eating, drinking, and being merry, and when that fails to satisfy, of attempting to find new ways of doing the same thing: getting gold plates, eating peacocks' tongues, all to whip up a flagging appetite so that the hours of the day and night would be filled without thought of the hollowness of it all.

Another way to fill the empty lives was to attempt to find meaning through the acceptance of new philosophies and religions which promised the individual some fulfillment. There was no dearth of these. The most prominent were Epicureanism as it was expounded to Rome by Lucretius in his long poem, *De Rerum Natura*, and as it was practiced by Horace and many others; Stoicism which was first explained by the author Seneca, and was practiced and written about further by the Emperor, Marcus Aurelius; and Neo-Platonism, which came the nearest to becoming a religion of any of these philosophies. In addition to these there were many cults: those of Isis, of Mithra, of the earth-mother, Cybele, and many others. Each of these gave the promise to the individual of some importance and purpose for himself, and converts were many who sought this fulfillment. Not the least of the religions which was brought to Rome and which gained a foothold there was Christianity.

Stoicism

Stoicism was the philosophy which probably had the widest influence in Rome, and which made its doctrines felt in many ways, one of which was in the development of the Roman legal system. For stoicism based its whole philosophy on a reasonable universe, the universe which the Ionian philosopher Heracleitus had described. Man is a part of this universe, and is himself reasonable. He bears within

himself a part of the *Logos*, which is his divine part. The whole purpose of man, in such a philosophy, is to cultivate this reason, or soul, and to preserve it intact from the good or evil fortunes of the world. Furthermore, since the world is a reasonable one, the things which happen to a person are a part of the whole, and are not to be emotionalized. The good man, according to this philosophy, is the one who denies all pains and pleasures of the flesh, since the flesh is of less importance than the reason. This last he cultivates as if it were divine. He faces the things he has to do resolutely, since these are a part of the universal reasonable order. This philosophy asserts the brotherhood of all men, since all men share in the divine spark, and all are a part of the great plan of the world. It is this belief that made Stoicism the basis for Roman law.

The Stoic philosophy accorded well with the Roman spirit and with the virtues of duty and simplicity. Since it recognized the brotherhood of men, it satisfied the need for unity in a vastly diversified population. In the same way it reconciled a society in which extremes of wealth and poverty existed side by side (two famous Stoics were Epictetus, a slave, and Marcus Aurelius, a Roman emperor) for both the slave and the emperor recognized his place as established in the orderly universe. Neither one would try to change his status in any way, but each would do his duties resolutely. Further, in a society in which man's condition was not always good, and in which misfortune was a frequent visitor, the stoic was steeled to accept all that came to him. His goal was to make himself entirely self-sufficient and self-contained. Stoicism was the noblest of the Roman philosophies. The greatest criticism which can be made of it is that it is a philosophy of complete acceptance. It is not a belief which allows the individual to take arms against a sea of troubles and by opposing end them. It is a belief which accepts evil but does little to remedy it.

Perhaps we can understand the Stoic philosophy by reading two of the *Meditations* of Marcus Aurelius. Many of these little paragraphs were written when the Emperor was leading armies against the enemies of Rome on the borders of the empire. It was a miserable life, even for an emperor, yet in the evenings he took time to write these paragraphs which yielded to him the consolations of his philosophy.

"Whatever this is that I am, it is a little flesh and breath, and the ruling part. Throw away thy books; no longer distract thyself: it is not allowed; but as if thou wast now dying despise the flesh, it is blood and bones and a network, a contexture of nerves, veins and arteries. See the breath also, what kind of a thing it is; air, and not always the same, but every moment sent out and again sucked in. The third then is the ruling part: consider thus: Thou art an old man; no longer let this be a slave, no longer be either dissatisfied with thy present lot, or shrink from the future."

"Every moment think steadily as a Roman and a man to do what thou hast in hand with perfect and simple dignity, and feeling of affection, and freedom, and justice; and to give thyself relief from all other thoughts. And thou wilt give thyself relief, if thou doest every act of thy life, as if it were the last, laying aside all carelessness and passionate aversion from the commands of reason, and all hypocrisy, and self-love, and discontent with the portion which has been given to thee. Thou seest how few the things are, the which if a man lays hold of, he is able to live a life which flows in quiet, and is like the existence of the gods; for the gods on their part will require nothing more from him who observes these things."

"Of the human life the time is a point, and the substance is in a flux, and the perception dull, and the composition of the whole body subject to putrefaction, and the soul of a whirl, and fortune hard to divine, and fame a thing devoid of judgment. And to say all in a word, everything which belongs to the body is a stream, and what belongs to the soul is a dream and vapour, and life is a warfare and a stranger's sojourn and after-fame is oblivion. What, then, is that which is able to conduct a man? One thing, and only one—philosophy. But this consists in keeping the spirit within a man free from violence and unharmed, superior to pains and pleasures, doing nothing without a purpose, nor yet falsely and with hypocrisy, not feeling the need of another man s doing or not doing anything; and besides, accepting all that happens, and all that is allotted, as coming from thence, wherever it is, from whence he himself came; and finally waiting for death with a cheerful mind, as being nothing else than a dissolution of the elements of which every living being is compounded. But if there is no harm to the elements themselves in each continually changing into another, why should a man have any apprehension about the change and dissolution of all the elements? For it is according to

nature, and nothing is evil which is according to nature."

Epicureanism

Epicureanism starts from an entirely different basis, and ends in almost the same position as does Stoicism, for Epicurus accepted the atomic world and the materialistic view of Democritus. All things occurred because of the almost chance drifting of atoms, according to Democritus and the Epicureans. This leads to a completely mechanistic world, a world in which there is no possibility for human planning and human foresight. In this philosophy individual happiness became the highest goal. This is essentially a statement that the world is a trap in which all men are caught, and the only thing that a man can do is to make the trap as comfortable as possible. For the individual Epicurean, then, the object of life is to make himself as self-sufficient as possible so that he will have to depend upon no one or no thing. Within the shell thus made, he must seek his own happiness; a happiness of moderation, of course, since excess of any sort may bring unpleasant reactions. The way of the Epicurean, then, is the way of isolation and moderation.

The chief difference in actual living which we can see between the Stoic and the Epicurean lies in the fact that the Stoic sees duty before him and goes resolutely and rationally forward to meet it. The Epicurean recognizes no duty but to himself and does only those jobs which will bring unhappiness if left undone.

Neo-Platonism

So far, the philosophies which have been discussed have little conception of a personal God, or of any God at all except the force of "reason" or "necessity." They have been philosophies which were practical and which served to guide men in their every day existence toward their conception of the good life. In other words, they are ethics rather than religions. The idea that men shall not or cannot live by bread alone works itself out in Roman history, for more and more mystic religions gained force in Rome, perhaps, if a rational explanation will suffice, because the life of the time was so unsatisfying and the sense of guilt so great, that the people sought some salvation and more perfect life, to be achieved after death.

Neo-Platonism was one of the early philosophies which developed toward a true religion, emphasizing spiritual qualities as well as ethics. As the name implies, this new faith originated with the doctrines of Plato, and came to Rome from the Academy, the still flourishing school in Athens which was founded by Plato. The Neo-Platonists started with the concept of *Ideas* as the only reality. The belief in the essence of the Good is almost the same as belief in God.

Now, said the Neo-Platonists, men can never know ideas in their pure form. For example, we must always appreciate and know beauty in some of its manifestations in a beautiful person, a beautiful landscape or a beautiful picture, but we can never imagine pure beauty apart from one of these things. To use another example, we can never imagine pure mind. We can only approach a knowledge of the mind as we see people acting as their mind dictates. That is, we see only the manifestations of mind; never the reality. So it is with Good (God, or Pure Idea), they said. For the reasons mentioned, the only reality, Pure Idea, is something which men can never conceive of on earth. The goal for man, then, is to approach as near as possible to an understanding of reality while he is on earth so that he may be fit to enter the City of Good upon his death and finally contemplate the True Reality.

Here, then, is the beginning of a true religion. It is dualistic, for it makes a distinction which is real and which can never be bridged between earth and heaven, flesh and spirit. With Neo-Platonism begins the idea of salvation and eternal life for those people who have lived this present life in contemplation and desire for true wisdom. The influence of this idea on Christianity can scarcely be over-emphasized, for it was St. Augustine, a Neo-Platonist in his youth, who built the foundation of doctrine for the early Roman Catholic Church in his great volume, *The City of God.*

Christianity, of course, was the religion which was to become the state religion of Rome, and the teachings of Jesus have furnished the framework of ideals for Western Europe and the Americas from late Roman times to the present. We wish to deal with these in a special section, however, and will not take them up here.

The Fall of Rome

In spite of the excellent work of the professionals in law and government, and in all other fields as well, the flaws of this type of culture revealed themselves in the Roman epoch. For two centuries the surface appearance of the Empire seemed solid, but rot and corruption at the very heart of the civilization could not support the smooth appearance. Eventually the hollow lives of the people, a hollowness created by the very professionalism which had been the glory of Rome, caused the whole structure to crumble and fall. Not even the great philosophies of Stoicism and Neo-Platonism, nor the Christian religion, could salvage the state from the wreckage. Rome fell, not so much from the attacks of the barbarian invaders as from the internal failure. It is interesting that at least once when the barbarians flooded into the city, most of the population was attending a gladiatorial spectacle. For about four centuries they had relied on their professionals to guard the city. By that time they could feel no sense of responsibility when professionalism failed.

EXERCISES

You have been reading about some of the philosophies current in Rome. Here are some statements, grossly exaggerated of course, from three different individuals; if you had to place them in some philosophical category in this last chapter, how would you label each one?

1. "After all, why shouldn't I follow my own opinion in everything I wish to do? I, myself, am the only standard . . . and if I get into difficulties, I guess I'll be able to talk my way out."

2. "I think I'll just sit in the sun—not too long, for that would be uncomfortable—and have a quiet drink. Not too much, of course, for that would be uncomfortable. I might as well enjoy what I can."

3. "My house burned down, my wife left me, and I lost my job when I broke my leg, but none of these things really matter; they are only indifferent external events, and cannot affect the real *me.*"

Roman Art: The Art of the State

A teacher of the mid-twentieth century, facing a group of college students, is almost beaten at the start when he tries to convince the students that the kind of art the Greeks practiced was in some way better than the kind of art the Romans used. The Roman statues look so "real"—just the way that the president of the First National Bank or local congressman would like to look. The Roman buildings look just like the county courthouse, and the usual student reaction is, "Gee, that's swell. It sure cost a lot of money." All this means that the American of the mid-twentieth century has the same type of mind and the same attitudes that the Roman had.

In the first place, the Romans were engineers, not artists. The Roman borrowed the primary creations of the Greeks and put them to work, for the glorification of the State, for the glorification of men who were wealthy enough to pay for it. It is significant that we can recall the names of at least a few of the Greek artists. We do not know the names of any Romans offhand; we only remember the names of the people who were wealthy enough to commission the art work. The most important commissioner of art works was the Roman State itself, for the police-state always has to sell its importance to the people, and one way to do the selling job is to erect great buildings and great monuments which make the onlooker feel small and insignificant.

In architecture, the Romans developed the arch— a form which they found already developed in the Near East—and put it to work. In the first place, they put it to work as the basic design for bridges and aqueducts. In this honest, useful labor, it and the Romans did a fine job. The bridges still carry traffic, and the aqueducts still carry water, and the arch is a clean design which suits these functions well.

The arch, however, developed a symbolic meaning. It resembles the yoke which an ox might wear as it pulled a plow or wagon. The Romans were quick to seize upon this symbolic meaning as a token of the subjugation of conquered peoples. The Roman general, planning his return from a campaign in Gaul or Asia or Africa would order an arch of triumph built for himself. Then, when he marched into Rome, the tribesmen whom he had conquered would trudge under his arch. The arch was more than that, though, for it had a psychological effect upon the people at home. The proportions of the arch were massive, so that the ordinary onlooker felt insignificant before it. The name of the general or emperor was always associated with the arch, so that the ordinary citizen was always reminded of his own unimportance and of the greatness of the general or emperor.

The Romans also borrowed the Doric, Ionic, and Corinthian orders of architecture from the conquered Greeks. In general, they preferred the Corinthian, and in the case of the Colosseum, they used all three and put Roman arches on top of these Greek columns. The first tier of arches here is Doric, the second Ionic, and the third is Corinthian, and a fourth tier of wood was later added. One can see the type of planning which went into the construction of this edifice: if one type of architecture is good, why not stack three good types on top of each other and thus achieve perfection?

The dome, an extension of the arch principle, was also developed by the Roman architects in order to roof over a large area and to provide indoor meeting space for large groups of people. A good example of the use of the dome is in the Pantheon at Rome.

Most of Roman sculpture was portrait sculpture. The artist who carved such a statue, like the present-day photographer, had two jobs to do. In the first place, the statue had to look like the subject, who was paying for the work. In the second place, the statue had to glamorize the subject by making him look handsome, or stern-and-powerful, or rich. Many of these statues were painted to make them even more realistic.

There is little Roman painting left, for painting is destroyed much more easily than buildings or statuary. That which remains is, like the sculpture, largely portrait work or mythological figures done in the Greek decadent style. Another form of wall decoration was the mosaic, a picture made by inlaying colored stones. We have numerous examples of this form of art, particularly in the houses of Pompeii and Herculaneum. These express the richness and luxury that the owners of the houses sought.

In general it may be said that Roman art had two functions: to achieve practical uses, as in aqueducts, bridges, and roads, and to impress the common man. As in all things Roman, it was eminently successful in both roles.

The Roman aqueduct near Nîmes, France, is an art form put to use to carry water across a river valley. It is purely functional here. Each arch, each stone, has a purpose. As a result, the aqueduct is also beautiful.

Ewing Galloway   PONT DU GARD NIMES, FRANCE

Roman Portrait Busts

Augustus Haranguing His Troops

This is the best of Roman portrait sculpture. The
lines are somewhat complicated, but the composition
is good. The face and figure are those of a driver and
leader of men. What is the difference in the Greek
and Roman idea of power? Compare this statue with
that of the Charioteer, taking each as the best symbol
of power produced in their respective cultures. The
little figure at Augustus' knee is Ascanius, symbol
of the mythical line of descent of the Romans.

Ewing Galloway   MARCUS VIPSANIUS AGRIPPA
LOUVRE, PARIS

AUGUSTUS
VATICAN, ROME

Ewing Galloway

COLOSSAL HEAD
OF CONSTANTINE   Ewing Galloway

Ewing Galloway   PANTHEON, ROME

A Greek temple facade (beauty) pasted on a Roman domed structure (utility). Is the result satisfying?

A state building designed as a place of amusement for the masses. This structure heaps the architectural forms of the Greeks, one on top of the other.

COLOSSEUM, ROME

Ewing Galloway   ARCH OF TITUS, ROME

The Arch of Titus is simple and fairly well proportioned, although the attic seems a little top-heavy. The Arch of Septimius Severus is too heavy, too highly decorated. This is typical military and totalitarian architecture.

Ewing Galloway   ARCH OF SEPTIMIUS SEVERUS, FORUM, ROME

The whole purpose of Roman art, particularly the triumphal arch, is best expressed in Vergil's famous lines:

Others, I ween,
Shall mould, more delicately, forms of bronze,
Lifelike, and shape the human face in stone;
But thou, O Roman, bend thy mind to rule
With strength thy people. This shall be thy art;
And to impose the terms and rules of peace;
To spare the vanquished, and subdue the
    proud.

VERGIL

Roman Music

Roman musical activities as described by Cicero, Seneca, Quintilianus and others occupied a rather important place in Roman life. The Romans had nothing original to contribute to music nor are there any extant musical documents or theoretical treatises; they were content to use the brass instruments of the Etruscans and the whole of Greek musical culture.

More instruments were used because there were more activities for which musical instruments had specific functions. The buccina, lituus, and tuba were all trumpet-like instruments associated with warfare and royal courts, functions reserved for trumpets until well into the seventeenth century. The hydraulis[1], originally a pipe organ of clear and delicate tone, was used in connection with gladiatorial contests, but with vastly increased air pressure resulting in a strident tone and a reputed range of three miles.[2]

Roman and Greek dramas still used music although the performers were usually Greek. The aulos (called tibia in Latin) and kithara continued to be employed as they were in Greece along with several varieties of percussion instruments. Nero, who should be mentioned in connection with music, had coins minted depicting him as a kithara player.

In summary, musical culture in Rome displays the same preoccupation with practicality and utility which characterizes the Roman Empire in general. Rome excelled in law, government, economics, engineering and the art of warfare, and built a mighty empire. The Greek empire of mind and spirit was taken over for what it was worth which, in the final analysis, was very little to the Romans and very much to later generations.

EXERCISES

Of course one needs to get some of the facts from this chapter. What were the architectural advances which the Romans made over the Greeks? What did the arch signify that made it especially important as a symbol for conquering generals? What were the two chief uses of Roman art? What is the etymology of the word *subjugate?*

1. Some comparisons are useful. Compare, for example, the statue of the Charioteer of Delphi in the Greek unit with the statue of Augustus here. The subject-matter is nearly the same. What are some significant differences? What do these differences reveal about the idea of beauty, or of strength, in the two cultures? Or compare the bust of Pericles with the head of Constantine and ask yourself the same questions.

2. On your campus there is probably a building called "Old Main," covered with ivy and tradition. Also some buildings have probably been built within the last few years. Compare the architecture of the two. Do you find any resemblances to qualities discussed in the text?

3. It is said at the first of this chapter that most Americans prefer Roman to Greek art. To what extent is this true? Why? Does the difference in the two campus buildings mentioned above suggest any change in American taste in the twentieth century?

ADDITIONAL READINGS

Again the student's attention is called to Gardner's *Art Through the Ages* and Cheyney's *World History of Art*. These will supplement the discussion and the examples given here. As always, one should read Raymond Stites, *The Arts and Man*, pp. 276-321. His discussion of art under the Romans is excellent.

---

[1]Hydraulis (Greek, hydor, water; aulos, pipe), invented c. 300 B.C. Actually a pipe organ with air pressure maintained through hydraulic pressure.

[2]The association of hydraulis with gladiatorial contests, especially those with assorted Christians and lions, delayed for many centuries the introduction of the pipe organ into Christian services. In general, the Roman manner of music caused this art form to have a lowly reputation among the early Christians.

TIME CHART FOR ROMAN CULTURE

Time	Government and Politics	Philosophy and Religion	Literature and Art
1000-500 B.C.	Period of kings, senate, and comitia curiata.	Worship of Janus, Tellus, and Vesta. A bargain religion.	
509 B.C.	Senate and comitia centuriata. Plebeian quest for equality: 1. Valerian Law—509 2. Office of Tribune—494 3. Twelve Tables—449 4. Comitia Tributa established 5. Plebiscites passed by comitia became law—287		Plautus 254-184 B.C. Terence 190-159 B.C.
270 B.C.	Italy united by Rome. Rome proceeds with world conquest. Punic Wars 264-146. Conquest under Republic ends 133.	The beginnings of Eastern cults, philosophies, and religions in Rome.	
133-49 B.C.	Critical period for Republic. Masses degenerate and flock to the city. Civil conflicts between rival generals and dictators.	Lucretius states Epicurean philosophy for Rome.	Cicero 106-43 B.C. Caesar 100-44 B.C. Lucretius 98-44 B.C. Catullus 87-54 B.C.
49 B.C.	Julius Caesar conquers Rome. Reforms of Caesar.		
30 B.C.	Octavius becomes first Roman emperor with title "Augustus."	Emperor worship. Seneca writes full statement of Stoicism.	Period of great architecture starts. Vergil 70-19 B.C. Horace 65-8 B.C. Livy 59 B.C. to A.D. 17
14-69 A.D.	The Julian Caesars.		Ovid 43 B.C. to A.D. 17
69-96 A.D.	The Flavian Caesars.		Petronius d.—66 A.D.
96-180 A.D. 180-	The Antoninus Caesars. The Army takes control. Central authority collapses.	The best people seek refuge in Epicureanism, Stoicism, Christianity, Judaism, Gnosticism, and in mystery cults. Complete formulation of Neo-Platonism as religion.	Martial 38-102 A.D. Juvenal 60-140 A.D. Marcus Aurelius 121-180 A.D. Plotinus 205-270 A.D.
337 A.D.	Constantine rules. Empire split between Constantinople and Rome.	Christianity becomes state religion.	
410 A.D. or 476 A.D.	Conventional date for fall of Rome. Alaric sacks city.	Great church fathers.	

The Aeneid, Book VI.

The Lower World

Publius Vergilius Maro

In the story of the journey of Aeneas, the Trojan hero has fled from Troy, and, after a great storm at sea which was caused by Juno, he and his people landed on the coast of North Africa. They made their way to Carthage, a land ruled by Queen Dido. In her court he told the story of the last days of the Trojan War and of the fall of Troy. He told how he gathered a group around him including his aged father, Anchises, his son Ascanius, and the household gods and fled from the coast of Asia Minor. He also told of their subsequent wanderings and of the death of Anchises.

In the meantime Dido has fallen in love with Aeneas, and he, as much as his duty will allow, with her. Fearful of what might come of this, Aeneas and his band fled to Sicily, and Dido built a great funeral pyre and cast herself upon it. In Sicily Aeneas left a good part of his group who were tired of wandering, and with a select band he pushed on to fulfill his destiny—the founding of the City of Rome. The group arrived in Italy after Palinurus, the steersman, was lost overboard. Long before, Aeneas had been told that he should consult the Cumaean Sibyl, a prophetess of Apollo, on his arrival, and that he should visit the underworld where he would meet the spirit of his father. This visit is presented here in full. After the visit the little group sailed up the Tiber and established a village and fort. They became engaged in a war with the Italian hero, Turnus, and finally vanquished him. Then Aeneas was ready to follow his destiny further by marrying Lavinia, daughter of King Latinus, and establishing the Roman Empire.

The selection given here presents the best of the Roman spirit. Notice, first, the difficulty of Aeneas' mission, yet his sense of duty drives him on. Notice the pathos which this professional spirit evokes in the meeting with Dido's spirit. Pride of race and family are present as Anchises points out the spirits who are to return to earth to found the great Roman families. Vergil is, for all practical purposes, writing the *Social Register* for the Rome of his own time. Finally one should notice the nine lines in which Anchises gives what seems to be the highest statement of the Roman ideal.

Since Dante used Vergil as his guide through Hell and Purgatory, it is interesting to note Vergil's influence on the *Divine Comedy*.

Mourning for Palinurus, he drives the fleet
To Cumae's coast-line; the prows are turned, the anchor
Let down, the beach is covered by the vessels.
Young in their eagerness for the land in the west,
They flash ashore; some seek the seeds of flame
Hidden in veins of flint, and others spoil
The woods of tinder, and show where water runs.
Aeneas, in devotion, seeks the heights
Where stands Apollo's temple, and the cave
Where the dread Sibyl dwells, Apollo's priestess,
With the great mind and heart, inspired revealer
Of things to come. They enter Diana's grove,
Pass underneath the roof of gold.

       The story
Has it that Daedalus fled from Minos' kingdom,[1]
Trusting himself to wings he made, and travelled
A course unknown to man, to the cold north,
Descending on this very summit; here,
Earth-bound again, he built a mighty temple,
Paying Apollo homage, the dedication
Of the oarage of his wings. On the temple doors
He carved, in bronze, Androgeos' death, and the payment
Enforced on Cecrops' children, seven sons
For sacrifice each year: there stands the urn,
The lots are drawn—facing this, over the sea,
Rises the land of Crete: the scene portrays
Pasiphae in cruel love, the bull
She took to her by cunning, and their offspring,
The mongrel Minotaur, half man, half monster,
The proof of lust unspeakable; and the toil
Of the house is shown, the labyrinthine maze
Which no one could have solved, but Daedalus
Pitied a princess' love, loosened the tangle,
Gave her a skein to guide her way. His boy,
Icarus, might have been here, in the picture,
And almost was—his father had made the effort
Once, and once more, and dropped his hands; he could
  not
Master his grief that much. The story held them;
They would have studied it longer, but Achates[2]
Came from his mission; with him came the priestess,
Deiphobe, daughter of Glaucus, who tends the temple
For Phoebus and Diana; she warned Aeneas:
"It is no such sights the time demands; far better
To offer sacrifice, seven chosen bullocks,
Seven chosen ewes, a herd without corruption."
They were prompt in their obedience, and the priestess
Summoned the Trojans to the lofty temple.

The rock's vast side is hollowed into a cavern,
With a hundred mouths, a hundred open portals,
Whence voices rush, the answers of the Sibyl.
They had reached the threshold, and the virgin cried:
"It is time to seek the fates; the god is here,
The god is here, behold him." And as she spoke
Before the entrance, her countenance and color
Changed, and her hair tossed loose, and her heart was
  heaving,
Her bosom swollen with frenzy; she seemed taller,
Her voice not human at all, as the god's presence
Drew nearer, and took hold on her. "Aeneas,"
She cried, "Aeneas, are you praying?
Are you being swift in prayer? Until you are,
The house of the gods will not be moved, nor open
Its mighty portals." More than her speech, her silence
Made the Trojans cold with terror, and Aeneas
Prayed from the depth of his heart: "Phoebus Apollo,
Compassionate ever, slayer of Achilles
Through aim of Paris' arrow, helper and guide
Over the seas, over the lands, the deserts,
The shoals and quicksands, now at last we have come
To Italy, we hold the lands which fled us:
Grant that thus far, no farther, a Trojan fortune
Attend our wandering. And spare us now,
All of you, gods and goddesses, who hated
Troy in the past, and Trojan glory. I beg you,
Most holy prophetess, in whose foreknowing
The future stands revealed, grant that the Trojans—
I ask with fate's permission—rest in Latium
Their wandering storm-tossed gods. I will build a temple,
In honor of Apollo and Diana,
Out of eternal marble, and ordain
Festivals in their honor, and for the Sibyl
A great shrine in our kingdom, and I will place there
The lots and mystic oracles for my people
With chosen priests to tend them. Only, priestess,
This once, I pray you, chant the sacred verses
With your own lips; do not trust them to the leaves,[3]
The mockery of the rushing wind's disorder."

---

[1]Daedalus was a mythical artist and inventor. Imprisoned by King Minos of Crete, he constructed wings for himself and his son Icarus and flew away. Icarus flew too near the sun and melted the wax wings. The other pieces of sculpture mentioned here show other incidents in Daedalus' life.

[2]The companion of Aeneas.

[3]The prophecies of this Cumaean Sibyl were usually written on leaves which the winds in the cave might scatter and confuse (v. Book III).

But the priestess, not yet subject to Apollo,
Went reeling through the cavern, wild, and storming
To throw the god, who presses, like a rider,
With bit and bridle and weight, tames her wild spirit,
Shapes her to his control. The doors fly open,
The hundred doors, of their own will, fly open,
And through the air the answer comes:—"O Trojans,
At last the dangers of the sea are over;
That course is run, but graver ones are waiting
On land. The sons of Dardanus⁴ will reach
The kingdom of Lavinia⁵—be easy
On that account—the sons of Dardanus, also,
Will wish they had not come there. War, I see,
Terrible war, and the river Tiber foaming
With streams of blood. There will be another Xanthus,
Another Simois,⁶ and Greek encampment,
Even another Achilles, born in Latium,
Himself a goddess' son. And Juno further
Will always be there: you will beg for mercy,
Be poor, turn everywhere for help. A woman
Will be the cause once more of so much evil,
A foreign bride, receptive to the Trojans,
A foreign marriage. Do not yield to evil,
Attack, attack, more boldly even than fortune
Seems to permit. An offering of safety,—
Incredible!—will come from a Greek city."

So, through the amplifiers of her cavern,
The hollow vaults, the Sibyl cast her warnings,
Riddles confused with truth; and Apollo rode her,
Reining her rage, and shaking her, and spurring
The fierceness of her heart. The frenzy dwindled,
A little, and her lips were still. Aeneas
Began:—"For me, no form of trouble, maiden,
Is new, or unexpected; all of this
I have known long since, lived in imagination.
One thing I ask: this is the gate of the kingdom,
So it is said, where Pluto reigns, the gloomy
Marsh where the water of Acheron⁷ runs over.
Teach me the way from here, open the portals
That I may go to my belovèd father,
Stand in his presence, talk with him. I brought him,
Once, on these shoulders, through a thousand weapons
And following fire, and foemen. He shared with me
The road, the sea, the menaces of heaven,
Things that an old man should not bear; he bore them,
Tired as he was. And he it was who told me
To come to you in humbleness. I beg you
Pity the son, the father. You have power,
Great priestess, over all; it is not for nothing

Hecate⁸ gave you this dominion over
Avernus' groves. If Orpheus could summon
Eurydice from the shadows with his music,
If Pollux could save his brother, coming, going,
Along this path,—why should I mention Theseus,
Why mention Hercules?⁹ I, too, descended
From the line of Jupiter." He clasped the altar,
Making his prayer, and she made answer to him:
"Son of Anchises, born of godly lineage,
By night, by day, the portals of dark Dis¹⁰
Stand open: it is easy, the descending
Down to Avernus. But to climb again,
To trace the footsteps back to the air above,
There lies the task, the toil. A few, beloved
By Jupiter, descended from the gods,
A few, in whom exalting virtue burned,
Have been permitted. Around the central woods
The black Cocytus glides, a sullen river;
But if such love is in your heart, such longing
For double crossing of the Stygian lake,
For double sight of Tartarus, learn first
What must be done. In a dark tree there hides
A bough, all golden, leaf and pliant stem,
Sacred to Proserpine.¹¹ This all the grove
Protects, and shadows cover it with darkness.
Until this bough, this bloom of light, is found,
No one receives his passport to the darkness
Whose queen requires this tribute. In succession,
After the bough is plucked, another grows,
Gold-green with the same metal. Raise the eyes,
Look up, reach up the hand, and it will follow
With ease, if fate is calling; otherwise,
No power, no steel, can loose it. Furthermore,
(Alas, you do not know this!), one of your men
Lies on the shore, unburied, a pollution

---

⁴The mythical founder of Troy.

⁵The daughter of the Italian King Latinus. Aeneas was later to marry her to establish his kingdom.

⁶Rivers near Troy that ran with blood during the Trojan War.

⁷This is the river that leads to Hades. Other rivers in the lower world are the Styx, which forms a boundary for the region, Cocytus, and Phlegethon, which serves as a barrier between the mild punishments and the more severe.

⁸Hecate is a very powerful goddess who, among many responsibilities, controlled the spirits of the dead. Avernus is a very deep pool surrounded by gloomy woods. Its depth and gloom inspired the idea that it led to the underworld.

⁹All of these are the names of mythical heroes who had descended into Hades and returned.

¹⁰Dis is another name for the underworld.

¹¹Proserpine, as wife of Pluto, is queen of the underworld.

To all the fleet, while you have come for counsel
Here to our threshold. Bury him with honor;
Black cattle slain in expiation for him
Must fall before you see the Stygian kingdoms,
The groves denied to living men."
                                        Aeneas,
With sadness in his eyes, and downcast heart,
Turned from the cave, and at his side Achates
Accompanied his anxious meditations.
They talked together: who could be the comrade
Named by the priestess, lying there unburied?
And they found him on dry sand; it was Misenus,
Aeolus' son, none better with the trumpet
To make men burn for warfare. He had been
Great Hector's man-at-arms; he was good in battle
With spear as well as horn, and after Hector
Had fallen to Achilles, he had followed
Aeneas, entering no meaner service.
Some foolishness came over him; he made
The ocean echo to the blare of his trumpet
That day, and challenged the sea-gods to a contest
In martial music, and Triton, jealous, caught him,
However unbelievable the story,
And held him down between the rocks, and drowned him
Under the foaming waves. His comrades mourned him,
Aeneas most of all, and in their sorrow
They carry out, in haste, the Sibyl's orders,
Construct the funeral altar, high as heaven,
They go to an old wood, and the pine-trees fall
Where wild beasts have their dens, and holm-oak rings
To the stroke of the axe, and oak and ash are riven
By the splitting wedge, and rowan-trees come rolling
Down the steep mountain-side. Aeneas helps them,
And cheers them on; studies the endless forest,
Takes thought, and prays: "If only we might see it,
That golden bough, here in the depth of the forest,
Bright on some tree. She told the truth, our priestess,
Too much, too bitter truth, about Misenus."
No sooner had he spoken than twin doves
Came flying down before him, and alighted
On the green ground. He knew his mother's birds,[12]
And made his prayer, rejoicing,—"Oh, be leaders,
Wherever the way, and guide me to the grove
Where the rich bough makes rich the shaded ground.
Help me, O goddess-mother!" And he paused,
Watching what sign they gave, what course they set.
The birds flew on a little, just ahead
Of the pursuing vision; when they came
To the jaws of dank Avernus, evil-smelling,

They rose aloft, then swooped down the bright air,
Perched on the double tree, where the off-color
Of gold was gleaming golden through the branches.
As mistletoe, in the cold winter, blossoms
With its strange foliage on an alien tree,
The yellow berry gilding the smooth branches,
Such was the vision of the gold in leaf
On the dark holm-oak, so the foil was rustling,
Rattling, almost, the bract in the soft wind
Stirring like metal. Aeneas broke it off
With eager grasp, and bore it to the Sibyl.
    Meanwhile, along the shore, the Trojans mourned,
Paying Misenus' dust the final honors.
A mighty pyre was raised, of pine and oak,
The sides hung with dark leaves, and somber cypress
Along the front, and gleaming arms above.
Some made the water hot, and some made ready
Bronze caldrons, shimmering over fire, and others
Lave and anoint the body, and with weeping
Lay on the bier his limbs, and place above them
Familiar garments, crimson color; and some
Take up the heavy burden, a sad office,
And, as their fathers did, they kept their eyes
Averted, as they brought the torches nearer.
They burn gifts with him, bowls of oil, and viands,
And frankincense; and when the flame is quiet
And the ashes settle to earth, they wash the embers
With wine, and slake the thirsty dust. The bones
Are placed in a bronze urn by Corynaeus,
Who, with pure water, thrice around his comrades
Made lustral cleansing, shaking gentle dew
From the fruitful branch of olive; and they said
Hail and farewell! And over him Aeneas
Erects a mighty tomb, with the hero's arms,
His oar and trumpet, where the mountain rises
Memorial for ever, and named Misenus.
    These rites performed, he hastened to the Sibyl.
There was a cavern, yawning wide and deep,
Jagged, below the darkness of the trees,
Beside the darkness of the lake. No bird
Could fly above it safely, with the vapor
Pouring from the black gulf (the Greeks have named it
Avernus, or A-Ornos, meaning *birdless*),
And here the priestess for the slaughter set
Four bullocks, black ones, poured the holy wine
Between the horns, and plucked the topmost bristles

---

[12]Aeneas' mother was Venus.

For the first offering to the sacred fire,
Calling on Hecate, a power in heaven,
A power in hell. Knives to the throat were driven,
The warm blood caught in bowls. Aeneas offered
A lamb, black-fleeced, to Night and her great sister,
A sterile heifer for the queen; for Dis
An altar in the night, and on the flames
The weight of heavy bulls, the fat oil pouring
Over the burning entrails. And at dawn,
Under their feet, earth seemed to shake and rumble,
The ridges move, and bitches bay in darkness,
As the presence neared. The Sibyl cried a warning,
"Keep off, keep off, whatever is unholy,
Depart from here! Courage, Aeneas; enter
The path, unsheathe the sword. The time is ready
For the brave heart." She strode out boldly, leading
Into the open cavern, and he followed.

  Gods of the world of spirit, silent shadows,
Chaos and Phlegethon, areas of silence,
Wide realms of dark, may it be right and proper
To tell what I have heard, this revelation
Of matters buried deep in earth and darkness!

  Vague forms in lonely darkness, they were going
Through void and shadow, through the empty realm
Like people in a forest, when the moonlight
Shifts with a baleful glimmer, and shadow covers
The sky, and all the colors turn to blackness.
At the first threshold, on the jaws of Orcus,
Grief and avenging Cares have set their couches,
And pale Diseases dwell, and sad Old Age,
Fear, evil-counselling Hunger, wretched Need,
Forms terrible to see, and Death, and Toil,
And Death's own brother, Sleep, and evil Joys,
Fantasies of the mind, and deadly War,
The Furies' iron chambers, Discord, raving,
Her snaky hair entwined in bloody bands.
An elm-tree loomed there, shadowy and huge,
The aged boughs outspread, beneath whose leaves,
Men say, the false dreams cling, thousands on thousands.
And there are monsters in the dooryard, Centaurs,
Scyllas, of double shape, the beast of Lerna,
Hissing most horribly, Briareus,
The hundred-handed giant, a Chimaera
Whose armament is fire, Harpies, and Gorgons,
A triple-bodied giant. In sudden panic
Aeneas drew his sword, the edge held forward,
Ready to rush and flail, however blindly,
Save that his wise companion warned him, saying

They had no substance, they were only phantoms
Flitting about, illusions without body.

  From here, the road turns off to Acheron,
River of Hell; here, thick with muddy whirling,
Cocytus boils with sand. Charon is here,
The guardian of these mingling waters, Charon,
Uncouth and filthy, on whose chin the hair
Is a tangled mat, whose eyes protrude, are burning,
Whose dirty cloak is knotted at the shoulder.
He poles a boat, tends to the sail, unaided,
Ferrying bodies in his rust-hued vessel.
Old, but a god's senility is awful
In its raw greenness. To the bank come thronging
Mothers and men, bodies of great-souled heroes,
Their life-time over, boys, unwedded maidens,
Young men whose fathers saw their pyres burning,
Thick as the forest leaves that fall in autumn
With early frost, thick as the birds to landfall
From over the seas, when the chill of the year compels
    them
To sunlight. There they stand, a host, imploring
To be taken over first. Their hands, in longing,
Reach out for the farther shore. But the gloomy boatman
Makes choice among them, taking some, and keeping
Others far back from the stream's edge. Aeneas,
Wondering, asks the Sibyl, "Why the crowding?
What are the spirits seeking? What distinction
Brings some across the livid stream, while others
Stay on the farther bank?" She answers, briefly:
"Son of Anchises, this is the awful river,
The Styx, by which the gods take oath; the boatman
Charon; those he takes with him are the buried,
Those he rejects, whose luck is out, the graveless.
It is not permitted him to take them over
The dreadful banks and hoarse-resounding waters
Till earth is cast upon their bones. They haunt
These shores a hundred restless years of waiting
Before they end postponement of the crossing."
Aeneas paused, in thoughtful mood, with pity
Over their lot's unevenness; and saw there,
Wanting the honor given the dead, and grieving,
Leucaspis, and Orontes, the Lycian captain,
Who had sailed from Troy across the stormy waters,
And drowned off Africa, with crew and vessel,
And there was Palinurus, once his pilot,
Who, not so long ago, had been swept over,
Watching the stars on the journey north from Carthage.
The murk was thick; Aeneas hardly knew him,

Sorrowful in that darkness, but made question:
"What god, O Palinurus, took you from us?
Who drowned you in the deep? Tell me. Apollo
Never before was false, and yet he told me
You would be safe across the seas, and come
Unharmed to Italy; what kind of promise
Was this, to fool me with?" But Palinurus
Gave him assurance:—"It was no god who drowned me,
No falsehood on Apollo's part, my captain,
But as I clung to the tiller, holding fast
To keep the course, as I should do, I felt it
Wrenched from the ship, and I fell with it, headlong.
By those rough seas I swear, I had less fear
On my account than for the ship, with rudder
And helmsman overboard, to drift at the mercy
Of rising seas. Three nights I rode the waters,
Three nights of storm, and from the crest of a wave,
On the fourth morning, sighted Italy,
I was swimming to land, I had almost reached it, heavy
In soaking garments; my cramped fingers struggled
To grasp the top of the rock, when barbarous people,
Ignorant men, mistaking me for booty,
Struck me with swords; waves hold me now, or winds
Roll me along the shore. By the light of heaven,
The lovely air, I beg you, by your father,
Your hope of young Iulus,[13] bring me rescue
Out of these evils, my unconquered leader!
Cast over my body earth—you have the power—
Return to Velia's harbor,—or there may be
Some other way—your mother is a goddess,
Else how would you be crossing this great river,
This Stygian swamp?—help a poor fellow, take me
Over the water with you, give a dead man
At least a place to rest in." But the Sibyl
Broke in upon him sternly:—"Palinurus,
Whence comes this mad desire? No man, unburied,
May see the Stygian waters, or Cocytus,
The Furies' dreadful river; no man may come
Unbidden to this bank. Give up the hope
That fate is changed by praying, but hear this,
A little comfort in your harsh misfortune:
Those neighboring people will make expiation,
Driven by signs from heaven, through their cities
And through their countryside; they will build a tomb,
Thereto bring offerings yearly, and the place
Shall take its name from you, Cape Palinurus."
So he was comforted a little, finding
Some happiness in the promise.

                                   And they went on,
Nearing the river, and from the stream the boatman
Beheld them cross the silent forest, nearer,
Turning their footsteps toward the bank. He challenged:—
"Whoever you are, O man in armor, coming
In this direction, halt where you are, and tell me
The reason why you come. This is the region
Of shadows, and of Sleep and drowsy Night;
I am not allowed to carry living bodies
In the Stygian boat; and I must say I was sorry
I ever accepted Hercules and Theseus
And Pirithous, and rowed them over the lake,
Though they were sons of gods and great in courage.
One of them dared to drag the guard of Hell,
Enchained, from Pluto's throne, shaking in terror,
The others to snatch our queen from Pluto's chamber."
The Sibyl answered briefly: "No such cunning
Is plotted here; our weapons bring no danger.
Be undisturbed: the hell-hound in his cavern
May bark forever, to keep the bloodless shadows
Frightened away from trespass; Proserpine,
Untouched, in pureness guard her uncle's threshold.
Trojan Aeneas, a man renowned for goodness,
Renowned for nerve in battle, is descending
To the lowest shades; he comes to find his father.
If such devotion has no meaning to you,
Look on this branch at least, and recognize it!"
And with the word she drew from under her mantle
The golden bough; his swollen wrath subsided.
No more was said; he saw the bough, and marvelled
At the holy gift, so long unseen; came sculling
The dark-blue boat to the shore, and drove the spirits,
Lining the thwarts, ashore, and cleared the gangway,
And took Aeneas aboard; as that big man
Stepped in, the leaky skiff groaned under the weight,
And the strained seams let in the muddy water,
But they made the crossing safely, seer and soldier,
To the far margin, colorless and shapeless,
Grey sedge and dark-brown ooze. They heard the baying
Of Cerberus, that great hound, in his cavern crouching,
Making the shore resound, as all three throats
Belled horribly; and serpents rose and bristled
Along the triple neck. The priestess threw him
A sop with honey and drugged meal; he opened
The ravenous throat, gulped, and subsided, filling
The den with his huge bulk. Aeneas, crossing,

---

[13]This is Aeneas' son, also known as Ascanius.

Passed on beyond the bank of the dread river
Whence none return.

          A wailing of thin voices [14]
Came to their ears, the souls of infants crying,
Those whom the day of darkness took from the breast
Before their share of living. And there were many
Whom some false sentence brought to death. Here Minos
Judges them once again; a silent jury
Reviews the evidence. And there are others,
Guilty of nothing, but who hated living,
The suicides. How gladly, now, they would suffer
Poverty, hardship, in the world of light!
But this is not permitted; they are bound
Nine times around by the black unlovely river;
Styx holds them fast.

          They came to the Fields of
  Mourning,
So-called, where those whom cruel love had wasted
Hid in secluded pathways, under myrtle,
And even in death were anxious. Procris, Phaedra,
Eriphyle, displaying wounds her son
Had given her, Caeneus, Laodamia,
Caeneus, a young man once, and now again
A young man, after having been a woman.
And here, new come from her own wound, was Dido, [15]
Wandering in the wood. The Trojan hero,
Standing near by, saw her, or thought he saw her,
Dim in the shadows, like the slender crescent
Of moon when cloud drifts over. Weeping, he greets
  her:—
"Unhappy Dido, so they told me truly
That your own hand had brought you death. Was I—
Alas!—the cause? I swear by all the stars,
By the world above, by everything held sacred
Here under the earth, unwillingly, O queen,
I left your kingdom. But the gods' commands,
Driving me now through these forsaken places,
This utter night, compelled me on. I could not
Believe my loss would cause so great a sorrow.
Linger a moment, do not leave me; whither,
Whom, are you fleeing? I am permitted only
This last word with you."

          But the queen, unmoving
As flint or marble, turned away, her eyes
Fixed on the ground: the tears were vain, the words,
Meant to be soothing, foolish; she turned away,
His enemy forever, to the shadows
Where Sychaeus, her former husband, took her

With love for love, and sorrow for her sorrow.
And still Aeneas wept for her, being troubled
By the injustice of her doom; his pity
Followed her going.

          They went on. They came
To the farthest fields, whose tenants are the warriors,
Illustrious throng. Here Tydeus came to meet him,
Parthenopaeus came, and pale Adrastus,
A fighter's ghost, and many, many others,
Mourned in the world above, and doomed in battle,
Leaders of Troy, in long array; Aeneas
Sighed as he saw them: Medon; Polyboetes,
The priest of Ceres; Glaucus; and Idaeus
Still keeping arms and chariot; three brothers,
Antenor's sons; Thersilochus; a host
To right and left of him, and when they see him,
One sight is not enough; they crowd around him,
Linger, and ask the reasons for his coming.
But Agamemnon's men, the Greek battalions,
Seeing him there, and his arms in shadow gleaming,
Tremble in panic, turn to flee for refuge,
As once they used to, toward their ships, but where
Are the ships now? They try to shout, in terror;
But only a thin and piping treble issues
To mock their mouths, wide-open.

          One he knew
Was here, Deiphobus, a son of Priam,
With his whole body mangled, and his features
Cruelly slashed, and both hands cut, and ears
Torn from his temples, and his nostrils slit
By shameful wounds. Aeneas hardly knew him,
Shivering there, and doing his best to hide
His marks of punishment; unhailed, he hailed him:—
"Deiphobus, great warrior, son of Teucer,
Whose cruel punishment was this? Whose license
Abused you so? I heard, it seems, a story
Of that last night, how you had fallen, weary
With killing Greeks at last; I built a tomb,
Although no body lay there, in your honor,
Three times I cried, aloud, over your spirit,
Where now your name and arms keep guard. I could not,
Leaving my country, find my friend, to give him
Proper interment in the earth he came from."

---

[14]Here and about 190 lines later you might compare
the sins and their punishments with the disposition Dante
makes of the souls in Hell in Canto XI of the *Inferno*.

[15]Dido, Queen of Carthage, filled with rage and grief,
had committed suicide when Aeneas sailed away from her
city.

And Priam's son replied:—"Nothing, dear comrade,
Was left undone; the dead man's shade was given
All ceremony due. It was my own fortune
And a Spartan woman's[16] deadliness that sunk me
Under these evils; she it was who left me
These souvenirs. You know how falsely happy
We were on that last night; I need not tell you.
When that dread horse came leaping over our walls,
Pregnant with soldiery, she led the dancing,
A solemn rite, she called it, with Trojan women
Screaming their bacchanals; she raised the torches
High on the citadel; she called the Greeks.
Then—I was worn with trouble, drugged in slumber,
Resting in our ill-omened bridal chamber,
With sleep as deep and sweet as death upon me—
Then she, that paragon of helpmates, deftly
Moved all the weapons from the house; my sword,
Even, she stole from underneath my pillow,
Opened the door, and called in Menelaus,
Hoping, no doubt, to please her loving husband,
To win forgetfulness of her old sinning.
It is quickly told: they broke into the chamber,
The two of them, and with them, as accomplice,
Ulysses came, the crime-contriving bastard.
O gods, pay back the Greeks; grant the petition
If goodness asks for vengeance! But you, Aeneas,
A living man—what chance has brought you here?
Vagrant of ocean, god-inspired,—which are you?
What chance has worn you down, to come, in sadness,
To these confusing sunless dwelling-places?"

While they were talking, Aurora's rosy car
Had halfway crossed the heaven; all their time
Might have been spent in converse, but the Sibyl
Hurried them forward:—"Night comes on, Aeneas;
We waste the hours with tears. We are at the cross-road,
Now; here we turn to the right, where the pathway leads
On to Elysium, under Pluto's ramparts.
Leftward is Tartarus, and retribution,
The terminal of the wicked, and their dungeon."
Deiphobus left them, saying, "O great priestess,
Do not be angry with me; I am going;
I shall not fail the roll-call of the shadows.
Pride of our race, go on; may better fortune
Attend you!" and, upon the word, he vanished.

As he looked back, Aeneas saw, to his left,
Wide walls beneath a cliff, a triple rampart,
A river running fire, Phlegethon's torrent,

Rocks roaring in its course, a gate, tremendous,
Pillars of adamant, a tower of iron,
Too strong for men, too strong for even gods
To batter down in warfare, and behind them
A Fury, sentinel in bloody garments,
Always on watch, by day, by night. He heard
Sobbing and groaning there, the crack of the lash,
The clank of iron, the sound of dragging shackles.
The noise was terrible; Aeneas halted,
Asking, "What forms of crime are these, O maiden?
What harrying punishment, what horrible outcry?"
She answered:—"O great leader of the Trojans,
I have never crossed that threshold of the wicked;
No pure soul is permitted entrance thither,
But Hecate, by whose order I was given
Charge of Avernus' groves, my guide, my teacher,
Told me how gods exact the toll of vengeance.
The monarch here, merciless Rhadamanthus,
Punishes guilt, and hears confession; he forces
Acknowledgment of crime; no man in the world,
No matter how cleverly he hides his evil,
No matter how much he smiles at his own slyness,
Can fend atonement off; the hour of death
Begins his sentence. Tisiphone, the Fury,
Leaps at the guilty with her scourge; her serpents
Are whips of menace as she calls her sisters.
Imagine the gates, on jarring hinge, rasp open,
You would see her in the doorway, a shape, a sentry,
Savage, implacable. Beyond, still fiercer,
The monstrous Hydra dwells; her fifty throats
Are black, and open wide, and Tartarus
Is black, and open wide, and it goes down
To darkness, sheer deep down, and twice the distance
That earth is from Olympus. At the bottom
The Titans crawl, Earth's oldest breed, hurled under
By thunderbolts; here lie the giant twins,
Aloeus' sons, who laid their hands on heaven
And tried to pull down Jove; Salmoneus here
Atones for high presumption,—it was he
Who aped Jove's noise and fire, wheeling his horses
Triumphant through his city in Elis, cheering
And shaking the torch, and claiming divine homage,
The arrogant fool, to think his brass was lightning,
His horny-footed horses beat out thunder!

---

[16]This is Helen of Troy. Vergil believes that she was
married to Deiphobus after Paris' death.

Jove showed him what real thunder was, what lightning
Spoke from immortal cloud, what whirlwind fury
Came sweeping from the heaven to overtake him.
Here Tityos, Earth's giant son, lies sprawling
Over nine acres, with a monstrous vulture
Gnawing, with crooked beak, vitals and liver
That grow as they are eaten; eternal anguish,
Eternal feast. Over another hangs
A rock, about to fall; and there are tables
Set for a banquet, gold with royal splendor,
But if a hand goes out to touch the viands,
The Fury drives it back with fire and yelling.
Why name them all, Pirithous, the Lapiths,
Ixion? The roll of crime would take forever.
Whoever, in his lifetime, hated his brother,
Or struck his father down; whoever cheated
A client, or was miserly—how many
Of these there seem to be!—whoever went
To treasonable war, or broke a promise
Made to his lord, whoever perished, slain
Over adultery, all these, walled in,
Wait here their punishment. Seek not to know
Too much about their doom. The stone is rolled,
The wheel keeps turning; Theseus forever
Sits in dejection; Phlegyas, accursed,
Cries through the halls forever: *Being warned,*
Learn justice; reverence the gods! The man
Who sold his country is here in hell; the man
Who altered laws for money; and a father
Who knew his daughter's bed. All of them dared,
And more than dared, achieved, unspeakable
Ambitions. If I had a hundred tongues,
A hundred iron throats, I could not tell
The fullness of their crime and punishment."
And then she added:—"Come: resume the journey,
Fulfill the mission; let us hurry onward.
I see the walls the Cyclops made, the portals
Under the archway, where, the orders tell us,
Our tribute must be set." They went together
Through the way's darkness, came to the doors, and
    halted,
And at the entrance Aeneas, having sprinkled
His body with fresh water, placed the bough
Golden before the threshold. The will of the goddess
Had been performed, the proper task completed.

  They came to happy places, the joyful dwelling,
The lovely greenery of the groves of the blessèd.

Here ampler air invests the fields with light,
Rose-colored, with familiar stars and sun.
Some grapple on the grassy wrestling-ground
In exercise and sport, and some are dancing,
And others singing; in his trailing robe
Orpheus strums the lyre; the seven clear notes
Accompany the dance, the song. And heroes
Are there, great-souled, born in the happier years,
Ilus,[17] Assaracus; the city's founder,
Prince Dardanus. Far off, Aeneas wonders,
Seeing the phantom arms, the chariots,
The spears fixed in the ground, the chargers browsing,
Unharnessed, over the plain. Whatever, living,
The men delighted in, whatever pleasure
Was theirs in horse and chariot, still holds them
Here under the world. To right and left, they banquet
In the green meadows, and a joyful chorus
Rises through groves of laurel, whence the river
Runs to the upper world. The band of heroes
Dwell here, all those whose mortal wounds were suffered
In fighting for the fatherland; and poets,
The good, the pure, the worthy of Apollo;
Those who discovered truth and made life nobler;
Those who served others—all, with snowy fillets
Binding their temples, throng the lovely valley.
And these the Sibyl questioned, most of all
Musaeus,[18] for he towered above the center
Of that great throng:—"O happy souls, O poet,
Where does Anchises dwell? For him we come here,
For him we have traversed Erebus' great rivers."
And he replied:—"It is all our home, the shady
Groves, and the streaming meadows, and the softness
Along the river-banks. No fixed abode
Is ours at all; but if it is your pleasure,
Cross over the ridge with me; I will guide you there
By easy going." And so Musaeus led them
And from the summit showed them fields, all shining,
And they went on over and down.

  Deep in a valley of green, father Anchises
Was watching, with deep earnestness, the spirits
Whose destiny was light, and counting them over,
All of his race to come, his dear descendants,
Their fates and fortunes and their works and ways,

---

[17]These are all ancestors of Aeneas, all former kings of
Troy.
  [18]A mythical poet and singer.

And as he saw Aeneas coming toward him
Over the meadow, his hands reached out with yearning,
He was moved to tears, and called:—"At last, my son,—
Have you really come, at last? and the long road nothing
To a son who loves his father? Do I, truly,
See you, and hear your voice? I was thinking so,
I was hoping so, I was counting off the days,
And I was right about it. O my son!
What a long journey, over land and water,
Yours must have been! What buffeting of danger!
I feared, so much, the Libyan realm would hurt you."

And his son answered:—"It was your spirit, father,
Your sorrowful shade, so often met, that led me
To find these portals. The ships ride safe at anchor,
Safe in the Tuscan sea. Embrace me, father;
Let hand join hand in love; do not forsake me."
And as he spoke, the tears streamed down. Three times
He reached out toward him, and three times the image
Fled like the breath of the wind or a dream on wings.

He saw, in a far valley, a separate grove
Where the woods stir and rustle, and a river,
The Lethe, gliding past the peaceful places,
And tribes of people thronging, hovering over,
Innumerable as the bees in summer
Working the bright-hued flowers, and the shining
Of the white lilies, murmuring and humming.
Aeneas, filled with wonder, asks the reason
For what he does not know, who are the people
In such a host, and to what river coming?
Anchises answers:—"These are spirits, ready
Once more for life; they drink of Lethe's water
The soothing potion of forgetfulness.
I have longed, for long, to show them to you, name them,
Our children's children; Italy discovered,
So much the greater happiness, my son."
"But, O my father, is it thinkable
That souls would leave this blessedness, be willing
A second time to bear the sluggish body,
Trade Paradise for earth? Alas, poor wretches,
Why such a mad desire for light?" Anchises
Gives detailed answer: "First, my son, a spirit
Sustains all matter, heaven and earth and ocean,
The moon, the stars; mind quickens mass, and moves it.
Hence comes the race of man, of beast, of wingèd
Creatures of air, of the strange shapes which ocean
Bears down below his mottled marble surface.
All these are blessed with energy from heaven;[19]

The seed of life is a spark of fire, but the body
A clod of earth, a clog, a mortal burden.
Hence humans fear, desire, grieve, and are joyful,
And even when life is over, all the evil
Ingrained so long, the adulterated mixture,
The plagues and pestilences of the body
Remain, persist. So there must be a cleansing,
By penalty, by punishment, by fire,
By sweep of wind, by water's absolution,
Before the guilt is gone. Each of us suffers
His own peculiar ghost. But the day comes
When we are sent through wide Elysium,
The Fields of the Blessed, a few of us, to linger
Until the turn of time, the wheel of ages,
Wears off the taint, and leaves the core of spirit
Pure sense, pure flame. A thousand years pass over
And the god calls the countless host to Lethe
Where memory is annulled, and souls are willing
Once more to enter into mortal bodies."

The discourse ended; the father drew his son
And his companion toward the hum, the center
Of the full host; they came to rising ground
Where all the long array was visible,
Anchises watching, noting, every comer.
"Glory to come, my son, illustrious spirits
Of Dardan lineage, Italian offspring,
Heirs of our name, begetters of our future!
These I will name for you and tell our fortunes:
First, leaning on a headless spear, and standing
Nearest the light, that youth, the first to rise
To the world above, is Silvius; his name
Is Alban; in his veins Italian blood
Will run with Trojan; he will be the son
Of your late age; Lavinia will bear him,
A king and sire of kings; from him our race
Will rule in Alba Longa.[20] Near him, Procas,
A glory to the Trojan race; and Capys,
And Numitor, and Silvius Aeneas,
Resembling you in name, in arms, in goodness,
If ever he wins the Alban kingdom over.
What fine young men they are! What strength, what
        prowess!
The civic oak already shades their foreheads.

---

[19]You might compare this with Dante's ideas on the same thing. See, for example, Purgatory, Cantos XVI and XVIII.

[20]One of the earliest of the Italian cities, near Rome. Supposedly founded by Ascanius.

These will found cities, Gabii, Fidenae,
Nomentum; they will crown the hills with towers
Above Collatia, Inuus fortress, Bola,
Cora, all names to be, thus far ungiven.
    "And there will be a son of Mars; his mother
Is Ilia, and his name is Romulus,
Assaracus' descendant. On his helmet
See, even now, twin plumes; his father's honor
Confers distinction on him for the world.
Under his auspices Rome, that glorious city,
Will bound her power by earth, her pride by heaven,
Happy in hero sons, one wall surrounding
Her seven hills, even as Cybele, riding
Through Phrygian cities, wears her crown of towers,
Rejoicing in her offspring, and embracing
A hundred children of the gods, her children,
Celestials, all of them, at home in heaven.
Turn the eyes now this way; behold the Romans,
Your very own. These are Iulus' children,
The race to come. One promise you have heard
Over and over: here is its fulfillment,
The son of a god, Augustus Caesar, founder
Of a new age of gold, in lands where Saturn
Ruled long ago; he will extend his empire
Beyond the Indies, beyond the normal measure
Of years and constellations, where high Atlas
Turns on his shoulders the star-studded world.
Maeotia[21] and the Caspian seas are trembling
As heaven's oracles predict his coming,
And all the seven mouths of Nile are troubled.
Not even Hercules, in all his travels,
Covered so much of the world, from Erymanthus
To Lerna; nor did Bacchus, driving his tigers
From Nysa's summit. How can hesitation
Keep us from deeds to make our prowess greater?
What fear can block us from Ausonian land?
    "And who is that one yonder, wearing the olive,
Holding the sacrifice? I recognize him,
That white-haired king of Rome, who comes from Cures,
A poor land, to a mighty empire, giver
Of law to the young town. His name is Numa.
Near him is Tullus; he will rouse to arms
A race grown sluggish, little used to triumph.
Beyond him Ancus, even now too boastful,
Too fond of popular favor. And then the Tarquins,
And the avenger Brutus, proud of spirit,
Restorer of the balance. He shall be
First holder of the consular power; his children

Will stir up wars again, and he, for freedom
And her sweet sake, will call down judgment on them,
Unhappy, however future men may praise him,
In love of country and intense ambition.
    "There are the Decii,[22] and there the Drusi,
A little farther off, and stern Torquatus,
The man with the axe, and Camillus, the regainer
Of standards lost. And see those two, resplendent
In equal arms, harmonious friendly spirits
Now, in the shadow of night, but if they ever
Come to the world of light, alas, what warfare,
What battle-lines, what slaughter they will fashion,
Each for the other, one from Alpine ramparts
Descending, and the other ranged against him
With armies from the east, father and son
Through marriage, Pompey and Caesar. O my children,
Cast out the thoughts of war, and do not murder
The flower of our country. O my son,
Whose line descends from heaven, let the sword
Fall from the hand, be leader in forbearing!
    "Yonder is one who, victor over Corinth,
Will ride in triumph home, famous for carnage
Inflicted on the Greeks; near him another,
Destroyer of old Argus and Mycenae
Where Agamemnon ruled; he will strike down
A king descended from Achilles; Pydna
Shall be revenge for Pallas' ruined temple,
For Trojan ancestors. Who would pass over,
Without a word, Cossus, or noble Cato,
The Gracchi, or those thunderbolts of warfare,
The Scipios, Libya's ruin, or Fabricius
Mighty with little, or Serranus, ploughing
The humble furrow? My tale must hurry on:
I see the Fabii next, and their great Quintus
Who brought us back an empire by delaying.
Others, no doubt, will better mould the bronze[23]
To the semblance of soft breathing, draw, from marble,
The living countenance; and others plead
With greater eloquence, or learn to measure,
Better than we, the pathways of the heaven,
The risings of the stars: remember, Roman,
To rule the people under law, to establish

_____

[21]These names merely signify that the empire will extend from one end to the other of the known world.

[22]These are the names of families who produced famous men in Rome's history.

[23]Probably these nine lines are a better expression of the best of the Roman spirit than can be found in any other place.

The way of peace, to battle down the haughty,
To spare the meek. Our fine arts, these, forever."

Anchises paused a moment, and they marvelled,
And he went on:—"See, how Marcellus triumphs,
Glorious over all, with the great trophies
Won when he slew the captain of the Gauls,
Leader victorious over leading foeman.
When Rome is in great trouble and confusion
He will establish order, Gaul and Carthage
Go down before his sword, and triple trophies
Be given Romulus in dedication."

There was a young man going with Marcellus,
Brilliant in shining armor, bright in beauty,
But sorrowful, with downcast eyes. Aeneas
Broke in, to ask his father: "Who is this youth
Attendant on the hero? A son of his?
One of his children's children? How the crowd
Murmurs and hums around him! what distinction,
What presence, in his person! But dark night
Hovers around his head with mournful shadow.
Who is he, father?" And Anchises answered:—
"Great sorrow for our people! O my son,
Ask not to know it. This one fate will only
Show to the world; he will not be permitted
Any long sojourn. Rome would be too mighty,
Too great in the gods' sight, were this gift hers.
What lamentation will the field of Mars
Raise to the city! Tiber, gliding by

The new-built tomb, the funeral state, bear witness!
No youth from Trojan stock will ever raise
His ancestors so high in hope, no Roman
Be such a cause for pride. Alas for goodness,
Alas for old-time honor, and the arm
Invincible in war! Against him no one,
Whether on foot or foaming horse, would come
In battle and depart unscathed. Poor boy,
If you should break the cruel fates; if only—
You are to be Marcellus. Let me scatter
Lilies, or dark-red flowers, bringing honor
To my descendant's shade; let the gift be offered,
However vain the tribute."

So through the whole wide realm they went together,
Anchises and his son; from fields of air
Learning and teaching of the fame and glory,
The wars to come, the toils to face, or flee from,
Latinus' city and the Latin peoples,
The love of what would be.

                                     There are two portals,
Twin gates of Sleep, one made of horn, where easy
Release is given true shades, the other gleaming
White ivory, whereby the false dreams issue
To the upper air. Aeneas and the Sibyl
Part from Anchises at the second portal.
He goes to the ships, again, rejoins his comrades,
Sails to Caieta's harbor, and the vessels
Rest on their mooring-lines.

Eclogue IV

Pubilius Vergilius Maro

Vergil's Fourth Eclogue, known as the "Pollio" from the name of the friend to whom it was addressed, and known also as "The Messianic Eclogue," was written in 40 B.C. to commemorate the birth of a child; but the identity of the child has eluded the scholars—there is no agreement among them. However, the high praise and the mystical allusions of the poet, strongly reminiscent of the very phrases of Isaiah in his prophecies of the Messiah, have connected the poem in the minds of many with the coming of the Christ. Early Christians found in the Eclogue corroboration of the Biblical prophecies, and thought of Vergil, consequently, as a "virtuous Pagan," one to whom had been vouchsafed some gleams of the advent of Christ. Vergil's reputation as a good, even holy, man, grew as the Middle Ages remembered his poem; his reputation increased, in folklore, as a magician and seer—possibly because of his birthplace, where witchcraft, necromancy, and magic were always a matter of popular concern. So strong was his reputation as a foreteller of Christ's birth that Dante saw fit to make him his "guide, philosopher, and friend" in the *Divine Comedy;* he was led by Vergil as far as the pagan could take him, to the very entrance of the earthly Paradise.

The student would do well to refresh his memory of the verses of Isaiah, especially in Chapters vii, ix, and xi, that have to do with vines and briers, "unto us a child is born," the concord among living things, and the like. There is no evidence that Vergil was acquainted with the writings of the Hebrew prophet.

Pastoral Muses of Sicily,
    now let us sing a loftier song;
    not all are pleased with country themes
        of orchard trees and lowly shrubs:
    if we sing in pastoral style,
        let it be a style still worthy of a consul's ear!

Now, even now, the last great age is coming in,
    foretold in the Cumaean Sybil's book;
The great cycle of the ages starts anew,
    as from the beginning;
Astraea returns, the maiden Justice;
    the Golden Age of Saturn comes again;
    a new generation is sent us from high heaven.

Diana,—Lucina, Light-Bringer—chaste goddess,
    look favorably upon the coming birth,
    the child for whom the old bad Iron Race yields
        to a new Golden one, rising over all the world:
    your brother Apollo begins his reign.

Pollio, in your term of office, even while you are consul,
    this Wonder of Time will begin his being;
    the majestic months commence their progress;
    under your leadership, Pollio,
    even if traces remain of our human guilt,
    new times will free earth from its abiding terror.

This child will live like a god;
    he will see gods and heroes mingling together,
    and himself will be seen of them a god and a hero;
    he will rule over a world made peaceful,
        with ancestral virtues.

For you, little child, the earth untilled
    will pour forth, as your first birthday-gifts,
    her plants and herbs; twining ivy,
    and valerian, and the arum lily,
        intermingling with the gay acanthus.

Of themselves the goats, untended, will return home,
    their udders swollen with milk;
    the herds will have no fear of mighty lions;
    your very cradle will run over with lovely flowers.
        The serpent will die, poison's treacherous plant
        will die;
    Oriental spice will spring up everywhere.

When you are old enough to read of great men,
    and the deeds of your fathers before you,
    when you understand the meaning of manliness,
    then will the harvest field turn yellow with volunteer
        grain,
    the reddening grape-cluster hang in the place of the
        profitless bramble,
    and tough old oaks will drip with honey-dew.

(Even then will linger some last vestiges
    of the wickedness of man;
    the lusting passion that delights
    to dare the sea with ships,
    to ring towns about with high walls,
    to scar the earth with furrows:
there will still be another Tiphys,
    piloting a new Argo that carries its chosen heroes;
there will still be wars; once again
    some great Achilles will be sent against another
        Troy . . .)

But when the maturing years find you fully grown,
    then even the trader will abandon the sea;
    no pine-masted vessels will barter wares;
    instead, everywhere the whole earth
        will of itself yield all things needful.
    No more will the ground suffer the harrow,
        nor the vine the pruning-hook;
    the stalwart plowman will remove the yoke from his
        oxen.

Wool will not have to learn the deception of lying dyes,
    for the ram in the meadows will himself
    change the color of his fleece,
    sometimes to soft purple, like the murex,
    sometimes to saffron yellow;
    of its own volition
        crimson will clothe the grazing lamb.

"Run on, such times as these!"
    —thus say the Gray Sisters over their spindles,
    agreeing in the fixed decree of destiny.

Go on, little child, to great honors;
    your hour is at hand, dear offspring of divinity,
    great fulfillment of Jove.
    See, earth bows its vaulted weight,
        the lands, the expanse of the sea, even the deep
            heavens;
    see how everything rejoices in the time that is to be!

With you for my theme, Orpheus, singer of Thrace, could
        not overcome me,
    though he were helped by his mother Calliope;
    nor Linus, howevermuch comely Apollo, his father,
        assisted him;

even Pan, if Arcadia his homeland judged him with
    me,
even Pan, with Arcadia judging, would admit him-
    self beaten!

Begin, then, little boy, by greeting your mother with a
    smile;
    she has waited thru the long weariness of many
        months.
    Learn to smile, little child—
    for one whom his parents have not smiled upon
no god deems worthy of his table, nor goddess of
    her couch.

Notes on the Fourth Eclogue

Line 1—"Pastoral"—it is interesting to note that the more sophisticated the civilization, the more urban and artificial the life of time, the greater the appeal of pastoral poetry, "the simple life," "back to nature." Vergil's age is a case in point; torn with the dissensions of civil strife and the growing importance of metropolitan Rome, the Italy of his day found satisfaction in "getting away from it all" thru the medium of the pastoral.

Line 9—"the cycle of the ages"—it is unnecessary to go into the ancient (Etruscan?) notion that the world-cycle moved thru successive stages back to a point identical with the beginning; the "Platonic Year," when even the stars and planets would return to their position as at Creation. Suffice it to say, Vergil does have some sort of cycle of world history in mind; the Ages of Gold, Silver, Brass, and Iron, returning eventually to a new Golden Age.

Line 19—"Pollio"—C. Asinus Pollio, Vergil's friend to whom the Eclogue is addressed, was a well-known public figure of the times; a general and adherent of Julius Caesar, he became consul in 40 B.C., and concluded the peace-treaty between Octavian and Antony, known as the Treaty of Brundisium. It has been suggested (but not proved) that the child of the Eclogue may have been one of Pollio's sons.

Line 54—"Tiphys"—the pilot of the Argo: Jason and the Argonauts, sailing after the Golden Fleece, suggest to the reader at once adventurousness and cupidity, bravery and selfishness.

Line 84—Orpheus, Linus, and Pan; the greatest singers of classical antiquity.

Line 89—the ending is apparently a mildly humorous good-luck charm: "Smile, baby, so that your parents will smile at you; unwanted, unwelcome children are Bad Luck, but smiling, happy, wanted ones are blessed."

On the Nature of Things

Titus Lucretius Carus

In the following passage, Lucretius discusses the rise of ambition, of republican forms of government, of religions, the discovery of metals, of garments, of agriculture, of singing and dancing, and finally of the total development of luxurious civilization. Notice how carefully he suggests a materialistic origin for all of these things.

At several points during the selection he makes general statements about the nature of men and of human motives. Can you piece these together to discover Lucretius' basic thoughts about human nature and human motives, and about the nature of the best life? From these would you say that the author was essentially an optimist, a pessimist, or something in between? Compare the ideas with some of those expressed by Cicero and by Marcus Aurelius.

More and more every day men who excelled in intellect and were of vigorous understanding, would kindly show others how to exchange their former way of living for new methods. Kings began to build towns and lay out a citadel as a place of strength and of refuge for themselves, and divided cattle and lands and gave to each man in proportion to his personal beauty and strength and intellect; for beauty and vigorous strength were much esteemed. Afterwards wealth was discovered and gold found out, which soon robbed of their honors strong and beautiful alike, for men however valiant and beautiful of person generally follow in the train of the richer man. But were a man to order his life by the rules of true reason, a frugal subsistence joined to a contented mind is for him great riches; for never is there any lack of a little. But men desired to be famous and powerful, in order that their fortunes might rest on a firm foundation and they might be able by their wealth to lead a tranquil life; but in vain, since in their struggle to mount up to the highest dignities they rendered their path one full of danger; and even if they reach it, yet envy like a thunderbolt sometimes strikes and dashes men down from the highest point with ignominy into noisome Tartarus; since the highest summits and those elevated above the level of other things are mostly blasted by envy as by a thunderbolt, so that far better it is to obey in peace and quiet than to wish to rule with power supreme and be the master of kingdoms. Therefore let men wear themselves out to no purpose and sweat drops of blood, as they struggle on along the straight road of ambition, since they gather their knowledge from the mouths of others and follow after things from hearsay rather than the dictates of their own feelings; and this prevails not now nor will prevail by and by any more than it has prevailed before.

Kings therefore being slain, the old majesty of thrones and proud sceptres were overthrown and laid in the dust, and the glorious badge of the sovereign head bloodstained beneath the feet of the rabble mourned for its high prerogative; for that is greedily trampled on which before was too much dreaded. It would come then in the end to the lees of uttermost disorder, each man seeking for himself empire and sovereignty. Next a portion of them taught men to elect legal officers, and drew up codes, to induce men to obey the laws. For mankind, tired out with a life of brute force, lay exhausted from its feuds; and therefore the more readily it submitted of its own free will to laws and stringent codes. For as each one moved by anger took measures to avenge himself with more severity than is now permitted by equitable laws, for this reason men grew sick of a life of brute force. Thence fear of punishment mars the prizes of life; for violence and wrong enclose all who commit them in their meshes and do mostly recoil on him whom they began; and it is not easy for him who by his deeds transgresses the terms of the public peace to pass a tranquil and a peaceful existence. For though he eludes God and man, yet he cannot but feel a misgiving that his secret can be kept forever; seeing that many by speaking in their dreams or in the wanderings of disease have often we are told betrayed themselves and have disclosed their hidden deeds of evil and their sins.

And now what cause has spread over great nations the worship of the divinities of the gods and filled towns with altars and led to the performance of stated sacred rites, rites not in fashion on solemn occasions and in solemn places, from which even now is implanted in mortals a shuddering awe which raises new temples of the gods over the whole earth and prompts men to crowd them on festive days, all this is not so difficult to explain in words. Even then in sooth the races of mortal men would see in waking mind glorious forms, would see them in sleep of yet more marvellous size of body. To these then they would attribute sense, because they seemed to move their limbs and to utter lofty words suitable to their glorious aspects and surpassing powers. And they would give them life everlasting, because their face would appear before them and their form abide; yes, and yet without all this because they would not believe that beings possessed of such powers could lightly be overcome by any force. And they would believe them to be pre-eminent in bliss, because none of them was ever troubled with the fear of death, and because at the same time in sleep they would see them perform many miracles, yet feel on their part no fatigue from the effort. Again they would see the system of heaven and the different seasons of the years come round in regular succession, and could not find out by what cause this was done; therefore they would seek a refuge in handing over all things to the gods and supposing all things to be guided by their nod. And they placed in heaven the abodes and realms of the gods, because night and moon are seen to roll through heaven; moon, day and night, and night's austere constellations and night-wandering of the sky and flying bodies of flame, clouds, sun, rains, snow, winds, lightnings, hail, and rapid rumblings and loud threatful thunderclaps.

O hapless race of men, when that they charged the gods with such acts and coupled with them bitter wrath! What groanings did they then beget for themselves, what wounds for us, what tears for our children's children! No act is it of piety to be often seen with veiled head to turn to a stone and approach every altar and fall prostrate on the ground and spread out the palms before the statues of the gods and sprinkle the altars with much blood of beasts and link vow on vow, but rather to be able to look on all things with a mind at peace. For when we turn our gaze on the heavenly quarters of the great upper world and ether fast above the glittering stars, and

direct our thoughts to the courses of the sun and moon, then into our breasts burdened with other ills that fear as well begins to exalt its reawakened head, the fear that we may haply find the power of the gods to be unlimited, able to wheel the bright stars in their varied motion; for lack of power to solve the question troubles the mind with doubts, whether there was ever a birth-time of the world, and whether likewise there is to be any end; how far the walls of the world can endure this strain of restless motion; or whether gifted by the grace of the gods with an everlasting existence they may glide on through a never-ending tract of time and defy the strong powers of immeasurable ages. Again who is there whose mind does not shrink into itself with fear of the gods, whose limbs do not cower in terror, when the parched earth rocks with the appalling thunder-stroke and rattling runs through the great heaven? Do not people and nations quake, and proud monarchs shrink into themselves smitten with fear of the gods, lest for any foul transgression or overweening work the heavy time of reckoning has arrived at its fulness? When, too, the utmost fury of the headstrong wind passes over the sea and sweeps over its waters the commander of a fleet together with his mighty legions and elephants, does he not draw near with vows to seek the mercy of the gods and ask in prayer with fear and trembling a lull in the winds and propitious gales; but all in vain, since often caught up in the furious hurricane he is borne none the less to the shoals of death? So constantly does some hidden power trample on human grandeur and is seen to tread under its heel and make sport for itself of the renowned rods and cruel axes.[1] Again when the whole earth rocks under their feet and towns tumble with the shock or doubtfully threaten to fall, what wonder that mortal men abase themselves and make over to the gods in things here on earth high prerogatives and marvellous powers, sufficient to govern all things?

To proceed, copper and gold and iron were discovered and at the same time weighty silver and the substance of lead, when fire with its heat had burnt up vast forests on the great hills, either by a discharge of heaven's lightning, or else because men waging with one another a forest-war had carried

[1]A bundle of rods enclosing an axe was the emblem of magisterial authority at Rome.

fire among the enemy in order to strike terror, or because drawn on by the goodness of the soil they would wish to clear rich fields, and bring the country into pasture, or else to destroy wild beasts and enrich themselves with the booty; for hunting with pitfall and with fire came into use before the practice of enclosing the lawn with nets and stirring it with dogs. Whatever the fact is, from whatever cause the heat of flame had swallowed up the forests with a frightful crackling from their very roots and had thoroughly baked the earth with fire, there would run from the boiling veins and collect into the hollows of the ground a stream of silver and gold, as well as of copper and lead. And when they saw these afterwards cool into lumps and glitter on the earth with a brilliant gleam, they would lift them up attracted by the bright and polished lustre, and they would see them to be moulded in a shape the same as the outline of the cavities in which each lay. Then it would strike them that these might be melted by heat and cast in any form or shape soever, and might by hammering out be brought to tapering points of any degree of sharpness and fineness, so as to furnish them with tools and enable them to cut the forests and hew timber and plane smooth the planks, and also to drill and pierce and bore, and they would set about these works just as much with silver and gold at first as with the overpowering strength of stout copper, but in vain, since their force would fail and give way and not be able like copper to stand the severe strain. At that time copper was in higher esteem and gold would be neglected on account of its uselessness, with its dull blunted edge; now copper lies neglected, gold has mounted up to the highest place of honor. Thus time as it goes round changes the seasons of things. That which was in esteem, falls at length into utter disrepute; and then another thing mounts up and issues out of its degraded state and every day is more and more coveted and blossoms forth high in honor when discovered and is in marvelous repute with men.

And now to find out by yourself in what way the nature of iron was discovered. Arms of old were hands, nails, and teeth, and stones and boughs broken off from the forest, and flame and fire, as soon as they had become known. Afterwards the force of iron and copper was discovered, and the use of copper was known before that of iron, as its nature is easier to work and it is found in greater quantity. With copper they would labor the soil of the earth, with copper stir up the billows of war and deal about the wide

gaping wounds and seize cattle and lands; for everything defenseless and unarmed would readily yield to them with arms in hand. Then by slow steps the sword of iron gained ground and the make of the copper sickle became a by-word; and with iron they began to plough through the earth's soil, and the struggles of wavering war were rendered equal . . . .

A garment tied on the body was in use before a dress of woven stuff. Woven stuff comes after iron, because iron is needed for weaving a web; and in no other way can such finely polished things be made, as heddles and spindles, shuttles and ringing yarnbeams. And nature impelled men to work up the wool before womankind; for the male sex in general far excells the other in skill and is much more ingenious; until the rugged countrymen so upbraided them with it, that they were glad to give it over into the hands of the women and take their share in supporting hard toil, and in such hard work hardened body and hands.

But nature parent of things was herself the first model of sowing and first gave rise to grafting, since berries and acorns dripping from the trees would put forth in due season swarms of young shoots underneath; and hence also came the fashion of inserting grafts in their stocks and planting in the ground young saplings over the fields. Next they would try another and yet another kind of tillage for their loved piece of land and would see the earth better the wild fruits through genial fostering and kindly cultivation, and they would force the forests to recede every day higher and higher up the hillside and yield the ground below to tilth, in order to have on the uplands and plains, meadows, tanks, runnels, cornfields, and glad vineyards, and allow a gray-green strip of olives to run between and mark divisions, spreading itself over hillocks and valleys and plains; just as you now see richly dight with varied beauty all the ground which they lay out and plant with rows of sweet fruit-trees, and enclose all round with plantations of other goodly trees.

But imitating with the mouth the clear notes of birds was in use long before men were able to sing in tune smooth-running verses and give pleasure to the ear. And the whistlings of the zephyr through the hollows of reeds first taught peasants to blow into hollow stalks. Then step by step they learned sweet plaintive ditties, which the pipe pours forth pressed by the fingers of the players, heard through pathless woods and forests and lawns, through the unfrequent-ed haunts of shepherds and abodes of unearthly calm. These things would soothe and gratify their minds when sated with food; for then all things of this kind are welcome. Often therefore stretched in groups on the soft grass beside a stream of water under the boughs of a high tree at no great cost they would pleasantly refresh their bodies, above all when the weather smiled and the seasons of the year painted the green grass with flowers. Then went round the jest, the tale, the peals of merry laughter; for the peasant muse was then in its glory; then frolick mirth would prompt to entwine head and shoulders with garlands plaited with flowers and leaves, and to advance in the dance out of step and move the limbs clumsily and with clumsy feet beat mother earth; which would occasion smiles and peals of merry laughter, because all these things then from their greater novelty and strangeness were in high repute, and the wakeful found a solace for want of sleep in this, in drawing out a variety of notes and going through tunes and running over the reeds with curving lip; whence even at the present day watchmen observe these traditions and have lately learned to keep the proper tune; and yet for all this receive not a jot more of enjoyment than erst the rugged race of sons of earth received. For that which we have in our hands, if we have known before nothing pleasanter, pleases above all and is thought to be the best;[2] and as a rule the later discovery of something better spoils the taste for the former things and changes the feelings in regard to all that has gone before. Thus began distaste for the acorn, thus were abandoned those sleeping places strawn with grass and enriched with leaves. The dress too of wild beasts' skin fell into neglect; though I can fancy that in those days it was found to arouse such jealousy that he who first wore it met his death by an ambuscado, and after all it was torn in pieces among them and drenched in blood, was utterly de-stroyed and could not be turned to any use. In those times therefore skins, now gold and purple plague men's lives with cares and wear them out

with war. And in this methinks the greater blame rests with us; but us it harms not in the least to do without a robe of purple, spangled with gold and large figures, if only we have a dress of the people to protect us. Mankind therefore ever toils vainly and to no purpose wastes life in groundless cares, because sure enough they have not learnt what is the true end of getting and up to what point genuine pleasure goes on increasing: this by slow degrees has carried life out into the deep sea and stirred up from their lowest depths the mighty billows of war.

But those watchful guardians sun and moon traversing with their light all around the great revolv-ing sphere of heaven taught men that the seasons of the year came round and that the system was carried on after a fixed plan and fixed order.

Already they would pass their life fenced about with strong towers, and the land, portioned out and marked off by boundaries, be tilled; the sea would be filled with ships scudding under sail; towns have auxiliaries and allies as stipulated by treaty, when poets began to consign the deeds of men to verse; and letters had not been invented long before. For this reason our age cannot look back to what has gone before, save where reason points out any traces.

Ships and tillage, walls, laws, roads, dress, and all such like things, all the prizes, all the elegancies too of life without exception, poems, pictures, and chisel-ling of fine-wrought statues, all these things practiced together with the acquired knowledge of the untiring mind taught men by slow degrees as they advanced on the way step by step. Thus time by degrees brings each several thing forth before men's eyes and reason raises it up into the borders of light; for things must be brought to light one after the other and in due order in the different arts, until these have reached their highest point of development.

[2]Notice throughout this piece the philosophic generaliza-tion which Lucretius makes. Try reading them together with-out the intervening descriptions and see if you can get a fairly complete picture of his philosophy.

Some Odes of Horace

Here are some questions to think about as you read the odes which
follow: As you know, Horace was an Epicurean. In the poems "To Licinius
Mureana," "To Leuconoe," and "To His Servant," what specific points of that
philosophy are mentioned? "To Aristius Fuscus" is a sort of love poem
(Lalage was Horace's current girl friend). How warm was Horace's passion?
In the poem "To Postumus" we get at least one of the ideas expressed
in the book of Ecclesiastes in the Bible. What do the two writers have in
common? What comments have you about the kind of life Horace leads
and advocates in these poems?

TO LICINIUS MUREANA

Receive, dear friend, the truths I teach;
So shalt thou live beyond the reach
    Of adverse Fortune's power;
Not always tempt the distant deep,
Nor always timorously creep
    Along the treacherous shore.

He that holds fast the golden mean,
And lives contentedly between
    The little and the great,
Feels not the wants that pinch the poor,
Nor plagues that haunt the rich man's door,
    Embittering all his state.

The tallest pines feel most the power
Of wintry blasts; the loftiest tower
    Comes heaviest to the ground;
The bolts that spare the mountain's side,
His cloud-capt eminence divide,
    And spread the ruin round.

The well informed philosopher
Rejoices with a wholesome fear,
    And hopes, in spite of pain;
If winter bellow from the north,
Soon the sweet spring comes dancing forth,
    And nature laughs again.

What if thine heaven be overcast?
The dark appearance will not last;
    Expect a brighter sky.
The god, that strings the silver bow,
Awakes sometimes the Muses too,
    And lays his arrows by.

If hindrances obstruct thy way,
Thy magnanimity display,
    And let thy strength be seen;
But oh! if Fortune fill thy sail
With more than a propitious gale,
    Take half thy canvas in.

TO ARISTIUS FUSCUS

The man, my friend, whose conscious heart
    With virtue's sacred ardour glows,
Nor taints with death th' envenomed dart,
    Nor needs the guard of Moorish bows.

O'er icy Caucasus he treads,
    O'er torrid Afric's faithless sands
Or where the famed Hydaspes spreads
    His liquid wealth through barbarous lands.

For while in Sabine forest charmed
    By Lalage, too far I strayed,
Me—singing careless and unarmed—
    A furious wolf approached—and fled.

No beast more dreadful ever stained
    Apulia's spacious wilds with gore,
No beast more fierce Numidia's land
    (The lion's thirsty parent) bore.

Place me where no soft summer gale
    Among the quivering branches sighs,
Where clouds condensed for ever veil
    With horrid gloom the frowning skies.

Place me beneath the burning zone,
    A clime denied to human race,
My flame for Lalage I'll own;
    Her voice, her smiles, my song shall grace.

TO LEUCONOE

Strive not, Leuconoe, to know what end
The gods above to me or thee will send;
Nor with astrologers consult at all,
That thou mayest better know what can befall;
Whether thou liv'st more winters, or thy last
Be this, which Tyrrhen waves 'gainst rock do cast.
Be wise! drink free, and in so short a space
Do not protracted hopes of life embrace,
Whilst we are talking, envious time doth slide:
This day's thine own; the next may be denied.

TO HIS SERVANT

Nay, nay, my boy—'tis not for me,
This studious pomp of Eastern luxury;
Give me no various garlands—fine
  With linden twine,
Nor seek, where latest lingering blows
  The solitary rose.
Earnest I beg—add not with toilsome pain,
One far-sought blossom to the myrtle plain,
For sure, the fragrant myrtle bough
  Looks seemliest on thy brow;
Nor me mis-seems, while, underneath the vine,
Close interweaved, I quaff the rosy wine.

TO POSTUMUS

How swiftly glide our flying years!
Alas! nor piety, nor tears
  Can stop the fleeting day;
Deep-furrowed wrinkles, posting age,
And death's unconquerable rage,
  Are strangers to delay.

Though every day a bull should bleed
To Pluto, bootless were the deed,
  The monarch tearless reigns,

Where vulture-tortured Tityus lies,
And triple Geryon's monstrous size
  The gloomy wave detains.

Whoever tastes of earthly food
Is doomed to pass the joyless flood.
  And hear the Stygian roar;
The sceptred king, who rules the earth,
The labouring hind, of humbler birth,
  Must reach the distant shore.

The broken surge of Adria's main,
Hoarse-sounding, we avoid in vain,
  And Mars in blood-stained arms;
The southern blast in vain we fear,
And autumn's life-annoying air
  With idle fears alarms;

For all must see Cocytus flow,
Whose gloomy water sadly slow
  Strays through the dreary soil.
The guilty maids, an ill-famed train!
And, Sisyphus, thy labours vain,
  Condemned to endless toil.

Your pleasing consort must be left,
And you of villas, lands, bereft,
  Must to the shades descend;
The cypress only, hated tree!
Of all thy much-loved groves, shall thee
  Its short-lived lord, attend.

Then shall your worthier heir discharge,
And set th' imprisoned casks at large,
  And dye the floor with wine,
So rich and precious, not the feasts
Of holy pontiffs cheer their guests
  With liquor more divine.

Given below are two of Horace's Odes, translated into the language of the mid-twentieth century. How modern they sound. Perhaps the idea of the first one, addressed to his former mistress, Pyrrha, is that it is better to have loved and lost than to have loved and kept. The second is a more conventional Epicurean thought. The translations were made by E. D. Graham and M. A. Crane.

On the bulletin board there's a picture of me
Luckily saved from disaster at sea
Donating my gear to the God of the Ocean.

Tonight, some boy smelling of after-shave lotion
Is making a play for you, Pyrrha, my fair,
Trying that innocent look with your hair.

His turn will come soon to complain of foul weather
If he thinks that after you're going together
You'll stay bland and easy as on this first date.

Until you up anchor, all dinghys look great.

The peace that the sailor seeks in the storm
And the rest that's the warrior's aim
Can't be purchased with wealth in any form
Nor, Grosphus, with power or fame.
The pauper who wants only what he can afford
Sleeps soundly. But he who would fly
To new fortunes, although he hastens aboard
Speedy vessels, sees his troubles stand by.

Fools nourish dreams of perfect joy;
I'll take less, having witnessed a hero
Die young and watched rotting old age destroy
Tithonus, reduced to a jibbering zero.
It may be *I* have just those things that *you* need
Amidst your horses, fine clothing, and cattle—
Subsistence, and joy from the poems I read,
And no jealous mob doing me battle.

unit **IV**

**some of the
teachings of Jesus**

The Impact of Christianity

It was pointed out in the preceding unit on Rome that life in the later years of the empire was a matter of increasing disillusionment and pessimism. Epicureanism is grounded on pessimism; Stoicism is at best a resignation to the evil of the world; popular cults provided little abiding satisfaction. The discontent and dissatisfaction were not found only among thinkers and philosophers, but were shared by the common people. A Roman epitaph found rather frequently reveals the spirit of cynicism and disillusion; it reads

I was not

I was

I am not

I do not care

One could scarcely go further in general world-weariness; yet the sentiment was not uncommon.

There were two conflicting tendencies during the period and earlier. One was the general disbelief in the old Olympian religion, and a cynical attitude toward emperor-worship; the intellectual was sceptical about religion in general. The other was, contradictorily, the appeal of mystical cults and religions, usually of Oriental origin: Mithraism, the worship of Isis, the cult of Cybele, and the like. However much scoffing or indifferent disregard there may have been at the upper level of society, the poor and uneducated were ready for the emotional appeal of any religiosity that softened their uncertainties and insecurities; there was need for comfort and reassurance.

The genius of the Greeks was intellectual rather than moral or spiritual, and the Romans had little to add on that score to what they inherited from the Greeks. Both peoples had advocated the life lived according to reason; for a Plato, an Aristotle, a Cato, such a life could be worthy and satisfying. But not many men in any generation are of such caliber; even those few are often felt to be wanting in human warmth. At best, the God whom Aristotle finds the sum of perfection is cold, distant, and aloof from the affairs of men: a noble concept, but, again, lacking warmth.

Reason, important as it is, has never been the only tool in man's possession. Call it emotion, belief, faith, there is something that is not in the same category. No man will seriously give six good reasons why he loves his beloved, for love is not "reasonable." That is not to say that it is necessarily contrary to reason; it simply moves in another category. That "something" beyond reason may be considered the compulsion of a moral ideal, or a yearning for spiritual satisfaction; it is more pronounced in some men than in others, but hardly ever totally absent in any individual. It is precisely such a range of human experience that the perhaps overly-intellectualized philosophical traditions of Greece and Rome failed to satisfy. Into this void came the teachings of Christ.

For two thousand years since that time, whether they have believed them or not, whether they have acted upon them or not, men throughout what was once called "Christendom" have been hearing the teachings of Jesus. What are the cardinal points of that teaching?—that One God (a Person, not an abstract idea nor a "principle") is not only the Creator, but the loving Father of all men; that all men are consequently the Sons of God, and as a result all men are brothers; that as Sons of God they are capable of better lives than they lead; that their human inadequacies, imperfections, and shortcomings (their "sinfulness") can be forgiven if they are repentant; that life is eternal, and death is not extinction; that "all the Law and the Prophets" hangs upon the joint commandment "Love thy God, and thy neighbor as thyself"; and that the intention, the act of the personality, is of greater importance than the deed, the act of the person.

Not the least of the appeals of Christianity is the joy and hope which it carries with it because of its doctrine of Christ as Redeemer. Theologically this may be explained in this way: because of the sin of Adam, mankind as a whole carried with it the taint of original sin, a sort of moral disease. But God, loving man, sought to redeem him. This was accomplished through the mystery of Incarnation in which God became Man, taking to Himself all of man's inherent guilt. Then, in Christ's mortal death, as man, the guilt is atoned, and man is set free. The possibility of man's salvation and eternal life with God from that moment on, lies before each man. In a world-weary and guilt-ridden time like that of the late Roman Empire, even as in our own time, such a possibility must bring hope and joy to the believer.

All of these teachings affect the world of here and now, for Christianity is a "social" religion; that is, its effects are seen in the daily acts of people in relation to other people. It is not essentially a religion in which the believers isolate themselves from others and seek individual salvation through private contemplation. Love must prompt the worshipper to present acts of love, mercy, and compassion as evidence of an inward change. The act of the believer in Christ cannot wait upon another world. If three words could be used to sum up this teaching, these three, with their many implications, might be those He addressed to Peter: "Feed my sheep."

Out of these teachings emerged certain concepts deeply rooted in the modern world. One was the gradual emergence of the importance of the human personality, a basic fundamental for democracy, carrying a religious sanction weightier than the speculations of the philosophers. The worth and dignity of the individual soul, and its responsibility to itself, has been a shaping influence in Western thought.

It is small wonder that Christianity spread from an obscure, remote province of the Roman Empire practically throughout the known world within the first century of its existence; its message of hope, joy, salvation, and a merciful and loving God in a world that knew only the sterner aspects of justice made its welcome assured. Encompassing the whole of life, and able to take to itself the good things of any civilization, Christianity could appropriate to itself the best of Greek thought, as well as the most notable product of Rome: its law and organization. With the passage of time, it produced such diverse offshoots as the elegance and beauty of Chartres Cathedral, the horror and brutality of the Inquisition; but its impact upon the Western world is fundamental.

It is not the purpose of this portion of the text to expound Christian doctrine, nor to attempt its interpretation. It is the purpose of this brief section only to present some of the words of Jesus as they are reported in the Gospels, and to let them speak for themselves.

The Sermon on the Mount

Seeing the crowds, he went up on the mountain, and when he sat down his disciples came to him. And he opened his mouth and taught them, saying:

"Blessed are the poor in spirit, for theirs is the kingdom of heaven.

"Blessed are those who mourn, for they shall be comforted.

"Blessed are the meek, for they shall inherit the earth.

"Blessed are those who hunger and thirst for righteousness, for they shall be satisfied.

"Blessed are the merciful, for they shall obtain mercy.

"Blessed are the pure in heart, for they shall see God.

"Blessed are the peacemakers, for they shall be called sons of God.

"Blessed are those who are persecuted for righteousness' sake, for theirs is the kingdom of heaven.

"Blessed are you when men revile you and persecute you and utter all kinds of evil against you falsely on my account. Rejoice and be glad, for your reward is great in heaven, for so men persecuted the prophets who were before you.

"You are the salt of the earth; but if salt has lost its taste, how can its saltness be restored? It is no longer good for anything except to be thrown out and trodden under foot by men.

"You are the light of the world. A city set on a hill cannot be hid. Nor do men light a lamp and put it under a bushel, but on a stand, and it gives light to all in the house. Let your light so shine before men, that they may see your good works and give glory to your Father who is in heaven.

"Think not that I have come to abolish the law and the prophets; I have come not to abolish them but to fulfill them. For truly, I say to you, till heaven and earth pass away, not an iota, not a dot, will pass from the law until all is accomplished. Whoever then relaxes one of the least of these commandments and teaches men so, shall be called least in the kingdom of heaven; but he who does them and teaches them shall be called great in the kingdom of heaven. For I tell you, unless your righteousness exceeds that of the scribes and Pharisees, you will never enter the kingdom of heaven.

"You have heard that it was said to the men of old, 'You shall not kill; and whoever kills shall be liable to judgment.' But I say to you that every one who is angry with his brother shall be liable to judgment; whoever insults his brother shall be liable to the council, and whoever says, 'You fool!' shall be liable to the hell of fire. So if you are offering your gift at the altar, and there remember that your brother has something against you, leave your gift there before the altar and go; first be reconciled to your brother, and then come and offer your gift. Make friends quickly with your accuser, while you are going with him to court, lest your accuser hand you over to the judge, and the judge to the guard, and you be put in prison; truly, I say to you, you will never get out till you have paid the last penny.

"You have heard that it was said, 'You shall not commit adultery.' But I say to you that every one who looks at a woman lustfully has already committed adultery with her in his heart. If your right eye causes you to sin, pluck it out and throw it away; it is better that you lose one of your members than that your whole body be thrown into hell. And if your right hand causes you to sin, cut it off and throw it away; it is better that you lose one of your members than that your whole body go into hell.

"It was also said, 'Whoever divorces his wife, let him give her a certificate of divorce.' But I say to you that every one who divorces his wife, except on the ground of unchastity, makes her an adulteress; and whoever marries a divorced woman commits adultery.

"Again you have heard that it was said to the men of old, 'You shall not swear falsely, but shall perform to the Lord what you have sworn.' But I say to you, do not swear at all, either by heaven, for it is the throne of God, or by the earth, for it is his footstool, or by Jerusalem, for it is the city of the great King. And do not swear by your head, for you cannot make one hair white or black. Let what you say be simply 'Yes' or 'No'; anything more than this comes from evil.

"You have heard that it was said, 'An eye for an eye and a tooth for a tooth.' But I say to you, Do not resist one who is evil. But if any one strikes you on the right cheek, turn to him the other also; and if any one would sue you and take your coat, let him have your cloak as well; and if any one forces you to go one mile, go with him two miles. Give to him who begs from you, and do not refuse him who would borrow from you.

"You have heard that it was said, 'You shall love your neighbor and hate your enemy.' But I say to you, Love your enemies and pray for those who persecute you, so that you may be sons of your Father who is in heaven; for he makes his sun rise on the evil and on the good, and sends rain on the just and on the unjust. For if you love those who love you, what reward have you? Do not even the tax collectors do the same? And if you salute only your brethren, what more are you doing than others? Do not even the Gentiles do the same? You, therefore, must be perfect, as your heavenly Father is perfect.

"Beware of practicing your piety before men in order to be seen by them; for then you will have no reward from your Father who is in heaven.

"Thus, when you give alms, sound no trumpet before you, as the hypocrites do in the synagogues and in the streets, that they may be praised by men. Truly, I say to you, they have their reward. But when you give alms, do not let your left hand know what your right hand is doing, so that your alms may be in secret; and your Father who sees in secret will reward you.

"And when you pray, you must not be like the hypocrites; for they love to stand and pray in the synagogues and at the street corners, that they may be seen by men. Truly, I say to you, they have their reward. But when you pray, go into your room and shut the door and pray to your Father who is in secret; and your Father who sees in secret will reward you.

"And in praying do not heap up empty phrases as the Gentiles do; for they think that they will be heard for their many words. Do not be like them, for your Father knows what you need before you ask him. Pray then like this:

'Our Father who art in heaven,
Hallowed be thy name.

Thy kingdom come,
Thy will be done,
    On earth as it is in heaven.
Give us this day our daily bread;
And forgive us our debts,
    As we also have forgiven our debtors;
And lead us not into temptation,
    But deliver us from evil.'

"For if you forgive men their trespasses, your heavenly Father also will forgive you; but if you do not forgive men their trespasses, neither will your Father forgive your trespasses.

"And when you fast, do not look dismal, like the hyprocrites, for they disfigure their faces that their fasting may be seen by men. Truly, I say to you, they have their reward. But when you fast, anoint your head and wash your face, that your fasting may not be seen by men but by your Father who is in secret; and your Father who sees in secret will reward you.

"Do not lay up for yourselves treasures on earth, where moth and rust consume and where thieves break in and steal, but lay up for yourselves treasures in heaven, where neither moth nor rust consumes and where thieves do not break in and steal; for where your treasure is, there will your heart be also.

"The eye is the lamp of the body. So, if your eye is sound, your whole body will be full of light; but if your eye is not sound, your whole body will be full of darkness. If then the light in you is darkness, how great is the darkness!

"No one can serve two masters; for either he will hate the one and love the other, or he will be devoted to the one and despise the other. You cannot serve God and mammon.

"Therefore I tell you, do not be anxious about your life, what you shall eat or what you shall drink, nor about your body, what you shall put on. Is not life more than food, and the body more than the clothing? Look at the birds of the air: they neither sow nor reap nor gather into barns, and yet your heavenly Father feeds them. Are you not of more value than they? And which of you by being anxious can add one cubit to his span of life? and why be anxious about clothing? Consider the lilies of the field, how they grow; they neither toil nor spin; yet I tell you, even Solomon in all his glory was not arrayed like one of these. But if God so clothes the grass of the field, which today is alive and tomorrow is thrown into the oven, will he not much more clothe you, O men of little faith? Therefore do not be anxious, saying, 'What shall we eat?' or 'What shall we drink?' or 'What shall we wear?' For the Gentiles seek all these things; and your heavenly Father knows that you need them all. But seek first his kingdom and his righteousness, and all these things shall be yours as well.

"Therefore do not be anxious about tomorrow, for tomorrow will be anxious for itself. Let the day's own trouble be sufficient for the day.

"Judge not, that you be not judged. For with the judgment you pronounce you will be judged, and the measure you give will be the measure you get. Why do you see the speck that is in your brother's eye, but do not notice the log that is in your own eye? Or how can you say to your brother, 'Let me take the speck out of your eye,' when there is the log in your own eye? you hypocrite, first take the log out of your own eye, and then you will see clearly to take the speck out of your brother's eye.

"Do not give dogs what is holy; and do not throw your pearls before swine, lest they trample them underfoot and turn to attack you.

"Ask, and it will be given you; seek, and you will find; knock, and it will be opened to you. For every one who asks receives, and he who seeks finds, and to him who knocks it will be opened. Or what man of you, if his son asks him for a loaf, will give him a stone? Or if he asks for a fish, will give him a serpent? If you then, who are evil, know how to give good gifts to your children, how much more will your Father who is in heaven give good things to those who ask him? So whatever you wish that men would do to you, do so to them; for this is the law and the prophets.

"Enter by the narrow gate; for the gate is wide and the way is easy, that leads to destruction, and those who enter by it are many. For the gate is narrow and the way is hard, that leads to life, and those who find it are few.

"Beware of false prophets, who come to you in sheep's clothing but inwardly are ravenous wolves. You will know them by their fruits. Are grapes gathered from thorns, or figs from thistles? So, every sound tree bears good fruit, but the bad tree bears evil fruit. A sound tree cannot bear evil fruit, nor can a bad tree bear good fruit. Every tree that does not bear good fruit is cut down and thrown into the fire. Thus you will know them by their fruits.

"Not every one who says to me, 'Lord, Lord,' shall enter the kingdom of heaven, but he who does the will of my Father who is in heaven. On that day many will say to me, 'Lord, Lord, did we not prophesy in your name, and cast out demons in your name, and do many mighty works in your name?' And then will I declare to them, 'I never knew you; depart from me, you evil-doers.'

"Every one then who hears these words of mine and does them will be like a wise man who built his house upon the rock; and the rain fell, and the floods came, and the winds blew and beat upon that house, but it did not fall, because it had been founded on the rock. And everyone who hears these words of mine and does not do them will be like a foolish man who built his house upon the sand; and the rain fell, and the floods came, and the winds blew and beat against the house, and it fell; and great was the fall of it."

And when Jesus finished these sayings, the crowds were astonished at his teaching, for he taught them as one who had authority, and not as their scribes.

Five Parables

I

"Therefore the kingdom of heaven may be compared to a king who wished to settle accounts with his servants. When he began the reckoning, one was brought to him who owed him ten thousand talents; and as he could not pay, his lord ordered him to be sold, with his wife and children and all that he had, and payment to be made. So the servant fell on his knees, imploring him, 'Lord, have patience with me, and I will pay you everything.' And out of pity for him the lord of that servant released him and forgave him the debt. But that same servant, as he went out, came upon one of his fellow servants who owed him a hundred denarii; and seizing him by the throat he said, 'Pay what you owe.' So his fellow servant fell down and besought him, 'Have patience with me, and I will pay you.' He refused and went and put him in prison till he should pay the debt. When his fellow servants saw what had taken place, they were greatly distressed, and they went and reported to their lord all that had taken place. Then his lord summoned him and said to him, 'You wicked servant! I forgave you all that debt because you besought me; and should not you have had mercy on your fellow servant, as I had mercy on you?' And in anger his lord delivered him to the jailers, till he should pay all his debt. So also my heavenly Father will do to every one of you, if you do not forgive your brother from your heart."

II

"For the kingdom of heaven is like a householder who went out early in the morning to hire laborers for his vineyard. After agreeing with the laborers for a denarius a day, he sent them into his vineyard. And going out about the third hour he saw others standing idle in the market place; and to them he said, 'You go into the vineyard too, and whatever is right I will give you.' So they went. Going out again about the sixth hour and the ninth hour, he did the same. And about the eleventh hour he went out and found others standing; and he said to them, 'Why do you stand here idle all day?' They said to him, 'Because no one has hired us.' He said to them, 'You go into the vineyard too.' And when evening came, the owner of the vineyard said to his steward, 'Call the laborers and pay them their wages, beginning with the last, up to the first.' And when those hired about the eleventh hour came, each of them received a denarius. Now when the first came, they thought they would receive more; but each of them also received a denarius. And on receiving it they grumbled at the householder, saying, 'These last worked only one hour, and you have made them equal to us who have borne the burden of the day and the scorching heat.' But he replied to one of them, 'Friend, I am doing you no wrong; did you not agree with me for a denarius? Take what belongs to you, and go; I choose to give to this last as I give to you. Am I not allowed to do what I chose with what belongs to me? Or do you begrudge my generosity?' So the last will be first, and the first last."

III

"A man was going down from Jerusalem to Jericho and he fell among robbers, who stripped him and beat him, and departed, leaving him half-dead. Now by chance a priest was going down that road; and when he saw him he passed by on the other side. So likewise a Levite, when he came to the place and saw him, passed by on the other side. But a Samaritan, as he journeyed, came to where he was; and when he saw him, he had compassion, and went to him and bound up his wounds, pouring on oil and wine; then he set him on his own beast and brought him to an inn, and took care of him. And the next day he took out two denarii and gave them to the innkeeper, saying, 'Take care of him; and whatever more you spend, I will repay you when I come back.' Which of these three, do you think, proved neighbor to the man who fell among the robbers?" He said, "The one who showed mercy on him." And Jesus said to him, "Go and do likewise."

IV

"There was a man who had two sons; and the younger of them said to his father, 'Father, give me the share of property that falls to me.' And he divided his living between them. Not many days later, the younger son gathered all he had and took his journey into a far country, and there he squandered his property in loose living. And when he had spent everything, a great famine arose in that country, and he began to be in want. So he went and joined himself to one of the citizens of that country, who sent him into his fields to feed swine. And he would gladly have fed on the pods that the swine ate; and no one gave him anything. But when he came to himself he said, 'How many of my father's hired servants have bread enough and to spare, but I perish here with hunger! I will arise and go to my father, and I will say to him, "Father, I have sinned against heaven and before you; I am no longer worthy to be called your son; treat me as one of your hired servants."' And he arose and came to his father. But while he was yet at a distance, his father saw him and had compassion, and ran and embraced him and kissed him. And the son said to him, 'Father, I have sinned against heaven and before you; I am no longer worthy to be called your son.' But the father said to his servants, 'Bring quickly the best robe, and put it on him; and put a ring on his hand, and shoes on his feet; and bring the fatted calf and kill it, and let us eat and make merry; for this my son was dead, and is alive again; he was lost, and is found.' And they began to make merry.

"Now his elder son was in the field; and as he came and drew near to the house, he heard music and dancing. And he called one of the servants and asked what this meant. And he said to him, 'Your brother has come, and your father has killed the fatted calf, because he has received him safe and sound.' But he was angry and refused to go in. His father came out and entreated him, but he answered his father, 'Lo, these many years I have served you, and I never disobeyed your command; yet you never gave me a kid, that I might make merry with my friends. But when this son of yours came, who has devoured your living with harlots, you killed for him the fatted calf!' And he said to him, 'Son, you are always with me, and all that is mine is yours. It was fitting to make merry and be glad, for this your brother was dead, and is alive; he was lost, and is found.'"

V

"For it [the Kingdom of Heaven] will be as when a man going on a journey called his servants and entrusted to them his property; to one he gave five talents, to another two, to another one, to each according to his ability. Then he went away. He who had received the five talents went at once and traded with them; and he made five talents more. So too, he who had the two talents made two talents more. But he who had received the one talent, went and dug in the ground and hid his master's money. Now after a long time the master of those servants came and settled accounts with them. And he who had received the five talents came forward, bringing five talents more, saying, 'Master, you delivered to me five talents; here I have made five talents more.' His master said to him, 'Well done, good and faithful servant; you have been faithful over a little, I will set you over much; enter into the joy of your master.' And he also who had the two talents came forward, saying, 'Master, you delivered to me two talents; here I have made two talents more.' His master said to him, 'Well done, good and faithful servant; you have been faithful over a little, I will set you over much; enter into the joy of your master.' He also who had received the one talent came forward, saying, 'Master, I knew you to be a hard man, reaping where you did not sow, and gathering where you did not winnow; so I was afraid, and I went and hid your talent in the ground. Here you have what is yours.' But his master answered him, 'You wicked and slothful servant! You knew that I reap where I have not sowed, and gather where I have not winnowed? Then you ought to have invested my money with the bankers, and at my coming I should have received what was my own with interest. So take the talent from him, and give it to him who has the ten talents. For to every one who has will more be given, and he will

have abundance; but from him who has not, even what he has will be taken away. And cast the worthless servant into the outer darkness; there men will weep and gnash their teeth.'"

EXERCISES

The East has always been fond of teaching by parable, the brief narrative that by comparison provides a way of getting at a truth. It is not quite like an algebraic problem, to be solved by substituting terms: "x=y, a=b", and the like. It is rather a way of stimulating the imagination, of getting at the point by *insight*. Jesus was following an ancient, well-established tradition in teaching by parables. These stories must be understood on an exceedingly literal level; they mean what they say; but they do not stop there—the mind goes on to seize upon the inherent likenesses, the points to be compared. Here are some questions over the parables in the text.

1. "The Wicked Servant." What prompted the action of the servant's lord, at the beginning and at the end? What is the specific fault of the servant? What was the point that Jesus was trying to convey?

2. "The Vineyard." Imagine a disciple of Plato, who wrote the whole treatise of *The Republic* in order to consider the question "What is Justice?", commenting upon this story. In two or three sentences, what would his opinion be? Imagine a disciple of Jesus trying to answer, again in two or three sentences. Where is the point of departure between the two?

3. "The Good Samaritan." Why does Jesus make a *Samaritan* the subject of his tale? In trying to modernize it, what word would you pick instead? (On second thought—better *not* answer that question!) What fault or shortcoming among His contemporaries was Jesus pointing out?

4. "The Prodigal Son." (It is always tempting to feel a great deal of sympathy for the elder brother in this story; you may find it interesting to look up Edwin Arlington Robinson's poem, "The Prodigal Son", in the *Nicodemus* volume, or in his Collected Works.) Suppose you try retelling the story from the point of view of the elder brother.

5. "The Talents." Which of the other parables is this most like? As a story, it is harsh and forbidding; how would you answer the argument that it does not portray a merciful and loving God?

6. It has been said earlier that the intention, the act of personality, is of more importance than the deed, the act of the person. Does this idea apply in any of these parables?

7. The selections given here are only a suggestion of the nature of Christianity. Fortunately, the Bible is the easiest of all books to come by. For the full development of the Christian churches as congregations, the student is encouraged to read the letters of St. Paul. For the wide variety of Christian tradition one might read the book of *Job,* and then *Ecclesiastes* with its echo of the decadent Greek tradition.

unit **V**

the pulls of
life and death
in the Middle Ages

The Dark Ages: Retreat to Certainty

The central problem of all our study is to examine the types of freedom which were established in each of the periods of the history of civilization in the West. The Middle Ages differs from all of the other cultures which we have studied in that it represents an almost completely new start for civilization in Europe.

With the gradual disappearance of the authority of the Roman Empire, most of the classical influence of the Graeco-Roman tradition disappeared. The remnants were roughly these: (1) the universal religious empire of the Roman Catholic Church which stood firm despite the crumbling secular authority; (2) the memory of the Roman Empire which had a brief burst of glory during the reign of Charlemagne and maintained a feeble flicker of light in the loose union which was called the Holy Roman Empire; and (3) a small amount of classical learning which was preserved in the monasteries. Beyond these there was nothing. The Roman cities became depopulated and fell into ruin. The people of Europe, grown used to the authority of the Roman professionals, were helpless in the face of a situation which demanded self-reliance. The first five hundred years of this thousand-year period truly represent a time of confusion.

The most obvious force which produced this confusion was the military devastation wrought by the tribesmen who swarmed over the entire continent of Europe. At the same time the Saracens from the East fought their way across northern Africa and up into Spain and France. Nothing stopped them, for the people had come to depend upon the Roman legions for protection. The first instinct of the people was to retreat, and the first five hundred years of this time tell the story of man's withdrawal.

Mumford[1] ably describes the line of retreat of the intellectuals. The world-weariness of the old Roman epoch was upon them, and the virile energies of the northern tribesmen stood in exact opposition to the ideas of balance of classical culture. The best way for the intellectuals lay in the monastic life where the processes of living were routinized, where there was protection from all forms of shock, a protection which was found in monasticism, with its easy balance between contemplation and physical labor.

For the common people, however, the monastic life was not possible or attractive. With the intellectual element of the population removed, the people were left to work out their own forms of retreat. With the exception of the few times when strong rulers emerged, the possibility of great empires was denied, for the building and maintaining of great empires demands keen wisdom and bold imagination, both of which were lacking in this time. The result was that small, local, self-sustaining units of government developed which were adequate for the minimum needs of the people.

Political and Economic Organization

At the time of the falling apart of Rome, one type of local organization had come into existence. This was the custom known as *precarium*. Under this custom, weak land-owners gave their land to a more powerful neighbor who, in return, promised protection and a bare living to the donor. It was this custom which furnished the pattern for the manorial system during the Middle Ages. The feudal system probably had its origin with the loose tribal fellowships of the Germanic tribes, which consisted simply of collections of men-at-arms who gathered about a chieftain. They promised to support the leader with their arms, and he, in turn, promised them the necessities of life. From these two, then, came the political and economic organization of Europe for the greater part of the Middle Ages.

Under the feudal system, a king, unable to defend all of his lands, divided them among powerful lords who promised him their allegiance and promised in addition to provide soldiers in case of a war, and acknowledged certain other obligations. These lords were vassals of the king. These vassals, unable to control the vast holdings which they gained, took subvassals, and these, in turn, took vassals unto themselves. The result of this vast subdivision of lands was that all the land was finally parcelled out, each piece with a lord over it, who, for all practical purposes, was the absolute ruler. This lord could establish his own courts and law, and in all ways govern his estates according to his own wishes. The only check was the allegiance which he owed to his lord. Because of this division, the feeling of nationality of people was almost completely lost, for each of the demesnes (holdings of a single lord) was complete within itself, and the horizons of the people extended no farther than the boundaries of the estate. A sense of nationality was further dimmed by the intricate network of allegiances which the feudal system brought about. Frequently a lord would hold land from several over-lords; sometimes a king would be the vassal of a lesser noble. Since wars between the nobles were the rule rather than the exception, allegiances frequently conflicted, and the duty of a vassal was hard to determine. Faulty as it was, however, the feudal system did provide government in a time when there was no man of sufficient strength to hold an entire nation or empire together.

Within the feudal system, the lowest member of the nobility held one demesne, and it was such an estate that formed the norm for human life, for the backbone of the entire social structure was agriculture, and the single estate was the unit for agricultural production. Indeed, it has been estimated that ninety per cent of the entire population of Europe were serfs living on such estates and engaged in farming. The remaining ten per cent of the people were about evenly split between the nobility and the clergy.

As a matter of protection, the people of the manor lived in a small village, usually surrounded by a wooden wall. The most prominent feature of such a village was the castle of the lord, surrounded by a moat or ditch. This was crossed by a drawbridge, which, as the name suggests, could be drawn up in times of war so that a besieging enemy would have to cross the moat without the help of a bridge. Overshadowing the gate, which could be closed with a heavy grated door called the portcullis, stood the donjon or tower, which was the main fortification. This was a massive structure, with walls many feet thick. The windows were small, as, of course, is necessary in such thick

---

[1]Lewis Mumford, *The Condition of Man*, pp. 76-107.

walls. It was possible to shoot arrows and throw flaming brands out of these windows, but they were so small that they provided poor targets for those outside. Within the castle wall, also, were sometimes a great hall and living chambers for the lord and his family. There were also buildings for the storage of arms and supplies, and usually a chapel. The castle, then, was both a residence and a fortress, designed to withstand a long siege.

Around the castle lay the land which supported it. This estate was divided into long strips of land which were cultivated by the serfs. The lord retained some land for his own use, though it, too, was cared for by the serfs, and the remainder was divided among these poor peasants. The little town stood in the middle of these fields. It usually contained the houses of the serfs, hovels without windows or chimneys, the lord's mill where the grain for the village was ground into flour, a wine-press, and the church which was cared for by the parish priest, whose lot was almost as bad as that of the serfs—indeed he was frequently drawn from that class.

Though the serfs did not own their land, they could not be deprived of it so long as they performed certain services for the lord. They promised a certain number of days of work in the lord's field. They might not marry without his consent. The women helped in baking, brewing, and sewing for the entire community. Each serf had to pay certain dues yearly to his lord, usually in the form of produce. Then, too, there were special obligations which the serf must pay on such special occasions as the marriage of the lord's daughter or the knighting of his son.

Much has been written on the subject of medieval agriculture. It was here that crop-rotation was first developed, with the three field system in which the entire estate was divided into three sections. Each serf held some strips of land in each of these sections. During one year, one section might be planted in wheat, another in oats, and the third allowed to lie fallow. These crops were rotated so that one section was allowed to lie fallow every third year. There was also a meadow held in common by all of the village on which the community herd was allowed to graze, and from which hay was harvested for the winter. Indicative of the efficiency of this agriculture was the fact that cows were frequently killed in the fall since there was insufficient hay to feed them throughout the

winter, and by spring the cattle were often so weak that they had to be carried to the meadow.

At least two things need to be noted about this society. In the first place, it was largely an agricultural and a fighting society. The chief obligations of vassals toward their lords were those of fighting and of providing men-at-arms. The village itself was designed for the purpose of protection against marauders. There were ample reasons for this, for this was a crude society, whose only concern was in preserving itself. The niceties of life were put aside in the sterner business of keeping alive.

A second characteristic of this society was its self-sufficiency. Within each village most of the necessities for a meager life were produced. The clothes for the community were made there; the food was grown and stored there. There was almost no necessity for going beyond the narrow limits of the manor; and for the average peasant, the world ended at the limits of the manor to which he was attached. Commerce was almost an impossibility, for robbers abounded on the roads; the roads themselves were bad; and the number of tolls and taxes which were collected on all roads and waterways made trade expensive and hazardous.

Following the fall of the Roman Empire, then, the people sought a form of life which would provide security and sureness in the midst of chaotic conditions with which they were not prepared to cope. The result was the establishment of governments over very small areas of land, each complete within itself. Here an absolute ruler held sway. It was the simplest societal development which we have yet seen. Yet it did accomplish its purpose. The duties of the serf were absolutely defined. He knew his rights to the community meadow and the community wood. His duties toward his lord were clearly established. He could not be removed from his land, which, though it produced little, yet kept him from starvation. Furthermore, the unit of government was sufficiently small that each individual could know of the workings of the whole system. It was an answer to the need for order and security when those were the greatest needs which people felt.

The Medieval Church

The Church was the most powerful organization of the time. With few exceptions, all people of western

Europe were members of it, and the salvation of each soul depended upon obedience to the dictates of the Church. At its head, as is still the case, was the Pope. Beneath him were a group of administrative assistants, the cardinals, and the papal legates or ambassadors. The churchmen who had direct control over the spiritual affairs of the people, the secular clergy, were the archbishops, the bishops, and the parish priests. In addition there were the holy men who lived under a strict rule of life, the "regular" clergy, the monks and friars.

The Church, though it was the supreme spiritual head of the western world, was also much interested in secular affairs. The Pope was the head of a state surrounding Rome, and most of the higher officials were lords and vassals of estates throughout Europe. The monasteries and abbeys were the centers of large estates. Thus the Church was a very rich organization and one whose duties consisted not only in saving souls, but in waging war, collecting taxes, and in managing vast farms.

Probably the organization of Christianity *as an institution* derived from the work of Christ, who gave the basic teachings; from Paul, who organized the early congregations; and from St. Augustine, who codified the theology of the church into a single, consistent body of doctrine. Augustine was a North African, a Bishop of Hippo who had lived in late Roman times (354-430). He had been a Neo-Platonist before he became a Christian, and his philosophy brings together much of Plato's thought as well as Christ's. Until the late Middle Ages, the doctrine which he formulated was the basic theology for the Church.

While the whole body of Augustine's philosophy can scarcely be touched here, three general conclusions and the reasons which lay back of them can be developed. They are (1) that the study of the physical world was a study of nothingness and consequently to be shunned; (2) that the purpose of man is to achieve salvation and unity with God, which can only be done through the mediation of the Church; and (3) that the Church itself is infallible.

To understand the first of these generalizations, it is necessary to remember at least one of the doctrines of Neo-Platonism. This was the theory of emanation. Accepting God as pure Idea (similar to Plato's essence of The Good), the Neo-Platonists said that the universal mind emanated from it. In human terms

the universal mind is the intellectual ability to understand such truths as that the sum of the angles of a triangle is always equal to 180 degrees, a truth which applies under all conditions to any and all triangles in Euclidean geometry. This, in turn, emanates the world soul, the life process, the difference between a living body and a corpse. From this, in turn, emanates the body and the physical world. Now, since God is the source of all, He is therefore the greatest reality, and men should seek to know that reality as directly as possible. Let us put it this way: Suppose that we want a drink of pure, clear water. And, let us suppose that it is impossible to catch any of the rain from heaven. Where would we go for our water? The least likely spot would be the cocoa-colored Mississippi at New Orleans (the physical world). Or we might think of filling our cup from one of the tributaries—let us say the Platte somewhere on the plains (the Universal Soul). But this, while better than the Mississippi, is still muddy and polluted. The best place to get our drink would be a clear mountain stream (the Universal Mind) which is as close as we get to the source of water. In the same way, says Augustine, we should not waste our time seeking reality at the level of the physical world whose emanation is cloudy. Instead, we should deal at least with the realm of universal ideas, and occasionally, by Divine Grace, we may be united with God himself.

Another support of the generalization that we should not be concerned with the things of the physical world lies in Augustine's philosophy of history. In this Augustine states that the purpose of history is the final separation of the City of God and the City of Satan. (Note the assumption that there *is* a purpose in history.) This purpose started in pre-history with the revolt of the angels and the casting out of Satan, and thus the creation of two domains, one of God, and the other of Satan. From the time of Adam's fall to the birth of Jesus, the two cities were greatly confused, and most people belonged to the City of Satan. Only a few of the Hebrews believed strongly in God and belonged to His city. Since the only purpose of history is the emergence of this city, the only history worth studying is that of the Hebrews, as contained in the Old Testament. The second stage in human history lies between the birth of Jesus and The Day of Judgment. Here, however, the two cities are more distinct, since the Christian Church had been established. It consists of those members

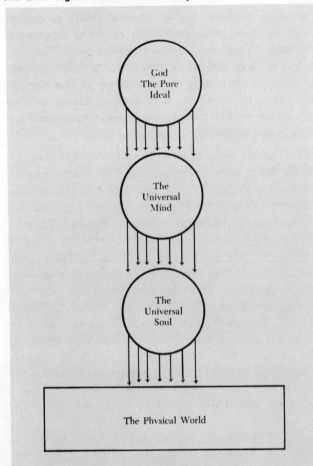

of the human race who have been redeemed by Jesus, so that all members of the City of God are also members of the Christian Church. The end of history will come with the final separation of the two cities, following the Day of Judgment. Thus the whole of history and all scientific studies were considered unimportant and leading away from the real purpose of history.

From the foregoing, it becomes evident that in this philosophy, the whole purpose of man is to be united with God. Man, created with free will, can choose either good or evil. Adam, the first man, and the essence and pattern of mankind (a Neo-Platonist concept), chose evil. Because Adam was not a man, but Man, all men are afflicted with a moral disease which causes them habitually to turn from God, and all are guilty of Adam's sin. Thus, man by himself cannot achieve his purpose. God, however, sent Christ to the earth to redeem mankind, and through Christ was established the Christian Church, to serve

as God's Vice-Regent here. Thus man can achieve his purpose only by membership in the Church.

The infallibility of the Church was proved by Augustine according to the doctrine of Apostolic Succession. According to this doctrine, the apostles were the first bishops of the church. Their authority descended directly through the generations of bishops who succeeded them. The question arose at this time about the efficacy of the sacraments when performed by priests of doubtful virtue. Still according to the doctrine of succession, the power to administer the sacraments lay in the office of bishop or priest rather than in the individual who administered them. Augustine recognized that with the decline of empire and the growth of the Church, there would be many unworthy men who would be attracted to the religious institution because of the power which it offered. With the development of the theory that the sacraments, even when administered by unworthy men, were efficacious, we have the infallibility of the Church established.

One question remains unsettled by Augustine. That was the nature of body and soul. Since the body is in the direct line of emanation from God, it must be good; and in point of fact, Augustine himself did not believe in dualism. On the other hand there was the idea coming directly from Plato, that the good man sought only the separation of soul from body. On this point, Augustine says,

What is man? Is he both of these (body and soul)? Or is he the body only, or the soul only? For although the things are two, soul and body, and although neither without the other could be called man, for the body would not be a man without the soul, nor again would the soul be man if there were not a body animated by it, still it is possible that one of these may be held to be man, and may be called so . . . This dispute is not easy to settle.

Augustine himself had no answer to this question. The other thinkers of the Middle Ages, seeking retreat from the world which was too much with them, denied the body and called it evil, accepting the view of Plato rather than that of Jesus. It is perhaps the most troublesome question of all the thousand years of this middle period, to be revived again in the battle of the universals, and not to be settled within the Church until St. Thomas. Outside of the Church, the battle and the discussion of this point continues to this day.

This is the theory on which the three great generalizations which were to serve as a foundation for the Church were built. There remained only the establishment of a firm organization to support and be supported by this doctrine. With the establishment of the Bishop of Rome as Pope, and with his political power, greater now than any wielded by Roman officialdom, particularly in dealing with the invading tribesmen who treated with the Bishop of Rome rather than with secular authorities and who spared Christian churches when they sacked the city, the church organization achieved the solidarity which it needed to impose its doctrine upon all the portions of the crumbled empire. This was an authority which was to grow until it reached its zenith about the year 1200, during the time of Pope Innocent III. While the Church never claimed actual authority over political rulers, yet kings and nobles were as anxious for heaven as the meanest serf, and it was the Church which, in the sacraments, held the keys to the kingdom. Thus the threat of excommunication was sufficient to bring kings, emperors, and barons to their knees before bishop and pope.

Medieval Science

The science of the time was synthesized with the doctrine of the Church until it is hard to separate them. The Ptolemaic system of astronomy was accepted, a system which placed the earth at the center of the universe. Around it, lay the orbits of the moon, the known planets, and the fixed stars. Then we come to the crystalline sphere, known as the *primum mobile*, beyond which lay the abode of God. The *primum mobile* was exactly what its name means, the first moved. According to the accepted theory, God was the mover, and the universe moved according to His will. The fixed stars, being nearest to Him were moved first, and all the rest of the heavenly bodies moved in accord, something like gears within gears. Finally, of course, the earth itself, and the men upon it, were affected by this movement.

Consequently the science of astrology was born, the science which attempted to determine the effect upon men of the movements of the stars, particularly the fixed stars in which were found the signs of the zodiac. If one accepts the principle of a First Mover, and the idea of Ptolemaic astronomy, the foundations of this pseudo-science are laid, and the rest follows as a matter of course. If one can determine how the stars are moved, and if one can know beforehand how such movement affects humans, then it is possible to make predictions from observed movements of stars. This was "judicial" astrology. "Natural" astrology was the actual observation of the heavens in order to determine the movements of the stars, to fix dates, and determine the calendar. Natural astrology, therefore, was much closer to modern astronomy than was the judicial branch.

It is impossible to go to any length in a description of the other branches of science. There was alchemy, which was the attempt to find a way of transmuting baser metals to gold. The more important experiments in medicine were in the attempt to find the Elixir of Life, a single remedy which would cure all diseases. Indeed, the foremost difficulty of all this time lay in the attempt to find perfection, to find certain answers to all questions. Thus the men who were interested in medicine tried to find the perfect remedy, while all around thousands were dying of diseases caused by filth and malnutrition. It was the attempt to do, in the sciences, the same thing that had been done in religious philosophy and in government: the discovery of answers which would fit exactly into the scheme of things and which would be completely solid and unyielding. The search for perfection and certainty obscured any partial answers which might have been found to questions of immediate interest, and the attempt to reconcile all knowledge to the doctrine of the Church, thus creating a perfect system, led to a distortion of the facts which was to hinder man's search for freedom through knowledge until centuries had passed and it was again possible to raise impertinent questions.

The attempt to reconcile all knowledge with the doctrine of the Church is easily illustrated in such stories of natural history as that one that the lion cub is born dead, and remains dead until its third day. At this point, the father comes and roars in its face, and wakens it to life. Thus, said the medieval natural historians, we have the symbolic representation of the death of Christ and His resurrection upon the third day. That the facts were false made little difference; it was the symbolism which mattered.

So, too, with the symbolism of numbers. The number seven became an almost magic number. It was the number of the Christian virtues, of the deadly sins, of the liberal arts, of the sacraments. So, too, did the numbers three and four develop mystic properties because of their significance in Christian thought.

Three was the number of the Trinity; and four was the number of the directions, of the elements—earth, air, fire, and water; of the qualities—hot, cold, moist, and dry; of the humours of man—sanguine, choleric, melancholic, and phlegmatic; the number and symbol of the idea of the macrocosm-microcosm (man's correspondence to the universe).

The great system of thought which was built in the Middle Ages was that of Scholasticism. This may be simply defined as the acknowledgment that the source of all knowledge lies in the Scriptures and in the writings of the Church fathers. From this source, any new knowledge may be derived by the use of Aristotelian logic. Thus the early church writings furnished the *material* to be thought about, and Aristotle furnished the *way of thinking*. This, it will be seen, goes back to Augustine, and his philosophy of history, for it limits all study to Christian sources. More than that, it limits study to the sources closest to God; again, an idea of St. Augustine.

It has been falsely claimed by some writers that the thinkers of the Middle Ages were of lesser ability than the thinkers either before or after them. Such a statement cannot be supported, for within this system was built a body of knowledge and a keenness of pure intellectuality which has seldom been equalled. The fault lay not with the men, but with the system which rested entirely upon authority, and which forbade any concern with the natural phenomena which surrounded men. Accepting the idea, as they did, that such phenomena were a part of the cloudiest emanation from God, their concern was entirely with pure intellect. The intellectual search for union with God, however appealing to the mind, did little to create a world of gracious living for men.

Thus, then, were the walls of the early Middle Ages built around men. The fall of Rome brought a need for protection, and the village of the Middle Ages built its wall. So, too, the need for security and for solidarity in every area of living called forth walls to hold out the darkness and the unknown. Within the political life, the feudal and manorial dues established certainty for each individual. On the manor, each man knew exactly what his status was, what he owed, and what rights he had. There, too, he was assured of a living—perhaps not a life—but at least enough food, clothing, and shelter to sustain his life. Thus was built the wall against armed foes and against the foes of need and want. In the face of the

great and final mystery, the mystery of life and death, was built the strong wall of the church doctrine, the infallible institution itself, and the sacraments which were the only sure way of life for an afterlife in heaven. In science, and particularly in the method of thought of scholasticism, there was another wall, a wall of authority which could not be questioned either in source or in method. There was no possibility for a lost or wandering mind. Within the framework of religion, of feudalism and manorialism, and of learning there were no dusty answers for either soul or body.

Expressions of Retreat in Works of Art of the Early Middle Ages

In the units of this study dealing with Greece and Rome, the ideal of classic art has already been discussed. Into this decadent civilization came the vigor and upward thrust of the Gothic man, the tribesman from northern Europe who ravaged what had once been the proud Roman empire. The spirit of these people is expressed in their mythology and in their hero stories.

Most of us are familiar with the mythology of these northern peoples. In this group of stories we find a group of "good" gods—Odin, Thor, Baldur, Freya, and others—in conflict with a race of giants, the Jotuns, who represent the ice and snow and bitter climate of the northern peoples. The "goodness" of gods, however, is relative. If we examine these deities, we find them to be gods of a warrior race. For example, the souls of some mortals were brought to dwell in Valhalla, the home of the gods, but those selected were the souls of the northern warriors who were slain in battle. There was no room in heaven for the kind or gentle or wise. Here came only the skull-crusher and bone-breaker, to spend eternity in hunting, warring, and in eating and drinking.

This same spirit is revealed in the hero stories of these Norsemen, of which we may take the epic poem *Beowulf* as an example. The very sound of the harsh lines, much smoothed and rounded in modern English translation, reveals something of the masculine vigor of the people. Consider, for example, the alliteration of crashing consonants in the line, "Bit his bone-frame, drank blood from his veins." This is a far cry from the epics of Greece and Rome in its very tone.

The story of *Beowulf* is almost equally harsh. It tells of Beowulf, a warrior from the south of Sweden who went to the court of his uncle in Denmark. There he slew a monster, Grendel, who had been devastating the uncle's kingdom. As a trophy of the fight, Beowulf brought home the arm and shoulder of the monster as it had been wrenched from the giant's torso. Following the victory, a great banquet was held in the hero's honor. Having eaten and drunk until they could hold no more, Beowulf and his men lay down on the floor of the banquet hall, their war-gear hanging by them, for the night's rest. But when all was quiet, Grendel's mother entered the hall, killed some of the men, and took the bloody arm and shoulder of her son back to the home which she had beneath the waters of a dismal fen.

On the next morning Beowulf set out and tracked Grendel's mother to the shore of a swamp. Fearlessly he donned his armor and plunged into the water, down to the opening of the cave. Here he grappled with the hag-monster and finally killed her with a weapon forged by the giants of old.

The last episode of the poem tells of Beowulf's last days when, as king or chief of his Swedish tribe, his own land was threatened by a dragon. As a warrior hero and leader, he went forth, killed the dragon, and was mortally wounded himself. The poem ends with his funeral pyre as a viking chieftain, and the construction of his tomb as a monument which would serve as a landmark for viking ships at sea.

Two other folk-epics illustrate the spirit of the earlier part of the Middle Ages. One of them is the *Song of Roland,* written in French about the time of the First Crusade (the 1090's), but concerned with events that happened (legendarily) three centuries before, in the days of Charlemagne. The persons of the story are Franks, the Germanic conquerors who gave their name to France; the central figure of the epic is Roland, the Emperor's nephew. The great event of the poem is the ambush by Saracens of the rearguard of Charlemagne's army in the passes of the Pyrenees at Roncevaux. The ambush was arranged by Roland's treacherous kinsmen Ganelon, inspired by envy and revenge. Roland and his companion Oliver, together with the militant Archbishop Turpin, are the last survivors of the Frankish host; they too are killed, facing overwhelming odds. One of the best-known episodes is that of Roland's refusal to blow his ivory horn, despite the urging of Oliver, to recall Charlemagne's host before the battle begins; when he realizes

that he and his Franks are doomed, he does at last blow three mighty blasts that Charlemagne hears, thirty leagues away, and the Emperor returns to rout the Saracens and avenge the death of Roland and his companions. The epic concludes with the trial and punishment of Ganelon.

It is a truly feudal poem, full of the vigorous, active, restless spirit of the Northern warrior. Roland is the man-at-arms, the warrior, unsoftened by the chivalry of later knighthood; he is a splendid barbarian, courageous in the face of overwhelming odds, loyal to his friends, utterly devoted to God, his spiritual overlord, and to Charlemagne, his temporal one. He is blood-brother to his earlier Northern kinsman, Beowulf: both heroes represent the all-out, do-or-die, "go-for-broke" spirit of the heroic age.

There are many magnificent scenes: the pathetic one in which the wounded Oliver, dazed and blinded by blood, strikes his best friend Roland, and the two are immediately reconciled; the striking one in which Roland tries to shatter his sword, "Durendal", against a rock lest it fall into paynim hands; for its hilt is a reliquary, with sacred and precious relics in it. Let us read only the one, the 176th stanza or "laisse" of the poem:

Count Roland lies under a pine tree,
Towards Spain has he turned his face.
Many things he recalls to remembrance:
How many lands, hero-like, he has won;
Sweet France; the men of his lineage;
Charlemagne his lord, who reared him.
At this he sighs and weeps, nor can he restrain himself.
But he does not wish to go into oblivion;
He confesses his fault, and prays God's mercy:
"True Father, Who never lies,
Who raised St. Lazarus from the dead,
Who preserved Daniel from the lions,
Keep my soul from all dangers,
Despite all the sins I have committed in my life!"
He raises towards God the glove from his right hand;
St. Gabriel from his hand receives it.
On his arms his head falls back;
His hands clasped, he goes to his end.
God sends his angel Cherubin
And St. Michael of the Peril;
Together with these comes St. Gabriel.
The count's soul they carry into Paradise.

The other is at once older and younger; it is the German tale called the *Niebelungenlied,* or "Song of the Niblungs." It was not written down in its present form until the 1200's, but its materials hark back to the days of Attila the Hun, in the fifth century. The Scandinavian version of the tale is known as the *Volsungasaga*; Wagner freely adapted the tale in his four music-dramas, *The Ring of the Niblungs.*

The epic is concerned with the hero Siegfried, who loved Kriemhild, sister of the Burgundian king, Gunther. In order to win her, Siegfried promised his help in Gunther's wooing of Brunhild, the warlike queen of a distant country. By magical means Siegfried assisted him in the feats of strength that won her. On their wedding night, Brunhild tied Gunther up in knots, and hung him behind the door; again it was Siegfried who came to the rescue, and on the second night, wrapped in his cloak of invisibility, wrestled with her and subdued her, without Brunhild's being aware that her adversary was Siegfried, not Gunther. How he took from her then a ring and a girdle, giving them to Kriemhild; how the two queens quarreled; how Kriemhild, in haughty anger, revealed the trick of Brunhild's conquest; and how Brunhild plotted revenge, is quickly recounted; the climax of the first part is the treacherous murder of Siegfried by Hagen, the loyal henchman of Gunther, and the villain of the piece. The last half of the story concerns Kriemhild's revenge against the Burgundians. Married, after many years, to Etzel (Attila), King of the Huns, she invites the Burgundians to visit her, and there follows a general massacre in which they are all slain, including Kriemhild.

One sees in these epics the warrior's world of the first half of the medieval period, its spirit of adventure, courage, bravery, harshness, and blood.

From these illustrations it is possible to catch a glimpse of the spirit which motivated these Gothic men. For contrast one may remember the spirit, let us say of Horace, who advised that when fortune became too strong (even good fortune), one should take half one's canvas in. The Gothic personality, in contrast, would sail his ship spreading all sails and driving the ship, with decks awash, either to glory or destruction.

Beowulf was never tender, never kind, never sympathetic. When his friends were slain in battle or in the great hall of Heorot, he never wept for them or extolled their virtues. Rather he swore vengeance and went forth to do it. He is the mighty warrior, the great adventurer. Such was the hero of the Germanic strain.

It was from this spirit as well as the general sense of insecurity which came as Roman authority disappeared that the men of the first five hundred years of the Middle Ages retreated. It was, of course, a retreat that would not end until the rough, intruding northern spirit was finally merged with the remains of the classic strain; a synthesis which would not come for many years. In the meantime, the only hope seemed to be in flight. What are some of the symptoms of this flight?

At least one interesting commentary on the retreat which took place during the early Middle Ages was the lack of individuality which we find. In all previous epochs which we have studied, we have noticed the emergence of individuality. In such periods a few men and women have stood out, head and shoulders above the crowd, as the great creators of their time. The names of the great Athenians have come to us, and we know them as well as we do the names of our own vice-presidents—or better! Yet in the vast early centuries of the Middle Ages, five centuries in time, all of Europe in space, very few individual names emerge. Not until comparatively late do the names of individual creators come forth, at first vaguely, as we have some of the names of the singers and composers of Germany, France, and Norman England. Yet we are not even too sure of these people, and the themes which they treated were old and glowing with the patina of much handling before their time.

What does this anonymity mean? It means simply that the spirit of the times smothered the individual. There is little reason to suppose that the creative impulse died among men. Whenever and wherever it has had a chance in human history, it has burst forth. Rather, in these middle times, the individual was not spurred by his experience. Probably because of the ban upon clearsighted examination of the world, he lacked the experience which evoked creative impulses: the desire to tell others of something he had felt, some truth which had suddenly become clear to him, some image of beauty which he had caught. Instead, the literature and the art is the expression of masses of people, worked over among them, and rising finally to expression as the group feeling, the group longing, the group ideal.

The group ideal of these times is perhaps best revealed in the religious literature, of which we have a great deal, a part of which deals with the lives of the saints. In all of these tales we see pictures of martyrs, eager to die for their faith, eager to shed the flesh which has held their true selves, their souls, with bonds of clay to this world. The more the body is hurt in this death, the greater the joy of the saint, the more holy he is. And yet one finds another strain here, perhaps the Gothic one which we have just discussed: a morbid delight in matters of the flesh. One recalls the tale of the murder of Thomas à Becket, with its too vivid description of the saint when his hair-shirt was removed, and of the desiccation of the flesh which had taken place beneath it. The delight of the teller is evident when he recounts the symptoms of leprosy, the disease sent as punishment to the murderers.

The morality play of *Everyman* belongs in the same literary time as the lives of the saints. Like those lives, it is literature with a lesson; literature for the instruction of the common people. What does it teach? The events of life which bring pleasure are evil, it tells us. Knowledge will carry us as far as the grave, as will our five wits, and even our beauty, but only our good deeds and our penance will go with us beyond that event. The entrance to heaven is kept, not by angels, but by an accountant who takes the record book of the individual, posts and makes double entries, and comes forth with the verdict: eternal bliss or eternal damnation. There is no middle ground.

Finally, the conception of a way of life in *Everyman* denies the human personality, since the individual has no chance to set his own purposes. The purpose is established from outside by the celestial accountants, and the fear of death is ever-present to frighten the individual into obedience. Man, in the early years of the Middle Ages, narrowing his living limits to the confines of the manor, governing himself according to the rules of feudalism, with his curiosity walled in by a religious philosophy which denied the value of investigation and experiment, and with his eyes turned to heaven rather than to the present life, built a set of walls around himself which offered the ultimate of certainty, though they shut off the possibilities of wide freedom more completely than had been true in any earlier cultural development.

Fortunately, such a condition cannot last while men retain a spark of their humanity. The narrow walls of this period served a purpose in that they did establish some security, and a measure of certainty that an animal existence could be maintained. With these assurances, men began to inquire, and to see the world about them. The thinkers of this epoch brought forth new facts and new ideas which were to shatter the walls, and in the later years of the Middle Ages bring forth a new balance and a new way of life. In the following chapter, these new ideas will be discussed.

Ideas Which Threatened
to Break Medieval Walls

In the assumptions made at the beginning of this study it was stated that freedom depended upon width of experience and upon a satisfactory discovery of meaning within that experience. It was pointed out in the same place that the characteristic of humanity lay in its creative powers and their use. It would seem from the previous chapter that in the Middle Ages, by the year 1000, the people had retreated to a point at which humanity and freedom were denied almost completely. People bartered their freedom and humanity for security and partial peace.

In the process they had built up feudalism for political protection. It narrowed most human horizons to the limits of one small estate, but yielded security from military violence within those limits. They had created manorialism as an economic system which never produced any more than a bare subsistence, but again made that secure in that the serf could not be removed from the land which was apportioned to him. Perhaps because of the very misery of life on earth, all eyes turned to the life of the soul after death, and the Church offered the one sure way of eternal bliss. For most of the people this involved, first, a despising of the desires of the flesh, and second, a firm belief that the way led through the sacraments of the church. Furthermore, it was bolstered and enforced by a fear of eternal damnation, quite as much as by the hope of eternal bliss. The Church, furthermore, with its elaborate system of philosophy based upon the beliefs of St. Augustine and the ensuing work of the scholastic philosophers not only encouraged the belief in heaven as the only goal, but discouraged natural curiosity about the world which lay about medieval men. The science of the time was limited by this narrow theology, and served as a buttress for it.

Smoldering beneath this structure of early medieval thought and organization lay unresolved conflicts which would someday demand settlement. We can list them here. The first was the normal desire of human beings for a good, gracious, and pleasant life here and now which was opposed to the accepted belief that such a life was probably evil. The second of the conflicts, one which had already been brought to the fore, was the conflict between Church and State in the government of secular matters. A third conflict, more deep-seated than either of the other two, lay between the two different culture-patterns which opposed each other at this time. The first one was the old and misunderstood Graeco-Roman tradition which survived from Italy, and which seemed triumphant in these early years of the Middle Ages. Opposed to it was the Celto-Germanic, Gothic, tradition which regarded life as a constant struggle. This last, while it was crude, rough, and barbaric, held the promise of more vigor than did the dying classic culture.

This last was perhaps the basic conflict of this whole time. Indeed, Dorothy Sayers points out that the basis for the two great political factions which struggled bitterly in Italy was a racial difference; originally the Guelfs were of indigenous Italian stock, while the Ghibellines descended from the Nordic invaders. The necessary integration of the energetic—often violent—northerners with the more rational but less active southern culture seems to underlie all of the other conflicts of the time.

These, then, were the conflicts. As always during such a period we have discoveries which tear the foundations from old institutions. So it was in the Middle Ages, for during the eleventh century came several facts, ideas, and discoveries which were to undermine the older culture and bring the conflicts to the surface where they would demand resolution. At least six new attitudes, discoveries, and forces can be named which disrupted the retreat and security which had been achieved during the first five hundred years of the period. They may be named as follows: first, the Crusades and the discovery of new ways of life; second, the domination of medieval life by women; third, the rise of cities; fourth, the realist-

nominalist controversy, called the "battle of universals"; fifth, the rediscovery of all of Aristotle's works; and sixth, the beginning of a new scientific attitude, signalized principally by the work of the friar, Roger Bacon. These new forces are to be discussed in this chapter.

The first Crusade occurred near the beginning of the eleventh century, and must have been an eye-opening experience to the crusaders, for throughout the dark period in European history, a relatively enlightened civilization had been maintained in the Near-East and throughout the Mohammedan lands. While this culture had been known in Europe before as a few travellers had come in contact with it, particularly in Spain, it was not until the time of the crusades that the possibility of a relatively luxurious way of life had been made known to many people in the West. As the soldiers returned, and told the tales of things which they had seen on their travels, perhaps bringing souvenirs home, as is the ancient custom of soldiers in all time, the demand for a better way of life spread throughout Europe.

Another important factor in making this new way of life possible was the development of cities.

Mumford attributes the development of towns and cities to three forces. One was the impetus given by feudalism itself, as the barons widened their holdings and sought men to protect them. It was natural that these men should be brought together to form an effective fighting force, and the lords, therefore, encouraged movement from the villages to larger towns. A second force which made the city possible was the increase of land devoted to agriculture, for at the beginning of the later Middle Ages vast areas of swamp-lands were drained, and forests were cut and more and more land was put to the plow. Since the city must depend upon its surrounding territory for its food, the increase in the food supply which resulted from this move was essential before the city could come into being and live. A third force which brought about the city was the development of markets by the monasteries. These institutions encouraged the people to bring their produce for exchange, and the holiness of the place insured peaceful transactions. Gradually the barter system gave way to a money system, and the market developed. Feudal lords, needing more and more money, encouraged this trend, for it made possible the collection of taxes and rents in money; and the lords were willing to extend privileges to the cities in order to increase their money revenues. Thus did the towns grow, and whatever the immediate forces which made them flourish, their development is but a symptom of a general stirring of the human spirit throughout Europe.

Throughout Europe the word went around, " City air is free air," for in the free cities the law was established that a serf who could maintain his residence for a year and a day became a free man. The serfs flocked to the cities. And in medieval times an unattached man was an outlaw. So men of common interests, interests centered about their trade, banded together in guilds. As these guilds—first craft guilds, later merchant guilds—became wealthy, the great guild halls flanked the great church to form a quadrangle about the open market place; these became the distinguishing feature of the medieval city. After the towns were founded came the great expansion of the merchants, plying their trade with the East, and returning to Europe with the silks and spices which they were able to buy there. Thus, in 1241, nearly three centuries after the first movement toward city growth, came the great Hanseatic League, the guild of merchants of the German coastal towns, uniting to carry on their trade. The cities, already founded, formed a safe outlet for their goods. Trade could be carried on. The increase in wealth, for Church, for the producers of goods in the craft guilds, and for the merchants was such that it found an outlet in processions and parades—the answer to the need for beauty in a world which had for centuries been sparse and bare.

Feudalism, according to Adams, was the code of men-at-arms. With these later Middle Ages, however, and especially in France, women succeeded to rule in the matter of ethics and behavior. The man was away from home for great stretches of time, trading, at the wars, wherever the affairs of the time called him. Women took over the manners of the time, manners which had been crude and rough under man's domination. If we must have a name by which to fix this movement in our memory, Adams gives us that of Eleanor of Guienne (1122-1202), Queen of France and Queen of England, and her daughter, Mary of Champagne and her granddaughter, Blanche of Castile. Certainly it was these women who established the Courts of Love, courts which were to write legal codes in all matters of etiquette. It was here that the rough codes of feudalism were transformed into the gentler modes of living and belief. This change may be seen in the contrast between Roland's lament over the fallen Franks at Roncevalles, representative of the ideals of feudalism, and the lament over the dead Lancelot, representative of the chivalrous knight. Roland, surveying the field of death where lie his comrades in arms, says:

> Lords and barons, now may God have mercy upon you, and grant Paradise to all your souls that you may rest among the blessed flowers. Man never saw better men of arms than ye were. Long and well, year in and year out, have you served me, and many wide lands have ye won for the glory of Charles. Was it to such an end that he nourished you? O France, fair land, today art thou made desolate by rude slaughter. Ye Frankish barons, I see you die through me, yet I can do naught to save and defend you. May God, who knows no lie, aid you!

Yet when Lancelot, the almost-perfect knight of chivalry, lies dead, we hear the following lament:

> Thou wert the courtliest knight that ever bare shield, and thou were the truest friend to thy lover that ever bestrode horse, and thou wert the truest lover among sinful men that ever loved woman, and thou wert the kindest man that ever struck with sword, and thou wert the goodliest person that ever came among the crowd of knights, and thou wert the meekest man and the gentlest that ever are in hall among ladies, and thou wert the sternest knight to thy mortal foe that ever put spear in breast.

From this we see the transformation from a fighting code to a courtly and courteous one. Both are found in the lament over Lancelot, but the virtues of mildness, of love, and of humility always stand before the virtues of strength or the recognition of human weakness.

Closely allied to the development of chivalry was the development of beauty and warmth within the Church. As has already been pointed out, the official doctrine of the Church was a vast intellectual monument. It centered in the Trinity—the Father, the Son, and the Holy Ghost—a Three who were always One, administering the cold and rigid justice which was found in the development of doctrine from the time of Augustine. For sinful men, justice is the last thing to be desired; and the medieval man, ridden by the absolutism and perfectionism of the time, was convinced that he was sinful. He sought not justice, but mercy; and for mercy he could only turn to the Woman, the Mother. Thus, as a part of the domination of woman which we have already noticed, developed the Cult of the Virgin.

This was the time of the building of cathedrals, and the power of the cult, almost an obsession with the people of the time, is shown in the number of cathedrals dedicated to Mary. Indeed, in France, one asks not how to get to the cathedral, but how to get to Notre Dame, the church of "Our Lady." The two are almost synonymous. As Adams points out:

> The measure of this devotion (to the Virgin), which proves to any religious American mind, beyond possible cavil, its serious and practical reality, is the money it cost. According to statistics, in the single century between 1170 and 1270, the French built 80 cathedrals and nearly five hundred churches of the cathedral class, which would have cost, according to an estimate made in 1840, more than five thousand millions to replace. Five thousand million francs is a thousand million dollars, and this covered only the great churches of a single century . . . The share of this capital which was—if one may use a commercial figure—invested in the Virgin cannot be fixed . . . but in a spiritual and artistic sense, it was almost the whole . . .
> Expenditure like this rests invariably on an economic idea . . . In the thirteenth (century) they trusted their money to the Queen of Heaven because of their belief in her power to repay it with interest in the life to come.[1]

Thus lay the power of the Virgin in bringing human understanding and human sympathy into the cold and austere structure of the doctrines of the Church. The last to be challenged of the great walls of medievalism was the way of thought which had built the walls: scholasticism. Up to this time there had been revolts from the whole structure, to be sure, as are found in the many heresies which gained wide acceptance: heresies so important that the Church, in 1229, established the Inquisition, both court and police force, pledged to detect heretical opinions wherever they existed, to obtain confession of the divergent views, to excommunicate and turn the heretic over to the civil courts for punishment. But in spite of these revolts, scholasticism stood until the end of the Middle Ages. The greatest challenge to this body and method of thought occurred in the "battle of universals," which had its beginnings just before 1100.

The scholastic philosophers took the position called "realism." That is, they believed that the *idea of a thing* was the only reality, existing before any particular created thing. The revolting group, known as the nominalists, held that there was no reality except in individual things, and that the idea was only a generalization, a name, created by the mind after experience with the particular objects. Thus the idea came after the particular object. The middle view, called the conceptualist, was that idea and matter exist only together, and cannot be separated. For this group, the idea exists in the things, and no other place.

To make this clear, let us use a homely example. Consider, for example, two or three chairs. One is a lounging chair, overstuffed; a second is a steel folding chair; a third is a straight-backed wooden chair. Looked at together, however, we call them all chairs, although they have very little in common. There must be, then, the *idea-chair*. Where did it come from? The "realists" stated that the idea chair existed before any particular chair was created. The "nominalists" said that the idea came only after we had experience with many different chairs, and is merely a creation of the mind. The "conceptualists" state that the idea and the form exist only in each other. The exact nature of the argument is beside the point, and it is unnecessary to labor it further. The point is that the nominalists, adopting an attitude somewhat like that of modern scientists, were saying that reality lay in the actual phenomena of the world: a serious threat to the structure of scholasticism.

Another threat lay in the work of one of the conceptualists, Peter Abelard, 1070-1142. Among Abelard's early writing was a work entitled *Sic et Non* (*Yes and No*). In this book he set down a number of theological questions, and by referring to the Scripture and the writings of the Church Fathers, showed that both positive and negative answers were given to the questions. Since it will be remembered that the Bible and the writings of the Fathers were regarded as the source of all knowledge, this pointing-out of discrepancies attacked the system at its very foundation.

Still another threat to scholasticism lay in the growth of what is now called the scientific method. The leading worker in this field was the Franciscan friar, Roger Bacon, who lived from 1214-1294. It was Bacon who said that the three worst arguments are "This is the way of our ancestors, this is the cus-

---

[1]Henry Adams, *Mont-Saint-Michel and Chartres*, (Boston, Houghton Mifflin Company, 1933) pp. 92-93.

tom, this is the common view." Such a spirit of doubting, together with the scientific observation which Bacon insisted upon, was bound to rock the entire doctrine built upon the idea that the things of the world are nothingness, and that true reality lies in God, the Pure Idea.

The final threat to scholasticism lay in the embarrassing recovery of all of the works of Aristotle. Up to this time, the only work which had been preserved was his logic, which, we again recall, was the method of scholasticism. Other works had been preserved by the Arabs, but had not been reintroduced into Europe. About the year 1200 other writings of Aristotle were translated from the Arabic into Latin, and were introduced into Europe. While there was a number of fine theological problems raised, the principal difficulty was that the new books brought with them a full-fledged science, which, while not accurate in its entirety, yet was based on observation. Clearly, here was trouble, when the great authority for scholasticism himself turned out to have been actively concerned with the observation of nature and a recording of facts which he saw about him. The first effort of the Church was to suppress the new works, but within a few years, expurgated editions of Aristotle were taught in all of the universities.

These, then, were the new ideas which brought the early Middle Ages into sharp focus. The ideas offered wider freedoms than men had known before in this time. The city offered mobility of the person, a freedom which had never been possible for the serf under manorial customs. The discoveries of new ways of life, and the development of ideals of chivalry, together with the cult of the Virgin, these helped to break down the old wall of austerity and other-worldliness which had been the code of life of the earlier time. But men were faced with a problem: How are these new ways compatible with what we have always known? In attempting to answer the question came the conflict which was noted at the first part of this chapter.

Chaucer, in his Prologue to the *Canterbury Tales*, illustrates this problem, though his tone and outlook are essentially realistic. While he is not seeking to illustrate anything, while he is trying only to describe an assortment of people, smiling at their too human weakness, yet he poses the problem, nevertheless. The basic nature of the gathering of the pilgrims is a case in point. The pilgrimage to the Shrine of

St. Thomas is, or should be, a religious exercise. Yet these people, or some of them, at any rate, seem to be there for an extended picnic, and nothing else. In the characters, again, we see the division of personality. On the one hand we have the poor Parson, on the other we see the Friar, the Summoner and the Pardoner, all of whom are devoted to the gratification of the flesh, and all of whom use their religious connections to make these gratifications possible.

In some instances we see the city men, the new class of merchants, lawyers, doctors, and guildsmen. While robbery and piracy were no longer carried on by the Celto-Germanic tribesmen, these men of the city embody much of the same spirit. Their aim is profit, and they will not be stopped by nice concerns of religion in order to achieve their purpose. They partake of the upsurging spirit which denies the balance of the old and mistaken Graeco-Roman tradition. Still another interesting group is composed of the knight, his son, and the prioress, who represent the ideals of chivalry, and of a religion which is turning from fear to beauty for its attractiveness. Chaucer draws no moral from this collection of people, nor does he attempt to state a problem with the exactness of a mathematician or a social worker. What does the reader make of the collection of medieval men and women?

Nowhere is the spiritual conflict of the time better illustrated than in the student songs, for the universities themselves were products of the new and stirring life. The pulls upon the personality are particularly evident in one of the student creeds in which the dying goliard burlesques the creed of the Church. With almost savage vigor he takes each word of the Church's creed and turns it to a flaunting of his vices and indulgences. One is reminded of the speech of Hamlet's mother, "Methinks the lady doth protest too much." Then the student faces the last moment and is gripped by a fear of the unknown to which he is committing himself: a fear which is supported by five hundred years of religious tradition. With an anguish which strikes home to the reader, he commits his soul to God and begs for the last sacrament of the Church.

Not only does the song of the dying university student illustrate for us the soul's dilemma of the time, but it was in the universities that the greatest of the new ideas were formulated, ideas which have already been described in the discussion of the battle of the universals. It is scarcely possible to present with sufficient clarity and force the chaos into which this battle threw philosophical circles and which spread from them down to the very foundation of medieval thinking.

Scholasticism had been the way of thinking of the time. All knowledge was derived from its sources and through its process. And suddenly this whole structure was shaken at its very foundation. Aristotle, who had given the structure its pattern of thought, was discovered to be one who had made careful study of the things and events of the world for their own sake. Such a man as Roger Bacon repudiated all of past knowledge. And the nominalists denied the whole idea of reality which had been accepted since the beginning of the epoch.

Through the methods of scholasticism had been evolved a body of knowledge in which people believed implicitly. It was, to its time, what the scientific method is to ours. The questioning of its methods and results were as earth shaking for the medieval mind as it would be to ours if a group of sound scholars were to announce that the scientific method of our time and all the knowledge which we had gained through its use were completely false. Imagine the consternation which such a position would make at the present time. The challenge to scholasticism was as important for the Middle Ages.

The questions and conflicts which these new ideas evoked were of the deepest significance. It would seem that it would be impossible to reconcile the differing positions, and that a period of balance would be impossible. Yet such a new synthesis, a new balance was achieved. In the next chapter we shall discuss the artistic works and the one great philosophical monument which were produced and which pointed ways to the "Medieval synthesis."

The Artists Propose New Designs for Living in the Middle Ages

At the end of this early time of conflict and disruption, then, the men of the Middle Ages were beset by four problems which threatened to disrupt the personality. In the first place we have seen the pulls of life and the pulls of death. The former term implies all of the ideas of pleasure and luxurious living which the time was able to support; the latter term carries with it the implications of living only for a hereafter of bliss in heaven, with mortification of the flesh as the way to achieve heavenly bliss. The first term implies hope and joy in the present life; the second implies that fear should be the dominant emotion in one's existence on earth.

The second problem was that of secular domination. As late as 1077 the Holy Roman Emperor Henry IV had knelt in the snow before the castle of Canossa, begging forgiveness of Pope Gregory VII. Such had been the power of the Church over the secular authorities. But the trend was not in this direction. Already the sense of nationalism was growing. Out of the international chaos was coming the sense of belonging to a nation, which was to be one of the glories of later epochs, as well as one of the plagues of the present one. By the end of the period of chaos, the strain of these two pulls was critical for the civilization of the time.

A third problem, like the first, was essentially a clash of personality. It was the difference between the Celto-Germanic Gothic temperament, such as we saw in *Beowulf*, with the old and lingering ideas of balance and order. Somehow these two forces needed to be brought into reconciliation. The latter was stagnant; the former represented only disorder and confusion. In terms of formal artistic values, we have here a contradiction as great as that between horizontal, essentially restful lines and vertical, energetic ones. Which was to become dominant in the new pattern for living?

The final problem was one which seems irreconcilable. It lies in the clash of philosophies of the time, for all of the rest of the old medieval pattern of life was shaped by the philosophical structure. Scholasticism made of the world an allegory, each symbol of which could be interpreted in religious terms. It denied the value of curiosity and of any study of the phenomena of the world, since the mother-lode of all knowledge lay in the Scriptures. The method of acquiring new knowledge was logic, the use of words and thought rather than investigation. With the coming of the nominalists, and with the scientific inquiries of Roger Bacon, however, this whole concept of the world was challenged. The new thinkers advocated a study of the things in the world which can be apprehended by our senses as valuable and important in themselves, not necessarily as allegories of the Divine Mind.

To sum it up in a word, the clash of the times came about in new secular ways of thinking and living which challenged the older religious and mystic ways. Where was the art that could bring these together in a new synthesis? Where were the men who could define new relationships between men and the universe, men and God, the individual man and society as a whole? Where could be found artists who could suggest new purposes for life since the old were so sorely challenged?

It would seem that this new synthesis came about in three places. In philosophy, it was St. Thomas Aquinas who built a new philosophic structure which could hold the divergent points of view. In architecture, the medieval Gothic cathedral furnished a synthesis at the point when the artist's skill and the function desired came together. Chartres Cathedral is the usual example of such building at its height. In literature, the new balance was suggested by Dante Alighieri in *The Divine Comedy*. Let us look briefly at the ways in which the synthesis was achieved in these three forms.

It cannot be our purpose here to go into detail in a discussion of the doctrines of St. Thomas. Rather, we shall here show how he reconciled some of the contradictions of the time. In discussing Thomas' thought, one can scarcely avoid using the symbol of the equilateral triangle as a representation of the individual person, of the nation, and of the universe, for all of his ideas seem to shape themselves around that symbol. It was no accident that this is also the symbol of the trinity of God; it may have been accident that it is also a shape which suggests both stability and upward motion. In its visual form it unifies the energy of the Celto-Germanic spirit with the desire for stability of the Graeco-Roman.

In Thomas' unification of Aristotelian thought with that of the Church, he accepted the central Aristotelian doctrine, similar to that of the conceptualists. This doctrine was that matter and form (or idea) cannot exist separately. Matter, he said, had only *potentiality*, that is the possibility of being itself, until it was entered into by the idea of the thing. Then it became that thing. For example, "clay" is not "brick," nor is there "brick" without "clay"; but when "clay," which has only *potentiality* by itself, is joined with the *form* or *idea* of "brick," then the "brick" exists. Next, he said, lower forms of existence are only matter in the formation of higher forms. And everything, he said, was moving, changing, growing, turning into something else. This movement is the movement toward perfection, which is God. Thus the First Mover, God, does not move things from behind, but is the purpose toward which all things are moving. Since things must desire the thing toward which they move, then the motive force is the Love of God.

It was with the doctrine of lower and higher forms, all in motion toward perfection, that Thomas brought together the conflict between the growing desire of people for natural knowledge and the doctrine of the Church that such knowledge was a study of nothingness, for, said Thomas, the highest human studies are philosophy and law. He considered philosophy as a study of the humanly-knowable laws for the discipline of the spirit, and law, of course, as the study of the rules for the governing of man's physical nature. Both, according to the Aristotelian concept of reality, are necessary and equal. To reach a knowledge of these subjects, a study of all forms and all matter is necessary. It is in this way that men attain their highest perfection—through knowledge.

Then, he continued, there is another realm of knowledge, complementary to philosophy. This is

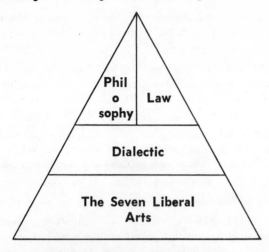

THOMAS' PLAN OF EDUCATION

theology, which has its source in God. It cannot be understood through natural learning, but only by revelation. The two, however, are not opposed to each other. Rather, a knowledge of philosophy leads to the possibility of receiving revelation and revelation presupposes a knowledge of philosophy. Finally, he said, that true knowledge, the union with the divine science, came only after death. It was the duty of man, therefore, during his life-time to acquire as much natural knowledge as possible that he might be fit to receive the final revelation of God after his death.

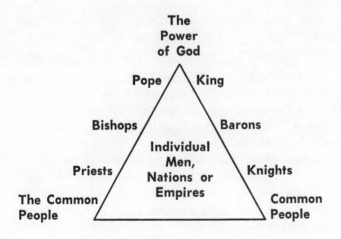

THE SEPARATE, EQUAL ROLES OF
CHURCH AND STATE

The settlement of the opposition of Church and State came with a justification of feudalism, on the basis of the lower forms constantly seeking the higher. However, in the governing of man he believed Church and State equal, with both the King and the Pope receiving their power directly from God. It was the duty of the king to administer God's laws for the physical nature of man; of the Pope and the Church to administer the law for the spirit of man.

The pull of life and death, perhaps the greatest question of all, was solved by St. Thomas, first with the Aristotelian doctrine of matter and form existing only when they were together and in each other. With this, and with Thomas' insistence that natural knowledge, gained through the use of human senses, was necessary for the perfection of the human being, he banished the dualism which had existed since the time of Augustine and the idea of the City of God. Hereafter both man's body and soul were necessary for his earthly perfection, the one as important as the other.

Thus it was that the Middle Ages, in this final great synthesis, found freedom and opened the way for man to develop himself, like the medieval city, outside of its early walls, yet still in keeping with the fundamental pattern. The way for science was now open, the hate for the body was banished, the state was recognized as one of the forms of order, leading to the highest order, that of the kingdom of God.

Without becoming too technical, this may suggest the kind of synthesis which was made in philosophy. For the common man, however, the involved thinking of the philosophers has little meaning. In the Middle Ages, it was the common man, as well as the serious thinker, who needed a solution to the problems which were splitting his personality.

For this common man, it is probable that the Gothic cathedral effected this synthesis. The thrust of the cathedral was upward. Standing before it, the beholder's eye moved up its great towers, impelled by the pointed arches, until the eye reached the spire which directed it even farther upward—toward heaven. In this way was the need for the other-worldly satisfied. So, too, did the figures in the stained-glass windows tell the stories of the Bible and the lives of saints and satisfy the religious needs of the time.

But there was more to the cathedral than that; for here was beauty. Not only did the windows preach the gospel, but their colors also brought joy to the beholder. The pageantry of the church was a thing of splendor, made colorful by the rich garments of the bishop and those who assisted him at the mass, by the heaviness of the perfume, and by the chant of the choir. All these brought richness to the life of the medieval man who sought such satisfaction in his day-to-day living. Even the task of building these cathedrals, a great communal effort shared alike by nobility, wealthy burghers, and the common men, furnished a creative outlet for the energies of these people of the Middle Ages.

Architecturally, the Gothic cathedral furnished a symbol of balance between classic and energetic. It achieved symmetry and unity. Yet it had the thrust, the upward push, which we have remarked as characteristic of the northern personality. The elongated statuary of the portals, the pointed arches, the flying buttresses, beautiful in themselves and symbolic of the desire to go upward beyond the limits which wall and column could support: all these are the marks of the Gothic.

In one other aspect the cathedral was the symbol of the synthesis of the Middle Ages, for it was here that the Cult of the Virgin reached its height. The sudden flowering of this cult may be ascribed to the sense of sin which obsessed the people, convinced as they were of their moral deformity from Adam, and of their weakness to withstand the pulls of the world around them. For them, the justice of the Trinity was a thing to flee from, and they fell back upon the mercy of the Mother. Miracles were needed to insure their salvation, and a whole body of literature has grown up to tell of the miracles wrought by the Gracious Lady. To quote Adams:

> To peasants, and beggars, and people in trouble, this sense of her power and calm is better than active sympathy. People who suffer beyond the formulas of expression—who are crushed into silence, and beyond pain—want no display of emotion—no bleeding heart—no weeping at the foot of the Cross—no hysterics—no phrases! They want to see God, and to know that He is watching over His own. How many women are there, in this mass of thirteenth century suppliants, who have lost children? Probably nearly all, for the death rate is very high in the conditions of medieval life. There are thousands of such women here, for it is precisely this class who come most; and probably every one of them has looked up to Mary in her great window, and has felt actual certainty, as though she saw with her own eyes—there in heaven, while she looked—

her own lost baby playing with the Christ-child at the Virgin's knee, as much at home as the saints, and much more at home than the kings. Before rising from her knees, every one of these women will have bent down and kissed the stone pavement in gratitude for Mary's mercy. The earth, she says, is a sorry place, and the best of it is bad enough . . . but there above is Mary in heaven who sees and hears me as I see her, and who keeps my little boy till I come; so I can wait with patience, more or less! Saints and prophets and martyrs are all very well, and Christ is very sublime and just, but Mary knows!

This worship of the woman brought comfort, solace, and understanding. For the nobleman, the joys of the world could be called courtesy and courteous love, all devoted to the woman and eventually to the Virgin. Here, for the man of noble birth, the natural desires could be regulated and channeled, put in the corsets of correct manners, which were dictated by the great ladies and their courts of love. And for the common man, the juggler, there was something else. There was escape from justice by throwing himself on mercy and upon the hope and expectation of miracles. The sins and errors which could in no way escape justice might be atoned through the mercy of the Mother of God. Even more, here we find a spiritual democracy; an outlet for the conscious or unconscious desire for equality within the unequal feudal system. This, of course, was a new desire for men, one which had grown up in the Middle Ages since the growth of cities, and the possibility of freedom and equality had dawned upon the mind of men who previously had assumed inequality to be the natural order. Men were not yet ready for equality on earth, however, but in the Virgin's sight, the juggler doing his tricks for her amusement was as important as the learned Friar, writing books according to the rules of scholasticism.

The cathedral was all these things to the common man of the Middle Ages. At the same time it provided beauty in the present life and inspiration to heaven. It curbed Gothic energy and heightened and vitalized classic stability. At its height, let us say at the time of the building of the older tower of Chartres, it represented the golden moment in the development of an art form, when the artist is able to do exactly what he has to do, when he has gained freedom in his medium.

In addition to the cathedral, there were other great syntheses of medieval life. We have already spoken of the great philosophic one of St. Thomas which brought the warring doctrines of the Church together into a single firm structure. Dante's *Commedia* in the realm of literature was the other.

For the present study, the important thing about the *Commedia* was the removal of the restrictions which earlier centuries had imposed on men. The goal and final purpose of man was still the attainment of heaven and the bliss of that afterlife, but man was left free to achieve this goal through his own power and the discipline of his own will. Dante's God was no accountant, such as we found in *Everyman*. Rather He was perfect Wisdom, which, in Dante's mind, was almost synonymous with Love. Man's purpose and goal, like the *enteleche* of Aristotle, was perfect union with this God. For Dante, this heavenly state is man's true home, which he must ever earn anew because of Adam's sin. Furthermore, man, while he is alive, cannot know the wisdom, or order, or love of God; for salvation, the final union with God, is still a matter of God's Grace rather than a result of man's effort. It is as if God's wisdom is a different category of wisdom from that of human beings, to which people may aspire, but to which they can be admitted only by the Will of God.

While men may not achieve union with God through their own efforts, they may prepare themselves for it by gaining the maturity which comes with earthly wisdom. This mature nature is called *innocence* by Dante, by which he meant the happy state of Adam before the Fall. It is for this reason that Dante places the Garden of Eden, the Earthly Paradise, at the top of the mountain of Purgatory. It is here that men, after having attained their full maturity, the sum total of human wisdom, may await the act of God which will transport them into the category beyond.

Dante's concept differs in another way from that of the author of *Everyman*. In that grim sermon-drama man is drawn to God through fear. With Dante mankind is a part of God's order, which is love; so it is through the pull of love that man works toward his great purpose. And with Dante, man has free will; the great choice is left squarely with him. On earth he may make his choice, and his choice, expressed in faith and works, becomes his destiny in the afterlife.

What are the choices? Since the way of God is discipline and orderliness, the way of Satan is dis-

order and lack of proportion. To choose this latter way is to sin. To understand this idea of sin is not difficult. Imagine a man being attracted to anything to such an extent that he forgets other things. Money and worldly goods are such an attraction; sex is another; the drive for power is still another; the desire for food or drink is another. We could mention many such things which, while not evil in themselves, can attract men so that they forget everything else. Dante and his Church imagine seven such fatal attractions. Now imagine a man who is attracted to food to such an extent that he becomes a glutton. He lives to eat, and even in his physical shape becomes a caricature, a grotesque, of what the human figure can and should be. Yet the man in question chooses that for himself; he wants to be that way, and has no hope nor desire to be anything else. That is the sort of thing which Dante considered as sinful. Such a person is destined for Hell, and the inscription which Dante envisions over the mouth of Hell, "Abandon Hope, all ye that enter here," is an expression of the state which the condemned ones have reached. In their choice, they have abandoned all hope and all desire to be anything or anywhere else. The punishments which Dante saw for the souls in Hell are symbolic of the nature which they have made for themselves. With the body removed, in other words, we see them exactly as they have made themselves to be. Step by descending step we traverse the cone of Hell, in each lower depth viewing the souls who are deeper and deeper in sin. Step by descending step we see these souls deprived of more and more freedom, until at the very bottom of the pit we find Satan, the greatest sinner of all, deprived of movement, frozen, as he is, in ice. So is he bound by his sins.

Emerging with Dante at the base of the mountain of Purgatory, we find another picture. Here are the souls who have erred, who have somehow strayed in their earthly lives from the path of wisdom. The difference is that these people still have hope; they aspire toward their own true selves and toward God. Their labors are difficult as they expiate their sin, but through all the labor they are joyous, for they know that the end will be full wisdom and maturity, the Garden of Eden, and the state of Earthly Paradise. The last of all the sins to atone for is lust, represented by a wall of flame through which the soul must pass before he attains innocence, and Dante in his vision hesitates before he goes through, and feels the fire sear him.

Finally in heaven, and guided by Beatrice, he receives instruction in theology, the science of God. It is here that he sees the perfect order of the whole universe, both of men and of angels. He sees the Church and its officers as the guardians of man's spirit and he sees the kings as equally important to God, for they maintain temporal order on earth. Here, too, he finds freedom, as opposed to the ever increasing bondage which he witnessed in Hell, for in Heaven, though the souls are symbolically assigned to different spheres as a result of their different capacities for virtue; yet they are actually free to pass through all the spheres and to approach the throne of God, itself. There is no bondage here.

Is this only a poem of death, or does Dante have something to say for men-alive? We believe that he has much to say to us. He says that men must make their choice, for which they have their own wills. If they choose wisely, they will choose a life of order and discipline. Throughout their life, they will gain knowledge, for that and its resultant wisdom will make men free. Finally, he tells us, man's studies should turn to philosophy and law, the fields of knowledge which represent the best possible concepts of order on earth, for the former disciplines and instructs the spirit, the latter has the same function in man's temporal dealings with other men. (One might well remember Plato and the idea of the philosopher-king here.) This life will be one which is joyously led, and which leads to the final realization of the true self when, by the Will of God, the soul is united with the Perfect Wisdom.

What has Dante brought together here? In the first place, he envisions a life at once balanced and aspiring. These are the Gothic and classic elements of the Middle Ages. He brings together the desire for broad worldly knowledge and religion, for his poem itself is scientific according to the science of his time, and he counsels the widest possible earthly knowledge as a necessary condition for heavenly bliss. He brings together the pulls of life and death, for his concept of the full life is one which is joyous and in which men use their full powers, yet use them as they aspire to the greatest possible happiness and freedom in the afterlife. Finally, he unites the rival claims of pope and king as he sees each, work-

ing God's will and God's order on earth, each in his own way and in his own place.

This is the final answer of the Middle Ages to the great question of man's search for freedom. It started with the building of walls, for men needed their protection. It has progressed through the stage where men found their walls no longer necessary for protection and found them cramping in the human desire for the good life. It emerges in a great synthesis in which human nature is free, by nature divine, but in which men have freedom of choice. The *Comedy* unites body and soul, in that the process of discipline, which the individual must choose for himself, is the discipline which must occur in the present life; a discipline, which in its order, produces freedom here and prepares the spirit for freedom in the afterlife. Particularly in the cathedrals and in the *Comedy* do we see the artist at work, proposing new answers to the great questions of mankind. It is upon these answers that the institutions are to be reshaped, and upon them that a new pattern for existence is to be built. What was the nature of human freedom within this new design?

The period of synthesis during the late Middle Ages was brief. Dante lived from 1265 to 1321. St. Thomas lived from 1225 to 1274. Chartres dates from the thirteenth century. Yet by the middle of the fifteenth century, the Renaissance had burst upon Europe. The forces which had challenged the old walls of life which had been built during the dark ages (the years 500 to 1000) were too strong to be held in check, and the secular spirit was to go ahead to new triumphs. But in those two hundred years, we can witness a new freedom toward which many world-weary people of the twentieth century look back with longing. It is worthy of at least a brief examination.

The single and fundamental characteristic of medieval freedom lies in the sense of unity which furnished strict rules for all types of human behavior, and yet which furnished complete individual freedom to create within those rules. This seems to be a paradox, a contradiction. At least it can be seen as a most delicate balance between individual aspiration and endeavor and community solidarity which offers stability.

Perhaps better than anywhere else, this balance can be seen in the art of the late Middle Ages. Consider, for example, the cathedral. Its pattern was extremely strict. It must be oriented, with the altar toward the east. It must be cruciform. Each part of the structure carried some symbolic meaning, so that the symbols must be exactly treated. All this was a part of the strict rule which governed art and life in the period of balance.

Yet consider the freedom of the individual within this rule. The stone-carver was free to do as he wanted. If he wanted to carve little fat angels or animals which he had seen or imagined, that was his decision. He could do as he felt. One sees much of this type of work on the *miserere* seats in the choir stall. Here a wood-carver thought that it would be fun to carve a pig playing a fiddle. No sooner thought of than started! Or somewhere else, the carver wished to caricature a fat burgher of the town. He could do it because he was a free man, working within the limits of the grand design. These were no machine-made units, to be put up as they came from the machine. They were the work of free and independent craftsmen, who could do what their imagination dictated and their hands could perform. Throughout medieval art, one sees this independent spirit working within the strict limits of rigid rules.

This same freedom within strict limits is found in all spheres of activity during the late Middle Ages. For example, the craftsman necessarily belonged to his guild. It was the association which regulated the quality of his work, the price which could be charged, and many other things. Beyond that, the guild served as an insurance and burial society for its members, a social group, and a dramatic society in that the mystery and miracle plays which amused and inspired the city-dwellers were functions of the guilds. The guild hall was not only a place of business, but was also a social center where banquets, weddings, and balls were held. The guild also regulated very strictly the membership within itself, and established strict rules for the training of the craftsmen. All these point to the strict communal regulation of the individual.

But within those limits, the member of a guild, the shoemakers, let us say, was absolutely free. He had his own shop, which was part of his home. He did his work only on order, so that when there was no business, he could lock up and take the members of his family, together with the apprentices and journeymen in his shop, and go for an outing in the country. Furthermore, and one suspects that this is the important aspect of the whole system, each pair

of shoes was an individual creation. The pride of craft and of creation entered into all of the work which was done, and the master craftsman developed a sense of pride in each item of his work. The very fact that he did the whole job, from heel to toe, from sole to the very top of the uppers, gave him a sense of responsibility and of pride.

The story of Our Lady's juggler reveals the same type of freedom within religion. The Catholic creed was strict, and its rules were absolute. But within them men were free. There was sufficient opportunity for individual practice of the religious observances to satisfy each person. Dante's idea of freedom as participation in the wisdom, the order, and the love of God are of great importance here. The man who was not free was the one who, by his own choices, had rendered himself inhuman in outward form and in nature. The order of God, however, was of sufficient latitude that men could make a comfortable life within it. In addition to this, there was the one provision of the Christian scheme of things which has always been a source of strength for that faith. This was the idea that a mistake does not mean inevitable damnation. Such an error may need purging, but it is only when one comes to a conscious desire for the way of evil that one is damned.

The concept of freedom in this period of balance in the Middle Ages, then, was one in which all the forces of the culture grouped themselves around the individual to give him support. Yet they did not hamper his freedom, his individuality, or his creativity as long as he stayed within the rules of that culture.

This balance, like all others which we have seen, is too delicate to last. Within a brief time, the secular forces which we have seen born during the Middle Ages were to triumph, breaking down the new designs which had been made by St. Thomas, by the architects of the great cathedrals, and by Dante. The stream of life was to quicken its rate of flow in a new epoch which we call the Renaissance.

EXERCISES

This chapter has presented a thesis about the Middle Ages: paradox and contradiction, the "Pulls of Life" and the "Pulls of Death," the Celto-Germanic dynamism and the Graeco-Roman conservatism. The student might find it profitable to list under one heading or the other the following pairs:

1. "Everyman"................"Aucassin and Nicolette"

What specific qualities in each make you respond as

you do? Can you cite an episode from each to justify your opinion?

2. The Franciscan Friars...............The Benedictine Monks

3. A portion of St. Francis' "Canticle of the Sun" reads thus:

My Lord be praised by brother sun
Who through the skies his course doth run,
And shines in brilliant splendor:
With brightness he doth fill the day
And signifies thy boundless sway.

My Lord be praised by sister moon
And all the stars that with her soon
Will point the glittering heavens.
Brothers wind, air, cloud, and calm
And weathers all, repeat the psalm.

By sister water be thou blessed,
Most humble, useful, precious, chaste;
Be praised by brother fire.
Jocund is he, robust and bright,
And strong to lighten all the night.

And here is a portion of another medieval hymn, the "Dies Irae"

Day of wrath, O day of mourning.
See fulfilled the prophet's warning,
Heaven and earth in ashes burning!

O what fear man's bosom rendeth
When from heaven the Judge descendeth,
On whose sentence all dependeth!

Wondrous sound the trumpet flingeth;
Through earth's sepulchers it ringeth;
All before the throne it bringeth.

Death is struck, and nature quaking,
All creation is awaking,
To its Judge an answer making.

To the book exactly worded,
Wherein all hath been recorded:
Thence shall judgment be awarded.

Of which of the selections in the text does this remind you? Which of the two would St. Augustine prefer? Why do you think so?

4. Here are some other pairs that might serve to tease you into thinking:

a. The "national epics"......Gawain and the Green
Knight

(*Beowulf, Song of
Roland, Niebelungenlied*)

b. Canterbury Cathedral ....The Tabard Inn

c. The Virgin Mary ....Eleanor of Aquitaine,
Blanche of Castile

d. William of Normandy, or Charlemagne..........
....St. Augustine

e. St. Francis' "marriage" to "Lady Poverty"....
..........his apology to "Brother Body" for having
so severely and ascetically
mistreated him

A Time Chart for the Middle Ages

The Middle Ages in Europe is roughly that period of a thousand years stretching from the year 500 to 1450. These dates, as always, are approximate. It is possible within this period, too, to make a division at about the year 1000. Before that time the people were chiefly concerned with the establishment of security following the fall of the Roman Empire. Following the turning point of the year 1000, the people turned their eyes forward and sought to give a graciousness and shapeliness to the forms they had created.

Indeed the Middle Ages may be viewed first as the search for any ways of life which would promise certainty. During the first five hundred years of the period, these were found in the development of the medieval church, which gave man a purpose and a way toward salvation; in the development of the feudal system which gave political security, and the manorial system which provided a meager fulfillment of the economic needs of the people; and a science which shut out most of the questioning which might bring disturbance to the mind. This science was used primarly in support of authoritarian religious beliefs.

The second five hundred years of the Middle Ages were devoted to the enrichment and decoration of the narrow limits which had been thus fixed. Feudalism, essentially a political and military institution, attached to itself the institution of chivalry. The Church, having established its doctrine and organization centered primarily upon death and the life everlasting, turned to the Cult of the Virgin which was to offer comfort in the present life, and to the building of great cathedrals, dedicated to the life eternal, but furnishing beauty and drama for life in this world. Scholarship, long preserved in the scriptoriums of the monasteries, now flowered in the development of the universities, and science began to concern itself with the realities of the present world. The dingy medieval village gave way to the city of the Middle Ages, and the narrow limits of geography of the dark ages were broken as crusades went to the Holy Land. Trading centers grew up to which were brought the riches and luxuries of the known world. Breaking the ties of feudalism, nations began to assume their identity. Music, art, and literature began to flourish. The course of some of these events is shown on the following chart.

TIME CHART FOR THE MIDDLE AGES

Important Political, Historical, and Military Events	Philosophical Events	Art, Music, and Literature
375-500 – Great invasions of Roman Empire by northern and eastern tribes. Asiatic Huns harry Germanic peoples	354-430 – Augustine formulated doctrine of Church based on Neo-Platonism	509-604 – Pope Gregory establishes Plain-song or Gregorian Chant
395 – Roman Empire split between East (Capitol: Constantinople) and West (Capitol: Rome or Ravenna)	395 – Christianity becomes Roman state religion under Emperor Constantine	
410-476 – Conventional dates for the fall of Rome. The city captured by tribes of Visigoths and Vandals		
465-511 – Clovis established line of Frankish kings and (496) becomes Christian	480-524 – Boethius, "Consolations of Philosophy" expresses Roman world-weariness	
509-604 – Pope Gregory defends Rome against invaders—establishes political power of the Church		

Maps Showing a Few Significant Territorial Changes

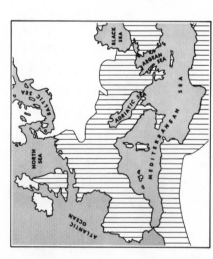

THE ROMAN EMPIRE c. 300 A.D.

INVASIONS OF THE ROMAN EMPIRE c. 500 A.D.

Maps Showing a Few Significant Territorial Changes

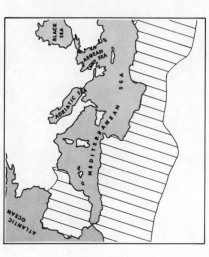

Spread of Mohammedanism c. 732 A.D.

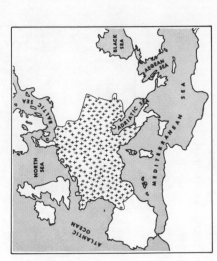

Charlemagne's Empire c. 800 A.D.

Important Political, Historical, and Military Events

570-632—Life of Mohammed

597—St. Augustine's mission to England

600-650—First development of Feudalism from northern tribal customs

732—Battle of Tours, Mohammedans checked in France, driven back to Spain

751—Pepin becomes King of Franks; establishes Carolingian rulers.

800—Charlemagne crowned Roman Emperor by Pope. Establishes precedent for Papal authcrity.

850-900—Decline of Frankish Kingdom. Further invasion of Northmen

900—Feudalism fully established in Europe

900-1000—Towns begin to spring up in Europe

1066—Norman invasion of England.

Philosophical Events

781— Charlemagne's Palace School established. Start of revival of learning

Art, Music, and Literature

700—Beginning of Romanesque architecture developed from basilica

c.900—Organum in music discussed by Odo of Cluny

900—Approximate beginning of stave architecture in Norway

291

Art, Music, and Literature

1000-1100—Full development of Romanesque architecture

1022-1084—Building of Abbey of Mont Saint Michel almost as we know it

1087-1127—First known troubadour—but secular music was already well established

1194—The beginning of building of the present Chartres Cathedral. The height of Gothic style 1170-1270—In France alone 80 cathedrals. 500 great churches built, almost all devoted to the Virgin. The height of the Cult of the Virgin

1240-1302—Cimabue, begins to paint figures naturalistically
1265-1321—Dante achieves "medieval synthesis" in "The Divine Comedy"

1276-1327—Painter Giotto continues trend toward naturalism
1300 onwards—Musical development of counterpoint, polyphony. Improvement of system of musical notation.

1313-1375 Boccaccio
1340-1400 — Geoffrey Chaucer "The Canterbury Tales"

Philosophical Events

1000-1100—The Battle of Universals; Realist-Nominalist Controversy

1079-1142 — Peter Abelard teaches in Paris, "Sic et Non"

1200—The first trickle of the main body of Aristotle's works enters Europe

1270—Formal founding of University of Paris. For at least 200 years groups of students had collected at Bologna, Salerno, etc. 1270—Introduction of all of Aristotle's works in Europe

1214-1294—Roger Bacon bases knowledge on study of physical world

1225-1274—Thomas Aquinas establishes Church doctrine on Aristotelian principles

Important Political, Historical, and Military Events

1077—Emperor Henry IV bows to Pope at Canossa

1100-1300—Period of Crusades

1154-1189—Rule of Henry II in England. Establishment of English common law

1150 onwards—Half Spain in Christian hands. Unification of Spain continues

1215—Magna Carta—law superior to king

1272—Rudolf of Hapsburg made Austrian king—start of the rise of the House of Hapsburg

1291—Revolt of Swiss Cantons. Start of democratic Switzerland
1295—English parliament established

1302—Estates General founded in France. A hint of democratic government

1337 to about 1440—Hundred Years War. England loses French lands. Great steps toward unification of both countries

Maps Showing a Few Significant Territorial Changes

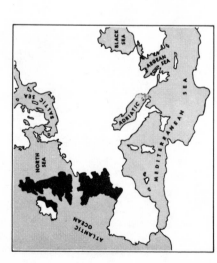

English and French Territories
about 1154

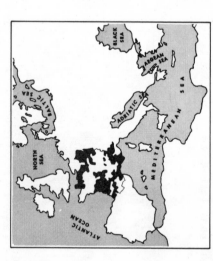

English and French Territories
about 1453

The Importance of Symbolism
in Medieval Art

Imagine yourself in one of the great European cathedrals of the thirteenth century. As you glance about, your eyes are filled with a profusion of details; everywhere you look is color, line, and pictorial representation. The stained glass windows offer a host of pictures—men and angels, animals and plants; the pillars, capitals, corbels, balustrades, brackets—all offer to your scrutiny the forms of flowers and growing things, the divers shapes of bird, beast, fish, or again the images of men, saints, and angels. Why?

"What is the meaning of the myriad forms of life? Appearance, or reality? . . . The Middle Ages were unanimous in their reply: the world is a symbol. As the idea of his work is in the mind of the artist, so the universe was in the thought of God from the beginning. . . . The world therefore may be defined as 'a thought of God realized through the Word.' If this be so, then in each being is hidden a divine thought; the world is a book written by the hand of God in which every creature is a word charged with meaning."[1]

Then foolish indeed would be the man who looked upon the forms and objects of the created world, yet saw nothing more than met the eye; the wise man, rather, would look upon this Book of God, finding hidden meanings in every "word," proceeding from the thing seen to the thing unseen, and wresting from Nature the very thoughts of God. He would say with Fra Lippo,

---

[1]Auguste Male, *Religious Art in France of the XIII Century*, p. 29.

". . . . This world's no blot for us,
Nor blank; it means intensely, and means good;
To find its meaning is my meat and drink."

Not that the phenomena of the physical world have value in themselves; not that the stone is important, but the sermon you find in it. The material world, seen in its proper light (proper, that is, to the man of the XIII Century) is but a shadow of the spiritual world; and to penetrate beyond material form to spiritual meaning is the only proper use of the world to the wise man.

The world of appearances, then, is but a picture-book, edifying mankind, instructing him, illustrating the one important concern of existence: namely, the Drama of God, the fall of man and his redemption in Christ. This, in short, is the pageant of the Church. What nobler function, then, has art, than to picture the natural world so that man may go beyond it, to deal with objects and things as they are,—symbols of eternal verities?

Such a point of view is not too easy for the modern to grasp; but it is a point of view that must be recognized, even if not wholly understood, if one is to find in the productions of the Middle Ages the intentions of the artists who created them. After all, it is much the same mood that prompted Walt Whitman to write about the grass,

"Or I guess it is the handkerchief of the Lord
A scented gift and remembrancer, designedly
    dropt,
Bearing the owner's name someway in the
    corners, that we may see and remark . . ."

As we look, then, upon the carvings, the paintings, the stained glass, we are to remember that our eyes, like those of the men who made them, are not to stop at the surface. We are to see the forms of nature as a code of spiritual meaning, the shape of things as symbols of religious import, leading always back to the Author of all things.

Even the physical appearance of the church building is symbolic. The building must be literally "oriented;" that is, the altar end must be the easternmost point: thus recalling to men's minds not only the direction of the Holy Land, our Lord's birthplace, but also the glory of the rising sun, symbolic of the Christ. Thus oriented, the cold, dark, north side represents the Old Testament; the light flooded, warm, southern side, the New. "The western facade—where the setting sun lights up the great scene of the eve-

ning of the world's history—is almost invariably reserved for a representation of the Last Judgment. The medieval doctors, with their curiously bad etymology, connected *occidens* (the west, cf. occidental) with the verb *occidere* (to kill), and the west became for them the region of death."[2]

The body of the church, wherein the congregation sat or kneeled, was known as the "nave" (Latin *navis*, ship or boat), reminding one that the church is indeed the "ship of souls," bearing men over the stormy waters of this world. Beyond the nave lies the chancel, where the choir is seated, and where pulpit and lectern (reading desk) stand; beyond the chancel, the sanctuary, where the altar is situated. Just so the church is divided symbolically: the Church Militant, the church in the world here and now, among the laity; the Church Expectant, the souls of those righteous ones who have died in the faith; and the Church Triumphant, the church as it will be after the Judgment, when God's purposes have been fulfilled. Between the nave and the chancel, separating laity from clergy, is a pierced screen or a heavy beam, stretching above the chancel steps. This is the "rood screen" or "rood beam," typifying the cross of Christ, and reminding the worshipper that before entering the Church Expectant or Church Triumphant, he, too, must pass under this yoke; he too must bear his cross.

One could go on endlessly about the significance of the architectural detail; the very appearance of the church building is fraught with meaning. Perhaps the detail of such symbolism could be strikingly seen in one last example: the shape of the baptismal font, for this bowl or basin was consistently made with eight sides. The reason? Eight is the number of regeneration (and baptism, of course, is the sacrament of regeneration). Does not the eighth tone of the scale begin the new octave? Did not six days suffice for the Creation, the seventh for rest, and the eighth mark the beginning of the new cycle? Does not eight follow the traditional seven which marks the limits of mortal man: his seven ages, the seven decades (three score years and ten) of his longevity? So detail piles upon detail; there is no item too small for consideration, no instance that does not lead beyond itself to some lesson that the busy mind of the beholder can discover and by which he may profit.

---

[2]Male, op. cit. p. 6.

In view, then, of the importance and the frequency of the use of symbols, let us consider some that are most often encountered.

One of the omnipresent symbols in the architecture and the painting of the Middle Ages is the central symbol of Christianity, the Cross. Not that Christianity has exclusive claim to the symbol; it was familiar for centuries, even millennia, before the birth of Jesus. Its variant forms, with various significations, can be found in all parts of the world. After all, it is one of the simplest geometric forms, the intersection of two lines; its very simplicity explains its appearance among Hindu and Eskimo, in China and North America. Its points represent the number four, a magical number amongst many peoples; the first square, the cardinal directions, the seasons, and in many theologies, the number of the rivers of the infernal or celestial regions, the four great winds; the list could be multiplied extensively. We still use a cross, quite without religious signification, as the sign of multiplication, the sign of addition, the sign manual of one who cannot write his name. "X marks the spot . . ."

(a) The Tau Cross appears in Christian art with some of its Egyptian connotation still clinging to it, for it is always the form used with St. Anthony of Egypt. If the cross is not actually in his hand, it appears as a T on his garments. Only rarely does the

DIAGRAM 1. COMMISSEE OR TAU

Tau form appear in pictures of the crucifixion as the cross of Jesus, but it is not unknown in this connection; however, it is frequently found as the type of cross on which the two thieves were crucified.

It is known also as the "Old Testament" or "Anticipatory" cross, for it was thought to be the sort used by Moses in the Wilderness. Thus it was frequently used in Advent season, foreshadowing the coming of Jesus. The heraldic device of the Cru-

saders' Kingdom of Jerusalem was a fourfold Tau Cross, or Cross Potent.

(b) The Latin Cross is perhaps the most familiar. Suggesting, as it does, the literal instrument of the Passion, it is also the symbol of Jesus Himself.

DIAGRAM 2. LATIN CROSS

(c) The Greek Cross, with its arms of equal length, is less literal than the Latin form; it carries the suggestion of "the four corners of the world," reminding the devout of the injunction, "Go ye into all the world." It is this cross that is represented on the top of the altar, in the center and altar corner, to symbolize the five wounds, in hands, feet, and side.

DIAGRAM 3. GREEK CROSS

(d) The Cross of St. Andrew, also known as the transverse cross, or cross saltire, is not only the mark of St. Andrew, and hence the Cross of Scotland; it also happens that St. Andrew's day determines the date of Advent, the beginning of the Christian year. Hence his is the cross of beginnings and of endings; it is also the cross of martyrdom and humility.

(e) The Maltese Cross resembles four spearheads with points touching. Early associated with St. John, it became the emblem of the Knights of St. John, or Knights Hospitalers. Its importance as a Christian

DIAGRAM 4.   MALTESE CROSS

symbol is its recall, through its eight points, of the Beatitudes. It is called also the cross of regeneration.

(f) The Celtic Cross is a particularly attractive form, developed in the north about the fourth century or later. It is less literal than the unadorned Latin Cross for the Circle of Eternity ring about its juncture is forward looking (the Life to Come) rather than backward looking (the Passion).

DIAGRAM 5.   CELTIC CROSS

The all-too-numerous other forms of the cross are beyond the scope of present mention, except, perhaps to point out the slender "reed" cross that is always associated with John the Baptist; one can always recognize it by its slenderness. Jesus is often portrayed carrying a "Resurrection" cross, a slender one with knobbed ends, the ends indicating that the suffering is over, the mission of the cross completed.

In conclusion, note the distinction between "cross" and "crucifix." The former is the plain geometrical figure; the latter a cross bearing a representation of the body of Christ.

One of the mysteries of Christian dogma is the mystery of the Trinity. It is very difficult to explain in

words the doctrine of the Triune God, God in three Persons. Small wonder that of St. Augustine there is told the story that one day, while meditating on the idea of the Trinity, he found a child on the sea shore, busily digging with a spoon, carrying water from the ocean to fill up the hole in the sands. Jokingly the Saint asked, "How long do you think it will take to put the whole ocean into that hole?" The child rose up, and revealed himself as an angel, and answered, "As long as will take your mortal mind to be filled with the mystery of the Trinity."

(a) But the medieval artist found great resource again in the use of the symbol. The triangle, simplest of geometrical forms, the first perfect figure, offers an excellent representation. Not only its decorative value,

DIAGRAM 6.   EQUILATERAL TRIANGLE

but its instructional worth, renders it the universal symbol in painting and architecture. Its simplest form is the equilateral triangle, often inscribed "Tersanctus": "Holy, holy, holy."

(b) Another representation is composed of three equal arcs of a circle, arranged in what is known as a triquetra. Its leaf-like beauty suggests at once unity and diversity, their continuity the eternity, and their interweaving the indivisibility of the Trinity.

DIAGRAM 7.   THE TRIQUETRA

(c) An interesting combination of circle and triangle is the familar trefoil. It is one of the symbols closest to the world of nature, leaf-like in shape, recalling St. Patrick and the shamrock that he used to exemplify the doctrine.

DIAGRAM 8.
THE TREFOIL

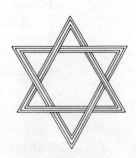

DIAGRAM 9.
TWO TRIANGLES

(d) The interwoven triangles, like a six-pointed star, is perhaps a Christian adaptation of the Shield (or Star) of David, an old Jewish device. This figure is also a symbol of creation, the triunitarian symbol of the triangles recalling that Son and Holy Ghost existed in and with the Father before worlds began.

(e) The last of these figures is "The Shield of the Holy Trinity," found particularly in the windows. It

How can the artist (and remember, in the Middle Ages he is no person set apart; he is the artisan, the maker of things—stone cutter or worker in glass), how can the artist be sure of representing a figure like that of the Christ so that it needs no label, so that its divinity is clear to every beholder? So difficult was the task that again he had recourse to symbols. In order to represent divinity and sanctity, a suggestion of light and radiance surrounds the head (sometimes the entire body) of the person. There was, during the medieval period, a strict convention in this code, revealing again that meticulous symbolization that is the point of our consideration; we should be aware of some of those conventions.

In the first place, the word so often used to describe this "glory" is incorrect; it is not a halo. Not until the strict conventions of the Middle Ages had gone into decline was this symbol rendered in perspective, like a golden band around the head.

The proper designation is "nimbus" and at its origin was used only to designate the Persons of the Trinity by placing behind them a simple circle of light. However, as the use of the symbol became more general, the Persons of the Trinity came to be marked by a nimbus that included a cross. This is the "tri-radiant" nimbus; three bands of light, one verti-

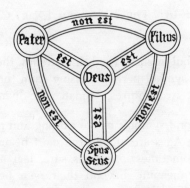

DIAGRAM 10. SHIELD OF THE HOLY TRINITY

DIAGRAM 11.
DECADENT TYPE

DIAGRAM 12.
TRI-RADIANT

is a vivid representation of the Athanasian Creed; read in any direction, its teaching is orthodox: "God is the Father," "The Father is not the Son," "The Son is God." Again one senses the mystery of unity in diversity.

cal, two horizontal, proceed from the head to the limits of the nimbus. Sometimes, as light-rays, they proceed beyond it. Occasionally diamond or "lozenge" shaped rays are shown in the nimbus. Infrequently one finds the nimbus strictly triangular. Then one knows the figure represented is that of God the Father.

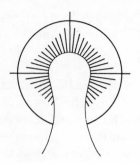

DIAGRAM 13.
LOZENGE SHAPE

DIAGRAM 14.
NIMBUS OF THE VIRGIN

The tri-radiant form, then, is restricted to the persons of the Trinity; but other forms of the nimbus appear to distinguish other saintly personages. Mary is often shown with a nimbus ringed inside with stars. There is always a single star in the nimbus of St. Dominic.

Translated, the phrase reads "Jesus Christ, Of God, the Son, Savior." It is the divinity of Christ and His mission as saviour that are important, and the recurrent symbol of the fish recalls this doctrine. (Webber mentions the curious employment of the mermaid as a

DIAGRAM 15. THE AUREOLE

DIAGRAM 16. THE FISH WITH I.X.θ.Y.C. REBUS

Christ-symbol in some English churches, the variation of the fish symbol perhaps arising from the desire to portray his two natures, human and divine.)

Sometimes the glory is enlarged to include the entire person; it is then properly called an aureole. Such a representation is most often used with God, Christ, or Holy Spirit; often with Mary, especially when she is represented holding the Divine Infant.

The floral symbols in the carving and painting of the Middle Ages are among the most beautiful of all symbols. Sometimes, one feels sure, leaf and flower have little meaning beyond their own beauty; Fra Lippo is still right:

One of the earliest and most curious symbols connected with Jesus is the fish. It is found in the first century on tombstones and elsewhere, as the mark of our Lord. It does not derive from the familiar miracle, but rather from an anagram upon a Greek phrase, the initial letters of which form the Greek word "icthys," or "fish." The phrase stresses two doctrinal points of great importance to the early Christian.

> If you get simple beauty and nought else,
>   You get about the best thing God invents.

But so strong is the tendency to make the flower a symbol that two are used here to illustrate the point: the "Rosa Mystica" and the Fleur-de-lys.

The Rose nearly always appears as a symbol of Mary, Mother of God. Its sweetness, purity, and

DIAGRAM 17. THE ROSE: MESSIANIC PROMISE

humility (for this is the wild rose, not the cultivated garden flower) are fitting reminders of the Mother of God. Many legends, like that of the "Christmas Rose," have grown up about this association. So strong is the connection between Mary and the rose that it has influenced the translation of a familiar hymn: We sing "Lo how a Rose," after the German hymn of the sixteenth century, "Es ist ein Reis entsprungen." *Reis* is not *Rose;* the poet was thinking of the "stem of Jesse," but we blithely insist upon the Rose. One also remembers, of course, the biblical "Rose of Sharon."

The fleur-de-lys is a conventional flower form. To most eyes, it always suggests the iris, with its erect, spear-like center, and the down-dropping side petals. However, it is supposed to be a conventionalization of the Annunciation lily. The fleur-de-lys was employed

DIAGRAM 18. FLEUR–DE–LYS

by the kings of France as their particular device, indicating their devotion to the Virgin; hence the association in our minds between the flower and kings of

France. In the Renaissance paintings of the Annunciation, there is almost without exception a pot or vase of lilies in the foreground. The fleur-de-lys was one of the most important decorative patterns of the Middle Ages, especially for what is known as "diaper-work," an over-all pattern against a solid ground.

Many are the figures of birds that one finds in the windows, paintings, and carvings of the medieval church. Small wonder, for is not a bird one of the symbols of the Holy Trinity? This, of course, is the dove, that portrays the Holy Ghost. Biblical reference portrayed the dove as emblematic of purity, peace, innocence; but, after the account of John's baptism of Jesus, when "The heavens opened, and the Spirit like a dove" descended upon Him, the reference of the dove is specifically to the Holy Ghost. The bird is often shown hovering above the head of Jesus.

One of the frequent bird-symbols is that of the phoenix. This mythical bird, having lived five hun-

DIAGRAM 19. THE PHOENIX: RESURRECTION

dred years, was supposed to fly to a spot in Arabia or Egypt, there to construct a funeral pyre of aromatic woods. Mounted on the pyre, the phoenix was consumed, to rise again out of its own ashes for a new cycle of life.

The phoenix is a natural symbol for the idea of resurrection; hence its association with the Risen Lord. Also, it may bring to the beholder's mind the "daily death" of which St. Paul speaks: "for as in Adam all die, even so in Christ shall all be made alive." The phoenix may also recall the sacrament of baptism and its regenerating power. Thus it applies not only specifically to Jesus, but to the hopes of every Christian.

Another of the bird-symbols found most frequently is the peacock. Spectacular and beautiful in its own right, the peacock yet has more than merely decorative significance. The Bestiaries had given rise to the notion that the peacock's flesh was not subject to decay: hence its fitness as a symbol of Jesus, who did

DIAGRAM 20. THE PEACOCK.
IMMORTALITY THROUGH JESUS CHRIST

DIAGRAM 21. THE AGNUS DEI
AND BANNER OF VICTORY

not suffer bodily corruption. Thus the peacock is a reminder of the Resurrection, and of immortality. Another meaning arises from the idea that the peacock moults its brilliant tail-feathers annually and renews his plumage more brilliant than before. This again is a regeneration symbol. The usual representation of the bird is that of the peacock standing on a globe, typifying the earth; the symbolism is obvious. The peacocks are often shown in pairs, with other symbols of Jesus like the Vine, the Vase (of the Waters of Life), or the Chi Rho monogram.

Numerous other bird-symbols could be cited, but these illustrate the point, that the value of the symbol is in proportion to the indefiniteness; it is better, symbolically, when not one, but many meanings are suggested by it.

An animal symbol of particular beauty and frequency is the "Agnus Dei," the Lamb of God. Although the immediate origin of the symbol is to be found in the words of John the Baptist, "Ecce Agnus Dei, qui tollit pecatta mundi" (Behold the Lamb of God Who taketh away the sins of the world), yet the sacrificial figure of the lamb makes the symbol almost inevitable even without John's words. The prophecies of Isaiah, the long familiarity of the lamb from the Passover sacrifice, and the New Testament references to the Shepherd and the flock render it a meaningful symbol. In the form of the Agnus Dei, the representation nearly always includes the three-rayed nimbus of divinity, and various other attributes are to be found

such as the resurrection cross or a book to suggest the Scriptures, or the four rivers to recall the four evangelists.

This is but one of the frequently found animal symbols. The lion is another one around whom was built a marvelous collection of myths and symbolic meanings. There are many others of equally interesting possibilities.

The final group of symbols is the group representing Christ and the Four Evangelists, from the porch of the cathedral at Chartres. This tympanum is pictured in the following chapter. It would be easy to dismiss the group of symbols by saying briefly that the winged man represents St. Matthew; the ox, St. Luke; the eagle, St. John; and the lion, St. Mark. So to deal with them misses the point and purpose of the whole consideration we have been giving these symbols. For the four beasts represent their respective gospels and carry additional meaning as well.

Why were these particular figures chosen for the evangels? St. Mark's gospel, after the introduction, begins with "The voice of one crying in the wilderness." Hence, the lion. St. Luke begins with an account of the offering in the temple of Zacharias, father of John. The ox comes from the type of sacrifice. Finally, St. John's lofty gospel is fittingly represented by the soaring eagle. As the eagle alone among the birds was said to look straight into the sun, so St. John looks into the heart of the Christian mystery. St. Matthew, because he traces the genealogy of Jesus, is represented by an earthly figure.

One can go much further with the symbolism represented in these figures. One might recall, for example, that these are the apocalyptic beasts which appear in the first chapter of Ezekiel. These symbols are also those of Christ himself. Nor does this exhaust the possibilities of these symbols; yet they cannot be further discussed at this point.

To summarize, there are two conclusions that have been the aim of this discussion. The first is the nature of medieval symbolic representation, and the attitude which prompts it. It insists upon the extrinsic values of the physical world, the view that things are important only as they instruct and edify the beholder in the growth of his spiritual life. Hence everything is to be regarded as a code of the Almighty, as if from the beginning of time He had intended to foreshadow in every object of His creation the Divine Drama of man's fall and redemption.

The second conclusion is that the cathedral (and by extension religious art in its various form) was the picture-book of the Middle Ages, addressed not only to the illiterate, but to all who were willing to delight in it. This is the "pull of the eternal" to all who received the faith. To sum up, we may quote Male again:

How much more vividly this must have been felt by the men of the Middle Ages. To them the cathedral was the sum of revelation. In it all the arts combined, speech, music, the living drama of the mysteries and the mute drama of sculpture. But it was something more than art, it was the white light before its division by the prism into multiple rays. Man, cramped by his social class or his trade, his nature disintegrated by his daily work and life, there renewed the sense of the unity of his being and regained equilibrium and harmony. The crowd assembled for the great festivals felt itself to be a living whole, and became the mystical body of Christ, its soul passing into His soul. The faithful were humanity, the cathedral was the world, and the spirit of God filled both man and all creation. St. Paul's words were realized and in God men lived and moved and had their being. Something of this was dimly felt by men of the Middle Ages when on a glorious Christmas or Easter-day, standing shoulder to shoulder, the whole city filled the immense church.[3]

_____

[3]Male, op. cit., p. 397.

18

Medieval Art Reveals the Conflict and Synthesis of the Time

The year 1000 came and went. No millennial disaster came with it: no dreaded Last Judgment, no signs and portents of the world's end. Contrary to the expectations of millions, life went on pretty much as before; but as if a new lease on life were in itself an energizing force, the acceleration of events after the year 1000 is remarkable. The long preparation for the Middle Ages reaches rapid culmination in the next 200 years. The most inclusive symbol of the Middle Ages (the Age of Faith, or the Gothic Period) is undoubtedly the Gothic cathedral of the twelfth century and after. It did not, however, come into being until three very different traditions met and blended.

The three traditions are the eastern Byzantine, the Roman, and the northern Celto-Germanic. The Byzantine tradition in Europe is quite properly associated with Italy, especially the city of Ravenna, although it is pointed out by Raymond Stites[1] that the folk wanderings of the Dark Ages had brought a considerable cross-fertilization between the northern Celto-Germanic tradition and the Near East. This influence is particularly noticeable in wall decorations and the like, which reveal themselves in the overall, patterns of nonnaturalistic designs found around doorways in early Norwegian churches, and which later appear as part of the "diaper-work" patterns in Gothic sculpture.

The Byzantine Tradition

The eastern style in art has a long tradition not only in Istanbul (Byzantium) but in Hellenistic

_____
[1]Raymond Stites, *The Arts and Man* (New York: McGraw-Hill Book Company, 1940), p. 366 ff.

Greece, including North Africa, and in Rome itself, but it expresses itself most forcefully in the Italian city of Ravenna where the Roman emperors resided during the fourth century, where the Gothic kings ruled during the latter part of that century, and where the capital of the Roman Empire was situated during Byzantine rule under Justinian in the fifth century. The art remains there in the churches, baptistries, and tombs of the various Christian sects which gathered in Ravenna during those years.

The great contribution of the eastern tradition in architecture is the central church, a church built around a dome, with the altar directly in the center under the dome. The Romans, of course, had used the dome, but usually on a circular building like the Pantheon. The pendentive dome (so-called because it seems to hang from above rather than built up from below) rises from a square area below it. The structural principle of the dome and pendentives is extremely complicated, but the dome itself arises from a drum which rests on the top of round arches which span the square area to be roofed. For the finest example of this type of architecture one should see pictures of the church of Hagia Sophia (Holy Wisdom) in Istanbul.

The second great contribution of the Byzantine style is its mosaic representation. The mosaic picture is made of thousands of pieces of colored stone or glass (tesserae) set close together to form a picture. The peculiar excellence of mosaic work lies in its quality of reflecting light. The tesserae themselves are finished with a hard, shiny surface. Furthermore, they are set in the wall, furnishing the surface of the wall, not flat, but with each one at a slight angle. Light from windows (few in these structures) and from candles and lamps is caught and reflected from the many facets of the mosaic picture, yielding a very rich and glowing effect. The accompanying picture of the Empress Theodora on the wall of the church of S. Vitale in Ravenna shows the Empress leading a procession of religious women toward the altar bearing gifts. The picture gives some idea of the mosaic are although even a colored picture fails to represent accurately the quality of light which is shed. It is interesting that the use of a gold background for the figures and the lack of depth in the picture is carried over in medieval painting.

The Romanesque Tradition

The Romanesque style descends directly from the Graeco-Roman tradition. It expresses itself in horizontal rather than vertical lines, in symmetry rather than emotional exuberance. The churches built in the Romanesque style continue the form of early Christian worship within the Roman Empire itself, following the pattern of the Roman basilica, or law court. The diagram below shows the essentials of the typical basilica structure.

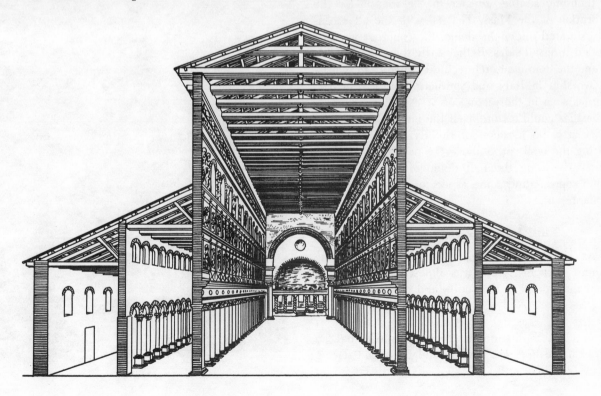

The features which one notices in the basilica are the long nave, flanked by side aisles. The ceiling may either be flat, as in the diagram, or rounded in a barrel vault (really a series of rounded arches supporting the roof, with the short space between arches roofed in the form of the rounded arch). One notices the many small columns which allow access to the side aisles, and support the wall and the roof above them. These small columns, marching down the length of the nave, provide a sense of rhythm and order, and at the same time lead the eye to the judge's seat at the end. The end of the building is rounded and is called the *apse* (from Greek *apsis,* or "wheel"). In church architecture, the altar was placed in the apse. Noticeable, too, is the triumphal arch just before one enters the apse, which came to symbolize the separation of the Church Militant (the nave, the church in this world) and the Church Triumphant. The lack of outside windows is also a feature of the basilica, since the heavy walls and the roof over the side aisles which is two-thirds the height of the building do not allow light to enter from the outside.

Since the Roman and the Byzantine traditions in art existed side-by-side and since the cultures represented by these traditions intermingled, the two traditions were rather quickly fused in the Middle Ages. The central-type church was not particularly satisfactory for the worship of the time since it made necessary the then-undesirable "theater in the round" for the celebration of the Mass. That is, with the altar centrally situated under the dome, the congregation surrounded it on all sides. Rather early then, the basilica became the dominant architectural structure for Christian worship in Italy and southern France. Furthermore, as seen in the picture of St. Apollinare Nuovo, the basilica could take to itself the interior decoration, particularly the mosaics, of the Byzantine tradition, utilizing the wall space above the nave columns, and particularly using the half dome of the apse for a mosaic representing some aspect of the Church Triumphant.

The Northern Tradition

As has been pointed out in Chapter 16, the northern spirit in Europe was almost the exact opposite of that found in the south, and the artistic tradition there reflected the difference in that spirit. Whereas the essential direction of the basilica was horizontal, with the dominant mood intellectual, in the north the line was vertical and the mood daring

and emotional. The Stave-Church of Norway demonstrates most of these principles. The architectural principle of such construction is relatively simple. Four ship's masts were placed in a square or rectangle, extending upward through the roof to support a sharply pointed tower. Around this skeleton the remainder of the structure and the walls were built of wood panels in a frame braced by ship-ribbing construction. The result is a building which looks like an arrow shot straight into the air. One can well make the point that in a climate where there is much snow, slanting roofs are necessary—but not *that* slanting. This was the architect's idea of beauty.

Another interesting feature of these churches is the exterior decoration consisting of long animal heads in wood, flung out vertically from the gables. Usually when we find such decoration, we also find function, as is the case with the gargoyles on the Gothic church which serve as rain spouts. On the mast churches no such function is apparent; they are purely decorative and illustrative of the wild emotionalism of the people who found them beautiful.

These then, the Byzantine and Romanesque traditions, already fused by the year 1000, and the Celto-Germanic spirit are the three traditions which were

Ewing Galloway   NORWEGIAN STAVE CHURCH

synthesized by Gothic architecture. In the remainder of the chapter we shall attempt to follow the main steps of this synthesis. Before approaching the architecture of the time, however, it might be well to discuss pictorial representation, including painting, and sculpture of the early medieval period.

Pictorial Representation and Wall Decoration

The wall decorations of the north consist of three principal patterns. These are the plant interweaves, animal interweaves, and the trumpet pattern. All these are nonrepresentational, for the plant and animal shapes are elongated and distorted until they are scarcely recognizable. The trumpet pattern starts with the shape of a trumpet, but from each point of the trumpet, another emerges. The designs given below represent this type of decoration. The lines seem

to be going in every possible direction, almost suggesting the element of confusion in the mind of the creator. Sometimes one even finds the human face or the human body caught up in the interweave of plant, animal, or winding trumpets, as if the human being were caught up in this maze of twisting lines.

The line of wall decorations from the south is essentially horizontal, as is suggested by the adaptation of the Greek key pattern given below. These people, sharing in the Graeco-Roman tradition, prized balance, peace, repose and logical predictability above other qualities in life. At least these art products would seem to indicate the truth of such a generalization.

The same overall design characteristic of the northern spirit and Byzantine as well, is found in many other areas of decoration. These designs are likely to be rich and lavish in the use of color. They exist for their own sake: lines, colors, and figures that appeal to the eye without having to mean something or be like something else.

One finds such ornamentation in the manuscripts of the medieval period, laboriously copied and brilliantly ornamented with flowing capital letters, floral borders, and carefully, colorfully drawn miniatures. Often the covers of such books are equally ornate, encrusted with gold and precious or semi-precious gems set in elaborate patterns.

The ornamental utensils of the time—coffers, jewel-cases, boxes—were also richly decorated. Enamel work and cloisonné were held in high favor. In such work, thin wires were set into a design; the spaces between were filled with gem-stones, or colored enamels, and then baked so that the whole design was fused together into a brilliant, glossy, colorful finish.

Wall decoration showed the Oriental influence, also, in the use of mosaics. We saw the use of mosaics among the Romans: picture or pattern formed by inlaying tiny colored stones or bits of glass in cement. Byzantine architecture abounds in their use and the Byzantine influence—always strong in Italy—extended such use of mosaic into the Romanesque churches. The mosaics of the medieval period are formalized, stylized, not particularly realistic; the features of the persons portrayed are conventionalized, their figures long and stiff. Little use is made of perspective; the whole composition is conceived of as a flat wall decoration, without the illusion of dimension; the background is generally a "ground" or surface of gold rather than a landscape or natural scene.

The painting of the early Middle Ages (before 1200) was extremely limited in nature. The greatest opportunity for a painter lay in the decoration of church walls, and we find many examples of religious scenes depicted either in fresco work (the pigment applied to wet plaster so the picture becomes a part of the wall itself) or in painting on the dry plaster, sometimes a combination of the two techniques. Most of this wall decoration harks back to the mosaic art which has already been touched upon, for the figures are flat, usually placed on a gold or blue ground, without the use of perspective.

Another type of painting appeared fairly early in France, and is best illustrated in the "Books of Hours" which were made for some of the great noblemen. The representation here is quite naturalistic, and marked by the use of beautiful color. The work here is like that of the illuminated manuscripts, miniature in size, and done with extreme delicacy.

It was not until the work of some of the Italian primitives that painting came into its own. Although one might well mention earlier artists, Giovanni Cimabue and Simone Martini in the 13th and 14th centuries represent this early work. Martini's "Annunciation" still shows the Byzantine influence very strongly in the gold background, the rather stiff arrangement of figures with the two personages in the side panels keeping the eye within the picture, and framing the angel and the virgin. There is, however, some beginning perspective here in the placement of the vase of lilies, and there is also the beginning of realistic portraiture. The tendency toward naturalism and humanism is revealed in several artists, Giotto among them. His works are so well known that it is more interesting to look at the Sassetta "Meeting of St. Anthony and St. Paul." The gold background typical of the Middle Ages is still here yet, it is broken by the forests which begin to look fairly naturalistic. Furthermore the artist is experimenting extensively with perspective in his use of the path to lead the eye into the background and the use of shadow within the cave to suggest depth. It is interesting that this picture almost uses a motion picture technique in that we have three portraits of St. Paul along the road. First we see him simply walking, next we see him greeted by a satyr and finally we have the meeting of the two saints. Of further interest is the naturalistic portraiture of the figures. While the nimbus is stylized, the faces of the figures are no longer generalized or conventionalized faces. Certainly the face of the satyr is as human as one could desire. In the meeting of the saints the figures are no longer stiff and straight. Instead they are bent in the saintly embrace to suggest motion and also to repeat the rhythm of the line of the cave mouth. This picture is still a far cry from the complete naturalism of the Renaissance and later. Yet we see here, as we do in Giotto's work, the breaking away from the conventions of the past.

Sculpture

For a number of reasons the art of sculpture was almost lost during the early Middle Ages, and revealed itself, as at Ravenna, in the capitals of columns, as carving for the decoration of thrones and tombs. Most of this carving is nonrepresentational, partly because of the Biblical injunction against the creation of graven images. The carving, therefore, usually consisted of symbolic figures such as those which have been mentioned earlier in the chapter on medieval symbolism.

The carving on sarcophagi, particularly during the height of feudalism, was of a much more naturalistic sort, representing the deceased person in ceremonial garments, of bishop or knight, lying in a pious posture with hands folded on chest, awaiting the heavenly journey.

It was not until the eleventh century and the triumph of the Romanesque basilica that sculpture began to come into its own again. The area called the tympanum (the area over a door and underneath an arch) offered the greatest opportunity for sculpture, and we find elaborate sculptural ideas developed in such edifices as the Abbey Church of La Madelaine at Vezelay.

This Romanesque sculpture was the beginning of the profusion of sculpture to be found in the Gothic churches. The accompanying pictures of the West Portal of Chartres Cathedral and the detail of the central portal and its tympanum suggest the wealth of sculpture in the Gothic building. On the columns themselves one finds statues of saints and kings and queens, with nonrepresentational diaper work below and on the columns between the statues. In the tympanum one sees the figure of Christ in glory in the *mandorla*, surrounded by the symbols of the authors of the four gospels. In the bands surrounding the tympanum all sorts of Biblical characters are represented.

Nor was the subject matter of sculpture limited to Biblical characters or the lives of saints. For example, on the door dedicated to the life of the Virgin, not only scenes depicting the Annunciation and the Birth of Christ, but also, surrounding the tympanum one finds figures representing the seven liberal arts, the traditional curriculum of the medieval schools and universities. The association here is that Mary (one remembers that this was the time of the Cult of the Virgin) was the master of all the liberal arts. Yet one feels that the sculptor found pleasure beyond the symbolic reference in creating these forms representing the learning of the time.

Underwood & Underwood WEST END, CATHEDRAL, CHARTRES

CATHEDRALE DE CHARTRES Ewing Galloway

One must notice that this sculptural work is not naturalistic. The figures on the columns are intentionally elongated to carry out the architectural idea; oftentimes the individual statues are squeezed to fit into the space allotted them, with a consequent loss in effect. In other words, sculpture on the Gothic cathedral was still subordinate to architecture. On the other hand, however, the Byzantine influence of mosaics and miniature painting has been assimilated, as has the inheritance from the wall decorations from the north. We see here, as in all other aspects of the Gothic church, the idea which we call the medieval synthesis.

Stained Glass

Certainly the most important of the arts except for architecture itself, was the art of the stained-glass windows of the twelfth century. As one stands within a cathedral such as the one at Chartres and sees the glory of one of the great rose windows with the lancets beneath it, glowing richly like jewels in the dark church, one realizes that this is about as close to pure beauty as man can come.

So much has been written on the art of stained glass that it is useless to do more here than picture it and make one or two suggestions about the technique. As in many other features of the cathedral, the windows were meant for religious teaching as well as beauty, and are intended to be read. The "reading" proceeds from bottom to top, reading the medallions (the fairly large sections of the windows) first across and then constantly upward. It is interesting that the donor of the window usually has left his sign, picture, or emblem at the bottom of the window before the story begins.

As for the technique of the stained glass, it is no far cry from mosaics to the creation of these windows that glorify the cathedrals and churches. The artist in glass used a technique similar to that of the cloisonné worker. He took small pieces of colored glass, fitting them into a framework of lead, to form his glowing pictures. The light of the sun streaming through these windows adds luminosity to color in a way that no other art achieves; and it is this effect of color and illumination that is the function of the stained–glass window far more than the carrying of mere pictorial effect. As Henry Adams writes, "The French held then (XII Century) that the first point in color decoration was color, and they never hesitated to put their color where they wanted it, or cared whether a green camel or a pink lion looked like a dog or a donkey provided they got their harmony or value. Everything except color was sacrificed to line in the large sense, but details of drawing were conventional and subordinate. So we laugh to see a knight with a blue face, on a green horse, that looks as though drawn by a four year old child, and probably the artist laughed too; but he was a colorist, and never sacrificed his color for a laugh."[2] Contemporary writers speak of the use of pulverized precious stones, and of fragments from mosaics, brought back by those who went on the Crusades, as giving the marvellous colors to XII Century glass. Certainly they were one of the most appealing and instructional elements of the churches; for, though the peasant, or even the nobleman, might not be able to read, he could see in the pictures the representations of the glories of heaven, the tortures of hell, and glowing examples of the Christian life on earth, not just in color, but in the living hues of light itself.

The Medieval Synthesis in the Gothic Cathedral

The Gothic cathedral is the crowning glory of the medieval period; in it one finds the stresses and strains dear to the restless North, resolved into a creation of great beauty, a synthesis of the Celto-Germanic, the Graeco-Roman, and the Byzantine-Oriental. In the pictures which follow, showing a change in the Romanesque, one can see the movement of the southern architecture toward the northern spirit.

Sant' Ambrogio in Milan represents the calmness and horizontal restfulness of the basilica structure. Later in France one sees this same basilican architecture move into the rather fortress-like structure of Notre Dame la Grande at Poitiers. One notices the rounded arches and the horizontal lines characteristic of Romanesque architecture. The profusion of sculpture on the facade and the rather stubby towers flanking the side aisles suggest the feudal fortress rather than the repose and quiet dignity of Sant' Ambrogio. The structure is still Romanesque, but the mood has changed significantly.

NOTRE DAME LA GRANDE,   Underwood & Underwood
POITIERS

At the time this development was taking place in Romanesque, a similar change was occurring in northern buildings. Moving from the stave-churches of Norway, we find the Norsemen in France constructing such edifices as Mont St. Michel on the coast of Normandy. The same thrusting, energetic spirit is still here, as it was in the early churches in Norway. This abbey church is built on a rock just off the coast of France; the material now is stone instead of wood. The goal still is for height. This is the church of St. Michel, the warrior, as much fortress as church, indeed the Church Militant. The heavenward impulse of the Middle Ages is nowhere more dramatically exemplified than in the upsurge of the Mont, which seems almost an assault on Heaven.

The top of the rock was not sliced off to provide level foundation; rather, the foundations were built out on a level with the summit to avoid sacrificing

---

[2]Henry Adams, *Mont St. Michel and Chartres*, p. 138.

COLORPLATE 6.   The Annunciation —[1333]—   Courtesy Uffizi Gallery, Florence
                Simone Martini e Lippo Memmi

COLORPLATE 7.   Empress Theodora and Retinue —[1534]—   Courtesy American Archives
                S. Vitale, Ravenna   of World Art, Inc.

COLORPLATE 8.   The Meeting of Saint Anthony and
Saint Paul by Sassetta and Assistant

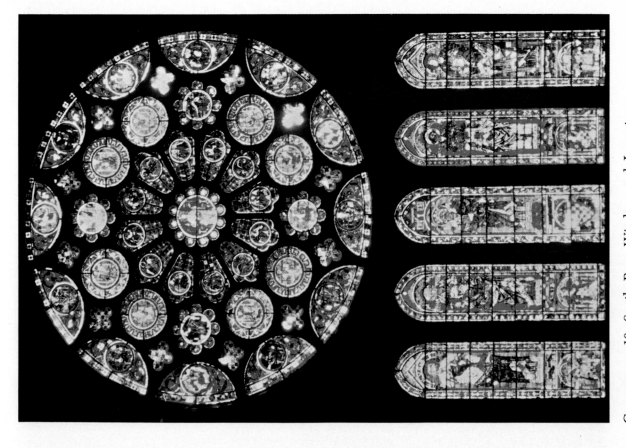

COLORPLATE 10. South Rose Window and Lancets—
Chartres Cathedral

COLORPLATE 9. Tree of Jessee—Chartres Cathedral

COLORPLATE 11. Death of the Virgin
Chartres Cathedral

Courtesy American Archives of World Art, Inc.

COLORPLATE 12. Nave, Notre Dame Cathedral, Paris
(Looking Toward Western Gallery)

1. The first question was satisfactorily dealt with when builders discovered the advantage of the pointed arch over the rounded arch. The principle of the arch is that of mutual support; the two halves lean upon each other so that the very force which would cause either half to fall is utilized to hold them upright. But the flatter the arch, the greater the "lateral thrust" at the springline—i.e., the greater sidewise push at the point it begins to turn upward. With the pointed arch, the lateral thrust is reduced; the push of its weight continues more nearly downward. Hence the more pointed the arch, the less tendency

MONT ST. MICHEL, FRANCE   Ewing Galloway

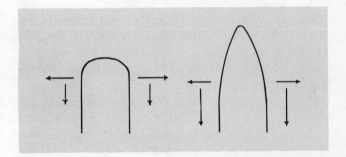

there is to push its supporting pier outwards, and the less need, consequently, to make the pier massive and heavy. Thus not only a mechanical difficulty is resolved, but an esthetic appeal is satisfied—the high, aspiring line of the leaping arch, with its greater verticality as well as height.

any height. Towers added in the thirteenth century proved too heavy and broke down the vaulting beneath. Other portions proved too weighty and collapsed their foundations in 1421. Restorations have repaired the damages, but the accidents are indicative of the restless medieval passion for height. And still, as we compare this structure with the stave-church, we are aware of a civilizing influence. The mood here has changed, as it did with the Romanesque. Gothic architecture brings these two spirits into one.

Simply as an architectural problem, the Gothic cathedral poses some difficult questions.

1. How can a building be constructed as tall as possible (in order to come literally as near to Heaven as it can, and in order to surpass the cathedrals of neighboring towns)?

2. If the height is increased, how can the weight be handled so that the wall does not buckle?

3. How can light be admitted into so vast and dark a structure, without weakening the walls?

4. How can so massive a building not only be kept from monotony, but made to serve the joint purpose of beauty and edification?

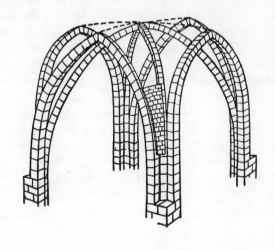

DIAGRAM SHOWING CONSTRUCTION
OF A GOTHIC VAULT

2. The pointed arch, obviously, does not eliminate weight and thrust, but merely distributes them differently. The Gothic style deals with the problem by propping or buttressing the piers of the pointed arch from the outside by means of another partial arch, known as a "flying buttress." At the springline of the pointed arch, the thrust is carried through the flying buttress outward and downward to the heavy buttresses outside the inner wall. Such support leaves space for windows in the upper walls of the nave.

3. Since most of the vertical thrust is carried by the massive central piers of the nave, there is no need for heavy masonry construction in the upper walls. Indeed, these too can be perforated and lightened by use of the pointed arch, leaving room for the tall, slender windows that are characteristic of the Gothic style. Thus the problem of "fenestration," or providing windows for admission of light into an otherwise gloomy interior, is again not merely a mechanical device, but an esthetic solution. Christian writers had always made much of the principle of light in their writings; light, radiance, provided a ready symbol for the Godhead. St. Augustine may reveal something of his Manichean background in his insistent employment of the figure of light. In any case, the structural necessity became one with the doctrinal idea in making the cathedral windows expressive of the very function of the church.

4. Huge edifices like the cathedrals, in the hands of builders who were still experimentally coping with structural problems for which they had no ready-made formula, could have become dull, factory-like structures, mechanically sound but esthetically uninteresting. That they did not is one of the triumphs of the Northern spirit in art. Rigidly limited by the nature of materials (stone, wood, glass) and held strictly by the uncompromising laws of mechanics, the builders yet managed to assert a remarkable degree of individuality within the limitations. Do the outside piers supporting the flying buttresses need weight for the downward thrust that is their function? Very well: but let that weight be disguised, by piling on their tops (adding still further to the downward thrust!) the heaven-pointing spires of crocket and finial (see illustration) carrying the eye ever upward

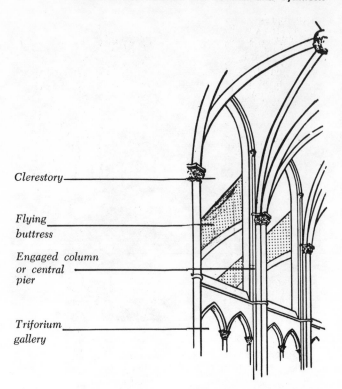

Clerestory

Flying buttress

Engaged column or central pier

Triforium gallery

THE DIAGRAM DEPICTS GOTHIC CONSTRUCTION, SHOWING THE TOP OF THE TRIFORIUM GALLERY, THE CLERESTORY (WINDOW AREA) MADE POSSIBLE BY THE USE OF THE ENGAGED COLUMNS FROM WHICH RIBS SPRING TO FORM THE CEILING VAULTING. THE SHADED AREA REPRESENTS TWO FLYING BUTTRESSES.

and adding a touch of delicacy through lacy carving. Do the slender engaged columns that are part of the central piers have a functional value in supporting weight? Good; let them also be decorative and instructive, by carving them into statues of saint and angel, Biblical and historical character, and relieved by surface-design of intricate carving. Do the lines of balustrade or cornice need relief from a too horizontal emphasis? Let them be decorated with *chimères* and grotesques (see illustration of Notre Dame cathedral) wnich not only break the horizontal, but in their very ugliness provide a contrast to the beauty of the building as a whole. And wherever stone can be cut or wood carved into beauty, let the lessons of nature, the symbols of God's world, occupy the eye and the mind of the beholder.

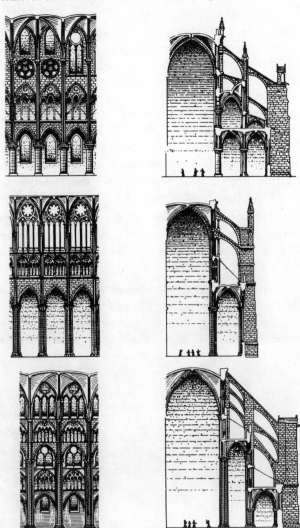

building, in its ornamentation, and by its function as a church, it reveals the medieval handling of the problem of the One and the Many, Unity and Diversity, the Particular and the General. The world is one, as an emanation from the Godhead; its parts—diverse and varied though they be—are yet related in intelligible order in the Divine Mind, an order which humans may glimpse even though they cannot wholly realize. Nothing, then, is unimportant; the little carved flower on the choir-stall, no less than the great Rose Window or the massive, heaven-soaring spires themselves, can lead man to a sense of the wholeness of the building, of life, of all creation.

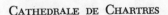

CATHEDRALE DE CHARTRES   Ewing Galloway

The cathedral, then, as the supreme work of art of the Middle Ages, is not only an architectural triumph; it is truly "the poor man's Bible," teaching in every stone and window, every carving and picture, the central concern of the life of the times. It is an expression of a way of life; the men (and women) who built it range through the entire social structure, from lord to serf; whatever their differences, here is common cause. In sheer weight of numbers, the cathedrals are enormously important: Henry Adams reports that in France alone, between 1170 and 1270, were built 80 cathedrals and nearly 500 churches of the cathedral class.[3] The cathedral is above all a concrete representation of the medieval synthesis: a strict pattern, within which is still left room for individual freedom. As a

---

[3]Henry Adams, *Mont St. Michael and Chartres*, p. 92.

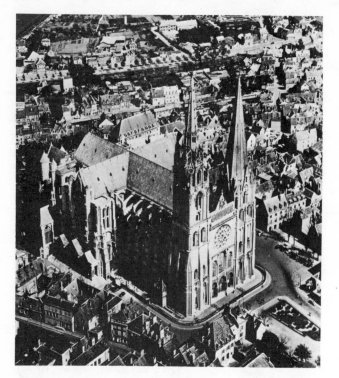

Ewing Galloway · VIEW OF CHARTRES FROM THE AIR, SHOWING CRUCIFORM STRUCTURE

Most perfect of all the medieval spires is the south tower of Chartres. The long, unbroken line from base to summit—the perfect transition from weight and massive bulk to the light, soaring pinnacle —the rightness and fitness of the whole, leave nothing to be desired. It does all that it is supposed to do, to draw the eye heavenward, and to complete its beauty in itself; and it does so without ostentation or distracting detail. There is nothing to take away, nothing to add. Here is the "medieval synthesis"; classical dignity, Gothic aspiration; the architect has given the fullest expression of his culture.

The studious ugliness of the *chimères* and grotesques is in part the humorous whim of the maker, in part the contrast to the no less studious beauty of the building as a whole.

These are purely decorative figures; there is no structural nor instructional need for them. They probably look the way they do, because someone wanted them to look that way! The carver is here free to express his own ideas, to create as he wishes.

NAVE OF CHARTRES, LOOKING EAST · Ewing Galloway

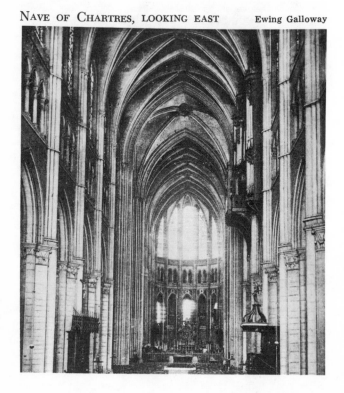

THE GRINNING DEVIL OF NOTRE DAME

Ewing Galloway

Medieval Music

Only the Christian church stood firm amidst the general confusion after the failure of Roman professionalism and the crumbling of secular authority. Along with the withdrawal to monastic life there was a movement to put the house in order, to reform and stabilize the organization of the church and to impose order on the great diversity of religious practices.

Pope Gregory I (590-604) was responsible for the organization and codification of the church's liturgical music (music associated with public worship). The unwieldy mass of traditional music, much of it of uncertain (pagan) origin, was reduced to a single large collection of melodies suitable for Christian worship.

Sacred Music

Gregorian chant[1] is the term usually applied to the nearly three thousand melodies which comprise the liturgical chant of the Roman Catholic church. Plainsong probably derives from Greek and Jewish sources. Some of the oriental characteristics can be traced to Jewish synagogue music, but similar characteristics appear in the music of ancient Greece.

The repertory of Gregorian chant falls into the two main classes of *mass* and *office*. The *mass* is the most solemn of Roman services. It represents the commemoration and symbolic repetition of the sacrifice of Christ on the cross. The *office hours* (Matins,

---

[1]Also called *plainsong* or occasionally, but more properly, *Roman chant.*

Vespers, Compline, etc.) include all the other daily services.

The mass consists of the *proper,* in which the texts vary by the liturgical calendar, and the *ordinary,* which uses the same texts throughout the church year. Both proper and ordinary have texts which are recited or spoken by the celebrants (clergy) or sung by the choir.[2] The complete mass is outlined below (italics indicate the sung portions of the text):

REFERENCE CHART: THE MASS

ORDINARY (same text)	PROPER (changing texts)
	1. *Introit*
2. *Kyrie*	
3. *Gloria*	
	4. Oratio (prayers, collect)
	5. Epistle
	6. Gradual
	7. *Alleluia* (or *Tract* during Lent)
	8. Gospel
9. *Credo*	
	10. *Offertory*
	11. Secret
	12. Preface
13. *Sanctus*	
14. Canon	
15. *Agnus dei*	
	16. *Communion*
	17. Post-communion
18. *Ite missa est* (or *Benedicamus Domino*)	

Recent modernization of the mass permits the incorporation of indigenous modern languages (in place of some of the Latin), layman participation and congregational singing. The traditional framework of the mass is not affected.

The melodies of Gregorian chant are analyzed by a theoretical system called the *eight church modes* (or *ecclesiastical modes*), a process similar to the Greater Perfect System, but in a much more simplified form. The eight church modes (also called the eight *tones*) helped categorize a body of music which had been in constant use for many centuries. Early Christian scholars tried to pattern their modal theory on the Greek model, but ended up with quite

a different system because of misconceptions resulting from an inadequate knowledge of Greek music and Greek theory.

The medieval theory of church modes still exists today, not only because of the continuing tradition of Gregorian chant, but also because thousands of secular modal melodies are still in constant use. According to modal theory (which from now on will be the church modes unless stated otherwise) there are four basic (*authentic*) modes: *Dorian, Phrygian, Lydian,* and *Mixolydian.* The four derivative (*plagal*) modes are the "lower" versions of the authentic modes: *Hypodorian, Hypophrygian, Hypolydian,* and *Hypomixolydian.*

So far this appears to follow the Greater Perfect System, but with an added *Hypomixolydian* mode. The difference becomes apparent when the systems are compared using the Hypodorian mode as an illustration:

Greater Perfect System

Hypodorian

Church Modes

Hypodorian

In the GPS the scale goes *down* in pitch (but *up* on the lyre). The ecclesiastical scale goes *up* in pitch; Gregorian chant is sung and there are no accompanying instruments. The systems go exactly in reverse throughout:

---

[2]High mass includes music; low mass usually does not.

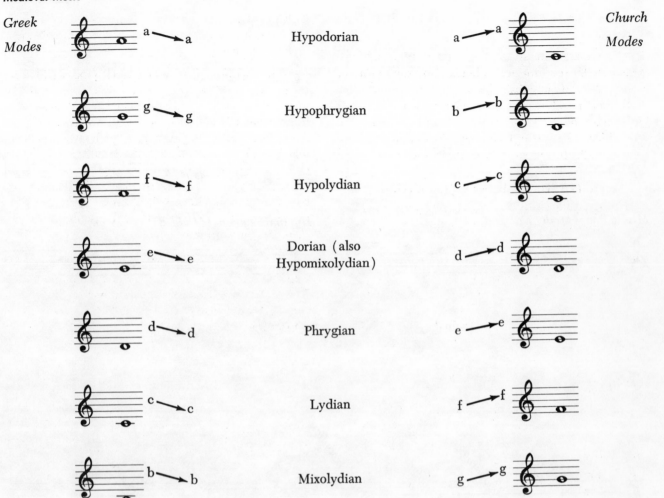

Greek Modes ... *Church Modes*

Greek Mode	Mode name	Church Mode
a → a	Hypodorian	a → a
g → g	Hypophrygian	b → b
f → f	Hypolydian	c → c
e → e	Dorian (also Hypomixolydian)	d → d
d → d	Phrygian	e → e
c → c	Lydian	f → f
b → b	Mixolydian	g → g

The church modes differ from the GPS in several other significant respects. The church modes are 1. diatonic only, 2. untransposed because there is no necessity for bringing unaccompanied vocal music within a fixed instrumental octave, and 3. tuned only in Pythagorean. Briefly stated, the manifold possibilities within the Greater Perfect System are sharply reduced to the four basic diatonic modes (Dorian, Phrygian, Lydian, Mixolydian) and one tuning.

Following is the complete modal system with accompanying explanations of the terminology:

REFERENCE CHART: CHURCH MODES

AUTHENTIC

Dorian (Mode 1)

PLAGAL

Hypodorian (Mode 2)

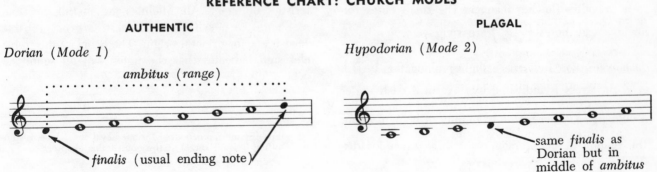

ambitus (range)

finalis (usual ending note)

same *finalis* as Dorian but in middle of *ambitus*

Phrygian (Mode 3)

Hypophrygian (Mode 4)

Lydian (Mode 5)

Hypolydian (Mode 6)

Mixolydian (Mode 7)

Hypomixolydian (Mode 8)

SUMMARY:

Number of mode

The following *Alleluias* which can be sung at Communion illustrate all eight modes as indicated by the Arabic numerals. All should be sung fairly rapidly in a smoothly flowing manner. The small notes following large notes (♩♪) are sung very lightly. A dash over a note indicates a slight prolongation (♪). A slight stress is indicated by a vertical dash under a note (♪). There is no unanimity of opinion about the singing of plainsong nor do these examples dis-play all the possibilities of performance practices; however, these eight short examples do illustrate both the complete modal system and a few of the characteristics of chant. All Alleluias are *melismatic*, several notes to a syllable, and many are of probable Jewish and/or oriental origin. The 8 below the treble clef sign indicates that the notes will all sound an octave lower.[3]

---

[3]For listening procedures for medieval music see Listening Outline (second stage) at the end of this chapter.

Gregorian Chant: *Alleluias*[4]

Total Time: 1:00

Medieval Notation

The prescribed notation for Gregorian chant is still the system developed during the Middle Ages. "For the proper execution of the chant, the manner of forming the notes and of linking them together, established by our forefathers and in constant and universal use in the Middle Ages, is of great importance and is recommended still as the norm for modern editions."[5]

Below is the previously cited Alleluia for Communion (Dorian mode) in medieval notation followed by the same chant in modern notation. These two examples obviously represent different stages of development of the same system. Because of the unique characteristics of plainsong the old notation is entirely adequate.

Gregorian Chant: *Alleluia*[6]

---

[4]*The Liber Usualis*, edited by the Benedictines of Solesmes, published by the Society of St. John the Evangelist, Desclée & Cie., printers to the Holy See and the Sacred Congregation of Rites, Tournai (Belgium), p. 96-7.

[5]*Ibid.*, p. x.

[6]*Ibid.*, p. 96.

Sacred monophonic music of the Middle Ages includes *Gregorian chant,* variations of chant such as *tropes* and *sequences,* and music associated with liturgical drama such as the *conductus.*

Gregorian Chant

Gregorian chant is *monophonic* (unison only), nonmetrical and rhythmically flexible because it is bound to the word rhythms of the text. Traditionally it is sung by a male soloist and a male chorus without accompaniment (a cappella).

The fluid and supple melodies of plainsong display a great range of melodic types and characteristics. In general, though there are many exceptions, the *range* is no more than one note larger than an octave (ninth). The melodic motion is usually stepwise (conjunct), and except for the octave large skips are quite rare.

Most chants are sung to prose texts with the great majority of these from the psalms. Other Scriptural texts are used, especially in Canticles, Introits and Graduals. The most significant non-Scriptural prose texts are in the ordinary of the mass: Kyrie, Gloria, Credo, Sanctus, Agnus Dei. In regard to text setting the melodies fall into three main classes: *syllabic* (one note to each syllable), *neumatic* (two to four notes to a syllable), and *melismatic* (still more notes to a syllable).

Following is the first item of Mass IV (also called *Missa Cunctipotens*), an example of tenth-century plainsong. The text is Greek with *Kyrie eleison* (Lord have mercy on us) sung three times (for the Holy Trinity), *Christe eleison* (Christ have mercy on us) sung three times, followed by three *Kyrie eleisons.* The chant is in mode 1 (Dorian) and is melismatic. The double dots before and after the double bars indicate that the section is to be repeated. Modal melodies do not always follow the "rules" by ending on the prescribed *finalis,* as is the case here. In terms of its musical form, the piece falls into three distinct sections which can be labeled a—b—c. All three sections have a note pattern of a—a—g—a at the beginning (commencing on the second note of section c) and sections a and b have identical cadences (ending patterns) of seven notes. Because there is no clear repetition of musical material the sectional pattern is a—b—c and the piece is described as *through-composed.*

Gregorian Chant
Kyrie IV: *Cunctipotens*[7]

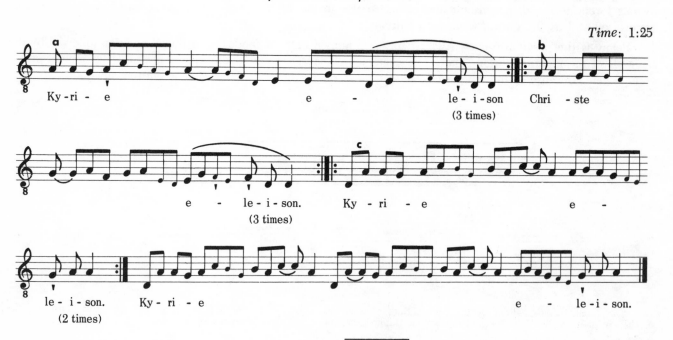

[7]*Ibid.,* p. 25.

Tropes

A *trope* (Latin, *tropus,* figure of speech) is a textual addition to an authorized text. Explanatory sentences and even whole poems were inserted between words of the original text. The longer melismatic passages which lent themselves to this procedure consequently became syllabic chants. The practice of troping reached its height during the Romanesque period, the ninth through thirteenth centuries.

Some historians explain troping as a natural desire toward continuing creativity in the face of unchanging texts authorized centuries earlier by Pope Gregory I. Another possible (and practical) explanation would consider troping as a method for remembering complicated melismatic passages. During the ninth century, and earlier, choirs had to sing the liturgy by memory after having learned the melodies by rote from monks who were sent out to the monasteries. At this time, music notation was in a low state of development and could provide only an approximation of the actual notes to be sung. Trying to remember a melody with many notes and few words must have been as trying for ninth-century musical amateurs as it is today.[8]

Troping was used most often with items of the Ordinary: Kyrie tropes, Gloria tropes and so forth. As troping became widespread it tended to overshadow some of the authorized texts with the consequence that all tropes were abolished by the Council of Trent (1543-63).

Following is the first part (section a) of the Kyrie IV illustrated above. Notes added to or removed from the original melody are indicated by parentheses.

A single Kyrie Eleison (Lord have mercy) now reads, in translation: "Omnipotent Father, Lord creator of all: have mercy upon us."

Sequences

A sequence is actually the oldest form of trope, an Alleluia trope. Many Alleluias are of oriental origin (at least in part) and end with a long melisma on the last syllable, which is where the sequence is added. This final section with its new poetry is then detached from the Alleluia to become a separate body of music. Extensive changes in the original melody are common after separation.

The sequence is of particular importance in western music because it apparently signifies the beginnings of music composition as such. From the ninth century onward there begins a gradual development of the creative individual (composer, artist, artisan) out of the collective society of the Middle Ages.

A large repertory of sequences and rhymed sequences threatened for a time to dominate traditional Gregorian chant. The Council of Trent also tried to abolish sequences, but met with such opposition that four sequences were permitted to remain in the repertory (with a fifth one, "Stabat Mater," added in 1727).

Kyrie-Trope: *Omnipotens*[9]

Time: :15

Om - ni - po-tens ge - ni -tor, De - us om - ni - um cre-a-tor: e -   lei - son.

---

[8]Guido of Arezzo (c. 995-1050) a Benedictine monk who, among other things, attempted to teach the liturgy to choirs of monks exclaimed in despair: "In our times, of all men, singers are the most foolish. . . . marvelous singers, and singer's pupils, though they sing every day for a hundred years, will never sing one antiphon, not even a short one, of themselves, without a master, losing enough time in singing to have learned thoroughly both sacred and secular letters." Oliver Strunk, *Source Readings in Music History* (New York: W. W. Norton & Company, Inc.), p. 117.

[9]A. Schubiger, *Die Sängerschule von St. Gallen* (1858), p. 40.

The oldest of the surviving sequences is the so-called Easter Sequence by Wipo (c. 1000-1050). Reproduced below is the first of four main sections of the sequence, in Dorian mode:

Sequence: *Victimae paschali laudes*[10]

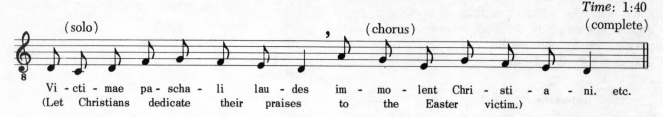

Vi - cti - mae pa - scha - li lau - des im - mo - lent Chri - sti - a - ni. etc.
(Let Christians dedicate their praises to the Easter victim.)

Liturgical Drama

Liturgical drama developed during the tenth and eleventh centuries from Introit tropes for Easter and Christmas written in dialogue form. Development continued until these plays became mysteries (fourteenth to sixteenth centuries) and finally, beginning in the sixteenth century, modern European drama.

The following excerpt from "The Play of the Three Kings" dates from about the late eleventh century. Some of the melodies were borrowed from plainsong, but some music was undoubtedly composed for the occasion. The mode is Dorian and the style, befitting a drama in which the text should be understood, is syllabic.

Liturgical Drama: *Infantem Vidimus*[11]

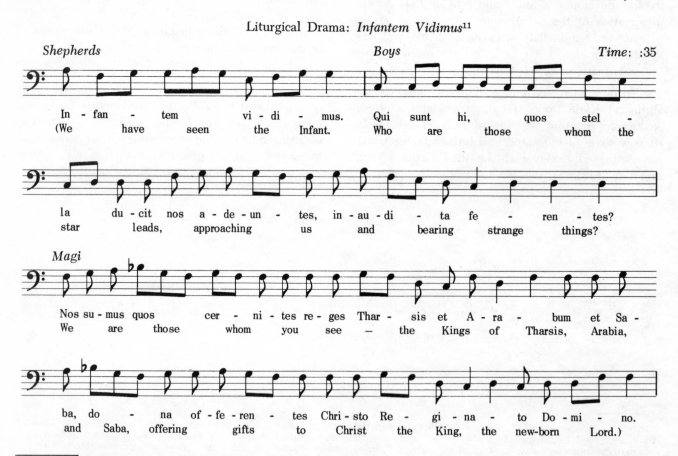

In - fan - tem vi - di - mus. Qui sunt hi, quos stel -
(We have seen the Infant. Who are those whom the

la du - cit nos a - de - un - tes, in - au - di - ta fe - ren - tes?
star leads, approaching us and bearing strange things?

Nos su - mus quos cer - ni - tes re - ges Thar - sis et A - ra - bum et Sa -
We are those whom you see — the Kings of Tharsis, Arabia,

ba, do - na of - fe - ren - tes Chri - sto Re - gi - na - to Do - mi - no.
and Saba, offering gifts to Christ the King, the new-born Lord.)

---

[10]*The Liber Usualis,* p. 780.

[11]Dom P. Schubiger, O.S.B., "Das liturgische Drama des Mittelalters und seine Musik," *Musikalische Spicilegien* (Berlin, 1876), p. 44 (citing Einsiedeln, *Stiftsbibliothek,* No. 367).

The *conductus,* a generic term for Latin lyric poetry of the twelfth and thirteenth centuries, is associated with the production of liturgical drama. It was sung as important characters in the play processed on and off the stage, for example, the Virgin Mary "conducted" on stage by an appropriate song. The conductus was the Latin counterpart of the secular style developed by troubadours and trouvères (see below under secular music).

Following is a *conductus* from "The Play of Daniel" in which the Virgin Mary is shown riding into the cathedral on an ass. The mode is Mixolydian (mode 7) and the style syllabic. A regular rhythmic organization replaces the free-flowing lines of plainsong, tropes and sequences. The conductus is *metrical* (quadruple meter in this case) as befits its function as processional music. Of the seven verses only the first verse is quoted.

Secular Music

If we are to evaluate secular music of the Middle Ages strictly on the basis of surviving manuscripts we would have to conclude that there was no secular music prior to the appearance of the first troubadour songs in c. 1100 A.D. In point of fact sacred music was written down by scholarly monks while secular music was not. The almost total dominance of the medieval church assured the preservation of accumulated knowledge which the church deemed important, and this did not include, among other things, secular music. Folk music survived as it always has (prior to modern recording techniques) solely as an oral tradition; they sang and played the notes that were never written down.

The *profession* of music could be practiced only in the church (choirs, choir masters, organists, composers) while the *practice* of music must have existed, as it has in every society, in the everyday lives of people, in their marrying, burying, working, fighting and dancing.

Troubadours

The *troubadours,* the aristocratic poet-musicians of Provence (southern France), began a tradition around 1100 A.D. which spread into northern France (*trouvères*) and Germany (*minnesingers*) before finally dying out with the *meistersingers* of sixteenth-century Germany. In a manner of speaking however, the troubadour tradition has never died out. The origins of the troubadours are obscure, but certainly bound up with the Age of Chivalry and the Crusades.

The institutions of chivalry probably began in the eleventh century as an occupation for the lower warrior class: the knights. At a time when the worst disorders of the so-called Dark Ages had ended, these warriors had little to occupy their attention since most were illiterate and theirs was a barren, isolated world of activities confined mainly to eating, drinking and fighting. Pope Urban II's call for the First Crusade in 1095 ultimately propelled Europe out of its cultural, economic and political isolation. Bored barons now had a Holy War on which to expend their energies. While the men were warring on the infidels, their women were quietly increasing their own importance in daily affairs outside the castle, which led to the development of the Virgin Cult in which women were credited with the idealized virtues of the Virgin Mary.

Conductus: *Song of the Ass*[12]

Time: :20

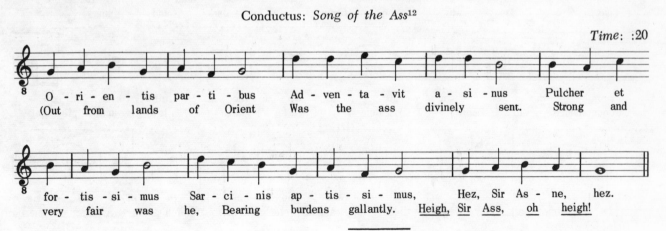

[12]G. M. Dreves, *Analecta hymnica* xx, 217, 257; H. C. Greene, *Speculum* vi.

Troubadours sang mostly of courtly love, of beautiful and virtuous ladies and brave and daring knights. Accompanied by a professional musician of the lower classes (*jongleur*, or *minstrel*) the troubadour traveled the countryside singing of love and romance and carrying the news in song between villages, manor houses, chateaus and castles.

Troubadour songs are generally *strophic*, using the same melody for each verse. The musical example below is a popular troubadour form called a *canso*. This version of the canso is made of four different phrases (called a, b, c, d) some of which are repeated to make a total of seven phrases. These seven phrases are grouped into three larger sections called

Troubadour Canso: *Be m'an perdut*[13]

Time: :45
Bernart de Ventadorn (d. 1195)

[13]C. Appel, *Bernart von Ventadorn* (Halle, 1915), Plate ix (citing Milan manuscript *Chansonnier G*, folio 14).

AAB. The following will indicate the basic plan of the piece. The lower case letters stand for the *phrase structure*, and the capital letters indicate the larger grouping called the *form* of the piece: $\begin{smallmatrix} A & A & B \\ ab, & ab, & cdb. \end{smallmatrix}$ All cansos have an AAB form. The piece given above is metrical (compound duple), but the mode is not clear because it has a strong tendency toward a diatonic scale of c–c. A number of these secular songs use this scale which will be described many centuries later as a *major scale* (c–d–e–f–g–a–b–c). Further unity is provided by a motive (labeled 1) which appears seven times. The language is Provençal, the language of medieval southern France (Provence).

Trouvères

By mid-twelfth century the troubadour influence had spread to northern France where Blondel de Nesles, minstrel to Richard-the-Lion-Hearted, was one of the first *trouvères*. Trouvère *chansons*, like the troubadour songs, were monophonic and probably unaccompanied. The *chansons*, however, were more clearly defined in their rhythmic and formal structures and in general more refined and elegant.

The following chanson is a *virelai* which has contrasting rotating patterns of words and music. The verse pattern of eight phrases can be described as *ab cd ef ab* or in larger units: $\begin{smallmatrix} A & B & C & A \\ ab & cd & ef & ab. \end{smallmatrix}$ The A section functions as a *refrain* which begins and ends the song. The music also has eight phrases, with a phrase structure of *ab cc ab ab*. Using larger units this can be described as $\begin{smallmatrix} A & B & A & A \\ ab & cc & ab & ab. \end{smallmatrix}$ There is a characteristic rhythmic pattern which appears twelve times: ♪♪ ♩ ♩. This virelai, in common with many trouvère songs, uses a scale of f–g–a–b♭–c–d–e–f. This can only be described as a clearcut *major mode*.[14]

Minnesingers

The German *minnesinger* tradition began about a century after the appearance of the first troubadour songs in Provence and persisted long after French secular music had changed to other forms. In medieval German *minne* means "love," but most *minnelieder* (literally "love songs") texts incline toward rather melancholy narration with much less concern for the amorous life. In keeping with German conservatism, minnelieder make less use of regular meters and more

use of the church modes. The favorite form was the *barform* (A–A–B), or exactly the same form used by troubadour *cansos* and trouvère *ballades*.[15]

Goliards

The *goliards* of the tenth through thirteenth centuries were wandering students, vagabonds, defrocked monks, minstrels, rascals, artists and dreamers, the medieval equivalent of today's disenchanted youth. Only one goliard melody was written in a musical notation which could be deciphered, but large collections of their poetry have been preserved, including the famous collection called "Carmina Burana." A sampling of the opening lines of a few poems from "Carmina Burana" clearly indicates the themes of most of their poetry:

"O fortune, variable as the moon"

"I lament fortune's blows"

"Were the world all mine from the sea to the Rhine, I would gladly forsake it all if the Queen of England were in my arms"

"In rage and bitterness I talk to myself"

"I am the Abbot of Cluny, and I spend my time with drinkers"

---

[14]The *major mode* differs from the church modes in two respects: 1. it has a *fixed* pattern of tones and semitones, and 2. there is only *one* major mode. In other words, a piece is in major or it is not.

A major scale is composed of two equal tetrachords (T–T–S) joined by a whole step:

C Major   F Major

The alter ego of the major is the *minor mode*, the other basic structure which makes up the so-called *major-minor system* which, during the seventeenth century, superseded the church modes. In the major-minor system all music is in either major or in minor. The eight church modes are reduced, in other words, to two: major or minor.

C major

C minor

[15]*Barform* is from the medieval German name, i.e., a "bar" has a form of A–A–B. The form is as old as the ancient Greek modes and persists to the present day, particularly in Lutheran chorales, for example, "A Mighty Fortress Is Our God." The same form is also used in the poetry of the *blues*.

Trouvère *Virelai: Or la truix*[16]

Time: :45

Or la truix trop du - re te, voir, voir! A ceu k'elle		
I find it hard to woo her, in - deed! Be - cause she		

est sim - ple te. Trop por ou - tre - cui - diés me taius,
is so simple. Much too presumptuous did I act,

cant je cu - doie es - tre cer - tains de ceu ke n'a ve-
E'n tho' it seem'd I was so sure of that which I shan't

rai des mois, oix, oix! C'est ceu - ke plus me ble - ce.
have so soon, a - las! T'is most - ly that which hurts me.

Or la truix trop du - re te, voir,
I find it hard to woo her, in -

voir! A ceu k'elle est sim - ple te.
deed! Because she is so simple.

"When we are in the tavern we don't care who has died"

"The God of Love flies everywhere"

"When a boy and a girl are alone together"

"Sweetest boy I give myself completely to you"

"Hail to thee, most beautiful"[17]

Harmony

At some unknown time and place during the eighth or ninth centuries (probably), experiments were begun which led to new directions in music. At this time, the entire liturgy consisted of mono-

[16]Bodleian Oxford, Douce 308, folio 226 and 237.
[17]Hans Spanke, "Der Codex Buranus als Liederbuch," *Zeitschrift für Musikwissenschaft* xiii (1931), p. 241.

phonic song, that is, Gregorian chant. What would happen if there were two or even three melodies sung at the same time? Text, rhythm, mode and timbre could possibly remain the same, but there would be one or more additional melodies. And so began the crude attempts at what became, by the sixteenth century, a vast repertory of complex and sophisticated music consisting essentially of four, six or even eight plainsongs sung simultaneously, and all skillfully blended to become the magnificent choral music of the High Renaissance.

The technique of writing simultaneous melodies is called *counterpoint,* and the resulting musical style is *polyphony. Counterpoint* (Latin, *punctus contra punctum,* note against note) is the skill involved in combining melodies, of putting "note against note." *Polyphony* (Greek, *poly,* many; *phonos,* voice) is a style of composition in which two or more melodies are sung or sounded together. The one-voice (monophonic) chant becomes a many-voiced composition (polyphonic).

Polyphony can be described as the *horizontal* aspect of harmony:

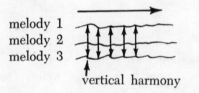

There is also a *vertical* harmony present in all polyphonic music inasmuch as notes are actually sounded together:

Emphasis on the vertical relationships of harmony did not develop until the seventeenth century.

Organum

Early polyphonic music was called *organum,* possibly in reference to the fact that the music was an "organized" addition to plainsong. Composers selected melodies from the liturgy and added notes below at a fixed interval.

Strict Organum

Organum of the Fifth: Beginning with a chant in Dorian mode, for example, composers added a

second voice a fifth below. The two voices then moved in parallel lines throughout, in *parallel fifths.*

Organum of the Fourth: The same principle was applied, but with the organizing voice a perfect fourth (P4) below the original plainsong melody.

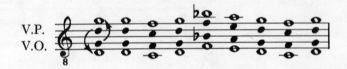

Composite Organum of the Fifth: Four parts could be obtained by writing organum of the fifth and then duplicating the *vox principalis* an octave lower and the *vox organalis* an octave higher.

Composite Organum of the Fourth: A different sound for four parts was produced by beginning with the interval of the perfect fourth.

V.P.
V.O.

The practice of strict organum probably did not last too long because composers sought ways of freeing the added melody from its strict dependence on the original chant. Their experiments included three different ways of achieving some independence for the added voice: *parallel, free* and *melismatic* organum.

Parallel Organum

The voices began together (in unison) after which the original plainsong moved up until it was a fourth above the organal voice and the two voices could move in parallel fourths. The voices came together to make a unison at cadences. This combined oblique and parallel motion can be diagrammed as follows:

and notated as follows:

Parallel Organum
Sequence: *Rex caeli, Domine*[18]

Free Organum

In their search for ways to make the added melody more independent composers hit on the idea of *contrary motion* (referred to as *free organum*). When the plainsong went *up* in pitch the organal voice would go *down* in pitch and vice versa, an idea which is still valid in polyphonic music. When the voices coincided (sounded notes together) the intervals were usually the preferred ones of octave, fifth, fourth or unison, all *perfect consonances* (as in Greek music). Voices could coincide on *thirds,* but these were *dissonances* at this time.

Following is an example of *free* (contrary motion) *organum.* The first and last sections of this piece are the original plainsong with *Agnus Dei* text. The music between the double bars is the Agnus Dei *trope.* When note stems go *up* the top voice (original chant) is indicated even though it is not always the higher voice. Stems go *down* to indicate the lower (organal) voice. The *intervals* formed where the two voices coincide are indicated by Arabic numerals above the staff. For a considerable length of time it was the custom for the choir to sing the plainsong and soloists the organum, and for obvious reasons: organum was harder to sing correctly. The piece is in mode 7 (Mixolydian).

――――――――――――

[18]M. Gerbert, *Scriptores* i (St. Blaise, 1784), p. 167.

Free Organum
Trope: *Agnus Dei*[19]

Time: :40
12th century

A - gnus De - i   qui tol - lis pec - ca - ta   mun - di; qui _____

_____   pi - us   es   fa - ctus,

pro - tho   plau - sti - sa - net   ut   a _____

ctus: mi - se - re - re   no - bis.

Melismatic Organum

Compositions in *melismatic organum* moved the original chant melody from the upper to the lower voice and made each note considerably longer in value. The organal (now the upper) voice sang elaborate melismas against the lower voice. The slowed-down chant is now called the *tenor* (Latin, *tenere*, to hold), because it "holds" onto the chant. The proper consonant intervals (unison, P4, P5, P8) occur where the voices coincide. Otherwise the top voice moves freely as a newly composed melody.

The following is a portion of melismatic organum in which the *tenor* holds each note so long that there are only eight notes in the tenor to eighty-five notes in the organal voice. The |o| indicates either a double whole-note or, as in this case, a long note of indefinite time value. The original chant was in Dorian mode, therefore the entire composition, solely on the basis of the tenor, is considered to be in the

Dorian mode. Determining the mode of a piece by the tenor line became the established method throughout the polyphonic period, through the sixteenth century. The piece is through-composed, but there are several motivic patterns in the organal voice.

Development of Polyphony

Beginning with the twelfth-century, polyphonic writing underwent rapid development. The notation of rhythm was improved by composers associated with the cathedral of Notre Dame in Paris as they began writing three-part compositions. Borrowing rhythmic modes from poetry (trochaic, iambic, dactylic, etc.) they wrote metrical music with two voices

_____

[19]Besseler, *Die Musik des Mittelalters* (Potsdam, 1931), p. 95.

Melismatic Organum: *Benedicamus Domino*[20]

Time: :35
12th century

etc.

above an elongated tenor. The tenor was now so drawn-out that it was usually played by an organ, the only instrument which could sustain the notes.

Organum: *Alleluya* (*Nativitas*)[21]

Time: 2:00
(Complete)
Perotin (12th century)

Triplum
(Treble)
Duplum

Tenor
(Instru-
ment)

etc.

Organs were used extensively in Byzantium during the early Middle Ages (along with kitharas and aulos) and were probably introduced into the western church during the ninth century. Since about the tenth century pipe organs have been the principle instrument for church music.

---

[20]F. Ludwig, transcription in G. Adler, *Handbuch der Musikgeschichte* (Frankfurt am Main, 1924), p. 148.
[21]Y. Rokseth, *Polyphonies du XIIIe sièclei* (Paris, 1935).

Motet

The *motet*, one of the most important forms of sacred music was developed in the thirteenth century. The text given in the example below in the tenor indicates only the source of the borrowed plainsong because the line is now played by an instrument. Above the tenor is a composed line with its own set of words, hence the name *motetus* (French, *le mot*, the word). The top voice, or *triplum* (treble) also had its own set of words which could be a different poem or even a different language. Increasing secularization led to motets such as the one illustrated with variations on the same love song (with borrowings from a trouvère song) sung in French by the *Triplum* and *Motetus*. The preferred consonances are still unison, P4, P5 and P8, but these apply only between adjoining voices. Strong dissonances against the third voice are common. The piece is in Dorian mode because the original plainsong was in mode 1. Titles of motets are given by using the opening lines of all three texts including the line that is played rather than sung. The meter is compound duple.

Motet

School of Notre Dame: *En non Diu!   Quant voi; Eius in Oriente*[22]   *Time*: 1:00
                                                                                              (Complete)

Secular Polyphonic Music

Secular influences became increasingly strong during the thirteenth and fourteenth centuries of the Gothic period. In addition to the secular texts of the motets there were polyphonic settings of the old troubadour-trouvère melodies and a growing literature of instrumental music for dancing. The *estampie* (Provençal, *estamper*, to stamp) was the most popular dance of the Gothic Age and also one of the oldest forms of instrumental music. It appeared in both monophonic and polyphonic versions. The monophonic *estampie* was usually performed by *pipe* and *tabor*.

The *pipe* was a *flageolet*, or small flute with three tone holes. It was held by the left hand and played by blowing directly into the mouthpiece. With his other hand the instrumentalist played a *tabor*, or small drum, and thus functioned as a one-man dance band.

The following monophonic *ductia* (shortened version of the *estampie*) is in the standard triple meter and *aa bb cc* form of the dance. The brackets above the numerals 1 and 2 are first and second endings. After the twelve-bar section a is played completely through the first ending, the section is repeated from the beginning, played through the second ending (omitting the first ending) and continued on into the next section.

Each of the three sections (a, b, c) is composed of three phrases of four bars each (4 + 4 + 4). Each section is repeated to give the complete form of *aa bb cc*. The phrase structure and form would diagram as follows:

---

[22]*Ibid.*

Section a 4 + 4 + 4 :‖ 4 ‖ (aa)

Section b 4 + 4 + 4 :‖ 4 ‖ (bb)

Section c 4 + 4 + 4 :‖ 4 ‖ (cc)

There is a b-flat standing after the clef sign at the beginning of each line. The b-flat is a *key signature* and indicates that every b in the piece is to be played as a b-flat. The practical reason for using a key signature is to avoid writing in so many sharps or flats, in this case, a flat in front of every b in the piece. The mode of the piece is *transposed Dorian* (g to g with a b-flat). With the rise again of instrumental music, the practice of transposing to fit instrumental ranges will obviously increase. *Dorian on g* (g Dorian) has the same arrangement of tones and semitones as *Dorian on d* (d Dorian):

g - a - b♭ - c - d - e - f - g

T S T T T S T

d - e - f - g - a - b - c - d

Ductia: *Danse Royale*[23]

Time: 1:05
13th century

———————

[23]P. Aubry, *Estampies et danses royales* (1906), p. 14.

Other instruments introduced into Gothic secular music included imports of Near Eastern origin such as the *lute, gittern, rebec, shawm* and *bagpipe*. The *lute* is a plucked string instrument with a pear-shaped body and a mellow resonant tone. It became the most popular instrument of the Renaissance.

The *gittern* (Greek, *kithara*) was a plucked string instrument with a boxlike body and a sharp bright tone. It was replaced by the *vihuela da mano* and in the fifteenth century by the *Spanish guitar*. Both the lute and gittern are mentioned for the first time in the thirteenth century epic poem *La Roman de la rose*.

The *rebec* (Arabian, *rabab*) was a bowed string instrument, or *fiddle*. Its most important characteristic was the sustained tone produced by bowing. Later developments led through the *vielle* to the *viol* to the modern *violin*.

The *shawm*, a loud double reed instrument, was a relative of the *aulos*. In conjunction with trumpets it was used mostly for ceremonial music. It was eventually replaced by the milder-toned *oboe*.

The *bagpipe*, of probable oriental or Near Eastern origin, appears in most cultures and is used for just about everything.

During the late fourteenth century the *flageolet* was replaced by a more developed form called the *recorder* which, in turn, was supplanted by the modern *flute* four centuries later.

Below is a two-part *estampie* with the parts labeled only as *Cantus Superior* and *Cantus Inferior*. They were to be played by any instruments that were available, a common practice in instrumental music until the eighteenth century. A partial key signature is used because the lower voice used b-flats while the upper part did not. The piece is in the major mode on f (F Major). The form of the complete piece is *a–b–c–c–c* of which only section a is given. It has two phrases of eight bars each (8 + 8).

The small note with a diagonal line through its stem (♪) in the example above is called a *grace note*. It is an ornamental embellishment of the melody and is played very rapidly. It is considered to have no time value although it does take a portion of the time value of the note which precedes it.

The Polyphonic Mass

As musical styles developed and flourished during the Gothic period, individual composers began

Estampie: Instrumental Dance[24]

Time: 1:20
13th century

[24]Wooldridge, *Early English Harmony* (London, 1897), plate 19.

achieving international reputations. Guillaume de Machaut, almost equally gifted as poet and composer of both sacred and secular music, is one of the first of the highly gifted artists who prepared the way for the so-called Renaissance man. He was the first to write a complete polyphonic setting of the ordinary of the Mass, a practice which was followed by every major composer through the sixteenth century and by many composers up to the present day.

The *tenor* of masses and motets is now referred to as the *cantus firmus* (fixed song). In its use as a basis for composition this pre-existing melody still stands as a kind of medieval authority for the composition of polyphonic sacred music. In many cases however, the *cantus firmus* is derived from a secular melody and the authority reduced to a convention, thus reflecting the waning of ecclesiastical control.

The selection below from Machaut's setting of the Mass illustrates several musical techniques:

1. *Syncopation.* This term refers to the deliberate disturbance of a normal beat and/or accent pattern. This is achieved by placing accents in unexpected places and/or by removing them from expected places. In a grouping of 8 eighth notes the expected accents would be on 1 and 5 .

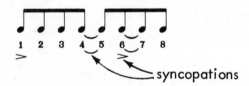

The rhythmic pattern below in measures two and four avoids the expected accent on the 5th eighth

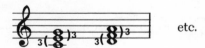

note (because of the tie) and shifts it over to the 6th eighth note (tied to the 7th eighth note) to give an off-beat accent to the music.

2. *Triadic harmony.* The *triad* is a harmonic construction, or *chord* which is made up of two or more superimposed thirds, for example, a third added above a bottom note (called the *root*) and another third added on top of that:

   etc.

The two thirds total up to a fifth $(3 + 3 = 5!)$ because the note in the middle is counted twice. *Tertiary harmony* (chords built in thirds) became the norm for composers until well into the twentieth century. In the Machaut piece triads are used in the middle of phrases and sections. The open chord of fifth plus

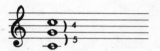

fourth is standard for beginning and ending sections but another century will see this open sound filled in to become a *triad* (plus an octave duplication for four part harmony):

3. *Cadences. Cadences* of this period frequently use a *double leading tone.* Two voices lead into the final chord by means of the smallest interval of a *half step* (semitone). In measures 6 and 7 e is a *leading tone* moving to f, and b leads to c: The symbol ⌒ is called a *fermata* and indicates a pause of indefinite length.

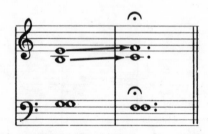

The following portion of the *Agnus Dei* is sung by the upper three voices and accompanied by an instrument on the *contratenor* part (as indicated by the absence of text). The mixed vocal-instrumental texture is characteristic of pre-Renaissance music.

Following is an outline of the major developments in music during the Middle Ages. The chart is of course greatly simplified in order to indicate general trends rather than details. Each period, style, and so forth begins approximately with the first letter of the word or phrase although there is no necessity for pinpointing precise dates even when they are

Mass: *Agnus Dei*[25]

Time: 1:20
(Complete)
Guillaume de Machaut (c. 1300-c. 1377)

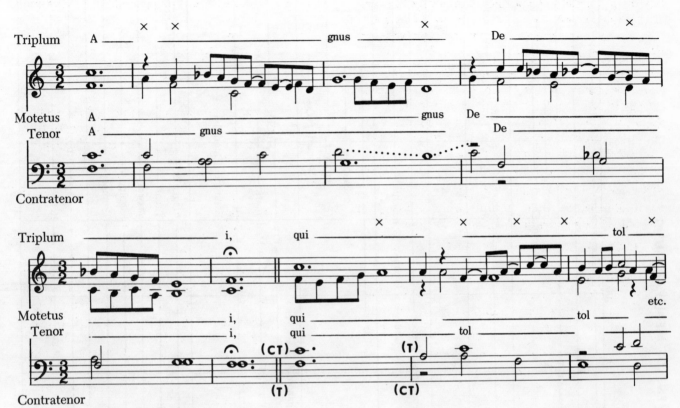

× = *triad*. (The notes of a triad may be moved up an octave without essentially affecting the triad sound, as in the first chord of measure 2).

known. Dotted lines indicate either prior development leading up to a specific musical instrument or, as with monasticism, the dissolution or waning influence of the institution. Arrows indicate continuing development or, as with the connection between feudalism and chivalry, one institution developing out of another.

LISTENING OUTLINE (2ND STAGE)

Note: This and subsequent outlines should be considered as guides to listening; they represent the *maximum* of things to listen for. There is no expectation that everyone or even anyone can actually hear all these items; however, one can follow the music with the outline and learn to systematize and objectify listening procedures.

1. Listening Outline
   a. Medium and Number of Performers
      (1) Vocal (specify voice parts)
          Text
      (2) Instrumental (specify instruments)
      (3) Combination (specify)
   b. Texture
      (1) Monophonic, homophonic, polyphonic, combination
      (2) Number of actual parts or voices (not necessarily the same as the number of performers)

[25]H. Besseler, *Die Musik des Mittelalters und der Renaissance* (Bücken, *Handbuch der Musikwissenschaft*), Potsdam, 1931, p. 149.

DEVELOPMENT OF MEDIEVAL MUSIC

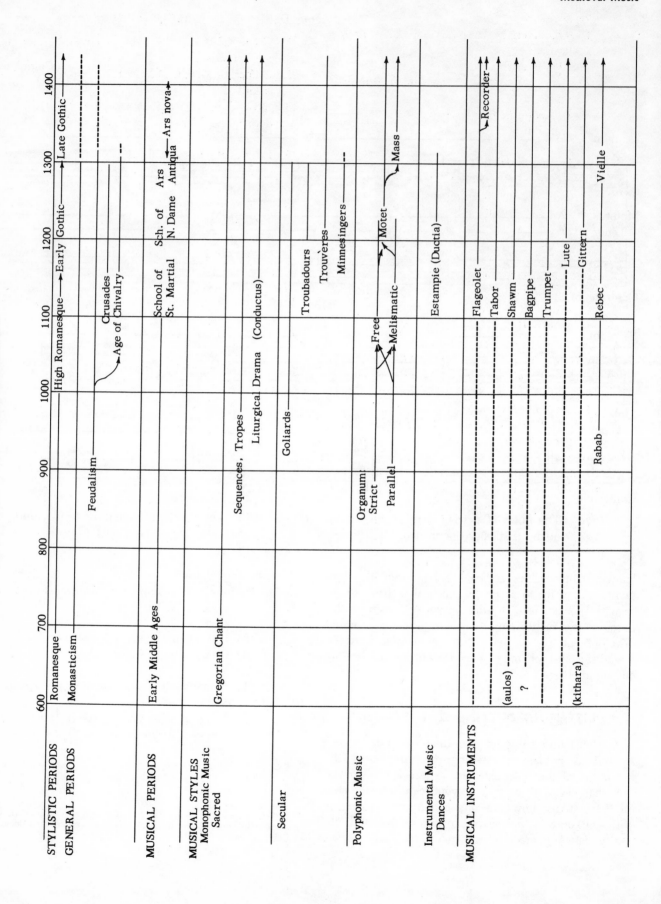

c. Construction
    (1) Characteristic intervals (melodic and/or harmonic)
    (2) Characteristic harmonies
    (3) Types of cadences (Landini, Burgundian, other)
        (a) Intermediate
        (b) Final
d. Form
    (1) Sacred, secular
    (2) Music: through-composed, barform, other
    (3) Text: through-composed, repeated, strophic, verse-refrain, other
e. Tonality
    (1) Modal
    (2) Major-minor
f. Notation (determined from the score)
    (1) Clef, time signature, tempo indication (if any)
g. Miscellaneous

2. Conclusions
    a. Possible Period: Ancient (600 B.C.-100 A.D.); Roman (100-600); Romanesque (600-1000); High Romanesque (1000-1150); Early Gothic (1150-1350); Late Gothic (1350-1450).
    b. Possible Style: Greek song, Gregorian chant, sequence, trope, liturgical drama, conductus, troubadour song, trouvère song, minnesinger song, goliard song, estampie, strict organum, parallel organum, free organum, melismatic organum, motet, mass movement.
    c. Possible National Origin: Greece, Rome, western Europe, northern France, southern France (Provence), Germany, Italy, other.

RECORD LIST

1. Gregorian Chant, "Eight Alleluias," apparently not recorded.
2. Gregorian Chant, "Kyrie IV: Cunctipotens," not recorded.
3. Kyrie-Trope: "Omnipotens," not recorded.
4. Sequence, "Victimae paschali laudes," *Masterpieces* (see Record List for Chapter 5).
5. Liturgical Drama: "Infantem vidimus," *Treasury of Early Music*, 4. volumes, Haydn Society 9100/9103; S-9100/9103 (referred to as *Treasury*).
6. Conductus: "Song of the Ass," not recorded.
7. Troubadour Canso: "Be m'an perdut," *Treasury*.
8. Trouvère Virelai: "Or la truix," *Masterpieces*.
9. Parallel Organum, Sequence: "Rex caeli Domino," *Masterpieces*.
10. Free Organum; Trope: "Agnus Dei," *Masterpieces*.
11. Melismatic Organum: "Benedicamus Domino," *Masterpieces*.
12. Perotin, Organum: "Alleluya (Nativitas)," *Masterpieces*.
13. School of Notre Dame, Motet: "En non Diu! Quant voi; Eius in Oriente," *Masterpieces*.
14. Ductia: "Danse Royale," not recorded.
15. Estampie: "Instrumental Dance," *Masterpieces*.
16. Machaut, Mass: "Agnus Dei," *Masterpieces*.

Also Recommended:

Music of Medieval France, Sacred and Secular (1200-1400), Bach Guild BG—656.
Ten Centuries of Music, 10—DGG KL—52/61; SKL—152/161.

Everyman

CHARACTERS

Everyman, God (Adonai), Death, Messenger, Fellowship, Cousin, Kindred, Goods, Good-Deeds, Discretion, Strength, Five-Wits, Beauty, Knowledge, Confession, Angel, Doctor.

HERE BEGINNETH A TREATISE HOW THE HIGH FATHER OF HEAVEN SENDETH DEATH TO SUMMON EVERY CREATURE TO COME AND GIVE ACCOUNT OF THEIR LIVES IN THIS WORLD AND IS IN MANNER OF A MORAL PLAY.

MESSENGER:
I pray you all give your audience,
And hear this matter with reverence,
By figure a moral play—
The *Summoning of Everyman* called it is,
That of our lives and ending shows
How transitory we be all day.
This matter is wondrous precious,
But the intent of it is more gracious,
And sweet to bear away.
The story saith,—Man, in the beginning,
Look well, and take good heed to the ending,
Be you never so gay!
Ye think sin in the beginning full sweet,
Which in the end causeth thy soul to weep,
When the body lieth in clay.
Here shall you see how *Fellowship* and *Jollity*,
Both *Strength, Pleasure,* and *Beauty,*
Will fade from thee as flower in May.
For ye shall hear, how our heaven king
Calleth *Everyman* to a general reckoning:
Give audience, and hear what he doth say.

GOD:
I perceive here in my majesty,
How that all creatures be to me unkind,
Living without dread in worldly prosperity:
Of ghostly sight the people be so blind,
Drowned in sin, they know me not for their God;
In worldly riches is all their mind,
They fear not my rightwiseness, the sharp rod;
My law that I shewed, when I for them died,
They forget clean, and shedding of my blood red;
I hanged between two, it cannot be denied;
To get them life I suffered to be dead;
I healed their feet, with thorns hurt was my head:

I could do no more than I did truly,
And now I see the people do clean forsake me.
They use the seven deadly sins damnable;
As pride, covetise, wrath, and lechery,
Now in the world be made commendable;
And thus they leave of angels the heavenly company;
Everyman liveth so after his own pleasure,
And yet of their life they be nothing sure:
I see the more that I them forbear
The worse they be from year to year;
All that liveth appaireth[1] fast,
Therefore I will in all the haste
Have a reckoning of Everyman's person
For and I leave the people thus alone
In their life and wicked tempests,
Verily they will become much worse than beasts;
For now one would by envy another up eat;
Charity they all do clean forget.
I hoped well that Everyman
In my glory should make his mansion,
And thereto I had them all elect;
But now I see, like traitors deject,
They thank me not for the pleasure that I to them
    meant
Nor yet for their being that I them have lent;
I proffered the people great multitude of mercy,
And few there be that asketh it heartily;
They be so combered with worldly riches,
That needs on them I must do justice,
On Everyman living without fear.
Where art thou, Death, thou mighty messenger?

DEATH:
Almighty God, I am here at your will,
Your commandment to fulfil.

GOD:
Go thou to Everyman,
And show him in my name
A pilgrimage he must on him take,
Which he in no wise may escape;
And that he bring with him a sure reckoning
Without delay or any tarrying.

DEATH:
Lord, I will in the world go run over all,
And cruelly outsearch both great and small;
Every man will I beset that liveth beastly
Out of God's laws, and dreadeth not folly:
He that loveth riches I will strike with my dart,
His sight to blind, and from heaven to depart,

---

[1] Is impaired.

Except that alms be his good friend,
In hell for to dwell, world without end.
Lo, yonder I see Everyman walking;
Full little he thinketh on my coming;
His mind is on fleshly lusts and his treasure,
And great pain it shall cause him to endure
Before the Lord Heaven King.
Everyman, stand still; whither art thou going
Thus gaily? Hast my Maker forgot?

EVERYMAN:
Why askst thou?
Wouldest thou wete?[2]

DEATH:
Yea, sir, I will show you;
In great haste I am sent to thee
From God out of his majesty.

EVERYMAN:
What, sent to me?

DEATH:
Yea, certainly.
Though thou have forget him here,
He thinketh on thee in the heavenly sphere,
As, or we depart, thou shalt know.

EVERYMAN:
What desireth God of me?

DEATH:
That shall I show thee;
A reckoning he will needs have
Without any longer respite.

EVERYMAN:
To give a reckoning longer leisure I crave;
This blind matter troubleth my wit.

DEATH:
On thee thou must take a long journey:
Therefore thy book of count with thee thou bring;
For turn again thou can not by no way,
And look thou be sure of thy reckoning:
For before God thou shalt answer, and show
Thy many bad deeds and good but a few;
How thou hast spent thy life, and in what wise,
Before the chief lord of paradise.
Have ado that we were in that way,
For, wete thou well, thou shalt make none attournay.[3]

EVERYMAN:
Full unready I am such reckoning to give.
I know thee not: what messenger art thou?

DEATH:
I am Death, that no man dreadeth.
For every man I rest and no man spareth;
For it is God's commandment
That all to me should be obedient.

EVERYMAN:
O Death, thou comest when I had thee least in mind,
In thy power it lieth me to save,
Yet of my good will I give thee, if ye will be kind,
Yea, a thousand pound shalt thou have,
And defer this matter till another day.

DEATH:
Everyman, it may not be by no way;
I set not by gold, silver, nor riches,
Ne by pope, emperor, king, duke, ne princes.
For and I would receive gifts great,
All the world I might get;
But my custom is clean contrary.
I give thee no respite: come hence, and not tarry.

EVERYMAN:
Alas, shall I have no longer respite?
I may say Death giveth no warning:
To think on thee, it maketh my heart sick,
For all unready is my book of reckoning.
But twelve year and I might have abiding,
My counting book I would make so clear,
That my reckoning I should not need to fear.
Wherefore, Death, I pray thee, for God's mercy,
Spare me till I be provided of remedy.

DEATH:
Thee availeth not to cry, weep, and pray:
But haste thee lightly that you were gone the journey.
And prove thy friends if thou can.
For, wete thou well, the tide abideth no man,
And in the world each living creature
For Adam's sin must die of nature.

EVERYMAN:
Death, if I should this pilgrimage take,
And my reckoning surely make,
Show me, for saint charity,
Should I not come again shortly?

---

[2]Know.
[3]Mediator.

DEATH:
No, Everyman; and thou be once there,
Thou mayst never more come here,
Trust me verily.

EVERYMAN:
O gracious God, in the high seat celestial,
Have mercy on me in this most need;
Shall I have no company from this vale terrestrial
Of mine acquaintance that way me to lead?

DEATH:
Yea, if any be so hardy,
That would go with thee and bear thee company.
Hie thee that you were gone to God's magnificence,
Thy reckoning to give before his presence.
What, weenest thou thy life is given thee,
And thy worldly goods also?

EVERYMAN:
I had wend so, verily.

DEATH:
Nay, nay; it was but lent thee;
For as soon as thou art go,
Another awhile shall have it, and then go therefro
Even as thou has done.
Everyman, thou art mad; thou hast thy wits five,
And here on earth will not amend thy life,
For suddenly I do come.

EVERYMAN:
O wretched caitiff, whither shall I flee,
That I might scape this endless sorrow!
Now, gentle Death, spare me till to-morrow,
That I may amend me
With good advisement.

DEATH:
Nay, thereto I will not consent,
Nor no man will I respite,
But to the heart suddenly I shall smite
Without any advisement.
And now out of thy sight I will me hie;
See thou make thee ready shortly,
For thou mayst say this is the day
That no man living may scape away.

EVERYMAN:
Alas, I may well weep with sighs deep;
Now have I no manner of company
To help me in my journey, and me to keep;
And also my writing is full unready.
How shall I do now for to excuse me?

I would to God I had never be gete![4]
To my soul a full great profit it had be;
For now I fear pains huge and great.
The time passeth; Lord, help that all wrought;
For though I mourn it availeth nought.
The day passeth, and is almost a-go;
I wot not well what for to do.
To whom were I best my complaint to make?
What, and I to Fellowship thereof spake,
And showed him of this sudden chance?
For in him is all mine affiance;
We have in the world so many a day
Be on good friends in sport and play.
I see him yonder, certainly;
I trust that he will bear me company;
Therefore to him will I speak to ease my sorrow.
Well met, good Fellowship, and good morrow!

FELLOWSHIP:
Everyman, good morrow by this day.
Sir, why lookest thou so piteously?
If any thing be amiss, I pray thee, me say,
That I may help to remedy.

EVERYMAN:
Yea, good Fellowship, yea,
I am in great jeopardy.

FELLOWSHIP:
My true friend, show to me your mind;
I will not forsake thee, unto my life's end,
In the way of good company.

EVERYMAN:
That was well spoken, and lovingly.

FELLOWSHIP:
Sir, I must needs know your heaviness;
I have pity to see you in any distress;
If any have ye wronged he shall revenged be,
Though I on the ground be slain for thee—
Though that I know before that I should die.

EVERYMAN:
Verily, Fellowship, gramercy.

FELLOWSHIP:
Tush! by thy thanks I set not a straw;
Show me your grief, and say no more.

EVERYMAN:
If I my heart should to you break,
And then you to turn your mind from me,

---

[4]Been gotten, been born.

And would not me comfort, when you hear me speak,
Then should I ten times sorrier be.

FELLOWSHIP:
Sir, I say as I will do in deed.

EVERYMAN:
Then be you a good friend at need:
I have found you true here before.

FELLOWSHIP:
And so ye shall evermore;
For, in faith, and thou go to Hell,
I will not forsake thee by the way!

EVERYMAN:
Ye speak like a good friend; I believe you well;
I shall deserve it, and I may.

FELLOWSHIP:
I speak of no deserving, by this day.
For he that will say and nothing do
Is not worthy with good company to go;
Therefore show me the grief of your mind,
As to your friend most loving and kind.

EVERYMAN:
I shall show you how it is;
Commanded I am to go a journey,
A long way, hard and dangerous,
And give a strait count without delay
Before the high judge Adonai.[5]
Wherefore I pray you, bear me company,
As ye have promised, in this journey.

FELLOWSHIP:
That is matter indeed! Promise is duty,
But, and I should take such a voyage on me,
I know it well, it should be to my pain:
Also it make me afeard, certain.
But let us take counsel here as well as we can,
For your words would fear a strong man.

EVERYMAN:
Why, ye said, If I had need,
Ye would me never forsake, quick nor dead,
Though it were to hell truly.

FELLOWSHIP:
So I said, certainly,
But such pleasures be set aside, thee sooth to say:
And also, if we took such a journey,
When should we come again?

EVERYMAN:
Nay, never again till the day of doom.

FELLOWSHIP:
In faith, then will not I come there!
Who hath you these tidings brought?

EVERYMAN:
Indeed, Death was with me here.

FELLOWSHIP:
Now, by God that all hath bought,
If Death were the messenger,
For no man that is living today
I will not go that loath journey—
Not for the father that begat me!

EVERYMAN:
Ye promised other wise, pardie.

FELLOWSHIP:
I wot well I say so truly
And yet if thou wilt eat, and drink, and make good
    cheer,
Or haunt to women, the lusty company,
I would not forsake you, while the day is clear,
Trust me verily!

EVERYMAN:
Yea, thereto ye would be ready;
To go to mirth, solace, and play
Your mind will sooner apply
Than to bear me company in my long journey.

FELLOWSHIP:
Now, in good faith, I will not that way.
But and thou wilt murder, or any man kill,
In that I will help thee with a good will!

EVERYMAN:
O that is a simple advice indeed!
Gentle fellow, help me in my necessity;
We have loved long, and now I need,
And now, gentle Fellowship, remember me.

FELLOWSHIP:
Whether ye have loved me or no,
By Saint John, I will not with thee go.

EVERYMAN:
Yet I pray thee, take the labour, and do so much
    for me
To bring me forward, for saint charity,
And comfort me till I come without the town.

---

[5]God.

FELLOWSHIP:

Nay, and thou would give me a new gown,

I will not a foot with thee go;

But and you had tarried I would not have left thee so.

And as now, God speed thee in thy journey,

For from thee I will depart as fast as I may.

EVERYMAN:

Whither away, Fellowship? Will you forsake me?

FELLOWSHIP:

Yea, by my fay, to God I betake thee.

EVERYMAN:

Farewell, good Fellowship; for this my heart is sore;

Adieu for ever, I shall see thee no more.

FELLOWSHIP:

In faith, Everyman, farewell now at the end;

For you I will remember that parting is mourning.

EVERYMAN:

Alack! shall we thus depart indeed?

Our Lady, help, without any more comfort,

Lo, Fellowship forsaketh me in my most need:

For help in this world whither shall I resort?

Fellowship herebefore with me would merry make;

And now little sorrow for me doth he take.

It is said, in prosperity men friends may find,

Which in adversity be full unkind.

Now whither for succour shall I flee,

Sith that Fellowship hath forsaken me?

To my kinsmen I will truly,

Praying them to help me in my necessity:

I believe that they will do so,

For kind will creep where it may not go.

Where be ye now, my friends and kinsmen?

KINDRED:

Here be we now at your commandment.

Cousin, I pray you show us your intent

In any wise, and not spare.

COUSIN:

Yea, Everyman, and to us declare

If ye be disposed to go any whither,

For wete you well, we will live and die together.

KINDRED:

In wealth and woe we will with you hold,

For over his kin a man may be bold.

EVERYMAN:

Gramercy, my friends and kinsmen kind.

Now shall I show you the grief of my mind:

I was commanded by a messenger,

That is an high king's chief officer;

He bade me go a pilgrimage to my pain,

And I know well I shall never come again;

Also I must give a reckoning straight,

For I have a great enemy, that hath me in wait,

Which intendeth me for to hinder.

KINDRED:

What account is that which ye must render?

That would I know.

EVERYMAN:

Of all my works I must show

How I have lived and my days spent;

Also of ill deeds, that I have used

In my time, sith life was me lent;

And of all virtues that I have refused.

Therefore I pray you go thither with me,

To help to make mine account, for saint charity.

COUSIN:

What, to go thither? Is that the matter?

Nay, Everyman, I had liefer fast bread and water

All this five year and more.

EVERYMAN:

Alas, that ever I was bore![6]

For now shall I never be merry

If that you forsake me.

KINDRED:

Ah, sir; what, ye be a merry man!

Take good heart to you, and make no moan.

But one thing I warn you, by Saint Anne,

As for me, ye shall go alone.

EVERYMAN:

My Cousin, will you not with me go?

COUSIN:

No, by our Lady; I have the cramp in my toe.

Trust not to me, for, so God me speed,

I will deceive you in your most need.

KINDRED:

It availeth not us to tice.

Ye shall have my maid with all my heart;

She loveth to go to feasts, there to be nice,

And to dance, and abroad to start:

I will give her leave to help you in that journey,

If that you and she may agree.

EVERYMAN:

Now show me the very effect of your mind.

Will you go with me, or abide behind?

_____

[6]Born.

KINDRED:
Abide behind? Yea, that I will and I may!
Therefore farewell until another day.

EVERYMAN:
How should I be merry or glad?
For fair promises to me make,
But when I have most need, they me forsake.
I am deceived; that maketh me sad.

COUSIN:
Cousin Everyman, farewell now,
For verily I will not go with you;
Also of mine own an unready reckoning
I have to account; therefore I make tarrying.
Now, God keep thee, for now I go.

EVERYMAN:
Ah, Jesus, is all come hereto?
Lo, fair words maketh fools feign;
They promise and nothing will do certain.
My kinsmen promised me faithfully
For to abide with me steadfastly,
And now fast away do they flee:
Even so Fellowship promised me.
What friend were best me of to provide?
I lose my time here longer to abide.
Yet in my mind a thing there is:—
All my life I have loved riches;
If that my goods now help me might,
He would make my heart full light.
I will speak to him in this distress.—
Where art thou, my Goods and riches?

GOODS:
Who calleth me? Everyman? What haste thou hast!
I lie here in corners, trussed and piled so high,
And in chests I am locked so fast,
Also sacked in bags, thou mayst see with thine eye,
I cannot stir; in packs low I lie.
What would ye have, lightly me say.

EVERYMAN:
Come hither, Good, in all the haste thou may,
For of counsel I must desire thee.

GOODS:
Sir, and ye in the world have trouble or adversity,
That can I help you to remedy shortly.

EVERYMAN:
It is another disease that grieveth me;
In this world it is not, I tell thee so.
I am sent for another way to go,
To give a straight account general

Before the highest Jupiter of all;
And all my life I have had joy and pleasure in thee.
Therefore I pray thee go with me,
For, peradventure, thou mayst before God Almighty
My reckoning help to clean and purify;
For it is said ever among,
That money maketh all right that is wrong.

GOODS:
Nay, Everyman, I sing another song,
I follow no man in such voyages;
For and I went with thee
Thou shouldst fare much the worse for me;
For because on me thou did set thy mind,
Thy reckoning I have made blotted and blind
That thine account thou cannot make truly;
And that hast thou for the love of me.

EVERYMAN:
That would grieve me full sore,
When I should come to that fearful answer.
Up, let us go thither together.

GOODS:
Nay, not so, I am too brittle, I may not endure;
I will follow no man one foot, be ye sure.

EVERYMAN:
Alas, I have thee loved, and had great pleasure
All my life-days on good and treasure.

GOODS:
That is to thy damnation without lesing,
For my love is contrary to the love everlasting
But if thou had me loved moderately during,
As, to the poor give part of me,
Then shouldst thou not in this dolour be,
Nor in this great sorrow and care.

EVERYMAN:
Lo, now was I deceived or I was ware,
And all I may wyte[7] my spending of time.

GOODS:
What, weenest thou that I am thine?

EVERYMAN:
I had wend so.

GOODS:
Nay, Everyman, I say no;
As for a while I was lent thee,
A season thou hast had me in prosperity;

---

[7]Blame.

My condition is man's soul to kill;
If I save one, a thousand I do spill;
Weenest thou that I will follow thee?
Nay, from this world, not verily.

EVERYMAN:
I had wend otherwise.

GOODS:
Therefore to thy soul Good is a thief;
For when thou art dead, this is my guise
Another to deceive in the same wise
As I have done thee, and all to his soul's reprief.

EVERYMAN:
O false Good, cursed thou be!
Thou traitor to God, that hast deceived me,
And caught me in thy snare.

GOODS:
Marry, thou brought thyself in care,
Whereof I am glad,
I must needs laugh, I cannot be sad.

EVERYMAN:
Ah, Good, thou hast had long my heartly love;
I gave thee that which should be the Lord's above.
But wilt thou not go with me in deed?
I pray thee truth to say.

GOODS:
No, so God me speed,
Therefore farewell, and have good day.

EVERYMAN:
O, to whom shall I make moan
For to go with me in that heavy journey?
First Fellowship said he would with me gone;
His words were very pleasant and gay,
But afterward he left me alone.
Then spake I to my kinsmen all in despair,
And also they gave me words fair,
They lacked no fair speaking,
But all forsake me in the ending.
Then went I to my Goods that I loved best,
In hope to have comfort, but there had I least:
For my Goods sharply did me tell
That he bringeth many into hell.
Then of myself I was ashamed,
And so I am worthy to be blamed;
Thus may I well myself hate,
Of whom shall I now counsel take?
I think that I shall never speed
Till that I go to my Good-Deed,
But alas, she is so weak,

That she can neither go nor speak,
Yet will I venture on her now.—
My Good-Deeds, where be you?

GOOD-DEEDS:
Here I lie cold on the ground;
Thy sins hath me sore bound,
That I cannot stir.

EVERYMAN:
O, Good-Deeds, I stand in fear;
I must you pray of counsel,
For help now should come right well.

GOOD-DEEDS:
Everyman, I have understanding
That ye be summoned account to make
Before Messias, of Jerusalem King;
And you do by me[8] that journey what[9] you will I
    take.

EVERYMAN:
Therefore I come to you, my moan to make;
I pray you, that ye will go with me.

GOOD-DEEDS:
I would full fain, but I cannot stand verily.

EVERYMAN:
Why, is there anything on you fall?

GOOD-DEEDS:
Yea, sir, I may thank you of all;
If ye had perfectly cheered me,
Your book of account now full ready had be.
Look, the books of your works and deeds eke;
Oh, see how they lie under the feet,
To your soul's heaviness.

EVERYMAN:
Our Lord Jesus, help me!
For one letter here I can not see.

GOOD-DEEDS:
There is a blind reckoning in time of distress!

EVERYMAN:
Good-Deeds, I pray you, help me in this need,
Or else I am for ever damned indeed;
Therefore help me to make reckoning
Before the redeemer of all thing,
That king is, and was, and ever shall.

---

[8]If you go by me.
[9]With.

GOOD-DEEDS:
Everyman, I am sorry of your fall,
And fain would I help you, and I were able.

EVERYMAN:
Good-Deeds, your counsel I pray you give me.

GOOD-DEEDS:
That shall I do verily;
Though that on my feet I may not go,
I have a sister, that shall with you also,
Called Knowledge, which shall with you abide,
To help you to make that dreadful reckoning.

KNOWLEDGE:
Everyman, I will go with thee, and be thy guide,
In thy most need to go by thy side.

EVERYMAN:
In good condition I am now in every thing,
And am wholly content with this good thing;
Thanked be God my Creator.

GOOD-DEEDS:
And when he hath brought thee there,
Where thou shalt heal thee of thy smart,
Then go you with your reckoning and your Good-
    Deeds together
For to make you joyful at heart
Before the blessed Trinity.

EVERYMAN:
My Good-Deeds, gramercy;
I am well content, certainly,
With your words sweet.

KNOWLEDGE:
Now go we together lovingly,
To Confession, that cleansing river.

EVERYMAN:
For joy I weep; I would we were there;
But, I pray you, give me cognition
Where dwelleth that holy man, Confession.

KNOWLEDGE:
In the house of salvation:
We shall find him in that place,
That shall us comfort by God's grace.
Lo, this is Confession; kneel down and ask mercy,
For he is in good conceit with God almighty.

EVERYMAN:
O glorious fountain that all uncleanness doth clarify,
Wash from me the spots of vices unclean,
That on me no sin may be seen;

I come with Knowledge for my redemption,
Repent with hearty and full contrition;
For I am commanded a pilgrimage to take,
And great accounts before God to make.
Now, I pray you, Shrift, mother of salvation,
Help my good deeds for my piteous exclamation.

CONFESSION:
I know your sorrow well, Everyman;
Because with Knowledge ye come to me,
I will you comfort as well as I can,
And a precious jewel I will give thee,
Called penance, wise voider of adversity;
Therewith shall your body chastised be,
With abstinence and perseverance in God's service:
Here shall you receive that scourge of me,
Which is penance strong, that ye must endure,
To remember thy Saviour was scourged for thee
With sharp scourges, and suffered it patiently;
So must thou, or thou scape that painful pilgrimage;
Knowledge, keep him in this voyage,
And by that time Good-Deeds will be with thee.
But in any wise, be sure of mercy,
For your time draweth fast, and ye will saved be;
Ask God mercy, and He will grant truly,
When with the scourge of penance man doth him
    bind,
The oil of forgiveness then shall he find.

EVERYMAN:
Thanked be God for his gracious work!
For now I will my penance begin;
This hath rejoiced and lighted my heart,
Though the knots be painful and hard within.

KNOWLEDGE:
Everyman, look your penance that ye fulfil,
What pain that ever it to you be,
And Knowledge shall give you counsel at will,
How your accounts ye shall make clearly.

EVERYMAN:
O eternal God, O heavenly figure,
O way of rightwiseness, O goodly vision,
Which descended down in a virgin pure
Because he would Everyman redeem,
Which Adam forfeited by his disobedience:
O blessed Godhead, elect and high-divine,
Forgive my grievous offence;
Here I cry thee mercy in this presence.
O ghostly treasure, O ransomer and redeemer
Of all the world, hope and conductor,

Mirror of joy, and founder of mercy,
Which illumineth heaven and earth thereby,
Hear my clamorous complaint, though it late be;
Receive my prayers; unworthy in this heavy life,
Though I be, a sinner most abominable,
Yet let my name be written in Moses' table;
O Mary, pray to the Maker of all thing,
Me for to help at my ending,
And save me from the power of my enemy,
For Death assaileth me strongly;
And, Lady, that I may be means of thy prayer
Of your Son's glory to be partaker,
By the means of his passion I it crave,
I beseech you, help my soul to save.—
Knowledge, give me the scourge of penance;
My flesh therewith shall give a quittance:
I will now begin, if God give me grace.

KNOWLEDGE:
Everyman, God give you time and space:
Thus I bequeath you in the hands of our Saviour,
Thus may you make your reckoning sure.

EVERYMAN:
In the name of the Holy Trinity,
My body sore punished shall be:
Take this, body, for the sin of the flesh;
Also thou delightest to go gay and fresh,
And in the way of damnation thou did me bring;
Therefore suffer now strokes and punishing.
Now of penance I will wade the water clear,
To save me from purgatory, that sharp fire.

GOOD-DEEDS:
I thank God, now I can walk and go;
And am delivered of my sickness and woe.
Therefore with Everyman I will go, and not spare;
His good works I will help him to declare.

KNOWLEDGE:
Now, Everyman, be merry and glad;
Your Good-Deeds cometh now; ye may not be sad;
Now is your Good-Deeds whole and sound,
Going upright upon the ground.

EVERYMAN:
My heart is light, and shall be evermore;
Now will I smite faster than I did before.

GOOD-DEEDS:
Everyman, pilgrim, my special friend,
Blessed be thou without end;
For thee is prepared the eternal glory.

Ye have me made whole and sound,
Therefore I will bide by thee in every stound.[10]

EVERYMAN:
Welcome, my Good-Deeds; now I hear thy voice,
I weep for very sweetness of love.

KNOWLEDGE:
Be no more sad, but ever rejoice,
God seeth thy living in his throne above;
Put on this garment to thy behove,
Which is wet with your tears,
Or else before God you may it miss,
When you to your journey's end come shall.

EVERYMAN:
Gentle Knowledge, what do you it call?

KNOWLEDGE:
It is a garment of sorrow:
From pain it will you borrow;
Contrition it is,
That getteth forgiveness;
It pleaseth God passing well.

GOOD-DEEDS:
Everyman, will you wear it for your heal?

EVERYMAN:
Now blessed be Jesu, Mary's Son!
For now have I on true contrition.
And let us go now without tarrying;
Good-Deeds, have we clear our reckoning?

GOOD-DEEDS:
Yea, indeed I have it here.

EVERYMAN:
Then I trust we need not fear;
Now, friends, let us not part in twain.

KNOWLEDGE:
Nay, Everyman, that will we not, certain.

GOOD-DEEDS:
Yet must thou lead with thee
Three persons of great might.

EVERYMAN:
Who should they be?

GOOD-DEEDS:
Discretion and Strength they hight,
And thy Beauty may not abide behind.

---

[10]Season.

KNOWLEDGE:
Also ye must call to mind
Your Five-wits as for your counsellors.

GOOD-DEEDS:
You must have them ready at all hours.

EVERYMAN:
How shall I get hither?

KNOWLEDGE:
You must call them all together,
And they will hear you incontinent.

EVERYMAN:
My friends, come hither and be present,
Discretion, Strength, my Five-wits, and Beauty.

BEAUTY:
Here at your will we be all ready.
What will ye that we should do?

GOOD-DEEDS:
That ye would with Everyman go,
And help him in his pilgrimage,
Advise you, will ye with him or not in that voyage?

STRENGTH:
We will bring him all thither,
To his help and comfort, ye may believe me.

DISCRETION:
So will we go with him all together.

EVERYMAN:
Almighty God, loved thou be,
I give thee laud that I have hither brought
Strength, Discretion, Beauty, and Five-wits; lack I
    nought;
And my Good-Deeds, with Knowledge clear,
All be in my company at my will here;
I desire no more to my business.

STRENGTH:
And I, Strength, will by you stand in distress,
Though thou would in battle fight on the ground.

FIVE-WITS:
And though it were through the world round,
We will not depart for sweet nor sour.

BEAUTY:
No more will I unto death's hour,
Whatsoever thereof befall.

DISCRETION:
Everyman, advise you first of all;
Go with a good advisement and deliberation;

We all give you virtuous monition
That all shall be well.

EVERYMAN:
My friends, hearken what I will tell:
I pray God reward you in his heavenly sphere.
Now hearken, all that be here
For I will make my testament
Here before you all present.
In alms half my good I will give with my hands twain
In the way of charity, with good intent,
And the other half still shall remain
In quiet to be returned there it ought to be.
This I do in despite of the fiend of hell
To go quite out of his peril
Ever after and this day.

KNOWLEDGE:
Everyman, hearken what I say;
Go to priesthood, I you advise,
And receive of him in any wise
The holy sacrament and ointment together;
Then shortly see ye turn again hither;
We will all abide you here.

FIVE-WITS:
Yea, Everyman, hie you that ye ready were,
There is no emperor, king, duke, ne baron,
That of God hath commission,
As hath the least priest in the world being;
For of the blessed sacraments pure and benign,
He beareth the keys and thereof hath the cure
For man's redemption, it is ever sure;
Which God for our soul's medicine
Gave us out of his heart with great pine;
Here in this transitory life, for thee and me
The blessed sacraments seven there be.
Baptism, confirmation, with priesthood good,
And the sacrament of God's precious flesh and blood,
Marriage, the holy extreme unction, and penance;
These seven be good to have in remembrance,
Gracious sacraments of high divinity.

EVERYMAN:
Fain would I receive that holy body
And meekly to my ghostly father I will go.

FIVE-WITS:
Everyman, that is the best that ye can do:
God will you to salvation bring,
For priesthood exceedeth all other thing;
To us Holy Scripture they do teach,
And converteth man from sin heaven to reach;

God hath to them more power given,
Than to any angel that is in heaven;
With five words he may consecrate
God's body in flesh and blood to make,
And handleth his maker between his hands;
The priest bindeth and unbindeth all bands,
Both in earth and in heaven;
Thou ministers all the sacraments seven;
Though we kissed thy feet thou were worthy;
Thou art surgeon that cureth sin deadly:
No remedy we find under God
But all only priesthood.
Everyman, God gave priests that dignity,
And setteth them in his stead among us to be;
Thus be they above angels in degree.

KNOWLEDGE:
If priests be good it is so surely;
But when Jesus hanged on the cross with great smart
There he gave, out of his blessed heart,
The same sacrament in great torment:
He sold them not to us, that Lord Omnipotent.
Therefore Saint Peter the apostle doth say
That Jesu's curse hath all they
Which God their Saviour do buy or sell,
Or they for any money do take or tell.
Sinful priests giveth the sinners example bad;
Their children sitteth by other men's fires, I have
    heard;
And some haunteth women's company,
With unclean life, as lusts of lechery:
These be with sin made blind.

FIVE-WITS:
I trust to God no such may we find;
Therefore let us priesthood honour,
And follow their doctrine for our souls' succour;
We be their sheep, and they shepherds be
By whom we all be kept in surety.
Peace, for yonder I see Everyman come,
Which hath made true satisfaction.

GOOD-DEEDS:
Methinketh it is he indeed.

EVERYMAN:
Now Jesu be our alder speed.[11]
I have received the sacrament for my redemption,
And then mine extreme unction:
Blessed be all they that counselled me to take it!
And now, friends, let us go without longer respite;

I thank God that ye have tarried so long.
Now set each of you on this rod your hand,
And shortly follow me:
I go before, there I would be; God be our guide.

STRENGTH:
Everyman, we will not from you go,
Till ye have gone this voyage long.

DISCRETION:
I, Discretion, will bide by you also.

KNOWLEDGE:
And though this pilgrimage be never so strong,
I will never part you fro:
Everyman, I will be as sure by thee
As ever I did by Judas Maccabee.

EVERYMAN:
Alas, I am so faint I may not stand,
My limbs under me do fold;
Friends, let us not turn again to this land,
Not for all the world's gold,
For into this cave must I creep
And turn to the earth and there to sleep.

BEAUTY:
What, into this grave? Alas!

EVERYMAN:
Yea, there shall you consume more and less.

BEAUTY:
And what, should I smother here?

EVERYMAN:
Yea, by my faith, and never more appear.
In this world live no more we shall,
But in heaven before the highest Lord of all.

BEAUTY:
I cross out all this; adieu by Saint John;
I take my cap in my lap and am gone.

EVERYMAN:
What, Beauty, whither will ye?

BEAUTY:
Peace, I am deaf; I look not behind me,
Not and thou would give me all the gold in thy chest.

EVERYMAN:
Alas, whereto may I trust?
Beauty goeth fast away hie;
She promised with me to live and die.

---

[11]Speed in help of all.

STRENGTH:
Everyman, I will thee also forsake and deny;
Thy game liketh me not at all.

EVERYMAN:
Why, then ye will forsake me all.
Sweet Strength, tarry a little space.

STRENGTH:
Nay, sir, by the rood of grace
Though thou weep till thy heart brast.

EVERYMAN:
Ye would ever bide by me, ye said.

STRENGTH:
Yea, I have you far enough conveyed;
Ye be old enough, I understand,
Your pilgrimage to take on hand;
I repent me that I hither came.

EVERYMAN:
Strength, you to displease I am to blame;
Will you break promise that is debt?

STRENGTH:
In faith, I care not;
Thou art but a fool to complain,
You spend your speech and waste your brain;
Go thrust thee into the ground.

EVERYMAN:
I had wend surer I should you have found.
He that trusteth in his Strength
She him deceiveth at the length.
Both Strength and Beauty forsaketh me,
Yet they promised me fair and lovingly.

DISCRETION:
Everyman, I will after Strength be gone,
As for me I will leave you alone.

EVERYMAN:
Why, Discretion, will ye forsake me?

DISCRETION:
Yea, in faith, I will go from thee,
For when Strength goeth before
I follow after evermore.

EVERYMAN:
Yet I pray thee, for the love of the Trinity,
Look in my grave once piteously.

DISCRETION:
Nay, so nigh will I not come.
Farewell, every one!

EVERYMAN:
O all thing faileth, save God alone;
Beauty, Strength, and Discretion;
For when Death bloweth his blast,
They all run from me full fast.

FIVE-WITS:
Everyman, my leave now of thee I take;
I will follow the other, for here I thee forsake.

EVERYMAN:
Alas! then may I wail and weep,
For I took you for my best friend.

FIVE-WITS:
I will no longer thee keep;
Now farewell, and there an end.

EVERYMAN:
O Jesu, help, all hath forsaken me!

GOOD-DEEDS:
Nay, Everyman, I will bide with thee,
I will not forsake thee indeed;
Thou shalt find me a good friend at need.

EVERYMAN:
Gramercy, Good-Deeds; now may I true friends see;
They have forsaken me every one;
I loved them better than my Good-Deeds alone.
Knowledge, will ye forsake me also?

KNOWLEDGE:
Yea, Everyman, when ye to death do go:
But not yet for no manner of danger.

EVERYMAN:
Gramercy, Knowledge, with all my heart.

KNOWLEDGE:
Nay, yet I will not from hence depart,
Till I see where ye shall be come.

EVERYMAN:
Methinketh, alas, that I must be gone
To make my reckoning and my debts pay,
For I see my time is nigh spent away.
Take example, all ye that this do hear or see,
How they that I loved best do forsake me,
Except my Good-Deeds that bideth truly.

GOOD-DEEDS:
All earthly things is but vanity:
Beauty, Strength, and Discretion, do man forsake,
Foolish friends and kinsmen, that fair spake,
All fleeth save Good-Deeds, and that am I.

EVERYMAN:

Have mercy on me, God most mighty;
And stand by me, thou Mother and Maid, holy Mary.

GOOD-DEEDS:

Fear not, I will speak for thee.

EVERYMAN:

Here I cry God mercy.

GOOD-DEEDS:

Short our end, and minish our pain;
Let us go and never come again.

EVERYMAN:

Into thy hands, Lord, my soul I commend;
Receive it, Lord, that it be not lost;
As thou me boughtest, so me defend,
And save me from the fiend's boast,
That I may appear with that blessed host
That shall be saved at the day of doom.
In manus tuas—of might's most
For ever—*commendo spiritum meum.*[12]

KNOWLEDGE:

Now hath he suffered that we all shall endure;
The Good-Deeds shall make all sure.
Now hath he made ending;
Methinketh that I hear angels sing
And make great joy and melody,
Where Everyman's soul received shall be.

ANGEL:

Come, excellent elect spouse to Jesu:
Hereabove thou shalt go

Because of thy singular virtue:
Now the soul is taken the body fro;
Thy reckoning is crystal-clear.
Now shalt thou into the heavenly sphere,
Unto the which all ye shall come
That liveth well before the day of doom.

DOCTOR:

This moral men may have in mind;
Ye hearers, take it of worth, old and young,
And forsake pride, for he deceiveth you in the end,
And remember Beauty, Five-wits, Strength, and Dis-
    cretion,
They all at the last do Everyman forsake,
Save his Good-Deeds, there doth he take.
But beware, and they be small
Before God, he hath not help at all.
None excuse may be there for Everyman:
Alas, how shall he do then?
For after death amends may no man make,
For then mercy and pity do him forsake.
If his reckoning be not clear when he do come,
God will say—*ite maledicti in ignem aeternum.*[13]
And he that hath his account whole and sound,
High in heaven he shall be crowned;
Unto which place God brings us all thither
That we may live body and soul together.
Thereto help the Trinity,
Amen, say ye, for saint Charity.

THUS ENDETH THIS MORALL PLAY OF
EVERYMAN.

---

[12]Into your hands I commend my spirit.
[13]Be damned to the eternal fire.

Aucassin and Nicolette

Who will deign to hear the song,
Solace of a captive's wrong,
Telling how two children met,
Aucassin and Nicolette;
How by grievous pains distraught,
Noble deeds the varlet wrought
For his love, and her bright face!
Sweet my rhyme, and full of grace,
Fair my tale, and debonair.
He who lists—though full of care,
Sore astonied, much amazed,
All cast down, by men mispraised,
Sick in body, sick in soul,
Hearing, shall be glad and whole,
So sweet the tale.

Now they say and tell and relate:

How the Count Bougars of Valence made war on Count Garin of Beaucaire, war so great, so wonderful, and so mortal, that never dawned the day but that he was at the gates and walls and barriers of the town, with a hundred knights and ten thousand men-at-arms, on foot and on horse. So he burned the Count's land, and spoiled his heritage, and dealt death to his men. The Count Garin of Beaucaire was full of years, and frail; he had long outworn his day. He had no heir, neither son nor daughter, save one only varlet, and he was such as I will tell you. Aucassin was the name of the lad. Fair he was, and pleasant to look upon, tall and shapely of body in every whit of him. His hair was golden, and curled in little rings about his head; he had grey and dancing eyes, a clear, oval face, a nose high and comely, and he was so gracious in all good graces that nought in him was found to blame, but good alone. But love, that high prince, so utterly had cast him down, that he cared not to become knight, neither to bear arms, nor to tilt at tourneys, nor yet to do aught that it became his name to do.

His father and his mother spake him thus, "Son, don now thy mail, mount thy horse, keep thy land, and render aid to thy men. Should they see thee amongst them, the better will the men-at-arms defend their bodies and their substance, thy fief[1] and mine."

"Father," said Aucassin, "why speakest thou in such fashion to me? May God give me nothing of my desire if I become knight, or mount to horse, or thrust into the press to strike other or be smitten down,

save only that thou give me Nicolette, my sweet friend, whom I love so well."

"Son," answered the father, "this may not be. Put Nicolette from mind. For Nicolette is but a captive maid, come hither from a far country, and the Viscount of this town bought her with money from the Saracens, and set her in this place. He hath nourished and baptized her, and held her at the font. On a near day he will give her to some young bachelor, who will gain her bread in all honor. With this what hast thou to do? Ask for a wife, and I will find thee the daughter of a king, or a count. Were he the richest man in France, his daughter shalt thou have, if so thou wilt."

"Faith, my father," said Aucassin, "what honor of this world would not Nicolette, my very sweet friend, most richly become! Were she Empress of Byzantium or of Allemaigne, or Queen of France or England, low enough would be her degree, so noble is she, so courteous and debonair, and gracious in all good graces."

Now is sung:
Aucassin was of Beaucaire,
Of the mighty castle there,
But his heart was ever set
On his fair friend, Nicolette.
Small he heeds his father's blame,
Or the harsh words of his dame:
"Fool, to weep the livelong day,
Nicolette trips light and gay.
Scouring she from far Carthage,
Bought of Paynims for a wage.
Since a wife beseems thee good,
Take a wife of wholesome blood."
"Mother, nought for this I care,
Nicolette is debonair;
Slim the body, fair the face,
Make my heart a lighted place;
Love has set her as my peer,
    Too sweet, my dear."

Now they say and tell and relate:

When the Count Garin of Beaucaire found that in nowise could he withdraw Aucassin his son from the love of Nicolette, he sought out the Viscount of the town, who was his man, and spake him thus, "Sir Count, send Nicolette your godchild straightly from this place. Cursed be the land wherefrom she was

---

[1]Fief—the demesne of the Count.

carried to this realm; for because of her I lose Aucassin, who will not become knight, nor do aught that it becometh knight to do. Know well that, were she once within my power, I would hurry her to the fire; and look well to yourself for you stand in utmost peril and fear."

"Sire," answered the Viscount, "this lies heavy upon me, that ever Aucassin goes and he comes seeking speech with my ward. I have bought her with my money, and nourished and baptized her, and held her at the font. Moreover, I am fain to give her to some young bachelor, who will gain her bread in all honor. With this Aucassin your son had nought to do. But since this is your will and your pleasure, I will send her to so far a country that nevermore shall he see her with his eyes."

"Walk warily," replied the Count Garin, "for great evil easily may fall to you of this." So they went their ways.

Now the Viscount was a very rich man, and had a rich palace standing within a garden. In a certain chamber of an upper floor he set Nicolette in ward, with an old woman to bear her company, and to watch; and he put there bread and meat and wine and all things for their need. Then he placed a seal upon the door, so that none might enter in, nor issue forth, save only that there was a window looking on the garden, strictly close, whereby they breathed a little fresh air.

Now is sung:

Nicolette is prisoned fast,
In a vaulted chamber cast,
Shaped and carven wondrous well,
Painted as by miracle.
At the marble casement stayed
On her elbow leaned the maid;
Golden showed her golden hair,
Softly curved her eyebrows rare,
Fair her face, and brightly flushed,
Sweeter maiden never blushed.
In the garden from her room
She might watch the roses bloom,
Hear the birds make tender moan;
Then she knew herself alone.
" 'Lack, great pity 'tis to place
Maid in such an evil case.
Aucassin, my liege, my squire,
Friend, and dear, and heart's desire,

Since thou dost not hate me quite,
Men have done me foul despite,
Sealed me in this vaulted room,
Thrust me to this bitter doom.
But by God, Our Lady's Son,
Soon will I from here begone,
    So it be won."

Now they say and tell and relate:

Nicolette was prisoned in the chamber, as you have heard and known. The cry and the haro[2] went through all the land that Nicolette was stolen away. Some said that she had fled the country, and some that the Count Garin of Beaucaire had done her to death. Whatever man may have rejoiced, Aucassin had no joy therein, so he sought out the Viscount of the town and spake him thus, "Sir Viscount, what have you done with Nicolette, my very sweet friend, the thing that most I love in all the world? Have you borne her off, or hidden her from my sight? Be sure that should I die hereof, my blood will be required of you, as is most just, for I am slain of your two hands; since you steal from me the thing that most I love in all the world."

"Fair sire," answered the Viscount, "put this from mind. Nicolette is a captive maid whom I brought here from a far country. For her price I trafficked with the Saracens, and I have bred and baptized her, and held her at the font. I have nourished her duly, and on a day will give her to some young bachelor who will gain her bread in honorable fashion. With this you have nought to do; but only to wed the daughter of some count or king. Beyond this, what profit would you have, had you become her lover, and taken her to your bed? Little enough would be your gain therefrom, for your soul would lie tormented in Hell all the days of all time, so that to Paradise never should you win."

"In Paradise what have I to do? I care not to enter, but only to have Nicolette, my very sweet friend, whom I love so dearly well. For into Paradise go none but such people as I will tell you of. There go those aged priests, and those old cripples, and the maimed, who all day long and all night cough before the altars, and in the crypts beneath the churches; those who go in worn old mantles and old tattered habits; who are naked, and barefoot, and full of

---

[2]Protest against injustice.

sores; who are dying of hunger and of thirst, of cold and of wretchedness. Such as these enter in Paradise, and with them have I nought to do. But in Hell will I go. For to Hell go the fair clerks and the fair knights who are slain in the tourney and the great wars, and the stout archer and the loyal man. With them will I go. And there go the fair and courteous ladies, who have friends, two or three, together with their wedded lords. And there pass the gold and the silver, the ermine and all rich furs, harpers and minstrels, and the happy of the world. With these will I go, so only that I have Nicolette, my very sweet friend, by my side."

"Truly," cried the Viscount, "you talk idly, for never shall you see her more; yea, and if perchance you spoke together, and your father heard thereof, he would burn both me and her in one fire and yourself might well have every fear."

"This lies heavy upon me," answered Aucassin. Thus he parted from the Viscount making great sorrow.

Now is sung:

Aucassin departed thus
Sad at heart and dolorous;
Gone is she, his fairest friend,
None may comfort give or mend,
None by counsel make good end.
To the palace turned he home,
Climbed the stair, and sought his room.
In the chamber all alone
Bitterly he made his moan,
Presently began to weep
For the love he might not keep.
"Nicolette, so gent, so sweet,
Fair the faring of thy feet,
Fair thy laughter, sweet thy speech,
Fair our playing each with each,
Fair thy clasping, fair thy kiss,
Yet it endeth all in this.
Since from me my love is ta'en
I misdoubt that I am slain;
    Sister, sweet friend."
Now they say and tell and relate:

Whilst Aucassin was in the chamber lamenting Nicolette, his friend, the Count Bougars of Valence, wishful to end the war, pressed on his quarrel, and setting his pikemen and horsemen in array, drew near the castle to take it by storm. Then the cry arose and the tumult; and the knights and the men-at-arms took their weapons, and hastened to the gates and the walls to defend the castle, and the burgesses climbed to the battlements, flinging quarrels[3] and sharpened darts upon the foe. Whilst the siege was so loud and perilous, the Count Garin of Beaucaire sought the chamber where Aucassin lay mourning, assotted upon[4] Nicolette, his very sweet friend, whom he loved so well.

"Ha, son," cried he, "craven art thou and shamed, that seest thy best and fairest castle so hardly beset. Know well that if thou lose it, thou art a naked man. Son, arm thyself lightly, mount the horse, keep thy land, aid thy men, hurtle into the press. Thou needest not to strike together, neither to be smitten down, but if they see thee amongst them, the better will they defend their goods and their bodies, thy land and mine; and thou art so stout and strong that very easily thou canst do this thing, as is but right."

"Father," answered Aucassin, "what sayest thou now? May God give me naught that I require of Him if I become a knight, or mount to horse, or thrust into the press to strike knight or to be smitten down, save only thou givest me Nicolette, my sweet friend, whom I love so well!"

"Son," replied the father, "this can never be. Rather will I suffer to lose my heritage, and go bare of all, than that thou shouldst have her, either as woman or as dame."

So he turned without farewell; but when Aucassin saw him part, he stayed him, saying, "Father, come now; I will make a true bargain with thee."

"What bargain, fair son?"

"I will arm me, and thrust into the press on such bargain as this: that if God bring me again safe and sound, thou wilt let me look on Nicolette, my sweet friend, so long that I may have with her two words or three, and kiss her only one time."

"I pledge my word to this," said the father. Of this covenant had Aucassin much joy.

Now is sung:

Aucassin the more was fain
Of the kiss he sought to gain,
Rather than his coffers hold

---

[3]Square-headed crossbow-bolt.
[4]Infatuated with.

A hundred thousand marks of gold.
At the call his squire drew near,
Armed him fast in battle gear;
Shirt and hauberk donned the lad,
Laced the helmet on his head,
Girt his golden-hilted sword—
Came the war-horse at his word—
Gripped the buckler and the lance,
At the stirrups cast a glance;
Then, most brave from plume to heel,
Pricked the charger with the steel,
Called to mind his absent dear,
Passed the gateway without fear
    Straight to the fight.

Now they say and tell and relate:

Aucassin was armed and horsed as you have heard. God, how bravely showed the shield about his neck, the helmet on his head, and the fringes of the baldric upon his left thigh! The lad was tall and strong, slender and comely to look upon; and the steed he bestrode was great and speedy, and fiercely had he charged clear of the gate. Now think not that he sought spoil of oxen and cattle, nor to smite others and himself escape. Nay, but of all this he took no heed. Another was with him; and he thought so dearly upon Nicolette, his fair friend, that the reins fell from his hand, and he struck never a blow. Then the charger, yet smarting from the spur, bore him into the battle, amidst the thickest of the foe, so that hands were laid upon him from every side, and he was made prisoner. Thus they spoiled him of shield and lance, and forthwith led him from the field a captive, questioning amongst themselves by what death he should be slain.

When Aucassin marked their words, "Ha, God!" cried he. "Sweet Creature, these are my mortal foes who lead me captive, and who soon will smite off my head; and when my head is smitten, never again may I have fair speech with Nicolette, my sweet friend, whom I hold so dear. Yet have I a good sword; and my horse is yet unblown. Now if I defend me not for her sake, may God keep her never, should she love me still!" The varlet was hardy and stout, and the charger he bestrode was right fierce. He plucked forth his sword, and smote suddenly on the right hand and on the left, cutting sheer through nasal and headpiece, gauntlet and arm, making such ruin around him as the wild boar deals when brought to bay by hounds in the wood, until he had struck down ten knights, and hurt seven more, and won clear of the *melee*, and rode back at utmost speed, sword in his hand.

The Count Bougars of Valence heard tell that his men were about to hang Aucassin, his foe, in shameful wise, so he hastened to the sight; and Aucassin passed him not by. His sword was yet in hand, and he struck the Count so fiercely upon the helm that the headpiece was cleft and shattered upon the head. So bewildered was he by the stroke that he tumbled to the ground, and. Aucassin stretched forth his hand, and took him, and led him captive by the nasal of the helmet, and delivered him to his father. "Father," said Aucassin, "behold the foe who wrought such war and mischief upon you! Twenty years hath this war endured, and none was there to bring it to an end."

"Fair son," replied his father, "better are such deeds as this than foolish dreams!"

"Father," returned Aucassin, "preach me no preachings; but carry out our bargain."

"Ha! What bargain, fair son?"

"How now, father, hast thou returned from the market? By my head, I will remember—whosoever may forget—so close is it to my heart! Didst thou not bargain with me, when I armed me and fared into the press, that if God brought me again safe and sound, thou wouldst grant me sight of Nicolette, my sweet friend, so long that I might have with her two words or three, and kiss her once? Such was the bargain; so be thou honest dealer."

"I!" cried the father. "God aid me never, should I keep such terms. Were she here, I would set her in the flames; and thou thyself might well have every fear."

"Is this the very end?" said Aucassin.

"So help me God," said his father, "yea!"

"Certes," said Aucassin, "grey hairs go ill with a lying tongue."

"Count of Valence," said Aucassin, "thou art my prisoner?"

"Sire," answered the Count, "it is verily and truly so."

"Give me thy hand," said Aucassin.

"Sire, as you wish!" So each took the other's hand.

"Plight me thy faith," said Aucassin, "that so long as thou drawest breath, never shall pass a day but thou shalt deal with my father in shameful fashion, either in goods or in person, if so thou canst."

"Sire, for God's love make me not a jest, but name me a price for my ransom. Whether you ask gold or silver, steed or palfrey, pelt or fur, hawk or hound, it shall be paid."

"What!" said Aucassin; "art thou not my prisoner?"

"Truly, sire," said the Count Bougars.

"God aid me never," quoth Aucassin, "but I send thy head flying, save thou plight me such faith as I said."

"In God's name," cried he, "I plight such affiance as seems most meet to thee." He pledged his troth; so Aucassin set him upon a horse, and brought him into a place of surety, himself riding by his side.

Now is sung:

When Count Garin knew his son
Aucassin still loved but one,
That his heart was ever set
Fondly on fond Nicolette,
Straight a prison he hath found,
Paved with marble, walled around,
Where in vault beneath the earth
Aucassin made little mirth,
But with wailing filled his cell
In such wise as now I tell
"Nicolette, white lily-flow'r,
Sweetest lady found in bow'r,
Sweet as grape that brimmeth up
Sweetness in the spiced cup,
On a day this chanced to you:
Out of Limousin there drew
One, a pilgrim, sore adread—
Lay in pain upon his bed,
Tossed, and took with fear his breath,
Very dolent, near to death—
Then you entered, pure and white,
Softly to the sick man's sight,
Raised the train that swept adown,
Raised the ermine-bordered gown,
Raised the smock, and bared to him,
Daintily, each lovely limb.
Then a wondrous thing befell.
Straight he rose up, sound and well,
Left his bed, took cross in hand,
Sought again his own dear land.
Lily-flow'r, so white, so sweet,
Fair the faring of thy feet,
Fair thy laughter, fair thy speech,
Fair our playing each with each!
Sweet thy kisses, soft thy touch!
All must love thee overmuch.
'Tis for thee that I am thrown
In this vaulted cell alone;
'Tis for thee that I attend
Death, that comes to make an end—
    For thee, sweet friend!

Now they say and tell and relate:

Aucassin was set in prison as you have heard tell, and Nicolette for her part was shut in the chamber. It was in the time of summer heat, in the month of May, when the days are warm, long and clear, and the night still and serene. Nicolette lay one night sleepless on her bed, and watched the moon shine brightly through the casement, and listened to the nightingale plain in the garden. Then she bethought her of Aucassin, her friend, whom she loved so well. She called also to mind the Count Garin of Beaucaire, her mortal foe, and feared greatly to remain, lest her hiding-place should be told to him, and she be put to death in some shameful fashion. She made certain that the old woman who held her in ward was sound asleep. So she rose, and wrapped herself in a very fair silk mantle, the best she had, and taking the sheets from her bed and the towels of her bath, knotted them together to make so long a rope as she was able, tied it about a pillar of the window, and slipped down into the garden. Then she took her skirt in both hands, the one before, and the other behind, and kilted her lightly against the dew which lay thickly upon the grass, and so passed through the garden. Her hair was golden, with little love-locks; her eyes blue and laughing; her face most dainty to see, with lips more vermeil than ever was rose or cherry in the time of summer heat; her teeth white and small; her breasts so firm that they showed beneath her vesture like two rounded nuts. So frail was she about the girdle that your two hands could have spanned her, and the daisies that she brake with her feet in passing showed altogether black against her instep and her flesh, so white was the fair young maiden.

She came to the postern, and unbarring the gate, issued forth upon the street of Beaucaire, taking heed to keep within the shadows, for the moon shone very bright, and thus she fared until she chanced upon the tower where her lover was prisoned. The tower was buttressed with pieces of wood in many places, and Nicolette hid herself amongst the pillars, wrapped close in her mantle. She set her face to a crevice of the tower, which was old and ruinous, and there she heard Aucassin weeping within, making great sorrow for the sweet friend whom he held so dear; and when she had hearkened awhile, she began to speak.

Now is sung:

Nicolette, so bright of face,
Leaned within this buttressed place,
Heard her lover weep within,
Marked the woe of Aucassin.
Then in words her thought she told:
"Aucassin, fond heart and bold,
What avails thine heart should ache
For a Paynim maiden's sake?
Ne'er may she become thy mate,
Since we prove thy father's hate,
Since thy kinsfolk hate me too;
What is left for me to do?
Nothing, but to seek the strand,
Pass o'er sea to some far land."
Shore she then one golden tress,
Thrust it in her love's duress;
Aucassin hath seen the gold
Shining bright in that dark hold,
Took the lock at her behest,
Kissed and placed it in his breast;
Then once more his eyes were wet
    For Nicolette.

Now they say and tell and relate:

When Aucassin heard Nicolette say that she would fare into another country, he was filled with anger. "Fair sweet friend," said he, "this be far from thee, for then wouldst thou have slain me. And the first man who saw thee, if so he might, would take thee forthwith and carry thee to his bed, and make thee his leman. Be sure that if thou wert found in any man's bed, save it be mine, I should not need a dagger to pierce my heart and slay me. Certes, no; wait would I not for a knife; but on the first wall or the nearest stone would I cast myself, and beat out my brains altogether. Better to die so foul a death as this than know thee to be in any man's bed, save mine."

"Aucassin," said she, "I doubt that thou lovest me less than thy words; and that my love is fonder than thine."

"Alack," cried Aucassin, "fair sweet friend, how can it be that thy love should be so great? Woman can not love man, as man loves woman; for woman's love is in the glance of her eye, and the blossom of her breast, and the tip of the toe of her foot; but the love of man is set deep in the hold of his heart, from whence it can not be torn away."

Whilst Aucassin and Nicolette were thus at odds together, the town watch entered the street, bearing naked swords beneath their mantles, for Count Garin had charged them strictly, once she were taken, to put her to death. The warder from his post upon the tower marked their approach, and as they drew near, heard them speaking of Nicolette, menacing her with death.

"God," said he, "it is great pity that so fair a damsel should be slain, and a rich alms should I give if I could warn her privily, and so she escape the snare; for of her death Aucassin, my liege, were dead already, and truly this were a piteous case."

Now is sung:

Brave the warder, full of guile,
Straight he sought some cunning wile:
Sought and found a song betime,
Raised this sweet and pleasant rhyme.
"Lady of the loyal mind,
Slender, gracious, very kind,
Gleaming head and golden hair,
Laughing lips and eyes of vair!
Easy, Lady, 'tis to tell
Two have speech who love full well.
Yet in peril are they met,
Set the snare, and spread the net.
Lo, the hunters draw this way,
Cloaked, with privy knives, to slay.
Ere the huntsmen spy the chase[5]
Let the quarry haste apace
    And keep her well."

Now they say and tell and relate:

"Ah," said Nicolette, "may the soul of thy father and of thy mother find sweetest rest, since in so fair and courteous a manner hast thou warned me. So God please, I will indeed keep myself close, and may He keep me too."

[5]Quarry.

She drew the folds of her cloak about her, and crouched in the darkness of the pillars till the watch had passed beyond; then she bade farewell to Aucassin, and bent her steps to the castle wall. The wall was very ruinous, and mended with timber, so she climbed the fence, and went her way till she found herself between wall and moat. Gazing below, she saw the fosse was very deep and perilous, and the maid had great fear.

"Ah, God," cried she, "sweet Creature, should I fall, my neck must be broken; and if I stay, tomorrow shall I be taken, and men will burn my body in a fire. Yet were it better to die, now, in this place, than to be made a show tomorrow in the market."

She crossed her brow, and let herself slide down into the moat, and when she reached the bottom, her fair feet and pretty hands, which had never learned that they could be hurt, were so bruised and wounded that the blood came from them in places a many; yet knew she neither ill nor dolor because of the mightiness of her fear. But if with pain she had entered in, still more it cost her to issue forth. She called to mind that it were death to tarry, and by chance found there a stake of sharpened wood, which those within the keep had flung forth in their defense of the tower. With this she cut herself a foothold, one step above the other, till with extreme labor she climbed forth from the moat. Now the forest lay but the distance of two bolts from a cross-bow, and ran some thirty leagues in length and breadth; moreover, within were many wild beasts and serpents. She feared these greatly, lest they should do her a mischief; but presently she remembered that should men lay hands upon her, they would lead her back to the city to burn her at the fire.

Now is sung:

Nicolette the fair, the fond,
Climbed the fosse and won beyond;
There she kneeled her, and implored
Very help of Christ the Lord.
"Father, King of majesty,
Where to turn I know not, I.
So, within the woodland gloom
Wolf and boar and lion roam,
Fearful things, with rav'ning maw,
Rending tusk and tooth and claw.
Yet, if all adread I stay,
Men will come at break of day,

Treat me to their heart's desire,
Burn my body in the fire.
But by God's dear majesty
Such a death I will not die;
Since I die, ah, better then
Trust the boar than trust to men.
Since all's evil, men and beast,
    Choose I the least."

Now they say and tell and relate:

Nicolette made great sorrow in such manner as you have heard. She commended herself to God's keeping, and fared on until she entered the forest. She kept upon the fringes of the woodland, for dread of the wild beasts and reptiles; and hiding herself within some thick bush, sleep overtook her, and she slept fast until six hours of the morn, when shepherds and herdsmen came from the city to lead their flocks to pasture between the wood and the river. The shepherds sat by a clear, sweet spring, which bubbled forth on the outskirts of the greenwood, and spreading a cloak upon the grass, set bread thereon. Whilst they ate together, Nicolette awoke at the song of the birds and the laughter, and hastened to the well.

"Fair children," said she, "God have you in His keeping."

"God bless you also," answered one who was more fluent of tongue than his companions.

"Fair child," said she, "do you know Aucassin, the son of Count Garin of this realm?"

"Yes, we know him well."

"So God keep you, pretty boy," said she, "as you tell him that within this wood there is a fair quarry for his hunting; and if he may take her, he would not part with one of her members for a hundred golden marks, nor for five hundred, nay, nor for aught that man can give."

Then looking upon her steadfastly, their hearts were troubled, the maid was so beautiful. "Will I tell him?" cried he who was readier of words than his companions. "Woe to him who speaks of it ever, or tells Aucassin what you say. You speak not truth but faery, for in all this forest there is no beast neither stag, nor lion, nor boar—one of whose legs would be worth two pence, or three at very best, and you talk of five hundred marks of gold! Woe betide him who believes your story, or shall spread it abroad! You are a fay, and no fit company for such as us; so pass upon your road."

"Ah, fair child," answered she, "yet you will do as I pray; for this beast is the only medicine that may heal Aucassin of his hurt. And I have here five sous in my purse; take them, and give him my message. For within three days must he hunt this chase and if within three days he find not the quarry, never may he cure him of his wound."

"By my faith," cried he, "we will take the money and if he comes this way, will give him your message; but certainly we will not go and look for him."

"As God pleases!" answered she. So she bade farewell to the shepherds, and went her way.

Now is sung:

Nicolette, as you heard tell,
Bade the shepherd lads farewell;
Through deep woodlands warily
Fared she 'neath the leafy tree,
Till the grass-grown way she trod
Brought her to a forest road,
Whence, like fingers on a hand,
Forked sev'n paths throughout the land.
There she called to heart her love,
There bethought her she would prove
Whether true her lover's vows.
Plucked she then young sapling boughs,
Grasses, leaves that branches yield,
Oak shoots, lilies of the field—
Built a lodge with frond and flow'r—
Fairest mason, fairest bow'r!
Swore then, by the truth of God,
Should her lover come that road,
Nor for love of her who made
Dream a little in its shade,
'Spite his oath, no true love, he
    Nor fond heart, she!

Now they say and tell and relate:

Nicolette built the lodge, as you have heard; very pretty it was and very dainty, and well furnished, both outside and in, with a tapestry of flowers and of leaves. Then she withdrew herself a little way from the bower, and hid within a thicket to spy what Aucassin would do. And the cry and the haro went through all the realm that Nicolette was lost; some had it that she was stolen away, and others that Count Garin had done her to death. Whoever had joy there-

of, Aucassin had little pleasure. His father, Count Garin, brought him out of his prison, and sent letters to the lords and ladies of those parts bidding them to a very rich feast, so that Aucassin, his son, might cease to dote. When the feast was at its merriest, Aucassin leaned against the musicians' gallery, sad and all discomforted. No laugh had he for any jest, since she whom most he loved was not amongst the ladies set in hall.

A certain knight marked his grief, and coming presently to him, said, "Aucassin, of such fever as yours, I, too, have been sick. I can give you good counsel, if you are willing to listen."

"Sir knight," said Aucassin, "great thanks! Good counsel, above all things, I would hear."

"Get to horse," said he; "take your pleasure in the woodland amongst flowers and bracken and the songs of the birds. Perchance (who knows?) you may hear some word of which you will be glad."

"Sir knight," answered Aucassin, "great thanks! This will I do." He left the hall privily, and went down-stairs to the stable where was his horse. He caused the charger to be saddled and bridled, then put foot in stirrup, mounted, and left the castle, riding till he entered the forest, and so by adventure came upon the well whereby the shepherd lads were sitting; and it was then about three hours after noon. They had spread a cloak upon the grass, and were eating their bread, with great mirth and jollity.

Now is sung:

Round about the well were set
Martin, Robin, Esmeret—
Jolly shepherds, gaily met—
Frulin, Jack, and Aubriet.
Laughed the one, "God keep in ward
Aucassin, our brave young lord—
Keep besides the damsel fair,
Blue of eye and gold of hair,
Gave us wherewithal to buy
Cate and sheath-knife presently,
Horn and quarter-staff and fruit,
Shepherd's pipe and country flute;
    God make him well!"

Now they say and tell and relate:

When Aucassin marked the song of the herdboys he called to heart Nicolette, his very sweet friend, whom he held so dear. He thought she must have passed that way, so he struck his horse with the spurs and came quickly to the shepherds.

"Fair children, God keep you!"

"God bless you!" replied he who was readier of tongue than his fellows.

"Fair children," said he, "tell over again the song that you told but now."

"We will not tell it," answered he who was more fluent of speech than the others. "Sorrow be his who sings it to you, fair sir!"

"Fair children," returned Aucassin, "do you not know me?"

"Oh, yes; we know that you are Aucassin, our young lord. But we are not your men; we belong to the Count."

"Fair children, sing me the song once more, I pray you!"

"By the Wounded Heart, what fine words! Why should I sing for you if I have no wish to do so? Why, the richest man in all the land—saving the presence of Count Garin—would not dare to drive my sheep and oxen and cows from out his wheat-field or his pasture, for fear of losing his eyes! Wherefore, then, should I sing for you if I have no wish to do so?"

"God keep you, fair children; yet you will do this thing for me. Take ten sous that I have in my purse."

"Sire, we will take the money; but I will not sing for you, since I have sworn not to do so. But I will tell it in plain prose, if such be your pleasure."

"As God pleases!" answered Aucassin. "Better the tale in prose than no story at all!"

"Sire, we were in this glade between six and nine of the morn, and were breaking our bread by the well, just as we are doing now, when a girl came by, the loveliest thing in all the world, so fair that we doubted her a fay, and she brimmed our wood with light. She gave us money, and made a bargain with us that if you came here we would tell you that you must hunt in this forest; for in it is such a quarry that if you may take her you would not part with one of her members for five hundred silver marks, nor for aught that man can give. For in the quest is so sweet a salve that if you take her you shall be cured of your wound; and within three days must

the chase be taken, for if she be not found by then, never will you see her more. Now go to your hunting if you will, and if you will not, let it go; for truly have I carried out my bargain with her."

"Fair children," cried Aucassin, "enough have you spoken; and may God set me on her track!"

Now is sung:

Aucassin's fond heart was moved
When this hidden word he proved
Sent him by the maid he loved.
Straight his charger he bestrode,
Bade farewell, and swiftly rode
Deep within the forest dim,
Saying o'er and o'er to him:
"Nicolette, so sweet, so good,
'Tis for you I search this wood—
Antler'd stag nor boar I chase—
Hot I follow on your trace.
Slender shape and deep blue eyes,
Dainty laughter, low replies,
Fledge the arrow in my heart.
Ah, to find you—ne'er to part!
Pray God give so fair an end,
   Sister, sweet friend!"

Now they say and tell and relate:

Aucassin rode through the wood in search of Nicolette, and the charger went right speedily. Do not think that the spines and the thorns were pitiful to him. Truly, it was not so; for his raiment was so torn that the least tattered of his garments could scarcely hold to his body, and the blood ran from his arms and legs and flanks in forty places, or at least in thirty, so that you could have followed after him by the blood which he left upon the grass. But he thought so fondly of Nicolette, his sweet friend, that he felt neither ill nor dolor. Thus all day long he searched the forest in this fashion, but might learn no news of her, and when it drew towards dusk, he commenced to weep because he had heard nothing. He rode at adventure down an old grass-grown road, and looking before him, saw a young man standing, such as I will tell you. Tall he was, and marvelously ugly and hideous. His head was big and blacker than smoked meat; the palm of your hand could easily have gone between his two eyes; he had very large cheeks and a monstrous flat nose with great nostrils; lips redder than uncooked flesh; teeth yellow and foul; he was shod with shoes and gaiters of bull's hide, bound about the leg with ropes to well above the knee; upon his back was a rough cloak; and he stood leaning on a huge club. Aucassin urged his steed towards him, but was all afeared when he saw him as he was.

"Fair brother, God keep you."

"God bless you too," said he.

"As God keeps you, what do you here?"

"What is that to you?" said he.

"Truly, naught," answered Aucassin. "I asked with no wish to do you wrong."

"And you, for what cause do you weep?" asked the other, "and make such heavy sorrow? Certainly, were I so rich a man as you are, not the whole world should make me shed a tear."

"Do you know me, then?" said Aucassin.

"Yes, well I know you to be Aucassin, the son of the Count, and if you will tell me why you weep, well, then I will tell what I do here."

"Certes," said Aucassin, "I will tell you with all my heart. I came this morning to hunt in the forest, and with a white grey-hound, the swiftest in the whole world. I have lost him, and that is why I weep."

"Hear him," cried he, "by the Sacred Heart, and you make all this lamentation for a filthy dog! Sorrow be his who shall esteem you more. Why, there is not a man of substance in these parts who would not give you ten or fifteen or twenty hounds—if so your father wishes—and be right glad to make you the gift. But for my part I have full reason to weep and cry aloud."

"And what is your grief, brother?"

"Sire, I will tell you. I was hired by a rich farmer to drive his plough, with a yoke of four oxen. Now three days ago, by great mischance, I lost the best of my bullocks, Roget, the very best ox in the plough. I have been looking for him ever since, and have neither eaten nor drunk for three days; since I dare not go back to the town, because men would put me into prison, as I have no money to pay for my loss. Of all the riches of the world I have nought but the rags upon my back. My poor old mother, too, who had nothing but one worn-out mattress, why, they have taken that from under her, and left her lying on the naked straw. That hurts me more than my own trouble. For money comes and money goes; if I have lost today, why, I may win tomorrow; and I will pay

for my ox when pay I can. Not for this will I wring my hands. And you—you weep aloud for a filthy cur. Sorrow take him who shall esteem you more."

"Certes, thou art a true comforter, fair brother, and blessed may you be. What is the worth of your bullock?"

"Sire, the villein demands twenty sous for his ox. I can not beat the price down by a single farthing."

"Hold out your hand," said Aucassin; "take these twenty sous which I have in my purse, and pay for your ox."

"Sire," answered the hind, "many thanks, and God grant you find that for which you seek."

So they parted from each other, and Aucassin rode upon his way. The night was beautiful and still, and so he fared along the forest path until he came to the seven cross-roads where Nicolette had builded her bower. Very pretty it was, and very dainty, and well furnished both outside and in, ceiling and floor, with arras and carpet of freshly plucked flowers; no sweeter habitation could man desire to see. When Aucassin came upon it, he reined back his horse sharply, and the moonbeams fell within the lodge.

"Dear God," cried Aucassin, "here was Nicolette, my sweet friend, and this has she builded with her fair white hands. For the sweetness of the house and for love of her, now will I dismount, and here will I refresh me this night."

He withdrew his foot from the stirrup, and the charger was tall and high. He dreamed so deeply on Nicolette, his very sweet friend, that he fell heavily upon a great stone, and his shoulder came from its socket. He knew himself to be grievously wounded, but he forced him to do all that he was able, and fastened his horse with the other hand to a thorn. Then he turned on his side, and crawled as best he might into the lodge. Looking through a crevice of the bower, he saw the stars shining in the sky, and one brighter than all the others, so he began to repeat—

Now is sung:

Little Star I gaze upon
Sweetly drawing to the moon.
In such golden haunt is set
Love, and bright-haired Nicolette.
God hath taken from our war
Beauty, like a shining star.

Ah, to reach her, though I fell
From her Heaven to my Hell!
Who were worthy such a thing,
Were he emperor or king?
Still you shine, oh perfect Star,
    Beyond, afar.

Now they say and tell and relate:

When Nicolette heard Aucassin speak these words, she hastened to him from where she was hidden near by. She entered in the bower, and clasping her arms about his neck, kissed and embraced him straitly. "Fair sweet friend, very glad am I to find you."

"And you, fair sweet friend, glad am I to meet." So they kissed, and held each other fast, and their joy was lovely to see.

"Ah, sweet friend," cried Aucassin, "it was but now that I was in grievous pain with my shoulder, but since I hold you close I feel neither sorrow nor wound."

Nicolette searched his hurt, and perceived that the shoulder was out of joint. She handled it so deftly with her white hands and used such skillful surgery, that by the grace of God (who loveth all true lovers) the shoulder came back to its place. Then she plucked flowers, and fresh grass and green leafage, and bound them tightly about the setting with the hem torn from her shift, and he was altogether healed.

"Aucassin," said she, "fair sweet friend, let us take thought together as to what must be done. If your father beats the wood tomorrow, and men take me, whatever may chance to you, certainly I shall be slain."

"Certes, fair sweet friend, the sorer grief would be mine. But so I may help, never shall you come to his hands." So he mounted to horse, and setting his love before him, held her fast in his arms, kissing her as he rode, and thus they came forth to the open fields.

Now is sung:

Aucassin, that loving squire,
Dainty fair to heart's desire,
Rode from out the forest dim
Clasping her he loved to him.
Placed upon the saddlebow
There he kissed her, chin and brow,
There embraced her, mouth and eyes.

But she spake him, sweetly wise:
"Love, a term to dalliance;
Since for us no home in France
See we Rome or far Byzance?"
"Sweet my love, all's one to me,
Dale or woodland, earth or sea;
Nothing care I where we ride
So I hold you at my side."
So, enlaced, the lovers went,
Skirting town and battlement,
Rocky scaur,[6] and quiet lawn;
Till one morning, with the dawn,
Broke the cliffs down to the shore,
Loud they heard the surges roar,
    Stood by the sea.

(From this point Aucassin and Nicolette were separated. After some adventures Aucassin returned to his home where he became Count of Beaucaire. Nicolette was taken to Carthage where she was recognized as the king's daughter and was to be married to a Moorish Prince. She ran away, however, and made her way to Beaucaire disguised as a minstrel.)

Now is sung:

'Neath the keep of strong Beaucaire
On a day of summer fair,
At his pleasure, Aucassin
Sat with baron, friend and kin.
Then upon the scent of flow'rs,
Song of birds, and golden hours,
Full of beauty, love, regret,
Stole the dream of Nicolette,
Came the tenderness of years;
So he drew apart in tears.
Then there entered to his eyes
Nicolette, in minstrel guise,
Touched the viol with the bow,
Sang as I will let you know.
"Lords and ladies, list to me,
High and low, of what degree;
Now I sing, for your delight,
Aucassin, that loyal knight,
And his fond friend, Nicolette.
Such the love betwixt them set
When his kinsfolk sought her head,
Fast he followed where she fled.
From their refuge in the keep

---

[6]Isolated cliff.

Paynims bore them o'er the deep.
Nought of him I know to end.
But for Nicolette, his friend,
Dear she is, desirable,
For her father loves her well;
Famous Carthage owns him king,
Where she has sweet cherishing.
Now, as lord he seeks for her,
Sultan, Caliph, proud Emir.
But the maid of these will none,
For she loves a dansellon,
Aucassin, who plighted troth.
Sworn has she some pretty oath
Ne'er shall she be wife or bride,
Never lie at baron's side
    Be he denied."

Now they say and tell and relate:

When Aucassin heard Nicolette sing in this fashion, he was glad at heart; so he drew her aside, and
asked, "Fair sweet friend," said Aucassin, "know you
nought of this Nicolette, whose ballad you have sung?"

"Sire, truly, yea; well I know her for the most loyal
of creatures, and as the most winning and modest of
maidens born. She is daughter to the King of Carthage, who took her when Aucassin also was taken,
and brought her to the city of Carthage, till he knew
for certain that she was his child, whereat he rejoiced
greatly. Any day he would give her for husband one
of the highest kings in all Spain; but rather would she
be hanged or burned than take him, however rich he
be."

"Ah, fair sweet friend," cried the Count Aucassin,
"if you would return to that country and persuade
her to have speech with me here, I would give you
of my riches more than you would dare to ask of me
or to take. Know that for love of her I choose not
to have a wife, however proud her race, but I stand
and wait; for never will there be wife of mine if it
be not she, and if I knew where to find her I should
not need to grope blindly for her thus."

"Sire," answered she, "if you will do these things,
I will go and seek her for your sake, and for hers
too; because to me she is very dear."

He pledged his word, and caused her to be given
twenty pounds. So she bade him farewell, and he
was weeping for the sweetness of Nicolette. And when
she saw his tears, "Sire," said she, "take it not so

much to heart; in so short a space will I bring her to
this town, and you shall see her with your eyes."

When Aucassin knew this, he rejoiced greatly. So
she parted from him, and fared in the town to the
house of the Viscountess, for the Viscount, her god-
father, was dead. There she lodged, and opened her
mind fully to the lady on all the business; and the
Viscountess recalled the past, and knew well that it
was Nicolette whom she had cherished. So she caused
the bath to be heated, and made her take her ease for
fully eight days. Then Nicolette sought an herb that
was called celandine, and washed herself therewith,
and became so fair as she had never been before. She
arrayed her in a rich silken gown from the lady's
goodly store, and seated herself in the chamber on a
rich stuff of broidered sendal; then she whispered the
dame, and begged her to fetch Aucassin, her friend.
This she did. When she reached the palace, lo,
Aucassin in tears, making great sorrow for the long
tarrying of Nicolette, his friend; and the lady called
to him, and said, "Aucassin, behave not so wildly;
but come with me, and I will show you that thing
you love best in all the world; for Nicolette, your
sweet friend, is here from a far country to seek her
love." So Aucassin was glad at heart.

Now is sung:
When he learned that in Beaucaire
Lodged his lady, sweet and fair,
Aucassin arose, and came
To her hostel, with the dame;
Entered in, and passed straightway
To the chamber where she lay.
When she saw him, Nicolette
Had such joy as never yet;
Sprang she lightly to her feet,
Swiftly came with welcome meet.
When he saw her, Aucassin
Oped both arms, and drew her in,
Clasped her close in fond embrace,
Kissed her eyes and kissed her face.
In such greeting sped the night,
Till, at dawning of the light,
Aucassin, with pomp most rare,
Crowned her Countess of Beaucaire.
Such delight these lovers met,
Aucassin and Nicolette.
Length of days and joy did win,
Nicolette and Aucassin;
Endeth song and tale I tell
    With marriage bell.

Songs and Poems of the Wandering Scholars

The pull of life was strong in the time when new ideas were breaking down the old medieval walls. And students (even those who were to become learned clergymen) were much the same in those days as they are now.

GAUDEAMUS IGITUR

Let us live, then, and be glad
  While young life's before us!
After youthful pastime had,
After old age, hard and sad,
  Earth will slumber o'er us.

Where are they who in this world
  Ere we kept, were keeping?
Go ye to the gods above;
Go to hell; inquire thereof;
  They are not; they are sleeping.

Brief is life, and brevity
  Briefly shall be ended;
Death comes like a whirlwind strong,
Bears us with his blast along;
  None shall be defended.

Live this university,
  Men that learning nourish;
Live each member of the same,
Long live all that bear its name,
  Let them ever flourish!

Live the commonwealth also,
  And the men that guide it!
Live our town in strength and health,
Founders, patrons, by whose wealth
  We are here provided!

Live all gods! A health to you,
  Melting maids and beauteous!
Live the wives and women too,
Gentle, loving, tender, true,
  Good, industrious, duteous!

Perish cares that pule and pine!
  Perish envious blamers!
Die the Devil, thine and mine!
Die the starch-neck Philistine!
  Scoffers and defamers!

LAURIGER HORATIUS

Horace with your laurel crowned,
Truly have you spoken;

Time, a-rush with leap and bound,
Devours and leaves us broken.

Where are now the flagons, full
Of sweet wine, honey-clear?
Where the smiles and shoves and frowns
Of blushing maiden dear?

Swift the young grape grows and swells;
So do comely lasses!
Lo, on the poet's head, the snows
Of the Time that passes!

What's the good of lasting fame,
If people think it sinful
Here and now to kiss a dame
And drink a jolly skinful!

A GOLIARD'S CREED

"A *goliard* is dying; the priest sent for in haste
speaks comfortable words; have comfort, good son:
let him but recite his Credo."[1]
That I will, Sir, and hear me now.
Credo—in dice I well believe,
That got me often bit and sup,
And many a time hath had me drunk,
And many a time delivered me
From every stitch and every penny.

In Deum—never with my will
Gave Him a thought nor ever will.
The other day I took a shirt
From a ribald and I diced it,
And lost, and never gave it back.
If I die, he can have mine.
Put it in writing, 'tis my will,
I would not like it were forgot.
Patrem—at St. Denis in France,
Good sir, I had a father once,

---

[1]The Creed being recited is as follows: I believe (credo) in God (in Deum) the Father (Patrem), Omnipotent (Omnipotentem), the Creator (Creatorem) of heaven (coeli) and earth (et terrae) . . . and in the resurrection (et . . . resurrectionem) of the body (corporis) and life everlasting (vitam aeternam). Amen.

Omnipotentem in his having,
Money and horses and fine wearing,
And by the dice that thieveth all things
I lost and gamed it all away . . . .
Creatorem who made all
I've denied - He has His will
Of me now. I know I'm dying,
Nothing here but bone and hide.
Coeli — of Heaven ever think?
Nay, but the wine that I could drink.

Et terrae - there was all my joy. . . .
(The burlesque recitation goes on to the final phrase)

Et corporis - the body's lust
I do perform. Sir Priest, I chafe
At thinking of that other life.
I tell you, 'tis not worth a straw.
And I would pray to the Lord God

That He will in no kind of way
Resurrectionem make of me,
So long as I may drench the place
With good wine where I'll be laid
And so pray I of all my friends
That if I can't, themselves will do't,
And leave me a full pot of wine
Which I may to the Judgment bring.

Vitam aeternam wilt Thou give,
O Lord God? wilt Thou forgive
All my evil, well I know it,
Amen. Priest, I now am through with't.
Through with life. Death hath its pain.
Too much . . . . too much . . . . This agony . . . .
I'm dying. I to God commend you.
I ask it of you—Pray for me."

Our Lady's Juggler

In this simple story one can see the hold and the charm of the Cult of the Virgin, especially for the simple people for whom chivalry on the one hand and philosophy on the other had no meaning.

In the days of King Louis there lived a poor juggler by the name of Barnabas, a native of Compiegne, who wandered from city to city performing tricks of skill and prowess.

On fair days he would lay down in the public square a worn and aged carpet, and after having attracted a group of children and idlers by certain amusing remarks which he had learned from an old juggler, and which he invariably repeated in the same fashion without altering a word, he would assume the strangest postures and balance a pewter plate on the tip of his nose. At first the crowd regarded him with indifference, but when, with his hands and head on the ground he threw into the air and caught with his feet six copper balls that glittered in the sunlight, or when, throwing himself back until his neck touched his heels, he assumed the form of a perfect wheel and in that position juggled with twelve knives, he elicited a murmer of admiration from his audience, and small coins rained on his carpet.

Still, Barnabas of Compiegne, like most of those who exist by their accomplishments, had a hard time making a living. Earning his bread by the sweat of his brow, he bore rather more than his share of those miseries we are all heir to through the fault of our Father Adam.

Besides, he was unable to work as much as he would have liked, for in order to exhibit his wonderful talents, he required—like the trees—the warmth of the sun and the heat of the day. In winter time he was no more than a tree stripped of its leaves, in fact, half-dead. The frozen earth was too hard for the juggler. Like the cicada mentioned by Marie de France, he suffered during the bad season from hunger and cold. But, since he had a simple heart, he suffered in silence.

He had never thought much about the origin of wealth nor about the inequality of human conditions. He firmly believed that if this world was evil the next could not but be good, and this faith upheld him. He was not like the clever fellows who sell their souls to the devil; he never took the name of God in vain; he lived the life of an honest man, and though he had no wife of his own, he did not covet his neighbor's, for woman is the enemy of strong men, as we learn by the story of Samson which is written in the Scriptures.

Verily, his mind was not turned in the direction of carnal desire, and it caused him far greater pain to renounce drinking than to forgo the pleasure of women. For, though he was not a drunkard, he enjoyed drinking when the weather was warm. He was a good man, fearing God, and devout in his adoration of the Holy Virgin. When he went into a church he never failed to kneel before the image of the Mother of God and to address her with his prayer:

"My Lady, watch over my life until it shall please God that I die, and when I am dead, see that I have the joys of Paradise."

One evening, after a day of rain, as he walked sad and bent with his juggling balls under his arm and his knives wrapped up in his old carpet seeking some barn where he might go supperless to bed, he saw a monk going in his direction, and respectfully saluted him. As they were both walking at the same pace, they fell into conversation.

"Friend," said the monk, "how does it happen that you are dressed all in green? Are you perchance going to play the part of the fool in some mystery?"[1]

"No, indeed, father," said Barnabas. "My name is Barnabas, and my business is that of juggler. It would be the finest calling in the world if I could eat every day."

"Friend Barnabas," answered the monk, "be careful what you say. There is no finer calling than the monastic. The priest celebrates the praise of God, the Virgin, and the saints; the life of a monk is a perpetual hymn to the Lord."

And Barnabas replied: "Father, I confess I spoke like an ignorant man. My estate cannot be compared

---

[1]Mystery—one of the religious dramas of the time.

to yours, and though there may be some merit in dancing and balancing a stick with a denier[2] on top of it on the end of your nose, it is in no wise comparable to your merit. Father, I wish I might, like you, sing the Office every day, especially the Office of the Very Holy Virgin, to whom I am specially and piously devoted. I would willingly give up the art by which I am known from Soissons to Beauvais, in more than six hundred cities and villages, in order to enter the monastic life."

The monk was touched by the simplicity of the juggler, and as he was not lacking in discernment, he recognized in Barnabas one of those well-disposed men of whom Our Lord has said, "Let peace be with them on earth." And he made answer therefore:

"Friend Barnabas, come with me and I will see that you enter the monastery of which I am the Prior. He who led Mary the Egyptian through the desert put me across your path in order that I might lead you to salvation."

Thus did Barnabas become a monk. In the monastery which he entered, the monks celebrated most magnificiently the cult of the Holy Virgin, each of them bringing to her service all the knowledge and skill which God had given him.

The Prior, for his part, wrote books, setting forth, according to the rules of scholasticism, all the virtues of the Mother of God. Brother Maurice copied these treatises with a cunning hand on pages of parchment, while Brother Alexandre decorated them with delicate miniatures representing the Queen of Heaven seated on the throne of Solomon, with four lions on guard at the foot of it. Around her head, which was encircled by a halo, flew seven doves, the seven gifts of the Holy Spirit: fear, piety, knowledge, power, judgment, intelligence, and wisdom. With her were six golden-haired virgins: Humility, Prudence, Retirement, Respect, Virginity, and Obedience. At her feet two little figures, shining white and quite naked, stood in suppliant attitudes. They were souls imploring, not in vain, Her all-powerful intercession for their salvation. On another page Brother Alexandre depicted Eve in the presence of Mary, that one might see at the same time sin and its redemption, woman humiliated, and the Virgin exalted. Among the other much prized pictures in his book were the Well of Living Waters, the Fountain, the Lily, the Moon, the Sun, and the Closed Garden, of which much is said in the Canticle; the Gate of Heaven and the City of God. These were all images of the Virgin.

Brother Marbode, too, was one of the cherished children of Mary. He was ever busy cutting images of stone, so that his beard, his eyebrows, and his hair were white with the dust, and his eyes perpetually swollen and full of tears. But he was a hardy and a happy man in his old age, and there was no doubt that the Queen of Paradise watched over the declining days of Her child. Marbode represented Her seated in a pulpit, Her forehead encircled by a halo, with an orb of pearls. He was at great pains to make the folds of Her robe cover the feet of Her of whom the prophet has said, "My beloved is like a closed garden."

At times he represented Her as a graceful child, and Her image seemed to say, "Lord, Thou art My Lord!"

There were also in the monastery poets who composed prose writings in Latin and hymns in honor of the Most Gracious Virgin Mary; there was, indeed, one among them—a Picard—who translated the Miracles of Our Lady into rimed verses in the vulgar tongue.

Perceiving so great a competition in praise and so fine a harvest of good works, Barnabas fell to lamenting his ignorance and simplicity.

"Alas!" he sighed as he walked by himself one day in the little garden shaded by the monastery wall, "I am so unhappy because I cannot, like my brothers, give worthy praise to the Holy Mother of God to whom I have consecrated all the love in my heart. Alas, I am a stupid fellow, without art, and for your service, Madame, I have no edifying sermons, no fine treatises nicely prepared according to the rules, no beautiful paintings, no cunningly carved statues, and no verses counted off by feet and marching in measure! Alas, I have nothing."

Thus did he lament and abandon himself to his misery.

One evening when the monks were talking together by way of diversion, he heard one of them tell of a monk who could not recite anything but the *Ave Maria*. He was scorned for his ignorance, but after he died there sprang from his mouth five roses, in honor of the five letters in the name Maria. Thus was his holiness made manifest.

In listening to this story, Barnabas was conscious once more of the Virgin's beneficence, but he was not

_____

[2]Denier—a small coin.

consoled by the example of the happy miracle, for his heart was full of zeal and he wanted to celebrate the glory of his Lady in Heaven.

He sought for a way in which to do this, but in vain, and each day brought him greater sorrow, until one morning he sprang joyously from his cot and ran to the chapel, where he remained alone for more than an hour. He returned thither again after dinner, and from that day onward he would go into the chapel every day the moment it was deserted, passing the greater part of the time which the other monks dedicated to the pursuit of the liberal arts and the sciences. He was no longer sad and he sighed no more. But such singular conduct aroused the curiosity of the other monks, and they asked themselves why Brother Barnabas retired alone so often, and the Prior, whose business it was to know everything that his monks were doing, determined to observe Barnabas. One day, therefore, when Barnabas was alone in the chapel, the Prior entered in company with two of the oldest brothers, in order to watch, through the bars of the door, what was going on within.

They saw Barnabas before the image of the Holy Virgin, his head on the floor and his feet in the air, juggling with six copper balls and twelve knives. In honor of the Holy Virgin he was performing the tricks which had in former days brought him the greatest fame. Not understanding that he was thus putting his best talents at the service of the Holy Virgin, the aged brothers cried out against such sacrilege. The Prior knew that Barnabas had a simple soul, but he believed that the man had lost his wits. All three set about to remove Barnabas from the chapel, when they saw the Virgin slowly descend from the altar and, with a fold of her blue mantle, wipe the sweat that streamed over the juggler's forehead.

Then the Prior, bowing his head down to the marble floor, repeated these words:

"Blessed are the pure in heart, for they shall see God."

"Amen," echoed the brothers, bowing down to the floor.

The Prolog to the Canterbury Tales
Goeffrey Chaucer

Chaucer gives us here a picture of some of the people of the late Middle Ages. Notice the shrewdness of his description: small references which reveal interesting qualities of the characters which one is apt to miss. The selection is included to give more than an interesting description of a group of people. A whole panorama of the late Middle Ages is presented.

When April with its sweet and welcome showers
The drought of March has pierced, and to the flowers
And every vein of growing things has sent
Life-giving moisture, wholesome nourishment;
When Zephyr,[1] too, has with his own sweet breath
Revived again in every wood and heath
The tender shoots, and when the northering sun
Has half his course into the Ram[2] now run,
And little song-birds make their melody
That sleep all thru the night with open eye
—So Nature urges them with her commands—
Then people long to go in pilgrim bands,
And palmers[3] once again to seek far strands
And distant shrines, well known in many lands:
Especially, from every county's end
Of England, Canterbury-ward they wend,
The holy blessed martyr[4] there to seek
Who was their help when they were ill or weak.

It happened in that season, on a day,
In Southwerk at the Tabard as I lay,
Ready my pilgrimage to undertake
To Canterbury, for my own soul's sake,
At night there came into that hostelry
Some nine-and-twenty in a company
Of various folk, who came by chance to fall
Into one group, and pilgrims were they all;
To Canterbury they all planned to ride.
The chambers and the stables there were wide,
And we were lodged in comfort, with the best.
And very soon—the sun now gone to rest—
So had I spoken with them, every one,
That I was of their fellowship anon,
And planned with them quite early to arise
To take our way, as I shall you advise:

—Nevertheless, while I have time and space,

Before I further in this story pace,
It seems to me both sensible and sound
To tell you in detail of all I found
About each one, just as it seemed to me,
And what they were, and what was their degree,
And tell what kind of costume they were in;
And at a knight, then, will I first begin.

KNIGHT

A knight there was, a worthy man,
Who from the time when that he first began
To ride on quests, had well loved chivalry,
Truth and honor, freedom and courtesy.
Full worthy was this man in his lord's war,
And therein had he ridden—none so far—
Thru Christendom, and heathen lands no less,
Always honored for his worthiness.
At Alexandria was he when it was won;
Many a time he had the board begun[5]
Above all other guests, in distant Prussia;
In Latvia[6] he fought, again in Russia,
No Christian man so oft, of his degree.
Against the Moors in Spain he fought, and he
In Africa and Asia Minor warred

---

[1]Zephyr—the west wind: here, the life-giving breath of Spring.

[2]Ram—the third sign of the zodiac, which the sun enters c. March 12 and leaves c. April 11 to enter Taurus. Chaucer is only saying that April is well-advanced; the date is about April 18.

[3]Palmers—pilgrims who had visited the Holy Lands bore palms as token of their pilgrimage.

[4]Martyr—Thomas à Becket, murdered in the cathedral at Canterbury in 1170, was canonized in 1173. His shrine was the great national shrine, and many stories of miraculous cures were told of it.

[5]He sat in the seat of honor, at the head of the table: a mark of distinction and worth.

Against the infidel; his mighty sword
Found service all about the Inland Sea;
At any noble action, there he'd be.
At mortal battles had he been—fifteen;
And for the faith he fought, at Tramyssene,
In tourney thrice, and each time slew his foe.
And this same worthy knight had been also
At one time with the lord of Palatye
Against another heathen land—Turkey;
And every time he held the topmost prize.
And yet, with all his courage, he was wise—
His conduct, meek as that of any maid.
No villainy had this man ever said
In all his life to any sort of wight.
He was a true, a perfect, gentle knight.
    —But, to tell you briefly his array,
His horse was good, but certainly not gay;
He wore a fustian garment (a gypoun)
All rust-and-armor stained (his haubergeon),
For he had just completed the last stage
Of travel, and at once made pilgrimage.

SQUIRE

With him was his son, a fine young Squire,
A lover and a lusty bachelor,
With locks as curly as if laid in press;
Near twenty years of age he was, I guess.
His stature was of ordinary length,
But agile, and revealing a great strength.
And he had ridden in the cavalry
In Flanders, in Artois, and Picardy,
And born him well, within his life's short space,
In hope that he might win his lady's grace.
Fancily clad in fashion's newest whim,
—One thought of flowering fields, on seeing him!—
Singing he was, or whistling, all the day:
He was as fresh as is the month of May.
His gown was short, with sleeves both long and wide;
He knew just how to sit a horse and ride,
To make up songs, and fit the words aright,
To joust, and dance, and draw, and even write.
So hot he loved (at least, so goes the tale)
He slept o'nights less than the nightingale!
Courteous was he, meek, in service able,
And carved before his father at the table;

YEOMAN

A yeoman had he—no other servants, tho,
As at that time; it pleased him to ride so—
And he was clad in coat and hood of green.
A sheaf of peacock arrows, bright and keen,

Under his belt he carried, gay but grim;
(He well knew how to keep his gear in trim—
His arrow never drooped with feathers low)
And in his hand he bore a mighty bow.
His head was cropped; his face the sun had burned;
Of woodcraft, every subtle trick he'd learned.
Upon his arm a bracer gay he wore
And by his side a sword and buckler bore,
And on the other side, a dagger gay,
As sharp as point of spear, well sheathed away.
A Christopher medal gleamed upon his breast;
His horn's green sling was hung across his chest.
He must have been a forester, I guess.

PRIORESS

There was also a nun, a Prioress,
Whose smile was sweetly simple, but not coy;[7]
Her greatest oath was but by good St. Loy;
And she was known as Madam Eglantine.
Full well she sang the services divine
Intoning thru her nose right properly.
And French she spoke, both well and carefully,
But Stratford-fashion, if the truth be told;
Parisian French she knew not—hers was old.
Her table-manners were well taught, withal;
She never from her lips let morsels fall,
Nor wet her fingers in the sauce too deep;
She knew just how to lift her food, to keep
A single drop from falling on her breast.
In etiquette she found the greatest zest.
Her upper lip she always wiped so clean
That in her cup there never could be seen
A speck of grease, when she had drunk her fill;
Fine manners at the table were her will.
And truly she was fond of harmless sport,
Pleasant, friendly, and of good report;
She took great pains the court to imitate,
Her manner formal, an affair of state;
For she would have men do her reverence.
But now, to tell about her moral sense,
So kindly was she and so piteous,
She wept, if ever that she saw a mouse
Caught in a trap, if it were dead, or bled.
Some little dogs she had, and these she fed
With roasted meat, or milk and good white bread.

---

[6]Probably he had fought in Latvia or Lithuania, with the Order of Teutonic Knights. Chaucer lists by name other scenes of the Knight's exploits: the main point is, they were associated with fighting for the faith rather than for gain. The Knight is very nearly the ideal knight of chivalry.

[7]Chaucer says her smiling *was* coy: but in his day the word meant "bashful," "modest," "retiring."

But sore she wept if one of them were dead,
Or if men hit one with a stick, to smart;
And all for her was conscience, tender heart.
Becomingly her wimple fell in pleat;
As blue as glass her eyes, her nose right neat;
Her mouth was very small, and soft, and red;
But certainly she had a fine forehead;
It was almost a span in breadth, I'd say—
She was not under-sized, in any way!
Quite stylish was the cloak the lady wore;
About her arm small coral beads she bore,
And they were interspersed with gauds[8] of green,
And therefrom hung a brooch of golden sheen,
Whereon was written first a crowned "A,"
And after, "Amor Vincit Omnia."
She had another nun, for company,
Who was her chaplain; and her priests were three.

MONK

A monk there was—th' administrative sort—
Outrider,—hunting was his favorite sport—
A manly man, to be an abbott able.
Full many a fancy horse he had in stable,
And when he rode, men could his bridle hear
Jingling in the whistling wind as clear
And just as loud as does the chapel-bell
Where this good lord was Keeper of the Cell.
The rule of Maurus or St. Benedict[9]
This monk considered old and over-strict.
He'd rather let the old things go their way.
And follow fashions of a newer day.
For texts he didn't give a well-plucked hen
That say that hunters are not holy men,
Nor that a monk who leaves his cloister's bounds
Is like a fish that's out of water—zounds!
—Why shouldn't monks go out of cloister?
Texts like that aren't worth an oyster!
And I said his views were good thereon.
Why should he study till his wits were gone
Upon a book in cloister, like a clerk,
Or labor with his hands, always at work,
As old St. Austin[10] bids? What good is served?
Let Austin have his work to him reserved!
And so this monk his hunting much preferred.
Greyhounds had he, swift as any bird;
In riding, and in hunting of the hare,
Was his delight—and for no cost he'd spare.
I saw his sleeves were fur-trimmed at the hand,
Expensively, the finest in the land;
And, to fasten up his hood beneath his chin.
He had a rich, elaborate, golden pin;

A love-knot in the larger end there was.
His head was bald, and shone as bright as glass;
As if anointed shone his ruddy face.
He was a lord right fat, and in good case.
His eyes were staring, rolling in his head,
Gleaming like the furnace-fires red.
His boots were supple, and his horse was great;
Now certainly, he was a fine prelate!
He was not pale as some poor starveling ghost.
A fat swan loved he best of any roast.
His palfrey was as brown as any berry.

FRIAR

A friar there was, a wanton man and merry;
A Limiter,[11] a most impressive one;
Indeed in all four orders there was none
Who knew so much of small talk, fine language;
And he had made right many a marriage
Of young girls at his own expense and hire;
A pillar of his order was this friar!
Familiar and full well beloved was he
With franklins[12] over all in his county,
For as confessor he had won renown
Far more than curates had in their possession
—His order licensed him to hear confession.
His hearing of confession was a pleasure,
His absolution always within measure;
The penance he imposed was never stern—
If something for himself he'd thereby earn!
For when to his poor order gifts were given,
It must be sign the givers were well shriven;
For such gifts, said this friar for his part,
Show clearly that a man is changed at heart.
For many men are hardened, it appears,
So that they find no outlet thru their tears;
Instead of tears and useless weeping, then,
The silver that they give will save such men.
He always kept his tippet[13] stuffed with knives
And pins to give to young attractive wives.
Certainly he had a merry note;

---

[8]Gauds—the large Paternoster beads marking off the sections of a rosary.

[9]St. Benedict and his disciple Maurus, founders of the Benedictine Order; St. Benedict established the famous monastery at Monte Cassino in 529.

[10]St. Augustine, Bishop of Hippo, was a great proponent of labor as part of the monastic life.

[11]A "Limiter" was a friar licensed to beg within a definite ("limited") region.

[12]Franklins were landholders of free, but not of noble, birth; they ranked below the gentry.

[13]Tippet—a long scarf; a handy substitute for pockets.

He knew well how to sing, and play a rote;[14]
At song-fests he would win the prize outright.
As any lily flower his neck was white.
And like a champion wrestler he was strong.
All the taverns, as he went along,
And every hostler, and barmaid, he knew,
Better than outcasts and the beggar-crew;
Because, to such a worthy man as he,
It was not fitting, you will all agree,
To have acquaintance with such worthless wretches;
Such contact brings no profit, nothing fetches. . . .
There is no gain in dealing with *canaille*,[15]
But with rich men, of social station high.
And thus, whenever profit would arise,
This friar was humble, courteous, and wise.
So virtuous a man was nowhere found;
And what a beggar, as he made his round!
Why, if a widow had no shoe to show,
So pleasant was his "In principio . . ."[16]
He'd have the widow's mite, before he went!
His income always went beyond his rent.
And he could play around like any whelp;
On love-days[17] he knew how to be of help.
He was not like a needy monk or scholar,
Threadbare, shabby, down to his last dollar;
But he was like a great man or a pope.
Of finest woolen was his semicope,[18]
That rounded like a bell out of its mold.
He lisped a little, if the truth he told,
To make his speech sound sweeter on his tongue;
And in his harping, after he had sung,
His twinkling eyes shone in his head as bright
As do the stars on cold and frosty night.
This worthy Limiter was called Hubert.

MERCHANT

The merchant, next:—with forked beard, and girt
In livery, high on his horse he sat,
Upon his head a Flemish beaver hat;
His boots were clasped up in the latest mode;
He spoke in serious fashion as he rode,
Referring always to his gains in gold.
He wished, he said, to have the sea patrolled
From Middleburgh across to Orewell.[19]
A money-changer, he could buy or sell;
This worthy man knew how his wits to set:
No one ever knew he was in debt,
So well he managed all the deals he made,
His sales and bargains, and his tricks of trade.
He was a worthy man, in every way;
But what his name, I never heard men say!

CLERK

A clerk of Oxford rode with us also,
Who turned to logic-study long ago;
His horse was lean and skinny as a rake,
And he was not so fat, I'll undertake!
But hollow-looking, hungry evermore;
Quite threadbare were the shabby clothes he wore,
For he had found as yet no benefice,
Nor was so worldly as to hold office.
For he had rather have, at his bed's head,
A score of books, all bound in black or red,
Of Aristotle and philosophy
Than rich robes, fiddle, or gay psaltery.
And yet philosophy, if truth be told,
Had brought him in but very little gold,
But all that willing friends to him had lent
On books and learning eagerly he spent;
When friends helped with his schooling, then for those
He'd pray in earnest, for their souls' repose.
Of study he took every care and heed;
Not a word he spoke more than was need;
Then what he said was formal, reverent,
Short and to the point, of high intent;
Pertaining unto virtue was his speech;
And gladly would he learn, and gladly teach.

SERGEANT-AT-LAW

A sergeant of the law, who used to go
Full many a time to St. Paul's portico,[20]
There was also, of richest excellence;
Discreet he was and of great reverence.
—At least he seemed so, for his words were wise.
He often sat as justice in assize,[21]

---

[14]Rote—a stringed instrument, sometimes played with a bow, sometimes with a fixed wheel like a hurdy-gurdy.

[15]Canaille—riff-raff, rabble.

[16]"In principio . . ."—the beginning of the Last Gospel. These verses were thought to have supernatural powers, and were used as greeting, blessing, and the like.

[17]"Love-days" were days set aside for settlement of disputes by arbitration; the clergy were often the judges.

[18]A short cape or cloak.

[19]The port of Middleburgh, just off the coast of Netherlands, was just opposite the English port of Harwich (then called "Orewell"). The merchant was probably engaged (among other things!) in the wool trade, and desired protection for his shipping.

[20]The porch of St. Paul's cathedral was a traditional meeting-place for lawyers.

[21]Assize: session of the court.

By full commission or in his own right.
His learning and his fame were more than slight,
So he had fees, and robes, abundantly.
Nowhere a greater purchaser[22] than he.
Provisions of the law so well he knew
That none could quibble with the deeds he drew.
But no one does as much as this man does—
And yet, he seemed much busier than he was . . .
From William's day[23] he knew each court decision
In every case, by heart, and with precision.
His documents were drawn up so that none
Could find a fault or loop-hole—not a one;
The Statutes he'd recite, and all by rote.
He rode quite simply in a medley coat,
Girt with a belt of striped silk. No more
I have to tell of what this Sergeant wore.

FRANKLIN

With him a franklin rode, whose beard was white
As any daisy, and his face was bright
And ruddy: sanguine, one would call the man.
He loved a wine-sop as the day began.
He liked to live in comfort and in joy;
Truly, he was Epicurus' boy,
Who stoutly held that comfort—that is, pleasure—
Was of happiness the only measure.
A householder, and a great, was he;
He was St. Julian[24] in his own country.
His bread and ale were uniformly fine;
No man was better stocked than he with wine;
Baked meats were never lacking at his place—
Both fish and flesh—or he'd have felt disgrace!
It snowed in his house both of meat and drink,
Of every good thing that a man can think.
According to the season of the year,
So changed his food, and all his table-cheer;
Fat partridges he kept on his preserve,
And fishponds stocked, his table well to serve.
Woe to the cook, unless his sauce were fine,
And sharp and tasty, and the meal on time!
His covered table was not put away
But stood in readiness the live-long day.
At session,[25] he was lord—no man stood higher—
And many a time he served as Knight-of-Shire.
He wore a knife, and purse—made all of silk—,
Hung from his girdle, white as morning milk.
He'd served as sheriff, and county auditor;
Nowhere was a more worthy vavasour.[26]

THE FIVE TRADESMEN

A haberdasher, and a carpenter,
A weaver, dyer, and an arras-maker,
—All these were clad in the same livery
Of one great dignified fraternity;
All fresh and new the gear they wore, it seemed;
Not with brass their knives and trimmings gleamed,
But silver, and fine work in every part;
Their belts and purses were in style, and smart.
Important citizens, enough, were all
These men, to sit on dais in guild-hall,
And anyone of them, it's safe to state,
Was wise enough to be a magistrate;
They certainly had goods enough, and rent;
And, I'm sure, their wives would give assent,
For otherwise they would have been in blame;
It's good to hear a "Madam" with one's name,
And lead the way at church, and to be seen
With mantle borne, as royal as a queen!

COOK

A cook was in their party, to prepare
Their favorite dishes, foods both rich and rare:
Chickens, marrow-bones, and tarts well-flavored.
Many a draught of London ale he'd savored.
He knew how to roast, boil, broil, and fry,
Make soups and sauces hot, and bake a pie.
A pity was it, so it seemed to me,
That on his shin an ulcerous sore had he.
His blanc-mange[27] would be rated with the best.

SHIPMAN

A shipman was there, living for to west
—For all I know he came from Dartmouth town.
He rode as best he could a nag; his gown
Of falding[28] rough hung clear down to his knee;

---

[22]Purchaser—a buyer of land. Does Chaucer imply that the Sergeant is desirous of becoming a landed gentleman, or that he is a land-speculator?

[23]The Sergeant knew the law clear back to the conquest—the statutes of William the Conqueror.

[24]St. Julian is the patron saint of hospitality.

[25]These were probably sessions of the Justices of the Peace, not the big assizes.

[26]Vavasour—a substantial landholder.

[27]Not like the modern pudding, but a compound of minced capon, almonds, cream, sugar, and flour!

[28]Falding—coarse woolen cloth with shaggy nap.

A dagger hanging on a lace had he
About his neck, beneath his arm and down.
Hot summer suns had made his hue all brown;
A boon companion was this salty tar.
He'd helped himself to many a good wine jar
From Bordeaux, while below his owners slept.
Fine scruple was a thing he never kept.
In sea-fights, if he got the upper hand,
By water he sent them home to every land.
But no man, in his skill to reckon tides,
His streams, his chance and all besides,
His harbors, and his moons, and navigation;
From Hull to Carthage had his reputation.
Bold he was, but wise, in undertaking;
Many a tempest set his beard to shaking!
And he knew all the havens as they were
From Gotland to the Cape of Finisterre,[29]
And every creek in Brittany and Spain.
His barge was called the good ship "Madeleine."

PHYSICIAN

A doctor of physic, known both far and near,
Was with us; nowhere could you find his peer,
In surgery or physic; what is more,
Well-grounded in astrology's deep lore,
He treated patients for the better part
By horoscope and such-like magic art.
For he knew how to forecast, by his spell,
The ascendant planets that would make them well.
He knew the cause of every malady,
Whether of cold or hot or moist or dry,[30]
Where engendered, from what humor traced;
He was a doctor of much skill and taste.
The cause once known, and of the source once sure,
He quickly brought the sick man to his cure.
And he had ready his apothecaries
To send him potent drugs and lectuaries—[31]
For each assisted other, gold to gain;
Their friendship was no new one, that is plain!
—This doctor knew old Esculapius,
The Greek Deiscorides, and ancient Rufus,
Hippocrates, Galen, Hali the Saracen,
Serapion, and Rhazes, Avicen,
Averroes, Bernard, Constantine,
Gatesden, Gilbert, John the Damascene.[32]
And in his diet temperate was he;
It was not full of superfluity,
But wholesome, one of healthful nourishment.
Bible-study was not this man's bent.

He dressed in costly colors, red and blue,
With taffeta and silken linings, too;
And yet he was a man to hate expense.
He kept what he had earned in pestilence;
And since, in physic, gold's a cordial, he
Found gold was what he loved especially!

WIFE OF BATH

A goodwife came from Bath, that ancient city,
But she was rather deaf; and that's a pity.
Her skill in making cloth, I hear, was such
That, as they say, she wove "to beat the Dutch."[33]
In all the parish never a woman came
To offering before this worthy dame—
But if there did, so much enraged was she
That she lost all her Christian charity!
Her kerchiefs were of finest weave, and dear;
They must have weighed a full ten pounds, or near,
That on a Sunday covered up her head.
Her hose[34] were fancy-fine, of scarlet red,
And tightly tied; her shoes were soft and new.
Her face was bold, and fair, and red of hue.
She was a worthy woman all her life;
To husbands five this woman had been wife,
Not counting other company in youth;
There's no need now to speak of that, in truth!
Three times to Jerusalem she'd been;
Full many a distant stream her feet were in . . .
To Rome she'd been, and gone to far Boulogne,
In Spain to Santiago, to Cologne;
She knew a lot of wandering by the way.
Gap-toothed this goodwife was, the truth to say.
Easily her ambling horse she sat,
With flowing wimple—on her head a hat
As broad as is a buckler or a shield;
A foot-mantle left her ample hips concealed;
And on her feet she wore well-sharpened spurs.
The gift of laughter and of fun was hers.

---

[29]That is, from Sweden to the western tip of France.

[30]The reference is to the theory of the "bodily humors," or fluids, and their effect on the health and temperament of the person.

[31]Lectuaries—more properly, electuaries. Medicine in a sticky or sirupy base, originally meant to be "licked up" by the patient!

[32]This impressive list is to indicate that the doctor was thoroughly versed in all the medical authorities, ancient and "modern." It seems curious to a modern reader to find among his qualifications that he is an excellent astrologer.

[33]Chaucer says "She passed hem of Ypres and of Gaunt" —the Low Countries were famous for textiles.

[34]Not stockings, but gaiters or leggings.

Love's remedies she knew, and not by chance;
She knew first-hand the art of that old dance.

PARSON

A good religious man went on this ride,
A parish priest, who served the countryside;
Poor in money, rich in holy work,
A very learned scholar was this clerk.
The gospel of Our Lord he strove to preach,
And tried his poor parishioners to teach.
Benign he was, hard-working, diligent,
In adverse seasons patiently content,
As he had proved on more than one occasion.
He did not threaten excommunication
When poor folk could not pay their tithes; instead,
The little that he had he'd share, his bread
As well as money, with a cheerful heart.
Contentment with a little was his art.
Tho wide his parish, houses far asunder,
He'd not neglect, in spite of rain or thunder,
The afflicted in mind, body, or estate,
The farthest in his parish, small or great;
Staff in hand, he'd visit them, on foot.
This fine example to his flock he put,
That first he acted; afterward he taught.
From out the Gospel these words he had caught.
This figure he had added thereunto:
"If fine gold rust, what shall poor iron do?"
For if the priest be foul, in whom we trust,
No wonder if the ignorant people rust;
A shame it is, and brings the priest to mock—
A shitty shepherd, tending a clean flock!
Rather should a priest example give,
By his clean living, how his sheep should live.
He never set his benefice to hire
And left his sheep encumbered in the mire,
Running up to London, to St. Paul's,
Singing paid requiems within those walls;
Nor in some brotherhood withdrew, alone;
But caring for his flock he stayed at home,
So that no wolf his helpless sheep might harry;
He was a shepherd, not a mercenary.
A virtuous man and holy was he, then,
Not arrogant in scolding sinful men,
Not haughty in his speech, or too divine,
But prudent in his teaching and benign.
To draw the folk to heaven by kindliness
And good example was his business.
But then, if any one were obstinate,
Whoever he was, of high or low estate,

He'd scold him sharply, raise a mighty row;
Nowhere was there a better priest, I vow.
No hankering after pomp and reverence,
No putting on of airs, and no pretence;
The lore of Christ and His apostles true
He taught; but what he preached, he'd do.

PLOWMAN

With him there was a plowman, his own brother,
Who'd loaded many a cart with dung; no other
Was a worker good and true as he,
Living in peace and perfect charity.
God he loved best, with his entire soul,
At all times, whether he knew joy or dole;
And next, as Christ commands, he loved his neighbor.
For he would thresh, or ditch, or dig, and labor
For Jesus' sake, without a thot of pay,
To help poor folk, if in his power it lay.
Cheerfully, in full, his tithes he paid
Both on his goods, and what by work he made.
In tabard clad, he rode an old gray mare.
—(A miller and a reeve were also there,
A summoner, also, and a pardoner,
A manciple and I—that's all there were.)

MILLER

The miller was a big and hefty lout,
Brawny, burly, big of bone, and stout.
Against all comers, as events turned out,
He won the ram[35] at every wrestling-bout,
Stocky, broad-shouldered, in build a battering-ram,
There was no door he couldn't tear from jamb
Or break it, running at it with his head.
His beard like any sow or fox was red,
And broad as any spade, and cut off short.
Right atop his nose he had a wart;
In it stood a little tuft of hairs,
Red as the bristles in an old sow's ears.
As for his nostrils, they were black and wide;
A sword and buckler bore he by his side.
His big mouth like a furnace needed stoking:
He was a jesting clown whose bawdy joking
Mostly ran to sin: it wasn't nice.
From the grain he ground he'd steal—and then toll
   thrice;
Good millers have a golden thumb, it's said . . .
A white coat, and a blue hood on his head,
He wore; and with his bagpipe's merry sound
He cheered us as we started, outward-bound.

---

[35]The customary wrestling prize.

MANCIPLE[36]

There was a manciple from the Inns of Court[37]
To whom all purchasers could well resort
To learn to buy supplies in large amount;
For whether he bought by cash, or on account,
He watched his dealings with so close an eye
That he came out ahead in every try.
Now is it not indeed by God's own grace
That he, uneducated, could outface
His masters—that heap of learned men?
His employers numbered three times ten,
Legal experts, with good sense endowed:
—There must have been a dozen in the crowd
Worthy to be stewards of rent or land
Of any lord in England, to help him stand
Within his income, if he only would,
In honor, out of debt, all to the good,
Or help him live as sparsely as desired:
Why, they could help a county, as required,
In any kind of case that might befall:—
And yet this manciple could beat them all.

REEVE

The reeve, a scrawny, peevish man was he;
His beard was shaved as close as close could be;
His hair was shorn off short around his ears,
His top docked like a priest's, so it appears.
His legs were very long and very lean,
Thin as a stick; no calf could there be seen.
He managed well the granary and bin;
No auditor could get ahead of him.
And he could estimate, by drought and rain,
The yield he could expect of seed and grain.
His lord's sheep, cows, and other stock,
The swine and horses, and the poultry-flock,
Were wholly in his hands to manage well,
And on his oath the reckoning to tell,
Ever since his lord reached twenty years.
No man could ever find him in arrears.
There was no agent, shepherd, hired hand,
Whose tricks he didn't know or understand;
They feared him, everyone, as they feared death.
His dwelling place stood fair upon the heath,
But sheltered was his place with green trees' shade.
Far better bargains than his lord he made;
Richly he had featherd his own nest.
He knew the way to please his master best,
By giving him, or lending, his own goods,
And getting not mere thanks, but coats and hoods.
In youth, he'd learned a trade—he was a wright;
In carpentry he was a skillful wight.

This reeve's good horse rode at an easy trot;
A dapple-gray he was; his name was Scot.
His long surcoat of Persian blue was made,
And by his side he bore a rusty blade.
Of Norfolk was this reeve of whom I tell,
From just outside a town called Baldeswell.
He tucked up all his garments like a friar,
And rode the hindmost: Such was his desire.

SUMMONER[38]

A summoner was there with us in that place,
Who had a fire-red cherubic face,
All pimply, full of whelks; his eyes were narrow,
And he was hot and lecherous as a sparrow,
With black and scabby brows, and scanty beard:
His was the sort of face that children feared.
There was no mercury nor brimstone, salve
Of tartar, lead, or borax, that could have
The strength to rid him of the lumps and knobs
Disfiguring his face in ugly gobs;
These acneous pimples covered both his cheeks.
And he was fond of garlic, onions, leeks;
He loved to drink strong wine, as red as blood;
Then spoke and cried as one demented would.
And having drunk his wine, and feeling gay,
Then not a word but Latin would he say;
—He knew a few expressions—two or three—
That he had picked up, out of some decree—
No wonder, for he heard it every day:
And everybody knows that even a jay
Can learn to call out "Wat!" as well as the Pope!
But when he tried with other things to cope,
His slender stock of learning would give out:
"Questio quid juris!"[39] he would shout.
He was a noble rascal, and a kind;
A better fellow would be hard to find.
He would arrange it, for a quart of wine,
For a friend of his to keep a concubine
The whole year thru, and never get in trouble;
Oh, he was very good at dealings double!
And if he liked a person whom he saw,
He'd teach that person not to stand in awe
Nor fear, for what he did, the archdeacon's curse—
Why, does a man's soul live within his purse?
Yet purse alone can suffer penalty:

---

[36]Steward, or purchasing agent.

[37]The lodgings of the lawyers.

[38]Process-server or bailiff for the ecclesiastical court, usually presided over by the archdeacon.

[39]"The question is, what part of the law applies?"—a lawyer's technicality.

"Purse is the archdeacon's hell," said he.
(But well I know he lied in saying so;
Such curses ought the guilty men forego.
As absolution saves, so curses slay;
From all *Significavits*,[40] stay away!)
And at his mercy, in his tender charge,
Were young folks of the diocese at large;
He knew their secrets; they were easily led.
He had set a garland on his head
So large it would have served for an ale-stake.[41]
A buckler he had made him of a cake.

PARDONER

With him a noble pardoner rode, his pal
And peer (his patron-house was Ronceval),[42]
Who straight from Rome had come—or so said he—
And loud he sang, "Come hither, love, to me!"
The summoner added, in the bass, a ground:
No trumpet had one half so loud a sound.
The pardoner had yellow hair, like wax,
That hung as limp as does a bunch of flax;
Stringily his locks hung from his head,
So that his shoulders were all overspread,
But thin it lay, in hanks there, one by one.
No hood he wore; he left it off, for fun,
Trussed up in his bag. It seemed to him
That thus he rode in fashion's latest whim,
Uncovered—save for cap—his head all bare.
Staring eyes he had, just like a hare.
A vernicle he'd sewed upon his cap.
His wallet lay before him, in his lap,
Brimful of pardons, hot from Rome, please note!
Small the voice he had, just like a goat.
He had no beard: nor ever would, in truth:
As it were fresh-shaved, his face was smooth;
I think he was a gelding—or a mare.
But of his trade, from Berwyck clear to Ware
Was never such a pardoner as this lad!

In his bag a pillow-case he had
Which—so he claimed—was once Our Lady's veil—
He said he had a fragment of the sail
That once St. Peter used, in days of yore,
Before Our Lord gave him new work, ashore!
He had a cross of latten,[43] set with stones,
And in a glass jar carried some pig's bones.
But with these silly "relics," when he spied
Some simple priest out in the country-side,
On such a day more money would he win
Than in two months the parson could fetch in;
And thus, with flattery and lying mock,
He'd fool the priest and all his simple flock.
But give the devil his due; for, when all's past,
In church he was a great ecclesiast;
Well knew he how to read a Bible story,
But especially well he sang the offertory;
For well he knew that when the song was sung,
He then would preach, and sharpen up his tongue,
To win their money from the gullible crowd;
That's why he sang so merrily and loud.
Now I've told you briefly, clause by clause,
The state, the number and array and cause
In which assembled was this company
In Southwerk at this noble hostelry
That's called the Tabard Inn, right near the Bell.

(And that is all that this book has to tell:
But Reader, while your interest still prevails,
Go read the rest of Chaucer's Canterbury Tales.)

---

[40]*Significavit*—the opening word in a summons to appear before the ecclesiastical court.

[41]Ale was advertised by a bunch of greens, hanging on a stake or pole above the door.

[42]A London hospital.

[43]Cheap metal.

The Divine Comedy
Dante Alighieri

At the outset, let us agree that reading the *Commedia* is no easy task. Dante himself recognized this when, in writing to a friend and patron, he said:

> The meaning of this work is not simple . . . for we obtain one meaning from the letter of it, and another from that which the letter signifies; and the first is called *literal,* but the other *allegorical* or *mystical* . . . .

> The subject of the whole work, then, taken in the literal sense is "the state of the soul after death straightforwardly affirmed," for the development of the whole work hinges on and about that. But, if, indeed, the work is taken *allegorically,* its subject is: "Man, as by good or ill deserts, in the exercise of his free choice, he becomes liable to rewarding or punishing justice."

On two scores, the rewards of reading the *Commedia* justify the effort. First, it represents the finest statement of the medieval synthesis that we have; it is comparable to Chartres Cathedral or the *Summa Theologica* of St. Thomas. Second, and more important, it presents one of the half-dozen very great insights into the nature and meaning of human life in all of literature or art. It is meaningful to us in the twentieth century not only as a great historical document, but as living literature.

Its form represents as tight a discipline as we know in literature, for it takes its shape around the number three. It is written in *terza rima,* a form preserved in the translations taken from the Hell and Purgatory as excerpts from those sections are given here. It is written in three great sections: Hell, Purgatory, and Heaven. Within the first of these sections we find one introductory canto, followed by thirty-three more cantos, and in each of the following sections thirty-three cantos are to be found. The sum is the number one hundred, the perfect and complete number.

Insofar as its meaning is concerned, the great poem will speak for itself, aided by the notes. We must understand, however, that Dante accepts the idea that all of nature is in motion, following the laws, the love, and the wisdom of God. Of all the orders of being, Man alone has both free will and the potentiality of turning from the way of God. With free will comes the responsibility of choosing and accepting the consequences of choice. No man can say that he is the irresponsible victim of heredity or environment. With the gift of intellect and free will, each man must assume the full weight of making choices, and he must, as well, accept the idea that his choices are important and that they do make a difference for others, and most particularly for himself.

THE GREATER IMAGES

DANTE in the *story* is always himself – the Florentine poet, philosopher, and politician, and the man who loved Beatrice. In the *allegory*, he is the image of every Christian sinner, and his pilgrimage is that which every soul must make, by one road or another, from the dark and solitary Wood of Error to the City of God.

VIRGIL is in the *story* the shade of the poet who, in the *Aeneid*, celebrated the origin and high destiny of the Roman Empire and its function in unifying the civilized world. In the Middle Ages he was looked upon as having been an unconscious prophet of Christianity and also (in popular tradition) as a great "White Magician", whose natural virtue gave him power among the dead. Dante's portrait of him has preserved traces of these medieval fancies, and also agrees very well with what we know of the gentle and charming characteristics of the real Virgil. In the *allegory*, Virgil is the image of Human Wisdom – the best that man can become in his own strength without the especial grace of God. He is the best of human philosophy, the best of human morality; he is also poetry and art, the best of human feeling and imagination. Virgil, as the image of these things, cannot himself enter Heaven or bring anyone else there (art and morality and philosophy cannot be made into substitutes for religion), but he can (and they can), under the direction of the Heavenly Wisdom, be used to awaken the soul to a realization of its own sinfulness, and can thereafter accompany and assist it towards that state of natural perfection in which it is again open to receive the immediate operation of Divine Grace.

BEATRICE remains in the *story* what she was in real life: the Florentine girl whom Dante loved from the first moment that he saw her, and in whom he seemed (as is sometimes the case with lovers) to see Heaven's glory walking the earth bodily. Because, for him, she was thus in fact the vehicle of the Glory – the earthly vessel in which the divine experience was carried – she is, in the *allegory*, from time to time likened to, or equated with, those other "God-bearers": the Church, and Divine Grace in the Church; the Blessed Virgin; even Christ Himself. She is the image by which Dante perceives all these, and her function in the poem is to bring him to that state in which he is able to perceive them directly; at the end of the *Paradiso* the image of Beatrice is – not replaced by, but – taken up into the images, successively, of the Church Triumphant; of Mary, the historic and universal God-bearer; and of God, in whom Image and Reality are one and the same. Beatrice thus represents for every man that person – or, more generally, that experience of the Not-self – which, by arousing his adoring love, has become for him the God-bearing image, the revelation of the presence of God.

HELL in the *story* is the place or condition of lost souls after death; it is pictured as a huge funnel-shaped pit, situated beneath the Northern Hemisphere and running down to the centre of the earth. In the *allegory*, it is the image of the deepening possibilities of evil within the soul. Similarly, the sinners who there remain fixed forever in the evil which they have obstinately chosen are also images of the perverted choice itself. For the *story*, they are historical or legendary personages, external to Dante (and to us); for the *allegory* they figure his (and our) disordered desires, seen and known to us as we plunge ever deeper into the hidden places of the self: every condemned sinner in the poem is thus the image of a self-condemned sin (actual or potential) in every man. Neither in the *story* nor in the *allegory* is Hell a place of punishment to which anybody is arbitrarily *sent*: it is the condition to which the soul reduces itself by a stubborn determination to evil, and in which it suffers the torment of its own perversions.

We must be careful to distinguish between Hell itself, taken literally, and the *vision of Hell* which is offered to Dante. Hell itself is not remedial; the dead who have chosen the "eternal exile" from God, and who thus experience the reality of their choice, cannot profit by that experience. In that sense, no living soul can enter Hell, since, however great the sin, repentance is always possible while there is life, even to the very moment of dying.[1] But the *vision of Hell*, which is remedial, is the soul's self-knowledge in all its evil potentialities – "the revelation of the nature of impenitent sin".[2]

PURGATORY in the *story*, as in Catholic theology, is the place or condition of redeemed souls after death, and is imagined by Dante as a lofty mountain on an island in the Southern Hemisphere. On its seven encircling cornices, the souls are purged successively of the taint of the seven deadly sins, and so made fit to ascend into the presence of God in Paradise. In the *allegory*, it is the image of repentance, by which the soul purges the guilt of sin in *this* life; and, similarly, the blessed spirits who willingly embrace its purifying pains figure the motions of the soul, eagerly confessing and making atonement for its sins.

PARADISE, in the same way, is, in the *story*, the place or condition, after death, of beatified souls in Heaven. Dante pictures it, first, under the figure of the ten Heavens of medieval astronomy and, secondly, under that of the Mystical Rose. He explains that, although the souls are shown as enjoying ascending degrees of bliss in the ten successive Heavens, all these are, in reality, one Heaven; nor is the bliss unequal, each soul being filled, according to its capacity, with all the joy it is able to experience. In the *allegory*, Paradise is the image of the soul in a state of grace, enjoying the foretaste of the Heaven which it knows to be its true home and city; and in the inhabitants of Paradise we may recognize the figure of the ascending stages by which it rises to the contemplation of the Beatific Vision.

THE EMPIRE AND THE CITY. Throughout the poem, we come across various images of the Empire of the City (Florence, Rome, and other cities of Italy, as well as the City and Empire of Dis in Hell, and the Eternal City or Heavenly Rome in Paradise). All these may be taken as expressing, in one way or another, what to-day we should perhaps more readily think of as the Community. Indeed, the whole *allegory* may be interpreted politically, in the widest sense of the word, as representing the way of salvation, not only for the individual man, but for Man-in-community. Civilizations, as well as persons, need to know the Hell within them and purge their sins before entering into a state of Grace, Justice, and Charity and so becoming the City of God on earth.

---

1. Unless, indeed, the will is so hardened in sin that the power to repent is destroyed, in which case the condition of the soul, even in this world, is literally a "living hell". Dante deals with this possibility in Canto XXXIII.
2. See P. H. Wicksteed: *From Vita Nuova to Paradiso*, from which the last few words are quoted.

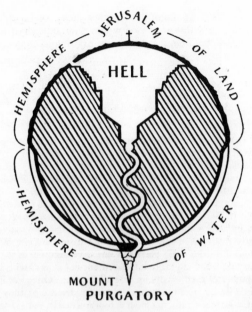

HELL

JERUSALEM — OF — LAND

HEMISPHERE

HEMISPHERE — OF — WATER

MOUNT
PURGATORY

CANTO I

THE STORY. *Dante finds that he has strayed from the right road and is lost in a Dark Wood. He tries to escape by climbing a beautiful Mountain, but is turned aside, first by a gambolling Leopard, then by a fierce Lion, and finally by a ravenous She-Wolf. As he is fleeing back into the Wood, he is stopped by the shade of Virgil, who tells him that he cannot hope to pass the Wolf and ascend the Mountain by that road. One day a Greyhound will come and drive the Wolf back to Hell; but the only course at present left open to Dante is to trust himself to Virgil, who will guide him by a longer way, leading through Hell and Purgatory. From there, a worthier spirit than Virgil (Beatrice) will lead him on to see the blessed souls in Paradise. Dante accepts Virgil as his "master, leader, and lord", and they set out together.*

Midway this way of life we're bound upon,
   I woke to find myself in a dark wood,
   Where the right road was wholly lost and gone.

4 Ay me! how hard to speak of it – that rude
   And rough and stubborn forest! the mere breath
   Of memory stirs the old fear in the blood;

7 It is so bitter, it goes nigh to death;
   Yet there I gained such good, that, to convey
   The tale, I'll write what else I found therewith.

10 How I got into it I cannot say,
   Because I was so heavy and full of sleep
   When first I stumbled from the narrow way;

13 But when at last I stood beneath a steep
   Hill's side, which closed that valley's wandering maze
   Whose dread had pierced me to the heart-root deep,

16 Then I looked up, and saw the morning rays
   Mantle its shoulder from that planet bright
   Which guides men's feet aright on all their ways;

19 And this a little quieted the affright
   That lurking in my bosom's lake had lain
   Through the long horror of that piteous night.

22 And as a swimmer, panting, from the main
   Heaves safe to shore, then turns to face the drive
   Of perilous seas, and looks, and looks again,

25 So, while my soul yet fled, did I contrive
   To turn and gaze on that dread pass once more
   Whence no man yet came ever out alive.

28 Weary of limb I rested a brief hour,
   Then rose and onward through the desert hied,
   So that the fixed foot always was the lower;

31 And see! not far from where the mountain-side
   First rose, a Leopard, nimble and light and fleet,
   Clothed in a fine furred pelt all dapple-dyed,

34 Came gambolling out, and skipped before my feet,
   Hindering me so, that from the forthright line
   Time and again I turned to beat retreat.

37 The morn was young, and in his native sign
   The Sun climbed with the stars whose glitterings
   Attended on him when the Love Divine

40 First moved those happy, prime-created things:
   So the sweet reason and the new-born day
   Filled me with hope and cheerful augurings

43 Of the bright beast so speckled and so gay;
   Yet not so much but that I fell to quaking
   At a fresh sight – a Lion in the way.

46 I saw him coming, swift and savage, making
   For me, head high, with ravenous hunger raving
   So that for dread the very air seemed shaking.

49 And next, a Wolf, gaunt with the famished craving
   Lodged ever in her horrible lean flank,
   The ancient cause of many men's enslaving; –

52 She was the worst – at that dread sight a blank
   Despair and whelming terror pinned me fast,
   Until all hope to scale the mountain sank.

55 Like one who loves the gains he has amassed,
   And meets the hour when he must lose his loot,
   Distracted in his mind and all aghast,

58 Even so was I, faced with that restless brute
   Which little by little edged and thrust me back,
   Back, to that place wherein the sun is mute.

61 Then, as I stumbled headlong down the track,
   Sudden a form was there, which dumbly crossed
   My path, as though grown voiceless from long lack

64 Of speech; and seeing it in that desert lost,
   "Have pity on me!" I hailed it as I ran,
   "Whate'er thou art – or very man, or ghost!"

67 It spoke: "No man, although I once was man;
   My parents' native land was Lombardy
   And both by citizenship were Mantuan.

70 *Sub Julio* born, though late in time, was I,
   And lived at Rome in good Augustus' days,
   When the false gods were worshipped ignorantly.

73 Poet was I, and tuned my verse to praise
   Anchises' righteous son, who sailed from Troy
   When Ilium's pride fell ruined down ablaze.

76 But thou – oh, why run back where fears destroy
  Peace? Why not climb the blissful mountain yonder,
  The cause and first beginning of all joy?"

79 "Canst thou be Virgil? thou that fount of splendour
  Whence poured so wide a stream of lordly speech?"
  Said I, and bowed my awe-struck head in wonder;

82 "Oh honour and light of poets all and each,
  Now let my great love stead me – the bent brow
  And long hours pondering all thy book can teach!

85 Thou art my master, and my author thou,
  From thee alone I learned the singing strain,
  The noble style, that does me honour now.

88 See there the beast that turned me back again –
  Save me from her, great sage – I fear her so,
  She shakes my blood through every pulse and vein."

91 "Nay, by another path thou needs must go
  If thou wilt ever leave this waste," he said,
  Looking upon me as I wept, "for lo!

94 The savage brute that makes thee cry for dread
  Lets no man pass this road of hers, but still
  Trammels him, till at last she lays him dead.

97 Vicious her nature is, and framed for ill;
  When crammed she craves more fiercely than before;
  Her raging greed can never gorge its fill.

100 With many a beast she mates, and shall with more,
  Until the Greyhound come, the Master-hound,
  And he shall slay her with a stroke right sore.

103 He'll not eat gold nor yet devour the ground;
  Wisdom and love and power his food shall be,
  His birthplace between Feltro and Feltro found;

106 Saviour he'll be to that low Italy
  For which Euryalus and Nisus died,
  Turnus and chaste Camilla, bloodily.

109 He'll hunt the Wolf through cities far and wide,
  Till in the end he hunt her back to Hell,
  Whence Envy first of all her leash untied.

112 But, as for thee, I think and deem it well
  Thou take me for thy guide, and pass with me
  Through an eternal place and terrible

115 Where thou shalt hear despairing cries, and see
  Long-parted souls that in their torments dire
  Howl for the second death perpetually.

118 Next, thou shalt gaze on those who in the fire
  Are happy, for they look to mount on high,
  In God's good time, up to the blissful quire;

121 To which glad place, a worthier spirit than I
  Must lead thy steps, if thou desire to come,
  With whom I'll leave thee then, and say good-bye;

124 For the Emperor of that high Imperium
  Wills not that I, once rebel to His crown,
  Into that city of His should lead men home.

127 Everywhere is His realm, but there His throne,
  There is His city and exalted seat:
  Thrice-blest whom there He chooses for His own!"

130 Then I to him: "Poet, I thee entreat,
  By that great God whom thou didst never know,
  Lead on, that I may free my wandering feet

133 From these snares and from worse; and I will go
  Along with thee, St Peter's Gate to find,
  And those whom thou portray'st as suffering so."

136 So he moved on; and I moved on behind.

THE IMAGES. *The Dark Wood* is the image of Sin or Error – not so much of any specific act of sin or intellectual perversion as of that spiritual condition called "hardness of heart", in which sinfulness has so taken possession of the soul as to render it incapable of turning to God, or even knowing which way to turn.

The Mountain, which on the mystical level is the image of the Soul's Ascent to God, is thus on the moral level the image of Repentance, by which the sinner returns to God. It can be ascended directly from "the right road", but not from the Dark Wood, because there the soul's cherished sins have become, as it were, externalized, and appear to it like demons or "beasts" with a will and power of their own, blocking all progress. Once lost in the Dark Wood, a man can only escape by so descending into himself that he sees his sin, not as an external obstacle, but as the will to chaos and death within him (Hell). Only when he has "died to sin" can he repent and purge it. Mount Purgatory and the Mountain of Canto I are, therefore, really one and the same mountain, as seen on the far side, and on this side, of the "death unto sin".

The Beasts. These are the images of sin. They may be identified with Lust, Pride, and Avarice respectively, or with the sins of Youth, Manhood, and Age; but they are perhaps best thought of as the images of the three *types* of sin which, if not repented, land the soul in one or other of the three main divisions of Hell (*v.* Canto XI).

The gay *Leopard* is the image of the self-indulgent sins – *Incontinence*; the fierce *Lion*, of the violent sins – *Bestiality*; the *She-Wolf* of the malicious sins, which involve *Fraud*.

The Greyhound has been much argued about. I think it has both an historical and a spiritual significance. Historically, it is perhaps the image of some hoped-for political saviour who should establish the just World-Empire. Spiritually, the Greyhound, which has the attributes of God ("wisdom, love, and power"), is probably the image of the reign of the Holy Ghost on earth – the visible Kingdom of God for which we pray in the Lord's Prayer (cf. *Purg.* xi. 7–9).

NOTES. l. 1: *midway*: i.e. at the age of 35, the middle point of man's earthly pilgrimage of three-score and ten years.

l. 17: *that planet bright*: the Sun. In medieval astronomy, the Earth was looked upon as being the centre of the universe, and the sun counted as a planet. In the *Comedy*, the Sun is often used as a figure for "the spiritual sun, which is God". (Dante: *Convivio*, iv. 12.)

l. 27: *whence no man yet came ever out alive*: Dante, as we shall see, is by no means "out" as yet; nor will he be, until he has passed through the "death unto sin".

l. 30: *so that the fixed foot always was the lower*: i.e. he was going uphill. In walking, there is always one fixed foot and one moving foot; in going uphill, the moving foot is brought *above*, and in going downhill *below*, the fixed foot.

l. 37: *in his native sign*: According to tradition, the Sun was in the Zodiacal sign of Aries (the Ram) at the moment of the creation. The Sun is in Aries from 21 March to 21 April: therefore the "sweet season" is that of spring. Later, we shall discover that the day is Good

Friday, and that the moon was full on the previous night. These indications do not precisely correspond to the actual Easter sky of 1300; Dante has merely described the astronomical phenomena typical of Eastertide.

ll. 63–4: *as though grown voiceless from long lack of speech*: i.e. the form is trying to speak to Dante, but cannot make itself heard. From the point of view of the *story*, I think this means that, being in fact that of a ghost, it cannot speak until Dante has established communication by addressing it first. *Allegorically*, we may take it in two ways: (1) on the historical level, it perhaps means that the wisdom and poetry of the classical age had been long neglected; (2) on the spiritual level, it undoubtedly means that Dante had sunk so deep into sin that the voice of reason, and even of poetry itself, had become faint and almost powerless to recall him.

l. 70: *sub Julio*: under Julius (Caesar). Virgil was born in 70 B.C. and had published none of his great poems before the murder of Julius in 44 B.C., so that he never enjoyed his patronage.

l. 87: *the noble style*: Dante, in 1300, was already a poet of considerable reputation for his love-lyrics and philosophic odes, though he had not as yet composed any narrative verse directly modelled upon the *Aeneid*. When he says that he owes to Virgil the "*bello stilo* which has won him honour", he can scarcely be referring to the style of his own *prose* works, whether in Latin or Italian, still less to that of the as yet unwritten *Comedy*. Presumably he means that he had studied to imitate, in his poems written in the vernacular, the elegance, concise power, and melodious rhythms of the Virgilian line.

l. 105: *between Feltro and Feltro*: This is a much-debated line. If the Greyhound represents a political "saviour", it may mean that his birthplace lies between Feltre in Venetia and Montefeltro in Romagna (i.e. in the valley of the Po). But some commentators think that "feltro" is not a geographical name at all, but simply that of a coarse cloth (felt, or frieze); in which case Dante would be expecting salvation to come from among those who wear the robe of poverty, and have renounced "gold and ground" – i.e. earthly possessions. We should perhaps translate: "In cloth of frieze his people shall be found".

l. 106: *low Italy*: The Italian word is *umile*, humble, which may mean either "low-lying", as opposed to "high Italy" among the Alps, or "humiliated", with reference to the degradation to which the country had been brought. In either case, the classical allusions which follow show that Dante meant Rome.

l. 114: *an eternal place and terrible*: Hell.

l. 117: *the second death*: this might mean "cry for a second death to put an end to their misery", but more probably means "cry out because of the pains of hell", in allusion to *Rev.* xx. 14.

ll. 118–19: *those who in the fire are happy*: the redeemed in Purgatory.

l. 134: *St Peter's Gate*: the gate by which redeemed souls are admitted to Purgatory (*Purg.* ix. 76 *sqq.*); not the gate of Heaven.

CANTO II

THE STORY. *Dante's attempts to climb the Mountain have taken the whole day and it is now Good Friday evening. Dante has not gone far before he loses heart and "begins to make excuse". To his specious arguments Virgil replies flatly: "This is mere cowardice;" and then tells how Beatrice, prompted by St Lucy at the instance of the Virgin Mary herself, descended into Limbo to entreat him to go to Dante's rescue. Thus encouraged, Dante pulls himself together, and they start off again.*

Day was departing and the dusk drew on,
   Loosing from labour every living thing
   Save me, in all the world; I – I alone –

Must gird me to the wars – rough travelling,
   And pity's sharp assault upon the heart –
   Which memory shall record, unfaltering;

7   Now, Muses, now, high Genius, do your part!
   And Memory, faithful scrivener to the eyes,
   Here show thy virtue, noble as thou art!

10   I soon began: "Poet – dear guide – 'twere wise
   Surely, to test my powers and weigh their worth
   Ere trusting me to this great enterprise.

13   Thou sayest, the author of young Silvius' birth,
   Did to the world immortal, mortal go,
   Clothed in the body of flesh he wore on earth –

16   Granted; if Hell's great Foeman deigned to show
   To *him* such favour, seeing the vast effect,
   And what and who has destined issue – no,

19   That need surprise no thoughtful intellect,
   Since to Rome's fostering city and empery
   High Heaven had sealed him as the father-elect;

22   Both these were there established, verily,
   To found that place, holy and dedicate,
   Wherein great Peter's heir should hold his See;

25   So that the deed thy verses celebrate
   Taught him the road to victory, and bestowed
   The Papal Mantle in its high estate.

28   Thither the Chosen Vessel, in like mode,
   Went afterward, and much confirmed thereby
   The faith that sets us on salvation's road.

31   But how should *I* go there? Who says so? Why?
   I'm not Aeneas, and I am not Paul!
   Who thinks me fit? Not others. And not I.

34   Say I submit, and go – suppose I fall
   Into some folly? Though I speak but ill,
   Thy better wisdom will construe it all."

37   As one who wills, and then unwills his will,
   Changing his mind with every changing whim,
   Till all his best intentions come to nil,

40   So I stood havering in that moorland dim,
   While through fond rifts of fancy oozed away
   The first quick zest that filled me to the brim.

43   "If I have grasped what thou dost seem to say,"
   The shade of greatness answered, "these doubts breed
   From sheer black cowardice, which day by day

46   Lays ambushes for men, checking the speed
   Of honourable purpose in mid-flight,
   As shapes half-seen startle a shying steed.

49   Well then, to rid thee of this foolish fright,
   Hear why I came, and learn whose eloquence
   Urged me to take compassion on thy plight.

52   While I was with the spirits who dwell suspense,
   A Lady summoned me – so blest, so rare,
   I begged her to command my diligence.

55   Her eyes outshone the firmament by far
   As she began, in her own gracious tongue,
   Gentle and low, as tongues of angels are:

58   'O courteous Mantuan soul, whose skill in song
   Keeps green on earth a fame that shall not end
   While motion rolls the turning spheres along!

61   A friend of mine, who is not Fortune's friend,
          Is hard beset upon the shadowy coast;
          Terrors and snares his fearful steps attend,

64   Driving him back; yea, and I fear almost
          I have risen too late to help – for I was told
          Such news of him in Heaven – he's too far lost.

67   But thou – go thou! Lift up thy voice of gold;
          Try every needful means to find and reach
          And free him, that my heart may rest consoled.

70   Beatrice am I, who thy good speed beseech;
          Love that first moved me from the blissful place
          Whither I'd fain return, now moves my speech.

73   Lo! when I stand before my Lord's bright face
          I'll praise thee many a time to Him.' Thereon
          She fell on silence; I replied apace:

76   'Excellent lady, for whose sake alone
          The breed of men exceeds all things that dwell
          Closed in the heaven whose circles narrowest run

79   To do thy bidding pleases me so well
          That were't already done, I should seem slow;
          I know thy wish, and more needs not to tell.

82   Yet say – how can thy blest feet bear to know
          This dark road downward to the dreadful centre,
          From that wide room which thou dost yearn for so?'

85   'Few words will serve (if thou desire to enter
          Thus far into our mystery),' she said,
          'To tell thee why I have no fear to venture.

88   Of hurtful things we ought to be afraid,
          But of no others, truly, inasmuch
          As these have nothing to give cause for dread;

91   My nature, by God's mercy, is made such
          As your calamities can nowise shake,
          Nor these dark fires have any power to touch.

94   Heaven hath a noble Lady, who doth take
          Ruth of this man thou goest to disensnare
          Such that high doom is cancelled for her sake.

97   She summoned Lucy to her side, and there
          Exhorted her: "Thy faithful votary
          Needs thee, and I commend him to thy care."

100   Lucy, the foe to every cruelty,
          Ran quickly and came and found me in my place
          Beside ancestral Rachel, crying to me:

103   "How now, how now, Beatrice, God's true praise!
          No help for him who once thy liegeman was,
          Quitting the common herd to win thy grace?

106   Dost thou not hear his piteous cries, alas?
          Dost thou not see death grapple him, on the river
          Whose furious rage no ocean can surpass?"

109   When I heard that, no living wight was ever
          So swift to seek his good or flee his fear
          As I from that high resting-place to sever

112   And speed me down, trusting my purpose dear
          To thee, and to thy golden rhetoric
          Which honours thee, and honours all who hear.'

115   She spoke; and as she turned from me the quick
          Tears starred the lustre of her eyes, which still
          Spurred on my going with a keener prick.

118   Therefore I sought thee out, as was her will,
          And brought thee safe off from that beast of prey
          Which barred thee from the short road up the hill.

121   What ails thee then? Why, why this dull delay?
          Why bring so white a liver to the deed?
          Why canst thou find no manhood to display

124   When three such blessed ladies deign to plead
          Thy cause at that supreme assize of right,
          And when my words promise thee such good speed?"

127   As little flowers, which all the frosty night
          Hung pinched and drooping, lift their stalks and fan
          Their blossoms out, touched by the warm white light,

130   So did my fainting powers; and therewith ran
          Such good, strong courage round about my heart
          That I spoke boldly out like a free man:

133   "O blessed she that stooped to take my part!
          O courteous thou, to obey her true-discerning
          Speech, and thus promptly to my rescue start!

136   Fired by thy words, my spirit now is burning
          So to go on, and see this venture through.
          I find my former stout resolve returning.

139   Forward! henceforth there's but one will for two,
          Thou master, and thou leader, and thou lord."
          I spoke; he moved; so, setting out anew,

142   I entered on that savage path and froward.

THE IMAGES. *Mary, The Blessed Virgin,* whom the Church calls *Theo-tokos* (Mother of God), is the historical and universal God-bearer, of whom Beatrice, like any other God-bearing image, is a particular type. Mary is thus, in an especial and supreme manner, the vessel of Divine Grace, as experienced in, and mediated through, the redeemed creation. (Note that the name of Mary, like the name of Christ, is never spoken in Hell.)

Lucìa (St Lucy), a virgin martyr of the third century, is the patron saint of those with weak sight, and chosen here as the image of Illuminating Grace. Mary, Beatrice, and Lucia are a threefold image of Divine Grace in its various manifestations.

Virgil's Mission. Dante is so far gone in sin and error that Divine Grace can no longer move him directly; but there is still something left in him which is capable of responding to the voice of poetry and of human reason; and this, under Grace, may yet be used to lead him back to God. In this profound and beautiful image, Dante places Religion, on the one hand, and human Art and Philosophy, on the other, in their just relationship.

NOTES. l. 7: Canto I forms, as it were, a prologue to the whole *Divine Comedy.* The actual *Inferno* (Hell) begins with Canto II; and here we have the invocation which, in each of the three books, prefaces the journey to Hell, Purgatory, and Paradise respectively. It is addressed, in the classic manner, to the Muses, to Genius, and to Memory, the Mother of the Muses. (As the story proceeds, Dante will invoke higher, and still higher aid; till the final invocation towards the end of the *Paradiso,* is made to God, the "supreme light" - Himself.)

l. 13: *the author of young Silvius' birth*: Aeneas; the allusion is to the sixth book of the *Aeneid*, which describes how Aeneas visits Hades and is told that he is to settle in Italy and so bring about the foundation of Rome, the seat both of the Empire and the Papacy.

l. 16: *Hell's great Foeman*: God.

l. 28: *the Chosen Vessel*: St Paul (*Acts* ix. 15). His vision of Hell is described in the fourth-century apocryphal book known as *The Apocalypse of Paul*, which Dante had evidently read. (See M. R. James: *The Apocryphal New Testament*.) There is probably also an allusion to 2 *Cor.* xii. 2.

l. 52: *the spirits who dwell suspense*: those of the virtuous pagans, who taste neither the bliss of salvation nor the pains of damnation, but dwell forever suspended between the two, in Limbo, the uppermost circle of Hell. (We shall meet them in Canto IV.)

l. 70: Of all this passage, Charles Williams says: "Beatrice has to ask [Virgil] to go; she cannot command him, though she puts her trust in his 'fair speech'. Religion itself cannot order poetry about; the grand art is wholly autonomous ... We should have been fortunate if the ministers of religion and poetry had always spoken to each other with such courtesy as these." (*The Figure of Beatrice*, p. 112.)

l. 78: *the heaven whose circles narrowest run*: The heaven of the Moon, the smallest and nearest to the Earth. (See note on *Dante's Universe*, p. 292.)

l. 91: *my nature, by God's mercy, is made such*: The souls of the blessed can still pity the self-inflicted misery of the wicked, but they can no longer be hurt or infected by it: "the action of pity will live for ever; the passion of pity will not". (C. S. Lewis: *The Great Divorce*, p. 111, where the subject is handled in a very illuminating way.)

l. 102: *ancestral Rachel*: Leah and Rachel, the two wives of Jacob, figure respectively the active and the contemplative life.

l. 107: *the river*: no literal river is intended; it is only a metaphor for human life.

l. 120: *the short road up the hill*: this line shows clearly that the "blissful Mountain" and Mount Purgatory are in reality one and the same; since the Beasts prevent Dante from taking "the short road", he is obliged to go by the long road – i.e. through Hell – to find the mountain again on the other side of the world.

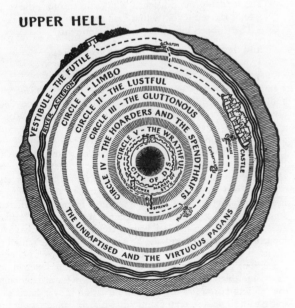

UPPER HELL

**INCONTINENCE –
THE SINS OF THE LEOPARD**

CANTO III

THE STORY. *Arriving at the gate of Hell, the Poets read the inscription upon its lintel. They enter and find themselves in the Vestibule of Hell, where the Futile run perpetually after a whirling standard. Passing quickly on, they reach the river Acheron. Here the souls of all the damned come at death to be ferried across by Charon, who refuses to take the living body of Dante till Virgil silences him with a word of power. While they are watching the departure of a boatload of souls the river banks are shaken by an earthquake so violent that Dante swoons away.*

THROUGH ME THE ROAD TO THE CITY OF DESOLATION,
  THROUGH ME THE ROAD TO SORROWS DIUTURNAL,
  THROUGH ME THE ROAD AMONG THE LOST CREATION.

4 JUSTICE MOVED MY GREAT MAKER; GOD ETERNAL
  WROUGHT ME: THE POWER, AND THE UNSEARCHABLY
  HIGH WISDOM, AND THE PRIMAL LOVE SUPERNAL.

7 NOTHING ERE I WAS MADE WAS MADE TO BE
  SAVE THINGS ETERNE, AND I ETERNE ABIDE;
  LAY DOWN ALL HOPE, YOU THAT GO IN BY ME.

10 These words, of sombre colour, I descried
  Writ on the lintel of a gateway; "Sir,
  This sentence is right hard for me," I cried.

13 And like a man of quick discernment: "Here
  Lay down all thy distrust," said he, "reject
  Dead from within thee every coward fear;

16 We've reached the place I told thee to expect,
  Where thou shouldst see the miserable race,
  Those who have lost the good of intellect."

19 He laid his hand on mine, and with a face
  So joyous that it comforted my quailing,
  Into the hidden things he led my ways.

22 Here sighing, and here crying, and loud railing
  Smote on the starless air, with lamentation,
  So that at first I wept to hear such wailing.

25 Tongues mixed and mingled, horrible execration,
  Shrill shrieks, hoarse groans, fierce yells and hideous blether
  And clapping of hands thereto, without cessation

28 Made tumult through the timeless night, that hither
  And thither drives in dizzying circles sped,
  As whirlwind whips the spinning sands together.

31 Whereat, with horror flapping round my head:
  "Master, what's this I hear? Who can they be,
  These people so distraught with grief?" I said.

34 And he replied: "The dismal company
  Of wretched spirits thus find their guerdon due
  Whose lives knew neither praise nor infamy;

37 They're mingled with that caitiff angel-crew
  Who against God rebelled not, nor to Him
  Were faithful, but to self alone were true;

40 Heaven cast them forth – their presence there would dim
  The light; deep Hell rejects so base a herd,
  Lest sin should boast itself because of them.

43 Then I: "But, Master, by what torment spurred
  Are they driven on to vent such bitter breath?"
  He answered: "I will tell thee in a word:

46 This dreary huddle has no hope of death,
Yet its blind life trails on so low and crass
That every other fate it envieth.

49 No reputation in the world it has,
Mercy and doom hold it alike in scorn –
Let us not speak of these; but look, and pass."

52 So I beheld, and lo! an ensign borne
Whirling, that span and ran, as in disdain
Of any rest; and there the folk forlorn

55 Rushed after it, in such an endless train,
It never would have entered in my head
There were so many men whom death had slain.

58 And when I'd noted here and there a shade
Whose face I knew, I saw and recognized
The coward spirit of the man who made

61 The great refusal; and that proof sufficed;
Here was that rabble, here without a doubt,
Whom God and whom His enemies despised.

64 This scum, who'd never lived, now fled about
Naked and goaded, for a swarm of fierce
Hornets and wasps stung all the wretched rout

67 Until their cheeks ran blood, whose slubbered smears,
Mingled with brine, around their footsteps fell,
Where loathly worms licked up their blood and tears.

70 Then I peered on ahead, and soon quite well
Made out the hither bank of a wide stream,
Where stood much people. "Sir," said I, "pray tell

73 Who these are, what their custom, why they seem
So eager to pass over and be gone –
If I may trust my sight in this pale gleam."

76 And he to me: "The whole shall be made known;
Only have patience till we stay our feet
On yonder sorrowful shore of Acheron."

79 Abashed, I dropped my eyes; and, lest unmeet
Chatter should vex him, held my tongue, and so
Paced on with him, in silence and discreet,

82 To the riverside. When from the far bank lo!
A boat shot forth, whose white-haired boatman old
Bawled as he came: "Woe to the wicked! Woe!

85 Never you hope to look on Heaven – behold!
I come to ferry you hence across the tide
To endless night, fierce fires and shramming cold.

88 And thou, the living man there! stand aside
From these who are dead!" I budged not, but abode;
So, when he saw me hold my ground, he cried:

91 "Away with thee! for by another road
And other ferries thou shalt make the shore,
Not here; a lighter skiff must bear thy load."

94 Then said my guide: "Charon, why wilt thou roar
And chafe in vain? Thus it is willed where power
And will are one; enough; ask thou no more."

97 This shut the shaggy mouth up of that sour
Infernal ferryman of the livid wash,
Only his flame-ringed eyeballs rolled a-glower.

100 But those outwearied, naked souls – how gash
And pale they grew, chattering their teeth for dread,
When first they felt his harsh tongue's cruel lash.

103 God they blaspheme, blaspheme their parents' bed,
The human race, the place, the time, the blood,
The seed that got them, and the womb that bred;

106 Then, huddling hugger-mugger, down they scud,
Dismally wailing, to the accursed strand
Which waits for every man that fears not God.

109 Charon, his eyes red like a burning brand,
Thumps with his oar the lingerers that delay,
And rounds them up, and beckons with his hand.

112 And as, by one and one, leaves drift away
In autumn, till the bough from which they fall
Sees the earth strewn with all its brave array,

115 So, from the bank there, one by one, drop all
Adam's ill seed, when signalled off the mark,
As drops the falcon to the falconer's call.

118 Away they're borne across the waters dark,
And ere they land that side the stream, anon
Fresh troops this side come flocking to embark.

121 Then said my courteous master: "See, my son,
All those that die beneath God's righteous ire
From every country come here every one.

124 They press to pass the river, for the fire
Of heavenly justice stings and spurs them so
That all their fear is changed into desire;

127 And by this passage, good souls never go;
Therefore, if Charon chide thee, do thou look
What this may mean – 'tis not so hard to know."

130 When he thus said, the dusky champaign shook
So terribly that, thinking on the event,
I feel the sweat pour off me like a brook.

133 The sodden ground belched wind, and through the rent
Shot the red levin, with a flash and sweep
That robbed me of my wits, incontinent;

136 And down I fell, as one that swoons on sleep.

THE IMAGES. Hell-Gate. High and wide and without bars (Inf. viii. 126), the door "whose threshold is denied to none" (Inf. xiv. 87) always waits to receive those who are astray in the Dark Wood. Anyone may enter if he so chooses, but if he does, he must abandon hope, since it leads nowhere but to the Città Dolente, the City of Desolation. In the story, Hell is filled with the souls of those who died with their wills set to enter by that gate; in the allegory, these souls are the images of sin in the self or in society.
The Vestibule was presumably suggested to Dante by the description in Aeneid vi. where, however, it is tenanted by rather a different set of people). It does not, I think, occur in any previous Christian eschatology. Heaven and Hell being states in which choice is permanently fixed, there must also be a state in which the refusal of choice is itself fixed, since to refuse choice is in fact to choose indecision. The Vestibule is the abode of the weather-cock mind, the vague tolerance which will neither approve nor condemn, the cautious cowardice for which no decision is ever final. The spirits rush aimlessly after the aimlessly whirling banner, stung and

goaded, as of old, by the thought that, in doing anything definite whatsoever, they are missing doing something else.

Acheron, "the joyless", first of the great rivers of Hell whose names Dante took from Virgil and Virgil from Homer. (See map, p. 84.)

Charon, the classical ferryman of the dead. Most of the monstrous organisms by which the functions of Hell are discharged are taken from Greek and Roman mythology. They are neither devils nor damned souls, but the images of perverted appetites, presiding over the circles appropriate to their natures.

NOTES. l. 1: *the City of Desolation* (*la citta dolente*; lit.: the sorrowful city). Hell, like Heaven, is represented under the figure sometimes of a city, and sometimes of an empire. Later on (Canto IX) we shall come to the actual city itself, which has its fortifications on the edge of the Sixth Circle, and comprises the whole of Nether Hell. At present we are only in Upper Hell, forming as it were the suburbs of the city and made up of the Vestibule and the first five circles. (See map, p. 84.)

ll. 4–6: *power ... wisdom supreme and primal love*: the attributes of the Trinity. "If there is God, if there is freewill, then man is able to choose the opposite of God. Power, Wisdom, Love, gave man freewill; therefore Power, Wisdom, Love, created the gate of hell and the possibility of hell." (Charles Williams: *The Figure of Beatrice*, p. 113.)

l. 8: *things eterne*: In Canto XXXIV Dante tells how Hell was made when Satan fell from Heaven: it was created "for the devil and his angels" (*Matt.* xxv. 41) and before it nothing was made except the "eternal things", i.e. the Angels and the Heavens.

l. 9: *lay down all hope*: For the soul that literally enters Hell there is no return, nor any passage to Purgatory and repentance. Dante is naturally disturbed (l. 12) by this warning. But what he is entering upon, while yet in this life, is not Hell but the vision of Hell, and for him there is a way out, provided he keeps his hope and faith. Accordingly, Virgil enjoins him (ll. 14–15) to reject doubt and fear.

l. 18: *the good of intellect*: In the *Convivio* Dante quotes Aristotle as saying: "truth is the good of the intellect". What the lost souls have lost is not the intellect itself, which still functions mechanically, but the *good* of the intellect: i.e. the knowledge of God, who is Truth. (For Dante, as for Aquinas, "intellect" does not mean what we call, colloquially, "braininess"; it means the whole "reasonable soul" of man.)

l. 16: *the great refusal*: Probably Celestine V, who, in 1294, at the age of 80, was made pope, but resigned the papacy five months later. His successor was Pope Boniface VIII, to whom Dante attributed many of the evils which had overtaken the Church.

ll. 91–2: *another road and other ferries*: souls destined for Heaven never cross Acheron; they assemble at the mouth of Tiber and are taken in a boat piloted by an angel to Mount Purgatory at the Antipodes (*Purg.* ii). Charon recognizes that Dante is a soul in Grace. (See ll. 127–9.)

l. 126: *all their fear is changed into desire*: This is another of the important passages in which Dante emphasizes that Hell is the soul's choice. The damned fear it and long for it, as in this life a man may hate the sin which makes him miserable, and yet obstinately seek and wallow in it.

CANTO IV

THE STORY. *Recovering from his swoon, Dante finds himself across Acheron and on the edge of the actual Pit of Hell. He follows Virgil into the First Circle – the Limbo where the Unbaptized and the Virtuous Pagans dwell "suspended", knowing no torment save exclusion from the positive bliss of God's presence. Virgil tells him of Christ's Harrowing of Hell, and then shows him the habitation of the great men of antiquity – poets, heroes, and philosophers.*

A heavy peal of thunder came to waken me
   Out of the stunning slumber that had bound me,
   Startling me up as though rude hands had shaken me.

4 I rose, and cast my rested eyes around me,
   Gazing intent to satisfy my wonder
   Concerning the strange place wherein I found me.

7 Hear truth: I stood on the steep brink whereunder
   Runs down the dolorous chasm of the Pit,
   Ringing with infinite groans like gathered thunder.

10 Deep, dense, and by no faintest glimmer lit
   It lay, and though I strained my sight to find
   Bottom, not one thing could I see in it.

13 "Down must we go, to that dark world and blind,"
   The poet said, turning on me a bleak
   Blanched face; "I will go first – come thou behind."

16 Then I, who had marked the colour of his cheek:
   "How can I go, when even thou art white
   For fear, who art wont to cheer me when I'm weak?"

19 But he: "Not so; the anguish infinite
   They suffer yonder paints my countenance
   With pity, which thou takest for affright;

22 Come, we have far to go; let us advance."
   So, entering, he made me enter, where
   The Pit's first circle makes circumference.

25 We heard no loud complaint, no crying there,
   No sound of grief except the sound of sighing
   Quivering for ever through the eternal air;

28 Grief, not for torment, but for loss undying,
   By women, men, and children sighed for so,
   Sorrowers thick-thronged, their sorrows multiplying.

31 Then my good guide: "Thou dost not ask me who
   These spirits are," said he, "whom thou perceivest?
   Ere going further, I would have thee know

34 They sinned not; yet their merit lacked its chiefest
   Fulfilment, lacking baptism, which is
   The gateway to the faith which thou believest;

37 Or, living before Christendom, their knees
   Paid not aright those tributes that belong
   To God; and I myself am one of these.

40 For such defects alone – no other wrong –
   We are lost; yet only by this grief offended:
   That, without hope, we ever live, and long."

43 Grief smote my heart to think, as he thus ended,
   What souls I knew, of great and sovran
   Virtue, who in that Limbo dwelt suspended.

46 "Tell me, sir – tell me, Master," I began
   (In hope some fresh assurance to be gleaning
   Of our sin-conquering Faith), "did any man

49 By his self-merit, or on another leaning,
   Ever fare forth from hence and come to be
   Among the blest?" He took my hidden meaning.

52 "When I was newly in this state," said he,
   "I saw One come in majesty and awe,
   And on His head were crowns of victory.

55   Our great first father's spirit He did withdraw,
       And righteous Abel, Noah who built the ark,
       Moses who gave and who obeyed the Law,

58   King David, Abraham the Patriarch,
       Israel with his father and generation,
       Rachel, for whom he did such deeds of mark,

61   With many another of His chosen nation;
       These did He bless; and know, that ere that day
       No human soul had ever seen salvation."

64   While he thus spake, we still made no delay,
       But passed the wood – I mean, the wood (as 'twere)
       Of souls ranged thick as trees. Being now some way –

67   Not far – from where I'd slept, I saw appear
       A light, which overcame the shadowy face
       Of gloom, and made a glowing hemisphere.

70   'Twas yet some distance on, yet I could trace
       So much as brought conviction to my heart
       That persons of great honour held that place.

73   "O thou that honour'st every science and art,
       Say, who are these whose honour gives them claim
       To different customs and a sphere apart?"

76   And he to me: "Their honourable name,
       Still in thy world resounding as it does,
       Wins here from Heaven the favour due to fame."

79   Meanwhile I heard a voice that cried out thus:
       "Honour the most high poet! his great shade,
       Which was departed, is returned to us."

82   It paused there, and was still; and lo! there made
       Toward us, four mighty shadows of the dead,
       Who in their mien nor grief nor joy displayed.

85   "Mark well the first of these," my master said,
       "Who in his right hand bears a naked sword
       And goes before the three as chief and head;

88   Homer is he, the poets' sovran lord;
       Next, Horace comes, the keen satirical;
       Ovid the third; and Lucan afterward.

91   Because I share with these that honourable
       Grand title the sole voice was heard to cry
       They do me honour, and therein do well."

94   Thus in their school assembled I, even I,
       Looked on the lords of loftiest song, whose style
       O'er all the rest goes soaring eagle-high.

97   When they had talked together a short while
       They all with signs of welcome turned my way,
       Which moved my master to a kindly smile;

100   And greater honour yet they did me – yea,
       Into their fellowship they deigned invite
       And make me sixth among such minds as they.

103   So we moved slowly onward toward the light
       In talk 'twere as unfitting to repeat
       Here, as to speak there was both fit and right.

196   And presently we reached a noble seat –
       A castle, girt with seven high walls around,
       And moated with a goodly rivulet

109   O'er which we went as though upon dry ground;
       With those wise men I passed the sevenfold gate
       Into a fresh green meadow, where we found

112   Persons with grave and tranquil eyes, and great
       Authority in their carriage and attitude,
       Who spoke but seldom and in voice sedate.

115   So here we walked aside a little, and stood
       Upon an open eminence, lit serene
       And clear, whence one and all might well be viewed.

118   Plain in my sight on the enamelled green
       All those grand spirits were shown me one by one –
       It thrills my heart to think what I have seen!

121   I saw Electra, saw with her anon
       Hector, Aeneas, many a Trojan peer,
       And hawk-eyed Caesar in his habergeon;

124   I saw Camilla and bold Penthesilea,
       On the other hand; Latinus on his throne
       Beside Lavinia his daughter dear;

127   Brutus, by whom proud Tarquin was o'erthrown,
       Marcia, Cornelia, Julia, Lucrece – and
       I saw great Saladin, aloof, alone.

130   Higher I raised my brows and further scanned,
       And saw the Master of the men who know
       Seated amid the philosophic band;

133   All do him honour and deep reverence show;
       Socrates, Plato, in the nearest room
       To him; Diogenes, Thales and Zeno,

136   Democritus, who held that all things come
       By chance; Empedocles, Anaxagoras wise,
       And Heraclitus, him that wept for doom;

139   Dioscorides, who named the qualities,
       Tully and Orpheus, Linus, and thereby
       Good Seneca, well-skilled to moralize;

142   Euclid the geometrician, Ptolemy,
       Galen, Hippocrates, and Avicen,
       Averroës who made the commentary –

145   Nay, but I tell not all that I saw then;
       The long theme drives me hard, and everywhere
       The wondrous truth outstrips my staggering pen.

148   The group of six dwindles to two; we fare
       Forth a new way, I and my guide withal,
       Out from that quiet to the quivering air,

151   And reach a place where nothing shines at all.

THE IMAGES. After those who refused choice come those without
    opportunity of choice. They could not, that is, choose Christ;
    they could, and did, choose human virtue, and for that they have
    their reward. (Pagans who chose evil by their own standards are
    judged by these standards – cf. *Rom*. ii. 8–15 – and are found
    lower down.) Here again, the souls "have what they chose";
    they enjoy that kind of after-life which they themselves imagined
    for the virtuous dead; their failure lay in not imagining better.
    They are lost (as Virgil says later, *Purg*. vii. 8) because they "had
    not faith" – primarily the Christian Faith, but also, more gener-
    ally, faith in the nature of things. The *allegory* is clear: it is the
    weakness of Humanism to fall short in the imagination of ecstasy;

at its best it is noble, reasonable, and cold, and however optimistic about a balanced happiness in this world, pessimistic about a rapturous eternity. Sometimes wistfully aware that others claim the experience of this positive bliss, the Humanist can neither accept it by faith, embrace it by hope, nor abandon himself to it in charity. Dante discusses the question further in the *Purgatory* (esp. Cantos VII and XXII) and makes his full doctrine explicit in *Paradise*, Cantos XIX–XX.

NOTES l. 7: *I stood on the steep brink*: It is disputed how Dante passed Acheron; the simplest explanation is that Charon, obedient to Virgil's "word of power", ferried him across during his swoon. Technically speaking, Dante had to describe a passage by boat in Canto VIII, and did not want to anticipate his effects; I think, however, he had also an allegorical reason for omitting the description here (see Canto VII. *Images: Path down Cliff*, p. 116). Note that the "peal of thunder" in l. 1 is not that which followed the lightning-flash at the end of Canto III, but (l. 9) the din issuing from the mouth of the Pit – an orchestra of discord, here blended into one confused roar, which, resolved into its component disharmonies, will accompany us to the bottom circle of Hell.

l. 53: *I saw One come*: The episode, based upon 1 *Peter* iii. 19, of Christ's descent into Limbo to rescue the souls of the patriarchs (the "Harrowing of Hell") was a favourite subject of medieval legend and drama. The crucifixion is reckoned as having occurred in A.D. 34, when Virgil had been dead fifty-three years. Note that the name of Christ is never spoken in Hell – He is always referred to by some periphrasis.

l. 55: *our great first father*: Adam.

l. 106: *a noble seat*: The scene is, I think, a medievalized version of the Elysian Fields, surrounded by "many-watered Eridanus". (*Aen.* vi. 659.) Detailed allegorical interpretations of the seven gates, walls, etc., have no great value.

l. 121: *Electra etc.*: Pride of place is given to the Trojans, founders of the Roman line; (Julius) Caesar is grouped with them as a descendant of Aeneas.

l. 129: *Saladin*: His inclusion here, along with Lucan, Averroës, and other A.D. personages who were not, strictly speaking, without opportunity of choice, perhaps tacitly indicates Dante's opinion about all those who, though living in touch with Christianity and practising all the moral virtues, find themselves sincerely unable to accept the Christian revelation.

l. 131: *the Master of the men who know*: Aristotle.

CANTO V

THE STORY. *Dante and Virgil descend from the First Circle to the Second (the first of the Circles of Incontinence). On the threshold sits Minos, the judge of Hell, assigning the souls to their appropriate places of torment. His opposition is overcome by Virgil's word of power, and the Poets enter the Circle, where the souls of the Lustful are tossed for ever upon a howling wind. After Virgil has pointed out a number of famous lovers, Dante speaks to the shade of Francesca da Rimini, who tells him her story.*

From the first circle thus I came descending
   To the second, which, in narrower compass turning,
   Holds greater woe, with outcry loud and rending.

There in the threshold, horrible and girning,
   Grim Minos sits, holding his ghastly session,
   And, as he girds him, sentencing and spurning;

7   For when the ill soul faces him, confession
   Pours out of it till nothing's left to tell;
   Whereon that connoisseur of all transgression

10   Assigns it to its proper place in hell,
   As many grades as he would have it fall,
   So oft he belts him round with his own tail.

13   Before him stands a throng continual;
   Each comes in turn to abye the fell arraign;
   They speak – they hear – they're whirled down one and all.

16   "Ho! thou that comest to the house of pain,"
   Cried Minos when he saw me, the appliance
   Of his dread powers suspending, "think again

19   How thou dost go, in whom is thy reliance;
   Be not deceived by the wide open door!"
   Then said my guide: "Wherefore this loud defiance?

22   Hinder not thou his fated way; be sure
   Hindrance is vain; thus it is willed where will
   And power are one; enough; ask now no more."

25   And now the sounds of grief begin to fill
   My ear; I'm come where cries of anguish smite
   My shrinking sense, and lamentation shrill –

28   A place made dumb of every glimmer of light,
   Which bellows like tempestuous ocean birling
   In the batter of a two-way wind's buffet and fight.

31   The blast of hell that never rests from whirling
   Harries the spirits along in the sweep of its swath,
   And vexes them, for ever beating and hurling.

34   When they are borne to the rim of the ruinous path
   With cry and wail and shriek they are caught by the gust,
   Railing and cursing the power of the Lord's wrath.

37   Into this torment carnal sinners are thrust,
   So I was told – the sinners who make their reason
   Bond thrall under the yoke of their lust.

40   Like as the starlings wheel in the wintry season
   In wide and clustering flocks wing-borne, wind-borne,
   Even so they go, the souls who did this treason,

43   Hither and thither, and up and down, outworn,
   Hopeless of any rest – rest, did I say?
   Of the least minishing of their pangs forlorn.

46   And as the cranes go chanting their harsh lay,
   Across the sky in long procession trailing,
   So I beheld some shadows borne my way,

49   Driven on the blast and uttering wail on wailing;
   Wherefore I said: "O Master, art thou able
   To name these spirits thrashed by the black wind's flailing?"

52   "Among this band," said he, "whose name and fable
   Thou seek'st to know, the first who yonder flies
   Was empress of many tongues, mistress of Babel.

55   She was so broken to lascivious vice
   She licensed lust by law, in hopes to cover
   Her scandal of unnumbered harlotries.

58   This was Semiramis; 'tis written of her
   That she was wife to Ninus and heiress, too,
   Who reigned in the land the Soldan now rules over.

61   Lo! she that slew herself for love, untrue
       To Sychaeus' ashes. Lo! tost on the blast,
       Voluptuous Cleopatra, whom love slew.

64   Look, look on Helen, for whose sake rolled past
       Long evil years. See great Achilles yonder,
       Who warred with love, and that war was his last.

67   See Paris, Tristram see!" And many – oh, wonder
       Many – a thousand more, he showed by name
       And pointing hand, whose life love rent asunder.

70   And when I had heard my Doctor tell the fame
       Of all those knights and ladies of long ago,
       I was pierced through with pity, and my head swam.

73   "Poet," said I, "fain would I speak those two
       That seem to ride as light as any foam,
       And hand in hand on the dark wind drifting go."

76   And he replied: "Wait till they nearer roam,
       And thou shalt see; summon them to thy side
       By the power of the love that leads them, and they will come."

79   So, as they eddied past on the whirling tide,
       I raised my voice: "O souls that wearily rove,
       Come to us, speak to us – if it be not denied."

82   And as desire wafts homeward dove with dove
       To their sweet nest, on raised and steady wing
       Down-dropping through the air, impelled by love,

85   So these from Dido's flock came fluttering
       And dropping toward us down the cruel wind,
       Such power was in my affectionate summoning.

88   "O living creature, gracious and so kind,
       Coming through this black air to visit us,
       Us, who in death the globe incarnadine,

91   Were the world's King our friend and might we thus
       Entreat, we would entreat Him for thy peace,
       That pitiest so our pangs dispiteous!

94   Hear all thou wilt, and speak as thou shalt please,
       And we will gladly speak with thee and hear,
       While the winds cease to howl, as they now cease.

97   There is a town upon the sea-coast, near
       Where Po with all his streams comes down to rest
       In ocean; I was born and nurtured there.

100 Love, that so soon takes hold in the gentle breast,
       Took this lad with the lovely body they tore
       From me; the way of it leaves me still distrest.

103 Love, that to no loved heart remits love's score,
       Took me with such great joy of him, that see!
       It holds me yet and never shall leave me more.

106 Love to a single death brought him and me;
       Cain's place lies waiting for our murderer now."
       These words came wafted to us plaintively.

109 Hearing those wounded souls, I bent my brow
       Downward, and thus bemused I let time pass,
       Till the poet said at length: "What thinkest thou?"

112 When I could answer, I began: "Alas!
       Sweet thoughts how many, and desire how great,
       Brought down these twain unto the dolorous pass!"

115 And then I turned to them: "Thy dreadful fate,
       Francesca, makes me weep, it so inspires
       Pity," said I, "and grief compassionate.

118 Tell me – in that time of sighing-sweet desires,
       How, and by what, did love his power disclose
       And grant you knowledge of your hidden fires?"

121 Then she to me: "The bitterest woe of woes
       Is to remember in our wretchedness
       Old happy times; and this thy Doctor knows;

124 Yet, if so dear desire thy heart possess
       To know that root of love which wrought our fall,
       I'll be as those who weep and who confess.

127 One day we read for pastime how in thrall
       Lord Lancelot lay to love, who loved the Queen;
       We were alone – we thought no harm at all.

130 As we read on, our eyes met now and then,
       And to our cheeks the changing colour started,
       But just one moment overcame us – when

133 We read of the smile, desired of lips long-thwarted,
       Such smile, by such a lover kissed away,
       He that may never more from me be parted

136 Trembling all over, kissed my mouth. I say
       The book was Galleot, Galleot the complying
       Ribald who wrote; we read no more that day."

139 While the one spirit thus spoke, the other's crying
       Wailed on me with a sound so lamentable,
       I swooned for pity like as I were dying,

142 And, as a dead man falling, down I fell.

THE IMAGES. *The Circles of Incontinence.* This and the next three
     circles are devoted to those who sinned less by deliberate choice
     of evil than by failure to make resolute choice of the good. Here
     are the sins of self-indulgence, weakness of will, and easy yielding
     to appetite – the "Sins of the Leopard".
The Lustful. The image here is sexual, though we need not confine
     the *allegory* to the sin of unchastity. Lust is a type of *shared* sin; at
     its best, and so long as it remains a sin of incontinence only, there
     is mutuality in it and exchange: although, in fact, mutual indul-
     gence only serves to push both parties along the road to Hell, it is
     not, in intention, wholly selfish. For this reason Dante, with per-
     fect orthodoxy, rates it as the least hateful of the deadly sins.
     (Sexual sins in which love and mutuality have no part find their
     place far below.)
Minos, a medievalized version of the classical Judge of the Under-
     world (see *Aen.* vi. 432). He may image an accusing conscience.
     The souls are damned on their own confession, for, Hell being the
     place of self-knowledge in sin, there can be no more self-decep-
     tion here. (Similarly, even in the circles of Fraud, all the shades
     tell Dante the truth about themselves; this is poetically convenient,
     but, given this conception of Hell, it must be so.) The *literally*
     damned, having lost "the good of the intellect", cannot profit by
     their self-knowledge; *allegorically,* for the living soul, this vision
     of the Hell in the self is the preliminary to repentance and restora-
     tion.
The Black Wind. As the lovers drifted into self-indulgence and were
     carried away by their passions, so now they drift for ever. The
     bright, voluptuous sin is now seen *as it is* – a howling darkness of
     helpless discomfort. (The "punishment" for sin is simply the sin

itself, experienced without illusion – though Dante does not work this out with mathematical rigidity in every circle.)

NOTES. l. 6: *as he girds him, sentencing*: as Dante explains in ll. 11–12, Minos girds himself so many times with his tail to indicate the number of the circle to which each soul is to go (cf. Canto XXVII. 124 and note).

l. 28: *a place made dumb of every glimmer of light* – (cf. Canto I. 60, "wherein the sun is mute"): Nevertheless, Dante is able to see the spirits. This is only one of many passages in which the poet conveys to us that the things he perceives during his journey are not perceived altogether by the mortal senses, but after another mode. (In *Purg.* xxi. 29, Virgil explains to another spirit that Dante "could not come alone, because he does not see after our manner, wherefore I was brought forth from Hell to guide him".) So, in the present case, Dante recognizes that the darkness is total, although he can see in the dark.

l. 61: *she that slew herself for love*: Dido.

l. 88: *O living creature*: The speaker is Francesca da Rimini. Like many of the personages in the *Comedy*, she does not directly name herself, but gives Dante particulars about her birthplace and history which enable him to recognize her. She was the daughter of Guido Vecchio di Polenta of Ravenna, and aunt to Guido Novello di Polenta, who was Dante's friend and host during the latter years of his life; so that her history was of topical interest to Dante's readers. For political reasons, she was married to the deformed Gianciotto, son of Malatesta da Verrucchio, lord of Rimini, but fell in love with his handsome younger brother Paolo, who became her lover. Her husband, having one day surprised them together, stabbed them both to death (1285).

l. 94: *hear all thou wilt*: Tender and beautiful as Dante's handling of Francesca is, he has sketched her with a deadly accuracy. All the good is there; the charm, the courtesy, the instant response to affection, the grateful eagerness to please; but also all the evil; the easy yielding, the inability to say No, the intense self-pity.

Of this, the most famous episode in the whole *Comedy*, Charles Williams writes: "It is always quoted as an example of Dante's tenderness. So, no doubt, it is, but it is not here for that reason. ... It has a much more important place; it presents the first tender, passionate, and half-excusable consent of the soul to sin. ... [Dante] so manages the description, he so heightens the excuse, that the excuse reveals itself as precisely the sin ... the persistent parleying with the occasion of sin, the sweet prolonged laziness of love, is the first surrender of the soul to Hell – small but certain. The formal sin here is the adultery of the two lovers; the poetic sin is their shrinking from the adult love demanded of them, and their refusal of the opportunity of glory." (*The Figure of Beatrice*, p. 118.)

l. 97: *a town upon the sea-coast*: Ravenna.

l. 102: *the way of it leaves me still distrest*: Either (1) the way of the murder, because the lovers were killed in the very act of sin and so had no time for repentance; or (2) the way in which their love came about. The story went that Paolo was sent to conduct the marriage negotiations, and that Francesca was tricked into consenting by being led to suppose that he, and not Gianciotto, was to be her bridegroom. In the same way, in the Arthurian romances, Queen Guinevere falls in love with Lancelot when he is sent to woo her on King Arthur's behalf; and it is this parallel which makes the tale of Lancelot so poignant for her and Paolo.

l. 107: *Cain's place*: Caina, so called after Cain; the first ring of the lowest circle in Hell, where lie those who were treacherous to their own kindred. (Canto XXXII.)

l. 123: *thy Doctor*: Virgil (see l. 70). Dante is probably thinking of Aeneas' words to Dido: *infandum, regina, jubes renovare dolorem* ... (O queen, thou dost bid me renew an unspeakable sorrow ...), *Aeneid* ii. 3.

l. 137: *the book was Galleot*: In the romance of *Lancelot du Lac*, Galleot (or Galehalt) acted as intermediary between Lancelot and Guinevere, and so in the Middle Ages his name, like that of Pandarus in the tale of *Troilus and Cressida*, became a synonym for a go-between. The sense of the passage is: "The book was a pander and so was he who wrote it".

CANTO VI

THE STORY. *Dante now finds himself in the Third Circle, where the Gluttonous lie wallowing in the mire, drenched by perpetual rain and mauled by the three-headed dog Cerberus. After Virgil has quieted Cerberus by throwing earth into his jaws, Dante talks to the shade of Ciacco, a Florentine, who prophesies some of the disasters which are about to befall Florence, and tells him where he will find certain other of their fellow-citizens. Virgil tells Dante what the condition of the spirits will be, after the Last Judgment.*

When consciousness returned, which had shut close
   The doors of sense, leaving me stupefied
   For pity of those sad kinsfolk and their woes,

4   New sufferings and new sufferers, far and wide,
   Where'er I move, or turn myself, or strain
   My curious eyes, are seen on every side.

7   I am now in the Third Circle: that of rain –
   One ceaseless, heavy, cold, accursed quench,
   Whose law and nature vary never a grain;

10   Huge hailstones, sleet and snow, and turbid drench
   Of water sluice down through the darkened air,
   And the soaked earth gives off a putrid stench.

13   Cerberus, the cruel, misshapen monster, there
   Bays in his triple gullet and doglike growls
   Over the wallowing shades; his eyeballs glare

16   A bloodshot crimson, and his bearded jowls
   Are greasy and black; pot-bellied, talon-heeled,
   He clutches and flays and rips and rends the souls.

19   They howl in the rain like hounds; they try to shield
   One flank with the other; with many a twist and squirm,
   The impious wretches writhe in the filthy field.

22   When Cerberus spied us coming, the great Worm,
   He gaped his mouths with all their fangs a-gloat,
   Bristling and quivering till no limb stood firm.

25   At once my guide, spreading both hands wide out,
   Scooped up whole fistfuls of the miry ground
   And shot them swiftly into each craving throat.

28   And as a ravenous and barking hound
   Falls dumb the moment he gets his teeth on food,
   And worries and bolts with never a thought beyond,

31   So did those beastly muzzles of the rude
   Fiend Cerberus, who so yells on the souls, they're all
   Half deafened – or they would be, if they could.

34   Then o'er the shades whom the rain's heavy fall
   Beats down, we forward went; and our feet trod
   Their nothingness, which seems corporeal.

37   These all lay grovelling flat upon the sod;
   Only, as we went by, a single shade
   Sat suddenly up, seeing us pass that road.

40   "O thou that through this Hell of ours art led,
        Look if thou know me, since thou wast, for sure,"
        Said he, "or ever I was unmade, made."

43   Then I to him: "Perchance thy torments sore
        Have changed thee out of knowledge – there's no trusting
        Sight, if I e'er set eyes on thee before.

46   But say, who are thou? brought by what ill lusting
        To such a pass and punishment as, meseems,
        Worse there may be, but nothing so disgusting?"

49   "Thy native city," said he, "where envy teems
        And swells so that already it brims the sack,
        Called me her own in the life where the light beams.

52   Ciacco you citizens nicknamed me – alack!
        Damnable gluttony was my soul's disease;
        See how I waste for it now in the rain's wrack.

55   And I, poor sinner, am not alone: all these
        Lie bound in the like penalty with me
        For the like offence." And there he held his peace,

58   And I at once began: "The misery
        Moves me to tears, Ciacco, and weighs me down.
        But tell me if thou canst, what end may be

61   In store for the people of our distracted town.
        Is there one just man left? And from what source
        To such foul head have these distempers grown?"

64   And he: "Long time their strife will run its course,
        And come to bloodshed; the wood party thence
        Will drive the other out with brutal force;

67   But within three brief suns their confidence
        Will have a fall, and t'other faction rise
        By help of one who now sits on the fence;

70   And these will lord it long with arrogant eyes,
        Crushing their foes with heavy loads indeed,
        For all their bitter shame and outraged cries.

73   Two righteous men there are, whom none will heed;
        Three sparks from Hell – Avarice, Envy, Pride –
        In all men's bosoms sowed the fiery seed."

76   His boding speech thus ended; so I cried:
        "Speak on, I beg thee! More, much more reveal!
        Tegghiaio, Farinata – how betide

79   Those worthy men? and Rusticucci's zeal?
        Arrigo, Mosca, and the rest as well
        Whose minds were still set on the public weal?

82   Where are they? Can I find them? Prithee tell –
        I am consumed with my desire to know –
        Feasting in Heaven, or poisoned here in Hell?"

85   He answered: "With the blacker spirits below,
        Dragged to the depth by other crimes abhorred;
        There shalt thou see them, if so deep thou go.

88   But when to the sweet world thou art restored,
        Recall my name to living memory;
        I'll tell no more, nor speak another word."

91   Therewith he squinted his straight gaze awry,
        Eyed me awhile, then, dropping down his head,
        Rolled over amid that sightless company.

94   Then spake my guide: "He'll rouse no more," he said,
        "Till the last loud angelic trumpet's sounding;
        For when the Enemy Power shall come arrayed

97   Each soul shall seek its own grave's mournful mounding,
        Put on once more its earthly flesh and feature,
        And hear the Doom eternally redounding."

100   Thus with slow steps I and my gentle teacher,
        Over that filthy sludge of souls and snow,
        Passed on, touching a little upon the nature

103   Of the life to come. "Master," said I, "this woe –
        Will it grow less, or still more fiercely burning
        With the Great Sentence, or remain just so?"

106   "Go to," said he, "hast thou forgot thy learning,
        Which hath it: The more perfect, the more keen,
        Whether for pleasure's or for pain's discerning?

109   Though true perfection never can be seen
        In these damned souls, they'll be more near complete
        After the Judgment than they yet have been."

112   So, with more talk which I need not repeat,
        We followed the road that rings that circle round,
        Till on the next descent we set our feet;

115   There Pluto, the great enemy, we found.

THE IMAGES. *The Gluttonous*: The surrender to sin which began with
mutual indulgence leads by an imperceptible degradation to solitary self-indulgence. Of this kind of sin, the Gluttons are chosen
as the image. Here is no reciprocity and no communication; each
soul grovels alone in the mud, without heeding his neighbours –
"a sightless company", Dante calls them.

The Rain. Gluttony (like the other self-indulgences it typifies) often
masquerades on earth as a warm, cosy, and indeed jolly kind of
sin; here it is seen as it is – a cold sensuality, a sodden and filthy
spiritual wretchedness.

Cerberus. In the *story*, Cerberus is the three-headed dog familiar to us
from Homer and Virgil and the tale of the Twelve Labours of
Hercules, who guards the threshold of the classical Hades. For the
allegory, he is the image of uncontrolled appetite; the Glutton,
whose appetite preyed upon people and things, is seen to be, in
fact, the helpless prey on which that appetite gluts itself.

NOTES. l. 7: *I am now in the Third Circle*: Once again, Dante does not
say how he got here: we may suppose that Virgil carried or assisted
him down before he had wholly recovered his senses.

    l. 22: *Worm*: This, in Old English as in Italian (*vermo*), is simply a
word for a monster, cf. the fairy-tale of "The Laidly Worm of
Spindleston Heugh", where it denotes a dragon.

    l. 26: *whole fistfuls of the miry ground*: To throw something into his
mouth was the traditional way of appeasing this particular guardian
of Hell – hence the phrase "to give a sop to Cerberus". In *Aeneid* vi,
the Sibyl who guides Aeneas through Hades brings a number of
cakes for the purpose. Here Virgil, not having made this provision,
makes use of the first substitute that comes to hand.

    l. 49: *thy native city*: Florence.

    l. 52: *Ciacco you citizens nicknamed me*: The word means "pig", and,
according to Boccacio, was the nickname of a Florentine gentleman
notorious for his gluttony.

    l. 61: *our distracted town*: i.e. Florence.

    l. 64: *long time their strife will run its course*: This is the first of
a number of passages dealing (under the guise of prophecy) with

political events in Italy, and especially in Florence, which took place after the supposed date of the Vision (1300). It refers to the struggle between the two Guelf parties (the Blacks and the Whites), and to the final expulsion of the Whites (including Dante) from Florence.

l. 65: *the wood party*: the Whites. The adjective *selvaggia* means either the "woodland" party (because certain of its leaders had come into Florence from the surrounding country) or the "savage" (i.e. uncultivated party) (as opposed to the more aristocratic Blacks). The English word "wood", which formerly had the meaning "mad, wild, savage", is thus a fairly exact equivalent of the ambiguous Italian.

The two parties "came to bloodshed" at the May-Day Festival of 1300, and the expulsion of the Black leaders took place shortly after. The Blacks returned in November 1301, with the help of Boniface VIII (the "sitter on the fence", l. 69), who till then had shown no decided preference for either party. The first decree banishing the Whites was published in January 1302, and the last in the latter half of the same year – all "within three suns" of the time at which Ciacco is supposed to be speaking.

l. 73: *two righteous men*: Dante is usually credited with meaning himself and his friend Guido Cavalcanti; but he does not say so, and we need not found a charge of self-righteousness on what he has not said.

ll. 78–80: *Tegghiaio ... Mosca*: The persons named are all distinguished Florentines. We shall meet Farinata in Canto X, Tegghiaio and Rusticucci in Canto XVI, and Mosca in Canto XXVIII. Arrigo is not mentioned again.

l. 96: *the Enemy Power*: This is the strangest and most terrible periphrasis used for Christ in these circles of the damned, who have chosen to know all goodness as antagonism and judgment.

l. 106: *thy learning*: the philosophy of Aristotle, as incorporated in the theology of St Thomas Aquinas. The souls will be "more perfect" after the Last Judgment because they will then be reunited to their bodies.

l. 115: *Pluto*: god of the wealth that springs from the soil, naturally came to be regarded as an "underground" deity, and from early times was apt to be identified with Hades (Dis). Dante, however, distinguishes him from Dis (Satan), and while making him an infernal power, retains his primitive character as a symbol of riches. There is perhaps also a fusion with Plutus, the "god of wealth" mentioned by Phaedrus. "The great enemy" is probably an allusion to I *Tim.* vi. 10.

CANTO VII

THE STORY. *At the entrance to the Fourth Circle, the poets are opposed by Pluto, and Virgil is again obliged to use a "word of power". In this circle, the Hoarders and the Spendthrifts roll huge rocks against one another, and here Virgil explains the nature and working of Luck (or Fortune). Then, crossing the circle, they descend the cliff to the Marsh of Styx, which forms the Fifth Circle and contains the Wrathful. Skirting its edge, they reach the foot of a tower.*

"*Papè Satan, papè Satan aleppe*,"
    Pluto 'gan gabble with his clucking tongue;
    My all-wise, gentle guide, to me unhappy

4   Said hearteningly: "Let no fears do thee wrong;
    He shall not stay thy journey down this steep;
    His powers, whate'er they be, are not so strong."

7   Then, turning him, and letting his glance sweep
    O'er that bloat face: "Peace, thou damned wolf!" said he,
    "Go, choke in thine own venom! To the deep,

10 Not without cause, we go. I say to thee,
    Thus it is willed on high, where Michaël
    Took vengeance on the proud adultery."

13 Then, as the sails bellying in the wind's swell
    Tumble a-tangle at crack of the snapping mast,
    Even so to earth the savage monster fell;

16 And we to the Fourth Circle downward passed,
    Skirting a new stretch of the grim abyss
    Where all the ills of all the world are cast.

19 God's justice! Who shall tell the agonies,
    Heaped thick and new before my shuddering glance?
    Why must our guilt smite us with strokes like this?

22 As waves against the encountering waves advance
    Above Charybdis, clashing with toppling crest,
    So must the folk here dance and counter-dance.

25 More than elsewhere, I saw them thronged and pressed
    This side and that, yelling with all their might,
    And shoving each a great weight with his chest.

28 They bump together, and where they bump, wheel right
    Round, and return, trundling their loads again,
    Shouting: "Why chuck away?" "Why grab so tight?"

31 Then round the dismal ring they pant and strain
    Back on both sides to where they first began
    Still as they go bawling their rude refrain;

34 And when they meet, then each re-treads his span,
    Half round the ring to joust in the other list;
    I felt quite shocked, and like a stricken man.

37 "Pray tell me, sir," said I, "all this – what is't?
    Who are these people? On our left I find
    Numberless tonsured heads; was each a priest?"

40 "In life," said he, "these were so squint of mind
    As in the handling of their wealth to use
    No moderation – none, in either kind;

43 That's plain, from their shrill yelpings of abuse
    At the ring's turn, where opposite degrees
    Of crime divide them into rival crews.

46 They whose pates boast no hairy canopies
    Are clerks – yea, popes and cardinals, in whom
    Covetousness hath made its masterpiece."

49 "Why, sir," said I, "surely there must be some
    Faces I know in all this gang, thus brought
    By these defilements to a common doom."

52 "Nay," he replied, "that is an empty thought;
    Living, their minds distinguished nothing; dead,
    They cannot be distinguished. In this sort

55 They'll butt and brawl for ever; when from bed
    The Last Trump wakes the body, these will be
    Raised with tight fists, and those stripped, hide and head.

58 Hoarding and squandering filched the bright world's glee
    Away, and set them to this tourney's shock,
    Whose charms need no embroidered words from me.

61 See now, my son, the fine and fleeting mock
    Of all those goods men wrangle for – the boon
    That is delivered into the hand of Luck;

64   For all the gold that is beneath the moon,
         Or ever was, could not avail to buy
         Repose for one of these weary souls – not one."

67   "Master, I would hear more of this," said I;
         "What is this Luck, whose talons take in hand
         All life's good things that go so pleasantly?"

70   Then he: "Ah, witless world! Behold the grand
         Folly of ignorance! Make thine ear attendant
         Now on my judgment of her, and understand.

73   He whose high wisdom's over all transcendent
         Stretched forth the Heavens, and guiding spirits supplied,
         So that each part to each part shines resplendent,

76   Spreading the light equal on every side;
         Likewise for earthly splendours He saw fit
         To ordain a general minister and guide,

79   By whom vain wealth, as time grew ripe for it,
         From race to race, from blood to blood, should pass,
         Far beyond hindrance of all human wit.

82   Wherefore some nations minish, some amass
         Great power, obedient to her subtle codes,
         Which are hidden, like the snake beneath the grass.

85   For her your science finds no measuring-rods;
         She in her realm provides, maintains, makes laws,
         And judges, as do in theirs the other gods.

88   Her permutations never know truce nor pause;
         Necessity lends her speed, so swift in fame
         Men come and go, and cause succeeds to cause.

91   Lo! this is she that hath so curst a name
         Even from those that should give praise to her –
         Luck, whom men senselessly revile and blame;

94   But she is blissful and she does not hear;
         She, with the other primal creatures gay,
         Tastes her own blessedness, and turns her sphere.

97   Come! to more piteous woes we must away;
         All stars that rose when I set out now sink,
         And the High Powers permit us no long stay."

100   So to the further edge we crossed the rink,
         Hard by a bubbling spring which, rising there,
         Cuts its own cleft and pours on down the brink.

103   Darker than any perse its waters were,
         And keeping company with the ripples dim
         We made our way down by that eerie stair.

106   A marsh there is called Styx, which the sad stream
         Forms when it finds the end of its descent
         Under the grey, malignant rock-foot grim;

109   And I, staring about with eyes intent,
         Saw mud-stained figures in the mire beneath,
         Naked, with looks of savage discontent,

112   At fisticuffs – not with fists alone, but with
         Their heads and heels, and with their bodies too,
         And tearing each other piecemeal with their teeth.

115   "Son," the kind master said, "here may'st thou view
         The souls of those who yielded them to wrath;
         Further, I'd have thee know and hold for true

118   That others lie plunged deep in this vile broth,
         Whose sighs – see there, wherever one may look –
         Come bubbling up to the top and make it froth.

121   Bogged there they say: 'Sullen were we – we took
         No joy of the pleasant air, no joy of the good
         Sun; our hearts smouldered with a sulky smoke;

124   Sullen we lie here now in the black mud.'
         This hymn they gurgle in their throats, for whole
         Words they can nowise frame." Thus we pursued

127   Our path round a wide arc of that ghast pool,
         Between the soggy marsh and arid shore,
         Still eyeing those who gulp the marish foul,

130   And reached at length the foot of a tall tower.

THE IMAGES. *The Hoarders and the Spendthrifts.* Mutual indulgence has already declined into selfish appetite; now, that appetite becomes aware of the incompatible and equally selfish appetites of other people. Indifference becomes mutual antagonism, imaged here by the antagonism between hoarding and squandering.

The Joust. Note the reappearance of community in a perverted form: these irrational appetites are united, after a fashion, by a common hatred, for the waging of a futile war. So nations, political parties, business combines, classes, gangs, etc., sometimes display a spurious comradeship in opposition.

The Wrathful. Community in sin is unstable: it soon disintegrates into an anarchy of hatred, all against all. Dante distinguishes two kinds of Wrath. The one is active and ferocious; it vents itself in sheer lust for inflicting pain and destruction – on other people, on itself, on anything and everything it meets. The other is passive and sullen, the withdrawal into a black sulkiness which can find no joy in God or man or the universe.

The Marsh. Both kinds of Wrath are figured as a muddy slough; on its surface, the active hatreds rend and snarl at one another; at the bottom, the sullen hatreds lie gurgling, unable even to express themselves for the rage that chokes them. This is the last of the Circles of Incontinence. This savage self-frustration is the end of that which had its tender and romantic beginnings in the dalliance of indulged passion.

The Path down the Cliff. For the first time, Dante's passage from one circle to the other is described in detail. We are not told at what precise point in the wilderness he found Hell-gate; one may encounter it at any moment. The crossing of Acheron – the image of the assent to sin – is made unconsciously. From Limbo to the Second Circle – from the lack of imagination that inhibits the will to the false imagination that saps it – the passage is easy and, as it were, unnoticed. From the Second Circle to the Third – from mutuality to separateness – the soul is carried as though in a dream. From the Third to the Fourth Circle the way is a little plainer – for as one continues in sin one becomes uneasily aware of inner antagonisms and resentments, though without any clear notion how they arise. But as antagonism turns to hatred, the steps of the downward path begin to be fearfully apparent. From this point on the descent is mapped out with inexorable clarity.

Styx – the name means "hateful" – is the second of the four chief rivers of Hell. It economically does double duty as the Fifth Circle and as the boundary between Upper and Nether Hell.

NOTES. l. 1: *Papè Satan aleppe*: Various attempts have been made to interpret this cryptic remark, but none of them is very convincing. One may safely conjecture that it is meant as an invocation to the Devil, and it is as well to leave it at that. Cf. Nimrod's jargon in Canto XXXI.

l. 12: *where Michaël took vengeance on the proud adultery*: The reference is to the Archangel Michael's war upon the rebellious angels (*Rev.* xii. 7–9). "Adultery" is used in the Biblical sense of unfaithfulness to God – as in "whoring after strange gods" (*Deut.* xxxi. 16, etc., and similar passages). "Proud", because Satan and his angels fell through pride.

l. 23: *Charybdis*: famous whirlpool near Messina.

l. 73 sqq.: *He whose high wisdom*: This is the first of the series of great discourses in which Dante gradually unfolds the plan of the spiritual and physical universe. The "guiding spirits" mentioned here are the celestial intelligences (angels) who control the heavenly spheres. *Luck* or *Fortune* is here conceived as a similar ministering spirit, whose function it is to control and distribute wealth and opportunity upon the earth. Virgil describes her under the familiar classical figure of a goddess with a wheel, or sphere, whose turning brings about the ups-and-downs of disaster and prosperity. By this figure Dante does not deny free will, or ascribe the course of history to blind chance: he says (*De Monarchia*, xii. 70): " ... fortune, which agency we better and more rightly call the divine providence".

l. 87: *the other gods*: i.e. the angels. Dante several times uses this name for them, and not only when Virgil is speaking.

l. 89: *necessity lends her speed*: Here again Dante does not mean that, in the pagan phrase, "the gods themselves are subject to necessity", but merely that, such is the brevity of human life, the changes of fortune must needs be swift.

l. 95: *primal creatures*: the celestial Intelligences, who were created, with the heavens themselves, directly by God, and not through secondary agencies (i.e. they were not evolved or generated).

l. 98: *all stars that rose ... now sink*: All the stars that were rising when Virgil first met Dante on Good Friday evening have passed the zenith and begun to set; i.e. it is now past midnight. (So long as the poets are descending into Hell the time is never indicated by the sun, but always by the changes of the night sky.)

l. 101: *a bubbling spring*: This is the water of the river Acheron, which, after forming a complete circle about Hell, runs underground beneath the first four circles, and now emerges again to pour down the cliff and form the river and marsh of Styx. (See map, p. 398).

CANTO VIII

THE STORY. *From the watch-tower on the edge of the marsh a beacon signals to the garrison of the City of Dis that Dante and Virgil are approaching, and a boat is sent to fetch them. Phlegyas ferries them across Styx. On the way they encounter Filippo Argenti, one of the Wrathful, who is recognized by Dante and tries to attack him. They draw near to the red-hot walls of the City and after a long circuit disembark at the gate. Virgil parleys with the Fallen Angels who are on guard there, but they slam the gate in his face. The two poets are obliged to wait for Divine assistance.*

I say, continuing, that ere we came
 To the tower's foot, our eyes had long been led
 To its summit, by two twinkling points of flame

4 Which we saw kindled there; while, far ahead,
 And almost out of eyeshot, we espied
 An answering beacon's flicker. So I said,

7 Turning to the well of wisdom at my side:
 "What does it say? What does that other light
 Wink back? Who make these signals?" He replied:

10 "Already across the water heaves in sight
 What's to be looked for from the signal's waft,
 So it be not veiled from thee by the blight

13 Of these marsh mists." I looked; and never shaft
 So swift from bowstring sped through the thin air
 As through those turbid waves a little craft

16 Came skimming toward us; one sole mariner
 Guided its course, who shouted from the prow:
 "Oho, thou wicked spirit! So thou art there!"

19 'Nay, Phlegyas, Phlegyas,' said my lord, "peace now!
 This time thou criest in vain; we are no meat
 For thee – thou hast but to ferry us o'er the slough."

22 As one who hears of some outrageous cheat
 Practised on him, and fumes and chokes with gall,
 So Phlegyas, thwarted, fumed at his defeat.

25 So then my guide embarked, and at his call
 I followed him; and not till I was in
 Did the boat seem to bear a load at all.

28 When we were set, the ancient vessel then
 Put forth at once, cleaving the water's grime
 Deeper than her wont, our voyage to begin;

31 And as we ran the channel of the dead slime
 There started up at me a mud-soaked head,
 Crying: "Who are thou, come here before thy time?"

34 "Tho' I come," said I, "I stay not; thou who art made
 So rank and beastly, who art thou?" "Go to;
 Thou seest that I am one who weep," he said.

37 And I: "Amid the weeping and the woe,
 Accursed spirit, do thou remain and rot!
 I know thee, filthy as thou art – I know."

40 Then he stretched out both hands to clutch the boat,
 But the master was on his guard and thrust him back,
 Crying: "Hence to the other dogs! Trouble him not!"

43 And after, laid his arms about my neck
 And kissed my face and said: "Indignant soul,
 Blessed is the womb that bare thee! This bold jack

46 Was an arrogant brute in the world, nor in his whole
 Life can remembrance find one sweetening touch;
 So must his raging spirit writhe here and roll.

49 Many who strut like kings up there are such
 As here shall wallow hog-like in the mud,
 Leaving behind nothing but foul reproach."

52 "Master," said I, "I tell thee, it were good
 If I might see this villain soused in the swill
 Before we have passed the lake – Oh, that I could!"

55 And he made answer: "Thou shalt gaze thy fill
 Or ever thou set eyes on the far shore;
 Herein 'tis fitting thou shouldst have thy will."

58 And soon I saw him set upon so sore
 By the muddy gang, with such a pulling and hauling,
 That I still praise and thank my God therefor.

61 "Have at Filippo Argenti!" they were bawling;
 "Loo! loo!" The shade of the fierce Florentine
 Turned on himself, biting with his teeth and mauling.

64 There left we him, as doth this tale of mine;
 For on my ears there smote a wailing cry,
 And I craned forward, eager to divine

67 Its meaning. "See, my son! it now draws nigh,"
    Said my good lord, "the city named of Dis,
    With its sad citizens, its great company."

70 And I: "Already I see its mosques arise
    Clear from the valley yonder – a red shell,
    As though drawn out of glowing furnaces."

73 And he replied: "The flames unquenchable
    That fire them from within thus make them burn
    Ruddy, as thou seest, in this, the nether Hell."

76 We now were come to the deep moats, which turn
    To gird that city all disconsolate,
    Whose walls appeared as they were made of iron.

79 A long way round we had to navigate
    Before we came to where the ferryman
    Roared: "Out with you now, for here's the gate!"

82 Thousand and more, thronging the barbican,
    I saw, of spirits fallen from Heaven, who cried
    Angrily: "Who goes there? why walks this man,

85 Undead, the kingdom of the dead?" My guide,
    Wary and wise, made signs to them, to show
    He sought a secret parley. Then, their pride

88 Abating somewhat, they called out: "Why, so!
    Come thou within, and bid that fellow begone –
    That rash intruder on our realm below.

91 Let him wend back his foolish way alone;
    See if he can; for thou with us shalt stay
    That through this nighted land hast led him on."

94 Reader, do but conceive of my dismay,
    Hearing these dreadful words! It seemed quite plain
    I nevermore should see the light of day.

97 "O Master dear, that seven times over again
    Hast brought me safely through," said I, "and freed
    From all the perils that in my path have lain,

100 Leave me not utterly undone! Indeed,
    If we may not go forward, pray let's quit,
    And hasten back together with all good speed!"

103 Then said my lord and leader: "Fear no whit;
    There's none at all can stay our steps, nor make thee
    Forbear the pass: such Power hath granted it.

106 Wait for me here; to cheerful thoughts betake thee;
    Feed thy faint heart with hope, and calm thy breast,
    For in this underworld I'll not forsake thee."

109 My gentle father's gone! I'm left distrest,
    Abandoned here! Horrid perhapses throng
    My doubtful mind, where yeas and noes contest.

112 His proffered terms I could not hear. Not long
    He'd stood in talk with them, when suddenly
    They all rushed jostling in again headlong,

115 Leaving him outside. So the enemy
    Slammed the gate in my master's face; who thus
    Turned him, and came with slow steps back to me.

118 His eyes were downcast, and his anxious brows
    Shorn of all boldness. Sighing he said: "What's here?
    Who dares forbid me the Mansions Dolorous?"

121 And then aloud to me: "Have thou no fear
    Though I be wroth; I'll win this trial of power,
    Whatever hindrance they contrive in there.

124 Their truculence is no new thing; once before
    'Twas tried at a less secret gate, whereon
    No bars remain for ever. Above that door

127 Thou sawest the dead title. And now comes one,
    This side already treading the steep abyss
    And guardless passing all the circles down,

130 That shall unbar to us the gates of Dis."

THE IMAGES. *Phlegyas* in Greek mythology was a king of Boeotia, son of Ares the war-god by a human mother. His daughter Coronis was loved by Apollo; whereupon Phlegyas in his rage set fire to Apollo's temple. Apollo killed him with his arrows, and he was condemned to torment in Hades. (See *Aen.* vi. 618.) He is thus an appropriate ferryman to ply between the Circle of the Wrathful and the City of the Impious.

The City of Dis. This comprises the whole of Nether Hell, and its ramparts, moated by the Styx, form a complete circle about the Pit. (See map, p. **393**.) The sins tormented within the City are those in which the will is actively involved (the sins of Violence and Fraud), and its iron walls are the image of a rigid and determined obstinacy in ill-doing.

Virgil's Repulse at the Gate. Humanism is always apt to underestimate, and to be baffled by, the deliberate will to evil. Neither is it any sure protection against Heresy. The *allegory* is further developed in the next canto.

NOTES. l. 3: *two twinkling points of flame*: to signal the approach of two passengers.

l. 18: *thou wicked spirit*: Phlegyas addresses only one of the poets; presumably because he (*a*) sees that Dante is not a shade, and (*b*) suspects Virgil of having brought him there for a felonious purpose (cf. Cantos IX. 54 and XII. 90).

l. 26: *not till I was in*: because of Dante's mortal weight.

l. 45: *blessed is the womb that bare thee*: It is important to understand this passage, since otherwise we may feel that Virgil is blasphemously encouraging Dante in very cruel and unchristian behaviour. We must distinguish here between the *literal* and *allegorical* meanings, which the poem fuses into a single image.

1. *Literally*. In Hell the soul is fixed eternally in that which it has chosen; it cannot, that is, enjoy there the good which it has rejected. Therefore, the reaction it calls forth from Dante can be no more than the reflection of what it has in itself. Thus Francesca calls forth that same easy pity which betrayed her to lust; Ciacco, the perfunctory pity which is all that the egotist can spare for his neighbours; the Hoarders and Spendthrifts, *because* they made no distinctions in life, are indistinguishable in eternity (Canto VII. 53, 54). But the Wrathful have rejected pity and chosen cruelty; therefore they can receive no pity, and goodness can only manifest itself to them as wrath, since they have chosen to know it so.

2. *Allegorically*. In the *vision* of Hell, the soul knows itself in a state of sin. Up to this moment Dante has only wondered, grieved, pitied, or trembled; now, for the first time, he sees (in the image of the damned soul) sin as it is – vile, degraded, and dangerous – and turns indignantly against it. For whatever inadequate and unworthy reasons, he accepts judgment and places himself on God's side. It is the first feeble stirring of the birth of Christ within the soul, and Virgil accordingly hails it with words that were used of Christ Himself. (*Luke* xi. 27.)

l. 61: *Filippo Argenti*: a Florentine knight of the Adimari family, of very violent temper, and so purse-proud that he is said to have had his horse shod with silver (hence the nickname "Argenti"). The Adimari were of the opposite faction to Dante and bitterly opposed his recall from banishment.

l. 68: *the city named of Dis*: i.e. named after Dis or Pluto, the King of Hell. Virgil uses the classical name; Dante, as a Christian, calls him Beelzebub, Satan, or Lucifer.

l. 70: *mosques*: Mohammedanism was looked on – correctly enough – by the Middle Ages as being a Christian heresy (see Canto XXVIII), and immediately inside the walls of Dis we shall, in fact, find the Circle of the Heretics. More generally, the "mosques" indicate that the City is devoted to a perverse and infidel cult.

l. 72: *glowing furnaces*: It is only in Nether Hell, below the walls of Dis, that we encounter any torment by fire.

l. 83: *spirits fallen from Heaven*: These are the rebel angels of Christian tradition; the classical monsters continue right down to the bottom of Hell, but here, in the Circles of the perverted will, we find also the more malignant spirits who knew the true God and opposed Him.

l. 125: *a less secret gate*: the gate of Hell, when the devils sought to oppose Christ's entrance into Limbo.

l. 127: *the dead title*: the inscription over Hell-gate. (Canto III. 1–6.)

NETHER HELL - 1

HERESY : VIOLENCE – THE SINS OF THE LION

CANTO IX

THE STORY. *Dante, alarmed by Virgil's anxiety, tactfully inquires of him whether he really knows the way through Hell, and gets a reassuring answer. The Furies appear and threaten to unloose Medusa. A noise like thunder announces the arrival of a Heavenly Messenger, who opens the gates of Dis and rebukes the demons. When he has departed, the Poets enter the City and find themselves in a great plain covered with the burning tombs of the Heretics.*

Seeing my face, and what a coward colour
    It turned when he came back, my guide was quick
    To put away his own unwonted pallor.

4 He stood and leaned intent, as who should prick
    His ear to hear, for far one could not see,
    So black the air was, and the fog so thick.

7 "Nay, somehow we must win this fight," said he;
    "If not ... That great self-proffered aid is lent;
    But oh! how long his coming seems to be!"

10 I saw too clearly how his first intent
    Was cloaked by what came after; what he said
    Was not what he'd designed, but different.

13 But none the less his speech increased my dread –
    For maybe I pieced out the broken phrase
    To a worse ending than was in his head.

16 "Did any ever, descending from that place
    Where loss of hope remains their only woe,
    Thread to its depth this hollow's dreary maze?"

19 I put this question. He replied: "Although
    'Tis rare that one of us should come this way
    Or undertake the journey I now go,

22 Yet once before I made it, truth to say,
    Conjured by cruel Erichtho, she whose spell
    Wont to call back the shades to their dead clay.

25 I was not long stripped of my mortal shell
    When she compelled me pass within yon wall
    To fetch a spirit from Judas' circle of Hell;

28 That is the deepest, darkest place of all,
    And farthest from high Heaven's all-moving gyre;
    I know the way; take heart – no ill shall fall.

31 On every side, the vast and reeking mire
    Surrounds this city of the woe-begot,
    Where now's no entering, save with wrath and ire ..."

34 And he went on, saying I know not what,
    For my whole being was drawn up with my eyes
    To where the tower's high battlements burned red-hot:

37 For there of a sudden I saw three shapes arise,
    Three hellish Furies, boltered all with blood;
    Their form and bearing were made woman-wise;

40 Vivid green hydras girt them, and a brood
    Of asps and adders, each a living tress,
    Writhed round the brows of that fell sisterhood.

43 And, knowing well those handmaids pitiless
    Who serve the Queen of everlasting woe:
    "Behold," said he, "the fierce Erinyes.

46 There on the right Alecto howls, and lo!
    Megaera on the left; betwixt them wails
    Tisiphone." And he was silent so.

49 They beat their breasts, and tore them with their nails,
    Shrieking so loud that, faint and tremulous,
    I clutched the poet; and they, with fiercer yells,

52 Cried: "Fetch Medusa!", glaring down on us,
    "Turn him to stone! Why did we not requite –
    Woe worth the day! – the assault of Theseus?"

55 "Turn thee about, and shut thine eyelids tight;
    If Gorgon show her face and thou thereon
    Look once, there's no returning to the light."

58 Thus cried the master; nor to my hands alone
    Would trust, but turned me himself, and urgently
    Pressed my palms close and covered them with his own.

61 O you whose intellects keep their sanity,
    Do you mark well the doctrine shrouded o'er
    By the strange verses with their mystery.

64 Then o'er that dull tide came the crash and roar
    Of an enormous and appalling sound,
    So that the ground shuddered from shore to shore;

67 A sound like the sound of a violent wind, around
    The time of opposing heats and the parched weather,
    When it sweeps on the forest and leaps with a sudden bound,

70 Shattering and scattering the boughs hither and thither;
    Superb with a tower of dust for harbinger
    It goes, while the wolves and herdsmen flee together.

73 He loosed my eyes: "Now look", said he, "see there,
    Yonder, beyond the foam of the ancient lake,
    Where the harsh marsh mist hangs thickest upon the air."

76 And as the frogs, spying the foeman snake,
    Go squattering over the pond, and dive, and sit
    Huddled in the mud, even so I saw them break

79 Apart, whole shoals of ruined spirits, and flit
    Scudding from the path of one who came to us,
    Walking the water of Styx with unwet feet.

82 His left hand, moving, fanned away the gross
    Air from his face, nor elsewise did he seem
    At all to find the way laborious.

85 And when I saw him, right well did I deem
    Him sent from Heaven, and turned me to my guide,
    Who signed me to be still and bow to him.

88 What scorn was in his look! He stood beside
    The gate, and touched it with a wand; it flew
    Open; there was no resistance; all stood wide.

91 "Outcasts of Heaven, despicable crew,"
    Said he, his feet set on the dreadful sill,
    "Why dwells this foolish insolence in you?

94 Why kick against the pricks of that great Will
    Whose purpose never can be overborne,
    And which hath oft increased your sorrows still?

97 Or say, what boots it at the Fates to spurn?
    Think how your Cerberus tried it, and yet bears
    The marks of it on jowl and throttle torn."

100 Then back he went by those foul thoroughfares,
    And unto us said nothing, but appeared
    Like one much pressed with weightier affairs

103 Than the cares of those before him. So we stirred
    Our footsteps citywards, with hearts reposed,
    Safely protected by the heavenly word.

106 Through the great ward we entered unopposed,
    And I, being all agog to learn what state
    Of things these huge defensive works enclosed,

109 Gazed round, the moment I had passed the gate,
    And saw a plain, stretched spacious on both sides,
    Filled with ill woes and torments desolate.

112 For as at Arles, where soft the slow Rhone slides,
    Or as at Pola, near Quarnaro's bay,
    That fences Italy with its washing tides,

115 The ground is all uneven with the array,
    On every hand, of countless sepulchres,
    So here; but in a far more bitter way:

118 For strewn among the tombs tall flames flared fierce,
    Heating them so white-hot as never burned
    Iron in the forge of any artificers.

121 The grave-slabs all were thrown back and upturned,
    And from within came forth such fearful crying,
    'Twas plain that here sad tortured spirits mourned.

124 "O Sir," said I, "who are the people lying
    In these grim coffers, whose sharp pains disclose
    Their presence to the ear by their sad sighing?"

127 And he: "The great heresiarchs, with all those,
    Of every sect, their followers; and much more
    The tombs lie laden than thou wouldst suppose.

130 Here like with like is laid; and their flames roar
    More and less hot within their monuments."
    Then we moved onward, and right-handed bore

133 Between those fires and the high battlements.

THE IMAGES. *The Furies* (*Erinyes*) in Greek mythology were the avenging goddesses who haunted those who had committed great crimes. In the *allegory*, they are the image of the fruitless remorse which does not lead to penitence.

Medusa was a *Gorgon* whose face was so terrible that anyone who looked upon it was turned to stone. In the *allegory*, she is the image of the despair which so hardens the heart that it becomes powerless to repent.

The Heavenly Messenger. He is, I think, the image of Divine revelation, (*a*) stirring the conscience, (*b*) safeguarding the mind against false doctrine.

The Heretics. See next canto.

NOTES. l. 8: *that great self-proffered aid is lent*: How Virgil summons this aid or knows of its coming is not stated; presumably he is aware that the help of Him who harrowed Hell is always available for a Christian soul in need.

l. 16: *descending from that place*, etc.: i.e. from Limbo.

l. 29: *high Heaven's all-moving gyre*: i.e. the *Primum Mobile*, the highest of the revolving heavens, which imparts motion to all the rest.

l. 44: *the Queen of everlasting woe*: Proserpine, or Persephone, queen of the classical underworld.

l. 54: *the assault of Theseus*: Theseus, king of Athens, tried to carry off Persephone from Hell; he failed, but was rescued by Hercules. The Furies mean that, if they had succeeded in punishing Theseus, other living men would have been deterred from venturing into the underworld, and they had better make an example of Dante.

l. 88: *what scorn was in his look!* In Hell, God's power is experienced only as judgment, alien and terrible.

l. 97: *what boots it at the Fates to spurn?* The Angel uses two forms of speech – one Christian, "that great Will", the other classical, "the Fates" – to denote the Divine power. The evil powers which he is addressing belong both to the Christian and to the pre-Christian mythology.

l. 98: *Cerberus*: As the last of his labours, Hercules brought Cerberus out of Hell, mauling his throat in the process.

l. 112: *Arles*: where in Dante's time the Rhone spread into a stagnant lake, contains many ancient tombs, said to be those of Charlemagne's soldiers slain in battle against the Saracens at Aleschans. *Pola* (on the Adriatic) is said to have formerly contained about 700 tombs of Slavonians, buried on the seashore.

CANTO X

THE STORY. *As the Poets are passing along beneath the city walls, Dante is hailed by Farinata from one of the burning tombs, and goes to speak to him. Their conversation is interrupted by Cavalcante dei Cavalcanti with a question about his son. Farinata prophesies Dante's exile and explains how the souls in Hell know nothing of the present, though they can remember the past and dimly foresee the future.*

Thus onward still, following a hidden track
    Between the city's ramparts and the fires,
    My master goes, and I go at his back.

4 "O sovran power, that through the impious gyres,"
    Said I, "dost wheel me as thou deemest well,
    Speak to me, satisfy my keen desires.

7 Those that find here their fiery burial,
    May they be seen? for nothing seems concealed;
    The lids are raised, and none stands sentinel."

10 And he: "All these shall be shut fast and sealed
    When from Jehoshaphat they come anew,
    Bringing their bodies now left far afield.

13 And hereabouts lie buried, close in view,
    Epicure and his followers – they who hold
    That when the body dies the soul dies too.

16 Hence that demand thou choosest to unfold
    May here and now be fully satisfied,
    Likewise thy hidden wish, to me untold."

19 "Alas," said I, "from thee I'd never hide
    One single thought, save that short speech is sweet,
    As thou hast warned me once or twice, dear guide."

22 "O Tuscan, walking thus with words discreet
    Alive through the city of fire, be it good to thee
    To turn thee hither awhile, and stay thy feet.

25 Thy native accent proves thee manifestly
    Born of the land I vexed with so great harm –
    A noble land, and too much vext, maybe."

28 This summons threw me into such alarm,
    Coming suddenly from a tomb, that in my dread
    I shrank up close against my escort's arm.

31 "Come, come, what art thou doing? Turn round," he said;
    "That's Farinata – look! he's risen to sight,
    And thou canst view him all, from waist to head."

34 Already my eyes were fixed on his; upright
    He had lifted him, strong-breasted, stony-fronted,
    Seeming to hold all Hell in deep despite;

37 And my good guide, with ready hands undaunted
    Thrusting me toward him through the tombs apace,
    Said: "In thy speech precision is what's wanted."

40 I reached the vault's foot, and he scanned my face
    A little while, and then said, with an air
    Almost contemptuous: "What's thy name and race?"

43 Being anxious to obey, I did not care
    To make a mystery, but told all out;
    He raised his brows a trifle, saying: "They were

46 Foes to me always, stubborn, fierce to flout
    Me and my house and party; I was quick
    To chase them, twice I put them to the rout."

49 "Quite true; and by that same arithmetic,"
    Said I, "they rallied all round and came back twice;
    Your side, it seems, have not yet learnt the trick."

52 Just then, close by him, I saw slowly rise
    Another shadow, visible down to the chin;
    It had got to its knees, I think. It moved its eyes

55 Round about me, as though it sought to win
    Sight of some person in my company;
    At last, when all such hope lay quenched within,

58 It wept: "If thy grand art has made thee free
    To walk at large in this blind prison of pain,
    Where is my son? why comes he not with thee?"

61 "I come not of myself," I answered plain,
    "He that waits yonder leads me on this road,
    For whom, perhaps, your Guido felt disdain."

64 The words he used, together with his mode
    Of torment, were sufficient to betray
    His name, as thus my pointed answer showed.

67 He leapt upright, crying: "What? what dost thou say?
    He felt? why felt? are life and feeling o'er?
    Looks he no longer on the pleasant day?"

70 Then, seeing me hesitate awhile before
    I made reply, he let himself suddenly fall
    Backward again, and showed his face no more.

73 But that great-hearted spirit, at whose call
    I'd stayed my steps, his countenance did not move,
    Nor bent his neck, nor stirred his side at all.

76 "And if," he spoke straight on where we broke off,
    "If they have missed the trick of it, I burn
    Less in this bed than with the thought thereof.

79 But thou, ere fifty times the light return
    To that queen's face who reigneth here below,
    Shalt find out just what that trick costs to learn.

82 But tell me why, as thou dost hope to go
    Back to the light, thy people make decrees
    So harsh against our house, and hate us so."

85 "That field of havoc and bloody butcheries,"
    I answered him, "when Arbia's stream ran red,
    Have filled our temple with these litanies."

88 He sighed before he spoke, and shook his head:
    "'Faith, I was not alone there, nor had gone
    In with the rest without good cause," he said;

91 "But when they made agreement, every one,
    To wipe out Florence, and I stood to plead
    Boldly for her – ay, there I was alone."

94 "Now, so may rest come some time to your seed,"
    Said I, "pray solve me this perplexity,
    Which ties my brains in a tight knot indeed.

97 It seems you can foresee and prophesy
    Events that time will bring, if I hear right,
    But with things present, you deal differently."

100   "We see," said he, "like men who are dim of sight,
      Things that are distant from us; just so far
      We still have gleams of the All-Guider's light.

103   But when these things draw near, or when they are,
      Our intellect is void, and your world's state
      Unknown, save some one bring us news from there.

106   Hence thou wilt see that all we can await
      Is the stark death of knowledge in us, then
      When time's last hour shall shut the future's gate."

109   At this my conscience smote me; I again
      Addressed him: "Tell that fallen shade, I pray,
      His son still walks the world of living men;

112   If I was silent when he asked me, say
      'Twas only that my wits were in a worry,
      Snared by that error which you've swept away."

115   And now my guide was calling me to hurry,
      Wherefore I urged the shade, with greater haste,
      To say who else was in that cemetery.

118   "I lie," said he, "with thousands; in this chest
      The second Frederick lies; our ranks include
      The Cardinal; I will not name the rest."

121   He spoke, and sank; returning to where stood
      The ancient poet, I pondered what they meant,
      Those words which seemed to bode me little good.

124   Then he moved on, and later, as we went,
      "Why so distraught?" said he. I set to work
      Answering his question to his full content.

127   Sagely he bade me: "See thou mind and mark
      Those adverse warnings; now to what I say – "
      And here he raised his finger – "prithee, hark!

130   When thou shalt stand bathed in the glorious ray
      Of her whose blest eyes see all things complete
      Thou'lt learn the meaning of thy life's whole way."

133   With that, leaving the wall, we turned our feet
      Towards the centre, by a path that ran
      Down to a vale, whose fumes rose high to greet

136   Our nostrils, even where the descent began.

THE IMAGES. *The Heretics.* "It is necessary to remember what Dante meant by heresy. He meant an obduracy of the mind; a spiritual state which defied, consciously, 'a power to which trust and obedience are due'; an intellectual obstinacy. A heretic, strictly, was a man who knew what he was doing; he accepted the Church, but at the same time he preferred his own judgment to that of the Church. This would seem to be impossible, except that it is apt to happen in all of us after our manner." (Charles Williams: *The Figure of Beatrice*, p. 125.)

    The tombs of the intellectually obdurate – iron without and fire within – thus fittingly open the circles of Nether Hell: the circles of deliberately willed sin.

NOTES. l. 11: *Jehoshaphat*: The belief that the Valley of Jehoshaphat would be the scene of the Last Judgment was derived from *Joel* iii. 2, 12.

    l. 18: *thy hidden wish, to me untold*: Virgil can often read Dante's thoughts, and sometimes seems to take a Sherlock-Holmes-like pleasure in surprising him by doing so. He knows that Dante's question covers an unspoken wish to see certain distinguished Florentines who had been followers of the school of Epicurus.

    ll, 22–7: *O Tuscan … thy native accent*: Dante is recognized as a Tuscan by his idiom and as a Florentine by his accent.

    l. 32: *Farinata*: This is Farinata degli Uberti, the famous leader of the Ghibellines in Florence, about whom Dante had already inquired of Ciacco (Canto VI. 78). After he and his party were banished in 1250, they allied themselves with the Siennese and, in 1260, lured the Florentine Guelfs into an ambush and defeated them with appalling slaughter at Montaperti, near the river Arbia.
The Guelfs, among whom were Dante's ancestors, fled from Florence. They never forgave Farinata, and when they returned to power, they razed the Uberti palaces to the ground and pronounced relentless decrees of exile against the whole family. Farinata was condemned for heresy in 1283.

    ll. 48–51: *twice … to the rout … they came back twice*: The first rout of the Guelfs was in 1248 and their first return in 1251. The second rout was at Montaperti in 1260, and the second and final return in 1266, after the Battle of Benevento, which extinguished the Ghibellines' hope of ever regaining power in Florence. (Note how Farinata's pride instantly evokes a corresponding pride in Dante.)

    l. 53: *another shadow*: Cavalcante dei Cavalcanti, a Guelf knight, noted, like Farinata, for his Epicureanism. His son, Guido Cavalcanti, was a fellow-poet and friend of Dante and son-in-law to Farinata.

    l. 58: *thy grand art* (lit.: "genius"): Cavalcante thinks that if poetical genius has enabled Dante to visit Hell in the flesh, his own poet-son should have been able to accompany his friend.

    l. 63: *your Guido felt disdain*: either because Guido, as a modern, despised classical poetry; or because, as a Guelf, he disliked Virgil's imperialism; or because, as a sceptic, he had no use for Virgil's religious piety: or all three. The passage has been much disputed. Note that, in speaking to Farinata and Cavalcante, Dante shows his respect by using the formal "you" in place of the familiar "thou".

    l. 70: *seeing me hesitate*: Dante is taken aback at finding that Cavalcante does not know whether Guido is alive or dead, and so does not answer immediately.

    l. 80: *queen … here below*: Proserpine, also identified with Hecate and Diana; the Moon (see Glossary). Fifty lunar months from the date of the vision (April 1300) bring us to the summer of 1304. Dante was banished in 1302, and the efforts of the White Guelfs to return to Florence were finally frustrated in July 1304.

    l. 87: *these litanies*: This may mean that prayers were offered in church for the downfall of the Ghibellines, or else that, when the Guelfs were in power, the decrees of exile were formally signed and published in the church of St John.

    l. 92: *to wipe out Florence*: After Montaperti, the wholesale destruction of Florence was voted by all the Ghibelline leaders except Farinata, who, drawing his sword, cried out that if they attempted it he was ready to lay down a thousand lives, if he had them, in defence of his native city; and Florence was accordingly spared.

    l. 108: *when time's last hour shall shut the future's gate*: "When earthly time ceases there will be nothing to know – nothing but the sin of the past and that sin in the present. … Charity has already failed here; presently prophecies and tongues and knowledge are to cease too." (Charles Williams: *The Figure of Beatrice*, p. 127.) Farinata's explanation clears up Dante's perplexity, and he hastens to convey to Cavalcante that his son is still alive. Guido's death was, however, so near in time that it had become veiled (l. 103) from the knowledge of the damned.

    l. 119: *the second Frederick*: the Emperor Frederick II (1194–1250).

    l. 120: *the Cardinal*: Ottaviano degli Ubaldini. (See Glossary.)

    l. 131: *her whose blest eyes*: Beatrice, under whose guidance Dante, in the Heaven of Mars, has the course of his life revealed to him by his ancestor Cacciaguida. (*Para*. xvi.)

CANTO XI

THE STORY. *While the Poets pause for a little on the brink of the descent to the Seventh Circle, Virgil explains to Dante the arrangement of Hell.*

Where a great cliff fell sheer, its beetling brow
 Ringed with huge jagged rocks, we reached the brink
 O'erhanging the still ghastlier dens below;

4 And here so overpowering was the stink
 The deep Abyss threw off, that we withdrew
 Staggered, and for a screen were forced to shrink

7 Behind a massive vault where, plain to view,
 Stood writ: "I hold Pope Anastasius,
 Lured by Photinus from the pathway true."

10 "We'll wait awhile," the master said, "that thus
 Our senses may grow used to this vile scent,
 And after that, it will not trouble us."

13 And I: "But let's not lose the time so spent;
 Think now what compensation thou canst find."
 "Surely," he answered, "such was my intent.

16 See now, my son: three narrowing circles wind
 Within these cliffs," thus he took up the tale,
 "Each under each, like those we've left behind.

19 Damned spirits fill them all; thou canst not fail
 To know them at a glance, though, if I state
 How and for what they're here pent up in jail.

22 Of all malicious wrong that earns Heaven's hate
 The end is injury; all such ends are won
 Either by force or fraud. Both perpetrate

25 Evil to others; but since man alone
 Is capable of fraud, God hates that worst;
 The fraudulent lie lowest, then, and groan

28 Deepest. Of these three circles, all the first
 Holds violent men; but as threefold may be
 Their victims, in three rings they are dispersed.

31 God, self, and neighbour – against all these three
 Force may be used; either to injure them
 Or theirs, as I shall show convincingly.

34 Man on his neighbour may bring death or mayhem
 By force; or damage his chattels, house, and lands
 By harsh extortions, pillage, or fire and flame;

37 So murderers, men who are violent of their hands,
 Robbers and plunderers, all find chastisement
 In the first ring, disposed in various bands.

40 Against themselves men may be violent,
 And their own lives or their own goods destroy;
 So they in the second ring in vain repent

43 Who rob themselves of your world, or make a toy
 Of fortune, gambling and wasting away their purse,
 And turn to weeping what was meant for joy.

46 Those men do violence to God, who curse
 And in their hearts deny Him, or defame
 His bounty and His Natural Universe;

49 So the third ring sets its seal on the double shame
 Of Sodom and of Cahors, and on the speech
 Of the froward heart, dishonouring God's great name.

52 Fraud, which gnaws every conscience, may be a breach
 Of trust against the confiding, or deceive
 Such as repose no confidence; though each

55 Is fraud, the latter sort seems but to cleave
 The general bond of love and Nature's tie;
 So the second circle opens to receive

58 Hypocrites, flatterers, dealers in sorcery,
 Panders and cheats, and all such filthy stuff,
 With theft, and simony and barratry.

61 Fraud of the other sort forgets both love
 Of kind, and that love too whence is begot
 The special trust that's over and above;

64 So, in the smallest circle, that dark spot,
 Core of the universe and throne of Dis,
 The traitors lie; and their worm dieth not."

67 "Master," said I, "how clear thy discourse is!
 It makes this gulf's arrangement plain as plain,
 With all its inmates; I quite follow this;

70 But tell me: all those others, whom the rain
 Beats, and the wind drives, and the sticky mire
 Bogs, and those brawlers with their shrill campaign –

73 Why dwell not they in the city red with fire
 If to God's wrath they too are fallen a prey?
 Or if not, wherefore is their plight so dire?"

76 "What error has seduced thy reason, pray?"
 Said he, "thou art not wont to be so dull;
 Or are thy wits woolgathering miles away?

79 Dost thou not mind the doctrine of thy school –
 Those pages where the *Ethics* tells of three
 Conditions contrary to Heaven's will and rule,

82 Incontinence, vice, and brute bestiality?
 And how incontinence offends God less
 Than the other two, and is less blameworthy?

85 If thou wilt think on what this teaching says,
 Bearing in mind what sort of sinners dwell
 Outside the city, and there endure distress,

88 Thou'lt see why they lie separate from these fell
 Spirits within, and why God's hammer-blow
 Of doom smites them with weight less terrible."

91 "O Sun that healest all dim sight, thou so
 Dost charm me in resolving of my doubt,
 To be perplexed is pleasant as to know.

94 Just once again," said I, "turn thee about
 To where thou spak'st of usury as a crime
 Against God's bounty – ravel me that knot out."

97 "Not in one place," said he, "but many a time
 Philosophy points out to who will learn,
 How Nature takes her course from the Sublime

100 Intellect and Its Art; note that; then turn
 The pages of thy *Physics*, and not far
 From the beginning, there shalt thou discern

103 How your Art, as it best can, follows her
 Like a pupil with his master; we may call
 This art of yours God's grandchild, as it were.

106 By Art and Nature, if thou well recall
   How Genesis begins, man ought to get
   His bread, and make prosperity for all.

109 But the usurer contrives a third way yet,
   And in herself and in her follower, Art,
   Scorns Nature, for his hope is elsewhere set.

112 Follow me now; I think we should depart;
   Horizon-high the twinkling Fishes swim,
   And the Wain's right over Caurus; we must start

115 Onward and downward, over the chasm's rim."

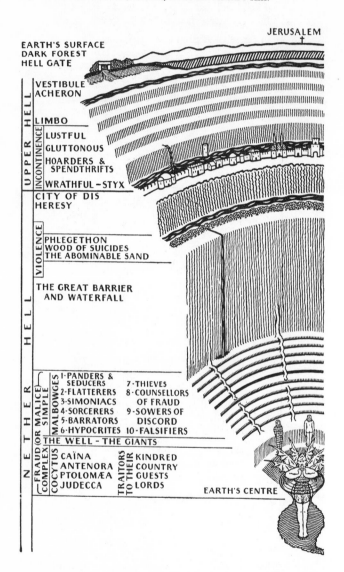

EARTH'S SURFACE
DARK FOREST
HELL GATE

JERUSALEM

UPPER HELL

INCONTINENCE

VESTIBULE
ACHERON

LIMBO
LUSTFUL
GLUTTONOUS
HOARDERS &
SPENDTHRIFTS
WRATHFUL – STYX
CITY OF DIS
HERESY

VIOLENCE

PHLEGETHON
WOOD OF SUICIDES
THE ABOMINABLE SAND

THE GREAT BARRIER
AND WATERFALL

NETHER HELL

FRAUD (OR MALICE)

SIMPLE

MALBOWGES

1·PANDERS &
   SEDUCERS
2·FLATTERERS
3·SIMONIACS
4·SORCERERS
5·BARRATORS
6·HYPOCRITES

7·THIEVES
8·COUNSELLORS
   OF FRAUD
9·SOWERS OF
   DISCORD
10·FALSIFIERS

THE WELL – THE GIANTS

COMPLEX

COCYTUS

CAÏNA
ANTENORA
PTOLOMÆA
JUDECCA

TRAITORS TO THEIR

KINDRED
COUNTRY
GUESTS
LORDS

EARTH'S CENTRE

THE IMAGES. The only image here is that of Hell itself. Dante's classification of sins is based chiefly on Aristotle, with a little assistance from Cicero. Aristotle divided wrong behaviour into three main kinds: (A) *Incontinence* (uncontrolled appetite); (B) *Bestiality* (perverted appetite); (C) *Malice* or *Vice* (abuse of the specifically human faculty of reason). Cicero declared that all injurious conduct acted by either (a) *Violence* or (b) *Fraud*. Combining these two classifications, Dante obtains three classes of sins: I. *Incontinence*; II *Violence* (or *Bestiality*); III. *Fraud* (or *Malice*).

These he subdivides and arranges in 7 Circles: 4 of Incontinence, 1 of Violence, and 2 of Fraud.

To these purely ethical categories of wrong *behaviour* he, as a Christian, adds 2 Circles of wrong *belief*: 1 of *Unbelief* (Limbo) and 1 of *Mischief* (the Heretics), making 9 Circles in all. Finally, he adds the Vestibule of the Futile, who have neither faith nor works; this, not being a Circle, bears no number.

Thus we get the 10 main divisions of Hell. In the other books of the *Comedy* we shall find the same numerical scheme of 3, made up by subdivision to 7; plus 2 (=9); plus 1 (=10). Hell, however, is complicated by still further subdivision. The Circle of *Violence* is again divided into 3 Rings; the Circle of Fraud Simple into 10 Bowges; and the Circle of Fraud Complex into 4 Regions. So that Hell contains a grand total of 24 divisions. (See section map.)

NOTES. l. 8: *Pope Anastasius*: Anastasius II (Pope 496–8); incurred the imputation of heresy by giving communion to Photinus, a deacon of Thessalonica in communion with the Church of Constantinople, which was at this time so at odds with the Western Church over the definition of the union of the two natures in Christ's one person. Dante probably got his information directly or indirectly from the *Liber Pontificalis*, a source hostile to Anastasius. (See Duchesne's edition, vol. i, p. 258.)

l. 16: *three narrowing circles*: i.e. the Circle of *Violence* (Circle 7) and the two Circles of *Fraud* (Circles 8 and 9). Virgil begins by describing that part of Nether Hell which still lies ahead. The circles get narrower as the Pit deepens.

l. 22: *malicious wrong*: the phrase "malicious" is here used generally to cover both Violence and Fraud; i.e. all deliberately injurious behaviour.

ll. 28–51: These lines describe the Circle of *Violence* (Circle 7), with its three component Rings devoted respectively to violence against (i) others, (ii) self, (iii) God.

l. 41: *their own lives or their own goods*: Property is regarded, in accordance with Roman law, as an extension of the personality. Consequently, to damage or destroy one's own or one's neighbour's goods is a sin of the same type as the damage and destruction of one's own or one's neighbour's body. Similarly (ll. 46–8), blasphemy against God's creation is blasphemy against God, for the creation belongs to Him.

l. 49: *the double shame of Sodom and of Cahors*: Sodomy (homosexual vice) is so named from *Genesis* xix. The "shame of Cahors" is Usury – so called from Cahors in the South of France, notorious for its many usurers in Dante's time. Ring iii thus punishes three sorts of violence against God: Sodomy, Usury, and Blasphemy.

ll. 52–66: Virgil now goes on to describe, successively, the two Circles of *Fraud*. There are two kinds of Fraud: the one (Fraud Simple, Circle 8) only betrays the confidence of humanity in general; the other (Fraud Complex, Circle 9) in addition betrays the confidence of those who had special reason to trust, and is, therefore, not merely fraudulent but treacherous.

l. 57: *the second circle*: i.e. the *second* in Nether Hell; the *first* Circle of *Fraud*; Circle 8 in the general scheme.

l. 61: *fraud of the other sort*: i.e. the treacherous sort – Circle 9.

l. 65: *Dis*: the classical king of Hades: i.e. Satan.

ll. 68 sqq.: *this gulf*: i.e. Nether Hell. Dante now asks about the people whom he had already seen in Upper Hell, and why they are not punished within the City of Dis. Virgil reminds him of the seventh chapter of Aristotle's *Ethics*, where incontinence is said to be less reprehensible than bestiality or malice, and treachery the worst conduct of all.

ll. 95 sqq.: *usury as a crime against God's bounty*: Dante's thought in this passage (which is that of the Medieval Church) is of such urgent relevance to-day that it is worth while to disentangle it from his (to us) rather odd and unfamiliar phraseology. What he is saying is that there are only two sources of real wealth: Nature and Art – or, as we should put it, Natural Resources and the Labour of Man. The buying and selling of Money as though it were a commodity creates only a spurious wealth, and results in injury to the earth (Nature) and the exploitation of labour (Art). The attitude to men and things which this implies is a kind of blasphemy; since Art derives from Nature, as Nature derives from God, so that contempt of them is contempt of Him.

l. 101: *thy Physics*: i.e. the *Physics* of Aristotle (ii. 2).

l. 107: *how Genesis begins*: "And the Lord God took the man, and put him into the garden of Eden" [put the resources of Nature at his disposal] "to dress it and to keep it" [that he might preserve and cultivate them by his art and labour]. (*Gen.* ii. 15.)

l. 113: *the twinkling Fishes*, etc.: Virgil again indicates the time by describing the position of the unseen stars. The Wain (the Plough, or Great Bear) is lying right over the abode of Caurus, the north-west wind, and the constellation of Pisces (the Fishes) is just rising over the horizon. This is the zodiacal sign which immediately precedes Aries (the Ram); and since the signs rise at two-hourly intervals, and the Sun is in Aries (Canto I. 37), it is now two hours before sunrise on Holy Saturday – i.e. about 4 A.M.

CANTO XII

THE STORY. *At the point where the sheer precipice leading down to the Seventh Circle is made negotiable by a pile of tumbled rock, Virgil and Dante are faced by the Minotaur. A taunt from Virgil throws him into a fit of blind fury, and while he is thrashing wildly about, the Poets slip past him. Virgil tells Dante how the rocks were dislodged by the earthquake which took place at the hour of Christ's descent into Limbo. At the foot of the cliff they come to Phlegethon, the river of boiling blood, in which the Violent against their Neighbours are immersed, and whose banks are guarded by Centaurs. At Virgil's request, Chiron, the chief Centaur, sends Nessus to guide them to the ford and carry Dante over on his back. On the way, Nessus points out a number of notable tyrants and robbers.*

The place we came to, to descend the brink from,
　　Was sheer crag; and there was a Thing there – making,
　　All told, a prospect any eye would shrink from.

4　Like the great landslide that rushed downward, shaking
　　The bank of Adige on this side Trent,
　　(Whether through faulty shoring or the earth's quaking)

7　So that the rock, down from the summit rent
　　Far as the plain, lies strewn, and one might crawl
　　From top to bottom by that unsure descent,

10　Such was the precipice; and there we spied,
　　Topping the cleft that split the rocky wall,
　　That which was wombed in the false heifer's side,

13　The infamy of Crete, stretched out a-sprawl;
　　And seeing us, he gnawed himself, like one
　　Inly devoured with spite and burning gall.

16　Then cried my Wisdom: "How now, hellion!
　　Thinkst thou the Duke of Athens comes anew,
　　That slew thee in the upper world? Begone,

19　Monster! not guided by thy sister's clue
　　Has this man come; only to see and know
　　Your punishments, he threads the circle through."

22　Then, as a bull pierced by the mortal blow
　　Breaks loose, and cannot go straight, but reels in the ring
　　Plunging wildly and staggering to and fro,

25　I saw the Minotaur fall a-floundering,
　　And my wary guide called: "Run! run for the pass!
　　Make good thy going now, while his rage has its fling."

28　So down we clambered by that steep crevasse
　　Of tumbled rock; and oft beneath my tread
　　The stones slipped shifting with my unwonted mass.

31　I went bemused; wherefore: "Perchance thy head
　　Puzzles at this great fissure here, watched o'er
　　By the furious brute I quelled just now," he said.

34　"I'd have thee know, when I went down before,
　　That other time, into Deep Hell this way,
　　The rock had not yet fallen; but now for sure

37　'Twas thus, if I judge rightly: on the day
　　When that great Prince to the First Circle above
　　Entered, and seized from Dis the mighty prey,

40　Shortly ere He came, the deep foul gulf did move
　　On all sides down to the centre, till I thought
　　The universe trembled in the throes of love,

43　Whereby, as some believe, the world's been brought
　　Oft-times to chaos; in that moment, here
　　And elsewhere, was these old rocks' ruin wrought.

46　But now look to the vale, for we draw near
　　The river of blood, where all those wretches boil
　　Whose violence filled the earth with pain and fear."

49　O blind, O rash and wicked lust of spoil,
　　That drives our short life with so keen a goad,
　　And steeps our life eternal in such broil!

52　I saw a river, curving full and broad
　　Arcwise, as though the whole plain's girth embracing.
　　Just as my guide had told me on the road;

55　And 'twixt the bank and it came centaurs racing
　　By one and one, their bows and quivers bearing
　　As when through the woods of the world they went a-chasing.

58　They checked their flight to watch us downward faring,
　　And three of the band wheeled out and stood a-row,
　　Their bows and chosen arrows first preparing;

61　And one cried out from far: "Hey! whither go
　　You on the cliff there? What's your penalty?
　　Speak where you stand; if not, I draw the bow."

64　The master shouted back: "That word shall be
　　For Chiron there; headstrong thou dost remain,
　　And so thou ever wast – the worse for thee."

67　Then, nudging me: "That's Nessus, who was slain
　　For fair Deïanira, and in the aftermath
　　With his own blood avenged his blood again.

70　Gazing upon his breast, betwixt them both,
　　Achilles' tutor, the great Chiron, stands;
　　The third is Pholus, once so full of wrath.

73　All round the fosse they speed in myriad bands,
　　Shooting at every soul that tries to lift
　　Higher out of the blood than doom demands."

76 We were near them now, those creatures snell and swift,
    And Chiron took an arrow, and with the notch
    Put back upon his jaws his snowy drift

79 Of beard, and having freed his great mouth: "Watch,"
    Said he to those who stood with him; "mark you
    How the feet of the one behind move what they touch?

82 Those of the dead are not used so to do,"
    And my good guide, now standing at his breast
    Where the two natures join, replied: "Quite true,

85 He is alive; so, on his lonely quest,
    Needs must I lead him through the vales of night;
    Necessity brings him here, not sport nor jest;

88 From the singing of alleluias in the light
    Came she who laid on me this novel charge;
    The man's no poacher, I'm no thievish sprite.

91 Now by the power that moves my steps at large
    On this wild way, lend us a courier
    Whom we may follow by the river's marge,

94 To show us where the ford is, and to bear
    This other upon his back across the tide,
    For he's no spirit to walk the empty air."

97 Then Chiron turned on his right flank, and cried:
    "Wheel round and guide them, Nessus; if you're met
    By another patrol, see that it stands aside."

100 So with this trusty escort, off we set
    Along the bank of the bubbling crimson flood,
    Whence the shrieks of the boiled rose shrill and desperate.

103 There saw I some – plunged eyebrow-deep they stood;
    And the great centaur said to me: "Behold
    Tyrants, who gave themselves to ravin and blood.

106 Here they bewail oppressions manifold;
    Alexander's here; Dionysius too, whose brute
    Fury long years vexed Sicily uncontrolled.

109 That forehead there, with locks as black as soot,
    Is Azzolino, and that fair-haired one
    Obizzo d' Este, he whose light was put

112 Out, up above there, by his stepson son."
    I turned here to the poet, who said, "Why, yes,
    He first, I second now, must guide thee on."

115 Further along, the centaur checked his pace
    Beside a second gang, who seemed to start
    Far as the throat from the stream's boiling race.

118 He showed one shade set by itself apart,
    Saying: "There stands the man who dared to smite,
    Even in the very bosom of God, the heart

121 They venerate still on Thames." Next, reared upright
    Both head and chest from the stream, another horde
    Appeared, full many known to me by sight.

124 Thus shallow and shallower still the red blood poured
    Till it was only deep enough to cook
    The feet; and here it was we passed the ford.

127 And the centaur said to me: "Now, prithee, look:
    Just as, this side, it ever grows less deep,
    On that, I'd have thee know, the boiling brook

130 Lowers its rocky bed, down-shelving steep,
    Until it comes full circle, and joins its ring
    There where the tyrants are condemned to weep.

133 Here doth the heavenly justice rack and wring
    Pyrrhus and Sextus; here it overbears
    That scourge of earth called Attila the King;

136 And here for ever it milks the trickling tears
    Squeezed by the scald from those rough highwaymen,
    The Pazzian and Cornetan Riniers."

139 With this he turned and crossed the ford again.

THE IMAGES. *The Circle of Violence.* From now to the end of Canto
    XVII we are in the circle devoted to *Violence* or *Bestiality* (the "sins
    of the Lion") which, together with the Circle of the Heretics,
    makes up the first division of Nether Hell.
The Minotaur and The Centaurs. In this and the next ring we find
    demon-guardians compounded of man and brute. They are the
    types of perverted appetite – the human reason subdued to animal
    passion. The Minotaur had the body of a man and the head of a
    bull; the Centaurs were half-man, half-horse.
Phlegethon – "the fiery" – is the third chief river of Hell. Like Acheron
    and Styx, it forms a complete circuit about the abyss, and it is deep
    at one side and shallow at the other. The sinners whose fiery
    passions caused them to shed man's blood are here plunged in that
    blood-bath for ever.

NOTES. l. 5: *the bank of Adige:* Dante likens the fall of rock to the
Slavini di Marco on the Adige between Trent and Verona. An early
commentator (Benvenuto da Imola) says that the comparison is very
apt, since before the landslide the bank was as sheer as the wall of a
house and absolutely unscalable; but afterwards it was just possible
to scramble down it.
    l. 13: *the infamy of Crete:* the Minotaur was the offspring of Pasi-
phaë (wife of Minos, king of Crete), who became enamoured of a
beautiful bull, and was brought to him in the effigy of a cow ("the
false heifer") made for her by the cunning artificer Daedalus. Minos
kept the Minotaur in the labyrinth at Cnossos. Later, having waged
a successful war against Athens, he compelled the Athenians to send
him a yearly tribute of seven youths and seven maidens to be devoured by the monster. The Minotaur was slain by Theseus, "the
Duke of Athens", who made his way back from the labyrinth by the
aid of a clue of thread given to him by Ariadne, daughter of Minos
and Pasiphaë.
    l. 34: *when I went down before:* Virgil's previous journey (Canto IX.
22) was made before the death of Christ.
    l. 39: *the mighty prey:* i.e. the souls of the patriarchs (Canto IV. 55
sqq.).
    l. 42: *the universe trembled in the throes of love,* etc.: Empedocles
taught that the universe was held together in tension by discord
among the elements; but that from time to time the motions of the
heavens brought about a state of harmony (love). When this happened, like matter flew to like, and the universe was once more
resolved into its original elements and so reduced to chaos.
    l. 47: *river of blood:* Phlegethon.
    l. 62: *what's your penalty?* The Centaurs mistake Dante and Virgil
for damned souls going to their allotted place of torment.
    l. 65: *Chiron:* the great Centaur to whom Achilles, Peleus, Theseus,
and other Greek heroes went to be tutored. He was famous for his
skill in hunting, gymnastics, medicine, music, and prophecy, and was
accounted the wisest and most just of the Centaurs. Accordingly,
though placing him among the guardians of Phlegethon, Dante has
given him the most amiable character of all the inhabitants of Hell.

l. 67: *Nessus*: This Centaur attempted to carry off Deïanira, the wife of Hercules, while taking her over a river on his back. Hercules killed him with an arrow, and the dying Nessus told Deïanira to take some of his blood, since it would act upon Hercules as a love-charm. Deïanira did so, and later, fearing that Hercules was falling in love with another woman, put on him a shirt steeped in the blood of Nessus. The blood was poisonous and, after suffering intolerable agonies, Hercules placed himself on a pyre of wood and had himself burned to death.

l. 72: *Pholus*: Little is known of him except that he also was killed by Hercules. The three Centaurs possibly typify three passions which may lead to violence: wrath, lust, and the will to dominate.

l. 88: *from the singing of alleluias ... came she*: i.e. Beatrice.

l. 90: *no poacher, and ... no thievish sprite*: Virgil means that he and Dante have not come, like Theseus or Orpheus, to try and rob Hell of any of its victims.

l. 112: *stepson son*: Actually his son; Dante calls him "stepson" because of his unnatural behaviour.

l. 120: *the heart they venerate still on Thames*: Prince Henry, son of Richard, Duke of Cornwall, and nephew to Henry III of England, was killed in the Cathedral at Viterbo, during High Mass ("in the very bosom of God"), by Guy, son of Simon de Montfort (1270). A statue of him, holding in its right hand the casket containing his heart, is said to have been placed on London Bridge.

l. 131: *until it comes full circle*: Apparently Dante and Virgil have made the full half-circle of Phlegethon, from the deep side where the tyrants stand to the shallow ford.

CANTO XIII

THE STORY. *The Poets enter a pathless Wood. Here Harpies sit shriek-ing among the withered trees, which enclose the souls of Suicides. Pier delle Vigne tells Dante his story, and also explains how these shades come to be changed into trees and what will happen to their bodies at the Last Day. The shades of two Profligates rush through the wood, pursued and torn by black hounds. Dante speaks to a bush containing the soul of a Florentine.*

Ere Nessus had regained the bank beyond
   We'd pushed into a forest, where no mark
   Of any beaten path was to be found.

4 No green here, but discoloured leaves and dark,
   No tender shoots, but writhen and gnarled and tough,
   No fruit, but poison-galls on the withered bark.

7 Wild beasts, from tilth and pasture slinking off
   'Twixt Cecina and Corveto, never come
   To lurk in scrub so tangled or so rough.

10 There the foul Harpies nest and are at home,
   Who chased the Trojans from the Strophades
   With dismal outcry ominous of doom.

13 Wide-winged like birds and lady-faced are these,
   With feathered belly broad and claws of steel;
   And there they sit and shriek on the strange trees.

16 And the good master thus began: "'Twere well,
   Ere going further, thou shouldst understand,
   Thou'rt now in the second ring, and shalt be, till

19 Thou comest to the abominable sand.
   But now, look well, and see a thing whose telling
   Might kill my credit with thee out of hand."

22 Already all round I heard a mournful wailing,
   But, seeing none to wail, I stopped short, blinking
   Bewilderedly, as though my wits were failing.

25 I think he must have thought that I was thinking
   That all these voices through the boles resounding
   Were those of folk who from our gaze hid shrinking,

28 Because he said: "If from these boughs abounding
   Thou wilt pluck off one small and single spray,
   Thy thoughts will stagger at their own dumbfounding."

31 So I put forth my hand a little way,
   And broke a branchlet from a thorn-tree tall;
   And the trunk cried out: "Why tear my limbs away?"

34 Then it grew dark with blood, and therewithal
   Cried out again: "Why dost thou rend my bones?
   Breathes there no pity in thy breast at all?

37 We that are turned to trees were human once;
   Nay, thou shouldst tender a more pious hand
   Though we had been the souls of scorpions."

40 As, when you burn one end of a green brand,
   Sap at the other oozes from the wood,
   Sizzling as the imprisoned airs expand,

43 So from that broken splint came words and blood
   At once: I dropped the twig, and like to one
   Rooted to the ground with terror, there I stood.

46 "O wounded soul," my sage replied anon,
   "Might I have brought him straightway to believe
   The thing he'd read of in my verse alone,

49 Never had he lifted finger to mischieve
   Thee thus; but 'twas incredible; so I
   Prompted his deed, for which myself must grieve.

52 But tell him who thou wast, that he may try
   For some amends, to right thee with mankind
   When, by permission, he returns on high."

55 To this the trunk made answer: "Words so kind
   Tempt me to speech; nor take it in ill part
   If at some length I'm lured to speak my mind.

58 I am he that held both keys of Frederick's heart,
   To lock and to unlock; and well I knew
   To turn them with so exquisite an art,

61 I kept his counsel and let few men through;
   Loyal to my glorious charge did I remain,
   And sacrificed my sleep and my strength too.

64 But that great harlot which can ne'er refrain
   From Caesar's household her adulterous eyes,
   The vice of kings' courts and their common bane,

67 Inflamed all hearts against me, and these likewise,
   Flaming, inflamed Augustus to distrust,
   Till my glad honours turned to obloquies.

70 So, in a scornful spirit of disgust,
   And thinking to escape from scorn by death,
   To my just self I made myself unjust;

73 But by these strange new roots my trunk beneath,
   Never to my most honourworthy lord,
   I swear to you, was I found false of faith;

76 And if to that bright world indeed restored
   One of you goes, oh, heal my memory,
   Which lies and bleeds from envy's venomed sword."

79   He paused there; and the poet said to me:
        "While he is mute, let not this moment go,
        But speak, and ask what more seems good to thee."

82   And I: "Ask thou, whate'er thou think'st will do
        My hunger good and satisfy me well;
        I cannot ask, pity unhearts me so."

85   Wherefore: "So may this man prove liberal,"
        Thus he resumed, "thine errand to perform,
        Imprisoned spirit, do thou be pleased to tell

88   How souls get cramped into this knotty form,
        And, if thou canst, if any shall do off
        These limbs one day and find release therefrom."

91   At this the trunk blew hard, and the windy puff
        After this wise soon whistled into speech:
        "You shall be answered with brief words enough.

94   When the wild soul leaps from the body, which
        Its own mad violence forces it to quit,
        Minos dispatches it down to the seventh ditch.

97   It falls in the wood; no place is picked for it,
        But as chance carries it, there it falls to be,
        And where it falls, it sprouts like a corn of wheat,

100   And grows to a sapling, and thence to a wild tree;
        Then the Harpies feed on its leaves, and the sharp bite
        Gives agony, and a vent to agony.

103   We shall take our flight, when all souls take their flight,
        To seek our spoils, but not to be rearrayed,
        For the spoils of the spoiler cannot be his by right;

106   Here shall we drag them, to this gloomy glade;
        Here shall they hang, each body evermore
        Borne on the thorn of its own self-slaughtering shade."

109   Thinking the trunk might wish to tell us more,
        We stood intent, when suddenly there came crashing
        On our astonished ears a wild uproar,

112   As the huntsman hears the boar and the chase dashing
        Down on his post like the noise of a hurricane,
        With trampling of beasts and all the branches smashing.

115   And lo! on the left of us came two that ran
        Naked and torn, with such a furious burst
        As snapped to flinders every forest fan.

118   "O death, come now, come quickly!" thus the first;
        And the second, finding himself outstripped in the rush,
        Cried: "Lano, thy legs were not so nimble erst

121   At the jousts of Toppo." So in the last push,
        His breath failing perhaps, he shot sidelong
        And made one group of himself and a thick bush.

124   And filling the woods behind them came a throng
        Of great black braches, fleet of foot and grim,
        And keen as greyhounds fresh-slipped from the thong;

127   They seized the skulker, and set their teeth in him,
        And rent him piecemeal, and away they went
        Carrying the wretched fragments limb by limb.

130   Then my guide drew me by the hand, and bent
        His steps to the poor bush, left mangled there,
        Gasping vain protests through each bleeding rent.

133   "O Jacomo," it cried, "of Sant' Andrea,
        Why make a screen of me? What was the good?
        Am I to blame for thy misspent career?"

136   Then said my gentle master when he stood
        Beside it: "Who wast thou, that through such tattered
        Wounds sighest out thy grief mingled with blood?"

139   "O spirits, who come in time to see me battered
        Thus shamefully, and all my foliage torn,"
        It said, "bring back the leaves that lie there scattered,

142   Gather them close beneath the shrub forlorn.
        My city was she that for the Baptist changed
        Her ancient patron, wherefore on her scorn

145   Still by his art he makes himself avenged;
        Yea, did not Arno's bridge even now retain
        Some image of the guardian she estranged,

148   Those citizens who built her walls again
        On the ashes left by Attila, had been baffled
        Wholly, and all their labour spent in vain;

151   I am one that made my own roof-tree my scaffold."

THE IMAGES. *The Wood.* This forms the Second Ring of the Circle of the Violent, and contains the souls of those who wantonly destroyed their own lives or their own goods, "turning to weeping what was meant for joy" (Canto XI. 45).

The Harpies. Here again we have a mixture of brute and human. The Harpies had the bodies of birds, long claws, and the faces of women pale with hunger. When Aeneas and his companions came to the Islands of the Strophades, the Harpies swooped down upon their food, devouring and defiling it (*Aen.* iii. 209 *sqq.*). They are the image of the "will to destruction".

The Bleeding Trees. The sin of Suicide is, in an especial manner, an insult to the body; so, here, the shades are deprived of even the semblance of the human form. As they refused life, they remain fixed in a dead and withered sterility. They are the image of the self-hatred which dries up the very sap of energy and makes all life infertile.

The Profligates. These are very different from the "Spendthrifts" of Canto VII, who were merely guilty of extravagance. The profligates here were men possessed by a depraved passion, who dissipated their goods for the sheer wanton lust of wreckage and disorder. They may be called the image of "gambling-fever" – or, more generally, the itch to destroy civilization, order, and reputation.

NOTES. l. 2: *we'd pushed into a forest*: Note that the three rings of Circle 7 are all on the same level.

l. 8: *'twixt Cecina and Corveto*: Cecina (a river in the province of Volterra) and Corveto (a small town on the river Marta) mark the boundaries of the Tuscan Maremma, where, in Dante's time, there were many dense forests full of wild animals.

l. 19: *the abominable sand*: Ring iii. (See Canto XIV.)

l. 48: *the thing he had read of in my verse alone*: i.e. in the *Aeneid* (iii. 22 *sqq.*). (This famous episode of the bleeding tree has been frequently imitated, not only by Dante, but notably also by Ariosto, Tasso, and Spenser.)

l. 58: *he that held both keys of Frederick's heart*: Pier delle Vigne, for many years chief counsellor to the Emperor Frederick II (mentioned in Canto X). Accused of conspiring against his master, he was disgraced, imprisoned, and blinded, and in despair took his own life.

l. 64: *that great harlot*: i.e. Envy. (See l. 78.)

l. 68: *Augustus*: i.e. Caesar = the Emperor.

l. 77: *heal my memory*: The fact that Dante places Pier in the Wood of the Suicides, and not among the traitors at the bottom of the Pit, shows that he believed him to have been falsely accused.

l. 102: *a vent to agony*: The trees can only utter when broken and bleeding. The Harpies, by tearing the leaves, make wounds from which issue the wails that puzzled Dante (ll. 22-7).

l. 105: *the spoils of the spoiler cannot be his by right*: (lit.: "it is not just that a man should have what he takes from himself") – Dante treats suicide as a kind of self-robbery (Canto XI. 43). Here he means, I think, that a robber cannot have a just title to the goods he has plundered.

l. 107: *here shall they hang*: Nowhere, perhaps, does Dante assert more clearly than in this moving and terrible image his conviction of the intimate and unbreakable bond between spirit and flesh. The Suicides willed the death of the flesh, but they cannot be rid of it: their eternity is an eternity of that death. (The absurd charge of heretically denying the resurrection of the body was brought against Dante on the strength of these lines, but only by those to whom the language of poetic imagery is a sealed book.)

l. 115: *two that ran*: "The first" is Lano of Siena; he belonged to a club of young rakes (referred to again in Canto XXIX), who sold up all their estates and "blued" the proceeds within twenty months. Lano then threw away his life in an encounter between the Sienese and Aretines at a ford called Pieve del Toppo (1288). "The second" is a Paduan, Jacomo di Sant' Andrea, who, not content with such pranks as playing ducks and drakes with gold pieces on the Lagoon at Venice, had a pleasant way of burning down his own and other people's houses for the fun of it. He is said to have been put to death in 1239 by Ezzelino.

l. 143: *my city*: Florence. Her "ancient patron" was Mars. When the Florentines were converted to Christianity they built the Church of St John Baptist on the site of the temple of Mars, and stowed the heathen statue away in a tower near the Arno. After the burning of the city by Totila (whom Dante, misled by some of the chroniclers, seems to have confused with Attila), the mutilated remains of the god were recovered from the river and set up on the Ponte Vecchio; and but for this, so the superstition ran, Florence could never have been rebuilt. Even so, it was said, Mars continued to vex the faithless city with continued internecine strife. But Dante may be covertly reproaching the Florentines with abandoning martial pursuits and concentrating on amassing the florins stamped with the Baptist's image.

l. 151: *one that made my own roof-tree my scaffold*: The speaker has been variously identified. Florence seems to have had a kind of "suicide-wave" about Dante's time; his son Jacopo observes that it is a special vice of the Florentines to hang themselves, "just as the people of Arezzo are given to throwing themselves down wells".

CANTO XIV

THE STORY. *In a desert of Burning Sand, under a rain of perpetual fire, Dante finds the Violent against God, Nature, and Art. The Violent against God lie supine, facing the Heaven which they insulted; among these is Capaneus, blasphemous and defiant in death as in life. The Poets pick their way carefully between the forest and the hot sand till they come to the edge of a boiling, red stream. Here Virgil explains the origin of all the rivers of Hell.*

Love of my native place with kind constraint
  Moving me, I brought back the scattered leaves
  To him whose voice already was grown faint;

Then on we went, to reach the bound which cleaves
  The second ring from the third, and saw appear
  A terrible art which justice here conceives.

7   I say, to make all this new matter clear,
      We reached a plain which spurns all foliage
      And every live plant from its surface sere.

10 The doleful wood garlands it like a hedge,
      As the sad moat garlands the wood around;
      And here we stayed our steps 'twixt edge and edge.

13 An arid, close-packed sand, in fashion found
      Not otherwise than that which once was trod
      By Cato's marching feet, such was the ground.

16 Fearful indeed art thou, vengeance of God!
      He that now reads what mine own eyes with awe
      Plainly beheld, well may he dread thy rod!

19 Great herds of naked spirits here I saw,
      Who all most wretchedly bewailed their lot,
      Seeming subjected to a diverse law.

22 Some on the ground lay supine in one spot,
      And some upon their hunkers squatted low,
      Others roamed ceaselessly and rested not;

25 Most numerous were the rovers to-and-fro;
      Of those that lay, the numbers were more small,
      But much the loudest were their cries of woe.

28 And slowly, slowly dropping over all
      The sand, there drifted down huge flakes of fire,
      As Alpine snows in windless weather fall.

31 Like as Alexander, in those torrider
      Regions of Ind, saw flaming fireballs shed
      Over his host, floating to earth entire,

34 So that his men and he took pains to tread
      The soil, trampling the blaze out with their feet,
      Since it was easier quenched before it spread,

37 Even so rained down the everlasting heat,
      And, as steel kindles tinder, kindled the sands,
      Redoubling pain; nor ever ceased the beat

40 And restless dance of miserable hands,
      Flapping away, now this side and now that,
      The raw smart of the still-fresh-biting brands.

43 I thus began: "Master, strong to frustrate
      All hostile things, save only indeed those grim
      Fiends who opposed our entrance at the gate,

46 Who is the shade that lies, mighty of limb,
      Contorted and contemptuous, scorning the flame,
      So that the rain seems not to ripen him?"

49 But he himself, soon as he heard me frame
      This question to my guide about him, cried:
      "That which in life I was, in death I am.

52 Though Jove tire out his armourer, who supplied
      His wrathful hand with the sharp thunder-stone
      That in my last day smote me through the side;

55 Though he tire all the rest out, one by one,
      In Mongibel's black stithy, and break them quite,
      Crying, 'To aid! Vulcan, lay on, lay on!'

58 As once before he cried at Phlegra's fight;
      Yea, though he crush me with his omnipotence,
      No merry vengeance shall his heart delight."

61 Then my guide spoke out with a vehemence
      Such as I never had heard him use before:
      "O Capaneus, since thy proud insolence

64   Will not be quenched, thy pains shall be the more;
    No torment save thine own hot rage could be
    A fitting cautery to thy rabid sore."

67   Then said with milder mouth, turning to me:
    "This was one of the seven kings who pressed
    The siege of Thebes; he held, and seemingly

70   Still holds, God light, and flouts Him with a jest;
    Yet, as I told him, his mad mouthings make
    A proper brooch for such a brazen breast.

73   Now follow me, and look to it that thou take
    No step upon the burning sand, but keep
    Thy feet close back against the woodland brake."

76   Silent we came where, from that forest deep,
    A little brook poured forth a bubbling jet
    Whose horrid redness makes my flesh still creep.

79   It was like that stream of the Bulicame, set
    Apart and shared by the women of the town;
    And straight out over the sand ran the rivulet.

82   Its bed, and both its shelving banks, and the crown
    Of the margins left and right, were turned to stone;
    Which made me think that here our path led down.

85   "Of all the marvels I as yet have shown
    Thine eyes, since first we entered by that door
    Of which the threshold is denied to none,

88   Nothing we've seen deserves thy wonder more
    Than this small stream which, flowing centreward,
    Puts out all flames above its either shore."

91   Thus said my guide; whom I at once implore
    Since he'd so whet my appetite to taste
    His food, immediately to spread the board.

94   "Far off amid the sea there lies a waste
    Country," said he, "called Crete, beneath whose king,
    Once on a long-lost time, the world was chaste.

97   A mount is there, named Ida; many a spring
    Laughed through its ferns of yore and the valleys smiled –
    Forsaken now, like some old, mouldering thing.

100   There Rhea once found safe cradling for her child,
    And to hide his cries, lest danger come to pass,
    Let fill the hills with Corybant clamours wild.

103   A great old man stands under the mountain's mass;
    Toward Damietta he keeps his shoulders holden,
    And he looks on Rome as though on a looking-glass.

106   He towers erect, and his head is purely golden,
    Of the silver fine his breast and arms and hands,
    Of brass down to the cleft his trunk is moulden,

109   And thence to the ground his legs are iron bands,
    Save that the right foot's baked of the earthen clay,
    And that is the foot upon which he chiefly stands.

112   All but the gold is cracked, and from the splay
    Of that great rift run tears gathering and dripping,
    Till out through the cavern floor they wear their way

115   Into this vale, from rock to rock down-dipping,
    Making Acheron, Styx and Phlegethon; then they take
    Their downward course, by this strait conduit slipping,

118   To where there is no more downward; there they make
    Cocytus; and what that's like I need not tell;
    For thine own eyes shall look on Cocytus lake."

121   Then I to him: "But, Master, if this rill
    Flows from our world, why is it only found
    Here on this bank, nor elsewhere visible?"

124   And he to me: "Thou knowest, the place is round;
    Though thou hast come a good long way, 'tis true,
    Still wheeling leftward toward the Pit's profound,

127   Thou hast not yet turned the full circle through;
    So why put on such a bewildered air
    If now and then we come upon something new?"

130   And I again: "Where's Lethe, sir? and where
    Is Phlegethon? The first thou leav'st aside,
    Tracing the second to that water there."

133   "Thy questions all delight me," he replied,
    "But for the one – thyself canst answer it:
    Think of the boiling of the blood-red tide.

136   And Lethe thou shalt see, far from this Pit,
    Where go the souls to wash them in its flood,
    Their guilt purged off, their penitence complete."

139   He added: "Come; it's time to leave the wood;
    See that thou follow closely where I tread;
    The margins burn not, they shall make our road,

142   And all the fires are quenched there overhead."

THE IMAGES. *The Sand.* "In these circles of the Violent the reader is peculiarly conscious of a sense of sterility. The bloody river, the dreary wood, the harsh sand, which compose them, to some extent are there as symbols of unfruitfulness" (Charles Williams: *The Figure of Beatrice*, p. 129). The images of the sand and burning rain are derived from the doom of Sodom and Gomorrah. (*Gen.* xix. 24.)

The Blasphemers. Capaneus the Blasphemer is chosen as the particular image of Violence against God: he is an image of Pride, which makes the soul obdurate under judgment. The arrangement of Hell, being classical, allots no special place to Pride (held by Christianity to be the root of all sin), but it offers a whole series of examples of Pride, each worse than the last, as the Pit deepens. Farinata's pride is dark and silent; that of Capaneus is loud and defiant, but not yet so wholly ignoble as that of Vanni Fucci (Canto XXV. 1), far down in the Eighth Circle.

NOTES. l. 3: *whose voice already was grown faint:* The small broken twigs were already clotted with blood, and the bush had no voice left.

l. 15: *Cato's marching feet:* The march of Cato of Utica through the Libyan desert in 47 B.C. is described in Lucan's *Pharsalia* ix. 411 *sqq.*

ll. 22 *sqq.: some lay ... some squatted ... others roamed:* the Violent against God, Art, and Nature respectively.

l. 31: *like as Alexander:* Dante seems to have taken this story about Alexander the Great from Albertus Magnus (*De Meteoris*), who in turn took it, with certain alterations, from the spurious *Letter of Alexander to Aristotle about the Marvels of the Indies.*

ll. 51 *sqq.: that which in life I was*, etc.: This is Capaneus, who took part in the war of the "Seven against Thebes" While scaling the city wall, he boasted that not even Jove could stop him, and was struck with a thunder-bolt. Dante read about him in the *Thebaïd* of Statius (the poet whom he afterwards meets in Purgatory).

l. 52: *his armourer:* Vulcan, the blacksmith of the gods, who had his forge in Mongibello (Mount Etna).

l. 58: *Phlegra's fight:* the battle in which the rebellious Titans were overthrown by the gods. (See Canto XXXI. 91 *sqq.*)

l. 70: *still holds God light:* Note again the double vocabulary (as in Canto IX. 94–9). Capaneus says "Jove"; Virgil says "God", meaning the same thing. The heathen are judged by their own standards.

l. 77: *a small brook*: This is the effluent of Phlegethon, which, after crossing the Wood of the Suicides, now runs across the Third Ring to plunge over the edge of the Pit. It has the property of petrifying the sand which forms its bed.

l. 79: *the Bulicame*: a hot sulphur-spring of reddish colour near Viterbo, part of whose waters were specially portioned off for use in the prostitutes' quarter.

l. 90: *puts out all flames*: The steam from the boiling river forms a cloud above the banks and quenches the flames. (Canto XV. I.)

ll. 95–6: *beneath whose king, … the world was chaste*: i.e. in the fabled "Golden Age" of Saturn, the mythical king of Crete.

l. 100: *Rhea*: wife of Saturn and mother by him of Jupiter. It had been prophesied to Saturn that he would be dethroned by his own son, and he therefore devoured all his children as soon as they were born. Rhea deceived him by wrapping a stone in swaddling-clothes, and fled with Jupiter to Mount Ida; when the child cried, she caused the Corybants (Bacchantes) to make a wild clamour so that Saturn should not hear him.

ll. 103 *sqq.*: *a great old man*, etc.: This *allegory* of the successively degenerating periods of history is founded in *Daniel* ii. 32 *sqq.*; the four ages of man (gold, silver, brass, iron) are taken from Ovid: *Metamorphoses* i. 89 *sqq.* Only the Golden Age gave no cause for tears. The feet of iron and clay may be respectively the Empire and the Church. The statue stands in the middle of the Mediterranean (the centre of civilization), looking from the old civilization of the East (Damietta) to the new civilization of the West (Rome).

l. 118: *no more downward*: the centre of the earth and of gravity. Cocytus (Canto XXXIV) is the last of the infernal rivers.

ll. 130 *sqq.*: *Lethe and … Phlegethon*: Virgil explains that Dante has already seen Phlegethon – it is the river of the tyrants, though its name was not mentioned in Canto XII. *Lethe* (the river of forgetfulness) flows to the Centre from the Earthly Paradise on Mount Purgatory on the other side of the world.

CANTO XV

THE STORY. *While crossing the Sand upon the dyke banking Phlegethon, Dante sees the Violent against Nature, who run perpetually, looking towards the human body against which they offended. He meets his old teacher, Brunetto Latini, whom he addresses with affectionate regret and deep gratitude for past benefits. Brunetto predicts Dante's ill-treatment at the hands of the Florentines.*

Now the hard margin bears us on, while steam
    From off the water makes a canopy
    Above, to fend the fire from bank and stream.

4   Just as the men of Flanders anxiously
    'Twixt Bruges and Wissant build their bulwarks wide
    Fearing the thrust and onset of the sea;

7   Or as the Paduans dyke up Brenta's tide
    To guard their towns and castles, ere the heat
    Loose down the snows from Chiarentana's side,

10 Such fashion were the brinks that banked the leat,
    Save that, whoe'er he was, their engineer
    In breadth and height had builded them less great.

13 Already we'd left the wood behind so far
    That I, had I turned back to view those glades,
    Could not have told their whereabouts; and here,

16 Hurrying close to the bank, a troop of shades
    Met us, who eyed us much as passers-by
    Eye one another when the daylight fades

19 To dusk and a new moon is in the sky,
    And knitting up their brows they squinnied at us
    Like an old tailor at the needle's eye.

22 Then, while the whole group peered upon me thus,
    One of them recognized me, who caught hard
    At my gown's hem, and cried: "O marvellous!"

25 When he put out his hand to me, I stared
    At his scorched face, searching him through and through,
    So that the shrivelled skin and features scarred

28 Might not mislead my memory: then I knew:
    And, stooping down to bring my face near his,
    I said: "What, you here, Ser Brunetto? you!"

31 And he: "My son, pray take it not amiss
    If now Brunetto Latini at thy side
    Turn back awhile, letting this troop dismiss."

34 "With all my heart I beg you to," I cried;
    "Or I'll sit down with you, as you like best,
    If he there will permit – for he's my guide."

37 "Oh, son," said he, "should one of our lot rest
    One second, a hundred years he must lie low,
    Nor even beat the flames back from his breast.

40 Therefore go on; I at thy skirts will go,
    And then rejoin my household, who thus race
    Forever lost, and weeping for their woe."

43 I durst not venture from the road to pace
    Beside him, so I walked with down-bent head,
    Like some devout soul in a holy place.

46 He thus began: "What chance or fate has led
    Thy footsteps here before thy final day?
    And who is this that guides thee?" So I said:

49 "Up in the sunlit life I lost my way
    In a dark vale, before my years had come
    To their full number. Only yesterday

52 At morn I turned my back upon its gloom;
    This other came, found me returning there,
    Stopped me, and by this path now leads me home."

55 And he made answer: "Follow but thy star;
    Thou canst not fail to win the glorious haven,
    If in glad life my judgment did not err.

58 Had I not died so soon, I would have given
    Counsel and aid to cheer thee in thy work,
    Seeing how favoured thou hast been by heaven.

61 But that ungrateful, that malignant folk
    Which formerly came down from Fiesole,
    And still is grained of mountain and hewn rock,

64 For thy good deeds will be thine enemy –
    With cause; for where the bitter sloes are rooted
    Is no fit orchard for the sweet fig-tree.

67 A blind people, and always so reputed,
    Proud, envious, covetous, since times remote;
    Cleanse off their customs lest thou be polluted.

70 Fortune has honours for thee – of such note,
    Both sides will seek to snatch thee and devour;
    But yet the good grass shall escape the goat.

73 Let Fiesole's wild beasts scratch up their sour
      Litter themselves from their rank native weed,
      Nor touch the plant, if any such can flower

76 Upon their midden, in whose sacred seed
      Survives the Roman line left there to dwell
      When this huge nest of vice began to breed."

79 I answered him: "Might I have had my will,
      Believe me, you'd not yet been thrust apart
      From human life; for I keep with me still,

82 Stamped on my mind, and now stabbing my heart,
      The dear, benign, paternal image of you,
      You living, you hourly teaching me the art

85 By which men grow immortal; know this too:
      I am so grateful, that while I breathe air
      My tongue shall speak the thanks which are your due.

88 Your words about my future I'll write fair,
      With other texts, to show to a wise lady
      Who'll gloss them, if I ever get to her.

91 This much I'd have you know: I can stand steady,
      So conscience chide not, facing unafraid
      Whatever Fortune brings, for I am ready.

94 Time and again I've heard these forecasts made;
      The whims of Luck shall find me undeterred,
      So let her ply her wheel, the churl his spade."

97 And when my master's ear had caught that word
      He turned right-face-about, and looked me straight
      In the eyes and said: "Well-heeded is well-heard."

100 Yet none the less I move on in debate
      With Ser Brunetto, asking him whose fame
      In all his band is widest and most great.

103 "Some," he replies, "it will be well to name;
      The rest we must pass over, for sheer dearth
      Of time – 'twould take too long to mention them.

106 All these, in brief, were clerks and men of worth
      In letters and in scholarship – none more so;
      And all defiled by one same taint on earth.

109 In that sad throng goes Francis of Accorso,
      And Priscian; could thy hunger have been sated
      By such scabbed meat, thou mightest have seen also

112 Him whom the Servant of servants once translated
      From Arno to Bacchiglione, where he left
      The body he'd unstrung and enervated.

115 I would say more, but must not; for a drift
      Of fresh dust rising from the sandy ground
      Warns me to cease and make my going swift;

118 Here come some folk with whom I mayn't be found;
      Keep handy my *Thesaurus*, where I yet
      Live on; I ask no more." Then he turned round,

121 And seemed like one of those who over the flat
      And open course in the fields beside Verona
      Run for the green cloth; and he seemed, at that,

124 Not like a loser, but the winning runner.

THE IMAGES. *The Sodomites* are chosen as the image of all pervese
vices which damage and corrupt the natural powers of the body.

(It is here, for instance, that Dante would probably place drug-
takers and the vicious type of alcoholics.) Their perpetual fruitless running forms a parallel, on a lower level, to the aimless
drifting of the Lustful in Canto v.

NOTES. ll. 4 *sqq.*: Dante compares the dykes to those built in the Low
Countries to keep out the sea, and to the embankments made by the
Paduans along the river Brenta to prevent flooding in spring, when
the river is swollen by melted snow from Chiarentana (probably
Carenzana, a mountain in the Trentino).

l. 11: *their engineer*: God is, of course, the supreme Architect of
Hell (Canto III. 4–6); but the constructional details would be supposed
to be carried out by some one of the "Intelligences" who are His
ministers. As we see from l. 23, the top of the dyke was about a man's
height from the sand.

l. 29: *to bring my face near his*: another reading, perhaps even more
attractive, has: "And reached my hand down to that face of his,
Saying ..."

l. 30: *Ser Brunetto*: Messer Brunetto Latini (*c.* 1220–94) was a
Florentine Guelf, a man of considerable learning. An early commentator says "that he was a neighbour of Dante and taught him a
great many things; that he did not care for the soul, as he was altogether worldly; that he sinned greatly in unnatural crime, and scoffed
much at the things of God and Holy Church" (Vernon). He wrote
in French a prose encyclopedia called *Le Livre dou Tresor* or *Thesaurus* (see l. 119), and an abridged version in Italian verse, *Il Tesoretto*.
Though he was an influence in Dante's early life, he was not a "tutor"
or "schoolmaster", but a man holding public office in the state, till he
was banished with other Guelfs after the Battle of Montaperti.

l. 56: *the glorious haven*: Brunetto seems to mistake Dante, and
think that he is only aspiring to lasting fame on earth, and says that, if
he himself had not died too soon, he would have helped him to
achieve perfection of knowledge.

ll. 61–79: According to Florentine tradition, Julius Caesar besieged
Catiline in Fiesole; when the city fell, the Romans built a new one –
Florence – on the Arno, to be peopled half by Fiesolans and half by
Romans. Dante attributes much of the strife and disorder in Florence
to this adulteration of the Roman stock by families from Fiesole and
the surrounding country (see *Para.* xvi. 67–9). "Blind Florentines"
was a proverbial reproach, whose origin is now lost in mists of
legend (cf. our "wise fools of Gotham").

l. 71: *both sides will seek to snatch thee*: i.e. Dante will be persecuted
by both parties.

l. 87: *my tongue shall speak the thanks which are your due:* The episode of Brunetto Latini gives the lie to the common assertion that
Dante put only his enemies in Hell. But while maintaining, on the
one hand, that personal feelings cannot remove the difference in
God's sight between right and wrong, he asserts, on the other, that,
as between man and man, nothing can ever remove the obligation to
acknowledge benefits received. "For ever and ever (derivation) must
be remembered, willingly praised, and ardently published before
earth and heaven. ... Such a loyalty is necessary to the life of the
City." (Charles Williams: *The Figure of Beatrice*, p. 130.)

l. 89: *to show to a wise lady*: Dante, remembering Virgil's words
(Canto X. 130–32), says he will ask Beatrice to explain all these prophecies about himself.

l. 96: *the churl his spade*: Let Luck turn her wheel, and the labourer
turn the soil – Dante shall remain as unmoved by the one as by the
other. Virgil seems not altogether to approve this parade of indifference, and warns Dante that he will do well to heed what is said to
him.

l. 112: *him whom the Servant of servants once translated*: Andrea dei
Mozzi. The title "Servant of the servants of God" is one of the official
titles of the Pope.

l. 121: *and seemed like one of those who ... run:* This foot-race, whose
prize was a piece of green cloth, was instituted to celebrate a Vero-
nese victory, and was run on the First Sunday in Lent

CANTO XVI

THE STORY. *Dante is already within earshot of the waterfall at the end
of the path, when he meets the shades of three distinguished Florentine
noblemen and gives them news of their city. At the edge of the cliff, Virgil
throws Dante's girdle into the gulf below, and in answer to this signal a
strange form comes swimming up towards them.*

Already I'd reached a place where the dull thrumming
    Of the water tumbling down to the circle below
    Was heard ahead like the sound of a beehive's humming,

4 When lo! three shadows, running all in a row,
    Broke from a company that across the sand
    Was passing under the rain of the burning woe.

7 They came towards us, crying with one voice: "Stand,
    Thou there, the fashion of whose dress would seem
    To make thee a native of our perverted land!"

10 O me! the marks I saw upon every limb,
    Branded in by the flames, old scars and new –
    It makes me heartsick only to think of them.

13 Heedful, my teacher heard those spirits through,
    Then turned his face my way: "Now wait," said he;
    "To those the utmost courtesy is due.

16 Were not this place by nature arrowy
    With fire, I'd say it was far more suitable
    That thou shouldst hurry to them than they to thee."

19 They raised their voices again when we stood still,
    Renewing their ancient wail; then, coming close,
    The three of them formed themselves into a wheel.

22 Like old-time champions, stript, oiled, on their toes
    Circling, and spying for vantage of hold and place
    Before getting down to clinches and to blows,

25 Just so they wheeled; but each one kept his gaze
    So fixed on me that all the time one way
    The feet went, and another way the face.

28 "Eh, though scorn prompt thee," one began to say,
    "Seeing our squalor, and scorched, filthy state,
    From us and from our prayers to turn away,

31 Let our great fame yet move thee to relate
    What man thou art, that free and dangerless
    Thus through deep Hell dost move thy living feet.

34 He in whose tracks I tread here, nevertheless,
    For all he now goes naked and peeled and scored,
    Was nobler in degree than thou couldst guess.

37 Grandson to good Gualdrada was this lord,
    He was called Guido Guerra, and his fame
    In life stood high with counsel and with sword.

40 He that behind me treads the sand and flame
    Was Tegghiai' Aldobrandi once; applause
    Up in your world should surely greet that name.

43 Here, partner in their pain, am I, who was
    Jacopo Rusticucci; of this woe
    My bestial wife's the first and foremost cause."

46 Could I have kept the fire off, there below,
    I'd have leapt down to them, and I declare
    I think my tutor would have let me go;

49 But I'd have burnt and baked me so, that fear
    Quite vanquished the good-will which made me yearn
    To clasp them to my bosom then and there.

52 So I began: "Indeed, indeed, not scorn
    But heartfelt grief to see your tribulation
    Pierced me, too deeply to be soon outworn,

55 When this my lord gave me an intimation
    Which made me think that I might look to gaze
    On men like you, and of such reputation.

58 Truly, your city's mine; I've heard your praise –
    Your deeds, your honoured names – rehearsed by all,
    And have with love rehearsed them all my days.

61 I'm one who, turning from the bitter gall,
    Seek the sweet fruit promised by my sure guide;
    But to the Centre I have first to fall."

64 "So may thy soul these many years abide
    Housed in thy body, and the after-light
    Of fame shine long behind thee," he replied,

67 "Tell us if in our city still burn bright
    Courage and courtesy, as they did of old,
    Or are their embers now extinguished quite?

70 For Guillim Borsier', but late enrolled
    With us, who runs in yon tormented train,
    Has much distressed us by the tales he's told."

73 "A glut of self-made men and quick-got gain
    Have bred excess in thee and pride, forsooth,
    O Florence! till e'en now thou criest for pain."

76 Thus I proclaimed aloud with lifted mouth;
    The three knew they were answered, each on each
    Looking, as men look when they hear the truth.

79 "If thou at other times canst thus enrich
    Men's ears," they all replied, "scot-free, as thus,
    Happy art thou, that hast the gift of speech!

82 Wherefore, if thou escape this place of loss
    And come to see the lovely stars again,
    Then, when thou shalt rejoice to say, 'I was,'

85 Look that thou speak of us to living men."
    Thereon they broke their wheel, and fled so fast,
    Their legs seemed wings; you could not say *Amen*

88 So quickly as across the sandy vast
    They vanished; only then my master stirred,
    Choosing to go. I followed. On we passed,

91 And went but a short way before we heard
    The sound of the water thundering down so close
    That had we spoken we'd scarce have heard a word.

94 As that first river that to the eastward flows
    From Monte Veso down to a mouth of its own,
    On the left slope of the Apennines (where it goes

97 By the name of Acquacheta, ere running down
    To its lower bed, and after that becomes
    Known by another name at Forlì town)

100   Resounds from the mountain-side as it drops and drums
  At the fall above St Benedict's, near the ground
  Where a thousand people should settle and have their homes,

103   So plunging over a steep chasm we found
  That dark-dyed water, bellowing with a din
  Such that the ear would soon be stunned with sound.

106   I was wearing a rope girdle, the same wherein
  I once, indeed, had nursed a fleeting hope
  To catch the leopard with the painted skin;

109   Now, at my guide's command, I loosed the rope
  And took it off, and held it out to him
  All neatly wound together and coiled up.

112   He took it, and leaning right-hand from the brim
  Of the Pit, he tossed it over the precipice,
  So that it dropped well out from the rocky rim.

115   "Surely some strange and novel thing will rise,"
  Said I to myself, "to answer this strange sign
  Which thus my master's following with his eyes."

118   Dear me! when one's with people who divine
  More than they see, and read one's thoughts right through,
  How careful one should be! My guide read mine:

121   "Oh, it will come," said he, "and quickly too,
  The thing I look for; what thy fancies frame
  There in thy head will soon be in thy view."

124   When truth looks like a lie, a man's to blame
  Not to sit still, if he can, and hold his tongue,
  Or he'll only cover his innocent head with shame;

127   But here I can't be silent; and by the song
  Of this my Comedy, Reader, hear me swear,
  So may my work find favour and live long,

130   That I beheld through that thick murky air
  Come swimming up a shape most marvellously
  Strange for even the stedfast heart to bear;

133   As he returns, that has gone down to free
  The anchor from whatever's fouling it,
  Or rock or other thing hid undersea,

136   Spreading his arms and gathering up his feet.

THE IMAGES. *The Rope Girdle.* Much controversy has raged about
this. For the *story*, it is perhaps enough to say that something was
needed to serve as a signal, and that the story-teller pitched upon
this as one of the few detachable objects which his characters
might be supposed to have about them. Dante, however, goes
out of his way to tell us (for the first time and rather surprisingly)
that he had once hoped to catch the Leopard of Canto I with the
rope. The Leopard is the image of the sins of Youth, or Incontinence; and it seems likely that the girdle has something to do with
Chastity – it may, e.g., symbolize some vow of chastity which
failed in its object. The Circles of Incontinence are now left behind, and the girdle is therefore available for another purpose.
This time it does "catch" something – a thing variegated and gay
like the Leopard, but infinitely more dangerous, brought up from
the Circles of Fraud. *Allegorically*, this may suggest that when the
earlier and more obvious temptations seem to have departed, they
may recur, disguised and more insidious, provoked by the very
safeguards originally erected against them.

NOTES. l. 2: *the water tumbling down*: The effluent of all the upper
rivers pours over the precipice, and runs either under or above ground
across the Eighth Circle, to reappear as Cocytus in the Ninth.

l. 8: *the fashion of whose dress*: The characteristic Florentine costume
– the straight gown (*lucco*) and hood (*capocchio*) – are familiar in all
the pictures of Dante.

l. 21: *formed themselves into a wheel*: These shades may not stop
running even for a moment (see Canto XV. 37–9) under a dire
penalty, so they adopt this method of remaining abreast of Dante.

ll. 37–45: The three persons named are all noble Florentine Guelfs.
Tegghiaio and Rusticucci are among the "worthy men" after whom
Dante inquired so anxiously of Ciacco (Canto VI. 78–80).

Just as the shades in Brunetto's group were all men of letters, these
are all persons of political importance; it appears from Canto XV. 118
that the various groups were not allowed to mix.

l. 76: *with lifted mouth*: Here, as again in Canto XIX, Dante marks
the difference between his private speech and his prophetic speech: he
lifts his head as though to proclaim the doom of Florence.

ll. 79–80: The shades acclaim Dante's powers of poetic inspiration,
but hint that his eloquence may some day cost him dear.

l. 84: *when thou shalt rejoice to say, "I was"*: i.e. when he will be glad
to remember that he once had this terrible experience.

l. 95: *down to a mouth of its own*: The Acquacheta, which from Forlì
onwards is called the Montone, was in Dante's time the first river rising in the Etruscan Alps to fall direct into the Adriatic, instead of into
the Po. (See map below.)

l. 102: *where a thousand people could settle*: This may refer to a
scheme of the Conti Guidi for settling a number of their vassals in
this district. (Some commentators think Dante means that the foundation of St Benedict's could have supported many more monks than
it actually did.)

l. 118: *people who divine ... one's thoughts*: cf. Cantos X. 18, XIII. 25,
etc.

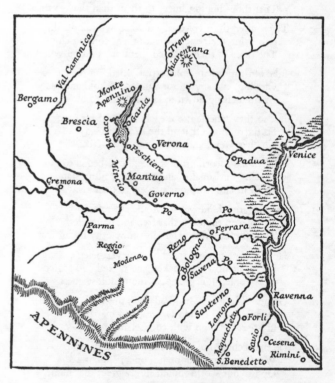

CANTO XVII

THE STORY. *Geryon, the monster called up from the Circles of Fraud,
alights on the edge of the precipice. While Virgil talks to him, Dante
goes to look at the shades of Usurers seated on the Burning Sand. The*

Poets then mount on Geryon's shoulders and are carried down over the
Great Barrier to the Eighth Circle.

"Behold the beast with stinging tail unfurled,
   That passes mountains and breaks weapon and wall;
   Behold him that pollutes the whole wide world."

4   Thus said my lord to me, and therewithal
   Made him a sign to bring him to aboard
   Near the path's end, but farther from the fall.

7   And on he came, that unclean image of Fraud,
   To ground upon the hard with head and chest,
   But not his tail, which still he left abroad.

10   His face was a just man's, it so expressed
   In every line a mild benignity;
   And like a wyvern's trunk was all the rest.

13   He had two fore-paws, shaggy arm-pit high,
   Whence breast and back and both flanks shimmered off,
   Painted with ring-knots and whorled tracery.

16   Nor Turk nor Tartar ever wrought coloured stuff
   So rainbow-trammed and broidered; never wore
   Arachne's web such dyes in warp and woof.

19   And as wherries many a time lie drawn ashore,
   Half in the water, half upon the strand,
   Or as the beaver plants him to wage war

22   At home there, in the guzzling Germans' land,
   So that worst beast of beastly kind hung clipped
   To the cliff whose curb of stone girdles the sand;

25   And all his tail quivered in the void and whipped
   Upward, twisting the venomed fork in air
   Wherewith, like a scorpion's tail, its point was tipped.

28   "Now," said my guide, "we must a little bear
   Aside, and make our way towards this same
   Malevolent brute that clings and crouches there."

31   So we descended on our right, and came
   Ten paces onward, skirting the cliff's face,
   To give a wide berth to the sand and flame,

34   And joined him thus; and when we reached the place,
   I saw some folk a little way ahead
   Sitting on the sand, near the empty edge of space;

37   Wherefore: "That thou mayst know," my master said,
   "All that there is to know about this ring,
   Go forward, view those shades and learn their state;

40   But do not linger too long parleying;
   While thou art gone I'll speak the beast, and borrow
   His sturdy back to speed our journeying."

43   So I went, all by myself, along the narrow
   Outermost brink of the seventh circle, and so
   Came where those people sat to dree their sorrow,

46   Which gushed from their eyes and made the sad tears flow;
   While this way and that they flapped their hands, for ease
   From the hot soil now, and now from the burning snow,

49   Behaving, in fact, exactly as one sees
   Dogs in the summer, scuffing with snout and paw,
   When they're eaten up with breeses and flies and fleas.

52   I looked at many thus scorched by the fiery flaw,
   And though I scanned their faces with utmost heed,
   There was no one there I recognized; but I saw

55   How, stamped with charge and tincture plain to read,
   About the neck of each a great purse hung,
   Whereon their eyes seemed still to fix and feed.

58   So as I went gazing upon the throng,
   I saw a purse display, azure on or,
   The gesture and form of a lion; further along

61   My eye pursued, and fell on one that bore
   A purse of blood-red gules, which had on it
   A goose whiter than curd; and yet one more

64   Beside him sat, who on his wallet white
   Showed a blue sow in farrow; this one cried
   To me: "What art thou doing in this pit?

67   Away! and learn (since thou hast not yet died),
   My neighbour Vitaliano shall come here
   To sit with me upon my left-hand side.

70   These Florentines keep bawling in my ear –
   I'm Paduan myself – all day they shout:
   'Let come, let come that knight without a peer

73   Who bears three goats upon his satchel stout!'"
   With that he writhed his mouth awry, and made
   A gross grimace, thrusting his tongue right out

76   Like an ox licking its nose. Then I, afraid
   To anger him who bade me make short stay
   By staying longer, left that sad brigade

79   And went to seek my guide without delay,
   And found him already mounted on the croup
   Of the fearsome beast. "Courage!" I heard him say,

82   "Such is the stair by which we have to stoop;
   I'll sit behind lest thou take harm from the tail,
   So do thou mount before; be bold now – up!"

85   Like one with the quartan fit on him, leaden-pale
   At the finger-nails already, and quaking faster
   At the mere sight of the shade, so did I quail

88   Hearing him; yet his hintings of disaster
   Shamed me to valour, as a hind may be
   Bold in the presence of an honoured master.

91   So I climbed to those dread shoulders obediently;
   "Only do" (I meant to say, but my voice somehow
   Wouldn't come out right) "please catch hold of me."

94   But he that at other times had not been slow
   In other straits to aid me, gripped me fast
   In his arms the moment I mounted, and held me now

97   Secure; and said: "Now move thee, Geryon! cast
   Thy circle wide, and wheel down gradually,
   Think of the strange new burden that thou hast."

100   And as a ship slips from her berth to sea
   Backing and backing, so did the beast begin
   To leave the bank; and when he felt quite free

103   He turned his tail to where his breast had been,
   Stretching it forth and wriggling like an eel,
   And with his paws gathered the thick air in.

106 No greater fear, methinks, did any feel
When Phaeton dropped the chariot-reins of the sun,
Firing the sky – we see the mark there still –

109 Nor when poor Icarus felt the hot wax run,
Unfeathering him, and heard his father calling,
"Alack! alack! thou fliest too high, my son!" –

112 Than I felt, finding myself in the void falling
With nothing but air all round, nothing to show,
No light, no sight but the sight of the beast appalling.

115 And on he goes, swimming and swimming slow,
Round and down, though I only know it by feeling
The wind come up and beat on my face from below.

118 And now I hear on the right as we spin wheeling
The noise of the cataract under us horribly roaring,
And I crane my head and look down with my senses reeling.

121 Then the terror of alighting seemed worse than the terror of soaring;
For I heard the wails and I saw the tall fires leap,
So that for fear I shrank back trembling and cowering.

124 And I saw – what before I could not see – the sweep
And swoop of our downward flight through the grand woes,
Which now drew near on every side of the deep.

127 And now, as a hawk that has long hung waiting does –
When, without any sight at all of lure or prey,
She makes the falconer cry: "She stoops!" and goes

130 Dropping down weary, then suddenly wheels away
In a hundred circlings, and sets her far aloof
From her master, sullen and scornful – so, I say,

133 Geryon set us down on the bottom rough,
A-foot at the foot of the cliff-face that surrounded
The chasm; and having shogged our burden off,

136 Brisker than bolt from bow away he bounded.

THE IMAGES. *Geryon.* In Greek mythology, Geryon was a monster who was killed by Hercules. He was usually represented as having a human form with three heads, or three conjoined bodies; but Dante has given him a shape compounded of three natures – human, bestial, and reptile. In the *allegory*, he is the image of Fraud, with "the face of a just man" and an iridescence of beautiful colour, but with the paws of a beast and a poisonous sting in his serpent's tail – an image which scarcely calls for interpretation.

The Usurers. These, as we have seen, are the image of the Violent against Nature and the Art derived from Nature; they sit looking upon the ground, because they have sinned against that and against the labour that should have cultivated its resources. The old commentator Gelli observes brilliantly that the Sodomites and Usurers are classed together because the first make sterile the natural instincts which result in fertility, while the second make fertile that which by its nature is sterile – i.e. they "make money breed". More generally, the Usurers may be taken as types of all economic and mechanical civilizations which multiply material luxuries at the expense of vital necessities and have no roots in the earth or in humanity.

NOTES. l. 12: *a wyvern's trunk*: Dante's word is *serpente*, which means any kind of reptile, with or without legs. I have rendered it here by "wyvern" – a fabulous creature with one pair of legs and a serpent's tail.

l. 18: *Arachne's web.*

l. 21: *as the beaver plants him*: The beaver was popularly supposed to angle for fish by sitting on the shore and dropping its tail into the water by way of bait. In Dante's time it was commonly found further south than it is to-day.

l. 31: *we descended on our right*: i.e. they descended from the dyke and went along at the extreme edge of the precipice, which was of stone (l. 24) and presumably outside the limits assigned by Providence to the fiery rain.

ll. 55 *sqq.*: *stamped with charge and tincture*: The various devices upon the Usurers' purses are the arms of men and families notorious for their usury. The Paduan who speaks in ll. 64–76 is Rinaldo dei Scrovegni, and Vitaliano dei Vitaliani, whom he mentions, is also a Paduan. The rest are Florentines: one of the Gianfigliazzi family, one of the Ubbriachi, and Giovanni Buiamonte dei Becchi (the "knight without a peer").

l. 75: *a gross grimace*: to taunt Dante with the number of Florentines among the Usurers.

l. 85: *the quartan fit*: i.e. the cold fit of the quartan ague, announcing itself by premonitory shiverings.

l. 107: *Phaeton*: the son of Phoebus; he asked his father to allow him to drive the chariot of the Sun, but was unable to control the horses, so that they started out of their course, burning the track of the Milky Way across the sky, and would have set fire to the earth, but that Jupiter intervened by killing Phaeton with a thunderbolt.

l. 109: *Icarus*: was the son of Daedalus. His father made him wings, which were fastened to his shoulders with wax. Icarus flew too near the sun, so that the wax melted and he fell into the Aegean Sea and was drowned.

NETHER HELL - 2

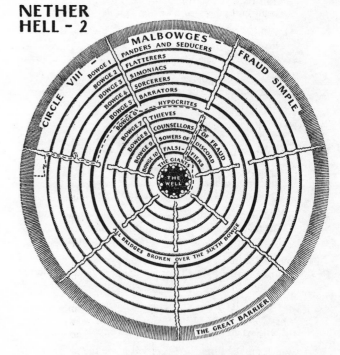

THE SINS OF THE WOLF

CANTO XVIII

THE STORY. *Dante now finds himself in the Eighth Circle (Malbowges), which is divided into ten trenches (bowges) containing those who committed Malicious Frauds upon mankind in general. The Poets walk along the edge of Bowge i, where Panders and Seducers run, in opposite directions, scourged by demons; and here Dante talks with Venedico Caccianemico of Bologna. As they cross the bridge over the bowge, they see the shade of Jason. Then they go on to the bridge over Bowge ii, where they see Thaïs, and Dante converses with another of the Flatterers who are here plunged in filth.*

There is in Hell a region that is called
    Malbowges; it is all of iron-grey stone,
    Like the huge barrier-rock with which it's walled.

4 Plumb in the middle of the dreadful cone
    There yawns a well, exceeding deep and wide,
    Whose form and fashion shall be told anon.

7 That which remains, then, of the foul Pit's side,
    Between the well and the foot of the craggy steep,
    Is a narrowing round, which ten great chasms divide.

10 As one may see the girding fosses deep
    Dug to defend a stronghold from the foe,
    Trench within trench about the castle-keep,

13 Such was the image here; and as men throw
    Their bridges outward from the fortress-wall,
    Crossing each moat to the far bank, just so

16 From the rock's base spring cliffs, spanning the fall
    Of dyke and ditch, to the central well, whose rim
    Cuts short their passage and unites them all.

19 When Geryon shook us off, 'twas in this grim
    Place that we found us; and the poet then
    Turned to the left, and I moved after him.

22 There, on our right, more anguished shades of men,
    New tortures and new torturers, I espied,
    Cramming the depth of this first bowge of ten.

25 In the bottom were naked sinners, who, our side
    The middle, moved to face us; on the other,
    Along with us, though with a swifter stride.

28 Just as the Romans, because of the great smother
    Of the Jubilee crowds, have thought of a good device
    For controlling the bridge, to make the traffic smoother,

31 So that on one side all must have their eyes
    On the Castle, and go to St Peter's; while all the throng
    On the other, towards the Mount moves contrariwise.

34 I saw horned fiends with heavy whips and strong
    Posted each side along the dismal rock,
    Who scourged their backs, and drove them on headlong.

37 Hey! how they made them skip at the first shock!
    How brisk they were to lift their legs and prance!
    Nobody stayed for the second or third stroke.

40 And as I was going, one of them caught my glance,
    And I promptly said to myself: "How now! who's he?
    Somewhere or other I've seen that countenance."

43 I stopped short, figuring out who this might be;
    And my good lord stopped too; then let me go
    Back a short way, to follow him and see.

46 The whipped shade hung his head, trying not to show
    His face; but little good he got thereby,
    For: "Hey, there! thou whose eyes are bent so low,

49 Thy name's Venedico – or thy features lie –
    Caccianemico, and I know thee well;
    What wormwood pickled such a rod," said I,

52 "To scrub thy back?" And he: "I would not tell,
    But for that voice of thine; those accents clear
    Remind me of the old life, and compel

55 My answer. I am the man who sold the fair
    Ghisola to the Marchese's lust; that's fact,
    However they tell the ugly tale up there.

58 I'm not alone here from Bologna; packed
    The place is with us; one could scarcely find
    More tongues saying 'Yep' for 'Yes' in all the tract

61 'Twixt Reno and Savena. Art inclined
    To call for proof? What witness need I join
    To the known witness of our covetous mind?"

64 And one of the fiends caught him a crack on the loin
    With the lash, even as he spoke, crying: "Away,
    Pander! there are no women here to coin!"

67 So to my escort I retraced my way,
    And soon we came, a few steps further wending,
    To where a great spur sprang from the barrier grey.

70 This we climbed lightly, and, right-handed bending,
    Crossed its rough crest, departing from that rout
    Of shades who run their circuits never-ending.

73 But, coming above the part that's tunnelled out
    To let the flogged pass under, "Stay" said he;
    "Let those who go the other way about

76 Strike on thine eyes; just now thou couldst not see
    Their faces, as we passed along the verge,
    For they were travelling the same road as we."

79 So from that ancient bridge we watched the surge
    Sweep on towards us of the wretched train
    On the farther side, chased likewise by the scourge.

82 "Look who comes here," my good guide said again
    Without my asking, "that great spirit of old,
    Who will not shed one tear for all his pain.

85 Is he not still right royal to behold?
    That's Jason, who by valour and by guile
    Bore from the Colchian strand the fleece of gold.

88 He took his way past Lemnos, where, short while
    Before, the pitiless bold women achieved
    The death of all the menfolk of their isle;

91 And there the young Hypsipyle received
    Tokens and fair false words, till, snared and shaken,
    She who deceived her fellows was deceived;

94 And there he left her, childing and forsaken;
    For those deceits he's sentenced to these woes,
    And for Medea too revenge is taken.

97 And with him every like deceiver goes.
    Suffice thee so much knowledge of this ditch
    And those whom its devouring jaws enclose."

100 Already we'd come to where the narrow ridge
    Crosses the second bank, and makes of it
    An abutment for the arch of the next bridge.

₁₀₃ Here we heard people in the farther pit
   Make a loud whimpering noise, and heard them cough,
   And slap themselves with their hands, and snuffle and spit.

₁₀₆ The banks were crusted with foul scum, thrown off
   By the fume, and caking there, till nose and eye
   Were vanquished with sight and reek of the noisome stuff.

₁₀₉ So deep the trench, that one could not espy
   Its bed save from the topmost cliff, which makes
   The keystone of the arch. We climbed; and I,

₁₁₂ Thence peering down, saw people in the lake's
   Foul bottom, plunged in dung, the which appeared
   Like human ordure running from a jakes.

₁₁₅ Searching its depths, I there made out a smeared
   Head – whether clerk or lay was hard to tell,
   It was so thickly plastered with the merd.

₁₁₈ "Why stand there gloating?" he began to yell,
   "Why stare at me more than the other scum?"
   "Because," said I, "if I remember well,

₁₂₁ I've seen thy face, dry-headed, up at home;
   Thou art Alessio Interminei, late
   Of Lucca – so, more eagerly than on some,

₁₂₄ I look on thee." He beat his pumpkin pate,
   And said: "The flatteries I spewed out apace
   With tireless tongue have sunk me to this state."

₁₂₇ Then said my guide: "Before we leave the place,
   Lean out a little further, that with full
   And perfect clearness thou may'st see the face

₁₃₀ Of that uncleanly and dishevelled trull
   Scratching with filthy nails, alternately
   Standing upright and crouching in the pool.

₁₃₃ That is the harlot Thaïs. 'To what degree,'
   Her leman asked, 'have I earned thanks, my love?'
   'O, to a very miracle,' said she.

₁₃₆ And having seen this, we have seen enough."

THE IMAGES. *The Eighth and Ninth Circles.* These are the Circles of *Fraud* or *Malice* – the "Sins of the Wolf".

Malbowges. The Eighth Circle is a huge funnel of rock, round which run, at irregular intervals, a series of deep, narrow trenches called "bowges" (*bolge*). From the foot of the Great Barrier at the top to the Well which forms the neck of the funnel run immense spurs of rock (like the ribs of an umbrella) raised above the general contour of the slope and forming bridges over the bowges. The maps on pp. 398 and 410 and the sketch on p. 415 show the arrangement, except, of course, that the distances from bowge to bowge are greater, and the rock-surfaces much steeper and craggier, than it is possible to suggest in small diagrams.

Malbowges is, I think, after a rather special manner, the image of the City in corruption: the progressive disintegration of every social relationship, personal and public. Sexuality, ecclesiastical and civil office, language, ownership, counsel, authority, psychic influence, and material interdependence – all the media of the community's exchange are perverted and falsified, till nothing remains but the descent into the final abyss where faith and trust are wholly and for ever extinguished.

The Panders and Seducers. In the Circles of Fraud (the abuse of the specifically human faculty of reason) the ministers of Hell are no longer mere embodied *appetites*, but actual devils, images of the perverted *intellect*. In the First Bowge, those who deliberately exploited the passions of others and so drove them to serve their own interests, are themselves driven and scourged. The image is a sexual one; but the Panders and Seducers *allegorically* figure the stimulation and exploitation of every kind of passion – e.g. rage or greed – by which one may make tools of other people.

The Flatterers. These, too, exploit others by playing upon their desires and fears; their especial weapon is that abuse and corruption of language which destroys communication between mind and mind. Here they are plunged in the slop and filth which they excreted upon the world. Dante did not live to see the full development of political propaganda, commercial advertisement, and sensational journalism, but he has prepared a place for them.

NOTES. l. 2: *Malbowges (Malebolge)*: The Italian word *bolgia* means (*a*) a trench in the ground; (*b*) a purse or pouch. *Malebolge* can thus be interpreted as either "evil pits" or "evil pouches"; and Dante puns on this double meaning (Canto XIX. 72). There is no English word which combines the two meanings; there is, however, an old word "bowge" meaning "pouch". This makes it possible to english *Malebolge* as "Malbowges" (which is, in all probability, the form which a medieval translator would have given it), and so to retain a suggestion of the pun about "pouching".

l. 6: *shall be told anon*: see Canto XXXI.

ll. 28–33: The fact that traffic control appears to Dante as a startling and ingenious novelty probably brings home to us, far more than his theology or his politics, the six hundred years which separate his times from ours. The year 1300 (the year of his vision) had been proclaimed by Pope Boniface VIII a Jubilee Year, and Rome was consequently crowded with pilgrims. For the better avoidance of congestion, the authorities (whose organization seems to have been remarkably efficient) adopted a rule of the road on the Bridge of Castello Sant' Angelo, so-called from the castle which stood at one end of it. The "Mount" at the other end was either the Janiculum or Monte Giordano. It will be noticed that in the First Bowge the rule is "keep to the right", as it is on the Continent to-day.

ll. 49–50: *Venedico Caccianemico*: a Bolognese Guelf. Ghisola was his own sister, and the Marchese was Obizzo d' Este (Canto XII. 111).

l. 51: *what wormwood*: lit.: "what has got thee into such a pickle (*pungenti salse*)?" The word *salse* means "*sauce*"; but it was also the name of a place near Bologna where criminals were flogged and executed, so that Dante's sauce is punning as well as pungent. I have done my best to supply a parallel allusion of a native and contemporary kind.

l. 57: *however they tell the ugly tale*: Presumably other, whitewashing, versions of the story, less disagreeable to the feelings of the powerful d' Este family, had been assiduously put about.

l. 60: "*yep*" (sipa) *for* "*yes*" (sì): an allusion to the Bolognese dialect. The Savena and Reno are rivers running west and east of Bologna.

l. 63: *the known witness of our covetous mind*: The Bolognese seem to have had a reputation for venality.

ll. 67 sqq.: *retraced my way*, etc.: The poets had turned left on entering Malbowges and walked along the edge of Bowge i. Then Dante retraced his steps to go after Caccianemico. Now he returns to where Virgil is waiting for him, and they continue their original course till they come to where the first rock-spur runs across their path at right angles and forms a bridge over the bowge. To cross the bridge they have to *climb* on to this spur and turn right so as to walk *along* it till they are over the spot where the rock is tunnelled out to let the bowge pass below it. From this, the crest of the arch, they look down on the sinners passing below, as one would watch trains from the middle of a railway bridge (see illustration, p. 415). Once this procedure has been clearly visualized, the reader will have very little trouble with the geography of Malbowges.

l. 86: *Jason*: the Greek hero who led the Argonauts to fetch the Golden Fleece from the hands of Aietes, king of Colchis. He was helped by the king's daughter, Medea, whom he persuaded to accompany him home to Iolcus. He married her, but afterwards deserted her for Creusa.

l. 88: *Lemnos*: When the women of Lemnos killed all the men in the island because they had brought home some Thracian concubines, Hypsipyle, the daughter of King Thosa, saved her father by a ruse (l. 93). On their way to Colchis, the Argonauts landed at Lemnos and Jason seduced Hypsipyle.

ll. 100–101: *the narrow ridge*, etc.: The spur runs straight on, forming bridges over all the bowges in succession. (See map, p. 410.)

l. 122: *Alessio Interminei*: Little is known of him, except that he was a member of a White Guelf family, and was notorious for his oily manners.

l. 133: *Thaïs*: The fulsome reply here quoted really belongs, not to the historical Thaïs, the Athenian courtesan, but to a character in Terence's play, *Eunuchus*, of the same name and profession. It is mentioned by Cicero, and Dante presumably took it from him, under the impression that it was historical. Note that Thaïs is not here because she is personally a harlot; the sin which has plunged her far below the Lustful, and even below the traffickers in flesh, is the prostitution of words – the medium of *intellectual* intercourse.

CANTO XIX

THE STORY. *In the Third Bowge of Malbowges, Dante sees the Simoniacs, plunged head-downwards in holes of the rock, with flames playing upon their feet. He talks to the shade of Pope Nicholas III, who prophesies that two of his successors will come to the same bad end as himself. Dante rebukes the avarice of the Papacy.*

O Simon Magus! O disciples of his!
   Miserable pimps and hucksters, that have sold
   The things of God, troth-plight to righteousness,

4 Into adultery for silver and gold;
   For you the trump must sound now – you are come
   To the bag: the third bowge has you in its hold.

7 Already we'd mounted over the next tomb,
   Scaling the cliff until we reached that part
   Whence a dropped line would hit the centre plumb.

10 O most high Wisdom, how exact an art
   Thou showest in heaven and earth and hell's profound;
   How just thy judgments, righteous as thou art!

13 I saw the gulley, both its banks and ground,
   Thickset with holes, all of the selfsame size,
   Pierced through the livid stone; and each was round,

16 Seeming nor more nor less wide to mine eyes
   Than those in my own beautiful St John,
   Made for the priests to stand in, to baptize;

19 Whereof, not many years back, I broke up one,
   To save a stifling youngster jammed in it;
   And by these presents be the true facts known.

22 From each hole's mouth stuck out a sinner's feet
   And legs up to the calf; but all the main
   Part of the body was hid within the pit.

25 The soles of them were all on fire, whence pain
   Made their joints quiver and thrash with such strong throes,
   They'd have snapped withies and hempen ropes in twain.

28 And as on oily matter the flame flows
   On the outer surface only, in lambent flashes,
   So did it here, flickering from heels to toes.

31 "Master, who is that writhing wretch, who lashes
   Out harder than all the rest of his company,"
   Said I, "and whom a ruddier fire washes?"

34 "If thou wouldst have me carry thee down," said he,
   "By the lower bank, his own lips shall afford
   News of his guilt, and make him known to thee."

37 "Thy pleasure is my choice; for thou art lord,"
   Said I, "and knowest I swerve not from thy will;
   Yea, knowest my heart, although I speak no word."

40 So to the fourth brink, and from thence downhill,
   Turning to the left, we clambered; and thus passed
   To the narrow and perforate bottom, my dear lord still

43 Loosing me not from his side, until at last
   He brought me close to the cleft, where he who made
   Such woeful play with his shanks was locked up fast.

46 "Oh thou, whoever thou art, unhappy shade,
   Heels over head thus planted like a stake,
   Speak if thou canst." This opening I essayed

49 And stood there like the friar who leans to take
   Confession from the treacherous murderer
   Quick-buried, who calls him back for respite's sake.

52 He cried aloud: "Already standing there?
   Art standing there already, Boniface?
   Why then, the writ has lied by many a year.

55 What! so soon sated with the gilded brass
   That nerved thee to betray and then to rape
   The Fairest among Women that ever was?"

58 Then I became like those who stand agape,
   Hearing remarks which seem to make no sense,
   Blank of retort for what seems jeer and jape.

61 But Virgil now broke in: "Tell him at once:
   'I am not who thou think'st, I am not he'";
   So I made answer in obedience.

64 At this the soul wrenched his feet furiously,
   Almost to spraining; then he sighed, and wept,
   Saying: "Why then, what dost thou ask of me?

67 Art so concerned to know my name, thou'st leapt
   These barriers just for that? Then truly know
   That the Great Mantle once my shoulders wrapped.

70 Son of the Bear was I, and thirsted so
   To advance the ursine litter that I pouched
   Coin up above, and pouched myself below.

73 Dragged down beneath my head lie others couched,
   My predecessors who simonized before,
   Now in the deep rock-fissures cowering crouched.

76 I too shall fall down thither and make one more
   When he shall come to stand here in my stead
   Whom my first sudden question took thee for.

79 But already have I been planted in this bed
   Longer with baked feet and thus topsy-turvy
   Than he shall stand flame-footed on his head;

82 For after him from the west comes one to serve ye
   With uglier acts, a lawless Shepherd indeed,
   Who'll cover us both – fit end for soul so scurvy;

85 He'll be another Jason, as we read
    The tale in Maccabees; as that controlled
    His king, so this shall bend France like a reed."

88 I know not whether I was here too bold,
    But in this strain my answer flowed out free:
    "Nay, tell me now how great a treasure of gold

91 Our Lord required of Peter, ere that He
    Committed the great Keys into his hand;
    Certes He nothing asked save 'Follow Me.'

94 Nor Peter nor the others made demand
    Of silver or gold when, in the lost soul's room,
    They chose Matthias to complete their band.

97 Then bide thou there; thou hast deserved thy doom;
    Do thou keep well those riches foully gained
    That against Charles made thee so venturesome.

100 And were it not that I am still constrained
    By veneration for the most high Keys
    Thou barest in glad life, I had not refrained

103 My tongue from yet more grievous words than these;
    Your avarice saddens the world, trampling on worth,
    Exalting the workers of iniquities.

106 Pastors like you the Evangelist shewed forth,
    Seeing her that sitteth on the floods committing
    Fornication with the kings of the earth;

109 Her, the seven-headed born, whose unremitting
    Witness uplifted in her ten horns thundered,
    While she yet pleased her Spouse with virtues fitting.

112 You deify silver and gold; how are you sundered
    In any fashion from the idolater,
    Save that he serves one god and you an hundred?

115 Ah, Constantine! what ills were gendered there –
    No, not from thy conversion, but the dower
    The first rich Pope received from thee as heir!"

118 While I thus chanted to him, such a sour
    Rage bit him – or perhaps his conscience stirred –
    He writhed and jerked his feet with all his power.

121 I think my guide approved of what he heard –
    I think so, since he patiently attended
    With a pleased smile to each outspoken word;

124 And after took me in both arms extended,
    And, when he had clasped me close upon his breast,
    Climbed back by the same road he had descended,

127 Nor wearied of the load that he embraced
    Till he had borne me to the arch's crown
    Linking the fourth and fifth banks; on that crest

130 He set at length his burden softly down,
    Soft on the steep, rough crag where even a goat
    Would find the way hard going; here was thrown

133 Open the view of yet another moat.

THE IMAGES. *The Simoniacs.* Simony is the sin of trafficking in holy things, e.g. the sale of sacraments or ecclesiastical offices. The sinners who thus made money for themselves out of what belongs to God are "pouched" in fiery pockets in the rock, head-downwards, because they reversed the proper order of things and subordinated the heavenly to the earthly. The image here is

ecclesiastical: we need not, however, suppose that, *allegorically*, the traffic in holy things is confined to medieval people or even to modern clergymen. A mercenary marriage, for example, is also the sale of a sacrament.

NOTES. l. 1: *Simon Magus*: after whom the sin of Simony is named (*Acts* viii. 9–24).

l. 17: *my own beautiful St John*: The Church of St John Baptist at Florence, where Dante himself was baptized, and of which he always thinks, in his exile, with homesick affection (cf. *Para.* xvi. 25; xxv. 5). The font in the Baptistery was surrounded by holes in which the officiating priests stood, so as not to be jostled by the crowd on days when a great number of babies were being baptized at once. (There is a similar font to this day at Pisa: see sketch, p. 415.) A small boy who was playing round the font one day got jammed in one of these holes, and was extricated by Dante, who took the responsibility of breaking down the marble surround. A garbled account of this story was apparently circulated, in which Dante no doubt figured as a sacrilegious destroyer of Church property – hence his determination to put the facts on record.

l. 34: *if thou wouldst have me carry thee down*: In this bowge (as also in Bowge x) Dante is taken down on to the floor of the ditch in order to speak to the sinners. The banks are too steep for him to descend in his mortal body unassisted, so Virgil carries him. They go right over the bridge first, and then down on the *inner* and *lower* side of the bowge, which (as Dante explains in Canto XXIII) is shorter and less steep than the upper (see sketch, p. 415).

l. 46: *whoever thou art*: The shade is Nicholas III, Pope 1277–80.

l. 50: *the treacherous murderer*: By Florentine law, assassins were executed by being planted head-downwards in a hole, which was then filled up. Dante likens his own attitude to that of the attendant priest, stooping down to hear the wretch's last confession – prolonged, to postpone the fatal moment as long as possible.

l. 53: *Boniface*: The shade thinks he is being addressed by Pope Boniface VIII. There appears to have been only one hole allotted to popes, each of whom remained with his burning feet protruding till his successor arrived to thrust him down lower and take his place.

l. 54: *the writ has lied*: Nicholas, like the other damned souls, can foresee the distant future, and, knowing that Boniface is not due to die till 1303, is amazed to find him (as he supposes) there already.

l. 57: *the Fairest among Women*: i.e. the Church, the Bride of God, identified with the "Spouse of Lebanon" (*Song of Songs*, i. 8, etc.).

l. 69: *the Great Mantle*: i.e. the Papal Mantle.

l. 70: *son of the Bear*: Nicholas was one of the Orsini family – *orsa* is the Italian for "bear" – hence the pun on the "ursine" litter.

l. 83: *a lawless Shepherd*: Pope Clement V, who came from Gascony (the West). Nicholas will hold the uppermost place for twenty-three years (1280–1303), but Boniface only for eleven (from his death in 1303 to that of Clement in 1314).

l. 85: *Jason*: See 2 *Maccabees* iv. 7 *sqq.* He bribed Antiochus Epiphanes to make him High Priest and to connive at pagan practices; similarly Clement V will rise to the papacy by the influence of Philip the Fair of France.

l. 89: *in this strain* (lit.: metre): Dante is now about to speak (as in Canto XVI) in his own character of prophetic poet, and so uses this word, and again the word "chanted" (l. 118), to mark the difference between his private and his prophetic utterance.

ll. 92–3: *the great Keys ... follow Me*: Matthew iv. 19; John xxi. 19.

ll. 94–6: *nor Peter nor the others, etc.*: when the Apostles chose Matthias to fill the place of Judas (*Acts* i. 13–26).

ll. 98–9: *those riches foully gained*: Having been thwarted in his ambitious scheme to marry his niece to Charles of Anjou, king of Sicily, Nicholas joined a conspiracy against Charles, which eventually resulted in the notorious massacre known as the Sicilian Vespers.

ll. 106 *sqq.*: *the Evangelist, etc.*: see *Revelation* xvii: The figure here is of the Church corrupted by avarice: the "seven heads" and "ten horns" are usually interpreted as signifying the Seven Sacraments and the Ten Commandments. (The attribution of the seven heads to the Woman, instead of to the Beast she sits on, is probably due to a misreading of the Vulgate.)

l. 115: *Constantine*: The allusion is to the so-called "Donation of Constantine", by which the first Christian Emperor was alleged to have transferred to the Papal See his temporal sovereignty over Italy. The document is undoubtedly a forgery; it is, however, true that it was Constantine's adoption of Christianity as the official Imperial religion which made it possible for the Church to make those claims to temporal power which led, in Dante's opinion, to so many political and ecclesiastical evils.

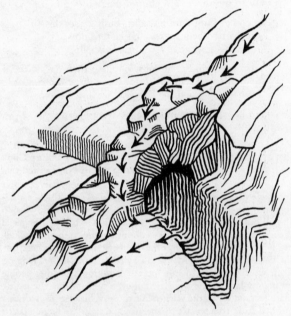

Bridge over Bowge iii, showing path taken by the poets (Canto XIX. 34 sqq. and note)

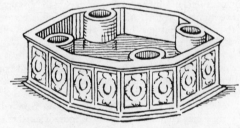

Font in the Baptistery at Pisa, showing the "holes" made for the priests to stand in (Canto XIX. 17 sqq. and note)

CANTO XX

THE STORY. *In the Fourth Bowge of the Eighth Circle Dante sees the Sorcerers, whose heads are twisted so that they can only look behind them, and who are therefore compelled to walk backwards. Virgil tells him about the origin of Mantua. The moon is setting as the Poets leave the bowge.*

New punishments behoves me sing in this
Twentieth canto of my first canticle,
Which tells of spirits sunk in the Abyss.

4 I now stood ready to observe the full
Extent of the new chasm thus laid bare,
Drenched as it was in tears most miserable.

7 Through the round vale I saw folk drawing near,
Weeping and silent, and at such slow pace
As Litany processions keep, up here,

10 And presently, when I had dropped my gaze
Lower than the head, I saw them strangely wried
'Twixt collar-bone and chin, so that the face

13 Of each was turned towards his own backside,
And backwards must they needs creep with their feet,
All power of looking forward being denied.

16 Perhaps some kind of paralytic fit
Could twist men so – such cases may have been;
I never saw it, nor can I credit it;

19 And, Reader, so God give thee grace to glean
Profit of my book, think if I could be left
Dry-eyed, when close before me I had seen

22 Our image so distorted, so bereft
Of dignity, that their eyes' brimming pools
Spilled down to bathe the buttocks at the cleft.

25 Truly I wept, leaned on the pinnacles
Of the hard rock; until my guide said, "Why!
And art thou too like all the other fools?

28 Here pity, or here piety, must die
If the other lives; who's wickeder than one
That's agonized by God's high equity?

31 Lift up, lift up thy head, and look upon
Him for whom once the earth gaped wide, before
The Thebans' eyes: 'Whither wilt thou begone,

34 Amphiaraüs? Why leavest thou the war?'
They cried; but he rushed down, and never stayed
Till he reached Minos, that o'er such hath power.

37 See how he makes a breast of's shoulder-blade!
Because he tried to see too far ahead,
He now looks backward and goes retrograde.

40 And lo you there Tiresias, who shed
His proper shape and altered every limb,
Changing his manhood for a womanhead,

43 So that he needs must smite the second time
His wand upon the twin and tangled snakes
To get his cock-feathers restored to him.

46 Aruns behind his breast back-forward makes;
In Luna's mountains, at whose foot the knave
Who dwells down in Carrara hoes and rakes,

49 He 'mid the white bright marbles had his cave;
There lived, and there looked out, with nought to screen
His view of starry heaven and ocean wave.

52 And she that veils her breasts, by thee unseen,
With her loose locks, and, viewed from where we stand,
Has on the far side all her hairy skin

55 Was Manto, she that searched through many a land
Ere settling in my birthplace; that's a tale
I'd like to tell – brief patience, then, command.

58 After her father passed beyond life's pale,
      When Bacchus' city lay in bondage thralled,
      Long years she wandered up hill and down dale.

61 High in fair Italy, where Almayn's walled
      By the Alps above the Tyrol, lies and dreams
      At the mountain's foot a lake, Benaco called;

64 For the water here of over a thousand streams,
      Meseems, that lave Mount Apennine, running apace
      'Twixt Garda and Val Camonica, spreads and brims

67 To a mere; and there in the midst of it lies a place
      That the bishop of Verona, and those of Trent
      And Brescia, if they passed that way, might bless.

70 Peschiera sits at the circling shore's descent,
      'Gainst Bergamese and Brescians built for cover,
      A goodly keep; there all the effluent

73 Benaco's bosom cannot hold, spills over,
      Slipping and lipping down, and sliding so
      Through verdant meads, a river and a rover –

76 Benaco called no more, but Mincio,
      From where the water first sets head to run,
      Down to Governo, where it joins the Po.

79 It finds a level, ere half its course is done,
      And there stagnates and spreads to a marshy fen,
      Rank and unwholesome in the summer sun.

82 Passing that road, the cruel witch-maiden
      Found in the marsh firm tracts of land, which lay
      Untilled and uninhabited of men;

85 There, shunning human contact, did she stay
      With her familiar household; there she plied
      Her arts; there lived; there left her empty clay.

88 After, the scattered folk from far and wide
      Drew to the spot, which lay defensibly,
      Being girded by the swamp on every side.

91 O'er those dead bones they built their city, to be
      For her sake named that chose the place out thus,
      Mantua, with no further augury.

94 Far more than now it once was populous,
      Ere Casalodi's folly fell to the sword
      Of Pinamonte, who was treacherous.

97 I charge thee then, if stories go abroad,
      Other than this, of how my city grew,
      Let no such lying tales the truth defraud."

100 "Master, for me thy teaching is so true
       And so compels belief, all other tales,"
       Said I, "were dust and ash compared thereto.

103 But tell me of this great crowd that yonder trails,
       If any worthy of note be now in sight;
       My mind harks back to that before all else."

106 He answered: "He whose chin-beard shows so white
       On his brown shoulders was a memorable
       Augur in Greece, what time the land was quite

109 Emptied of males, so that you'd scarce be able
       To find a cradling boy; he set the time,
       With Calchas, for the cutting of the first cable;

112 Eurypylus his name; and my sublime
       Tragedy sings him somewhere – thou'lt recall
       The place, that hast by heart the whole long rhyme.

115 That other there, who looks so lean and small
       In the flanks, was Michael Scott, who verily
       Knew every trick of the art magical.

118 Lo! Guy Bonatti; lo! Asdente – he
       May well wish now that he had stuck to his last,
       But he repents too late; and yonder see

121 The witch-wives, miserable women who cast
       Needle and spindle and shuttle away for skill
       With mommets and philtres; there they all go past.

124 But come! Cain with his thorn-bush strides the sill
       Of the two hemispheres; his lantern now
       Already dips to the wave below Seville;

127 And yesternight the moon was full, as thou
       Shouldst well remember, for throughout thy stay
       In the deep wood she harmed thee not, I trow."

130 Thus he; and while he spake we went our way.

THE IMAGES. *The Sorcerers.* The primary image of sorcery here is that of the fortune-tellers, who, having attempted to usurp God's prerogative by prying into the future, are now so twisted that eyes and feet face in opposite directions. More generally, there is an image of the twisted nature of all magical art, which is a deformation of knowledge, and especially of the psychic powers, to an end outside the unity of the creation in God. It is in especial the misuse of knowledge so as to dominate environment (including not only material things but the personalities of others) for the benefit of the ego. Magic to-day takes many forms, ranging from actual Satanism to attempts at "conditioning" other people by manipulating their psyches; but even when it uses the legitimate techniques of the scientist or the psychiatrist, it is distinguished from true science by the "twisted sight", which looks to self instead of to God for the source and direction of its power.

NOTES. l. 22: *our image so distorted*: "Dante weeps, not now for any personal discovery in Hell, but from sheer misery at the physical contortion of the human form. ... All is gone awry; all is perverted – and so much so that his pity has here no place." (Charles Williams: *The Figure of Beatrice*, p. 136.)

l. 28: *here pity, or here piety, must die* (lit.: "Here *pietà* lives when it is wholly dead"): the word *pietà* means both "pity" and "piety"; I have had to expand Dante's epigrammatic phrase to give the full force of the equivoque.

ll. 29–30: *who's wickeder*, etc.: These two lines, again, have a double significance: they may be rendered: "Who is more wicked than (the sinner) who is (here) tormented by God's judgment?" or "Who is more wicked than one who is tormented by (i.e. passionately protests against) God's judgment (as here exhibited)?" I have no doubt that *both* meanings are intended. Pity and piety are here mutually exclusive: it is necessary to acquiesce in judgment if one is not to become (by sympathy) partaker in the sin.

The rebuke which Dante here puts into Virgil's mouth may have been suggested by passages in the fourth-century *Apocalypse of Paul*: "And I wept and said: Woe unto men! woe unto the sinners! ... And the angel answered and said unto me: Wherefore weepest thou? Art thou more merciful than the Lord God which is blessed for ever, who hath established the judgment and left every man of his own will to choose good and evil and to do as pleaseth him?" (M. R. James: *Apocryphal New Testament*, p. 546; and see also p. 543.)

l. 34: *Amphiaraüs*: one of the "Seven against Thebes". Having foreseen his own death, he tried to escape taking part in the war; but his wife Eriphyle betrayed him, and while fleeing from the pursuit of Polynices, he was swallowed up by an earthquake. (See Statius: *Thebaïd* viii. 147 *sqq.*)

l. 40: *Tiresias*: a Theban prophet. In his youth he found a pair of snakes twined together and struck them with his stick to separate them: whereupon he found himself changed into a woman, and so remained for seven years, until, having similarly separated another pair of snakes, he regained his manhood. (See Ovid: *Metam.* iii.)

l. 46: *Aruns*: an Etruscan augur (see Lucan: *Pharsalia* i. 584–8). Luna (Luni), near the mouth of the Macra, is called by Pliny the first city in Etruria. The mountains of Carrara, above Luna, are famous for their white marble.

l. 55: *Manto*: the daughter of Tiresias. The founding of Mantua by Manto is mentioned in *Aeneid* x. 198–200.

l. 59: *Bacchus' city*: Thebes, the legendary birthplace of Bacchus.

l. 61: *Almayn*: Germany.

l. 63: *Benaco*: now called Lake Garda.

l. 65: *Mount Apennine*: not the Apennine range, but a single mountain. (See map, p.408.)

l. 68: *the bishop of Verona … Trent and Brescia*: the three dioceses met on an island in the lake.

l. 95: *Casalodi*: In 1272 the Brescian counts of Casalodi who were Guelfs, seized Mantua. Their rule was greatly resented; and Alberto di Casalodi foolishly let himself be persuaded by Pinamonte dei Buonaccorsi, a Mantuan, to appease the people by banishing all the unpopular nobles of his party. As soon as he had done so, Pinamonte put himself at the head of the citizens, and drove out the Casalodi with great slaughter.

l. 109: *emptied of males*: i.e. when all the Greeks had departed to the siege of Troy. Eurypylus is associated with Calchas in *Aen.* ii. 110 *sqq.* (See Glossary: "Eurypylus".)

l. 116: *Michael Scott*: the famous wizard of Balwearie mentioned in Scott's *Lay of the Last Minstrel*.

l. 118: *Bonatti … Asdente*: Bonatti of Forlì was an astrologer; Asdente, a shoemaker of Parma, who set up as a soothsayer.

l. 123: *mommets and philtres*: waxen images and magic potions made of herbs. Here Dante touches on magical arts even more dangerous than soothsaying; for the philtres were used to obtain power over the wills of others, and the waxen images were pierced with nails or melted before the fire to bring about the death of the victim.

l. 124: *Cain with his thorn-bush*: i.e. the Man in the Moon (cf. Shakespeare: *M.N.D.* iii. 1; v. 1, where Moon appears with a lantern and a thorn-bush). The Moon is now setting; i.e. it is about 6.52 A.M. on Saturday.

CANTO XXI

THE STORY. *In the Fifth Bowge, Barrators, who made money by trafficking in public offices, are plunged in Boiling Pitch, guarded by demons with sharp hooks. Virgil crosses the bridge and goes down to parley with the demons. Belzecue, the chief demon, says that the spur of rock which the Poets have been following was broken by an earthquake (at the moment of Christ's entry into Hell) and no longer bridges the Sixth Bowge; but he will give them an escort of ten demons to "see them safe as far as the bridge which is still unbroken". In this disagreeable company, Virgil and Dante set off along the lower brink of the Bowge.*

And so we passed along from bridge to bridge,
  With other talk, whereof my Comedy
  Cares not to tell, until we topped the ridge;

4 And there we stayed our steps awhile, to see
  Malbowges' next ravine, and wailings all
  Vain: and most marvellous dark it seemed to be.

7 For as at Venice, in the Arsenal
  In winter-time, they boil the gummy pitch
  To caulk such ships as need an overhaul,

10 Now that they cannot sail – instead of which
  One builds him a new boat, one toils to plug
  Seams strained by many a voyage, others stitch

13 Canvas to patch a tattered jib or lug,
  Hammer at the prow, hammer at the stern, or twine
  Ropes, or shave oars, refit and make all snug –

16 So, not by fire, but by the art divine,
  A thick pitch boiled down there, spattering the brink
  With viscous glue; I saw this, but therein

19 Nothing; only great bubbles black as ink
  Would rise and burst there; or the seething tide
  Heave up all over, and settle again, and sink.

22 And while I stood intent to gaze, my guide,
  Suddenly crying to me, "Look out! look out!"
  Caught me where I stood, and pulled me to his side.

25 O then I turned, as one who turns about,
  Longing to see the thing he has to shun,
  Dares not, and dares, and, dashed with hideous doubt,

28 Casts a look back and still goes fleeing on;
  And there behind us I beheld a grim
  Black fiend come over the rock-ridge at a run.

31 Wow! what a grisly look he had on him!
  How fierce his rush! And, skimming with spread wing,
  How swift of foot he seemed! how light of limb!

34 On high-hunched shoulders he was carrying
  A wretched sinner, hoist by haunch and hip,
  Clutching each ankle by the sinew-string.

37 "Bridge ho!" he bawled, "Our own Hellrakership!
  Here's an alderman of St Zita's coming down;
  Go souse him, while I make another trip

40 For more; they're barrators all in that good town –
  Except Bonturo, hey? – I've packed it stiff
  With fellows who'd swear black's white for half-a-crown."

43 He tossed him in, and over the flinty cliff
  Wheeled off; and never did mastiff run so hot
  And hard on the trail, unleashed to follow a thief.

46 Down bobbed the sinner, then up in a writhing knot;
  But the fiends beneath the archway yelled as he rose up:
  "No Sacred Face will help thee here! it's not

49 A Serchio bathing-party! Now then, toes up
  And dive!'Ware hooks! To save thyself a jabbing,
  Stay in the pitch, nor dare to poke thy nose up!"

52 Then, with a hundred prongs clawing and stabbing:
  "Go cut thy capers! Try down there to do
  Subsurface deals and secret money-grabbing!"

55 Just so, cooks make their scullions prod the stew
  With forks, to thrust the flesh well down within
  The cauldron, lest it float above the brew.

58   Then the good master: "Better not be seen,"
         Said he; "so crouch well down in some embrasure
         Behind a crag, to serve thee for a screen;

61   And whatsoever outrage or displeasure
         They do to me, fear nothing; I have faced
         Frays of this sort before, and have their measure."

64   He passed the bridgehead then; but when he placed
         His foot on the sixth bank, good need had he
         Of a bold front; for with such furious haste

67   And concentrated venom of savagery
         As dogs rush out upon some harmless tramp
         Who stops, alarmed, to falter out his plea,

70   Out dashed the demons lurking under the ramp,
         Each flourishing in his face a hideous hook;
         But he: "Hands off! ere grappling-iron or cramp

73   Touch me, send one to hear me speak; then look
         You take good counsel, before any of you
         Try to dispose of me by hook or crook!"

76   This checked them; and they cried: "Send Belzecue!"
         And one moved forward, snarling as he went:
         "What good does he imagine this will do?"

79   "Dost thou think, Belzecue, that I had bent
         My footsteps thus far hither," the master said,
         "Safe against all your harms, were I not sent

82   By will divine, by fates propitious led?
         Let me pass on; 'tis willed in Heaven that I
         Should guide another by this pathway dread."

85   At this the fiend, crestfallen utterly,
         Let fall his grappling-iron at his feet,
         Crying to the rest: "Strike not! he must go by."

88   My guide called up: "Thou, cowering there discreet,
         Hid mousey-mouse among the splintery, cracked
         Crags of the bridge, come down! all's safe for it."

91   I rose and ran to him, and sure I slacked
         Not speed; for the fiends pressed forward, and grave doubt
         Seized me, for fear they might not keep the pact.

94   So I once saw the footmen, who marched out
         Under treaty from Caprona, look and feel
         Nervous, with all their foes ringed round about.

97   I pressed close to my guide from head to heel,
         Cringing, and keeping a sharp eye upon
         Their looks, which were by no means amiable.

100 They lowered their hooks to the ready, and, "Just for fun,"
         Says one, "shall I tickle his rump for him?" "Yes, try it,"
         Says another, "nick him and prick him, boy – go on!"

103 But the other devil, the one that stood in diet
         Still with my escort, turned him instant round,
         Saying: "Now Scaramallion! quiet, quiet!"

106 And then to us: "By this cliff 'twill be found
         Impossible to proceed, for the sixth arch
         Lies at the bottom, shattered to the ground.

109 If you're determined to pursue your march,
         Follow the bank; a span quite free from block
         Or fall, lies handy to reward your search;

112 But this – why, yesterday, five hours by the clock
         From now, 'twas just twelve hundred, sixty and six
         Years since the road was rent by earthquake shock.

115 I'm sending a squad your way, to fork and fix
         Any rash soul who may be taking the air;
         Why not go with them? They will play no tricks.

118 Stand forward, Hacklespur and Hellkin there!"
         He then began, "and Harrowhound as well,
         And your decurion shall be Barbiger;

121 Let Libbicock go too, and Dragonel,
         Guttlehog of the tusks, and Grabbersnitch
         And raving Rubicant and Farfarel

124 Take a good look all round the boiling pitch;
         See these two safe, as far as to the spit
         That runs unbroken on from ditch to ditch."

127 "Sir, I don't like the looks of this one bit,"
         Said I; "no escort, please; let's go alone,
         If thou know'st how – for I've no stomach to it!

130 Where is thy wonted caution? Ugh! they frown,
         They grind their teeth – dost thou not see them? Lo,
         How they threat mischief, with their brows drawn down!"

133 But he: "I'd have thee firmer-minded; no,
         Let them go grind and gnash their teeth to suit
         Their mood; 'tis the broiled souls they glare at so."

136 They by the left bank wheeling chose their route;
         But first in signal to their captain each
         Thrust out his tongue; and, taking the salute,

139 He promptly made a bugle of his breech.

THE IMAGES. *The Barrators and the Pitch.* The Barrators are to the
City what the Simoniacs are to the Church: they make profit out
of the trust reposed in them by the community; and what they
sell is justice. As the Simoniacs are imbedded in the burning rock,
so these are plunged beneath the black and boiling stream, for
their dealings were secret. Money stuck to their fingers: so now
the defilement of the pitch sticks fast to them.

NOTES. *Cantos XXI and XXII.* The mood of these two cantos – a mixture of savage satire and tearing high spirits – is unlike anything else
in the *Comedy*, and is a little disconcerting to the more solemn-minded
of Dante's admirers. Artistically, this grim burlesque is of great value
as an interlude in the ever-deepening descent from horror to horror;
but Dante had also personal reasons for letting his pen rip at this point,
since an accusation of barratry was the pretext upon which he was
banished from Florence. (I have translated rather more freely here
than elsewhere, in order to keep up the pace of the original.)

l. 7: *at Venice, in the Arsenal:* Venice, in the Middle Ages, was a
great sea-power, and the old Arsenal, built in 1104, was one of the
most important shipyards in Europe.

l. 35: *a wretched sinner:* One old commentator identifies him as an
alderman called Martino Bottaio, who died in 1300.

l. 37: *our own Hellrakership* (lit.: *Malebranche* of our bridge): Dante
calls the demons in this bowge *Malebranche* = Evil Claws, which I
have rendered "Hellrakers".

l. 38: *St Zita's:* i.e. Lucca, whose patron saint was St Zita.

l. 41: *except Bonturo:* This is sarcasm, since Bonturo Dati was
especially notorious for his barratry.

l. 48: *Sacred Face:* an ancient wooden figure of Christ, revered at
Lucca, and invoked in time of need.

l. 49: *Serchio*: a river near Lucca.

l. 65: *the sixth bank*: i.e. the lower bank of the Fifth Bowge, which is also the upper bank of the Sixth.

l. 76: *Belzecue*: In Italian, *Malacoda* = Evil Tail. The names of the demons in the Fifth Bowge are thought by some to contain allusions to various Florentine officials who were Dante's enemies; but even if they do, the average English reader cannot get much fun out of it at this time of day. I have therefore englished most of the names for the greater convenience of rhyme and metre.

l. 82: *by will divine, by fates propitious*: Notice once again the double terminology, as in Canto IX. 94–7 and Canto XIV. 52 and 70.

l. 88: *cowering there*: Dante's comic terror in this bowge is, characteristically, a double-edged gibe at himself and his accusers.

l. 95: *Caprona*: This Pisan fortress was taken by the Tuscan Guelfs in 1289, and Dante, apparently, took part in the operation.

ll. 112–14: *five hours by the clock from now*, etc.: The earthquake is that which followed the Crucifixion and is mentioned by Virgil as having heralded Christ's entry into Hell and caused the landslide on the cliff between the Sixth and Seventh Circles (Canto XII. 34–45). According to the Synoptists, it took place at the ninth hour (3 P.M.); this would make the conversation with Belzecue take place five hours earlier, i.e. at 10 A.M.

l. 113: *twelve hundred, sixty and six*: The Crucifixion is reckoned as having taken place A.D. 34.

l. 125–6: *safe, as far as to the spit that runs unbroken*: As will be seen later (Canto XXIII), the safe-conduct is less valuable than it might appear, and the malicious grimaces of the demons show that they have taken these instructions in the spirit in which they were meant.

CANTO XXII

THE STORY. *As the party proceeds along the bank of the bowge, the devils fork a Barrator up out of the pitch, who tells the Poets who he is and mentions the names of some of his fellow-sinners. By a trick he eludes the devils who are preparing to tear him to pieces; whereupon his captors quarrel among themselves and two of them fall into the pitch.*

I have seen horsemen moving camp, and beating
  The muster and assault, seen troops advancing,
  And sometimes with uncommon haste retreating,

4 Seen forays in your land, and coursers prancing,
  O Aretines! and I've beheld some grandish
  Tilts run and tourneys fought, with banners dancing,

7 And fife and drum, and signal-flares a-brandish
  From towers, and cars with tintinnabulation
  Of bells, and things both native and outlandish;

10 But to so strange a trumpet's proclamation
  I ne'er saw move or infantry or cavalry,
  Or ship by sea-mark or by constellation.

13 Well, off we started with that bunch of devilry;
  Queer company – but there! "with saints at church,
  And at the inn with roisterers and revelry".

16 Meanwhile, my eyes were wholly bent to search
  The pitch, to learn the custom of that moat
  And those who wallowed in the scald and smirch.

19 And very like the dolphins, when they float
  Hump-backed, to warn poor seamen of the heightening
  Storm, that they may prepare to save the boat,

22 So now and then, to get a little slightening
  Of pain, some miserable wretch would hulk
  His back up, and pop down again like lightning.

25 Others lay round about like frogs, that skulk
  At the stream's edge, just noses out of shelter,
  The water hiding all their limbs and bulk, –

28 Till Barbiger arrived; then, in a welter
  Of fear, with unanimity quite clannish,
  They shot into the hot-pot helter-skelter.

31 I saw – and from my memory cannot banish
  The horrid thrill – one soul remain a squatter,
  As one frog will at times, when others vanish;

34 And Grabbersnitch, the nearest truant-spotter,
  Hooked him by the clogged hair, and up he came,
  Looking to me exactly like an otter.

37 (I could pick all the fiends out now by name;
  I'd watched while they were chosen, noted how
  They called each other, and made sure of them.)

40 "Claws, claws there, Rubicant! we've got him now!
  Worry him, worry him, flay him high and low!"
  Yelled all the demon-guardians of the slough.

43 "O master, if thou canst, contrive to know
  Who is this wretched criminal," I said,
  "Thus fallen into the clutches of the foe."

46 My guide drew near to him thus hard-bested,
  And asked him whence he came; he said: "Navarre;
  In that same kingdom was I born and bred.

49 My mother placed me servant to a peer,
  For he that got me was a ribald knave,
  A spendthrift of himself and of his gear.

52 Next, I was good King Tibbald's man, and gave
  My mind to jobbery; now, I job no more,
  But foot the bill this hotter side the grave."

55 Here Guttlehog, who, like a savage boar,
  Carried great tushes either side his jaws,
  Let the wretch feel how deep the fangs could score.

58 'Twas cat and mouse – ten cats with cruel claws!
  But Barbiger, with both arms seizing him,
  Cried: "Back! I'll do the grabbing!" In the pause

61 He leered round at my lord, and said with grim
  Relish: "Any further questions? Ask away!
  Quick – before some one tears him limb from limb!"

64 So then my guide: "Name if thou canst, I pray,
  Some Latian rogues among these tarry throngs."
  And he: "But now, I left one such – or, nay,

67 One that to a near-neighbouring isle belongs;
  Would I lay hid beside him still! – I'd mock
  At threatening claws, and ugly tusks, and prongs."

70 "We've stood too much of this!" cried Libbicock,
  And from his arm, making a sudden snatch,
  Ripped off a sinewy gobbet with his hook.

73 Then Dragonel was fain to have a catch
  At the dangling legs; which made their leader spin
  Round with ferocious haste, and looks to match.

76 When they were somewhat calmer, and the din
  Died down, my guide, turning to him who still
  Stared upon his own mangled flesh and skin,

79   Asked promptly: "Who was he, whom in an ill
        Hour thou didst quit, thou sayest, to seek the brink?"
        "'Twas Fra Gomita, the ineffable

82   Scamp of Gallura, corruption's very sink,"
        Said he; "he held his lord's foes in his power,
        And earned their praise – earned it right well, I think;

85   'The golden key,' says he, 'undid the door';
        But all his jobs were jobbed; no petty jobbery
        For him – he was a sovereign barrator.

88   With him's Don Michael Zanche, artist in robbery
        From Logodor'; their tongues, going clack-clack-clack
        About Sardinia, kick up a ceaseless bobbery.

91   O look! that fiend there grinning at me! alack,
        He frightens me! – I've plenty more to tell,
        But sure he'll flay my scalp or skin my back!"

94   Then their huge prefect turned on Farfarel,
        Whose eyes were rolling in the act to pounce,
        Crying: "Hop off, thou filthy bird of hell!"

97   "Are there no souls from other lands or towns,"
        The quivering wretch went on, "you'd like to see?
        Tuscans? or Lombards? I'll get them here at once.

100 Let but the Hellrakers draw back a wee
        Bit from the shore, so that they need not fear
        Reprisals, and for one poor little me

103 I'll fetch up seven, just sitting quietly here
        And whistling, as it is our wont to do
        When one pops out and finds the coast is clear."

106 Harrowhound shook his head and scornful threw
        His snout up: "That's a dirty trick," said he,
        "He's thought of, to get back beneath the brew."

109 "Trickster I am, and what a trick 'twill be,"
        Said he who had every dodge at his command,
        "Luring my neighbours to worse misery!"

112 Here Hellkin got completely out of hand
        And burst out: "If thou stoop to hit the ditch
        I need not gallop after thee by land,

115 I have my wings to soar above the pitch;
        We'll leave the crest and hide behind the bank –
        Are ten heads best, or one? We'll show thee which!"

118 New sport, good Reader! hear this merry prank!
        The silly demons turned their eyes away –
        And he who first held back now led the rank.

121 The Navarrese chose well the time to play;
        He dug his toes in hard, then, quick as thought,
        Dived; and so baulked the sportsmen of their prey.

124 Then all were stung with guilt, and he who taught
        The rest to play the fool was angriest;
        He swooped off to pursue him, shouting: "Caught!"

127 But all in vain; no wings could fly so fast
        As fear; the quarry plunged; the hunter rose,
        Skimming the surface with uplifted breast.

130 Just as the wild-duck, with the falcon close
        Upon her, all of a sudden dives down quick,
        And up he skirrs again, foiled and morose.

133 Hacklespur, who was furious at the trick,
        Went rushing after, hoping very much
        The sinner would escape, that he might pick

136 A quarrel; so when he saw the jobber touch
        Surface and vanish, he turned his claws on his brother-
        Fiend, and they grappled over the ditch in a clutch.

139 But Hellkin was a hawk as good as another
        To fight back tooth and nail; so, scratching and chewing,
        They both dropped down plumb in the boiling smother.

142 The heat at once unlocked them; their undoing
        Came when they tried to rise; they struggled, fluttering
        With helpless wings clogged stiff by the tarry glueing.

145 Barbiger, who with the others stood there spluttering
        With rage, sent four across to the farthermost
        Bank with their draghooks; so the band flew scuttering

148 This side and that, each to some vantage-post
        Whence they could reach their drags to the pair half-strangled
        And baked already beneath the scummy crust;

151 And there we left them, floundering and entangled.

THE IMAGES. *The Tricked and Quarrelling Demons.* Though it may present an appearance of solidarity, Satan's kingdom is divided against itself and cannot stand, for it has no true order, and fear is its only discipline. Moreover, in the long run, the devil is a fool: trickery preys on trickery and cruelty on cruelty.

NOTES. ll. 1 *sqq.*: *I have seen horsemen*, etc.: The Battle of Campaldino (1289) was fought between the Guelfs (headed by Florence) and the Ghibellines (headed by Arezzo). The Florentine forces, among whom Dante was, were thrown into confusion by the first charge of the Aretines; but the Guelfs rallied and eventually defeated the Ghibellines with great slaughter, and the rest of the campaign was fought on Aretine territory.
  l. 6: *tilts run and tourneys fought*: A *tilt* was an encounter between two knights across a barrier; a *tourney* or *tournament* was an "all-in" encounter between equal parties of knights in open field.
  l. 8: *cars with tintinnabulation of bells*: In Dante's time, each Italian city had a car (*carroccio*), or war-chariot. It was gaily painted, drawn by oxen, and furnished with a bell, and served as a rallying-point in battle.
  ll. 19–21: *dolphins*: This common belief about dolphins is mentioned in a popular Italian version of Brunetto Latini's *Thesaurus*, and elsewhere.
  l. 44: *who is this wretched criminal*: Tradition says that this is a certain Spaniard, named Ciampolo, or Gian Polo.
  l. 52: *King Tibbald*: Teobaldo II (Count Thibaut V of Champagne), king of Navarre (1253–70).
  l. 65: *Latian*: a native of Lower Italy. (Dante never uses the word "Italian", but speaks only of Tuscans, Lombards, etc., in the north and Latians in the south.)
  l. 67: *a near-neighbouring isle*: Sardinia.
  l. 81: *Fra Gomita*: Sardinia at that time belonged to Pisa, and Gomita was judge of the province of Gallura, under Nino Visconti of Pisa, who put up with his peculations until he found that he had been bribed to let some prisoners escape, whereupon he had him hanged.
  l. 88: *Michael Zanche*: Vicar of Logodoro under Enzo, king of Sardinia, who was a natural son of Frederick II. About 1290 he was murdered by his son-in-law, Branca d' Oria, whom we shall hear of in Canto XXXIII. 134–47.

CANTO XXIII

THE STORY. *The angry demons pursue the Poets, who are forced to escape by scrambling down the upper bank of Bowge vi. Here they find the Hypocrites, walking in Gilded Cloaks lined with lead. They talk to two Jovial Friars from Bologna, and see the shade of Caiaphas crucified upon the ground.*

Silent, apart, companionless we went,
   One going on before and one behind,
   Like Friars Minor on a journey bent.

4 And Aesop's fable came into my mind
   As I was pondering on the late affray –
   I mean the frog-and-mouse one; for you'll find

6 That if with an attentive mind you lay
   Their heads and tails together, the two things
   Are just as much alike as Yes and Yea.

10 And, as one fancy from another springs
   Sometimes, this started a new train of thought
   Which doubled my first fears and flutterings.

13 I argued thus: "These demons have been brought,
   Through us, to a most mortifying plight –
   Tricked, knocked about, made fools of, set at naught;

16 If rage be added to their natural spite
   They'll come for us, pursuing on our heel
   Like greyhounds on the hare, teeth bared to bite."

19 I kept on looking backward, and could feel
   My hair already bristling on my head;
   "Master," said I, "unless thou canst conceal

22 Thyself and me, I'm very much afraid
   Of the Hellrakers; they're after us; I see
   And imagine it so, I can hear them now," I said.

25 "If I were made of looking-glass," said he,
   "My outward image scarce could mirror thine
   So jump as I mirror thine image inwardly.

28 Even now thy mind came entering into mine,
   Its living likeness both in act and face;
   So to one single purpose we'll combine

31 The two; if on our right-hand side this place
   So slopes that we can manage to descend
   To the next bowge, we'll flee the imagined chase."

34 Thus he resolved. He'd hardly made an end,
   When lo! I saw them, close at hand, and making
   To seize us, swooping on wide wings careened.

37 Then my master caught me up, like a mother, waking
   To the roar and crackle of fire, who sees the flare,
   And snatches her child from the cradle and runs, taking

40 More thought for him than herself, and will not spare
   A moment even so much as to cast a shift
   About her body, but flees naked and bare;

43 And over the flinty ridge of the great rift
   He slithered and slid with his back to the hanging spill
   Of the rock that walls one side of the next cleft.

46 Never yet did water run to the mill
   So swift and sure, where the head-race rushes on
   Through the narrow sluice to hit the floats of the wheel,

49 As down that bank my master went at a run,
   Carrying me off, hugged closely to his breast,
   Truly not like a comrade, but a son.

52 And his foot had scarce touched bottom, when on the crest
   Above us, there they were! But he, at large
   In the other chasm, could set his fears at rest;

55 For that high provident Will which gave them charge
   Over the fifth moat, curbs them with constraint,
   So that they have no power to pass its verge.

58 And now we saw a people decked with paint,
   Who trod their circling way with tear and groan
   And slow, slow steps, seeming subdued and faint.

61 They all wore cloaks, with deep hoods forward thrown
   Over their eyes, and shaped in fashion quite
   Like the great cowls the monks wear at Cologne;

64 Outwardly they were gilded dazzling-bright,
   But all within was lead, and, weighed thereby,
   King Frederick's copes would have seemed feather-light.

67 O weary mantle for eternity!
   Once more we turned to the left, and by their side
   Paced on, intent upon their mournful cry.

70 But crushed 'neath that vast load those sad folk plied
   Such slow feet that abreast of us we found
   Fresh company with every changing stride.

73 Wherefore: "Try now to find some soul renowned
   In name or deed, and as we forward fare,"
   I begged my guide, "pray cast thine eyes around."

76 And, hearing the Tuscan tongue, some one, somewhere
   Behind us cried: "Stay, stay now! slack your speed,
   You two that run so fast through this dark air,

79 And I, maybe, can furnish what you need."
   My guide looked round, and then to me said: "Good!
   Wait here, and then at his own pace proceed."

82 I stopped, and saw two toiling on, who showed,
   By looks, much haste of mind to get beside me,
   Though cumbered by the great load and strait road.

85 But when at length they reached us, then they eyed me
   Askance for a long time before they spoke;
   Then turned to each other, saying, while still they spied me:

88 "That one seems living – his throat moves to the stroke
   Of the breath and the blood; besides, if they are dead,
   What favour exempts them from the heavy cloak?"

91 And then to me: "O Tuscan, strangely led
   To the sad college of hypocrites, do not scorn
   To tell us who thou art," the spirits said.

94 I answered them: "I was bred up and born
   In the great city on Arno's lovely stream,
   And wear the body that I've always worn.

97 But who are you, whose cheeks are seen to teem
   Such distillation of grief? What comfortless
   Garments of guilt upon your shoulders gleam?"

100 And one replied: "Our orange-gilded dress
   Is leaden, and so heavy that its weight
   Wrings out these creakings from the balances.

103   Two Jovial Friars were we; our city-state
        Bologna; Catalano was my name,
        His, Loderingo; we were designate

106   By thine own city, to keep peace and tame
        Faction, as one sole judge is wont to do;
        What peace we kept, Gardingo can proclaim."

109   "Friars," I began, "the miseries that you –"
        But broke off short, seeing one lie crucified
        There on the ground, with three stakes stricken through;

112   Who, when he saw me, writhed himself, and sighed
        Most bitterly in his beard; and seeing me make
        A questioning sign, Friar Catalan replied:

115   "He thou dost gaze on, pierced by the triple stake,
        Counselled the Pharisees 'twas expedient
        One man should suffer for the people's sake.

118   Naked, transverse, barring the road's extent,
        He lies; and all who pass, with all their load
        Must tread him down; such is his punishment.

121   In this same ditch lie stretched in this same mode
        His father-in-law, and all the Sanhedrim
        Whose counsel sowed for the Jews the seed of blood."

124   Then I saw Virgil stand and marvel at him
        Thus racked for ever on the shameful cross
        In the everlasting exile. He to them

127   Turning him, then addressed the Friars thus:
        "May it so please you, if your rule permit,
        To tell us if, on this right side the fosse,

130   Be any gap to take us out of it,
        That we need not compel any of the Black
        Angels to extricate us from this pit."

133   "Nearer than thou hop'st," the Friar answered back,
        "There lies a rock, part of the mighty spur
        That springs from the great wall, and makes a track

136   O'er all the cruel moats save this, for here
        The arch is down; but you could scale the rock,
        Whose ruins are piled from the floor to the barrier."

139   My guide stood with bent head and downward look
        Awhile; then said: "He gave us bad advice,
        Who spears the sinners yonder with his hook."

142   And the Friar: "I heard the devil's iniquities
        Much canvassed at Bologna; among the rest
        'Twas said, he was a liar and father of lies."

145   My guide with raking steps strode off in haste,
        Troubled in his looks, and showing some small heat
        Of anger; so I left those spirits oppressed,

148   Following in the prints of the belovèd feet.

THE IMAGES. *The Leaden Cloaks.* The image of Hypocrisy, present-
ing a brilliant show and weighing like lead so as to make spiritual
progress impossible, scarcely needs interpretation.

Caiaphas. This image lends itself peculiarly well to Dante's fourfold
system of interpretation.   (1) *Literal*: the
punishment of Caiaphas after death; (2) *Allegorical*: the condition
of the Jews in this world, being identified with the Image they
rejected and the suffering they inflicted – "crucified for ever in the
eternal exile"; (3) *Moral*: the condition in this life of the man who

sacrifices his inner truth to expediency (e.g. his true vocation to
money-making, or his true love to a politic alliance), and to
whom the rejected good becomes at once a heaven from which
he is exiled and a rack on which he suffers; (4) *Anagogical*: the
state, here and hereafter, of the soul which rejects God, and which
can know God only as wrath and terror, while at the same time
it suffers the agony of eternal separation from God, who is its only
true good.

NOTES. l. 3: *Friars Minor*: the Franciscans.

l. 4: *Aesop's fable*: A frog offers to carry a mouse across a pond, tied
to its leg. Half-way over, the frog treacherously dives, drowning the
mouse. A hawk swoops down and devours both. The fable is found
in most of the medieval collections attributed to Aesop. In one version
the mouse escapes, and this may have been the one Dante had in mind.
The mouse = Ciampolo; the frog = Hellkin; the hawk = Hacklespur.

l. 9: *Yes and Yea*: In the Italian *mo* and *issa*, two words both meaning
"now".

l. 25: *looking-glass*: lit.: "leaded glass", mirrors being then made
with a backing of lead. Virgil is saying that his own feelings are a
perfect reflection of Dante's, both in face (appearance of alarm) and
act (recoil from danger); so they will combine their fears and form a
common resolution: viz. flight.

l. 31: *on our right-hand side*: They had already crossed the intervening space and were walking along the upper edge of Bowge vi.

l. 54: *the other chasm*: i.e. the Sixth Bowge.

l. 58: *decked with paint*: Some commentators think this means that
the faces of the hypocrites were "made up"; but since this could hardly
have been apparent to Dante at the first glance, because of the deep
hoods they wore, it seems more likely that it refers to the brilliant
colour of their cloaks (l. 64).

l. 63: *at Cologne*: Several old commentators relate a story that the
monks of Cologne once grew so arrogant that they made formal
request to the Pope to be allowed to wear scarlet robes, with silver
girdles and spurs. To punish their pride, the Pope commanded, on
the contrary, that they should wear especially ample robes of very
common material. Some editors for "Cologne" read "Cluny".

l. 66: *King Frederick's copes*: Frederick II was said to have punished
traitors by wrapping them in lead and throwing them into a hot
cauldron.

l. 88: *his throat moves*: We may notice the various ways by which
Dante's living body is distinguished from the apparent bodies of the
shades: in the twilight of Hell his weight sinks Phlegyas' boat "deeper
than her wont" (Canto VIII) and dislodges stones (Canto XII); his
throat moves when he breathes and speaks, as here; a blow from his
foot surprises the souls by its heaviness (Canto XXXII. 90); in Purgatory, where the sun shines, he alone casts a shadow (*Purg.* iii. 16
sqq., etc.).

l. 92: *college of hypocrites*: The word "college" here means only
"company".

l. 95: *the great city on Arno's lovely stream*: i.e. Florence.

l. 103: *Jovial Friars*: the nickname of the *Ordo militiae beatae Mariae*,
a religious order of knights founded in 1261. Its objects were to promote reconciliation, protect widows and poor persons, etc.; but its
rule was so lax that before long it became a scandal and was sup-
pressed.

ll. 105–8: *designate by thine own city*: Catalano de' Malavolti (a Guelf)
and Loderingo di Landolo (a Ghibelline), both from Bologna, were
in 1266 appointed jointly to the office of *podesta* of Florence, in the
hope that they might keep the peace and administer justice impartial-
ly; but all that came of their administration was a particularly savage
anti-Ghibelline rising, in which the palaces of the Uberti, in the
Gardingo, were sacked and burned.

l. 116: *counselled the Pharisees*: John xi. 49, 50.

l. 122: *his father-in-law*: Annas. (John xviii. 13.)

l. 124: *I saw Virgil ... marvel at him*: Virgil had not, of course, seen Caiaphas on his previous journey through Hell (see Canto IX. 19–30), which was made before the time of Christ.

l. 140: *he gave us bad advise*: Belzecue (Canto XXI. 123–6) had bidden the demons see the poets safe "as far as the unbroken bridge", which, he implied, was near at hand. But the next bridge is broken also, and it now dawns on Virgil that no "unbroken bridge" exists, and that the devil was sending them under a worthless safeguard on a fool's errand. (N.B. In the map on p. 410, the poets are shown as having already passed another bridgehead unawares on their way between Bowges v and vi; this liberty being taken to gain a little more room for the lettering.)

CANTO XXIV

THE STORY. *After an arduous climb from the bottom of Bowge vi, the Poets gain the arch of the seventh bridge. They hear voices from below, but it is too dark to see anything, so they cross to the far side and go down. The Seventh Bowge is filled with monstrous reptiles, among whom are the shades of Thieves. A Thief is stung by a serpent, reduced to ashes, and then restored to his former shape. He reveals himself to be Vanni Fucci of Pistoia, tells his story, and predicts the overthrow of the Florentine Whites.*

What time the Sun, in the year's early youth,
   Beneath Aquarius rinses his bright hair,
   And nights begin to dwindle toward the south;

4 When on the ground the hoar-frost copies fair
   Her snow-white sister's image, though her pen,
   Soon losing temper, leaves brief traces there;

7 The hind, no fodder in his empty bin,
   Wakes and looks forth; he sees the countryside
   All white, slaps a despairing thigh, and then

10 Back to his cot; and nowhere can abide,
   Nothing begin, but roams about the place,
   Grieving, poor soul! Once more he peeps outside,

13 And hope revives – the world has changed its face
   In that short time; away, then, to the pasture
   He takes his crook, and drives his lambs to graze.

16 Just so I felt distressed, to see my master
   So much put out; in just so brief a while
   To salve my sore there came the healing plaster;

19 For when we reached the arch's broken pile
   He turned towards me with the look I knew
   First at the mountain's foot – his old, sweet smile.

22 Opening his arms – but seeming first to do
   Some careful planning, and scanning of the rock –
   He seized and lifted me; then, like a true

25 And conscientious workman, who takes stock,
   And thinks things out ahead, expending great
   Pains, he would hoist me over one big block,

28 And when I was up, choose out another straight,
   Saying: "Now climb this spike – now this – take heed
   To test it first; make sure 'twill bear thy weight."

31 No path was that for one in cloak of lead!
   For even we – he weightless, I pushed on –
   From crag to crag made arduous way indeed.

34 Had not the nether of those banks of stone
   Been shorter than the upper – I can't tell
   How he'd have fared, but I should have been done.

37 But since toward the mouth of the central well
   Malbowges' sides form one continuous slope,
   It follows that in each succeeding vale

40 One bank must rise and the other bank must drop;
   And howsoever, we clambered till we got
   To the last jag, level with the barrier-top.

43 My lungs were so pumped out, I just had not
   Breath to go on; nor did I try, but came
   Scramblingly up and sat down on the spot.

46 "Put off this sloth," the master said, "for shame!
   Sitting on feather-pillows, lying reclined
   Beneath the blanket is no way to fame –

49 Fame, without which man's life wastes out of mind,
   Leaving on earth no more memorial
   Than foam in water or smoke upon the wind.

52 Rise up; control thy panting breath, and call
   The soul to aid, that wins in every fight,
   Save the dull flesh should drag it to a fall.

55 More stairs remain to climb – a longer flight;
   Merely to quit that crew suffices not;
   Dost take my meaning? Act, and profit by it."

58 So up I scrambled, making myself out
   Less breathless than I really felt; wherefore:
   "Lead on," said I, "I'm resolute and stout."

61 And on we went, scaling the flinty scaur,
   Which was rugged, narrow, and awkward in the ascent,
   And very much steeper than the one before.

64 Not wishing to seem weak, I spoke as I went;
   Whereon a voice rose from the ditch below,
   Which sounded like a voice that was not meant

67 For speech; what it was saying I do not know,
   Though already I stood on the crown of the bridge across
   The moat; but whoever it was seemed angry; so

70 I craned to see; but the darkness was so gross
   No living eye could pierce its heavy pall.
   "Master," said I, "do please go over the fosse

73 To the other bank and let's descend the wall;
   From hence I hear, but cannot understand,
   And look below, but cannot see at all."

76 "My sole reply," said he, "to that demand
   Is action; when a fit request is made
   Silence and deeds should follow out of hand."

79 So over we went and down, where the bridge's head
   Stooping to the eighth barrier, hits the brink of it,
   And now at last the chasm lay displayed;

82 And the most loathsome welter filled the sink of it –
   A mass of serpents, so diverse and daunting,
   My blood still turns to water when I think of it.

85 Let the great Libyan desert cease from vaunting
   Her cenchrid and chalydra broods, nor boast
   The amphisbenes, pareas and jacules haunting

88   Her sands; she never spawned so vile a host
     Of plagues, nor all the land of Ethiope,
     Nor that which lies along the Red Sea coast.

91   Amid this cruel and repulsive crop
     Of monsters, naked men ran terrified,
     Hopeless of hiding-hole or heliotrope;

94   Their hands were held behind their backs and tied
     With snakes, whose head and tail transfixed the loin,
     Writhing in knots convolved on the hither side.

97   And lo! as one came running near our coign
     Of vantage on the bank, a snake in a flash
     Leapt up and stung him where neck and shoulder join.

100   Never did writer with a single dash
     Of the pen write "o" or "i" so swift as he
     Took fire, and burned, and crumbled away to ash.

103   But as he lay on the ground dispersedly,
     All by itself the dust gathered and stirred
     And grew to its former shape immediately.

106   So wise men say the sole Arabian bird,
     The phoenix, dies and is reborn from fire
     When her five-hundredth year is near expired;

109   Living, nor herb nor grain is food for her,
     Only amomum and dropping incense-gums,
     And her last swathings are of nard and myrrh.

112   As one who falls, nor knows how the fit comes,
     By diabolic power, or oppilation
     That chokes the brain with stupefying fumes,

115   Who, when he rises, stares in consternation
     All round, bewildered by his late hard throes,
     With rolling eyes and anguished suspiration,

118   So seemed that wretched sinner when he rose.
     Stern is thy hand, Divine omnipotence,
     That in thy vengeance rainest down such blows!

121   Then my guide asked him who he was, and whence;
     And he: "From Tuscany I came pelting in
     To this fierce gullet, and no long time since.

124   I loved to live as beasts live and not men,
     Mule that I was! – Vanni Fucci, absolute
     Beast; and Pistoia was my fitting den."

127   I told my guide: "Bid him not budge a foot,
     But say what brought him here; – I've only seen him
     An evil-tempered, bloody-minded brute."

130   The sinner heard; nor did he try to screen him,
     Nor feign, but turned on me his mind and face,
     Showing a dismal shame at work within him.

133   "That thou," said he, "shouldst catch me in this place
     And see me so, torments me worse than leaving
     The other life, and doubles my disgrace.

136   Yet answer thee I must, without deceiving:
     I'm thrust so low, because I stole the treasure
     Of the sacristy; for which fine piece of thieving

139   Others were falsely blamed and put in seizure;
     But lest, if ever thou escape these drear
     Abodes, this picture should afford thee pleasure,

142   I'll tell thee something; prick thine ears and hear:
     Pistoia shall purge out the party Black;
     New men, new laws in Florence shall appear;

145   From Valdimagra Mars shall bring a stack
     Of vapour rolled in clouds turbid as night,
     And with impetuous storm and tempest-wrack

148   Over Piceno's field all shall rage the fight,
     Whence he shall suddenly rend the mists apart
     Striking a blow to stagger every White;

151   And so I tell thee; may it break thy heart."

THE IMAGES. *The Thieves.* Two cantos are devoted to the Thieves, the full nature of whose punishment is not fully developed till we get to Canto xxv. The old commentators point out the likeness between the subtle serpent and the creeping thief; in this canto we can already see how, as in life the thief stole other men's goods, so here he is himself robbed of his very semblance. One must always remember that to the mind of the Middle Ages a man's lawful property was an extension of his personality (see Canto xi. 41, note) – an exterior body, as it were, and, like that body, a sacred trust to be used and not abused, either by himself or by others. This accounts for the severe view which Dante takes of offences against property.

NOTES. ll. 1–3: *the year's early youth*, etc.: The Sun is in Aquarius (the Water-Carrier) from 21 January to 21 February; the year is just passing out of "childhood" into early "youth" – i.e. from winter to spring. As the Sun moves daily higher into the north, the "nights" (the point of the heavens opposed to the sun) begin to pass away southward, and grow shorter.

ll. 5–6: *her pen, soon losing temper*: Hoar-frost melts more quickly than snow.

ll. 34–5: *the nether ... shorter than the upper*: See diagram.

l. 42: *level with the barrier-top*: They have climbed to the top of the lower wall of the bowge, and have still to climb up the side of the spur and reach the arch of the next bridge.

l. 55: *more stairs remain to climb*: primarily, the spur; but Virgil is probably hinting that, even when the whole descent into Hell is accomplished, there remains the steep ascent to Purgatory. To renounce sin is not all: the active work of purgation remains to be done before (if Dante takes his meaning) he can be reunited with Beatrice.

l. 63: *the one before*: i.e. the spur which they had been following from the First Bowge to the Fifth.

ll. 85 sqq.: *the great Libyan desert*, etc.: This list of reptilian monsters is taken from Lucan's *Pharsalia* (ix. 708–21); cf. Milton: *Paradise Lost*, x. 519–28.

l. 93: *heliotrope*: a kind of chalcedony, supposed to make the wearer invisible.

l. 94: *their hands were ... tied*: because they had been used for "picking and stealing".

ll. 107 sqq.: *the phoenix*: Legend has it that there was only one phoenix in all the world. Every 500 years she built herself a nest of myrrh and spices. When this had been kindled by the heat of the Arabian sun, she fanned the flames with her wings till she was wholly consumed, and was afterwards reborn from the ashes.

l. 110: *amomum*: a genus of aromatic plants, which includes cardamoms, etc.

ll. 112 sqq.: *one who falls*: Dante is probably describing an epileptic fit.

l. 125: *Vanni Fucci*: This notorious ruffian was a Black Guelf from Pistoia. With two accomplices he stole the treasure of San Jacopo from the Church of San Zeno (1293). For this crime an innocent man (Rampino dei Foresi) was arrested, but Vanni Fucci (who had fled the city) laid an information against the person who had acted as receiver. The latter was hanged and Rampino set at liberty.

l. 126: *Pistoia was my fitting den*: Pistoia was infamous as the birthplace of the feud between Blacks and Whites.

l. 128: *say what brought him here*: i.e. to the Bowge of the Thieves; for Dante had only known him as a "man of blood", and might have expected to find him in the Marsh of the Wrathful or the Boiling River.

ll. 142 *sqq.*: In May 1301, the Florentine Whites assisted the Pistoian Whites to rid Pistoia of the Blacks, who then took refuge in Florence, joined the Black party there, and in November, when Charles of Valois entered the city, helped in their turn to expel the Whites from Florence. "Piceno's field" is probably the battle in which the Florentine and Lucchese Blacks, under the command of Moroëllo Malaspina (the "stack of vapour"), Lord of Lunigiana in the Valdimagra, captured the White stronghold of Serravalle.

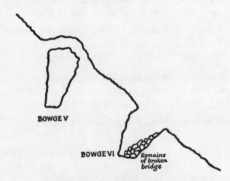

BOWGE V

BOWGE VI *Remains of broken bridge*

Diagram to illustrate Canto XXIV. 34–5

CANTO XXV

THE STORY. *Vanni Fucci defies God and flees, pursued by the monster Cacus. Three more spirits arrive, and the Poets watch while one of them becomes blended with the form of a reptile containing the spirit of a fourth, and the second exchanges shapes with yet another transformed Thief.*

This said, the thief lifted his hands on high,
  Making the figs with both his thumbs, and shrieking:
  "The fico for Thee, God! take that, say I!"

4 At once I liked the snakes; for one came sneaking
  About his throat, and wreathed itself around
  As though to say: "I will not have thee speaking";

7 Another wrapped his arms, and once more bound
  All fast in front, knotting the coils till he
  Could give no jog, they were so tightly wound.

10 Pistoia, O Pistoia! well were thee
  To burn thyself to ashes and perish all,
  Whose crimes outgo thy criminal ancestry!

13 Through all Hell's sable gyres funereal
  I saw no spirit so proud against the Lord –
  No, not that king who fell from the Theban wall –

16 As this; he fled without another word;
  And I saw a centaur galloping in a storm
  Of wrath: "Where, where's this insolent wretch?" he roared.

19 Maremma, methinks, breeds no such serpent-swarm
  As from his crupper writhed in hideous play
  To where horse-withers join with human form.

22 Behind his head, crouched on his shoulders, lay
  A dragon with spread wings, whose burning breath
  Set fire to all that crossed him on the way.

25 "Lo, Cacus!" said my guide, "who dwelt beneath
  Mount Aventine's high rock, and spilt abroad
  Full many a time a lake of blood and death.

28 He with his brethren goes not one same road,
  For when his knavish hand drew to his den
  His neighbour's kine, he wrought a theft by fraud,

31 Whereby his crooked courses ended, when
  Hercules with his club rained on him nigh
  One hundred blows, whereof he felt not ten."

34 While he thus spake, the centaur thundered by,
  And at the same time, close beneath us, three
  Spirits arrived, whom nor my guide nor I

37 Noticed, until they shouted: "Who are ye?"
  So we broke off the tale, to pay attention
  To them. Just who they were I could not see;

40 But, as so often haps, by intervention
  Of chance, or other such occasion-bringer,
  One of them, as they spoke, was moved to mention

43 Another, saying: "Why does Cianfa linger?
  Where is he?" So, to bid my guide give ear,
  From chin to nose I laid a warning finger.

46 Reader, if thou discredit what is here
  Set down, no wonder; for I hesitate
  Myself, who saw it all as clear as clear.

49 Lo! while I gazed, there darted up a great
  Six-leggèd worm, and leapt with all its claws
  On one of them from in front, and seized him straight;

52 Clasping his middle with its middle paws,
  Along his arms it made its fore-paws reach,
  And clenched its teeth tightly in both his jaws;

55 Hind-legs to thighs it fastened, each to each,
  And after, thrust its tail betwixt the two,
  Up-bent upon his loins behind the breech.

58 Ivy to oak so rooted never grew
  As limb by limb that monstrous beast obscene
  Cling him about, and close and closer drew,

61 Till like hot wax they stuck; and, melting in,
  Their tints began to mingle and to run,
  And neither seemed to be what it had been;

64 Just as when paper burns you see a dun
  Brown hue go creeping up before the flare,
  Not black as yet, although the white has gone.

67 The other two cried out, left gaping there:
  "O me, Agnel! how thou art changed!" they said;
  "Nor 'tother nor which! nor single nor a pair!"

70 Two heads already had become one head,
  We saw two faces fuse themselves, to weld
  One countenance whence both the first had fled;

73 Into two arms the four fore-quarters swelled;
Legs and thighs, breast and belly, blent and knit
Such nightmare limbs as never eye beheld;

76 All former forms wholly extinct in it,
The perverse image – both at once and neither –
Reeled slowly out of sight on languid feet.

79 And just as a lizard, with a quick, slick slither,
Flicks across the highway from hedge to hedge,
Fleeter than a flash, in the battering dog-day weather,

82 A fiery little monster, livid, in a rage,
Black as any peppercorn, came and made a dart
At the guts of the others, and leaping to engage

85 One of the pair, it pierced him at the part
Through which we first draw food; then loosed its grip
And fell before him, outstretched and apart.

88 The stung thief stared, but no word passed his lip;
He stood, foot-fixed, rigid in every limb,
Yawning, as though o'ercome by fever or sleep.

91 He eyed the monster and the monster him;
From this one's mouth, from that one's wound, a trail
Of smoke poured out; meeting, they merged their stream.

94 Let Lucan whisht now with his wondrous tale
Of poor Sabellus and Nasidius,
And wait to hear the wonder that befel;

97 Whisht Ovid! though he metamorphosed thus
Cadmus and Arethusa to a snake
And fountain, I need not be envious;

100 He never undertook in verse to make
Two natures interchanging, eye to eye,
Substance and form by mutual give-and-take

103 For with strange corresponding symmetry,
The monster's tail forked to a double tine;
The shade's feet clave together, till by and by

106 Legs, thighs and all so fused that never a sign
Could be discerned of seam, or junction scarred,
Or suture anywhere along the line;

109 The cloven tail put on the image marred
And lost in the other, and the reptile's skin
Softened all over, while the man's grew hard.

112 I saw the arms at the arm-pits shrivel in;
And the brute's fore-feet, which were stubby and stout,
As the other's shortened, lengthen and grow thin.

115 The hind-feet, intertwined, began to sprout
Into the member which men keep concealed,
Whence, in the thief, two nasty paws shot out.

118 The smoke with counter-change of colour wheeled
Re-dyeing both; the hair was stript and sown
So that one head grew shag, the other peeled.

121 One of them rose erect and one dropped down,
Yet never shifting the fixed, evil stare
Wherein each made the other's face his own.

124 The erect one's snout bulged temple-wards, and there
Out of the superfluity of stuff,
From each flat cheek-bone there emerged an ear;

127 Part went not back, but stayed in front, whereof
The extra matter formed a nose to adorn
The face, and proper lips made thick enough.

130 He that lay prostrate had his features drawn
Forth to a muzzle, and inside his head
He pulled his ears, as a snail pulls her horn;

133 The tongue once whole and apt for speech was splayed
Into a fork; in the forked tongue the split
Closed; and the smoke subsided. Then the shade

136 Now brutified, fled off with hiss and spit
Along the valley; the other, in a crack,
Chattering and sputtering, sped off after it;

139 Then suddenly turned on it his new-made back,
Bawling to his fellow: "I'll see Buoso range,
Crawling as I crawled, all around the track!"

142 Thus I saw change, re-change and interchange
The seventh moat's ballast; if my pen has erred,
Pray pardon me: 'twas all so new and strange.

145 And though my vision was perplexed and blurred,
My mind distraught, the prompt celerity
With which those flying sinners disappeared

148 Was no disguise for Limping Puccio – he
Was the only one, in fact, who did not turn
Into something else, of the original three;

151 The other was he that made Gaville mourn.

THE IMAGES. In this canto we see how the Thieves, who made no distinction between *meum* and *tuum* – between the "mine" and the "thine" – cannot call their forms or their personalities their own; for in Hell's horrible parody of exchange the "I" and the "thou" fluctuate and are lost.

NOTES. l. 2: *the figs*: an obscene and insulting gesture, made by thrusting the thumb between the first and second fingers.
l. 12: *thy criminal ancestry*: alluding to the tradition that Pistoia was founded by the remnants of Catiline's army.
l. 15: *that king who fell from the Theban wall*: Capaneus. (See Canto XIV. 51 and note.)
l. 25: *Cacus*: This giant was not really a Centaur; Dante was probably misled by Virgil's calling him "semi-human". He stole the oxen of Geryon, which Hercules was bringing from Spain as one of his Twelve Labours, and dragged them backwards into his cave so as to leave a misleading set of hoof-prints; but Hercules heard them bellowing, killed Cacus, and recovered his property.
l. 28: *his brethren*: the Centaurs of Circle 7, Ring i (Canto XII). Cacus added theft to his crimes of bloodshed, and is therefore placed in this lower circle.
l. 33: *whereof he felt not ten*: because he died after the first nine.
l. 35: *close beneath us*: It seems clear that the poets did not go right down to the floor of the bowge among the serpents. They either remained on the top of the bank or (as is perhaps more probable from Canto XXVI. 13–15) came part of the way down.
ll. 35–6: *three spirits*: Agnello dei Brunelleschi, Buoso degli Abati (or possibly the Buoso dei Donati mentioned in Canto XXX. 44), and Puccio dei Galigai. These, together with Cianfa dei Donati and Francesco Guercio dei Cavalcanti, who appear in the form of serpents, are the five Florentine nobles who, in this canto, confusingly exchange shapes.
ll. 49–50: *a great six-leggèd worm*: This is Cianfa dei Donati, the missing member of the party, who has been changed into a reptile.

l. 68: *Agnel*: This is Agnello dei Brunelleschi.

l. 82: *a little fiery monster*: This is Francesco Guercio dei Cavalcanti, whom Dante does not identify till the last line of the canto.

l. 85: *one of them*: This is Buoso degli Abati (or dei Donati).

ll. 85–6: *the part through which we first draw food*: the navel.

l. 94: *Lucan*: in his *Pharsalia*, tells how, on Cato's march through the Libyan desert, two of his soldiers were stung by serpents. One, Sabellus, dissolved away into a puddle of liquid flesh; the other, Nasidius, swelled up into a shapeless mass that burst his coat of mail.

l. 97: *Ovid*: See *Metamorphoses* iv. 563 *sqq*., and v. 572 *sqq*.

ll. 135–6: *the shade now brutified*: i.e. Buoso.

l. 137: *the other*: i.e. Francesco dei Cavalcanti, now restored to human form.

l. 148: *Limping Puccio* (Puccio Sciancato): this is Puccio dei Galigai. Dante did not at first (l. 39) know him, but recognized him by his limp when he ran off.

l. 151: *that made Gaville mourn*: Francesco dei Cavalcanti was killed by the inhabitants of this village in the Arno Valley, and his kinsmen avenged his death on the villagers.

A summary of these various transformations may be a convenience:

(1) *Agnello*: appears as a man, and is blended with

(2) *Cianfa*, who appears as a six-legged monster.

(3) *Buoso*: appears first as a man, and changes shapes with

(4) *Francesco*, who appears first as a four-legged "lizard".

(5) *Puccio*: remains unchanged.

CANTO XXVI

THE STORY. *Dante, with bitter irony, reproaches Florence. The Poets climb up and along the rugged spur to the arch of the next bridge, from which they see the Counsellors of Fraud moving along the floor of the Eighth Bowge, each wrapped in a tall flame. Virgil stops the twin-flame which contains the souls of Ulysses and Diomede, and compels Ulysses to tell the story of his last voyage.*

Florence, rejoice, because thy soaring fame
    Beats its broad wings across both land and sea,
    And all the deep of Hell rings with thy name!

4 Five of thy noble townsmen did I see
    Among the thieves; which makes me blush anew,
    And mighty little honour it does to thee.

7 But if toward the morning men dream true,
    Thou must ere long abide the bitter boon
    That Prato craves for thee, and others too;

10 Nay, were't already here, 'twere none too soon;
    Let come what must come, quickly – I shall find
    The burden heavier as the years roll on.

13 We left that place; and by the stones that bind
    The brink, which made the stair for our descent,
    My guide climbed back, and drew me up behind.

16 So on our solitary way we went,
    Up crags, up boulders, where the foot in vain
    Might seek to speed, unless the hand were lent.

19 I sorrowed then; I sorrow now again,
    Pondering the things I saw, and curb my hot
    Spirit with an unwontedly strong rein

22 For fear it run where virtue guide it not,
    Lest, if kind star or greater grace have blest
    Me with good gifts, I mar my own fair lot.

25 Now, thickly clustered, – as the peasant at rest
    On some hill-side, when he whose rays illume
    The world conceals his burning countenance least,

28 What time the flies go and mosquitoes come,
    Looks down the vale and sees the fire-flies sprinkling
    Fields where he tills or brings the vintage home –

31 So thick and bright I saw the eighth moat twinkling
    With wandering fires, soon as the arching road
    Laid bare the bottom of the deep rock-wrinkling.

34 Such as the chariot of Elijah showed
    When he the bears avenged beheld it rise,
    And straight to Heaven the rearing steeds upstrode,

37 For he could not so follow it with his eyes
    But that at last it seemed a bodiless fire
    Like a little shining cloud high in the skies,

40 So through that gulf moved every flaming spire;
    For though none shows the theft, each, like a thief,
    Conceals a pilfered sinner. To admire,

43 I craned so tip-toe from the bridge, that if
    I had not clutched a rock I'd have gone over,
    Needing no push to send me down the cliff.

46 Seeing me thus intently lean and hover,
    My guide said: "In those flames the spirits go
    Shrouded, with their own torment for their cover."

49 "Now thou hast told me, sir," said I, "I know
    The truth for sure; but I'd already guessed,
    And meant to ask – thinking it must be so –

52 Who walks in that tall fire cleft at the crest
    As though it crowned the pyre where those great foes,
    His brother and Eteocles, were placed?"

55 "Tormented there," said he, "Ulysses goes
    With Diomede, for as they ran one course,
    Sharing their wrath, they share the avenging throes.

58 In fire they mourn the trickery of the horse,
    That opened up the gates through which the high
    Seed of the Romans issued forth perforce;

61 There mourn the cheat by which betrayed to die
    Deïdamia wails Achilles still;
    And the Palladium is avenged thereby."

64 Then I: "O Master! if these sparks have skill
    To speak, I pray, and re-pray that each prayer
    May count with thee for prayers innumerable,

67 Deny me not to tarry a moment here
    Until the horned flame come; how much I long
    And lean to it I think thee well aware."

70 And he to me: "That wish is nowise wrong,
    But worthy of high praise; gladly indeed
    I grant it; but do thou refrain thy tongue

73 And let me speak to them; for I can read
    The question in thy mind; and they, being Greek,
    Haply might scorn thy speech and pay no heed."

76 So, when by time and place the twin-fire peak,
    As to my guide seemed fitting, had come on,
    In this form conjuring it, I heard him speak:

79 "You that within one flame go two as one,
By whatsoever I merited once of you,
By whatsoever I merited under the sun

82 When I sang the high songs, whether little or great my due,
Stand; and let one of you say what distant bourne,
When he voyaged to loss and death, he voyaged unto."

85 Then of that age-old fire the loftier horn
Began to mutter and move, as a wavering flame
Wrestles against the wind and is over-worn;

88 And, like a speaking tongue vibrant to frame
Language, the tip of it flickering to and fro
Threw out a voice and answered: "When I came

91 From Circe at last, who would not let me go,
But twelve months near Caieta hindered me
Before Aeneas ever named it so,

94 No tenderness for my son, nor piety
To my old father, nor the wedded love
That should have comforted Penelope

97 Could conquer in me the restless itch to rove
And rummage through the world exploring it,
All human worth and wickedness to prove.

100 So on the deep and open sea I set
Forth, with a single ship and that small band
Of comrades that had never left me yet.

103 Far as Morocco, far as Spain I scanned
Both shores; I saw the island of the Sardi,
And all that sea, and every wave-girt land.

106 I and my fellows were grown old and tardy
Or ere we made the straits where Hercules
Set up his marks, that none should prove so hardy

109 To venture the uncharted distances;
Ceuta I'd left to larboard, sailing by,
Seville I now left in the starboard seas.

112 'Brothers,' said I, 'that have come valiantly
Through hundred thousand jeopardies undergone
To reach the West, you will not now deny

115 To this last little vigil left to run
Of feeling life, the new experience
Of the uninhabited world behind the sun.

118 Think of your breed; for brutish ignorance
Your mettle was not made; you were made men,
To follow after knowledge and excellence.'

121 My little speech made every one so keen
To forge ahead, that even if I'd tried
I hardly think I could have held them in.

124 So, with our poop shouldering the dawn, we plied,
Making our oars wings to the witless flight,
And steadily gaining on the larboard side.

127 Already the other pole was up by night
With all its stars, and ours had sunk so low,
It rose no more from the ocean-floor to sight;

130 Five times we had seen the light kindle and grow
Beneath the moon, and five times wane away,
Since to the deep we had set course to go,

133 When at long last hove up a mountain, grey
With distance, and so lofty and so steep,
I never had seen the like on any day.

136 Then we rejoiced; but soon we had to weep,
For out of the unknown land there blew foul weather,
And a whirlwind struck the forepart of the ship;

139 And three times round she went in a roaring smother
With all the waters; at the fourth, the poop
Rose, and the prow went down, as pleased Another,

142 And over our heads the hollow seas closed up."

THE IMAGES. *The Counsellors of Fraud.* The sinners in Bowge viii are not men who deceived those whom they counselled, but men who counselled others to practise fraud. The Thieves in the bowge above stole material goods; these are spiritual thieves, who rob other men of their integrity. This explains, I think, the name which Dante gives to their punishment.

The Thievish Fire: The fire which torments also conceals the Counsellors of Fraud, for theirs was a furtive sin (Lat.: *furtivus*, from *fur*, thief). And as they sinned with their tongues, so now speech has to pass through the tongue of the tormenting and thievish flame.

NOTES. l. 9: *Prato*: Cardinal Nicholas of Prato was sent to Florence in 1304 by Pope Benedict XI in hopes of reconciling the hostile factions. Finding all his efforts wasted, he said, "Since you refuse to be blessed, remain accursed," and laid the city under an interdict. Various disasters which happened shortly afterwards – the collapse of a bridge, killing a vast number of people, and a terrible fire in which over 2000 houses were destroyed and many great families ruined – were attributed to the curse of the Church.

ll. 20–24: Dante realizes that he, like the Counsellors, has been blessed by fate ("kind star") or Providence ("greater grace") with great intellectual gifts, and must, therefore, take particular care not to abuse them.

l. 26: *when he whose rays*, etc.: i.e. in summer, when the days are longest.

l. 28: *what time the flies go and mosquitoes come*: i.e. at dusk.

l. 35: *he the bears avenged*: Elisha. (2 Kings ii. 11–12, 23–4.)

l. 54: *Eteocles*: The war of the Seven against Thebes arose from the rival claims of Eteocles and his brother Polynices, the sons of Oedipus, to the throne. They killed each other in battle, and were placed on one pyre; but, even so, such was their mutual hatred that their very flames would not mingle. (Statius: *Thebaïd* xii, 429 *sqq.*)

ll. 55–6: *Ulysses ... Diomede*: the Greek heroes who fought against Troy. The "crafty Ulysses" (Odysseus) advised the stratagem of the Wooden Horse, by which Greek soldiers were smuggled into Troy to open the gates to the besiegers; and also the theft of the sacred statue of Pallas (the Palladium) on which the safety of Troy was held to depend. Thetis, the mother of Achilles, knowing that he would perish if he went to Troy, concealed him at the court of the king of Scyros, disguised as a woman; but he seduced the king's daughter, Deïdamia, who bore him a son. Ulysses discovered his hiding-place and persuaded him to go to Troy; whereupon Deïdamia died of grief.

ll. 74–5: *they: being Greek ... might scorn thy speech*: The great Greek heroes would despise Dante, as an Italian (i.e. a descendant of the defeated Trojans).

l. 78: *in this form*: Virgil is also an Italian; but he has the power, which Dante has not, of compelling the spirits. We must remember that Virgil, in the Middle Ages, was thought of as a "White Magician", and though the power he uses is not what we should nowadays call "magic" in any evil sense, what follows is in fact a *formal conjura-*

tion. Notice that, since Virgil is here only gratifying Dante's laudable curiosity, he does not use any of those great "words of power" by which he overcame the ministers of Hell in the name of high Heaven (cf. Cantos III. 95; v. 23; VII. 11, etc.), but relies on his own power, which is twofold: (1) the native virtue of a good man who, though not in the Grace of Christ, is yet fulfilling a Divine commission "under the Protection"; (2) the claim of the Poet upon the souls who are indebted to him for their fame in the world.

ll. 80–83: "*By whatsoever ... stand and ... say*": This is the *forma* – the form, or formula – of conjuration: a twice-repeated obsecration, "by whatsoever ..." (naming the claim which constitutes the point of psychic contact between the master and the spirits), followed by a command: "stand ... speak". In the next canto we shall see that the spirits cannot depart until he dismisses them (Canto XXVII. 3) and a few lines later (Canto XXVII. 21) we shall be given the *forma* of the "licence to depart".

l. 83: *one of you*: i.e. Ulysses. Notice that, unlike the other spirits with whom the poets talk, Ulysses never addresses them personally. Compelled by the conjuration, his narrative reels off automatically like a gramophone record and then stops.

The voyage of Ulysses, perhaps the most beautiful thing in the whole *Inferno*, derives from no classical source, and appears to be Dante's own invention. It may have been suggested to him by the Celtic voyages of Maelduin and St Brendan. It influenced Tasso (*Ger. Lib.* Canto XV), and furnished Tennyson with the theme for his poem *Ulysses*.

l. 91: *Circe*: the sorceress who detained Ulysses on his way from Troy to Ithaca, after turning several of his companions into swine. (See *Odyssey*, Bk. x.)

l. 92: *Caieta* (Gaeta): a town on the south coast of Italy, said to have been so named by Aeneas after his old nurse, who died and was buried there. (*Aen.* VII. 1–4.)

l. 96: *Penelope*: the faithful wife of Ulysses.

l. 104: *the island of the Sardi*: Sardinia.

l. 108: *his marks*: The Pillars of Hercules were looked upon as the limit of the habitable globe, and the sun was imagined setting close behind them.

ll. 127 sqq.: *the other pole*, etc.: The voyagers had crossed the equator and made so much leeway south that the Southern Celestial Pole stood high in the heavens with all its attendant constellations; consequently, not only was our Pole Star beneath the northern horizon, but the Arctic constellations (the Great and Little Bears, etc.), which in this hemisphere never set, there never rose.

l. 133: *a mountain*: This is the mountain of the Earthly Paradise, which, after Christ's Harrowing of Hell, becomes Mount Purgatory – the only land, according to Dante, in the Southern Hemisphere. (See Canto XXXIV. 122–3, note.)

l. 141: *as pleased Another*: i.e. as pleased God.

CANTO XXVII

THE STORY. *The spirit of Guido da Montefeltro asks for news of Romagna, and, being answered, tells his story.*

Erect and quiet now, its utterance done,
　　The tall flame stood; and presently, dismissed
　　By the sweet poet's licence, it passed on;

4　When lo! our eyes were drawn towards the crest
　　Of a new flame, coming behind its fellow,
　　By the strange muffled roarings it expressed.

7　As the Sicilian bull, first made to bellow
　　(And that was justice) by his cries whose tool
　　Tuned the vile instrument and made it mellow,

10　Bellowed with its victim's voice, until the bull,
　　Though brass throughout, appeared itself to roar,
　　Pierced through with torments unendurable,

13　So, finding at the start no way nor door
　　Out of the fire, the sad words were translated
　　Into fire's native speech; but when they wore

16　Their way up to the tip and had vibrated
　　That, with the same vibration given to them
　　By the tongue, as they passed out articulated,

19　We heard it say: "O thou at whom I aim
　　My voice, who saidst in speech of Lombardy:
　　'Go now; I vex thee with no further claim';

22　Though I have come a little late maybe,
　　Speak to me! let it not irk thee to be stayed,
　　For see! I burn, and yet it irks not me.

25　If thou into this blind realm of the dead
　　Art fall'n but now from those sweet Latian shores
　　Whence I brought all my sins here on my head,

28　Tell me, have the Romagnols peace or wars?
　　For I was of the mountains there, between
　　Urbino and the yoke whence Tiber pours."

31　Now as I leaned there still, intent and keen,
　　My leader touched my side, and said: "Go to;
　　This one is Latian, so do thou begin."

34　I had my answer all prepared, and so
　　Made no delay but carried the talk on,
　　Saying: "O spirit hidden there below,

37　Not now, nor ever, has thy Romagna known
　　Times when her tyrants' hearts were free from feud,
　　But open strife just now I there left none.

40　Ravenna stands as many a year she's stood;
　　The Eagle of Polenta, with broad vans
　　Stretched o'er Cervia, sits and guards his brood.

43　She that piled up the slaughtered hordes of France,
　　Having endured such stubborn siege and strong,
　　Is back beneath the Green Claws' governance.

46　The Mastiffs of Verrucchio old and young,
　　That mauled Montagna with such murderous mouth,
　　Flesh their keen teeth where they have fleshed them long.

49　Beside Lamone and Santerno both,
　　The cities serve the white-laired Lioncel
　　Who changes sides as he turns north or south.

52　The town where Savio bathes the city-wall,
　　Lying betwixt the mountains and the plain,
　　Like as she lies, so lives 'twixt free and thrall.

55　And now, pray tell, so may thy name remain
　　Green upon earth, who wast thou? No deny
　　Was made to thee; deny us not again."

58　So when the flame had roared confusedly
　　After its wont awhile, it started quaking
　　Its sharp point to and fro, and breathed reply

61　As follows: "If I thought that I were making
　　Answer to one that might return to view
　　The world, this flame should evermore cease shaking.

64   But since from this abyss, if I hear true,
         None ever came alive, I have no fear
         Of infamy, but give thee answer due.

67   A man of arms was I, turned Cordelier,
         Thinking, thus girt, to make amends for ill,
         And my whole hope had been fulfilled, I swear,

70   But for the High Priest – may he rot in Hell! –
         Who thrust me back in the old evil mesh;
         And how and why hearken! for I will tell.

73   While I was still that shape of bone and flesh
         In which my mother moulded me at birth
         My deeds were foxy and not lionish;

76   I knew each winding way, each covert earth,
         And used such art and cunning in deceit
         That to the ends of the world the sound went forth.

79   But when I reached the age when it is meet
         For every mariner, with his port in sight,
         To lower sail and gather in the sheet,

82   That which had pleased offended me; contrite,
         Confessed, I took the habit, O, and these
         Good means of grace had served to set me right.

85   But he, the Prince of the modern Pharisees,
         Having a war to wage by Lateran –
         Not against Jews, nor Moslem enemies,

88   For every foe he had was Christian,
         Not one had marched on Acre, none had bought
         Or sold within the realm of the Soldan –

91   Reckless of his High Office, setting at naught
         Both his own priesthood and that girdle of mine
         Which once made lean the wearer, – this man sought

94   Me out, as in Soracte Constantine
         Sought Silvester to cure his leprosy,
         Even so, as a skilled leech to medicine

97   The fever of his pride, he sent for me,
         Demanding counsel; I with dubious brow
         Sat mute – his words seemed drunken lunacy.

100   But then he said: 'Fear nothing; here and now
         I absolve thee in advance; therefore speak out,
         Teach me how to lay Palestrina low.

103   Thou knowest I have the power to open or shut
         The gates of Heaven, for those High Keys are twain,
         The Keys my predecessor cherished not.'

106   Then he showed weighty cause, till to refrain
         Seemed worse than speech. 'Father, since thou straightway,'
         Said I, 'dost cleanse me of the guilty stain

109   I must contract, why then, to hold thy sway
         Victor triumphant in the Holy See,
         Promise great things; promise, and do not pay.'

112   Later, I died, and Francis came for me;
         But one of the Black Cherubs cried, 'Beware
         Thou wrong me not! Hands off! He's not for thee;

115   He must go join my servitors down there;
         He counselled fraud – that was his contribution
         To Hell; since then I've had him by the hair.

118   Absolved uncontrite means no absolution;
         Nor can one will at once sin and contrition,
         The contradiction bars the false conclusion.'

121   O what a waking! when with fierce derision
         He seized on wretched me, saying: 'I'll be bound
         Thou didst not think that I was a logician.'

124   He haled me off to Minos; eight times round
         His scaly back the monster twined his tail,
         And in his rage he bit it; then he found

127   Against me, saying: 'Here's a criminal
         For the thievish fire.' So was I lost, so borne
         Where, as thou seest, thus clothed I walk and wail."

130   Its story told, the flame began to mourn
         Anew, and sorrowing passed away from us,
         Twisting and tossing with its pointed horn;

133   And we went on, my guide and I, to cross
         The bridge that o'er the following chasm lies,
         Where those who make division and purchase thus

136   A load of guilt, receive their merchandise.

NOTES. ll. 2–3: *dismissed by the sweet poet's licence*: These lines make it clear that the conjured spirits cannot move without the formal permission of the Master. (See note, Canto XXVI. 80–83.)

l. 7: *the Sicilian bull*: This instrument of torture was made by Perillus for Phalaris, the Sicilian tyrant. The victims were roasted alive in it, and their yells, issuing through the brazen mouth, were supposed to sound like the bull bellowing. Phalaris, with grisly humour, tried the invention out on Perillus. (Ovid: *Ars Amat.* i. 635–6.)

ll. 13–18: This rather complicated description becomes easily intelligible if one thinks how words spoken into a telephone are transmitted as electrical waves and retranslated into speech by vibrating the receiver at the other end of the line.

ll. 20–21: *who saidst in speech of Lombardy: "Go now"*, etc.: This is the *forma* of the "licence to depart" – "*issa ten va, più non t' adizzo*" – "now go, I vex thee no further". (The fact that Virgil uses "speech of Lombardy" shows that it was not the difference of language that would have prevented the Greeks from paying attention to Dante).

l. 29: *I was of the mountains there*: The speaker is the great Ghibelline leader, Guido da Montefeltro (1223–98) of Romagna.

l. 40: *Ravenna*: The lords of Polenta, who bore an eagle on their coat of arms, ruled Ravenna from 1270 to 1441. In 1300 the head of the family was Guido Vecchio ("the elder"), uncle to Dante's friend Guido Novello ("the younger"); his territory had already been extended to cover Cervia, a town about twelve miles south of Ravenna.

l. 43: *She that piled up the … hordes of France*: Forlì; its successful defence against French troops sent by Pope Martin IV (1282) was conducted by Guido da Montefeltro himself. In 1300 it was ruled by Sinibaldo degli Ordelaffi, whose arms were a lion, vert.

l. 46: *The Mastiffs of Verrucchio*: Malatesta and his son Malatestino of Rimini. They were Black Guelfs; Montagna dei Parcitati, whom they took prisoner (1295) and murdered, was a Ghibelline of the same city.

l. 48: *there*: in Verruchio, family seat of the lords of Rimini.

l. 50: *the white-haired Lioncel*: Mainardo Pagano (*d*. 1302), whose arms were a lion, azure, on a field, argent. He was lord of Faenza on the Lamone and of Imola on the Santerno (see map, p. 173); and is said to have behaved like a Ghibelline in Romagna (to the south) and a Guelf in Tuscany (to the north).

l. 52: *where Savio bathes the city-wall*: Cesna (between Forlì and
Rimini) was continually changing its government, but was in 1300
comparatively free from tyranny, under the rule of its own officers.

ll. 56-7: *No deny ... deny us not*: i.e. "We have answered your
question; now answer ours."

ll. 61-6: Guido cannot see that Dante is alive, and supposes him to
be one of the damned souls on its way to its own place (*cf.* Cantos
XII. 62; XXVIII. 42-5, etc.). Dante does not undeceive him, but leaves
the Counsellor of Fraud to his self-deception (see note on Canto
VIII. 45). Generally speaking, the shades in the Circles of Fraud, unlike
those in the circles above, do not want to have their stories made
known in the world.

l. 67: *Cordelier*: a friar, wearing the cord of the Franciscan Order,
which Guido entered in 1296.

l. 70: *the High Priest*: i.e. the Pope (Boniface VIII).

l. 86: *a war to wage by Lateran*: The long and embittered feud between
Boniface and the Colonna family broke out into open warfare in
1297.

l. 89: *Acre*: the last stronghold that remained to the Christians in
Palestine after the Crusades was retaken in 1291 by the Saracens,
with the aid of renegade Jews and of Christian merchants who
treacherously supplied them with contraband of war.

l. 94: *in Soracte*: The legend was that when the Emperor Constantine was stricken with leprosy for his persecution of Christians, he
summoned Pope Silvester from his refuge in Soracte, and was converted and cured by him, making the alleged "Donation of Constantine" (see Canto XIX. 115, note) as a thank-offering.

l. 102: *Palestrina* (or Penestrino): The forces of the Colonna had
retired to this stronghold. On Guido's advice, the Pope offered them
an amnesty, and when they had surrendered on those conditions,
razed the place to the ground.

l. 105: *my predecessor*: Celestine V. (See Canto III, 60, note.)

l. 112: *Francis*: i.e St Francis of Assisi, founder of the Franciscan
Order.

ll. 118-20: "Contrition is necessary if the absolution is to be valid;
but a man cannot be contrite for a sin at the same time that he is in-
tending to commit it, since this involves a contradiction in logic (i.e.
one cannot both will and not-will the same thing at the same time);
therefore the absolution obtained in these circumstances is invalid".

l. 124: *eight times round*: indicating the Eighth Circle (see Canto V.
10-12), and adding "the Thievish Fire" to show which bowge of it.

CANTO XXVIII

THE STORY. *From the bridge over the Ninth Bowge the Poets look
down upon the Sowers of Discord, who are continually smitten asunder
by a Demon with a sword. Dante is addressed by Mahomet and Pier da
Medicina, who send messages of warning to people on earth. He sees
Curio and Mosca, and finally Bertrand de Born.*

Who, though with words unshackled from the rhymes,
    Could yet tell full the tale of wounds and blood
    Now shown me, let him try ten thousand times?

4 Truly all tongues would fail, for neither could
    The mind avail, nor any speech be found
    For things not to be named nor understood.

7 If in one single place were gathered round
    All those whose life-blood in the days of yore
    Made outcry from Apulia's fateful ground,

10 Victims of Trojan frays, and that long war
    Whose spoil was heaped so high with rings of gold,
    As Livy tells, who errs not; those that bore

13 The hammering brunt of battle, being bold
    'Gainst Robert Guiscard to make stand on stand;
    And they whose bones still whiten in the mould

16 Of Ceperan', where all the Apulian band
    Turned traitors, and on Tagliacozzo's field
    Won by old Alard, weaponless and outmanned;

19 If each should show his bleeding limbs unhealed,
    Pierced, lopt and maimed, 'twere nothing, nothing whatever
    To that ghast sight in the ninth bowge revealed.

22 No cask stove in by cant or middle ever
    So gaped as one I saw there, from the chin
    Down to the fart-hole split as by a cleaver.

25 His tripes hung by his heels; the pluck and spleen
    Showed with the liver and the sordid sack
    That turns to dung the food it swallows in.

28 I stood and stared; he saw me and stared back;
    Then with his hands wrenched open his own breast,
    Crying: "See how I rend myself! what rack

31 Mangles Mahomet! Weeping without rest
    Ali before me goes, his whole face slit
    By one great stroke upward from chin to crest.

34 All these whom thou beholdest in the pit
    Were sowers of scandal, sowers of schism abroad
    While they yet lived; therefore they now go split.

37 Back yonder stands a fiend, by whom we're scored
    Thus cruelly; and over and over again
    He puts us to the edge of the sharp sword

40 As we crawl through our bitter round of pain;
    For ere we come before him to be bruised
    Anew, the gashed flesh reunites its grain.

43 But who art thou that dalliest there bemused
    Up on the rock-spur – doubtless to delay
    Going to thy pangs self-judged and self-accused?"

46 "Nor dead as yet, nor brought here as a prey
    To torment by his guilt," my master said,
    "But to gain full experience of the Way

49 He comes; wherefore behoves him to be led –
    And this is true as that I speak to thee –
    Gyre after gyre through Hell, by me who am dead."

52 And, hearing him, stock-still to look on me
    Souls by the hundred stood in the valley of stone,
    And in amaze forgot their agony.

55 "Well, go then, thou that shalt behold the sun
    Belike ere long – let Fra Dolcino know,
    Unless he is in haste to follow me down,

58 He must well arm himself against the snow
    With victuals, lest the Novarese starve him out,
    Who else might find him hard to overthrow."

61 Thus unto me Mahomet, with one foot
    Lifted to leave us; having said, he straight
    Stretched it to earth and went his dreary route.

64 Then one with gullet pierced and nose shorn flat
      Off to the very eyebrows, and who bare
      Only a single ear upon his pate,

67 Having remained with all the rest to stare,
      Before the rest opened his weasand now,
      Which outwardly ran crimson everywhere,

70 And said: "O thou whom guilt condemns not, thou
      Whom I have seen up there in Italy
      Unless some likeness written in thy brow

73 Deceives me; if thou e'er return to see
      Once more the lovely plain that slopes between
      Vercelli and Marcabò, then think of me,

76 Of Pier da Medicina; and tell those twain,
      Ser Guido and Angiolello, Fano's best,
      That, if our foresight here be not all vain,

79 They'll be flung overboard and drowned, in the unblest
      Passage near La Cattolica, by the embargo
      Laid on their lives at a false lord's behest.

82 Neptune ne'er saw so foul a crime, such cargo
      Of wickedness 'twixt Cyprus and Majorca
      Ne'er passed, no pirate-crew, no men of Argo

85 Could show the like. That one-eyed mischief-worker
      Whose land there's one here with me in this vale
      Wishes he'd never seen, that smooth-tongued talker

88 Shall lure them to a parley, and when they sail
      Deal so with them that they shall have no need
      Of vow or prayer against Focara's gale."

91 Then I to him: "Tell me, so may I speed
      Thy message up to the world as thou dost seek,
      Who's he whose eyes brought him that bitter meed?"

94 At once he laid his hand upon the cheek
      Of a fellow-shade, and pulled his jaws apart,
      Saying: "Look! this is he; he cannot speak.

97 This outcast quenched the doubt in Caesar's heart:
      'To men prepared delays are dangerous';
      Thus he gave sign for civil strife to start."

100 O how deject to me, how dolorous
      Seemed Curio, with his tongue hacked from his throat,
      He that of speech was so adventurous!

103 And one that had both hands cut off upsmote
      The bloody stumps through the thick air and black,
      Sprinkling his face with many a filthy clot,

106 And cried: "Think, too, on Mosca, Mosca alack!
      Who said: 'What's done is ended,' and thereby
      For Tuscany sowed seed of ruin and wrack."

109 "And death to all thy kindred," added I;
      Whereat, heaping despair upon despair,
      He fled, like one made mad with misery.

112 But I remained to watch the throng, and there
      I saw a thing I'd hesitate to tell
      Without more proof – indeed, I should not dare,

115 Did not a blameless conscience stead me well –
      That trusty squire that harnesses a man
      In his own virtue like a coat of mail.

118 Truly I saw – it seems to me I can
      See still – I saw a headless trunk that sped
      Running towards me as the others ran;

121 And by the hair it held the severed head
      Swung, as one swings a lantern, in its hand;
      And that caught sight of us: "Ay me!" it said.

124 Itself was its own lamp, you understand,
      And two in one and one in two it was,
      But how – He only knows who thus ordained!

127 And when it reached our bridge, I saw it toss
      Arm up and head together, with design
      To bring the words it uttered near to us;

130 Which were: "O breathing soul, brought here to win
      Sight of the dead, behold this grievous thing,
      See if there be any sorrow like to mine.

133 And know, if news of me thou seek to bring
      Yonder, Bertrand de Born am I, whose fell
      Counsel, warping the mind of the Young King

136 Like Absalom with David, made rebel
      Son against father, father against son,
      Deadly as the malice of Achitophel.

139 Because I sundered those that should be one,
      I'm doomed, woe worth the day! to bear my brain
      Cleft from the trunk whence all its life should run;

142 Thus is my measure measured to me again."

THE IMAGES. *The Sowers of Discord*. Three types are shown: fomenters of (1) religious schism (Mahomet; Ali), (2) civil strife (de Medicina; Curio), (3) family disunion (Mosca; Bertrand).

They appear in the Circle of Fraud because their sin is primarily of the intellect. They are the fanatics of party, seeing the world in a false perspective, and ready to rip up the whole fabric of society to gratify a sectional egotism.

The Sundering Sword. The image here is sufficiently obvious. Note how it is adapted to suit the various types of crime.

NOTES. l. 9: *Apulia's fatal ground*: The region in south-east Italy where all the wars and battles alluded to in this passage took place.

l. 10: *Trojan frays*: Wars of the Romans (Trojans) against the Samnites (343–290 B.C.); *that long war*, etc.: the Punic Wars (264–146 B.C.).

l. 11: *rings of gold*: According to Livy, so many Romans were killed at the Battle of Cannae, in the second Punic War, that three bushels of golden rings were collected from their bodies.

l. 14: *Robert Guiscard*: combated Greeks and Saracens (1015–85).

l. 16: *Ceperan(o)*: The Apulian barons, under Manfred, deserted at the pass of Ceperano, and let Charles of Anjou through to defeat Manfred at Benevento (1266).

l. 17: *Tagliacozzo*: where Charles of Anjou defeated Manfred's nephew, Conradin; by the advice of Alard de Valéry, he allowed two-thirds of his army to retreat, and then, with his reserve troops, annihilated the enemy who had scattered in search of plunder.

l. 31: *Mahomet*: classed as a Christian schismatic.

l. 32: *Ali*: the nephew of Mahomet, was himself the figurehead of an internal schism within the following of the Prophet himself.

l. 42: *the gashed flesh reunites*: We may suppose that in all cases where damned souls are mangled or mutilated (e.g. by Cerberus in the Third Circle or by the "black braches" in the Wood of the Suicides) the shadowy flesh is thus restored; but Dante, with great artistic tact, says nothing about it until, at this point, he can use it to make a ghastly and grotesque effect. He hints at it again in Canto XXXIV. 60.

l. 56: *Fra Dolcino*: Head of a sect, the "Apostolic Brethren", rightly or wrongly condemned as schismatic. In 1305 Pope Clement V ordered a crusade against the Brethren, and after holding out for a year and a day in the hills near Novara, they were forced to surrender. Dolcino was burnt at Vercelli in 1307.

l. 76: *Pier da Medicina*: whose intrigues were instrumental in fomenting the feud between the houses of Polenta and Malatesta in Romagna. His methods were to disseminate scandal and misrepresentation – hence he is shown mutilated in the eavesdropping ear, the lying throat, and the inquisitive nose.

l. 77: *Guido* (del Cassero) *and Angiolello* (da Calignano): two noblemen of Fano, were invited to a conference at La Cattolica, on the Adriatic, by Malatestino of Rimini, who had them treacherously drowned off the headland of Focara, notorious for its dangerous winds.

l. 84: *men of Argo*: lit.: the Argolican race, i.e. the Greeks, always famous for piracy. But there may be a specific reference to the crime of the Argonauts, who murdered Absyrtus and threw his body into the sea on their return from Colchis.

l. 85: *that one-eyed mischief-worker*: Malatestino of Rimini.

l. 93: *that bitter meed*: referring back to ll. 86–7. It was by Curio's advice that Julius Caesar crossed the Rubicon (near Rimini), which at that time (49 B.C.) was the frontier between Italy and Cis-Alpine Gaul, and so declared war on the Republic.

l. 98: *to men prepared*, etc.: Quoted from Lucan: *Pharsalia* (i. 281).

l. 106: *Mosca*: The great Guelf-Ghibelline feud in Florence flared up over a family quarrel. Buondelmonte dei Buondelmonti, who was betrothed to a girl of the Amadei, jilted her for one of the Donati. When her kinsfolk were debating how best to avenge the slight, Mosca dei Lamberti said: "What's done is ended" (i.e. "stone dead hath no fellow"). Buondelmonte was accordingly murdered; the whole city took sides; and thenceforward Florence was distracted by the disputes of the rival factions.

l. 134: *Bertrand de Born*: (c. 1140–1215), the warrior and troubadour, was lord of Hautefort (Altaforte) in Perigord. According to his Provençal biographers, he fomented the quarrel between Henry II of England and his son Prince Henry, "the Young King" (so-called because he was crowned during his father's lifetime). For Absalom and Achitophel, see 2 *Samuel* xv–xvii. Bertrand is decapitated because to part father and son is like severing the head from the body.

CANTO XXIX

THE STORY. *Dante lingers, expecting to see a kinsman of his in the Ninth Bowge; but Virgil says he has already passed by unnoticed. They cross the next bridge and descend into Bowge x, where the Falsifiers lie stricken with hideous diseases. Dante talks with an old friend, Capocchio.*

My eyes were grown so maudlin with the plight
　　Of all these people racked with wounds and woe,
　　They longed to linger weeping at the sight;

4　But Virgil said: "How now! Why dost thou grow
　　Rooted to gaze? Why is thy vision drowned
　　Among these smitten shades? Thou didst not so

7　At the other moats. Dost think that thou art bound
　　To catalogue them all? Come, use thy wit;
　　Consider, this fosse is twenty-two miles round,

10　And already the moon is underneath our feet;
　　Short grows the time allowed, and on our way
　　There's more to see than thou hast seen as yet."

13　"Hadst thou but waited," I began to say,
　　"To find out what it was I was looking for,
　　I think perhaps thou wouldst have let me stay."

16　My guide, however, had started on before,
　　And I trailed after, making my reply
　　And adding: "Somewhere on that rocky floor,

19　I think, among the throng that held my eye,
　　A spirit of my own blood runs damnified,
　　Weeping the guilt that there is priced so high."

22　"Let not thy mind," the master then replied,
　　"Henceforth distract itself upon that fellow;
　　Thou hast other things to think of – let him bide:

25　I saw him, close beneath the bridge's hollow,
　　Pointing at thee, and threatening with bent fist,
　　And heard him called by name Geri del Bello.

28　Just at that moment thou wast hard intent
　　On him that dwelt in Altaforte; hence
　　Thou didst not look his way, and so he went."

31　"Alas, dear Sir! his death by violence,"
　　Said I, "still unavenged by any of them
　　Who shared the affront, has rankled to this sense

34　Of deep resentment; wherefore, as I deem,
　　He went away and would not speak to me;
　　And all the more for that, I pity him."

37　Thus we talked up the cliff, till presently
　　The next moat's bottom came in sight, – or would
　　Have come in sight had there been light to see.

40　There, from the crossing-span's high altitude,
　　Malbowges' final cloister all appears
　　Thrown open, with its sad lay-brotherhood;

43　And there, such arrowy shrieks, such lancing spears
　　Of anguish, barbed with pity, pierced me through,
　　I had to clamp my hands upon my ears.

46　Could all disease, all dog-day plagues that stew
　　In Valdichiana's spitals, all fever-drench
　　Drained from Maremma and Sardinia, spew

49　Their horrors all together in one trench –
　　Like that, so this: suffering, and running sore
　　Of gangrened limbs, and putrefying stench.

52　Down that last bank of the long cliff we bore,
　　Still turning left; and now as I drew near,
　　I saw more vividly to the very core

55　That pit wherein the High Lord's minister,
　　Infallible Justice, dooms to pains condign
　　The falsifiers she registers down here.

58　No sadder sight was seen, as I divine, –
　　Even in Aegina, when wrath knew no term,
　　But the whole people in that air malign

61　Sickened, and beasts, down to the littlest worm,
　　Dropped dead, till in the end the ancient race
　　Had to be born anew, as poets affirm,

64　From seed of ants – than in that dreadful place
　　The sight of the spirits strewn through the dark valley,
　　Heaped here, heaped there, enduring their distress.

67 This on the back, and that upon the belly
One of another lay, while some crawled round
The dismal road, all-fours, lethargically.

70 So step by step we went, nor uttered sound,
To see and hear those sick souls in their pains,
Who could not lift their bodies from the ground.

73 I saw two sitting, propped like a couple of pans
Set to warm by the fireside, back to back,
And blotched from head to foot with scabs and blains.

76 And I ne'er saw curry-comb plied by ostler's jack
Or groom, in a frenzy because his master's waiting,
Or because he is kept up late and wants to pack

79 Bedwards, to match the furious rasping and grating
With which they curried their own hide with their nails,
Maddened by the itch that still finds no abating.

82 The nail went stripping down the scurfy shales,
Just as a scullion's knife will strip a bream,
Or any other fish with great coarse scales.

85 "Thou that dost take thy finger-nails to trim
Thy coat, and sometimes," thus my guide began
To one of these, "for pincers usest them,

88 Tell us, so may thy claws outlast the span
Of all eternity to do their task,
Is any one here within a Latian man?"

91 "We who confront thee in this hideous mask
Are Latians both," one answered in a wail,
"But who art thou? and wherefore dost thou ask?"

94 "I am one who comes descending, vale by vale,
To lead this living man," my guide averred,
"And all my business is to show him Hell."

97 Their mutual propping broke; startled, they stirred
And turned towards me trembling; others too
Turned when they caught the echo of his word.

100 Then my kind master courteously withdrew
To give me place: "Whate'er thou wilt," he said,
"Ask them." And since he urged me so to do

103 I thus began: "So may your names not fade,
In that first world, from human memory,
But live for many suns, be not afraid

106 To tell me who and whence you both may be,
Nor let your sad and shameful state prevent
Your free unfolding of yourselves to me."

109 "I'm Aretine, and to the stake was sent
By Alberto of Siena; yet," said one,
"What caused my death caused not this punishment.

112 It's true I told the fool one day for fun:
'I can take wings and fly,' and he – an ass
Full of wild whims, with addled wits, or none –

115 Would have me teach him how; and just because
I could not make him Daedalus, why, then
He had me burned, by one who, more or less,

118 Fathered him; but to this last bowge of ten
Unerring Minos doomed me for the art
Alchemic, which I practised among men."

121 "Was ever race so frivolous of heart,"
Said I to the poet, "as the Sienese?
I think they could give even the French a start

124 And a beating." Whereupon the second of these
Leprous shades joined in: "Except, no doubt,
Stricca, renowned for his economies,

127 And Niccolò, of course, who first found out
How to make cloves a costly cult and passion
In the garden where such seeds take root and sprout;

130 Oh – and except the club where Caccia d'Ascian
Lost woods and vineyards, and the ingenious
Abbagliato, like a man of fashion,

133 Displayed his wit. Wouldst know who backs thee thus
Against Siena? Come, focus thy glance,
Get my face clear; thou'lt not be at a loss

136 To know Capocchio's shadowy countenance,
Transmuter of metals, alchemist, and – a feature
Which, if I eye thee hard, thou wilt at once

139 Recall – a most consummate ape of nature."

THE IMAGES. *The Falsifiers.* The Tenth Bowge shows us the images of those who falsified things, words, money, and persons. This canto deals with the falsifiers of things, typified by the Alchemists (transmuters of metals). They may be taken to figure every kind of deceiver who tampers with the basic commodities by which society lives – the adulterators of food and drugs, jerry-builders, manufacturers of shoddy, and so forth – as well, of course, as the baseness of the individual self consenting to such dishonesty.

The Valley of Disease. For the *allegory*, this is at one level the image of the corrupt heart which acknowledges no obligation to keep faith with its fellow-men; at another, it is the image of a diseased society in the last stages of its mortal sickness and already necrosing. Every value it has is false; it alternates between a deadly lethargy and a raving insanity. Malbowges began with the sale of the sexual relationship, and went on to the sale of Church and State; now, the very money is itself corrupted, every affirmation has become perjury, and every identity a lie; no medium of exchange remains, and the "general bond of love and nature's tie" (Canto XI. 56) is utterly dissolved.

NOTES. l. 9: *twenty-two miles round*: Various attempts have been made to calculate the exact proportions of Malbowges from the indications in this and the next canto; but I think it is best just to bear in mind that Hell extends from a little below the Earth's surface to its centre, and that the Great Barrier comes about half-way down; and so leave imagination to fill in the details of this colossal scheme.

l. 10: *the moon is underneath our feet*: it is about 1 P.M.

l. 27: *Geri del Bello*: a cousin of Dante's father. He is said to have delighted in making mischief, and to have been killed by a member of the Sacchetti family, which he had set by the ears. The customary vendetta for his death seems not to have been carried out by his kinsmen – or, at any rate, not before 1300.

l. 29: *him that dwelt in Altaforte*: Bertrand de Born.

ll. 47–9: *Valdichiana ... Maremma and Sardinia*: All these districts were reckoned extremely unhealthy, especially in summer; Valdichiana (in Tuscany, between the mouths of the Chiana) and Maremma being full of marshy and malarial swamps.

l. 59: *Aegina*: The story of the pestilence sent by Juno, and of how Jupiter re-peopled the island by turning ants into men, is told by Ovid. (*Metam.* vii. 523–657.)

l. 110: *said one*: The speaker is Griffolino d'Arezzo, a physicist, who, by promising all kinds of miracles, extracted large sums of money from a foolish young man, Albero, reputed to be the son of the Bishop of Siena. His dupe eventually complained to the Bishop, who had Griffolino burnt as a sorcerer. The offence which brings him to the Tenth Bowge is, however, not alchemy considered as a magical art (which would be punished in Bowge iv), but alchemy in its more practical application – viz. the falsification of commodities. (For Daedalus, see Canto XVII. 109, note.)

ll. 125 *sqq.*: *Except, no doubt, Stricca*: As in Canto XXI. 41, the "except" is ironical. The four noblemen named all belonged to the "Spendthrifts' Club" in Siena, of which Lano was also a member (see Canto XIII. 115, note). Niccolò dei Salembeni specialized in the invention of dishes prepared with costly spices.

l. 136: *Capocchio*: is said to have been a friend and fellow-student of Dante's, and to be called an "ape of nature" on account of his powers either as a draughtsman or as a mimic. If the latter, then his saying, "If I eye thee hard", perhaps means that at this point he indulged in some characteristic facial gesture which Dante could not fail to recognize – he gave him, so to speak, a "George Robey look".

CANTO XXX

THE STORY. *The shades of Myrrha and Gianni Schicchi are pointed out by Griffolino. Dante becomes intent upon a quarrel between Adam of Brescia and Sinon of Troy, and earns a memorable rebuke from Virgil.*

When Juno was incensed for Semele,
And wreaking vengeance on the Theban race,
As her sharp strokes had shown repeatedly,

4 So fierce a madness seized on Athamas
That, seeing his wife go with her two young sons
One on each arm: "Spread nets, nets at the pass,

7 We'll take the lioness and the whelps at once!"
He roared aloud; then, grasping in his wild
And pitiless clutch one of those little ones,

10 Baby Learchus, as he crowed and smiled,
He whirled him round and dashed him on a stone;
She fled, and drowned herself with the other child.

13 And when, by Fortune's hostile hand o'erthrown,
The towering pride of Troy fell to the ground,
Kingdom and king together ruining down,

16 Sad Hecuba, forlorn and captive bound,
After she'd seen Polyxena lie slain,
After, poor hapless mother, she had found

19 Polydorus dead by the seashore, fell insane
And howled like a dog, so fearfully distraught
Was she, so wrenched out of her mind with pain.

22 Yet Theban or Trojan furies never wrought
Such cruel frenzy, even in the maddened breast
Of a brute, still less in any of human sort,

25 As I saw in two shades, naked, pale, possessed,
Who ran, like a rutting boar that has made escape
From the sty, biting and savaging all the rest.

28 One of them fell on Capocchio, catching his nape
In its teeth, and dragging him prostrate, so that it made
His belly on the rough rock-bottom scour and scrape.

31 The Aretine, left trembling, turned dismayed
To me: "That's Gianni Schicchi, that hell-hound there;
He's rabid, he bites whatever he sees," he said.

34 "So may thou 'scape the other's teeth, declare
Its name," said I; "prithee be good enough –
Quick! ere it dart away and disappear."

37 And he: "There doth the ancient spirit rove
Of criminal Myrrha, who cast amorous eyes
On her own father with unlawful love,

40 And in a borrowed frame and false disguise
Went in to him to do a deed of shame;
As he that fled but now, to win the prize

43 'Queen of the Stable', lent his own false frame
To Buoso de' Donati, and made a will
In legal form, and forged it in his name."

46 So when that rabid pair, on whom I still
Kept my gaze fixed, had passed, I turned about
To view those other spirits born for ill;

49 And saw one there whose shape was like a lute,
Had but his legs, between the groin and haunch,
Where the fork comes, been lopt off at the root.

52 The heavy dropsy, whose indigested bunch
Of humours bloats the swollen frame within,
Till the face bears no proportion to the paunch,

55 Puffed his parched lips apart, with stiffened skin
Drawn tight, as the hectic gapes, one dry lip curled
Upward by thirst, the other toward the chin.

58 "O you," said he, "that through this grisly world
Walk free from punishment – I can't think why –
Look now and hear; behold the torments hurled

61 On Master Adam! All that wealth could buy
Was mine; and now, one drop of water fills
My craving mind – one drop! O misery!

64 The little brooks that ripple from the hills
Of the green Casentin to Arno river,
Suppling their channels with their cooling rills,

67 Are in my eyes and in my ears for ever;
And not for naught – their image dries me more
Than the disease that wastes my face's favour.

70 Strict, searching justice balances my score:
The very land I sinned in has been turned
To account, to make my sighs more swiftly pour.

73 Romena's there, the city where I learned
To falsify the Baptist's coin; up yonder,
For the offence, I was condemned and burned.

76 But might I here see Guido or Alexander
Damned, or their brother, I would not miss that sight
For all the water in the fount of Branda.

79 One's here already, if those mad spirits are right
Who circle all the track; but what's the good
Of that to me, whose legs are tied so tight?

82 Were I but still so active that I could
Drag myself only an inch in a hundred years,
I'd be on the road by now, be sure I would,

85 To seek out from all these sufferers
Disfigured and maimed, though it's half a mile across
And eleven miles round at least, from all one hears.

88 They brought me into this gang of ruin and loss,
They caused me coin the florins that brought me hither,
Whose gold contained three carats by weight of dross."

91 Then I to him: "What shades lie there together
Rolled in a heap on thy right – that abject pair
Who smoke as a washed hand smokes in wintry weather?"

94 "When I tumbled into this coop I found them there,"
Said he, "and they've never given a turn or kick,
Nor will to all eternity, I dare swear.

97 Sinon of Troy is one, the lying Greek;
One, the false wife who lyingly accused
Joseph; their burning fever makes them reek."

100 Then, vexed belike to hear his name thus used
Slightingly, one of those shadows seemed to come
To life and fetched him a walloping blow, fist closed,

103 On the rigid belly, which thudded back like a drum;
So Master Adam lammed him over the face
With an arm as hard as his own, and hit him plumb.

106 "See now," said he, "though I cannot shift my place,
Because my legs are heavy, yet if need be
My arm is free, and I keep it ready, in case."

109 And he: "It was not so ready and not so free
When they haled thee off to the fire; it was free to do
Thy dirty job of coining – there I agree."

112 Then he of the dropsy: "Now thou speakest true;
But when at Troy they called on thee to tell
The truth, thy truthfulness was less in view."

115 "If I spoke false, thy coins were false as well;
I uttered but one lie," quoth Sinon, "thou
Hast uttered more than any fiend in hell."

118 "Perjurer, think of the horse, think of thy vow
Forsworn," retorted the blown belly; "howl
For grief to think the whole world knows it now."

121 "Howl for the thirst that cracks thy tongue, the foul
Water that bloats thy paunch," the Greek replied,
"To a hedge that walls thine eyes and hides thy jowl."

124 To whom the coiner: "Ay, thy mouth gapes wide
As ever with evil words; if I feel thirst,
And watery humours stuff me up inside,

127 Thou burnest, and thy head aches fit to burst;
Hadst thou Narcissus' mirror there, we'd see
Thee lap it up and need no prompting first."

130 I was all agog and listening eagerly,
When the master said: "Yes, feast thine eyes; go on;
A little more, and I shall quarrel with thee."

133 And when I heard him use that angry tone
To me, I turned to him so on fire with shame,
It comes over me still, though all these years have flown.

136 And like a man who dreams a dreadful dream,
And dreams he would it were a dream indeed,
Longing for that which is, with eager aim

139 As though 'twere not; so I, speechless to plead
For pardon, pleaded all the while with him
By my distress, and did not know I did.

142 "Less shame would wash away a greater crime
Than thine has been"; so said my gentle guide;
"Think no more of it; but another time,

145 Imagine I'm still standing at thy side
Whenever Fortune, in thy wayfaring,
Brings thee where people wrangle thus and chide;

148 It's vulgar to enjoy that kind of thing."

THE IMAGES. *The Falsifiers.* In this canto we have the images of impersonators (falsifiers of person), perjurers (falsifiers of words), and coiners (falsifiers of money).

NOTES. ll. 1 sqq.: *when Juno was incensed*, etc.: Semele, daughter of Cadmus, king of Thebes, became by Jupiter the mother of Bacchus. Among other acts of revenge upon the royal house, Juno sent a homicidal madness upon Athamas, the husband of Semele's sister Ino. (Ovid: *Metam.* iv. 512–30.)

ll. 13 sqq.: *and when, by Fortune's hostile hand*, etc.: Hecuba was the wife of Priam, king of Troy. After the fall of the city, she and her daughter Polyxena were carried away captive to Greece. Having seen Polyxena sacrificed at the tomb of Achilles, she found on the shore the body of her son Polydorus, treacherously murdered by Polymnestor, king of Thrace, to whom she had entrusted him for safe keeping. (Ovid: *Metam.* xiii. 404–575.)

l. 31: *the Aretine*: i.e. Griffolino.

l. 32: *Gianni Schicchi*: a Florentine of the Cavalcanti family. When Buoso Donati (see Canto xxv. 140, note) died, his son Simone was haunted with the fear that he might have left a will restoring some of the property he had unjustly acquired. Before making the death known, he consulted Gianni Schicchi, who, being a very clever mimic, offered to dress up as Buoso and dictate a new will in Simone's favour. This he did, taking the opportunity to bequeath himself a handsome legacy and the best mare in the stables.

l. 38: *Myrrha*: The story of her crime is told by Ovid (*Metam.* x. 298 sqq.)

l. 42: *he that fled but now*: i.e. Gianni Schicchi; "Queen of the Stud" was the name of the mare.

l. 61: *Master Adam*: a native of Brescia who was employed by the Counts Guidi of Romena to counterfeit the gold florins of Florence. He was burnt in 1281. The coining was on a large scale, and the whole currency of Tuscany was seriously affected.

l. 65: *the green Casentin*: The Casentino is the beautiful hill district of the Upper Arno, where Romena, the castle of the Conti Guidi, was situated.

l. 74: *the Baptist's coin*: the Florentine florin bore the image of St John Baptist, patron saint of the city (see Canto xiii. 143, note), on one side and a lily-flower on the other.

l. 76: *Guido or Alexander ... or their brother* (Aghinolfo): i.e. the Conti Guidi.

l. 78: *the fount of Branda*: There was a famous fountain of this name at Siena; but Master Adam probably means the one at Romena.

l. 97: *Sinon of Troy*: the Greek spy, who, by a lying story backed up by the most solemn oaths, persuaded the Trojans to bring the Wooden Horse into Troy. (See Canto xxvi. 55, note.)

l. 98: *the false wife*: Potiphar's wife. (*Gen.* xxxix. 6–23.)

l. 128: *Narcissus' mirror*: water. Narcissus fell in love with his own reflection in a pool, and, pining away, was transformed into a flower.

l. 148: *vulgar*: The Italian word *basso* is rather stronger than the English "vulgar" – it means "base" as well; perhaps the most exact equivalent would be the colloquial use of "low".

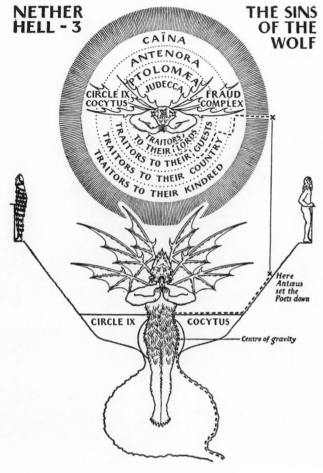

CAÏNA
ANTENORA
PTOLOMÆA
JUDECCA
CIRCLE IX   FRAUD
COCYTUS   COMPLEX
TRAITORS TO THEIR LORDS
TRAITORS TO THEIR GUESTS
TRAITORS TO THEIR COUNTRY
TRAITORS TO THEIR KINDRED

Here
Antæus
set the
Poets down

CIRCLE IX   COCYTUS

Centre of gravity

CANTO XXXI

THE STORY. *Dante and Virgil now reach the Well at the bottom of the abyss, round which stand the Giants, visible from the waist up above its rim. They see Nimrod and Ephialtes, and are lowered over the edge of the Well by Antaeus.*

The self-same tongue that first had wounded me,
    Bringing the scarlet blood to both my cheeks,
    Thus to my sore applied the remedy;

4 Even so, Achilles' lance was wont to mix
    Good gifts with ill, as erst his sire's had done,
    Hurting and healing; so the old tale speaks.

7 We went our way, turning our backs upon
    That mournful vale, up by its girdling bound,
    And silent paced across the bank of stone;

10 And less than day, and less than night, all round
    It gloomed; my eyes, strained forward on our course,
    Saw little; but I heard a high horn sound

13 So loud, it made all thunder seem but hoarse;
    Whereby to one sole spot my gaze was led,
    Following the clamour backward to its source:

16 When Charlemayn, in rout and ruin red,
    Lost all the peerage of the holy war
    The horn of Roland sounded not so dread.

19 And when I'd gazed that way a little more
    I seemed to see a plump of tall towers looming;
    "Master," said I, "what town lies on before?"

22 "Thou striv'st to see too far amid these glooming
    Shadows," said he: "this makes thy fancy err,
    Concluding falsely from thy false assuming;

25 Full well shalt thou perceive, when thou art there,
    How strangely distance can delude the eye:
    Therefore spur on thy steps the speedier."

28 But after that, he took me lovingly
    By the hand, and said: "Nay now, before we go,
    I'll tell thee, lest the strange reality

31 Surprise thee out of measure; therefore know,
    These are not towers, but giants, set in a ring,
    And hid from the navel down in the well below."

34 And, just as when a mist is vanishing,
    Little by little the eye reshapes anew
    The outlines hid by the crowded vapouring,

37 So, as that thick, gross air we journeyed through,
    Little by little drawing nigh the well,
    My error left me, and my terror grew.

40 As Montereggion's ring-shaped citadel
    Has all its circling rampart crowned with towers,
    Even so, with half their bodies the horrible

43 Giants, whom Jove, when the thunder rolls and lowers,
    Threatens from heaven, girded the well's high rim,
    Turreting it – the tall and terrible powers.

46 Already I made out one huge face, the dim
    Shoulders and breast and part of the belly, and close
    Hung at his sides, both monstrous arms of him.

49 Nature in truth did wisely when she chose
    To leave off making such vast animals
    And let Mars lack executives like those;

52 If she repents not elephants or whales,
    Whoso looks subtly at the case will find
    How prudently her judgment trims the scales;

55 For where the instrument of thinking mind
    Is joined to strength and malice, man's defence
    Cannot avail to meet those powers combined.

58 As large and long his face seemed, to my sense,
    As Peter's Pine at Rome, and every bone
    Appeared to be proportionately immense,

61 So that the bank which aproned him from zone
    To foot, still showed so much, three Friesians
    Might vainly boast to lay a finger on

64 His hair; for from the place at which a man's
    Mantle is buckled, downward, you may call me
    Liar if he measured not fully thirty spans.

67 "*Rafel maı amech zabi almi*"
    The savage mouth began at once to howl,
    Such was the sweetest and the only psalm he

70 Could sing. "Stick to thy horn, thou stupid soul,"
    My guide called up; "use that to vent thy breast
    When rage or other passions through thee roll.

73 Feel at thy neck and find the baldrick laced
   That girds it on thee; see, O spirit confused,
   The horn itself that hoops thy monstrous chest.''

76 And then to me: ''Himself he hath accused;
   That's Nimrod, by whose fault the gracious bands
   Of common speech throughout the world were loosed.

79 We'll waste no words, but leave him where he stands,
   For all speech is to him as is to all
   That jargon of his which no one understands.''

82 So, turning to the left beside the wall,
   We went perhaps a cross-bow shot, to find
   A second giant, still more fierce and tall.

85 I do not know what master hand could bind
   Him thus, but there he stood, his left hand bound
   Fast down before him, and the right behind,

88 By an iron chain, which held him closely wound
   Down from the neck; and on the part displayed
   Above the brink the turns went five times round.

91 ''So proud a spirit was this,'' my leader said,
   ''He dared to match his strength against high Jove,
   And in this fashion his reward is paid.

94 Ephialtes is his name, who greatly strove
   When the giants made the gods tremble for fright;
   The arms he brandished then no longer move.''

97 ''Were it but possible, I wish my sight,''
   Said I, ''could once experience and take in
   Briareus' huge unmeasurable might.''

100 ''Not far from hence,'' he answered, ''thou shalt win
    Sight of Antaeus, who speaks and wears no chain;
    And he shall bear us to the bottom of sin.

103 Very far off is he whom thou wouldst fain
    Behold; like this he's fettered, and doth look
    As this one looks, but twice as fierce again.''

106 No terrible earthquake-trembling ever took
    And shook a tower so mightily as forthwith
    Huge Ephialtes in his fury shook;

109 And never had I been so afraid of death –
    For which no more was needed save the fear,
    But that I saw the chains, and dared draw breath.

112 So on we went; and presently drew near
    Antaeus; seven cloth-yards above the well,
    Without the head, his towering bulk rose sheer.

115 ''Thou that of old within the fateful vale
    That made the name of Scipio ever-glorious,
    When Hannibal with all his host turned tail,

118 Didst ravish by thy prowess meritorious
    A thousand lions; thou whose aid, 'twould seem,
    Might well have made the sons of earth victorious

121 Hadst thou allied thee with thy brethren's team,
    Pray be not loth, but lower us to the deep,
    Where the great cold locks up Cocytus' stream.

124 Make us not go to Typhon; let not slip
    Thy chance to Tityus; for this man can give
    That which is craved for here; curl not thy lip,

127 But stoop; for he's alive, and can retrieve
    Thy fame on earth, where he expects – so Grace
    Call him not early home – long years to live.''

130 Thus spake the master; he, all eagerness,
    Stretched those enormous hands out to my guide
    Whence Hercules endured so great distress.

133 And when he felt them grasp him, Virgil cried
    To me: ''Come here and let me take thee!'' So
    He clasped me and made one bunch of us twined and tied.

136 As Carisenda looks, when one stands below
    On the leaning side, and watches a passing cloud
    Drift over against the slant of it, swimming slow,

139 Antaeus looked to me, as I watched him bowed
    Ready to stoop; and that was a moment such
    That I heartily wished we might travel another road.

142 But he set us lightly down in the deep whose clutch
    Holds Judas and holds Lucifer pent fast;
    Nor in that stooping posture lingered much,

145 But swung him up, as in a ship the mast.

THE IMAGES. *The Giants.* From the point of view of the *story*, it is easy to see that Dante placed the Giants here, not merely to furnish a means of transport from Malbowges to the depth of the Well, but, artistically, to provide a little light relief between the sickening horrors of the last bowges of Fraud Simple and the still greater, but wholly different, horrors of the pit of Treachery. But *allegorically*, what do they signify? In one sense they are images of Pride; the Giants who rebelled against Jove typify the pride of Satan who rebelled against God. But they may also, I think, be taken as the images of the blind forces which remain in the soul, and in society, when the ''general bond of love'' is dissolved and the ''good of the intellect'' wholly withdrawn, and when nothing remains but blocks of primitive mass-emotion, fit to be the ''executives of Mars'' and the tools of treachery. Nimrod is a braggart stupidity; Ephialtes, a senseless rage; Antaeus, a brainless vanity: one may call them the doom of nonsense, violence, and triviality, overtaking a civilization in which the whole natural order is abrogated.

NOTES. l. 4: *Achilles' lance*: Peleus, the father of Achilles, gave to his son a lance, whose wound could be healed only by sprinkling with rust from the lance-head itself. (See Ovid: *Remed. Amor.* 47–8; Chaucer, *Squire's Tale*, 231–2; Shakespeare, 2 *Hen. VI.* v. i, etc.)

l. 16: *Charlemayn*: When Charlemagne was returning from fighting the Saracens in Spain, his rearguard, led by his nephew Roland and the Twelve Peers, was betrayed to the enemy by Ganelon (see Canto XXXII. 122), and slaughtered at the Pass of Roncevaux in the Pyrenees. With almost his last breath, Roland blew his horn Olifant so loud that Charlemagne, eight miles away, heard it and returned to avenge his Peerage.

l. 40: *Montereggion*: A castle about six miles from Siena, surmounted by twelve turrets.

l. 59: *Peter's Pine*: A bronze image of a pine-tree, about $7\frac{1}{2}$ ft. high, which, in Dante's time, stood under a canopy outside the old basilica of St Peter in Rome, but was later removed to the Vatican. Much ingenuity has been expended on calculating the height of the Giants; we may take them to average 50 or 60 ft.

l. 62: *Friesians*: The men of Friesland were celebrated for their immense stature.

l. 67: *Rafel maï amech zabi almi*: In view of Virgil's express warning (ll. 80–81), the strenuous efforts of commentators to make sense of this remark seem rather a waste of energy. My own impression, for what it is worth, is that if Dante did not make up this gibberish out of his own head, it may have been suggested to him by some conjuring book, for its diction and rhythm are curiously reminiscent of the garbled language of popular charms.

l. 77: *Nimrod*: "and the beginning of his kingdom was Babel" (*Gen.* x. 9–10). For the story of the building of Babel and the confusion of languages see *Genesis* xi. In making Nimrod a giant, Dante follows St Augustine. (*De Civ. Dei* xvi. 3.) He is given a horn because he was "a mighty hunter before the Lord".

l. 85: *what master hand*: cf. Canto xv. 11 and note.

l. 94: *Ephialtes*: son of Neptune (the sea); one of the giants who fought against the gods, threatening to pile Mount Ossa upon Olympus, and Mount Pelion upon Ossa. They were slain by Apollo.

l. 99: *Briareus*: son of Tellus (the earth), another giant who fought against the Olympians (*Aen.* x. 565 *sqq.*). According to Homer and Virgil, he had a hundred arms and fifty heads; but Dante merely calls him here to have followed Statius, who (*Theb.* ii. 596) merely calls him "immense", and Lucan, who (*Phars.* iv. 596) refers to "fierce Briareus".

ll. 101–21: *Antaeus*: son of Neptune and Tellus – a giant who was invincible so long as he was in contact with his mother Earth. Hercules eventually overcame him by lifting him from the ground and squeezing him to death in mid-air (see l. 132 of this canto). Antaeus is left unchained because he was not one of the giants who fought against the gods. His exploit with the lions took place near Zama in Libya, where Hannibal was defeated by Scipio. Dante took all these details about Antaeus from Lucan's *Pharsalia* (iv. 593–660).

ll. 124–5: *Typhon ... Tityus*: two more of the sons of Tellus, who offended against Jupiter. All these earth-giants and sea-giants seem originally to have been personifications of elemental natural forces.

l. 136: *Carisenda*: a leaning tower at Bologna. When one stands beneath one of these towers and looks up, an optical illusion is produced as though it were about to fall upon one; and this illusion is strengthened if a cloud happens to be moving across in the opposite direction to the apparent movement.

CANTO XXXII

THE STORY. *The Ninth Circle is the frozen Lake of Cocytus, which fills the bottom of the Pit, and holds the souls of the Traitors. In the outermost region, Caïna, are the betrayers of their own kindred, plunged to the neck in ice; here Dante sees the Alberti brothers, and speaks with Camicion dei Pazzi. In the next, Antenora, he sees and lays violent hands on Bocca degli Abati, who names various other betrayers of their country; and a little further on he comes upon two other shades, frozen together in the same hole, one of whom is gnawing the head of the other.*

Had I but rhymes rugged and harsh and hoarse,
  Fit for the hideous hole on which the weight
  Of all those rocks grinds downward course by course,

4 I might press out my matter's juice complete;
  As 'tis, I tremble lest the telling mar
  The tale; for, truly, to describe the great

7 Fundament of the world is very far
  From being a task for idle wits at play,
  Or infant tongues that pipe *mamma*, *papa*.

10 But may those heavenly ladies aid my lay
  That helped Amphion wall high Thebes with stone,
  Lest from the truth my wandering verses stray.

13 O well for you, dregs of damnation, thrown
  In that last sink which words are weak to tell,
  Had you lived as sheep or goats in the world of the sun!

16 When we were down in the deep of the darkling well,
  Under the feet of the giant and yet more low,
  And I still gazed up at the towering walls of Hell,

19 I heard it said: "Take heed how thou dost go,
  For fear thy feet should trample as they pass
  On the heads of the weary brotherhood of woe."

22 I turned and saw, stretched out before my face
  And 'neath my feet, a lake so bound with ice,
  It did not look like water but like glass.

25 Danube in Austria never could disguise
  His wintry course beneath a shroud so thick
  As this, nor Tanaïs under frozen skies

28 Afar; if Pietrapan or Tambernic
  Had crashed full weight on it, the very rim
  Would not have given so much as even a creak.

31 And as with muzzles peeping from the stream
  The frogs sit croaking in the time of year
  When gleaning haunts the peasant-woman's dream,

34 So, wedged in ice to the point at which appear
  The hues of shame, livid, and with their teeth
  Chattering like storks, the dismal shades stood here.

37 Their heads were bowed toward the ice beneath,
  Their eyes attest their grief; their mouths proclaim
  The bitter airs that through that dungeon breathe.

40 My gaze roamed round awhile, and, when it came
  Back to my feet, found two shades so close pressed,
  The hair was mingled on the heads of them.

43 I said: "You two, thus cramponed breast to breast,
  Tell me who you are." They heaved their necks a-strain
  To see me; and as they stood with faces raised,

46 Their eyes, which were but inly wet till then,
  Gushed at the lids; at once the fierce frost blocked
  The tears between and sealed them shut again.

49 Never was wood to wood so rigid locked
  By clamps of iron; like butting goats they jarred
  Their heads together, by helpless fury rocked.

52 Then one who'd lost both ears from off his scarred
  Head with the cold, still keeping his face down,
  Cried out: "Why dost thou stare at us so hard?

55 Wouldst learn who those two are? Then be it known,
  They and their father Albert held the valley
  From which the waters of Bisenzio run;

58 Both of them issued from one mother's belly,
  Nor shalt thou find, search all Caïna through,
  Two shades more fit to stand here fixt in jelly;

61 Not him whose breast and shadow at one blow
  Were pierced together by the sword of Arthur,
  Not Focaccia, nor this other who

64 So blocks me with his head I see no farther,
  Called Sassol Mascheroni – if thou be
  Tuscan, thou know'st him; and I'll tell thee, rather

67 Than thou shouldst plague me for more speech with thee,
  I'm Camicion de' Pazzi, and I wait
  Till Carlin come to make excuse for me."

70 Then I saw thousand faces, and thousands yet,
Made doggish with the cold; so that for dread
I shudder, and always shall, whenever I set

73 Eyes on a frozen pool; and as we made
Towards the centre where all weights down-weigh,
And I was shivering in the eternal shade,

76 Whether 'twas will, fate, chance, I cannot say,
But threading through the heads, I struck my heel
Hard on a face that stood athwart my way.

79 "Why trample me? What for?" it clamoured shrill;
"Art come to make the vengeance I endure
For Montaperti more vindictive still?"

82 "Master!" I cried, "wait for me! I adjure
Thee, wait! Then hurry me on as thou shalt choose;
But I think I know who it is, and I must make sure."

85 The master stopped; and while the shade let loose
Volleys of oaths: "Who art thou, cursing so
And treating people to such foul abuse?"

88 Said I; and he: "Nay, who art thou, to go
Through Antenora, kicking people's faces?
Thou might'st be living, 'twas so shrewd a blow."

91 "Living I am," said I; "do thou sing praises
For that; if thou seek fame, I'll give thee it,
Writing thy name with other notable cases."

94 "All I demand is just the opposite;
Be off, and pester me no more," he said;
"To try such wheedling here shows little wit."

97 At that I grasped the scruff behind his head:
"Thou'lt either tell thy name, or have thy hair
Stripped from thy scalp," I panted, "shred by shred."

100 "Pluck it all out," said he; "I'll not declare
My name, nor show my face, though thou insist
And break my head a thousand times, I swear."

103 I'd got his hair twined tightly in my fist
Already, and wrenched away a tuft or two,
He yelping, head down, stubborn to resist,

106 When another called: "Hey, Bocca, what's to do?
Don't thy jaws make enough infernal clatter
But, what the devil! must thou start barking too?"

109 "There, that's enough," said I, "thou filthy traitor;
Thou need'st not speak; but to thy shame I'll see
The whole world hears true tidings of this matter."

112 "Away, and publish what thou wilt!" said he;
"But prithee do not fail to advertise
That chatterbox there, if thou from hence go free.

115 He wails the Frenchmen's *argent*, treason's price;
'Him of Duera,' thou shalt say, 'right clear
I saw, where sinners are preserved in ice.'

118 And if they should inquire who else was there,
Close by thee's Beccarìa, whose throat was cut
By Florentines; Gianni de' Soldanier

121 Is somewhat further on, I fancy, put
With Ganelon, and Tibbald, who undid
Faenza's gates when sleeping eyes were shut."

124 And when we'd left him, in that icy bed,
I saw two frozen together in one hole
So that the one head capped the other head;

127 And as starved men tear bread, this tore the poll
Of the one beneath, chewing with ravenous jaw,
Where brain meets marrow, just beneath the skull.

130 With no more furious zest did Tydeus gnaw
The scalp of Menalippus, than he ate
The brain-pan and the other tissues raw.

133 "O thou that in such bestial wise dost sate
Thy rage on him thou munchest, tell me why;
On this condition," I said, "that if thy hate

136 Seem justified, I undertake that I,
Knowing who you are, and knowing all his crime,
Will see thee righted in the world on high,

139 Unless my tongue wither before the time."

THE IMAGES. *Cocytus*. Beneath the clamour, beneath the monotonous circlings, beneath the fires of Hell, here at the centre of the lost soul and the lost city, lie the silence and the rigidity and the eternal frozen cold. It is perhaps the greatest image in the whole *Inferno*. "Dante," says Charles Williams, "scatters phrases on the *difference* of the place. It is treachery, but it is also ... cruelty; the traitor is cruel" (*The Figure of Beatrice*, p. 143). A cold and cruel egotism, gradually striking inward till even the lingering passions of hatred and destruction are frozen into immobility – that is the final state of sin. The conception is, I think, Dante's own; although the *Apocalypse of Paul* mentions a number of cold torments, these are indiscriminately mingled with the torments by fire, and their placing has no structural significance. (It is interesting, however, that in the seventeenth century, the witches who claimed to have had to do with Satan sometimes reported that he was ice-cold.)

Cocytus, the "river of mourning", is the fourth of the great infernal rivers. Caïna is named from Cain who slew his brother (*Gen.* iv.); Antenora, from Antenor of Troy who, according to medieval tradition, betrayed his city to the Greeks.

NOTES. l. 10: *those heavenly ladies*: The Muses. Amphion played so bewitchingly upon the lyre that the stones of Mount Cithaeron were drawn to hear him, and built themselves up into the walls of Thebes.

l. 17: *under the feet of the giant and yet more low*: Antaeus, as we have seen, was about 50–60 ft. high; therefore his feet cannot have been more than 30 ft. or so below the edge of the well. The latter was, however, "exceeding deep" (Canto XVIII. 5), and Dante here makes it clear that they descended to a considerable depth below the feet of the giant. We must suppose that there was, first, a sheer thirty-foot drop, followed by a rather less steep descent which it was possible to negotiate on foot (see sketch, p. 437). I get the impression that Dante clambered down backwards, as one gets down a ladder; and consequently did not see where he had got to until Virgil's voice (l. 19) caused him to turn round (l. 22).

l. 27: *Tanais*: the Don.

l. 28: *Pietrapan or Tambernic*: Pietrapana: a corruption of Petra Apuana, a mountain in north-west Tuscany. Tambernic: either the *Frusta Gora*, near Tovarnicho, in Slavonia, or the Javornic in Carniola.

ll. 34–5: *to the point at which appear the hues of shame*: i.e. up to the neck.

l. 56: *they and their father Albert*: These are Napoleone and Alessandro degli Alberti, Counts of Mangona, who slew each other in a quarrel over their possessions in the valley of the river Bisenzio, a tributary of the Arno. One was a Guelf, the other a Ghibelline.

ll. 61–2: *him whose breast and shadow … were pierced*: Mordred the traitor, who attempted to usurp the throne of Arthur. In their last fight, Arthur smote him so fiercely that when the lance was withdrawn the sun shone through the wound and broke the shadow of his body.

l. 63: *Focaccìa*: one of the Cancellieri family of Pistoia. He is said. to have cut off the hand of one of his cousins and cut his uncle's throat, and thus to have started the family feud from which the Black and White Guelf factions had their origin.

l. 65: *Sassol Mascheroni*: One of the Toschi of Florence, who treacherously murdered his uncle's only son and seized the inheritance.

ll. 68–9: *Camicion de' Pazzi*: of Valdarno, murdered his kinsman Ubertino. *Carlino* dei Pazzi, another member of the family, was bribed by the Blacks to surrender the castle of Piantravigne, which he was holding for the Whites – and, having pocketed the bribe, sold it back to the Whites again. Camicion means that his own crimes will seem comparatively excusable beside that of Carlino (who is presumably destined for Antenora). It will be noticed that the shades of the Traitors, though inclined to be reticent about their own affairs, are only too eager to denounce each other, and pour out strings of names without even being asked. (Compare Bocca, ll. 113–23; and contrast, e.g. Farinata, Canto x. 118–20.)

ll. 73–4: *as we made towards the centre*: They are now entering Antenora (l. 89). There is no line of demarcation between the regions of Cocytus, but as we go on we find the sinners plunged more deeply in the ice.

l. 81: *Montaperti*: The speaker, Bocca degli Abati, was a Ghibelline; but in the Battle of Montaperti (see Canto x. 85, note) he fought on the Guelf side and, at the most critical moment, came treacherously up behind the standard-bearer of the Florentine cavalry and cut off his hand, bringing down the standard and throwing the Florentines into a panic which lost them the day.

l. 90: *thou might'st be living*: i.e. the blow is heavier than the speaker can account for, as coming from another shade, which he supposes Dante to be.

ll. 97 *sqq.*: For the significance of Dante's ferocious behaviour, see Canto VIII. 45, note; treachery is cruel, and cruelty calls forth cruelty.

l. 114: *that chatterbox there*: Buoso da Duera; he was in command of the Ghibellines assembled to repel the French forces who were marching through Lombardy to link up with Charles of Anjou, and sold the passage of the Oglio to Guy de Montfort. Bocca uses the French word for money (*argent*) by way of rubbing in the accusation.

l. 122: *Ganelon*: see Canto XXXI. 16, note. *Tibbald*: one of the Zambrasi family of Faenza. He had a vendetta against the Lambertazzi, a Ghibelline Bolognese family who had taken refuge in Faenza, and in 1280 opened the gates of the city to the Bolognese Guelfs.

l. 130: *Tydeus*: king of Calydon, one of the "Seven against Thebes". Being himself mortally wounded by Menalippus, he yet killed his opponent, and, having ordered his head to be struck off, gnawed the scalp and tore out the brains. (Statius: *Theb.* viii. 740–63.)

CANTO XXXIII

THE STORY. *Having heard Count Ugolino's ghastly story of his death by famine, the Poets pass on to Ptolomaea, where Fra Alberigo is cheated by Dante into telling him about himself and Branca d' Oria and others who enjoy the terrible "privilege" of Ptolomaea.*

Lifting his mouth up from the horrid feast,
  The sinner wiped it on the hair that grew
  Atop the head whose rear he had laid waste;

4 Then he began: "Thou bid'st me to renew
  A grief so desperate that the thought alone,
  Before I voice it, cracks my heart in two.

7 Yet, if indeed my words, like seedlings sown,
  Shall fruit, to shame this traitor whom I tear,
  Then shalt thou see me speak and weep in one.

10 What man thou art, or what hath brought thee here
  I know not; but I judge thee Florentine,
  If I can trust the witness of my ear.

13 First learn our names: I was Count Ugolin,
  And he, Archbishop Roger; hearken well
  Wherefore I use him thus, this neighbour of mine.

16 That once I trusted him, and that I fell
  Into the snare that he contrived somehow,
  And so was seized and slain, I need not tell.

19 What thou canst not have learned, I'll tell thee now:
  How bitter cruel my death was; hear, and then,
  If he has done me injury, judge thou.

22 A narrow loophole in the dreadful den
  Called 'Famine' after me, and which, meseems,
  Shall be a dungeon yet for many men,

25 Had filtered through to me the pallid gleams
  Of many changing moons, before one night
  Unveiled the future to my haunted dreams.

28 I saw this man, a lord and master of might,
  Chasing the wolf and wolf-cubs on the hill
  Which shuts out Lucca from the Pisans' sight.

31 His hounds were savage, swift and keen of skill,
  And many a Sismund, Gualand and Lanfranc,
  Like huntsmen, rode before him to the kill.

34 I saw how father and sons wearied and sank
  After a short quick run; I saw the dread
  Sharp teeth that tore at bleeding throat and flank.

37 And waking early ere the dawn was red
  I heard my sons, who were with me, in their sleep
  Weeping aloud and crying out for bread.

40 Think what my heart misgave; and if thou keep
  From tears, thou art right cruel; if thou for this
  Weep not, at what then art thou wont to weep?

43 By now they'd waked; the hour at which our mess
  Was daily brought drew near; ill dreams had stirred
  Our hearts and filled us with unquietness.

46 Then at the foot of that grim tower I heard
  Men nailing up the gate, far down below;
  I gazed in my sons' eyes without a word;

49 I wept not; I seemed turned to stone all through;
  They wept; I heard my little Anselm say:
  'Father, what's come to thee? Why look'st thou so?'

52 I shed no tear, nor answered, all that day
  Nor the next night, until another sun
  Rose on the world. And when the first faint ray

55 Stole through into that dismal cell of stone,
  And eyeing those four faces I could see
  In every one the image of my own,

58 I gnawed at both my hands for misery;
  And they, who thought it was for hunger plain
  And simple, rose at once and said to me:

61 'O Father, it will give us much less pain
  If thou wilt feed on us; thy gift at birth
  Was this sad flesh, strip thou it off again.'

64   To spare them grief I calmed myself. Hard earth,
        Hadst thou no pity? couldst thou not gape wide?
        That day and next we all sat mute. The fourth,

67   Crept slowly in on us. Then Gaddo cried,
        And dropped down at my feet: 'My father, why
        Dost thou not help me?' So he said, and died.

70   As thou dost see me here, I saw him die,
        And one by one the other three died too,
        From the fifth day to the sixth. Already I

73   Was blind; I took to fumbling them over; two
        Long days I groped there, calling on the dead;
        Then famine did what sorrow could not do."

76   He ceased, and rolled his eyes asquint, and sped
        To plant his teeth, which, like a dog's, were strong
        Upon the bone, back in the wretched head.

79   O Pisa! scandal of all folk whose tongue
        In our fair country speaks the sound of *sì*,
        Since thy dull neighbours will not smite such wrong

82   With vengeance, move Gorgona from the sea,
        Caprara move, and dam up Arno's mouth,
        Till every living soul is drowned in thee!

85   For though Count Ugolin in very truth
        Betrayed thee of thy castles, it was crime
        To torture those poor children; tender youth,

88   O crüel city, Thebes of modern time,
        Made Hugh and Il Brigata innocent
        And the other two whose names are in my rhyme.

91   We passed; and found, as further on we went,
        A people fettered in the frost's rough grip,
        Flat on their backs, instead of forward bent.

94   There the mere weeping will not let them weep,
        For grief, which finds no outlet at the eyes,
        Turns inward to make anguish drive more deep;

97   For their first tears freeze to a lump of ice
        Which like a crystal mask fills all the space
        Beneath the brows and plugs the orifice.

100 And now, although, as from a calloused place,
        By reason of the cold that pinched me so,
        All feeling had departed from my face,

103 I felt as 'twere a wind begin to blow.
        Wherefore I said: "Master, what makes it move?
        Is not all heat extinguished here below?"

106 "Thine eyes," said he, "shall answer soon enough;
        We're coming to the place from which the blast
        Pours down, and thou shalt see the cause thereof."

109 And one of the wretched whom the frost holds fast
        Cried out: "O souls so wicked that of all
        The posts of Hell you hold the very last,

112 Rend from my face this rigid corporal,
        That I may vent my stuffed heart at my eyes
        Once, though the tears refreeze before they fall."

115 Then I: "Tell me thy name: that is my price
        For help; and if I do not set thee free,
        May I be sent to the bottom of the ice."

118 And he: "I am Friar Alberigo, he
        Of the fruits of the ill garden; in this bed
        Dates for my figs are given back to me."

121 "How now," said I, "art thou already dead?"
        And in reply: "Nay, how my body fares
        In the upper world I do not know," he said.

124 "Such privilege this Ptolomaea bears
        That oft the soul falls down here ere the day
        When Atropos compels it with her shears.

127 And, if it will persuade thee take away
        These glazing tears by which my face is screened,
        Know, when a soul has chosen to betray,

130 As I did, straight it's ousted by a fiend,
        Who takes and rules the body till the full
        Term of its years has circled to an end.

133 The soul drops down into this cistern-pool;
        Belike the shade wintering behind me here
        Still has a body on earth – it's probable

136 Thou'lt know, if thou art new come down from there;
        He is Ser Branca d' Oria; in this pit's
        Cold storage he has lain this many a year."

139 "I think," said I, "that these are pure deceits,
        For Branca d' Oria has by no means died;
        He wears his clothes and sleeps and drinks and eats."

142 "Up in that moat where the Hellrakers bide,"
        He answere "Michael Zanche'd not yet come
        To boil and bubble in the tarry tide

145 When this man left a devil in his room,
        In his flesh and that kinsman's flesh, whom he
        Joined with himself in treachery, and in doom.

148 And now, do thou stretch forth thy hand to me,
        Undo my eyes." And I undid them not,
        And churlishness to him was courtesy.

152 O Genoa, where hearts corrupt and rot,
        Lost to all decency! will no man hound
        Thy whole tribe from the earth and purge this blot?

154 For with Romagna's vilest spirit I found
        One of such rank deeds, such a Genoan,
        His soul bathes in Cocytus, while on ground

157 His body walks and seems a living man.

THE IMAGES. *Ugolin and Roger* are the last of those pairs of shades who image partnership in sin. In each case, only one of them speaks. Francesca speaks of the sharing of the sin, and offers excuses for Paolo along with herself. Ulysses ignores Diomede (partnership is lost). Ugolin justifies himself at Roger's expense (treachery can share nothing but a mutual hatred). There is a deliberate parallel between the Paolo-Francesca pair and the Ugolin-Roger pair: in both cases the lines that introduce their respective stories are drawn from the same passage of Virgil, and there are other, minor, correspondences. This is Dante's way of indicating that here in the ice of Cocytus we have the last state of the corruption of love; that every devouring passion, sexual or otherwise, that sets itself against the order of God and the City, bears in itself the seeds of treachery and a devouring passion of destruction.

Ptolomaea. This third region of Cocytus is probably named after Ptolemy, captain of Jericho, who invited Simon the High Priest and his sons to a banquet and there slew them (I *Maccabees* xvi).

Here lie the Traitors to Hospitality. They who denied the most primitive of human sanctities are now almost sealed off from humanity; they cannot even weep. And they are dead to humanity before they die; that which seems to live in them on earth is only a devil in human form – the man in them has withdrawn out of reach into the cold damnation.

NOTES. ll. 4–9: Compare with Canto v. 121–6, and both with *Aeneid* ii. 3, 10–13.

l. 13: *Count Ugolin*: Count Ugolino della Gherardesca and his grandson, Nino dei Visconti (whom we shall meet in *Purg.* viii), were respectively the heads of the two Guelf parties which in 1288 held power in Pisa. To get rid of Nino, Ugolino allied himself with the Archbishop, Ruggieri (Roger) degli Ubaldini. But as soon as Nino was driven out, the Archbishop, seeing the Guelfs thus weakened, turned on Ugolino and imprisoned him with four of his sons and grandsons in a tower subsequently named "the Tower of Famine". There they remained till March 1289, when the Archbishop ordered the tower to be locked and the keys thrown into the river. (Dante's word (*chiavar*), however, probably means "nail up" – a sound more alarming to the prisoners.) After eight days the tower was opened and all the victims found dead of starvation.

l. 29: *the wolf and wolf-cubs*: i.e. Ugolino and his children. *The hill that shuts out Lucca* is the Monte di San Giuliano, half-way between Pisa and Lucca.

l. 32: *Sismund, Gualand and Lanfranc*: Ghibelline families of Pisa.

l. 34: *father and sons*: Actually, the youths imprisoned with Ugolino were his own two youngest sons, Gaddo and Uguccione (Hugh), and his two grandsons, Nino (surnamed *il Brigata*) and Anselm. All except Anselm were young men rather than "children" or "boys" as Dante represents them. Anselm was 15.

ll. 72–3: *already I was blind*: "from grief", say some commentators; but Dante knew, I think, that one of the effects of starvation is to produce blindness.

l. 75: *then famine did what sorrow could not do*: i.e. kill him.

l. 80: *speaks the sound of* sì: i.e. all who speak Italian. The various romance-languages were distinguished by the word used for "Yes", that of Northern France being the *langue d'oïl* (*oui*); that of Southern France, the *langue d'oc*; that of Italy, the *lingua di sì*.

ll. 82–3: *Gorgona … Caprara*: These two islands near the mouth of the Arno then belonged to Pisa.

ll. 85–6: *in very truth betrayed thee of thy castles*: Ugolino was accused of treachery in ceding certain Pisan strongholds to the Florentines and Lucchese. Others think he had no choice but to do so; Dante's words are ambiguous, but in any case Ugolino's treacherous conspiracy with Ruggieri against Nino, by which he betrayed both his party and his city, would have sufficed to bring him to Antenora.

l. 91: *as further on we went*: They are now passing into Ptolomaea.

l. 105: *is not all heat extinguished*: Dante knows that winds are caused by differences of temperature in the atmosphere, and wants to know how, in this region of absolute cold, there can be wind without heat. Virgil replies that he will see the cause of it later on. (Canto XXXIV. 46–51.)

l. 110: *O souls so wicked*: The speaker thinks that Dante and Virgil are damned souls going down to the Circle of Judecca.

l. 117: *to the bottom of the ice*: Treachery calls forth treachery; Dante knows that he *is* going to the bottom – though not in the sense the shade supposes.

ll. 118–20; *Friar Alberigo*: a "Jovial Friar" of the Manfredi family of Faenza. His younger brother, Manfred, struck him in the face in the course of a dispute. Alberigo pretended to forgive and forget, and later on invited Manfred and one of his sons to a dinner. When it was

time for the dessert he called out: "Bring on the fruit!" This was the signal for armed servants to rush in and kill Manfred and his son. The "fruit of the ill garden" is probably an allusion to this. "To receive dates for one's figs" is a Tuscan expression meaning "to get back one's own with interest", "to be given tit for tat".

l. 126: *Atropos*: the Fate who cuts the thread of life.

l. 137: *Ser Branca d' Oria*: a Ghibelline of Genoa, who invited his father-in-law, Michael Zanche (see Canto XXII. 88), to a banquet and there, with the help of a nephew, murdered him. Dante says that Zanche had not yet reached the Bowge of the Barrators before the traitor's body had been taken over by a devil and his soul fallen to Ptolomaea – i.e. he was damned in the moment of committing – or perhaps even of assenting to – the treachery.

l. 146: *that kinsman*: i.e. the nephew.

l. 149: *and I undid them not*: The chorus of indignant comment about Dante's behaviour becomes so loud at this point that I feel obliged to repeat that it arises from a misunderstanding of the *allegory*, and once more refer to Canto VIII. 45, note.

CANTO XXXIV

THE STORY. *After passing over the region of Judecca, where the Traitors to their Lords are wholly immersed in the ice, the Poets see Dis (Satan) devouring the shades of Judas, Brutus, and Cassius. They clamber along his body until, passing through the centre of the Earth, they emerge into a rocky cavern. From here they follow the stream of Lethe upwards until it brings them out on the island of Mount Purgatory in the Antipodes.*

"*Vexilla regis prodeunt inferni*
  Encountering us; canst thou distinguish him,
  Look forward," said the master, "as we journey."

4 As, when a thick mist breathes, or when the rim
  Of night creeps up across our hemisphere,
  A turning windmill looms in the distance dim,

7 I thought I saw a shadowy mass appear;
  Then shrank behind my leader from the blast,
  Because there was no other cabin here.

10 I stood (with fear I write it) where at last
  The shades, quite covered by the frozen sheet,
  Gleamed through the ice like straws in crystal glassed;

13 Some lie at length and others stand in it,
  This one upon his head, and that upright,
  Another like a bow bent face to feet.

16 And when we had come so far that it seemed right
  To my dear master, he should let me see
  That creature fairest once of the sons of light,

19 He moved him from before me and halted me,
  And said: "Behold now Dis! behold the place
  Where thou must steel thy soul with constancy."

22 How cold I grew, how faint with fearfulness,
  Ask me not, Reader; I shall not waste breath
  Telling what words are powerless to express;

25 This was not life, and yet it was not death;
  If thou hast wit to think how I might fare
  Bereft of both, let fancy aid thy faith.

28 The Emperor of the sorrowful realm was there,
  Out of the girding ice he stood breast-high,
  And to his arm alone the giants were

31 Less comparable than to a giant I;
  Judge then how huge the stature of the whole
  That to so huge a part bears symmetry.

34 If he was once as fair as now he's foul,
And dared outface his Maker in rebellion,
Well may he be the fount of all our dole.

37 And marvel 'twas, out-marvelling a million,
When I beheld three faces in his head;
The one in front was scarlet like vermilion;

40 And two, mid-centred on the shoulders, made
Union with this, and each with either fellow
Knit at the crest, in triune junction wed.

43 The right was of a hue 'twixt white and yellow;
The left was coloured like the men who dwell
Where Nile runs down from source to sandy shallow.

46 From under each sprang two great wings that well
Befitted such a monstrous bird as that;
I ne'er saw ship with such a spread of sail.

49 Plumeless and like the pinions of a bat
Their fashion was; and as they flapped and whipped
Three winds went rushing over the icy flat

52 And froze up all Cocytus; and he wept
From his six eyes, and down his triple chin
Runnels of tears and bloody slaver dripped.

55 Each mouth devoured a sinner clenched within,
Frayed by the fangs like flax beneath a brake;
Three at a time he tortured them for sin.

58 But all the bites the one in front might take
Were nothing to the claws that flayed his hide
And sometimes stripped his back to the last flake.

61 "That wretch up there whom keenest pangs divide
Is Judas called Iscariot," said my lord,
"His head within, his jerking legs outside;

64 As for the pair whose heads hang hitherward:
From the black mouth the limbs of Brutus sprawl –
See how he writhes and utters never a word;

67 And strong-thewed Cassius is his fellow-thrall.
But come; for night is rising on the world
Once more; we must depart; we have seen all."

70 Then, as he bade, about his neck I curled
My arms and clasped him. And he spied the time
And place; and when the wings were wide unfurled

73 Set him upon the shaggy flanks to climb,
And thus from shag to shag descended down
'Twixt matted hair and crusts of frozen rime.

76 And when we had come to where the huge thigh-bone
Rides in its socket at the haunch's swell,
My guide, with labour and great exertion,

79 Turned head to where his feet had been, and fell
To hoisting himself up upon the hair,
So that I thought us mounting back to Hell.

82 "Hold fast to me, for by so steep a stair,"
My master said, panting like one forspent,
"Needs must we quit this realm of all despair."

85 At length, emerging through a rocky vent,
He perched me sitting on the rim of the cup
And crawled out after, heedful how he went.

88 I raised my eyes, thinking to see the top
Of Lucifer, as I had left him last;
But only saw his great legs sticking up.

91 And if I stood dumbfounded and aghast,
Let those thick-witted gentry judge and say,
Who do not see what point it was I'd passed.

94 "Up on thy legs!" the master said; "the way
Is long, the road rough going for the feet,
And at mid-terce already stands the day."

97 The place we stood in was by no means fit
For a king's palace, but a natural prison,
With a vile floor, and very badly lit.

100 "One moment, sir," said I, when I had risen;
"Before I pluck myself from the Abyss,
Lighten my darkness with a word in season.

103 Kindly explain; what's happened to the ice?
What's turned him upside-down? or in an hour
Thus whirled the sun from dusk to dawning skies?"

106 "Thou think'st," he said, "thou standest as before)
Yon side the centre, where I grasped the hair
Of the ill Worm that pierces the world's core.

109 So long as I descended, thou wast there;
But when I turned, then was the point passed by
Toward which all weight bears down from everywhere.

112 The other hemisphere doth o'er thee lie –
Antipodal to that which land roofs in,
And under whose meridian came to die

115 The Man born sinless and who did no sin;
Thou hast thy feet upon a little sphere
Of whose far side Judecca forms the skin.

118 When it is evening there, it's morning here;
And he whose pelt our ladder was, stands still
Fixt in the self-same place, and does not stir.

121 This side the world from out high Heaven he fell;
The land which here stood forth fled back dismayed,
Pulling the sea upon her like a veil,

124 And sought our hemisphere; with equal dread,
Belike, that peak of earth which still is found
This side, rushed up, and so this void was made."

127 There is a place low down there underground,
As far from Belzebub as his tomb's deep,
Not known to sight, but only by the sound

130 Of a small stream which trickles down the steep,
Hollowing its channel, where with gentle fall
And devious course its wandering waters creep.

133 By that hid way my guide and I withal,
Back to the lit world from the darkened dens
Toiled upward, caring for no rest at all,

136 He first, I following; till my straining sense
Glimpsed the bright burden of the heavenly cars
Through a round hole; by this we climbed, and thence

139 Came forth, to look once more upon the stars.

THE IMAGES. *Judecca*. The region of the Traitors to sworn allegiance is called Judecca after Judas, who betrayed Our Lord.

Here, cut off from every contact and every means of expression, those who committed the final treason lie wholly submerged.

Judas, Brutus and Cassius. Judas, obviously enough, is the image of the betrayal of God. To us, with our minds dominated by Shakespeare and by "democratic" ideas, the presence here of Brutus and Cassius needs some explanation. To understand it, we must get rid of all political notions in the narrow sense. We should notice, first, that Dante's attitude to Julius Caesar is ambivalent. *Personally*, as a pagan, Julius is in Limbo (Canto IV. 123). *Politically*, his rise to power involved the making of civil war, and Curio, who advised him to cross the Rubicon, is in the Eighth Circle of Hell (Canto XXVIII. 97–102 and note). But, although Julius was never actually Emperor, he was the founder of the Roman Empire, and *by his function*, therefore, he images that institution which, in Dante's view, was divinely appointed to govern the world. Thus Brutus and Cassius, by their breach of sworn allegiance to Caesar, were Traitors to the Empire, i.e. to World-order. Consequently, just as Judas figures treason against God, so Brutus and Cassius figure treason against Man-in-Society; or we may say that we have here   images of treason against the Divine and the Secular government of the world.

Dis, so Virgil calls him; Dis, or Pluto, being the name of the King of the Classical Underworld. But to Dante he is Satan or Lucifer or Beelzebub – or, as we say, the Devil. "He can see it now – that which monotonously resents and repels, that which despairs. ... Milton imagined Satan, but an active Satan; this is beyond it, this is passive except for its longing. Shakespeare imagined treachery; this is treachery raised to an infinite cannibalism. Treachery gnaws treachery, and so inevitably. It is the imagination of the freezing of every conception, an experience of which neither life nor death can know, and which is yet quite certain, if it is willed." (Charles Williams: *The Figure of Beatrice*, p. 144.)

NOTES. l. 1: *Vexilla regis prodeunt inferni*: "The banners of the King of Hell go forth". This, with the addition of the word *inferni* (of Hell), is the first line of the Latin hymn which we know best as "The royal banners forward go".

l. 28: *fairest once of the sons of light*: referring to Satan's original status as one of the brightest of the Cherubim.

l. 28: *the Emperor*: "Dante uses the word with the full meaning of its perversion" (Charles Williams). In Canto II, he refers to God as "the Emperor of the Imperium on high"; this is the Emperor of the realm below, who gives his name to the "sorrowful City". (Canto VIII. 68.)

l. 38: *three faces*: The three faces, red, yellow, and black, are thought to suggest Satan's dominion over the three races of the world: the red, the European (the race of Japhet); the yellow, the Asiatic (the race of Shem); the black, the African (the race of Ham). But they are also, undoubtedly, a blasphemous anti-type of the Blessed Trinity: Hatred, Ignorance, Impotence as against Love, Wisdom, Power.

l. 46: *from under each sprang two great wings*: Satan was a fallen cherub, and retains, in a hideous and perverted form, the six wings which belong to his original rank.

ll. 51–2: *three winds ... and froze up all Cocytus*: see Canto XXXIII. 103–108.

l. 68: *night is rising on the world*: it is about 6 P.M.

l. 74: *from shag to shag descended*: Satan's body is shaggy like that of a satyr, according to a well-known medieval convention. The poets clamber down him, feet-first, as one descends a ladder, working their way through the points where the thick pelt prevents the ice from adhering close to the surface of his body. (We must remember the enormous height of Satan – somewhere about 1000 or 1500 ft. at a rough calculation.)

l. 79: *turned head to ... feet*, etc.: They have been descending feet-first; now they turn themselves topsy-turvy and go *up* again, head-first.

l. 93: *what point it was I'd passed*: Since Dante proceeds to take the sting out of "thick-witted" by admitting that he himself was completely bewildered, we may perhaps, without offence, explain that the "point" was the centre of gravity, which was situated precisely at Satan's navel. The sketch on p. 437 will make all these geographical complexities clear.

l. 96: *mid-terce*: Terce, the first of the four canonical divisions of the day, lasted from sunrise (6 A.M. at the equinox) till 9 A.M.; mid-terce would therefore be about 7.30 A.M.

l. 103: *Kindly explain*: Dante wants to know (1) why Satan is apparently upside-down; (2) how it is that, having started their descent of Satan about 6 P.M., they have, after about an hour and a half of climbing, apparently arrived at the following morning. Virgil explains that (1) having passed the centre, they are now in the Southern Hemisphere, so that "up" and "down" are reversed, and (2) they are now going by southern time, so that day and night are reversed. Purgatory stands on the opposite meridian to Jerusalem; therefore Purgatory time is twelve hours behind Jerusalem time; i.e. it is now 7.30 A.M. on Holy Saturday, all over again.

l. 108: *the ill Worm*: Satan. At the centre of the Earth is a little sphere (see l. 116, and look at the sketch), and Satan's body is run through this, like a knitting-needle through an orange, with his head out at one end and his legs at the other.

l. 113: *that which land roofs in*: the Northern Hemisphere, which, according to St Augustine and most medieval geographers, contained all the land in the world.

l. 114: *under whose meridian*: the meridian of Jerusalem, where Christ ("the Man born sinless") was crucified.

ll. 116–17: *a little sphere*, etc.: See Sketch, p. 437.

ll. 121 sqq.: *This side the world*: i.e. the southern side. When Satan fell from Heaven, two things happened. (1) The dry land, which until then had occupied the Southern Hemisphere, fled in horror from before him, and fetched up in the Northern Hemisphere; while the ocean poured in from all sides to fill the gap. (2) The inner bowels of the Earth, to avoid contact with him, rushed upwards towards the south, and there formed the island and mountain at the top of which was the Earthly Paradise, ready for the reception of Man, and which, after Hell's Harrowing became Mount Purgatory. This, according to Dante, is the only land in the Southern Hemisphere. The hollow thus left in the middle of the Earth is the core of Hell, together with the space in which Dante and Virgil are now standing – the "tomb" of Satan. From this a winding passage leads up to the surface of the Antipodes. By this passage the river Lethe descends, and up it the poets now make their way.

l. 130: *a small stream*: This is Lethe, the river of oblivion, whose springs are in the Earthly Paradise. They are moving against it – i.e. towards recollection.

Overtone Series

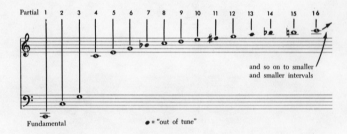

Partial 1 2 3 4 5 6 7 8 9 10 11 12 13 14 15 16

and so on to smaller
and smaller intervals

Fundamental   ● = "out of tune"

1. The numbers of the partials also give the ratio of one pitch to another; from second partial to first partial is 2/1 or a P8, third to second partials is 3/2 or a P5, etc.

2. The "out of tune" notes are not commonly used in the music of western civilization. They are, however, part and parcel of other musical systems (Hindu, Arabic, etc.) and are therefore "in tune" in these systems.

3. The overtone series can be easily demonstrated and should be tried by everyone in order to understand the acoustical principles The piano is not the perfect demonstration instrument since it uses an adjusted tuning (equal temperament) rather than portions of the natural scale (except for the octave). It is reasonably close to the overtone series and will provide an adequate demonstration.

    a. Find the fundamental pitch (Great C), press gently (do not sound the note) and hold the key down. This "opens" the string. Strike the second partial (small c) sharply and release it immediately. The second partial is now sounding on the fundamental string. Release the lower key and the tone stops.

    b. Again press gently on the fundamental note and hold the key down. Strike the third partial (g) nptalo.

and immediately release. The g is now sounding on the open C string which is vibrating in three segments.

c. Press and hold the fundamental and strike, one after another the second, third, fourth and fifth partials (c–g–c^1–e^1) and listen to all four notes sounding on this one open string.

d. Hold the fundamental string open and strike all the partials one after another up the overtone series and hear the tones become softer as they rise higher in the series.

e. Now press and hold the notes c^1–e^1–g^1. Strike the fundamental note very sharply and listen to the tones you are holding come to life as they begin to vibrate in sympathy with the partials in the fundamental string.

4. The ♮ sign in front of the fifteenth partial is called a *natural sign*. Its function is to cancel out the flat which was used to make b-flat for the fourteenth partial.

Pythagorean Theory

A. Pythagoras devised the single procedure of adding fifths and subtracting octaves to determine the ratios between all notes of a scale. Following is an illustration of the pitches obtained by dividing the string into four parts (1;2;3;4):

○ = known pitches

● = pitches to be located

1. To begin the process add a fifth to g to get d^1 and then move d^1 down to d by subtracting an octave (2/1).[1]

$$\frac{c \text{ to } g}{3/2} + \frac{g \text{ to } d^1}{3/2 \ (3/2 \times 3/2)} = \frac{c \text{ to } d^1}{9/4}$$

Then substract the octave (d to d^1) from c to d^1 to get c to d:

$$\frac{c \text{ to } d^1}{9/4} - \frac{d \text{ to } d^1}{2/1 \ (9/4 \times 1/2)} = \frac{c \text{ to } d}{9/8}$$

c to d is therefore 9/8 (9 parts of the string to 8 parts of the string). If the full string sounds c then d will be located as illustrated:

---

[1]Ratios are *not* fractions; they are relationships. When *adding* ratios multiple straight across. When subtracting ratios *invert* the second ratio (the one being subtracted) and then multiply straight across. Always reduce to the smallest figures by factoring out.

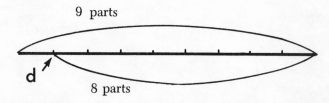

2. To find *a* go up another fifth from d^1 and subtract the octave g to g^1:

$$\frac{\text{g to } d^1}{3/2} + \frac{d^1 \text{ to } a^1}{3/2 \,(3/2 \times 3/2)} = \frac{\text{g to } a^1}{9/4} -$$

$$\frac{\text{g to } g^1}{2/1 \,(9/4 \times 1/2)} = \frac{\text{g to } a}{9/8}$$

The scale will now look like this:

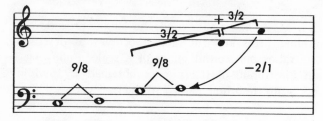

3. Next add up successive fifths from c to g to d^1 to a^1 to e^2 and then subtract *two* octaves $(2 \times 2/1 = 4/1)$ to bring e^2 down to e, thus giving the ratio for c to e.

$$\frac{\text{c to g}}{3/2} \underset{(\times)}{+} \frac{\text{g to } d^1}{3/2} = \frac{\text{c to } d^1}{9/4} \underset{(\times)}{+} \frac{d^1 \text{ to } a^1}{3/2} =$$

$$\frac{\text{c to } a^1}{27/8} \underset{(\times)}{+} \frac{a^1 \text{ to } e^2}{3/2} = \frac{\text{c to } e^2}{81/16}$$

$$\frac{\text{c to } e^2}{81/16} - \frac{2 \text{ octaves}}{4/1 \,(81/16 \times 1/4)} = \frac{\text{c to e}}{81/64}$$

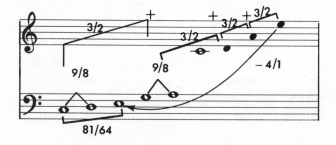

4. To get c to b add b^2 to the four fifths already added up

$$\frac{(\text{c to g to } d^1 \text{ to } a^1 \text{ to } e^2)}{81/16} \underset{(\times)}{+} \frac{b^2}{3/2} = \frac{\text{c to } b^2}{243/32} -$$

$$\frac{2 \text{ octaves}}{4/1 \,(243/32 \times 1/4)} = \frac{\text{c to b}}{243/128}$$

This gives the following known ratios to this point:

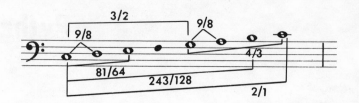

B. The computation can be completed by continuing to add fifths and subtract octaves until all relationships are known; however, enough information is now available to be able to add and subtract ratios within the octave and thus determine the remaining relationships.

1. To find the ratio of d to e subtract c to d from c to e:

$$\frac{\text{c to e}}{81/64} - \frac{\text{c to d}}{9/8} \left(\frac{\cancel{9}}{\cancel{81/64}} \times \frac{1}{\cancel{8/9}}\right) = \frac{\text{d to e}}{9/8}$$

2. c to f is a P4 because it has the same number of semitones (five) as g to c^1. The ratio is therefore 4/3.

3. To find e to f subtract c to e (81/64) from c to f (4/3).

$$\frac{\text{c to f}}{4/3} - \frac{\text{c to e}}{81/64} \,(4/3 \times 64/81) = \quad 256/243$$
$$\text{or e to f.}$$

4. a to b is found by adding g to a (9/8) to c to g (3/2) to get c to a.

$$\frac{\text{c to g}}{3/2} \underset{(\times)}{+} \frac{\text{g to a}}{9/8} = \frac{\text{c to a}}{27/16}$$

Then subtract c to a (27/16) from c to b (243/128).

$$\underset{243/128}{\text{c to b}} - \underset{27/16}{\text{c to a}} \left(\overset{9}{\underset{8}{243/128}} \times \overset{1}{\underset{1}{16/27}} \right) = \underset{9/8}{\text{a to b}}$$

The known ratios to this point are now:

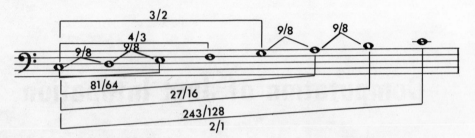

The note-to-note ratios still to be determined are e to f, f to g and b to c.

5. To determine e to f subtract c to e (81/64) from c to f (4/3).

$$\underset{4/3}{\text{c to f}} - \underset{81/64}{\text{c to e}} \quad (4/3 \times 64/81) = \underset{256/243}{\text{e to f}}$$

6. f to g is obtained by subtracting c to f (4/3) from c to g (3/2):

$$\underset{3/2}{\text{c to g}} - \underset{4/3}{\text{c to f}} \quad (3/2 \times 3/4) = \underset{9/8}{\text{f to g}}$$

7. For b to c¹ subtract c to b (243/128) from c to c¹ (2/1).

$$\underset{2/1}{\text{c to c}^1} - \underset{243/128}{\text{c to b}} \quad (2/1 \times 128/243) = \underset{256/243}{\text{b to c}^i}$$

The completed scale is:

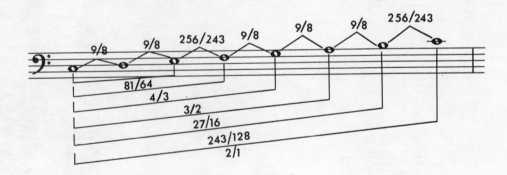

The Greeks used far more tonal materials than the eight notes (with their ratios) that are illustrated here, including sharps, flats and other notes that are not even utilized in the western world; however, this brief summary of the tuning process (Pythagorean) for a diatonic scale does serve to illustrate the procedures.

Computation of Just Intonation

Just Intonation is based essentially on the first six partials of the overtone series. Using these six partials (1:2:3:4:5:6) these intervals can be assumed:

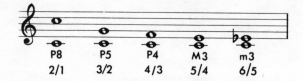

P8	P5	P4	M3	m3
2/1	3/2	4/3	5/4	6/5

With so many known ratios there are of course many mathematical procedures which will determine the remaining intervals. Following is one way to do it.

1. Subtract C–E (5/4) from C–F (4/3) to get E–F:

$$4/3 - 5/4 \ (4/3 \times 4/5) = 16/15$$

2. Subtract E–F (16/15) from E–G (6/5) to get F–G:

$$6/5 - 16/15 \ (6/5 \times 15/16) = 9/8$$

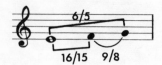

452

Up to this point the ratios look like this:

3. To find D–E subtract E–G (6/5) from D–G (4/3):

$$4/3 - 6/5 \;(4/3 \times 5/6) = 10/9$$

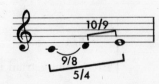

4. To find C–D subtract D–E (10/9) from C–E (5/4):

$$5/4 - 10/9 \;(5/4 \times 9/10) = 9/8$$

The note-to-note ratios are now:

5. To get B–C subtract G–B (5/4) from G–C (4/3):

$$4/3 - 5/4 \;(4/3 \times 4/5) = 16/15$$

6. For A–B subtract B–C (16/15) from A–C (6/5):

$$6/5 - 16/15 \;(6/5 \times 15/16) = 9/8$$

7. To find G–A subtract A–B (9/8) from G–B (5/4):

$$5/4 - 9/8 \;(5/4 \times 8/9) = 10/9$$

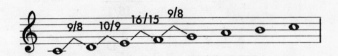

The note-to-note ratios are now complete:

Using the ratios of the just scale we can now check the ratios and therefore the tuning of each triad in the scale.

a. Major Triads: C–E–G, F–A–C, G–B–D

$$1.\;C{-}E{-}G = \quad \frac{C - E}{9/8 + 10/9} = 5/4 \quad \frac{E - G}{16/15 + 9/8} = 6/5 \quad \frac{C - E}{5/4} + \frac{E - G}{6/5} = 3/2$$

All of the intervals correlate with the overtone series and the C Major triad is in perfect tune. By following the same procedures it will be found that the F Major and G Major triads are also in perfect tune.

b. Minor Triads: D–F–A, E–G–B

1. $E-G-B = \dfrac{E-G}{16/15 + 9/8} = 6/5$

   $\dfrac{G-B}{10/9 + 9/8} = 5/4 \qquad \dfrac{E-G}{6/5} +$

   $\dfrac{G-B}{5/4} = 3/2$

The E minor triad is also in perfect tune.

2. $D-F-A = \dfrac{D-F}{10/9 + 16/15} = 32/27$

   $\dfrac{F-A}{9/8 + 10/9} = 5/4 \qquad \dfrac{D-F}{32/27} +$

   $\dfrac{F-A}{5/4} = 40/27$

The two thirds should add up to the 3/2 fifth. Therefore if we subtract 40/27 from 3/2 we can determine the extent of the discrepancy:

$$3/2 - 40/27 \; (3/2 \times 27/40)$$
$$3/2 \times 27/40 = 81/80$$

This ratio of 81/80 is called a tuning discrepancy, or *comma*. Pythagorean, Just Intonation and all other systems using natural ratios (from the overtone system) have commas because, among other reasons, all intervals when divided harmonically divide unevenly:

An octave divides into a P5 and a P4.

$$3/2 + 4/3 = 2/1$$

A P5 divides into a M3 and a m3.

$$5/4 + 6/5 = 3/2$$

A M3 divides into Major seconds of different sizes.

$$\overset{\text{M2}}{9/8} + \overset{\text{M2}}{10/9} = 5/4$$

The division continues into ever smaller but still differently sized intervals.

If intervals of a whole step come in two different sizes then half steps also come in two different sizes, for example, 16/15 and 25/24. The only practical solution is to make all half steps the same size so instruments with fixed pitches such as piano and organ can play all types of music. This is exactly what *equal temperament* does. Only the octave on the piano is in perfect tune (2/1). All the half steps, and therefore all the intervals, are slightly out of tune. All the half steps are the same size: C♯ is the same note as D♭, D♯ as E♭ and so forth.

A piano keyboard with all naturally tuned notes would have eighteen notes to an octave, instead of twelve. No one has yet determined an effective way to increase the notes on a piano keyboard by fifty per cent and still be able to build and to play such an instrument.